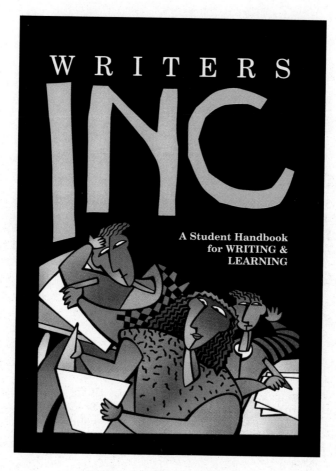

WRITERS INC

A Student Handbook for WRITING & LEARNING

Written and Compiled by

Patrick Sebranek, Verne Meyer, and Dave Kemper

WRITE SOURCE

GREAT SOURCE EDUCATION GROUP

a Houghton Mifflin Company
Wilmington, Massachusetts

W R I T E R S

INC

Acknowledgements

Writers INC is a reality because of the help and advice of a number of people, among them: Tom Gilding, Chris Johnson, Rita Sullivan, Mary Ann Hoff, Ken Taylor, Carol Domblewski, Connie Stephens, Laura Bachman, Dawn Weis, Colleen Biehn, John VanRys, Kim Rylaarsdam, Randy VanderMey, and Bev Jessen. Also, several of our students allowed us to use their papers as samples in the handbook: Monica, John, Ann, Kris, Lisa, Amy, Lynn, and Susie. We thank them all.

Editorial: Lois Krenzke, Dave Kemper, Pat Sebranek

Book Design: Julie Sebranek

Production: Sherry Gordon

Illustration: Chris Krenzke

Printed in the United States of America

International Standard Book Number: 0-669-38812-2 (hardcover)

8 9 10 11 12 -RRDC- 01 00 99 98 97 96

International Standard Book Number: 0-669-38813-0 (softcover)

8 9 10 11 12 -RRDC- 01 00 99 98 97 96

Using the Handbook

Your *Writers INC* emphasizes writing, a challenge for people of all ages. But the handbook does not stop with writing. It also provides information on reading techniques, vocabulary building, study skills, note taking, speaking, thinking, you name it.

In addition, the **Almanac** at the back of the book provides many extras like full-color maps, traffic signs, the periodic table of the elements, and a copy of the Constitution of the United States.

The **Table of Contents** near the front of the handbook gives you a list of the major sections and the chapters found under those sections. It also tells you the topic number on which each unit begins.

The **Index** at the back of *Writers INC* is one of its most useful parts. It is arranged in alphabetical order and includes every specific topic discussed in the handbook. The numbers after each word in the index are topic numbers, not page numbers. Since there are often many topics on one page, we've used topic numbers to help you find information more quickly.

Look through the **Body** of your handbook and notice the wide variety of material. Notice in particular the material that will be most useful to you— then use it. Here's a preview of what you'll find inside:

Table of
Contents

TOP 10

Reasons to Write

10. To become a wealthy author

9. To impress a certain guy or girl

8. To compose *creative* excuses

7. To fill up your notebook

6. *To be different*

5. To become a better thinker and learner

4. To share your experiences and ideas

3. **To improve your performance in school**

2. To get you ready for the next step

1. To help you shape a meaningful life

002 A "Fixed" List

As you can tell, this list is fixed. The first five ideas are really pretty lame reasons to write. The second five are a different story. They tell us just how important writing really is and why we should care about improving our own writing.

Reason No. 5: To become a better thinker and learner. Writing about new ideas and concepts helps you explore and analyze them, which in turn helps them become part of your own thinking. As writer Ray Bradbury once said, writing "lets the world burn through you."

Reason No. 4: To share your experiences and ideas. Writing helps you establish your place in the world. It satisfies your need to explain, invent, and persuade. The more you write, the better you will be able to share your thoughts and feelings with those around you. So get into a regular writing routine. Write in a journal, in a notebook, on the back of an envelope—just write!

Reason No. 3: To improve your performance in school. Writing about your course work can help you get better grades in just about any class. Is writing your ticket to the honor roll? Maybe, maybe not. But it is your ticket to improvement and feeling better about school.

Reason No. 2: To get you ready for the next step. How far you go in school—be it high school, tech school, or college—really depends upon your ability to take charge of your own learning. Every bit of extra effort you put into your writing and learning now will make you a better student next month, next semester, next year, forever.

Reason No. 1: To help you shape a meaningful life. A lot of what is important to you right now is surface stuff: wearing the right clothes, hanging out with certain people, doing the right things. Pardon the expression, but there is a whole lot more to life than any of these things. You will understand what I mean once you start writing and learning for yourself.

So what does Writers INC have to do with all of this?

Writers INC is a portable resource loaded with all sorts of great information—writing guidelines, models, thinking strategies, test-taking skills, maps, and much more. What you won't find are any exercises or assignments, not a one. So repeat after me: *Writers INC* is not just another textbook. Say it again! Then note the subtitle on the cover: *A Student Handbook for Writing & Learning*. Get it? *Writers INC* is a guide to your *own* writing and learning. It will help you become an interested, and interesting, student of learning now and for years to come.

The Writing Process

"Writing is mind traveling, destination unknown."

Mind Traveling

003   Read the bold statement above; read it again; repeat it after every meal; have it tattooed on your arm. And by all means remember it every time you write. Let this statement be your constant reminder that when you write, you are often involved in uncharted thinking and exploring. For example, at the beginning of the process, you may be searching for possible subjects related to your assignment. At another point, you may be experimenting with different ways to write about one of these subjects. Later on, you may be searching for the perfect idea to tie all of your main points together.

004 Writing to Discover

These examples illustrate the following important point: Writing is not trying to figure out everything you want to say *before* you put pen to paper or fingers to the keyboard. Attempting to work in this way will result in having very little to say, or worse yet, in having nothing to say at all. (Ever hear of writer's block?) Writing almost always works best when it springs from the discoveries you make *during* the process. That's why it is important to keep your pen moving or your keyboard clicking. You open up your mind to your best ideas when you keep the words flowing.

Remember: Writing is mind traveling, destination unknown. Make this statement your writing motto, and step into the writing process expecting to surprise yourself with the discoveries you make.

what's ahead?   The three pages that follow in this opening chapter review the basic steps in the writing process (and in mind traveling). The next chapter (011-015) provides an example of one writer's work in progress so you can see firsthand how the process works. The remaining chapters in this section list specific skills and strategies you can apply to your writing at different steps in the process.

> "Writing to me is a voyage, an odyssey, a discovery, because I'm never certain of precisely what I will find."
>
> —Gabriel Fielding

005 Understanding the Process

The basic steps in the writing process discussed in your handbook cover different aspects of mind traveling. **Prewriting** helps you select and shape a subject for writing. **Writing the First Draft** helps you connect all of your thoughts about your subject. It is your first complete look at a developing piece of writing. **Revising** helps you make changes in your writing until it says what you want it to say. **Editing and Proofreading** help you check your revised writing for correctness and prepare it for publication. **Publishing** helps you evaluate the effectiveness of your work. Sharing a finished piece of writing with your classmates is one form of publishing; submitting your work to a school newspaper or magazine is another.

Setting the Stage

Before you use this section, it's important that you understand four main points about the writing process.

- **Experience shapes writing.** Each of life's experiences becomes part of what you know, what you think, and what you have to say. Your mind is a storehouse for these past experiences, as well as a creative processor for your thoughts of today and tomorrow. Writing is the process of capturing those thoughts and experiences on paper.

- **Writing never follows a straight path.** Writing is a backward as well as a forward activity, so don't expect to move neatly and efficiently through the steps in the writing process. Mind traveling by its very nature includes detours, wrong turns, and repeat visits.

- **Each assignment presents unique challenges.** For one composition, you might search high and low for an interesting subject. For another composition, you might do a lot of collecting and reviewing before you find an interesting way to write about a subject. For still another, you might be ready to write your first draft almost immediately.

- **Each writer works differently.** Some writers work more in their heads, while others work more on paper. Some writers need to talk about their writing early on, while others would rather keep their ideas to themselves. Your own writing personality will develop as you become more and more experienced.

 All of the guidelines and strategies included in this section won't necessarily make you a better writer. Real improvement comes from writing regularly, experimenting with a number of different forms, and addressing a number of different audiences.

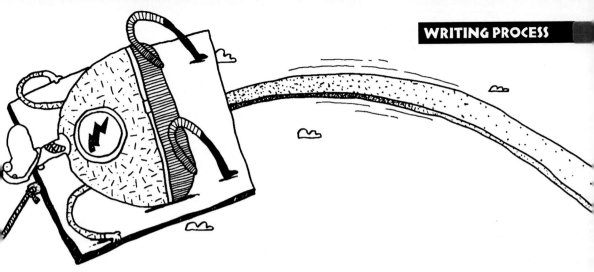

The Process in Action

The next two pages provide a basic look at the writing process in action. Use this information as a general guide whenever you write.

006 Prewriting

1. Find an interesting idea to write about—one that meets the requirements of the assignment and lends itself to worthwhile mind traveling.

2. Begin your subject search with free writing, clustering, or another selecting activity. (See 017-018.)

3. Learn as much as you can about a potential subject. (See 021-022.)

4. Take a close look at your prewriting progress to see whether or not you have a solid interest in your subject. If one subject leads to a dead end, drop it and search for another one.

5. Once you have a topic, find an interesting way (a focus) to write about it. (See 024-025.)

6. Think about an overall plan or design for organizing your writing. This plan can be anything from a brief list to a detailed outline. (See 026.)

007 Writing the First Draft

1. Write the first draft while your prewriting is still fresh in your mind.

2. Give your opening paragraph special attention to set the right tone for your writing. (See 030.)

3. Refer to your plan or outline (if you have one) for the main part of your writing, but be flexible. A more interesting route may unfold as you write.

4. Keep writing until you come to a natural stopping point. Don't worry about corrections at this point. Concentrate on developing your ideas.

5. Remember that your first draft is your first look at a developing writing idea. (You may find it necessary to write more than one draft of an emerging writing idea.)

008 Revising

1. Review your first draft to make sure you understand which parts work and which parts need to be changed.

2. Add, cut, reword, or rearrange the ideas in your writing. Your writing should answer many of the questions your readers may have about your subject. (See 036.)

3. Check your writing for opportunities you may have missed to make it as meaningful and lively as possible. (See 039.)

4. Review (or write) the opening and closing paragraphs. They should help tie everything together in your paper.

5. Refine the style of your writing. Your ideas should sound interesting, colorful, and natural. (See 041.)

6. Ask your classmates to react to your writing. (See 042-048.)

009 Editing and Proofreading

1. Reread your final draft aloud to test it for sense and sound. Replace any words, phrases, or sentences that are awkward or confusing.

2. Then check for errors in usage, punctuation, capitalization, spelling, and grammar.

3. Have a dictionary, thesaurus, and your *Writers INC* handbook close at hand as you work.

4. Ask a reliable editor—a friend, classmate, teacher, or parent—to check your writing for errors you may have missed.

5. Prepare (write, type, or keyboard) a neat final copy of your writing. Follow the guidelines for a final draft established by your teacher.

6. Proofread the final draft for errors before submitting it for publication.

010 Publishing

1. Share your finished product with your writing group and teacher. (Have copies of your work available for group members.)

2. Listen carefully to their reactions to your work. Take brief notes so you can refer to their comments the next time you write.

3. Decide if you are going to include the writing in your portfolio. Follow the guidelines established by your teacher.

4. Consider submitting your work to a school, local, or national publication. Make sure to follow the necessary requirements for submitting manuscripts. (See 058.)

"As soon as you connect with your true subject, you will write."

—Joyce Carol Oates

One Writer's Process

For one of her writing assignments, Barb Anderson was asked to write a reminiscence of school life. Here's how she used the writing process to develop her work.

011 Prewriting: Searching and Selecting

Barb started her subject search by freely listing highlights or impressions from her years in elementary school. As her list developed, two writing ideas caught her attention: the balance beam in her kindergarten classroom and the student teacher in her third-grade class. Then, when she eventually focused her attention on sixth grade, she knew she had connected with her true subject. She wanted to write about a special reading experience.

012 Shaping the Experience

To gather basic details related to this experience, Barb answered the 5 W's of writing *(Who? What? Where? When?* and *Why?).*

Who: teacher, Mr. Erickson; kids in sixth grade; the boy and his two dogs in the best book ever

What: reading out loud to us, like we were little kids again; *Where the Red Fern Grows*

Where: gathered around the teacher's chair; sat on the floor

When: everyday after recess; instead of starting math class right away; always wanted him to read more . . . take more time

Why: Mr. Erickson must've known we'd love it . . . must've wanted us to learn again to love books, like when we were little kids

Barb could have tried another shaping activity like free writing. (See 021.) However, after her initial gathering, she felt more than ready to write her first draft. (See the next page.)

013 Writing the First Draft

Barb's answer to the *Why?* question (on the previous page) gave her an effective starting point for her first draft. She discusses her feelings about reading *before* sixth grade. She then describes how she was introduced to *Where the Red Fern Grows*. (The opening part of her draft follows.)

The writer shares early reading memories.

When I was a child, I was read to by my mother and grandmother. My books, such as Peter Rabbit, were very important to me. But by the time I was 10 or 11, books had lost there magic, and I read only what was required in school. My sixth-grade teacher changed all of that.

She continues by writing freely about the main part of her reminiscence.

I hurryed in from recess with the rest of the sixth graders. We all took our assigned seats and settled down to begin our next subject, math. Mr. Erickson was very strict, so we all knew we must be quiet and ready to begin. But, today day, Mr. Erickson did not open his math book. He simply stood up and calmly told us to gather around his chair at the front of the room. "You want us to sit on the floor?" one boy asked. Oh yes, that is exactly what our teacher wanted. I haven't done anything this childish since second grade, I thought, but I guess this is better then math. "Today, we will begin to read a book entitled <u>Where the Red Fern Grows</u>," Mr. Erickson began. Each day we

Details about the actions of the class bring the experience to life.

were going to have a read-aloud. Day after day, we took in the story of a boy and his two dogs. Mr. Erickson no longer had to ask us to sit at the front of the room; we were already their, crowded around his chair, anxiously waiting for more of this heart warming story we begged our teacher to read longer and he would smile, close the book, and tell us there would be more tomorrow. . . .

014 Revising the First Draft

After reading and reviewing her first draft, the writer finds a number of ways to improve it for content and style. Her goal is to create a clear and interesting story for her readers. Here are some of the changes she makes.

The writer adds an adjective (young) and changes the first main verb (read) to the active voice.

She realizes this sentence is off the subject and deletes it.

For interest and clarity, she adds an idea.

When I was a ~~young~~ child, ~~I was read to by~~ my mother and grandmother ~~read to me often.~~ My books, such as Peter Rabbit, were very important to me. But by the time I was 10 or 11, books had lost there magic, and I read only what was required in school. My sixth-grade teacher changed all of that.

One day

I hurried in from recess with the rest of the sixth graders. We all took our assigned seats and settled down to begin our next subject, math. ~~Mr. Erickson was very strict, so we all knew we must be quiet and ready to begin.~~ But, today day, Mr. Erickson did not open his math book. He simply stood up and calmly told us to gather around his chair at the front of the room. "You want us to sit on the floor?" one boy asked. Oh yes, that is exactly what our teacher wanted. I ~~haven't~~ hadn't done anything ~~this~~ that childish since second grade, ~~I thought,~~ but ~~I guess this is~~ anything was better then math. "Today, we will begin to read a book entitled <u>Where the Red Fern Grows</u>," Mr. Erickson began. Each day we were going to have a read-aloud. Day after day, we took in With each new installment, our interest grew. the story of a boy and his two dogs. Mr. Erickson no longer had to ask us to sit at the front of the room; we were already their, crowded around his chair, anxiously waiting for more of this heart warming story . We we begged our teacher to read longer and he would smile, close the book, and tell us there would be more tomorrow. . . .

015 Editing and Proofreading

In this step, Barb makes sure that all of the sentences "work" in her revised writing. She also makes sure that her writing is free of careless errors. (She will proofread her writing for errors one last time after producing a final draft.)

The writer corrects a common usage error.

She combines two sentences to improve the flow of the writing.

After checking a dictionary, the writer discovers that "heartwarming" is one word.

When I was a young child, my mother and grandmother read to me often. My books, such as Peter Rabbit, were very important to me. But by the time I was 10 or 11, books had lost ~~there~~ *their* magic, and I read only what was required in school. My sixth-grade teacher changed all of that.

One day I ~~hurryed~~ *hurried* in from recess with the rest of the sixth graders, ~~We~~ *and we* all took our assigned seats and settled down to begin our next subject, math. But, today ~~day~~, Mr. Erickson did not open his math book. He simply stood up and calmly told us to gather around his chair at the front of the room. "You want us to sit on the floor?" one boy asked. Oh yes, that is exactly what our teacher wanted. I hadn't done anything that childish since second grade, but anything was better ~~then~~ *than* math. "Today, we will begin to read a book entitled Where the Red Fern Grows," Mr. Erickson began. Each day we were going to have a read-aloud.

Day after day, we took in the story of a boy and his two dogs. With each new installment, our interest grew. Mr. Erickson no longer had to ask us to sit at the front of the room; we were already ~~their~~ *there*, crowded around his chair, anxiously waiting for more of this ~~heart warming~~ *heartwarming* story. We begged our teacher to read longer, and he would smile, close the book, and tell us there would be more tomorrow. . . .

"There are few experiences quite so satisfactory as getting a good idea. . . . You're pleased with it and feel good. It may not be right, but at least you can try it out."

—Lancelot L. White

A Guide to Prewriting

016   Selecting, shaping, focusing, and planning are key components in the prewriting process. You **select** a meaningful subject that reflects your personal needs or interests (and meets the requirements of your assignment). You **shape** your thoughts about this subject to understand it better. You **focus** your attention on a specific part of the subject that you would like to write about. You then may **plan** some of your basic writing moves before you start your first draft.

Listed below is a guide to different prewriting strategies. Whenever you have a question about your prewriting (selecting a subject, perhaps), turn to the appropriate strategy for help.

On the following pages:

017 Guidelines for Selecting a Subject

The following activities will help you find a worthwhile subject for your writing. Read through the entire list before you choose an activity to begin your subject search.

1. **Journal Writing** Write on a regular basis in a journal. Explore your personal feelings, develop your thoughts, and record the happenings of each day. Underline ideas in your personal writing that you would like to explore in writing assignments.

2. **Free Writing** Write nonstop for 10 minutes to discover possible writing ideas. Begin writing with a particular focus in mind; otherwise, pick up on something that has recently attracted your attention.

3. **Clustering** Begin a cluster with a nucleus word (like *pollution*) related to your writing topic or assignment. Then record or cluster ideas around the nucleus word. Circle each idea as you write it, and draw a line connecting it to the closest related idea.

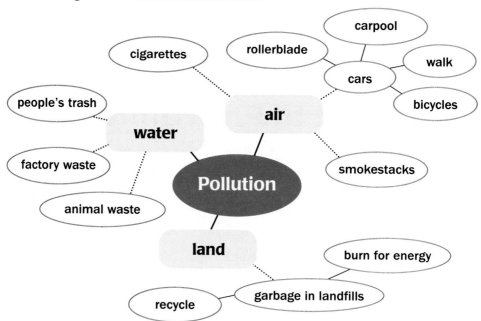

Note • After 3 or 4 minutes of clustering, scan your cluster for a word or an idea to explore in a free writing. A specific writing subject should begin to emerge during this writing.

4. **Listing** Freely listing ideas as they come to mind is another effective technique for finding a writing subject. Begin with an idea or a key word related to your assignment and simply start listing words. Brainstorming, listing ideas with members of a group, is an effective way to search for writing ideas.

018 **5. Imaginary Dialogue** Create an imaginary dialogue between you and someone else or between two strangers. The subject of this dialogue should be related to your writing assignment. Continue the conversation as long as you can, or until a possible writing idea begins to unfold.

6. Sentence Completion Complete an open-ended sentence in as many ways as you can. Try to word your sentence so that it leads to a subject you can use for a particular writing assignment:

I wonder how . . .	I hope our school . . .	Our grading system . . .
Too many people . . .	I just learned . . .	Television is . . .
The good thing about . . .	One place I enjoy . . .	Cars can be . . .

Note • Try alternating responses with a friend or classmate and work from each other's ideas.

7. Reflecting, Participating, and Listening Think about possible writing ideas as you read, as you ride (or drive) to school, and as you wait in the cafeteria line. Watch for unusual events, persons, objects, or conversations. Participate in activities related to your writing assignment. Interview someone who is knowledgeable or experienced about a writing idea. Also talk with family members and friends about possible subjects.

8. Using the "Essentials of Life Checklist" Below you will find a checklist of the major categories into which most essential things in our lives are divided. The checklist provides an endless variety of subject possibilities. Consider the first category, clothing. It could lead to the following writing ideas:

- the changing fashions in school clothing
- clothing as a statement ("we are what we wear")
- a clothing fad
- a favorite piece of clothing

019 # Essentials of Life Checklist

clothing	communication	exercise	health/medicine
housing	purpose/goals	community	entertainment
food	measurement	arts/music	literature/books
exercise	machines	faith/religion	recreation/hobby
education	intelligence	trade/money	personality/identity
family	agriculture	heat/fuel	natural resources
friends	environment	rules/laws	tools/utensils
love	science	freedom/rights	plants/vegetation
senses	energy	land/property	work/occupation

> "The faster I write the better my output. If I'm going slow, I'm in trouble. It means I'm pushing the words, instead of being pulled by them."
>
> —Raymond Chandler

020 Guidelines for Free Writing

Reminders . . .

- **Thoughts are constantly passing through your mind;** you never have nothing on your mind.
- **Free writing helps you get these thoughts down on paper.**
- **Free writing is also a way to develop these thoughts;** you do this by adding details and making meaning out of them.
- **Many things seem awkward or difficult when you first try them;** free writing will probably be no different.
- **Just stick with it and don't be discouraged.**

The Process . . .

- **Write nonstop and record whatever comes into your mind.** (Write for at least 10 minutes if possible.)
- **If you have a particular topic in mind, begin writing about it.** Otherwise, pick up on anything that comes to mind and begin writing.
- **Don't stop to judge, edit, or correct your writing;** that will come later.
- **Keep writing even when you think you have exhausted all of your ideas.** Switch to another mode of thought (sensory, memory, reflective) if necessary, but keep writing.
- **When a particular topic seems to be working, stick with it;** record as many specific details as possible. If your ideas dry up, look for a new idea in your free writing or begin a new nonstop writing.

Hint: Carry your journal with you and write freely in it whenever you have an idea you don't want to forget, or even when you simply have nothing else to do. These free writings will help you become a better writer.

The Result . . .

- **Review your writings and underline the ideas you like.** These ideas will often serve as the basis for more formal writings.
- **Make sure a free-writing idea meets the requirements of an assignment;** also make sure it's one you feel good about sharing.
- **Determine exactly what you plan (or are required) to write about;** add specific details as necessary. (This may require a second free writing.)
- **Listen to and read the free writings of others;** learn from them.

021 Guidelines for Searching and Shaping a Subject

The following activities will help you develop your subjects for writing. If you already have a good "feel" for a particular writing subject, you might attempt only one of the activities. If you need to explore your idea in some detail and time permits, you might attempt two or more of the activities.

Free Writing At this point, you can approach free writing in two different ways. You can do a focused free writing to see how many ideas come to mind about your subject as you write, or you can approach your free writing as if it were an instant version of the finished product. An instant version will give you a good feel for your subject and will also tell you how much you know or need to find out about it.

Clustering Try clustering again, this time with your subject as the nucleus word. This clustering will naturally be more focused or structured than your earlier prewriting cluster since you now have a specific subject in mind. (See 017 for a model cluster.)

5 W's of Writing Answer the 5 W's—Who? What? Where? When? and Why?—to identify basic information about your subject. (You can add How? to the list for even better coverage.)

Directed Free Writing Do a variation of free writing by selecting one of the six thinking modes below and writing whatever comes to mind. (Repeat the process as often as you need to, selecting a different mode each time.)

Describe it. What do you see, hear, feel, smell, taste . . . ?

Compare it. What is it like? What is it different from?

Associate it. What connections between this and something else come to mind?

Analyze it. What parts does it have? How do they work (or not work) together?

Apply it. What can you do with it? How can you use it?

Argue for or against it. What do you like about it? Not like about it? What are its good points? Its bad points?

Imaginary Dialogue Create an imaginary dialogue between two people in which your specific subject is the topic of the conversation. The two speakers should build on each other's comments or give them a new "spin."

Audience Appeal Select a specific audience to address in an exploratory writing. Consider a group of preschoolers, a live television audience, readers of a popular teen magazine, a panel of experts, the local school board . . .

Structured Questions Answering structured questions will help you understand what is important or unique about your writing idea.

   a. What makes your subject different from others that are similar to it?
   b. How is your subject changing?
   c. How does your subject fit into his or her (its) world or environment?
   d. What larger group is your subject a part of? What are the features of this larger group?
   e. What features make your subject part of this larger group?
   f. What features make your subject different from this group?
   g. What other questions can you think of?

Offbeat (Unstructured) Questions Creating and answering offbeat questions will help you see your writing idea in different ways. The sample questions that follow suggest a number of offbeat ways to look at different types of writing subjects.

Writing About a Person
● What type of clothing is he (she) like?
● What does his (her) menu look like?

Writing About a Place
● What is the place's best sense (sight, smell, hearing, etc.)?
● Where does this place go for advice?

Writing About an Object
● What does this object look like upside down?
● What kind of shadow does it cast?

Writing About an Issue or Event
● What kind of car would you drive to this event?
● What machine does it most resemble?

Writing to Persuade
● What clubs or organizations would your argument or viewpoint join?
● Would your argument take the stairs or the elevator?

Writing to Explain a Process
● What restaurant is this process like?
● Where in a hardware store would this process feel most at home?

Writing a Narrative
● What fruit does this story resemble?
● What would your great-grandmother say about this story?

 Consider answering your structured and unstructured questions in the form of mini-free writings (5 minutes) to unlock creative ideas. You might also consider answering your questions with the help of a friend or writing group.

023 Taking Inventory of Your Thoughts

Let's say you still don't feel comfortable with your subject after thinking and writing about it. That is, you've done some searching and you've discovered some interesting things about your writing idea, but you still don't feel ready to write a first draft. Now may be a good time to see how well you match up with your subject.

After carefully considering the questions that follow, you should be able to decide whether to move ahead or look for another approach or even another subject.

Assignment: What are the specific requirements of this assignment?

Do I have enough time to do a good job with this subject?

Self: How committed am I to my writing subject?

What can I learn or gain if I continue writing on this topic?

Subject: How much do I now know about this subject?

Is additional information available?

Have I tried any of the searching activities? (See 021-022.)

Purpose: Why am I writing?

Do I want to inform, entertain, explain, or persuade?

Audience: Who is my audience and what response do I want from them?

How much do they care or already know about this subject?

How can I get my audience interested in my ideas?

Form: In what form could I present my ideas: story, essay, poem, personal narrative, parody, interview? (See 135.)

Can I think of an especially interesting way to lead into my paper?

> "An effective piece of writing has focus. There is a controlling vision that orders what is being said."
>
> —Donald Murray

024 Focusing Your Efforts

Sooner or later you will feel the urge to say to your readers exactly what you think and what you alone are best suited to say about a particular subject. This idea or feeling should be your focus. A **focus** is a meaningful and interesting way to write about your subject.

025 Forming a Focus Statement

State your focus in a sentence that you feel effectively expresses what you want to explore in your essay. A focus statement usually expresses a specific feeling about a subject or highlights a specific feature of it. Write as many versions as it takes to come up with a sentence that establishes the right tone and direction for your writing. Use the following formula if you have trouble forming that statement:

> **Formula:** A specific subject *(Bungee jumping)*
> + a specific feeling or feature *(stretches safety to the limit)*
> = an effective focus or thesis statement.

Note • A focus statement is often called a *thesis statement*. It is also similar to a topic sentence, the controlling idea in a paragraph. (See 103.)

026 Designing a Writing Plan

With a clear focus in mind, you may be ready to start your first draft. If so, have a nice trip. If, however, you are a careful mind traveler, or your subject is quite complex, you may need to design a writing plan before you start your first draft. Your plan can be anything from a brief list of ideas to a detailed sentence outline. (See 119.) Use the guidelines that follow to help you plan and organize your writing:

1. Study your focus statement. It may suggest a logical method of organization for your writing.

2. Review all of the facts and details you have produced so far to see if an overall pattern of organization begins to emerge.

3. Consider the methods of organization listed in the handbook. (See 112.)

4. Organize your ideas in some kind of list, cluster, or outline.

5. If nothing seems to work, consider gathering more information, or simply write your first draft to see what unfolds.

"The first draft is a discovery draft—a vision of what might be."

—Donald Murray

A Guide to Drafting

027   This is it. You're into your first draft, your first complete look at your writing idea. All of your searching and planning have led up to this point. Write as much of your first draft as possible in your first sitting while all of your prewriting is still fresh in your mind. Refer to your planning notes as you write, but be flexible. A more interesting path of travel may unfold during the drafting process. Concentrate on developing your ideas, not on producing neat copy. Remember that first drafts are often called *rough* drafts. Keep these additional points in mind during the drafting stage:

- ◉ Speak naturally and honestly so the real you comes through in your writing.
- ◉ Pay special attention to your opening paragraph. It should grab your readers' attention and identify the focus of your writing.
- ◉ Develop the main part of your draft with as much detail as possible.
- ◉ Continue writing until you make all of your main points, or you come to a logical stopping point.

If you get stuck at any point during the drafting process, turn to the appropriate strategy listed below for help.

On the following pages:

028 Writing Naturally

Write naturally. Be yourself, they say. But, you say, I don't like the way I "naturally" write. It never sounds natural, for one thing. Sometimes it even sounds dumb or boring. Don't worry. Your writing will seem natural and pleasing if you keep one thought above all others: **The writer is never alone.** Your writing is one-half of a conversation with a reader you invent. Talk to your "silent partner."

1. **Clustering and free writing can help you write in your true "voice."**

2. **Know your subject.**
   A good knowledge base makes the job of drafting much easier.

3. **Be honest; don't try to fake it.**
   Readers are drawn to writers who are honest and trustworthy.

4. **Be personally involved in your writing.**
   Share your personal thoughts and feelings; make connections between your subject and your own experience.

5. **Be at ease; don't rush or nervously bounce around.**
   Think about what you've already said—repeat it in your mind or on paper—and let that help you decide what you should say next.

> "Voice is the imprint of ourselves in our writing. Take the voice away . . . and there's no writing, just words following words."
>
> —Donald Graves

029 A Natural Writing Style in Action

To develop a natural writing style, write about subjects that genuinely interest you, and tell good stories about these subjects, stories that share real feelings and specific details. The following excerpt from "The Bike" by Tony Rogers speaks naturally. As you will see, he genuinely cares about his subject and is able to bring it to life for his readers. (The writer capitalizes "The Bike" throughout the narrative.)

The Bike hung from its own spot in the ceiling next to the big front window, away from the other bikes. Dad and I would stare up at the glossy paint and shimmering spokes as the wheels spun lazily around. My eyes would travel along The Bike's exquisite lines and trace through the intricate pattern of bolts and springs that all joined together to form a brake or a shift lever. The price was written in black marker on a cardboard rectangle and knotted with twine to the handlebars. It was steep. The price was one that would typically accompany such a work of art, or a particularly rare vintage wine. Suddenly The Bike escaped like smoke through my fingers. Dad had seen the glint in my eye, but, "It's just too expensive," he said.

030 Writing an Opening or Lead Paragraph

Writing your opening or lead paragraph should help clarify your thinking on your writing subject, and it should set a number of things in motion: It should (1) point the way into your essay, (2) spark your readers' interest, (3) commit you to a certain language, and (4) establish a frame, or form, for your writing. It is one of the most important elements of each composition you write. Several possible starting points are listed below.

- Begin with a funny story to set a humorous tone.
- Challenge your readers with a thought-provoking question.
- Open with an impressive or fitting quotation.
- Offer a little "sip" of the conclusion to get your readers' attention.
- List all your main points and treat your subject in a very serious, straightforward manner.
- Provide a dramatic or eye-opening statement.
- Come up with an angle that none of your readers have seen before.

Remember: The angle you use in your opening will affect the direction and style of your entire piece of writing. This is why your opening, your angle, is so important.

031 Sample Opening Paragraph

In the following sample opening, student writer Donna Actie begins with four dramatic ideas that immediately get the readers' attention. She then challenges readers with a thought-provoking question: "Why do so many of us have problems at school?" In her brief analysis of this question, the writer identifies the subject of her essay, the dangers of lead poisoning.

Get the Lead Out!

Low grades on exams. Failing classes. Lack of interest in school. Plans of dropping out. Why do so many of us have problems at school? There are many reasons: drugs, poverty, poor schools . . . But there's another reason you may not have heard about—lead poisoning. Recent studies indicate that young children exposed to even low levels of lead often face major difficulties later in life.

If you have been successful in writing an opening paragraph, you should have a pretty good idea of how the rest of your first draft will develop. Your opening paragraph should also establish the tone for the rest of your writing. In the sample above, the writer has clearly established a serious tone to reflect the seriousness of her subject.

 INSIDE info

A form usually unfolds naturally as you write, so don't worry if you can't see too far into your first draft. Remember that your destination is often unknown in mind traveling. That's part of the fun of taking the trip in the first place.

032 Selecting a Method of Development

Chris bought the first pair of shoes she tried on. The style, the color, and the fit were that good. Larry tried on five pairs of shoes before he found what he was looking for. Not unusual. Sometimes we know that the first thing we try on is right for us; other times we aren't so sure. The same holds true with the way you develop your ideas in a piece of writing. At times, the first method that comes to mind will be the logical approach. (Narration, for example, is the method you would use when sharing a reminiscence.) At other times, you will have to do some comparison shopping before you feel comfortable with a method for developing your writing.

Several methods are listed here. Any one of them can help you shape your writing. You may choose to . . .

<u>narrate:</u> tell a story or re-create an experience. (See 105 and 283-293.)

<u>describe:</u> tell in detail how something or someone appeared. (See 106 and 297-298.)

<u>define:</u> clarify or explain the meaning of a term, idea, or concept. (See 363-364.)

<u>explain:</u> prove a point by providing specific examples or reasons.

<u>analyze:</u> break down a thing or a process into its parts and subparts.

<u>classify:</u> divide a large and complex set of things into smaller groups and identify each group.

<u>compare:</u> measure one thing against something more or less like it, or explain something new or complex by using an analogy to something quite familiar. (See 359-360.)

<u>argue:</u> use logic and evidence to prove that something is true or that something should be done. (See 365-367.)

 INSIDE info

In a longer composition you might begin with one method of development, but utilize other methods once you get into the piece. For example, in an essay of definition, you may, among other things, attempt to classify your subject, compare it to something similar, and share a brief story (anecdote) about it.

033 Bringing Your Writing to a Close

Sometimes your writing will come to an effective stopping point after the last main point is made. Whenever that is the case, don't try to tack on a closing paragraph. Leave well enough alone.

Closing paragraphs are important when you feel it is necessary to tie up any loose ends or clarify certain points in the body of your writing. You may also want to leave readers with a final thought that helps them see the importance of your message. Experiment with a number of possible endings before you settle on one. (For ideas, check the endings of the models in "Forms of Writing.")

"It's never perfect when I write it down the first time, or the second time, or the fifth time. But it always gets better as I go over it and over it."

—Jane Yolen

A Guide to Revising

034   The first step in the revising process is to review your first draft to see how you feel about it . . . and to see how much work you have ahead of you. Use these questions as a basic guide when you review a first draft:

- Is the content interesting and worth sharing?
- Is the style natural and effective in getting my message across?
- Are there any major gaps or soft spots in my writing?
- How can I improve what I have done so far?

035 Improving Your Writing

Once you have a good feel for your first draft, you're ready to turn it into a more complete and effective piece of writing. In very basic terms, that is what revising is all about—making changes in your writing until it says exactly what you want it to say. How many changes you make depends on the quality of your first draft and your commitment to your writing. Someone once asked writer Ernest Hemingway why he rewrote one of his endings 27 times. Hemingway answered, "It wasn't right." (That's commitment.)

Whenever you have a specific question about revising a piece of writing, turn to one of the strategies listed below for help.

On the following pages:

> "I work on a word processor for the first drafts, but for revisions, I always print out a copy . . . and do my corrections by hand."
>
> —Betsy Byars

036 Using Basic Revising Strategies

Making the Right Moves

No writer gets it right the first time. Few writers get it right the second time. In fact, professional writers often have to write a number of revisions before they are satisfied with their work. Don't be surprised if you have to do the same. The guidelines that follow will help you work your first draft into shape once you read and review it:

◉ **First, look at the big picture.** Take it all in. Decide if there is a focus or main idea either stated or suggested in your writing. If you can't find the focus, write one. Or, if your original thinking on your subject has changed, write a new focus statement.

◉ **Then, look at specific chunks of information** in your writing and reorder them, if you feel they could be arranged more effectively.

◉ **Also, cut information** that doesn't support your focus; **add information** if you feel additional points need to be made. Make sure that your writing answers the basic questions your readers may have; **rewrite parts** that aren't as clear as you would like them to be.

◉ **Finally,** look very closely at your writing style and **refine it** so your ideas are interesting, colorful, and smooth reading.

Remember that the paragraph is the basic unit of information in almost all academic writing. Each of your paragraphs should develop an important point related to your subject. In addition, each paragraph should serve as an effective link to the information that comes before it and after it.

037 Revising on the Run

Writer Peter Elbow recommends "cut-and-paste revising" when you have very little time to make changes in your writing. For example, let's say you are working on an in-class writing assignment, and you have only 15 minutes to revise your writing. The five steps that follow describe this quick revising technique:

1. Don't add any new information to your writing.
2. Remove unnecessary facts and details.
3. Find the best possible information and go with it.
4. Put the pieces in the best possible order.
5. Do what little rewriting is necessary.

⬤038 The R-R-R-R-Revising Strategy

The 5-R's strategy covers everything from reading the first draft to reworking parts of the writing, from reflecting on the changes you make to refining or polishing the revised copy. (If you're looking for an in-depth revising strategy, you've just found it.)

READ: Sometimes it's hard to keep an open mind when you read your first draft. You need to put some distance between yourself and your writing.

- Whenever possible, put your writing aside for a day or two.
- Read it out loud.
- Ask others (family, friends, classmates) to read it out loud to you.
- Listen to your writing: How does it sound? What does it say?

REACT: Here are six questions that will help you react to your own writing on the second or third read-through:

- What parts of my writing work for me?
- Do all of these parts work together? Are they logical?
- Do all the parts point to one idea? What is the main idea?
- Do the parts say what I want them to say?
- Have I arranged the parts in the best possible order?
- Where do I need to go from here?

REWORK: Reworking your writing means making changes until all of the parts work equally well. There is usually plenty of reworking to do in the early stages of writing.

REFLECT: One of the best ways of keeping track of your revising progress is to write comments in the margins of your paper. Margins are the perfect place for you to explore your feelings concerning what you have written. Here are some guidelines:

- Explore your thoughts freely and naturally.
- Note what you plan to cut, move, explain further, and so on.
- Reflect upon the changes you make. (How do they work?)
- If you are unsure of what to do, write down a question to solve later.

REFINE: Refining is putting some style into your written copy—shining up your thoughts and words. Here's what you can do:

- Read your paper out loud to make sure that you haven't missed anything.
- Listen for both the clarity and quality of your words and sentences.
- Make the final adjustments so your writing reads smoothly and clearly.

039 Making Your Writing More Interesting

Escaping the "Badlands"

The later stage of revising is one of the most important in the whole composing process. Why? Because here you can escape the "badlands" of writing—those stretches of uninspired words and ideas that can make writing seem boring. Use these questions as a guide to check for problem areas.

1. **Is your topic worn-out?** "My Weekend at the State Tournament," for example. With a new twist you can revive it: "March Madness!"

2. **Is your purpose stale?** If you have been writing merely to please a teacher or to get a good grade, start again. But this time try writing to learn something or to trigger a particular emotion in your readers. You may find your new purpose refreshing.

3. **Is your voice predictable or fake?** If it is ("A good time was had by all"), start again. This time, be honest. Be real.

4. **Does your first draft sound boring?** Maybe it's boring because it pays an equal amount of attention to everything. Shorten some parts by summarizing them; lengthen others by explaining. If you're sharing a story, skim through the less significant parts by "telling" what happened; then focus on the more important parts by "showing" what happened. Summarize and explain. Tell and show. These powerful shaping tools help you control your writing.

5. **Does your essay follow the "formula" too closely?** The "Five-Paragraph Essay" (Introduction, Three Main Points, Conclusion) provides you with an important organizing frame to build on. However, if this frame is followed too closely, it may actually get in the way. So read your draft again, and the first time your inner voice starts saying "formula, formula," cross out some words and start blazing a more unpredictable trail.

 INSIDE info

Think of revising as a special opportunity rather than a chore. Try a number of different things to make your writing come to life. If you need to refuel your thinking at any point during the revising process, consider using one of the prewriting activities listed in the handbook.

Reviewing the Opening and Closing Paragraphs

After making changes in the body of your writing, you may need to change the opening paragraph as well. Make sure that it draws your reader into the main part of your paper and accurately introduces the focus of your writing. (See 030.) Also review (or write) the closing paragraph for your essay. The closing should tie up any loose ends left in the body of your paper and remind readers of the importance of your subject. Remember, however, that it may not be necessary to add a closing paragraph if your writing comes to an effective stopping point after the last main point is made.

⟨040⟩ Using the Right Level of Language
T-Shirts or Tuxedoes?

As you revise, be sure your word choice sticks to an appropriate level of language or diction. Your choice of words should reflect and reinforce the purpose of a particular writing assignment. For example, you might write a story in which jazzy street language or **slang** is appropriate.

> Darrell is about 22 and fits the "livin' phat" myth: mad money, gear, phat car, and a beeper.
>
> This little herb thinks he is so bad and that he's down with everybody.

Or, you might write a composition in which the **informal English** (also known as colloquial English) used in casual conversation is the best choice. Informal English is characterized by contractions, sentence fragments, popular expressions (you know, like, forget it), cliches (like a chicken with its head cut off), and frequent references to oneself (I couldn't quite figure out . . .).

> We weren't afraid to admit we were scared silly when the cops stopped us that time. Who wouldn't be?

Or you might write an essay or a research paper in which the word choice meets the standards of **semiformal English**. When writing is published, it usually is edited to meet such standards. In semiformal English, slang and conversational phrases are replaced by more carefully chosen words:

> Semiformal English, such as you are reading in this sentence, is worded correctly and cautiously so that it can withstand repeated readings without seeming tiresome, sloppy, or cute.

Note • For special purposes, like permanent documents or specialized instruction manuals, formal or technical diction may be required.

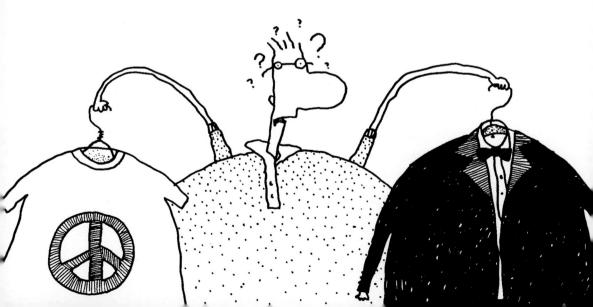

> "Advice to young writers? Always the same advice: learn to trust your own judgment, learn inner independence, learn to trust that time will sort the good from the bad."
>
> —Doris Lessing

041 Checking the Style of Your Writing

Don't worry too much about style as long as you still face major questions concerning the content, focus, and organization of your writing. All of the reviewing, reworking, and refining that you do will naturally bear the stamp of your personal style. But at some point, you will want to look closely at your writing to make sure that all of your ideas speak clearly and effectively.

What follows is a list of basic reminders that will help you check your writing for style. (Refer to "Style" in the index for more information.)

1. **Write clearly.** Clarity is the foundation of good writing. Until your ideas are clearly expressed, nothing else really matters.

2. **Strive for simplicity.** Essayist E. B. White advises young writers to "approach style by way of simplicity, plainness, orderliness, and sincerity." That's good advice from one of America's most stylish writers.

3. **Know when your writing doesn't work.** Watch for sentences that all sound the same and sentences that hang limp like wet wash. Rely on your writer's sixth sense to help you sort the good from the bad in your writing.

4. **Know when to cut.** And as writer Kurt Vonnegut says, "Have the guts to do it." Cut any words and phrases that don't strengthen your sentences and any sentences that don't strengthen your paragraphs.

5. **Write with details** (examples, figures of speech, anecdotes, etc.). Writing without details is like baking bread without yeast. One of the most important ingredients is missing. But be careful. Your writing will sound forced if you overdo the details.

6. **Write with specific nouns and verbs.** Writing with specific nouns (Bruce Springsteen) and verbs (swaggers) gives your writing energy. Writing with vague nouns (man) and weak verbs (is, are, was, were, etc.) forces you to use a lot of modifiers.

7. **Write active, forward-moving sentences.** Make it clear in your sentences that your subject is doing something (Anita asked . . . , He rebelled . . . , Marine biologists discovered . . . , A new theory states . . .).

 INSIDE info

Many of the writers considered to be the best stylists write in an "invisible" style. That is, their thoughts and ideas always come first, and their language, though it may be interesting or colorful, never draws attention to itself.

042 Group Advising and Revising

All writers can benefit from an interested audience, especially one that offers constructive and honest advice during a writing project. And who could make a better audience than your fellow writers? Some of you might already work in writing groups, so you know the value of writers sharing their work. Others of you might want to start a writing group so you, too, can experience the benefits.

How exactly can a writing group help you? For starters, your fellow writers can tell you what does and doesn't work for them in your writing. This feedback is valuable throughout the writing process; but it is especially helpful early in the revising process so you can find out if your writing idea is one others would really be interested in reading about.

Some experts go so far as to say that talking about writing is *the* most important step in the process of writing. By sharing ideas and concerns, a community spirit will develop, a spirit that will help make writing a meaningful and exciting process of learning rather than just another assignment. This enthusiasm is bound to have a positive effect on the final product.

> "At first, I thought, 'Why bother?' What did we know about writing? I resented the group discussions about my writing and offered very few suggestions for the others. It took me awhile to realize that in my small group we were talking about what we each really needed right now, for this paper. That was something even the teacher couldn't tell me."
>
> —Paul, a student

043 Maintaining Good Relations

To maintain good relations among group members, focus your comments on specific things you see and hear in the writing. For example, an observation such as "I noticed many 'There is' statements in your opening" will mean much more to a writer than a general, personal comment such as "Your opening is so boring" or "Put some life into your opening." The specific observation helps the writer see a problem without hurting his or her confidence.

Give praise when praise is due, but base it on something you observe or feel in the writing. For example, here is a meaningful compliment based on a specific observation: "The series of questions and answers is an effective way to organize your essay." And here is an example of an honest, helpful reaction to a piece of writing: "There is an energy in this writing that I really like."

take note At first, your observations may seem limited. You may only be able to comment on the nice sound the writing has, a surprising detail, the length or brevity of the writing, or a point you don't understand. Fine. Just keep trying—and listening. Your ability to make a variety of observations will naturally improve with practice.

044 Writing Group Guidelines

The guidelines that follow will help you conduct effective group revising sessions.

The Author/Writer

◉ **Come prepared with a substantial piece of writing.** Prepare a copy for each group member if this is part of normal group procedure.

◉ **Introduce your writing.** However, don't say too much; let your writing do the talking.

◉ **Read your copy out loud.** Speak confidently and clearly.

◉ **As the group reacts to your writing, listen carefully and take brief notes.** Don't be defensive about your writing, since this will stop some members from commenting honestly about your work. Answer all of their questions.

◉ **If you have some special concerns or problems, share these with your fellow writers.**

The Group Members

◉ **Listen carefully as the writer reads.** Take notes, but make them brief so that you don't miss part of the reading. You may find it more helpful to listen to the entire work, and then do a mini-free writing immediately after the reading. (There are other reaction methods to choose from, as well. See 045-048 for four strategies.)

◉ **Keep your comments positive and constructive.**

◉ **Focus your comments as much as you can on specific things you observe in the writing.**

◉ **Ask questions of the author:** "Why? How? What do you mean when you say . . . ?" And answer questions the author might have for you.

◉ **Listen to other comments and add to them.** In this way, you help each other become better writers.

Group Revising Strategies

CRITIQUING A PAPER

A Checklist for Critiquing a Paper

Use the checklist that follows to help you evaluate compositions during group revising sessions.

Purpose: Does the writer have a clear purpose in mind? That is, is it clear that the writer is trying to entertain, to inform, to persuade, etc.?

Audience: Does the writing address a specific audience? And will the readers understand and appreciate this subject?

Form: Is the subject presented in an effective or appropriate form?

Content: Does the writer consider the subject from a number of angles? For example, does he or she try to compare, classify, define, and/or analyze the writing idea?

Writing Devices: Does the writing include any figures of speech, anecdotes, dialogue, specific examples, etc.? Which ones are most effective?

Voice: Does the writing sound sincere and honest? That is, do you "hear" the writer when you read his or her paper?

Personal Thoughts and Comments: Does the writer include any personal thoughts or comments in the writing? Are they needed or desirable?

Purpose Again: Does the writing succeed in making a person smile, nod, or react in some other way? What is especially good about the writing?

REACTING TO WRITING

Peter Elbow, in *Writing Without Teachers,* offers four types of reactions group members might have to a piece of writing: *pointing, summarizing, telling,* and *showing.* **Pointing** refers to a reaction in which a group member "points out" words, phrases, or ideas in the writing that make a positive or negative impression on him or her. **Summarizing** refers to a reader's general reaction or understanding of the writing. It may be a list of main ideas, a sentence, or a word that gets at the heart of the writing.

Telling refers to readers expressing what happens as they read a piece: first this happens, then this happens, later this happens, and so on. **Showing** refers to feelings expressed about the piece. Elbow suggests that readers express these feelings metaphorically. A reader might, for example, refer to something in the writing as if it were a voice quality, a color, a shape, a type of clothing, etc. ("Why do I feel like I've been lectured to in this essay?" or "Your writing has a neat, tailored quality to it.")

047 ## GOOD WRITING: A MATTER OF CHOICE

What makes for good writing? Six basic points appear on the lists of most experienced writers. Use these points as a guide during group revising sessions. Good writing is . . .

- **original** (the subject or the way the subject is covered is lively and energized),
- **organized** (the ideas are presented in a sensible order),
- **detailed** (the details are specific and colorful),
- **clear** (the sentences clearly and smoothly move the writing forward),
- **correct** (the final product is clean and correct),
- and **effective** (the writing is interesting and informative).

048 ## FEELING YOUR OAQS

Here's a simple and effective four-step scheme you can use to comment on early drafts in group revising sessions:

Observe
Appreciate
Question
Suggest

- **Observe** means to notice what another person's essay is designed to do, and to say something about that design, or purpose. For example, you might say, "Even though you are writing about your boyfriend, it appears that you are trying to get a message across to your parents."

- **Appreciate** means to praise something in the writing that impresses or pleases you. You can find something to appreciate in any piece of writing. For example, you might say, "You have a wonderful main idea" or "With your description, I can actually see his broken tooth."

- **Question** means to ask whatever you want to know after you've read the essay. You might ask for background information, or a definition, or an interpretation, or an explanation. For example, you might say, "Why didn't you tell us what happened when you got to the emergency room?"

- **Suggest** means to give thoughtful advice about possible changes. Offer this advice honestly and courteously. Be specific, and be positive. For example, you might say, "With a little more physical detail—especially sound and smell—your third paragraph could be the highlight of the whole essay. What do you think?"

"No iron can pierce the heart with such force as a period put just at the right place."

—Isaac Babel

A Guide to Editing and Proofreading

049   There comes a point in any writing project (like a fast approaching due date) when you must prepare it for publication. At this point you must edit and proofread your revised writing so that it speaks clearly and accurately. Your first main concern when editing is to replace any words, phrases, and sentences that sound awkward or confusing. Then you should check your writing for spelling, usage, mechanics, and grammar errors.

050 Working Smart

    Make sure to ask a classmate or teacher to help you edit your writing. Also make sure to have all of the necessary editing tools on hand (handbook, dictionary, thesaurus, computer spell checker, etc.) when you work. Follow any guidelines provided by your teacher when preparing your final draft. Then proofread your finished product for errors before submitting it.

    The checklists and strategies listed below will help you edit and proofread your work. (The "Editing Checklist" focuses primarily on sentence style and clarity. The "Proofreading Checklist" focuses on spelling, usage, mechanics, and grammar errors.)

On the following pages:

051 Editing Checklist

Have you ever used a shopping or study list? Isn't it helpful to have your thoughts organized? The following checklist should help you each time you edit your writing. You might think of it as a "chopping" list, but it's really more: chopping, connecting, rearranging, polishing. . . .

1. Read your final draft aloud to test it for sense and sound. Better yet, have someone read it aloud to you. Listen carefully as he or she reads. Your writing should read smoothly and naturally. If it doesn't, you have more editing to do.

2. Does each sentence express a complete thought? Does each paragraph have an overall point or purpose?

3. Have you used different sentence types and lengths? Are any sentences too long and rambling? Do you use too many short, choppy sentences?

4. Have you used a variety of sentence beginnings? Watch out for too many sentences that begin with the same pronoun or article (*I, My, The, There,* etc.).

5. Check each simple sentence for effective use of modifiers, especially prepositional phrases, participial phrases, and appositives. Have you punctuated these modifiers correctly?

6. Check your compound sentences. Do they contain two equal ideas, and is the logical relationship between the two ideas expressed by the proper conjunction (*and* versus *but* versus *or* . . .)?

7. What about your complex sentences? Have you used the most appropriate subordinating conjunction (*although, before, because, since, when, while,* etc.) or relative pronoun (*that, who, which,* etc.) to connect the two clauses in these sentences?

8. Make sure your writing is concise and to the point. Have you omitted slang, wordiness, and flowery language? Strive for simplicity and clarity in your writing.

9. Is your writing fresh and original? Have you avoided overused words and phrases? If not, substitute nouns, verbs, and adjectives that are specific, vivid, and colorful.

10. Replace any words or phrases that may be awkward, confusing, or misleading.

052 Cut, Clarify, Condense

Would you like an easy and effective strategy for fixing problems with wording? Try the 3 C's of editing.

Editing Code:

- **CUT** [brackets]

  If you find a section in your writing that seems unnecessary or wordy, put brackets around it. If you later decide that this section is definitely unneeded, cut it.

- **CLARIFY** 〰〰〰

  If you see something confusing or unclear in your writing, put a wavy line under it. Then, when you go back to this section, reword it or add to it.

- **CONDENSE** (parentheses)

  If you come across part of your writing that is wordy or over-explained, put a set of parentheses around it. Then rewrite this section so that it reads more simply and clearly.

053 Testing Your Sentences

Another effective editing strategy is to test your sentences for variety, verb choice, and length. Here's how you can carry out this strategy:

- In one column on a piece of paper, list the opening words in each of your sentences. (Then decide if you need to vary some of your sentence beginnings.)

- In another column, list the verbs in each sentence. (Then decide if you need to replace any overused verbs—*is, are, see, look,* etc.—with more vivid ones.)

- In a third column, identify the number of words in each sentence. (Then decide if you need to change the length of some of your sentences.)

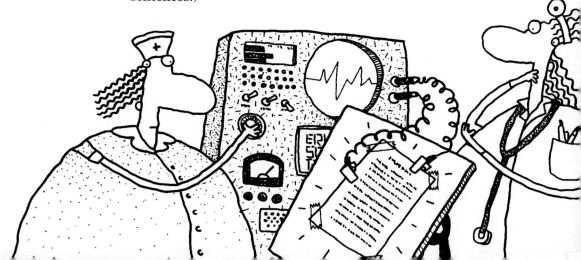

054 Proofreading Checklist

The following guidelines will help you check your writing for spelling, usage, mechanics, and grammar errors before you share it.

1. Have you spelled all your words correctly? Here are some tips:
   - Read your writing backward and aloud—one word at a time—so you focus on each word.
   - Circle each word you are unsure of.
   - For help, consult the list of commonly misspelled words in your handbook index under "Spelling, Commonly misspelled." (For additional help, check a dictionary.)

2. Does each sentence end with a punctuation mark?

3. Are coordinating conjunctions (*and, but, or, so,* etc.) in compound sentences preceded by a comma? Have you used commas to set off items listed in a series, after introductory clauses, and so on?

4. Have you used apostrophes to show possession or to mark contractions?

5. Is all dialogue or written conversation properly punctuated?

6. Do all complete sentences in general copy or in dialogue begin with a capital letter?

7. Have you capitalized the proper names of people, places, and things?

8. Have you misused any of the commonly mixed pairs of words: there/their/they're; accept/except? (Refer to the section "Using the Right Word" in your handbook or look in the index under "Usage, mixed pairs.")

9. Have you used any words, phrases, or sentences that may confuse the reader?

10. Do your subjects and verbs agree in number?

11. Do your pronouns agree with their antecedents?

12. Have you used any sentence fragments, run-ons, or rambling sentences?

13. Have you chosen an appropriate title if one is needed?

14. Is your paper labeled correctly with your name and the class's name?

15. Does the form meet the requirements of the assignment?

"Writing becomes real when it has an audience."

—Tom Liner

A Guide to Publishing

055   Publishing is the driving force behind writing. It makes all of your planning, drafting, and revising worth the effort. It helps you stay with a piece of writing longer and produce your best efforts. Publishing is to a writer what an exhibit is to an artist or a live performance is to a musician. It is why you have worked so hard in the first place—to create a finished product that effectively expresses your thoughts, feelings, and ideas.

056 Sharing Your Work

The most immediate and, by far, the most helpful form of publishing is sharing a finished piece with your writing group and teacher. Their reactions and responses to your work are invaluable to your growth as a writer. As writer and teacher Tom Liner says, "You learn ways to make your writing more effective by seeing its effect on others."

Submitting selected pieces to your school newspaper or literary magazine is another important form of publishing. The possibility of seeing a story or poem in print is a great incentive to produce your best work. Then, if you're really adventurous, you may want to submit a finished piece to a real-world publication, perhaps your daily newspaper or favorite magazine. But be forewarned: Your chances of getting published in a large-market publication are slim. Read through the list below for more publishing ideas.

- ◉ Include certain pieces in your writing portfolio.
- ◉ Enter a writing contest.
- ◉ Submit your work to a young writers' conference.
- ◉ Self-publish collections of your writing.
- ◉ Exhibit selections in a literary/art fair or in a class-project display.
- ◉ Establish an alternative forum for your work.

057 Preparing a Writing Portfolio

A portfolio is a collection of your best writing that you submit for assessment. It is different from the traditional writing folder (also known as a working folder) that contains writing in various stages of completion. Portfolios contain only your finished work. Compiling a portfolio allows you to participate in the assessment process. You decide what writing to include; you reflect upon your writing progress; you make sure that all the right pieces are in all the right places. You are pretty much in control.

What You Should Include

Most writing portfolios contain the following basic components. (Check with your teacher for the specific requirements.)

- A **table of contents** listing the information included in your portfolio.

- An **opening essay** or **letter** detailing the story behind your portfolio (how you compiled it, how you feel about it, what it means to you, etc.).

- A **specified number of finished pieces** representing your best writing in the class. Your teacher may require you to include all of your planning, drafting, and revising work for one or more of these pieces.

- A **best "other" piece** related to your work in another content area.

- A **cover sheet** attached to each piece of writing discussing the reason for its selection, the amount of work that went into it, and so on.

- **Evaluation sheets** or **checklists** charting, among other things, the basic skills you have mastered as well as the skills you still need to work on. Your teacher will supply these sheets.

How You Should Work

1. Keep track of all of your writing (including planning notes and drafts) throughout the term. This way, when it comes to compiling your portfolio, you will have the necessary pieces to work with.

2. Make sure that you understand all of the specific requirements for your portfolio.

3. Work with an expandable or pocket-type folder. You will avoid dog-eared or ripped pages if you keep the components in a "safe environment."

4. Maintain a regular working schedule. It will be impossible to produce an effective portfolio if you approach it as a last-minute project.

5. Develop a feeling of pride in your portfolio. Allow it to reflect as positive an image of yourself as possible. Look your best!

 INSIDE info

The guidelines provided on this page deal with a portfolio that showcases your abilities as a writer. You would normally submit this type of portfolio prior to a semester- or final-grading period.

058 Submitting a Manuscript

Q. What types of writing can I submit?

A. There are potential markets for all types of writing—essays, articles, short stories, plays, poems, children's books, novels, and so on. Newspapers, of course, will be more interested in essays and articles. With magazines, it depends. Some magazines publish nonfiction, fiction, and poetry; others focus exclusively on nonfiction.

Tip: Check the *Writer's Market* (Cincinnati, Writer's Digest Books, 1995) to find out who publishes what. If your school library doesn't have this resource, your city library will.

Q. Where should I submit my work?

A. You will probably have better success if you try to publish your work locally. Your area newspaper may invite submissions, as may your local historical society, arts council, and church for their publications. If you're interested in submitting something to a major-market publication, turn again to the *Writer's Market*. It lists almost every conceivable market (4,000, in fact), including a special section devoted exclusively to teen and young adult publications.

Q. How should I submit my work?

A. Check the publication's masthead for guidelines pertaining to submissions, or simply call the publication. (The masthead is the small print on one of the opening pages identifying key personnel, subscription rates, address, etc.) Most publications expect you to include . . .

- a brief cover letter (addressed to a specific editor) identifying the title of your piece, the word count, and so on;

- a neatly printed copy of your work with your name on each page—double-spaced and paper-clipped;

- and a SASE (self-addressed stamped envelope) large enough for your manuscript so it can be returned after it has been read.

Q. What should I expect?

A. First, you should expect to wait a long time to hear from the publication. (It may take up to two or three months.) Second, you should not be surprised or disappointed if your manuscript is not accepted. View your submission as a learning process, and keep writing and submitting.

The Basic Elements of Writing

"Easy writing makes hard reading."

—Ernest Hemingway

Writing with Style

059   Think about your hair. This morning when you first yawned into the mirror, you had to choose: Shall I wash my hair? Shall I comb it? Shall I blow it dry? Shall I use mousse, gel, or spritz? Shall I try something new? Shall I braid it, rubber-band it, slick it, or just leave it? Do I want my football number shaved in back or shall I get a Mohawk? Whatever you do—or don't do—that is your style.

Your writing style, similarly, comes from a series of choices that makes your writing yours. It is your words, your sentences, and your paragraphs—nobody else's. Fortunately, as a writer, you don't have to change your style every month or two to be in fashion. Your writing will always be in style if you do everything possible to make sure that it sounds like you, an honest and interested writer.

Think of Your Readers

Why is it important to write with style? "Do so, if for no other reason, out of respect for your readers," says novelist Kurt Vonnegut. If your writing is dull and predictable, your readers will think that you don't care about your subject, or about them. They, in turn, will show little interest in your writing. On the other hand, if you speak honestly in your writing, and engage your reader's interest, he or she will appreciate everything you have to say.

what's ahead?   The first part of this chapter discusses traits of an effective style and common ailments of style. What follows are explanations of many important techniques that add style to your writing: showing versus telling, making comparisons, using strong, colorful words, and using repetition.

060 Traits of an Effective Style

View the growth of your personal style as a lifelong challenge and each new writing project as a chance to improve upon it. Set a high standard for yourself. If you want your style to live, as writers say, you must always reach for something higher than before. Evaluate your writing style in a particular piece of writing using the following traits as a guide. (Also see 041.)

Focus ● Stylistic writing displays a clear focus or purpose. It stems from a specific feeling you have about your subject. It attempts to entertain, explain, surprise, or persuade. It uses one word when one word will do, one sentence when one sentence will do. It is clearly under your control.

Concreteness ● Stylistic writing is precise and colorful. It helps readers see, hear, and feel things. Instead of general terms like *animal, sea creature, emotion,* or *Mexican sauce,* it contains specific ones like *schnauzer, bottlenose dolphin, heartfelt admiration,* or *tongue-numbing salsa.*

Vitality ● Stylistic writing is lively. It crackles with energy. Instead of a lazy, "just-get-it-done" feeling, it shows signs of emotion and intensity. To achieve vitality in your writing, speak honestly about your subject, share personal experiences, and provide plenty of interesting information.

Originality ● Stylistic writing is fresh and original. It involves risk taking, perhaps using a negative definition (what something is not) or a poetic expression to make an important point. It may also involve purposely breaking a rule, perhaps using a sentence fragment or a long, rambling idea for dramatic effect.

Grace ● Stylistic writing contains no unnecessary bumps or rough spots. It links important ideas from sentence to sentence and from paragraph to paragraph. It reads smoothly and clearly from start to finish. Grace is achieved by working and reworking your ideas many, many times.

Commitment ● Stylistic writing begins and ends with commitment. If you feel strongly about a writing idea—be it your love for a guitar or your strong attachment to a keepsake—you're ready to give it the proper attention.

Common Ailments of Style

061 Primer Style

The Ailment: If your writing contains many short sentences, one right after another, it may sound like a grade-school textbook, or "primer."

> Our policy for makeup assignments is unfair. The teachers go strictly by the rules. They don't care about the amount of work you have. They don't care about your other activities. You must complete missing work within three school days. No credit is given after that.

The Cure: The main cure is to combine some of your ideas into longer, smoother-reading sentences. Here's the same passage revised:

> When it comes to makeup assignments, our teachers go strictly by the rules. They don't care about the amount of work you have or about your other responsibilities. You must complete missing work within three school days; otherwise, you receive no credit.

062 Passive Voice

The Ailment: If your writing seems slow moving and impersonal, you may have used too many passive verbs. With passive verbs, the subject of the sentence is the receiver of the action: *The sky was struck by lightning.* Here's an example passage written in the passive voice:

> Our biology teacher was greatly loved by us. He was often asked for extra help, which was always given. He was visited by his students before and after school and often was the object of our personal jokes and sincere praises.

The Cure: Unless you need a passive verb, change it to the active voice: *Lightning struck the sky.* Here is the passage written in the active voice:

> We loved our biology teacher. We were always asking for extra help, and he was always willing to give it. Students often dropped in before or after school to visit, study, or play a practical joke.

063 Insecurity

The Ailment: Does your writing contain many qualifiers (*to be perfectly honest, to tell the truth,* etc.) or intensifiers (*really, truly,* etc.)? These words and phrases may suggest that you lack confidence in your ideas:

> I totally and completely agree with Mr. Grim about changing the school's drug policy, but that's only my opinion.

The Cure: Visualize yourself standing before an audience and say exactly what you mean. Here is the revised example:

> I agree with Mr. Grim about changing our school's drug policy.

For other ailments of style, see "Wordiness" (095), "Flowery Language" (091), "Jargon" (093), and "Cliche" (096).

064 Showing Versus Telling

Writer Donald Murray suggests that you put people in your writing whose actions communicate important ideas for you. Brief "slices of life" add spark to your writing. They allow you to **show** your readers something in a lively and interesting manner rather than **tell** them matter-of-factly.

Example No. 1:

In the following passage, student writer Sheila Maldonado shares a slice of life about her Coney Island (New York) neighborhood:

> Under the boardwalk, a few homeless people find shelter; they hang up sheets and lay out their old clothes, empty cans, and plastic bags full of things they've collected on the streets. Even though the boardwalk doesn't provide them with walls, it does give them a roof over their heads. In the winter, they make fires on the beach and keep warm in tents. Some of them even have dogs, strays that probably approached them for food one day and stayed.

Discussion: This brief story shows us real people doing real things. It helps bring part of Coney Island alive for readers. It is much more revealing than a basic telling statement like "Some homeless people live around Coney Island."

Example No. 2:

In this passage, professional writer Mary Anne Hoff shares the story of a visitor to her childhood home, North Dakota:

> His "bee-yoo-tee-ful" stopped me short. This lanky Mr. Sophisticate from just outside Paris was describing the North Dakota prairie. The wild grasses and big sky, the black-eyed Susan and sagebrush, the hum of dog days were new to him. Now all he could say as he lay exhausted in Mother's recliner was "bee-yoo-tee-ful."
>
> Two days later we all huddled around a book about Paris, every picture in full color. Suddenly our guest pointed to a photo and repeated "bee-yoo-tee-ful." It was the Champs Elysee at night. The Champs Elysee and the North Dakota prairie described with the same word? My prairie and a Parisian street linked? That was when I knew I would like him.

Discussion: Notice how much more effective this story is than a telling state-ment like "A visitor helped me see my North Dakota home in a new way." All of the wonderful details help readers share in the experience.

INSIDE info

How do you show in writing? Think in terms of the 5 W's and H *(who? what? when? where? why?* and *how?).* Make sure that your brief stories answer these questions. Also think in terms of the three different types of details: sensory, memory, and reflective. (See 111.)

"Metaphors create tension and excitement by producing new connections, and in doing so reveal a truth about the world we had not previously recognized."

—Gabriele Rico

065 Writing Metaphorically

A **metaphor** connects an idea or image in your writing to something new and unexpected and creates a powerful picture for your readers. (Remember that a metaphor connects two ideas without using *like* or *as.*) In the following examples, notice how the basic ideas come to life when they are stated metaphorically:

Basic Idea: My performance was a real disappointment.

Stated Metaphorically:

> My performance was a real choke sandwich, all peanut butter and no jelly.

Basic Idea: Our mothers were strong.

Stated Metaphorically:

> Our mothers were headragged generals.   —Alice Walker

Extending a Metaphor

Sometimes a metaphor can serve as the unifying element throughout a series of sentences. Extending a metaphor in this way helps you expand or clarify an idea in your writing. You can use an **extended metaphor** to describe a scene, an event, a character, or a feeling. Notice how a metaphor (using references to cloth to describe a family reunion) is effectively extended in the following passage:

> The **loose ends** of my family were **reknitted** at our July reunion. Whatever feelings had been **torn** over my older brother's divorce, whatever emotions had **frayed** over my grandmother's lingering illness, they were **mended** in a long day of boating, fishing, and board games played quietly under the river oaks.

Note ● Extending a metaphor works best for special effect. If this technique is overused, it will sound forced or artificial.

Making Metaphors Work

- **Create original comparisons:** The student who wrote "Demi Moore's last movie sent me to the moon" has spent too much time gazing into space and not enough time creating fresh comparisons.
- **Be clear in your thinking:** The student who wrote "Homelessness is a thorn in the city's image" has created a confusing figure of speech. Homelessness may be a thorn in the city's side, but not in its image.
- **Be consistent:** The reporter who wrote "In the final debate, Senator Jones dodged each of his opponent's accusations and eventually scored the winning shot" has created a *mixed metaphor.* He shifts from one comparison (boxing) to another (basketball).

066 Using Strong, Colorful Words

Suppose, in your mind, you see a soaring power forward, with the ball held high in his right hand, slam home a dunk shot. Now, suppose you write "The forward scored a basket." How clearly do you think you have communicated this thought? Obviously, not very clearly. By using specific words, you can create clear and colorful word pictures for your reader.

067 **Choose specific nouns:** Some nouns are general *(car, jacket, animal)* and give the reader a vague, uninteresting picture. Other nouns are specific *(Mustang, aviator's jacket, raccoon)* and give the reader a much clearer, more detailed picture. In the chart that follows, the first word in each category is a general noun. The second word is more specific. Finally, each word at the bottom of the chart is clearly a specific noun. These last nouns are the type that can make your writing clear and colorful.

General to Specific Nouns

person	*place*	*thing*	*idea*
woman	park	drink	pain
writer	baseball park	nutritious drink	headache
Toni Morrison	Yankee Stadium	grapefruit juice	migraine

068 **Use vivid verbs:** Like nouns, verbs can be too general to create a vivid word picture. For example, the verb *looked* does not say the same thing as *stared, glared, glanced, peeked,* or *inspected.* The statement "Ms. Shaw *glared* at the two goof-offs" is much more vivid and interesting than "Ms. Shaw *looked* at the two goof-offs."

⦿ Whenever possible, use a verb that is strong enough to stand alone without the help of an adverb.

> Verb and adverb: Joan sat down on the couch.
>
> **Vivid verb:**   Joan plopped on the couch.

⦿ Avoid overusing the "to be" verbs *(is, are, was, were . . .).* Also avoid overusing *would, could,* or *should.* Often a better verb can be made from another word in the same sentence.

> A "to be" verb: Yolanda is someone who plans for the future.
>
> **A stronger verb:**   Yolanda plans for the future.

⦿ Use active rather than passive verbs. (Use passive verbs only if you want to downplay who is performing the action in a sentence. See 062.)

> Passive verb: Another deep pass was launched by Gerald.
>
> **Active verb:**   Gerald launched another deep pass.

⦿ Use verbs that show rather than tell. (See 064.)

> A verb that tells: Greta is very tall.
>
> **A verb that shows:**   Greta towers over her teammates.

069 **Select specific adjectives:** Use precise, colorful adjectives to describe the nouns in your writing. Strong adjectives can help make the nouns you choose even more interesting and clear to the reader. For example, when describing your uncle's new car as a *"sleek, red* convertible," you are using adjectives to give the reader a clearer picture of the car.

- ◉ Avoid using adjectives that carry little meaning: *neat, big, pretty, small, cute, fun, bad, nice, good, dumb, great, funny,* etc.

    Overused adjective: The **neat** house on the square belongs to an architect.

    Specific adjective: The **Victorian** house on the square belongs to an architect.

- ◉ Use adjectives selectively. If your writing contains too many adjectives, they will simply get in the way and lose their effectiveness.

    Too many adjectives: A tall, shocking column of thick, yellow smoke marked the exact spot where the unexpected explosion had occurred.

    Revised: A column of thick, yellow smoke marked the spot where the unexpected explosion had occurred.

070 **Include specific adverbs:** Use adverbs when you think they can help describe the action in a sentence. For example, the statement "Mayor Meyer *reluctantly* agreed to meet the protesters" is more specific than "Mayor Meyer agreed to meet the protesters." Don't, however, use a verb and an adverb when a single vivid verb would be better. (See 068.)

071 **Use the "right" words:** The words in your writing should not only be specific and colorful, but they should also have the right feeling, or *connotation*. The connotation of a word is what it suggests or implies beyond its literal meaning. Notice how the underlined words in the following passage connote positive, almost magical feelings about the subject, the writer's boyhood town. (Reprinted from *Good Old Boy* by Willie Morris with permission from Yoknaptawpha Press, Oxford, Mississippi.)

> [Yazoo City] was a lazy town, stretched out on its hills and its flat streets in a summer sun; [it was] a dreamy place, always green and lush except for the four cold months at the beginning and end of each year. It was heavy with leafy smells, and in springtime there was a perfume in the air that made you dizzy if you breathed too much.

072 Using Repetition

Another important stylistic technique is to repeat similar grammatical structures (words, phrases, or ideas) for the purpose of rhythm, emphasis, and unity. When used effectively, **repetition** can do more to improve your style of writing than just about any other technique.

The key point to remember when using repetition is to keep the words or ideas *parallel,* or stated in the same way. (As you read the examples below, you will see parallelism in action.)

For Rhythm and Balance: Notice in each of the sentences below how smoothly the repeated words or phrases flow from one to the next. They are in perfect balance.

> **The chimpanzee, the orangutan,** and **the baboon** are three of the most intelligent subhuman primates.

> My brother's room is full of **smelly sweatshirts, wrinkled shorts,** and **dirty socks**.

> Jumal **wants to graduate from college, become a volunteer medic,** and **work in the African sub-Sahara**.

For Emphasis and Effect: Notice in the passages below how the repetition of a basic sentence structure adds intensity to the writing.

> Dad and Mr. Harmel danced in the rain. **They waltzed cheek to cheek; they schottisched side by side; they do-si-doed arm in arm.** Because the drought had broken, the wheat would grow.

> **We shall fight on the beaches, we shall fight on the landing grounds, we shall fight in the fields and in the streets, we shall fight in the hills; we shall never surrender.**
> —Winston Churchill

For Unity and Organization: Notice in the passage below how repetition is used to unify and organize all of the ideas. (This passage is from *The Land Remembers* by Ben Logan. Copyright © 1975 by Ben T. Logan. Reprinted by permission of Northwood Press/Heartland Press.)

> **Let the smell of mint touch me.** I am kneeling along a little stream, the water numbing my hands as I reach for a trout. I feel the fish arch and struggle. I let go, pulling watercress from the water instead.

> **Let me see a certain color** and I am standing beside the threshing machine, grain cascading through my hands. The seeds we planted when snow was spitting down have multiplied a hundred times, returning in a stream of bright gold, still warm with the sunlight of the fields.

> **Let me hear an odd whirring.** I am deep in the woods, following an elusive sound, looking in vain for a last passenger pigeon, a feathered lightning I have never seen, unwilling to believe no person will ever see one again.

"A writer is not someone who expresses his thoughts, his passion, or his imagination in sentences but someone who thinks sentences."

—Roland Barthes

Writing Sentences

073   Let's start with some good news: You don't have to be a grammar expert to write effective sentences. Yes, you have to know the basic rules, but rules are secondary to the real thing. You learn the most about sentences by experiencing them—by seeing them in print (in the books and magazines you read) and by writing regularly (in a variety of forms).

    And now for some more good news: This chapter provides a quick, easy-to-use set of guidelines for writing clear, effective sentences. It's the place to turn whenever you have a question about sentence sense.

On the following pages:

074 Combining Sentences

Most sentences contain several basic ideas that work together to form a complete thought. For example, if you were to write a sentence about a tornado that struck a small town without warning, causing damage, injury, and death, you would actually be working with six different ideas. Each of these ideas could be written as a separate sentence:

1. There was a tornado.
2. The tornado struck a small town.
3. The tornado struck without warning.
4. The tornado caused a great deal of damage.
5. The tornado caused a number of serious injuries.
6. The tornado caused several deaths.

Of course, you wouldn't express each idea separately like this. Instead, you would combine these ideas into longer, more detailed sentences. **Sentence combining** is one of the most effective writing techniques you can practice. It is generally carried out in the following ways:

1. Use a **series** to combine three or more similar ideas.

> The tornado struck the small town without warning, causing **extensive damage, numerous injuries,** and **several deaths**.

2. Use a **relative pronoun** *(who, whose, that, which)* to introduce the subordinate (less important) ideas.

> The tornado, **which was completely unexpected,** swept through the small town, causing extensive damage, numerous injuries, and several deaths.

3. Use an **introductory phrase** or **clause** for the less important ideas.

> **Because the tornado was completely unexpected,** it caused extensive damage, numerous injuries, and several deaths.

4. Use a **participial phrase** *(-ing, -ed)* at the beginning or end of a sentence.

> The tornado swept through the small town without warning, **leaving behind a trail of death and destruction**.

5. Use a **semicolon**. (Also use a conjunctive adverb if appropriate.)

> The tornado swept through the small town without warning; **as a result,** it caused extensive damage, numerous injuries, and several deaths.

6. Repeat a **key word** or phrase to emphasize an idea.

> The tornado left a permanent **scar** on the small town, a **scar** of destruction, injury, and death.

7. Use a **correlative conjunction** *(either, or; not only, but also)* to compare or contrast two ideas in a sentence.

> The tornado inflicted **not only** immense property damage, **but also** immeasurable human suffering.

8. Use an **appositive** (a word or phrase that renames) to emphasize an idea.

> A single incident—**a tornado that came without warning**—changed the face of the small town forever.

075 Modeling Sentences

What you will find if you study the sentences of your favorite authors may surprise you. You may find sentences that seem to flow on forever, sentences that are so direct that they hit you right between the eyes, sentences that sort of sneak up on you, and "sentences" that aren't by definition complete thoughts. (Writers do occasionally break the rules.)

Generally speaking, most popular authors write in a relaxed, somewhat informal style. This style is characterized by sentences with a lot of personality, rhythm, and varied structures.

The Modeling Process

You will want to try imitating certain sentences in your own writing because you like the way they sound or the way they make a point. This process is sometimes called **modeling**. Like sentence combining, sentence modeling can help you improve your writing style. Here's how you can get started:

- ◉ **Reserve** a special section in your notebook or journal to list effective sentences you come across in your reading.
- ◉ **List** the well-made sentences (or short passages) that you come across in your reading. Focus on sentences that flow smoothly, that use effective descriptive words, that contain original figures of speech (metaphor, simile, personification, etc.).
- ◉ **Study** each sentence so you know how it is put together. Read it out loud. Look for phrases and clauses set off by commas. Also focus on word endings (*-ing, -ed,* etc.) and on the location of articles (*a, an, the*) and prepositions (*to, by, of,* etc.).
- ◉ **Write** your own version of a sentence by imitating it part by part. Try to use the same word endings, articles, and prepositions, but work in your own nouns, verbs, and modifiers. (Your imitation does not have to be exact.) If possible, practice writing a number of different versions.
- ◉ **Continue** imitating a number of different sentences to help you fine-tune your sense of sentence style. The more you practice, the better able you will be to write well-made sentences in your own essays and stories.

The Process in Action

Study the following interesting sentence:

> He has a thin face with sharp features and a couple of eyes burning with truth oil. 　　　　　　　　　　　　　　　　　　—Tom Wolfe

Now look carefully at the modeled version: (Compare it part by part to the original sentence. Can you see how the imitation was carried out?)

> He has an athletic body with a sinewy contour and a couple of arms bulging with weight-room dedication.

Expanding Sentences

Details seem to spill out of accomplished writers' minds naturally as their writing develops. We, as readers, marvel at how effectively they are able to **expand** a basic idea with engaging details. We envy good writers because of this special ability, and we wish we could write in the same way.

076 Cumulative Sentences

The specific type of sentence that marks an accomplished and stylistic writer is the *cumulative sentence.* What you normally find in a cumulative sentence is a main idea that is expanded by modifying words, phrases, or clauses. In this type of sentence, the details accumulate or build after the main clause, creating a stylistic, image-rich thought. (See 760 for more information.) Here's a sample cumulative sentence: (The main idea is in italics.)

> *Julie was studying at the kitchen table,* memorizing a list of vocabulary words, completely focused, intent on acing tomorrow's Spanish quiz.

Discussion: Notice how each new modifier adds another level of meaning to the sentence. Three modifying phrases have been added. Also notice that each new modifier is set off by a comma. (When you write expanded sentences, plan on using a lot of commas.) Here's another sample sentence:

> *Tony is laughing,* halfheartedly, with her hands on her face, looking puzzled.

Discussion: Notice in this example that one of the modifiers is a single word *(halfheartedly).* Also note how each modifier adds to the flow or the rhythm of the sentence.

077 Expanding with Details

When you practice expanding sentences on your own, remember that there are five basic ways to extend a main idea:

- **individual words:** *halfheartedly*
- **prepositional phrases:** *with her hands on her face*
- **participial (-*ing* or -*ed*) phrases:** *looking puzzled*
- **subordinate clauses:** *while her friend talks*
- **relative clauses:** *who isn't laughing at all*

 It will take time and effort on your part to write stylistic sentences. First, make sure to practice modeling sentences (see the previous page). Second, make sure to practice sentence expanding following our advice above. And third, become a regular reader and writer. This last step is probably the most important. You must immerse yourself in the language in order to understand its richness, its textures, and its rhythms.

"To err is human, but when the eraser wears out ahead of the pencil, you're overdoing it."

—J. Jenkins

Writing Complete Sentences

078 With a few exceptions in special situations, you should use complete sentences when you write. By definition, a complete sentence expresses a complete thought. However, a sentence may actually contain several ideas, not just one. The trick is getting those ideas to work together to form a clear, interesting sentence that expresses your exact meaning.

Among the most common errors that writers make when attempting to write complete and effective sentences are **fragments, comma splices, run-ons,** and **rambling sentences.**

079 A **fragment** is a group of words used as a sentence. It is not a sentence, though, because it lacks a subject, a verb, or some other essential part. That missing part causes it to be an incomplete thought.

Fragment: Lettuce all over the table. (This phrase lacks a verb.)

Sentence: Lettuce flew all over the table.

Fragment: When Herbie served the salad. (This clause does not convey a complete thought. We need to know what happened "when Herbie served the salad.")

Sentence: When Herbie served the salad, lettuce flew all over the table.

Fragment: Kate asked, "Is that what you call a tossed salad?" Laughing and scooping up a pile of lettuce. (This is a sentence followed by a fragment. This error can be corrected by combining the fragment with the sentence.)

Sentence: Laughing and scooping up a pile of lettuce, Kate asked, "Is that what you call a tossed salad?"

---

take note ▶ When you write dialogue, fragments are not mistakes. In fact, they are often preferable to complete sentences because that's how people talk:

"Hey, Rico. My house?"

"Yeah, right. On Tuesday afternoon."

"Whatever."

080 A **comma splice** is a mistake made when two independent clauses are connected ("spliced") with only a comma. The comma is not enough: a period, semicolon, or conjunction is needed.

Splice:	The concert crowd had been waiting in the hot sun for two hours, many were beginning to show their impatience by chanting and clapping.
Corrected:	The concert crowd had been waiting in the hot sun for two hours, and many were beginning to show their impatience by chanting and clapping. **(Coordinating conjunction** *and* **has been added.)**
Corrected:	The concert crowd had been waiting in the hot sun for two hours; many were beginning to show their impatience by chanting and clapping. **(Comma has been changed to a semicolon.)**

081 A **rambling sentence** is one that seems to go on and on. It is often the result of the overuse of the word *and*.

Rambling:	The intruder entered through the window and moved sideways down the hall and under a stairwell and he stood waiting in the shadows.
Corrected:	The intruder entered through the window. He moved sideways down the hall and under a stairwell where he stood, waiting in the shadows.

082 A **run-on sentence** is actually two sentences joined without adequate punctuation or a connecting word.

Run-on:	I thought the ride would never end my eyes were crossed, and my fingers were numb.

I thought the ride would never end. My eyes were crossed, and my fingers were numb.

> "If any man wishes to write a clear style, let him first be clear in his thoughts."
> — Johann Wolfgang von Goethe

083 Writing Clear Sentences

Writing is thinking. Before you can write clearly, you must think clearly. Nothing is more frustrating for the reader than writing that has to be reread just to understand its basic meaning.

Look carefully at the common errors that follow. Do you recognize any of them as errors you sometimes make in your own writing? If so, use this section as a checklist when you revise. Conquering these errors will help to make your writing clear and readable.

084 An **incomplete comparison** is the result of leaving out a word or words that are necessary to show exactly what is being compared to what.

Incomplete: I get along better with Rosa than my sister. (Do you mean that you get along better with Rosa than you get along with your sister? . . . or that you get along better with Rosa than your sister does?)

Clear: I get along better with Rosa than my sister does.

085 **Ambiguous wording** is wording that is unclear because it has two or more possible meanings. It often occurs when sentences are combined.

Ambiguous: Mike decided to take his new convertible to the drive-in movie, which turned out to be a real horror story. (What turned out to be a real horror story—Mike's taking his new convertible to the drive-in, or the movie?)

Clear: Mike decided to take his new convertible to the drive-in movie, a decision that turned out to be a real horror story.

086 An **indefinite reference** is a problem caused by careless use of pronouns. As a result, the reader is not sure what the pronoun(s) is referring to.

Indefinite: In *To Kill a Mockingbird,* **she** describes the problems faced by Atticus Finch and his family. (Who is **she**?)

Clear: In *To Kill a Mockingbird,* the author, Harper Lee, describes the problems faced by Atticus Finch and his family.

Indefinite: As he pulled his car up to the service window, **it** made a strange rattling sound. (Which rattled, the car or the window?)

Clear: His car made a strange rattling sound as he pulled up to the service window.

087 <u>Misplaced</u> **modifiers** are modifiers that have been placed incorrectly; therefore, the meaning of the sentence is not clear.

Misplaced: We have an assortment of combs for physically active people with unbreakable teeth. (People with unbreakable teeth?)

Corrected: For physically active people, we have an assortment of combs with unbreakable teeth.

For physically active people, we have an assortment of combs with unbreakable teeth.

088 <u>Dangling</u> **modifiers** are modifiers that appear to modify the wrong word or a word that isn't in the sentence.

Dangling: Trying desperately to get under the fence, Paul's mother called him. (The phrase *Trying desperately to get under the fence* appears to modify Paul's mother.)

Corrected: Trying desperately to get under the fence, Paul heard his mother call him. (Here the phrase modifies *Paul.*)

Dangling: After standing in line for five hours, the manager announced that all the tickets had been sold. (In this sentence, it appears as if the manager had been *standing in line for five hours.*)

Corrected: After standing in line for five hours, Ian heard the manager announce that all the tickets had been sold. (Now the phrase clearly modifies the person who has been standing in line: *Ian.*)

> "Read over your compositions and, when you meet a passage which you think is particularly fine, strike it out."
>
> — Samuel Johnson

089 Writing Natural Sentences

Samuel Johnson, a noted writer of the eighteenth century, was undoubtedly talking about one of the greatest temptations facing writers—to use lots of words (big words, clever words, fancy words). For some reason, we get into our heads the idea that writing simply, is not writing effectively. Nothing could be further from the truth.

The very best writing is ordinary and natural, not fancy or artificial. That's why it is so important to master the art of free writing. It is your best chance at a personal style. A personal voice will produce natural, honest passages you will not have to strike out. Learn from the following samples, which are wordy and artificial.

090 **Deadwood** is wording that fills up lots of space but does not add anything important or new to the overall meaning.

Wordy: At this point in time, I feel the study needs additional work before the subcommittee can recommend it be resubmitted for consideration.

Concise: The study needs more work.

091 **Flowery language** is writing that uses more or bigger words than needed. It is writing that often contains too many adjectives or adverbs.

Flowery: The cool, fresh breeze, which came like a storm in the night, lifted me to the exhilarating heights from which I had been previously suppressed by the incandescent cloud in the learning center.

Concise: The cool breeze was a refreshing change from the muggy classroom air.

092 A **trite expression** is one that is overused and stale; as a result, it sounds neither sincere nor natural.

Trite: It gives me a great deal of pleasure to present to you this plaque as a token of our appreciation. Let me read it.

Natural: The words on this plaque speak for all of us.

093 **Jargon** is language used in a certain profession or by a particular group of people. It is usually very technical and not at all natural.

Jargon: I'm having conceptual difficulty with these employee mandates.

Natural: I don't understand these work orders.

094 A **euphemism** is a word or phrase that is substituted for another because it is considered a less offensive way of saying something. (Avoid overusing euphemisms.)

Euphemism: I am so *exasperated* that I could *expectorate*.

Natural: I am so mad, I could spit.

095 **Wordiness** occurs when a word (or a synonym for that word) is repeated unnecessarily.

Redundant: He had a way of keeping my attention by the way he raised and lowered his voice on every single word he spoke.

Concise: He kept my attention by raising and lowering his voice when he spoke.

Double
Subject: Some people they don't use their voices as well as they could. (Drop *they*, since *people* is the only subject needed.)

Concise: Some people don't use their voices as well as they could.

Tautology: *widow woman, descend down, audible to the ear, return back, unite together, final outcome* (Each phrase says the same thing twice.)

096 A **cliche** is an overused word or phrase that springs quickly to mind but just as quickly bores the user and the audience. A cliche gives the reader nothing new or original to think about—no new insight into the subject.

Cliche: Her face was as red as a beet.

Natural: Her face flushed, turning first a rosy pink, then a red too deep to hide.

cliches to avoid

after all is said and done	food for thought
beat around the bush	grin and bear it
believe it or not	in a nutshell
best foot forward	in one ear and out the other
better late than never	in the nick of time
calm before the storm	last but not least
cart before the horse	lesser of two evils
chalk up a victory	more than meets the eye
come through with flying colors	no time like the present
crying shame	put your foot in your mouth
don't rock the boat	quiet enough to hear a pin drop
drop in the bucket	raining cats and dogs
easier said than done	see eye to eye
face the music	shot in the arm
fish out of water	sink or swim
flat as a pancake	so far, so good

> "You can be a little ungrammatical if you come from the right part of the country."
>
> —Robert Frost

097 Writing Acceptable Sentences

What Robert Frost says is very true. Much of the color and charm of literature comes from the everyday habits, customs—and especially the speech—of its characters. Keep that in mind when you write fiction of any kind. However, when you write essays, reports, and most other assignments, keep in mind that it's just as important to use language that is correct and appropriate.

098 **Substandard (nonstandard) language** is language that is often acceptable in everyday conversation, but seldom in formal writing (except fiction).

Colloquial:	Avoid the use of colloquial language such as *go with, wait up.* Can I go with? (Substandard) Can I go with you? (Standard)
Double preposition:	Avoid the use of certain double prepositions: *off of, off to, in on.* Reggie went off to the movies. (Substandard) Reggie went to the movies. (Standard)
Substitution:	Avoid substituting *and* for *to* in formal writing. Try and get here on time. (Substandard) Try to get here on time. (Standard) Avoid substituting *of* for *have* when combining with *could, would, should,* or *might.* I should of studied for that test. (Substandard) I should have studied for that test. (Standard)
Slang:	Avoid the use of slang or any "in" words. Hey, dude, what's happenin'? (Substandard)

099 **Double negative** is a sentence that contains two negative words. Because two negatives make a positive, this type of sentence can take on a meaning opposite of what is intended. Usually, it just sounds bad.

Awkward:	I haven't got no money. (This actually says—after taking out the two negatives that are now a positive—I have got money.)
Corrected:	I haven't got any money. / I have no money.

Note ● Do not use *hardly, barely,* or *scarcely* with a negative; the result is a double negative.

100 **Shift in construction** is a change in the structure or style midway through a sentence. (Also see "Agreement of Subject and Verb" in the handbook index.)

Shift in number: When *a person* goes shopping for a used car, *he or she* (not *they*) must be careful not to get a lemon.

Shift in tense: The trunk should be checked to see that it *contains* a jack and a spare tire that *are* (not *should be*) in good shape.

Shift in person: *One* must be careful to watch for heavy, white exhaust or *one* (not *you*) can end up with real engine problems.

Shift in voice: As you continue to look for the right car (active voice), many freshly painted ones are sure to be seen (passive voice).

Corrected: As you continue to look for the right car, you are sure to see many freshly painted ones. (Both verbs are in the active voice.)

101 **Inconsistent (unparallel) construction** occurs when the kind of words or phrases being used changes in the middle of a sentence.

Inconsistent: In my hometown, the people pass the time shooting bow, pitching horseshoes, and at softball games. (The sentence switches from the *-ing* words, shoot*ing* and pitch*ing,* to *at softball games.*)

Consistent: In my hometown, the people pass the time shooting bow, pitching horseshoes, and playing softball. (Now all three things being discussed are *-ing* words—they are consistent, or parallel.)

the **bottom** line

Use sentence combining, modeling, and expanding to build your sentences; use the four guidelines below to build them correctly:

- ◉ **Be Complete** Avoid fragments, comma splices, run-ons, and rambling sentences.

- ◉ **Be Clear** Avoid incomplete comparisons, ambiguous wording, indefinite references, and misplaced and dangling modifiers.

- ◉ **Be Natural** Avoid deadwood, flowery language, euphemisms, wordiness, trite expressions, jargon, and cliches.

- ◉ **Be Grammatically Correct** Avoid substandard language, double negatives, shifts in construction, and inconsistent construction.

"The paragraph [is] a mini-essay; it is also a maxi-sentence."

—Donald Hall

Writing Paragraphs

102 The **paragraph** is a unit of thought. It can be compared to a building block that is made up of separate, smaller units (called *sentences*). Paragraphs help the reader to follow your thinking as you describe, support, or explain your specific topic or idea.

103 The Topic Sentence

A Starting Point

Most paragraphs contain a sentence somewhere that states (or strongly suggests) the focus or topic of the paragraph. This sentence is sometimes called the **topic sentence** and is often found at or near the beginning of the paragraph, although it can appear in the middle or at the end.

In a tightly organized paragraph, every sentence is closely related to the topic sentence, bringing a sense of unity and clarity to your writing. As you work your way through your overall topic or idea, you move from one paragraph (or unit of thought) to the next. Eventually you will tie all the paragraphs together into an essay, report, analysis, critique, or other type of composition calling for highly organized writing.

A Simple Formula

A well-written **topic sentence** tells your reader what your subject is and what you plan to say about it. Here's a simple formula to follow:

Music helps people relax.

Formula: A limited topic *(Music)*
+ a specific impression *(helps people relax)*
= a topic sentence.

104 Writing a Paragraph

Quick Guide

Each paragraph you write should stand on its own and say something worthwhile. Readers want information; they want to learn something. Readers want to be entertained; they appreciate interesting details and colorful word pictures. Readers want writing that is original; they want writing that has a voice and personality. Here are some tips to help you give your readers what they want:

1. If you haven't already been assigned a topic, select one that interests you (and your reader) and can be covered in one paragraph.

2. For your paragraph, write a topic sentence that clearly states your topic and a specific impression. (See 103.)

3. List the details you plan to cover in your paragraph. Be sure to consider both personal details and details from other sources. (See 110 and 111.)

4. Write your paragraph as honestly and naturally as you can. Let your own personality and creativity be your guide, along with (of course) your topic sentence.

5. If you are having difficulty putting your thoughts into a logical order, refer to the "Methods of Arranging Details," 112, for help.

6. Use a variety of sentence beginnings, lengths, and types. (See "Adding Variety," 113.) Don't, however, worry about variety until after you have all your ideas down in writing.

7. Also make sure that your sentences read smoothly and connect well with one another. (See "Combining Sentences," 074, and "Transitions and Linking Words," 115.)

8. Once the first draft of your paragraph is complete, check it over to be sure your topic reads clearly from start to finish and that all your sentences belong in the paragraph. (See "Paragraph Unity," 109.)

9. If necessary, add a final sentence (a concluding or clincher sentence) to bring your paragraph to a logical stopping point.

10. Proofread your paragraph carefully for usage, punctuation, spelling, and so on.

Types of Paragraphs

There are four types of paragraphs: *narrative, descriptive, expository,* and *persuasive.* (Notice how the details support each topic sentence.)

105 A **narrative paragraph** tells a story of one kind or another. It should have a clear progression—a beginning, a middle, and an end.

> In first grade I learned some of the harsh realities of life. I found out that circuses aren't all they're supposed to be. We were going to the circus for our class trip, and I was really excited about it because I had never been to one before. Our class worked for weeks on a circus train made of shoe boxes, and Carrie Kaske told me her mom had fainted once when she saw the lion trainer. The day of the trip finally came, and my wonderful circus turned out to be nothing but one disappointment after another. I couldn't see much of anything for that matter. I could just barely make out some tiny figures scurrying around in the three rings that seemed to be a hundred miles away from my seat. After the first half hour, all I wanted to do was buy a Pepsi and a monkey-on-a-stick and get out of there. Of course, nothing in life is that easy. We weren't allowed to buy anything; so I couldn't have my souvenir, and instead of a cold Pepsi to quench my thirst, I had warm, curdled milk that the room mothers had so thoughtfully brought along. I returned to school tired and a little wiser. I remember looking at our little circus train on the window ledge and thinking that I'd rather sit and watch it do nothing than go to another circus.

106 A **descriptive paragraph** is one in which the sentences work together to present a single, clear picture (description) of a person, place, thing, or idea. (See "Writing About a Person, . . . Place, . . . Object," 136-138.)

> My Uncle John is normally a likable and friendly man, but when there is a group of people and one of those instant cameras around, he becomes a real pest. No matter what the occasion, even something as uneventful as a few of our relatives getting together for a visit after work, Uncle John appoints himself official photographer. He spends the whole time with one eye looking through the lens and the other scoping out the potential subjects for his pictures. In most situations, taking pictures is a great way to spend some time and have a little fun, but when Uncle John is pushing the button, it's quite another story. He doesn't believe in candids. Instead, Uncle John insists upon interrupting all activity to persuade his prey to pose for his pictures. In return, he gets photographs of people arranged in neat rows smiling through clenched teeth. Although we have tried again and again to convince Uncle John that his old, traditional methods of photography aren't necessarily the best, he continues to insist that we "Come over here, so I can take your picture." About the only solution is to convince Uncle John that he should be in some of these pictures and that you'd be happy to snap a few. Then, once you get the camera in your hands, don't stop shooting until all the film is gone.

107 An **expository paragraph** is one that presents facts, gives directions, defines terms, and so on. This type of writing can be used when you wish to present or explain facts or ideas.

> Braille is a system of communication used by the blind. It was developed by Louis Braille, a blind French student, in 1824. The code consists of an alphabet using combinations of small raised dots. The dots are imprinted on paper and can be felt, and thus read, by running the fingers across the page. The basic unit of the code is called a "cell" that is two dots wide and three dots high. Each letter is formed by different combinations of these dots. Numbers, punctuation marks, and even a system for writing music are also expressed by using different arrangements. These small dots, which may seem insignificant to the sighted, have opened up the entire world of books and reading for the blind.

108 A **persuasive paragraph** is one that presents information to support or prove a point. It expresses an opinion and tries to convince the reader that the opinion is correct or valid.

> Capital punishment should be abolished for three major reasons. First, common sense tells me that two wrongs don't make a right. To kill someone convicted of murder contradicts the reasoning behind the law that taking another's life is wrong. The state is committing the same violent, dehumanizing act it is condemning. Second, the death penalty is not an effective deterrent. Numerous studies show that murder is usually the result of a complex psychological and sociological problem and that most murderers do not contemplate the consequences of their act; or, if they do, any penalty is seen as a far-off possibility. The offense, on the other hand, brings immediate gratification. The third and most serious objection is that death is final and cannot be altered. Errors in deciding guilt or innocence will always be present in our system of trial by jury. There is too great a risk that innocent people will be put to death. Official records show that it has already happened in the past. For these reasons, I feel capital punishment should be replaced with a system that puts all doubt on the side of life—not death.

 INSIDE info   You will find a number of other special paragraphs throughout your handbook. Here is a partial list:

- The **summary paragraph** (500)
- The **introductory paragraph** (117)
- The **concluding paragraph** (033)
- The **one-paragraph essay answer** (507)
- The **paragraph of definition** (547)

109 Paragraph Unity

Every sentence in a paragraph should be closely related to the topic sentence and fit in well with the other sentences. This relationship brings a sense of **unity** to the paragraph. Notice how all but one of the sentences in the paragraph below fit smoothly and logically. The boldfaced sentence is simply not needed; it disrupts the flow of the paragraph and distracts the reader from the point that is being made. Once the boldfaced sentence has been removed, the paragraph reads smoothly and clearly from start to finish.

General Sherman and his men devised ingenious methods for the wrecking of the Southern railroad. They first used a portable rail-lifter that consisted of a chain with a hook on one end and a large iron ring on the other. The hook would be placed under the rail and a small pole put through the ring. By bracing the pole on the ground, a group of soldiers could lift the rail from the ties. **There is no way they could have lifted the rails without this added leverage.** The rails, which were made of a flimsy type of steel, could be heated and easily twisted into almost any shape. Initially, Sherman and his men took the heated rails and twisted them around nearby trees into what they called "Sherman's hairpins." After it was pointed out that the Confederates might be able to straighten these rails and use them again, Sherman's men devised a new system. They again heated the rails, but this time they used huge wrenches on either end and twisted in opposite directions. This process left a useless, licorice-shaped rail.

110 Paragraph Details

Levels of Detail

A well-written paragraph is made up of three levels of detail. It's good to be aware of the function of each of these levels so that you can check your own paragraphs for appropriate details. Here is a brief description and a model of each:

- **Level 1**
  Controlling sentences name and control the topic.
  General Sherman and his men devised ingenious methods for the wrecking of the Southern railroad.

- **Level 2**
  Clarifying sentences help make the topic clearer.
  They first used a portable rail-lifter that consisted of a chain with a hook on one end and a large iron ring on the other.

- **Level 3**
  Completing sentences add specific details that explain or describe the topic to the reader.
  The hook would be placed under the rail and a small pole put through the ring. By bracing the pole on the ground, a group of soldiers could lift the rail from the ties. The rails, which were made of a flimsy type of steel, could be heated and easily twisted into almost any shape.

⬤111 Types of Details

Personal Details

When you are attempting to add specific details to your paragraphs, you should begin with personal details—those sensory, memory, and reflective details you have stored inside. These are the details that come to mind naturally, the kind you don't really think much about. At times, though, it can be useful to stop and think about the kinds of details you are using. The following explanations and models may help you do that.

Sensory details are those that come to you through the senses *(smell, touch, taste, hearing, and sight)*. Sensory details are especially important when you are attempting to describe something you are observing (or have observed) firsthand.

> I could feel the warmth of the kerosene stove and smell its penetrating odor even before I opened the squeaky door leading to his third-floor apartment.

Memory details are those that you recall from past experiences. Often, memory details will come to you in the form of mental pictures or images, which you can use to build strong, colorful descriptions.

> I can remember as a kid how I walked the noisy, wooden stairway to his attic room and how he was always waiting at the half-opened door to take the newspaper from my shaking hand.

Reflective details are those that come to mind as you wonder about or reflect on something (*I wish, hope, dream, wonder,* etc.). Reflective details bring a strong personality to your writing and allow you to write about the way things might have been or may yet be.

> I wonder if he ever knew how frightened I was then and how I imagined there to be all varieties of evil on the other side of that half-opened door— beyond the kerosene stove.

Details from Other Sources

After you have gathered all your personal details about the topic, you may then want to add details—*facts, figures, reasons, examples*—from other sources. You can find these "secondhand" details in a number of ways:

● **First**, you can simply ask another person—a parent, neighbor, teacher—anyone who has interesting information or experiences to share.

● **Second**, you can ask an "expert," someone who is knowledgeable on the topic.

● **Third**, you can gather details from magazines, newspapers, books, videotapes, and so on, in your media center or library.

● **Finally**, you can use a computer to tap into a wide range of informational services.

112 Methods of Arranging Details

If your writing is flowing smoothly, it will most likely have an inner logic or natural direction that will hold it together for the reader. However, if necessary, you can purposely arrange the details in your paragraph in any of several basic ways:

- **Chronological** *(time)* **order** is effective for narrating personal experiences, summarizing steps, and explaining events. Details are arranged in the order in which they happen.

- **Order of location** is useful for many types of descriptions. It helps provide unity by arranging details left to right, right to left, top to bottom, edge to center, the distant to the near, and so on.

- **Illustration** *(deduction:* general to specific) is a method of arrangement in which you first state a general idea (topic sentence) and follow with specific reasons, examples, facts, and details to support the general idea.

- **Climax** *(induction:* specific to general) is a method of arrangement in which you present details followed by a general statement or conclusion drawn from the specific information provided. (If a topic sentence is used, it is placed at the end.)

- **Cause and effect** arrangement helps you make connections between a result and the events that preceded it. The general statement (a result or cause) can be supported by specific effects, or the general statement (an effect) can be supported by specific causes. (See 361-362 for guidelines and a model essay.)

- **Comparison** is a method of arrangement in which you measure one subject against another subject that is often more familiar. State the main point of the comparison early and present the likenesses (details) in a clear, organized fashion. (See 548-551.) **Contrast** uses details to measure the differences between two subjects.

- **Definition** or **classification** can be used when explaining a term or concept (a machine, theory, game, etc.). Begin by placing the subject in the appropriate class, and then provide details that show how your term or concept is different from others in the same class. Do not include more than a few features, or distinctions, in one paragraph. (See 546 and 552.)

take note ⟶ The transitions listed in your handbook (115) can help you tie your points together smoothly, whether you use one of the methods explained above or simply follow your own natural method of arranging details.

⓵⓵⓷ Adding Variety

You can bring interest, emphasis, and balance to your paragraph writing by using a variety of words and sentence types. Here are some suggestions:

Word Variety

- Use your own vocabulary as much as possible. Your best words will be those that sound as if you are simply talking to your reader.
- Use synonyms to avoid the monotony of using the same words or phrases over and over again.

Sentence Variety

- Vary your sentence beginnings. Rather than beginning each sentence with the subject, use modifiers, phrases, and clauses instead.
- Vary the length of your sentences to suit the topic and tone of your paragraph. Short, concise sentences, for example, are appropriate for explaining complex ideas or for adding feeling or dramatic effect. Longer sentences help to show the relationship between ideas and usually read more smoothly.
- Vary the arrangement of the material within each sentence by using different kinds and types of sentences. (See 757-760.)

Notice the change in tone and maturity of the paragraph below after some of the repeated words (in boldface) have been eliminated or replaced (by the words in parentheses). Also notice the variety of sentence beginnings, lengths, and types.

January in northern Wisconsin can be **bitter cold**. The temperature is often 20 to 30 degrees below zero. If the wind also blows, the result can be a windchill of 70 to 80 degrees below. **That's cold!** (eliminate altogether) It is so **cold** (frigid) at times that you can't go outside for fear of having some real problems with **the cold hurting your hands or face** (frostbite). On these **really cold** (face-numbing) days, people are warned against traveling except for an emergency. If the **cold** (arctic-like weather) continues for more than a couple of days, almost all traffic stops. You cannot trust your car to keep running even if it does start. Too often a car will stall in the middle of nowhere, leaving a traveler stranded in the **extreme cold** (frozen air). About the only way to beat the **incredible cold** of a northern Wisconsin winter is to huddle around the fireplace and dream of the warm, sunny days of summer.

a closer look Look for variety in the words and sentences of other sample paragraphs in this chapter and throughout the handbook. Always keep in mind, though, that your words and sentences should not get in the way of what you're trying to say. If your paragraph is clear and effective, don't change it just to add variety.

⑪ Reviewing Paragraphs in Essays
Quick Guide

Look at each paragraph in your essays and other longer writings in two ways: first, as an individual unit and, second, as one part of the whole piece. (Use the paragraph symbol [¶] to indicate where each paragraph begins as you review your writing. This will remind you to indent each new paragraph in your final copy.)

1. Each paragraph should say enough to stand on its own. One way to check the effectiveness of a paragraph is to imagine a title for it, as if it were the only thing you had written. Another way is to form a simple question that the paragraph answers clearly. (If one of your paragraphs doesn't pass either of these tests, consider revising it or leaving it out.)

2. Change, rearrange, or delete any sentences that take away from the effectiveness of each paragraph. All of the sentences in a paragraph should be clear, meaningful, and smooth reading.

3. Consider arranging your opening paragraph like an inverted pyramid. That is, start with general statements that get the reader's attention, and then state the specific subject, or thesis, in the last sentence or two.

Note • If you feel your opening paragraph is effectively structured in another way, leave it alone.

4. The concluding paragraph often begins with a general review of the important ideas discussed in the essay, and ends with a statement that reminds the reader of the overall importance of the paper.

5. All of the paragraphs in the body of your paper should help develop your thesis (main idea) in some way. A paragraph might explain, define, compare, or classify information to support your thesis statement. Another paragraph might relate a personal experience or recent incident that adds to or clarifies your main idea.

6. Transitions should be used to connect one paragraph to the next. They unify the paragraphs, and they make your writing easier for the reader to follow and understand. (See 115.)

7. The bottom line? If you want readers to "stand up" and listen to your writing—whether one paragarph or many—you must make it worth reading. Readers want to learn something and be entertained in the process. Readers want writing that is original and clearly moves from one point to the next. And readers want to hear the real voice of the writer, you.

Transitions and Linking Words

Words that can be used to **show location**:

above	away from	beyond	into	over
across	behind	by	near	throughout
against	below	down	off	to the right
along	beneath	in back of	onto	under
among	beside	in front of	on top of	
around	between	inside	outside	

Words that can be used to **show time**:

about	first	meanwhile	soon	then
after	second	today	later	next
at	third	tomorrow	afterward	as soon as
before	till	next week	immediately	when
during	until	yesterday	finally	

Words that can be used to **compare things** (show similarities):

in the same way	likewise	as
similarly	like	also

Words that can be used to **contrast things** (show differences):

but	otherwise	although	on the other hand
however	yet	still	even though

Words that can be used to **emphasize a point**:

again	for this reason	truly
to repeat	to emphasize	in fact

Words that can be used to **conclude** or **summarize**:

as a result	finally	in conclusion	to sum up
therefore	last	in summary	all in all

Words that can be used to **add information**:

again	another	for instance	finally
also	and	moreover	as well
additionally	besides	next	along with
in addition	for example	likewise	equally important

Words that can be used to **clarify**:

in other words	for instance	that is	put another way

"To write about people, you have to know people; to write about blood-hounds, you have to know bloodhounds; to write about the Loch Ness monster, you have to find out about it."

—James Thurber

Writing Basic Essays

The essay is the basic form of writing assigned in all academic areas. You write essays about important concepts covered in your reading and class discussions. You research related topics. You compose procedure (how-to) papers. You take essay tests. Anytime you are asked to inform, explain, analyze, or write persuasively about a subject, you are developing an essay. Basic essays usually contain at least three to five paragraphs.

Building a Knowledge Base

Begin the essay-writing process by selecting a subject that genuinely interests you (and meets the requirements of your assignment). Then learn as much as you can about this subject by collecting a wide variety of facts and details.

Once you have a good knowledge base, you're ready to develop your essay. Are you expected to inform your readers about your subject? Fine. Then present your findings as clearly and completely as you can. Are you expected to persuade your readers to accept your position on a subject? In that case, support your point of view using the facts and figures you have gathered. The key in either situation is to work with solid information. Always remember that effective essays begin and end with information.

what's ahead? The first part of this chapter discusses the main elements in the development of an essay: structure, organization, and support. On the pages that follow, you will find writing guidelines and a model for a basic expository essay and for a persuasive essay. Also included in this chapter are two interesting extras: a graphic organizer for planning (124) and tips for personalizing an essay (128-129). Note • Refer to "Academic Writing" (354-370) for more guidelines and models.

117 The Importance of Structure

The basic essay has a tight structure; that is, it contains an opening paragraph, several developmental paragraphs, and a closing paragraph.

Beginning

Your **opening paragraph** should accomplish two things: It should gain your reader's interest in your subject, and it should identify the focus or thesis that you will develop in the main part of your essay. Remember that the focus identifies the specific part of your subject that you will write about. (See 024-025 for more about your focus or *thesis statement.*)

There are several ways to draw your reader's attention to your subject. Five effective techniques are listed here.

- ◉ Open with a series of questions about the topic.
- ◉ Provide an interesting story or anecdote about the subject.
- ◉ Present a startling or unusual fact or figure.
- ◉ Quote a well-known person or literary work.
- ◉ Define an important, subject-related term.

Middle

The **developmental paragraphs** are at the heart of the essay. They must clearly and logically support your thesis. If, for instance, you are going to present information about paper recycling, each developmental paragraph in your essay should discuss an important element related to that subject.

It's important that these paragraphs are arranged in the best possible way—chronologically, by order of importance, or by an order of your own making. (See 112 for methods of arrangement.) It's also important that your paragraphs flow smoothly from one to the next. To achieve this flow, make sure that the first sentence in each new paragraph serves as an effective link to the preceding paragraph. Transitions like *in addition, on the other hand,* and *as a result* are often used for this purpose. (See 115.)

---

take note   Start a new paragraph whenever there is a shift or change in the essay. This change is called a *paragraph shift* and can take place for any of four basic reasons:

1. a change in emphasis or ideas
2. a change in time
3. a change in speakers
4. a change in place or setting

Ending

The **closing** or summary paragraph should tie all of the important points in the essay together and draw a final conclusion for the reader. It should leave the reader with a clear understanding of the essay topic.

The Importance of Organization

118 The Topic Outline

A **topic outline** is a listing of the topics to be covered in a piece of writing; it contains no specific details. Topics are stated in words and phrases rather than complete sentences. This makes the topic outline useful for short essays. It is always a good idea to begin your outlining task by placing your thesis statement, or controlling idea, at the top of your paper. This will serve as a reminder of the specific topic you are going to be outlining and later writing about. Use the standard format shown in the example for labeling the lines of your outline. Do not attempt to outline your opening or closing paragraph unless specifically told to do so.

Introduction
I. Paper recycling big business
   A. Industry involved
   B. Recyclable paper plentiful
   C. Countries buy wastepaper
II. Simple process
   A. Collect and sort paper
   B. Form a pulp
   C. Dry pulp to make paper
   D. New paper used in many ways
III. Some papers not recyclable
   A. Glossy, envelopes, glued papers
   B. Must be sorted out
   C. New process coming for glossy paper
Conclusion

119 The Sentence Outline

The **sentence outline** not only contains the major points to be covered but lists supporting details as well. It is used for longer, more formal writing assignments; each point should, therefore, be written as a complete sentence.

Introduction
I. Paper recycling is a booming business today.
   A. Industry believes recycling paper makes good sense.
   B. A large supply of recyclable paper is thrown away by Americans.
   C. Taiwan actually buys paper waste from the U.S.
II. Paper recycling is a simple process.
   A. Paper is collected and sorted.
   B. Paper is mixed with water and chemicals to form pulp.
   C. Pulp is dried and new paper is formed.
   D. The new paper is used for a wide range of products.
III. Some types of paper cannot be recycled presently.
   A. Equipment cannot handle glossy paper, envelopes, glued papers, etc.
   B. These types must be sorted out.
   C. A new technology is being perfected that will make glossy papers recyclable.
Conclusion

120 The Importance of Support

Believe it or not, writing is a privilege. But with this privilege comes the responsibility of supporting and developing your main points with facts, quotations, and examples. Without this kind of evidence, your readers will not take your writing seriously. Here's how it's done.

Using Facts

In the model persuasive essay in this chapter, the writer asks if metal detectors are the answer to student safety. He makes this statement: "The answer to this question for Somerset High School is, I believe, 'no.' " Here are two supporting facts he presents to get the reader to accept his opinion:

1. The only weapons found so far at SHS have been knives.
2. We've had very few weapon-related expulsions compared to other area campuses.

Using Quotations

A quotation from an expert can go a long way toward lending support. For example, in an essay about sports and children, a writer made this claim: "Competitive sports can be harmful for preschoolers." Later, he shared this supporting quotation to help convince the reader:

> Dr. M. Jones recently reported, "The high stress of athletic training and conditioning in youngsters can damage their bone structure."

Using Examples

Examples will strengthen your writing by making it more concrete. In the model expository essay in this chapter, the writer states, "Paper recycling has truly become part of the daily lives of many Americans." Here are two of the examples the writer uses to prove his statement is true:

1. Recyclable paper is collected at home (curbside) and at the office.
2. Americans recycled 20 million tons of paper last year.

121 **Guidelines for Writing an Expository Essay**

Informing Your Readers

Discussion: Write an expository essay presenting information about a subject of personal interest. Your goal will be to share facts, explaining them as necessary, and guiding your reader to a clear understanding of your subject. Gather facts by referring to at least two different sources—books or periodicals. Do your best to prepare an essay that reads smoothly from the opening paragraph to the closing thought. Refer to the model essay that follows and the guidelines below to help you with your writing.

Searching and Selecting

1. **Searching** • Think of a subject you would like to know more about. Consider subjects related to your course work, as well as interests outside of school. Page through textbooks or newspapers, or brainstorm for ideas with other classmates. Make a list of possible subjects.

2. **Selecting** • Look over your list and focus your attention on interesting subjects that you know you can find plenty of facts about—either in a textbook, reference book, or magazine. Now choose your favorite.

Generating the Text

3. **Collecting** • Find at least two good sources of information and begin reading. List important facts as you come across them. (Don't worry about their order at this point.) To be certain you understand the information you're collecting, use your own words as much as possible.

4. **Planning** • Review your facts, looking for a main idea or impression that could serve as the focus or thesis of your essay. Once you identify a possible focus, write it out in a sentence. Next, put a check mark by the facts and details that support this idea. Then plan and organize your writing accordingly. You may find it helpful at this point to prepare an outline. (See 118.)

Writing and Revising

5. **Writing** • Develop your first draft according to your planning and organizing. Devote extra time to your opening paragraph, which should catch your reader's attention and identify the focus of your writing.

6. **Revising** • Carefully review your first draft, making sure that the main idea you had intended to share has, in fact, been clearly put forth. Also make sure that you have effectively supported this idea and that your writing flows smoothly. (See topic 128 for more ideas.)

Evaluating

Is the essay well organized?

Do the facts effectively support the focus?

Will readers appreciate the treatment of this subject?

122 Expository Essay

The purpose of an **expository essay** is to present important information about a specific subject. In the following example, student writer Todd Michaels shares timely information about paper recycling. You will notice that his essay follows the traditional five-paragraph pattern (opening paragraph, three developmental paragraphs, and closing paragraph).

Paper Recycling

From large paper chutes at the office to home curbside collection, paper recycling has become an everyday thing. Americans have changed their throwaway attitude for a recycling consciousness, and they are recycling in record numbers. Last year 20 million tons of paper were recycled— a substantial increase from the previous year. Paper recycling has truly become part of the daily lives of many Americans.

Paper recycling has indeed become a big deal, and a big business. Today, industry recycles paper not just because it is a good thing to do, but because it makes good business sense. Since Americans throw away more paper than anything else, there is much to be gained by recycling paper. For example, Fort Howard Corporation of Green Bay, Wisconsin, produces bathroom tissue made entirely of recycled paper. The company recycles enough paper each year to cover 100 acres 18 feet deep (Grove 104). Foreign countries are even buying our paper waste. If you see a MADE IN TAIWAN tag on a manufactured paper product, in another life it was probably a newspaper in America. Taiwan buys all of its paper from the United States.

The process of paper recycling is a simple one. First, paper is collected and sorted. Recyclable paper includes typing paper, newspaper, cardboard boxes, scrap paper, index cards, and computer printouts. This recyclable paper is dumped into a vat of water and chemicals. A large spinning blade mixes the paper to a pulp. This pulp is dried on screens, and the new paper is formed on cylinders. Items made from this new recycled paper include newspapers, cereal and shoe boxes, toilet tissue, paper towels, building insulation, egg cartons, and even livestock bedding.

The focus or thesis statement is clearly presented.

Specific facts are used to support main points.

The writer clearly explains the recycling process.

123

Each developmental paragraph addresses a specific aspect of recycling.

Not all types of paper can be recycled, however. Recycling equipment at this time cannot handle envelopes, carbon paper, glossy paper, photographs, or paper with scotch tape, glue, or staples attached. These types of paper must be sorted out. Advancements are being made, though, to accommodate these items. Recycling equipment currently is being perfected that will remove ink from glossy magazine and catalog paper, enabling it to be recycled.

The closing line reminds the reader of the importance of the subject.

Although landfills are still filling up with over two-thirds of our recyclable waste, paper recycling has become a success story. While only 18 percent of metal cans and 2 percent of plastics are recycled, 40 percent of recyclable paper is, in fact, recycled. Five thousand community programs exist nationwide for the recycling of paper products, and big business has discovered the advantages of a product-material that can be reused up to eight times. Recycling fever hasn't been as high in the United States since World War II, when people in a wartime situation felt it was their duty to recycle. Perhaps people today have realized that the world is in a different kind of emergency situation, and that, again, it is their duty to recycle. @

124 Another Look at Organization

Using a Graphic Organizer

Using an outline is an exact, tight way to organize your writing. Using a graphic organizer is a looser way—like laying your main ideas and details down on the table and looking them over. The following graphic organizer was used to plan the model persuasive essay in this chapter (126). The focus of this essay appears in the oval. Each main point listed under this focus completes a "because" statement. For example, "No metal detectors are needed at Somerset High School *because* they may cause problems." Finally, supporting details are placed in boxes below the main points.

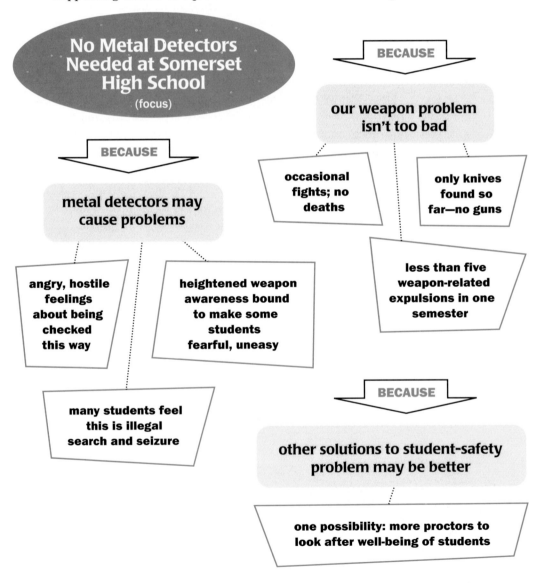

125 Guidelines for Writing a Persuasive Essay
Convincing Your Readers

Discussion: Write a persuasive essay in which you try to convince your readers to think the way you do about a subject. To accomplish this goal, you will have to support your opinion using effective facts and details. Naturally, it is important that you choose a subject of personal interest—something you feel strongly about. Your subject should also be current and somewhat controversial. Refer to the model that follows and the guidelines below to help you with your essay.

Searching and Selecting

1. **Searching** • With three or four classmates, brainstorm a list of possible problems. These may be school problems, community problems, national problems, and so on. Page through newspapers and review your class notes to get your brains working.

2. **Selecting** • Choose one subject that you feel most strongly about. Perhaps you disagree with the steps being taken to solve a certain problem—you have a better idea. Perhaps you have a solution for a problem no one else seems to be addressing. Just remember to select a subject you have a definite opinion about.

Generating the Text

3. **Collecting** • Gather facts in support of your opinion. (Good sources of information may range from local newspapers to national news magazines to special-interest periodicals.) Become aware of opinions different from your own, so that you can address these in your writing (I know some people feel that . . . ; however, . . .).

4. **Planning** • Think carefully and logically about your opinion and the reasons behind it. Write a statement of purpose for your essay, explaining your opinion and what you will try to prove in your composition. This will be the focus or thesis of your writing. Next, make a plan for organizing your ideas and details into a clear, convincing essay.

Writing and Revising

5. **Writing** • Develop your first draft according to your planning and organizing, but feel free to add points that did not occur to you previously.

6. **Revising** • Carefully review your first draft. If you haven't been convincing enough, fix your essay—by adding information, rearranging what's there, and deleting unnecessary details. (See 129 for more ideas.)

Evaluating

Has the focus (opinion) been clearly set forth?

Do the facts effectively support the writer's opinion?

Will the readers be convinced to share (or at least respect) the writer's opinion?

126 Persuasive Essay

The purpose of a **persuasive essay** is to convince readers to accept a particular point of view on a subject. It is based on clear thinking and effective information. The following model by student writer David Schoen was published in the Inland Valley (CA) *Daily Bulletin* on March 29, 1993. Even if you find yourself disagreeing with this student's views, note the persuasive elements he has used. (The names of the schools are fictitious.)

The opening paragraph gains the reader's attention.

The writer's position (focus) is identified here.

The writer addresses different sides of the issue.

No Metal Detectors Needed

If you haven't noticed, the arms race is heating up. But this is a different sort of arms race. It's a race to rid the schools of arms. And the weapon of choice is the metal detector.

The tension accompanying a recent deadly shooting at a high school in Los Angeles has spread to the Fairfield County High School District, where some schools have decided to use metal detectors. But are metal detectors the answer for every school? The answer to this question for Somerset High School is, I believe, "no."

On our campus, the only weapons found have been knives. There haven't been any deaths on campus and very few of the expulsions that take place are weapon related. In fact, we had less than five such expulsions during the first semester. To some, that is five too many, but it's next to nothing compared to other schools. Somerset has a good record when it comes to the safety of the students. For this reason, SHS doesn't need metal detectors.

An important question needs to be explored: Can Somerset ensure the future safety of its students? I happen to believe it can. Admittedly an occasional fight erupts. What high school doesn't have fights? But SHS isn't dangerous enough to warrant the purchase of a metal detector. While a metal detector might cut down on weapons being brought on campus, we need to remember that running a metal detector up and down someone's body may initiate feelings of anger and hostility—the exact feelings that may lead to fights and violence. Yet these are the activities that metal detectors are supposed to prevent.

It is interesting to note that most weapon-related expulsions involved students who were carrying weapons for defense purposes. These were not students who intended to hurt anyone. In fact, quite the opposite is true. These students were carrying weapons because they felt unsafe. Most of the students that I have talked to believe that metal

127

A reasonable
solution is
proposed.

The writer's
position is
reaffirmed.

detectors are a violation of the Fourth Amendment, dealing with illegal search and seizure. However, something has to be done to ensure everyone's safety.

Here is my solution. We have about 2,600 students with 10 people looking out for their well-being on campus. That's not enough eyes for that many students. We need to hire more proctors or disciplinarians. I understand that with budget cuts this action may be difficult. I also understand that a metal detector would actually be cheaper than hiring more staff. But putting a metal detector on campus will heighten weapon awareness. If students become more conscious of weapons at school, fear and uneasiness may follow. This situation is exactly what we are trying to prevent.

The school administration should save Somerset the trouble that would be caused if a metal detector were used. We have no significant weapons problem on our campus. We should ensure everyone's safety, but within reason. If something isn't broken, it doesn't need to be fixed.

Personalizing the Basic Essay

If, after reviewing the first draft of your essay, you feel that it needs more energy or spark, try one or more of the following activities. Each one is guaranteed to refuel your thinking.

128 **For Expository Essays**

◉ **Write a negative definition of your subject** (what it is not). Then expand upon this definition in a free writing, working in thoughts and ideas as they come to mind. Fresh ideas are bound to develop.

◉ **Compare your subject to a similar one** that may be more (or less) familiar to you. Work with this comparison for a while to see what you can discover.

◉ **Ask yourself, "What am I trying to say here?"** And then answer the question in your mind or out loud. Pick up on anything that sounds better than the way you initially expressed yourself.

◉ **Reexamine your subject from a number of different angles.** (See 021-022 for ideas.)

◉ **Bend the rules** (if your teacher allows it). If you don't feel like starting with a typical opening paragraph, open in a way that feels right to you—perhaps with a personal story that got you interested in the subject in the first place.

129 **For Persuasive Essays**

◉ **Write freely about your subject** from the opposite point of view. Or exaggerate or downplay the seriousness of your subject in a free writing. This exercise may help you see your subject in new ways.

◉ **Step back and reassess your feelings about your subject.** Do you still feel that your position is an effective one? Can you effectively present this position to your readers? *Remember:* You can't be convincing unless you have "you" on your side.

◉ **Talk about your subject with someone new**. How about your guidance counselor, your grandmother, or your younger brother? What are their feelings about your subject and why do they feel this way? Listen carefully. Test your own position and reasons on them.

◉ **Gather more facts and details if necessary.** But this time try to find new sources of information, new points of view. How about a national newspaper like the *New York Times* or a magazine devoted to senior citizens or young learners?

◉ **Rethink the arrangement of the ideas in your essay.** How would your essay sound if you placed your best argument first instead of last? What would happen if you started with a strong argument against your position? Mix and match, cut and paste. You may come up with a more effective arrangement of ideas.

"I love being a writer. What I can't stand is the paperwork."

—Peter De Vries

Writer's Resource

130 In the writing process section of your handbook, it's mentioned that your own writing personality will develop as you become more experienced. Well, let's not wait until you gain more experience. How would you classify your writing personality right now?

Personality Plus

Are you a free spirit, ready and willing to write on just about any topic, at any time? Or are you more methodical, a clock puncher, interested in keeping track of each writing move as you go along? Then again, are you a detail person, wrapped up in the terminology of writing. (What is my *purpose?* Should I add a *modifier?*) Still again, are you a visionary, experimenting with many different forms of writing? Or are you . . .

In all probability, your writing personality doesn't fit into any one category. Maybe you're a free-spirited visionary, or how about a free-spirited detail person? (Is that possible?) No matter how you approach writing, you'll find valuable information in this chapter. Topics, terms, forms, charts, and guidelines—there's something here for everyone.

what's ahead? Here's what you'll find in the "Writer's Resource": (Make a point of becoming familiar with each part.)

- **Your Basic Writing and Thinking Moves**
  (a chart connecting thinking and writing)

- **Writing Topics** (lists and lists of writing ideas)

- **Writing Terms** (a glossary for quick reference)

- **A Survey of Writing Forms**
  (a chart classifying the different forms)

- **Writing About a Person, Place, Object**
  (guidelines for exploring and writing)

131 **Your Basic Writing and Thinking Moves**

OBSERVE

| Watch | Listen | Taste | Feel | Smell | Perceive (sense it) |

GATHER

| Collect observations | Use personal experiences | Free-write, cluster, list | Brainstorm with others | Interview others | Read, write, draw |

QUESTION

| Ask: Who? What? When? Where? Why? | Ask: How? How much? | Wonder what if . . . Why not? | Look into, investigate, survey |

FOCUS

| Find a main point or center of interest | Identify or define the key problem or issue | Select a way to approach the issue | Set a simple goal or purpose |

ORGANIZE

| Distinguish the whole from the part | Put in meaningful order | Compare, contrast | Give reasons | Group, classify | Pro/Con (for/against) |

ANALYZE

| Select best idea(s) or feature(s) | Relate it to other things | What caused it? What did it cause? | See patterns, relationships, connections |

IMAGINE

| See from another point of view | Create new ideas, alternatives | Experiment, invent, design | Infer (draw conclusions) | Hypothesize (make an educated guess) | Predict, estimate |

RETHINK

| Restate: "What I really mean is . . ." | Reconsider: What are the results? | Re-examine: Look for weaknesses | Rearrange: Change the order | Revise: Review rules, goals, models | Restructure: See from new perspective |

EVALUATE

| Judge: Is it understandable? Is it clear? Accurate? Concise? | Criticize: Is it effective? Workable? Interesting? | Persuade: Is it worthwhile? Practical? Logical? | Argue: What are the advantages? Disadvantages? |

132 Descriptive

Person: friend, teacher, relative, classmate, minister (priest, rabbi), co-worker, neighbor, teammate, coach, entertainer, politician, sister, brother, bus driver, an older person, a younger person, a baby, someone who taught you well, someone who spends time with you, someone you wish you were more like, someone who always bugs you

Place: school, neighborhood, old neighborhood, the beach, the park, the hangout, home, your room, your garage, your basement, the attic, a rooftop, the alley, the bowling alley, a classroom, the theater, the locker room, the store, a restaurant, the library, a church, a stadium, the office, the zoo, the study hall, the cafeteria, the hallway, the barn

Thing: a billboard, a bulletin board, a poster, a photograph, a camera, a machine, a computer, a video game, a music video, a musical instrument, a tool, a monkey wrench, a monkey, a pet, a pet peeve, a bus, a boat, a book, a car, a cat, a camp, a dog, a drawing, a diary, a model, a miniature, a muppet

Narrative

stage fright, just last week, on the bus, learning a lesson, learning to drive, the trip, a kind act, homesick, Christmas, Hanukkah, a big mistake, odd field trips, studying, a reunion, a special party, getting lost, being late, asking for help, after school, Friday night, getting hurt, success, flirting, an embarrassing moment, staying overnight, moving, the big game, building a _____, the first day of _____, the last day of _____, a miserable time, all wet, running away, being alone, getting caught, cleaning it up, a practical joke, being punished, staying after, a special conference, the school play, being a friend

Expository

How to . . . wash a car, make a taco, improve your memory, get a job, make a legal petition, care for a pet, prevent accidents, entertain a child, impress your teacher, earn extra money, get in shape, study for a test, conserve energy, take a good picture

How to operate . . . control . . . run . . .

How to choose . . . select . . . pick . . .

How to build . . . grow . . . create . . .

How to fix . . . clean . . . wash . . .

How to protect . . . warn . . . save . . .

The causes of . . . acid rain, rust, hiccups, snoring, inflation, northern lights, shinsplints, dropouts, tornadoes, birth defects, cheating, child abuse

Kinds of . . . music, crowds, friends, teachers, love, intelligence, rules, compliments, commercials, punishment, censorship, dreams, happiness, neighbors, pollution, poetry, taxes, clouds, stereos, heroes, chores, homework, pain, vacations, communication, clocks

Definition of . . . rock 'n' roll, best friend, poverty, generation gap, greed, agent, a good time, hassle, a disabled person, government, a radical, a conservative, metric system, soul, school, brain, nerd, grandmother, arthritis, loyalty, antibiotic, CPR, kosher

Persuasive

safety in the home, girls in all sports, organ transplants, homework, study halls, capital punishment, the speed limit, smoking in public places, air bags, shoplifting, gun control, courtroom television, graduation requirements, students on school boards, final exams, four-day workweek, public housing, a career in the armed forces, teen centers, something that's unfair, something that needs improving, something that everyone should have to see or do, something . . .

133 Writing Terms

Argumentation: Writing or speaking in which reasons or arguments are presented in a logical way.

Arrangement: The order in which details are placed or arranged in a piece of writing.

Audience: Those people who read or hear what you have written.

Balance: The arranging of words or phrases so that two ideas are given equal emphasis in a sentence or paragraph; a pleasing rhythm created when a pattern is repeated in a sentence.

Body: The writing between the introduction and conclusion that develops the main idea.

Brainstorming: Collecting ideas by thinking freely and openly about all the possibilities; used most often with groups.

Case Study: The story of one individual whose experiences speak for the experiences of a larger group of people.

Central idea: The main point or purpose of a piece of writing, often stated in a thesis statement or topic sentence.

Clincher sentence: The sentence that summarizes the point being made in a paragraph, usually located last.

Coherence: The arrangement of ideas in such a way that the reader can easily follow from one point to the next.

Composition: A process in which several different ideas are combined into one unified piece of writing.

Data: Information that is accepted as being true—facts, figures, examples—and from which conclusions can be drawn.

Deductive reasoning: The act of reasoning from a general idea to a specific point or conclusion.

Description: Writing that paints a colorful picture of a person, a place, a thing, or an idea using concrete, vivid details.

Details: The words used to describe a person, convince an audience, explain a process, or in some way support the central idea; to be effective, details should be vivid, colorful, and appeal to the senses.

Emphasis: Placing greater stress on the most important idea in a piece of writing by giving it special treatment; emphasis can be achieved by placing the important idea in a special position, by repeating a key word or phrase, or by simply writing more about this idea than the others.

Essay: A piece of prose writing in which ideas on a single topic are presented, explained, argued, or described in an interesting way.

Exposition: Writing that explains.

Extended definition: Writing that goes beyond a simple definition of a term in order to stress a point; it can cover several paragraphs and include personal definitions and experiences, similes and metaphors, quotations, and even verse.

Figurative language: Language that goes beyond the normal meaning of the words used; writing in which a figure of speech is used to heighten or color the meaning.

Focus: Concentrating on a specific subject to give it emphasis or clarity.

Form: The arrangement of the details into a pattern or style; the way in which the content of writing is organized.

Free writing: Writing openly and freely on any topic; focused free writing is writing openly on a specific topic or angle.

Generalization: An idea or statement that emphasizes the general characteristics rather than the specific details of a subject.

Grammar: The study of the structure and features of a language; it usually consists of rules and standards that are to be followed to produce acceptable writing and speaking.

Idiom: A phrase or expression that means something different from what the words actually say. An idiom is usually understandable to a particular group of people. (Example: using *over his head* for *didn't understand*)

Illustration: Writing that uses an experience to make a point or clarify an idea.

Inductive reasoning: Reasoning that leads one to a conclusion or generalization after examining specific examples or facts; drawing generalizations from specific evidence.

Inverted sentence: A sentence in which the normal word order is inverted or switched; usually the verb comes before the subject.

Issue: A point or question to be decided.

Journal: A daily record of thoughts, impressions, and autobiographical information; a journal is often a source of ideas for writing.

134 **Juxtaposition:** Placing two ideas (words or pictures) side by side so that their closeness creates a new, often ironic meaning.

Limiting the subject: Narrowing the subject to a specific topic that is suitable for the writing or speaking task.

Literal: The actual or dictionary meaning of a word; language that means exactly what it appears to mean.

Loaded words: Words that are slanted for or against the subject.

Logic: The science of correct reasoning; correctly using facts, examples, and reasons to support your point.

Modifier: A word, phrase, or clause that limits or describes another word or group of words. (See "Adjective" and "Adverb" in the index.)

Narration: Writing that tells a story or recounts an event.

Objective: Relating information in an impersonal manner; without feelings or opinions.

Observation: Paying close attention to people, places, things, and events to collect details for later use.

Overview: A general idea of what is to be covered in a piece of writing.

Personal narrative: Personal writing that covers an event in the writer's life; it often contains personal comments and observations as well as a description of the event.

Persuasion: Writing that is meant to change a reader's thinking or action.

Poetic license: The freedom a writer has to bend the rules of writing to achieve a certain effect.

Point of view: The position or angle from which a story is told.

Premise: A statement or point that serves as the basis of a discussion or debate.

Process: A method of doing something that involves several steps or stages; the writing process involves prewriting, composing, revising, and proofreading.

Profile: Writing that reveals an individual or re-creates a time period, using interviews and research.

Prose: Writing or speaking in the usual or ordinary form; prose becomes poetry when it takes on rhyme and rhythm.

Purpose: The specific reason a person has for writing; the goal of writing.

Reminiscence: Writing that focuses on a memorable past experience.

Report: A writing that results from gathering, investigating, and organizing facts and thoughts on a topic.

Revision: Changing a piece of writing to improve it in style or content.

Spontaneous: Doing, thinking, or writing without planning. (See "Free writing," 020.)

Subjective: Thinking or writing that includes personal feelings, attitudes, and opinions.

Syntax: The order and relationship of words in a sentence.

Theme: The central idea in a piece of writing (lengthy writings may have several themes); a term used to describe a short essay.

Thesis statement: A statement of the purpose, intent, or main idea of an essay.

Tone: The writer's attitude toward the subject; a writer's tone can be serious, sarcastic, tongue-in-cheek, solemn, objective, etc.

Topic: The specific subject of a piece of writing.

Transitions: Words or phrases that help tie ideas together.

Unity: A sense of oneness; writing in which each sentence helps to develop the main idea.

Universal: A topic or idea that applies to everyone.

Usage: The way in which people use language; language is generally considered to be standard (formal and informal) or nonstandard. Only standard usage is acceptable in writing.

Vivid details: Details that appeal to the senses and help the reader see, feel, smell, taste, and hear the subject being written about.

135 A Survey of Writing Forms

The chart that follows classifies the different forms of writing in one of six ways. (See 277-397 for guidelines and models.) Experiment with all forms of writing, moving freely between "categories." An essay, for example, can (and should) be creative as well as informative.

PERSONAL WRITING

Remembering & Sharing
Exploring, free flowing
Promotes writing fluency

Journals • Reminiscences • Logs • Diaries •
Personal Essays and Narratives • Listing •
Free Writing • Clustering • Brainstorming

SUBJECT WRITING

Searching & Reporting
Investigating
Broadens writing
  experiences

Descriptions • Profiles • Case Studies •
Firsthand Experiences • Summary Reports •
Eyewitness Accounts • Observation Reports •
Personal Research Reports • Interviews

CREATIVE WRITING

Inventing & Imitating
Reshaping ideas
Encourages creativity

Poems • Myths • Plays • Stories •
Anecdotes • Songs • Ads • Jokes •
Parodies • Character Sketches

REFLECTIVE WRITING

Reflecting & Speculating
Searching for meaning
  in experiences
Reinforces complex
  thinking

Essays of Illustration • Dialogues of Ideas •
Essays of Explanation • Essays of Reflection •
Position Papers • Personal Commentaries •
Responses to Literature • Editorials •
Essays of Opposing Ideas • Pet Peeves

ACADEMIC WRITING

Informing & Analyzing
Shaping information into
  clear essays
Develops organizing skills

Essays of Information • Essays to Compare •
Essays of Definition • Cause/Effect Essays •
Problem/Solution Essays • Summaries •
Essays of Argumentation • Paragraphs/Essays

BUSINESS WRITING

Questioning & Answering
Writing to get a job done
Builds real-world writing

Letters of Inquiry • Résumés • Memos •
Letters of Application • Messages •
Follow-Up Letters • Writing Instructions

⒀⒍ Writing About a Person

Whenever possible, write about someone you know—or would like to know. Follow the steps in the writing process, using the suggested prewriting techniques to gather as much information and as many specific details as you can. The suggestions that follow will help you think about your topic on a variety of levels.

1. **Observe** • Begin gathering details by observing the person you are describing; notice in particular those details of personality and character that set your subject apart from other people.

2. **Investigate** • Talk to your subject (in person, by phone, or by letter). Have some specific questions ready ahead of time, but be prepared to add or follow up as you go along. What are your subject's goals, dreams, attitudes, concerns, pet peeves, hobbies . . . ? Quote your subject directly whenever possible (use a tape recorder). Read about your subject if she or he is well known and not available for an interview.

3. **Define** • Determine what type of person it is you are describing (child/adult, student/professional, shy/mischievous, friend/stranger) and how he or she is like other people of the same type.

4. **Describe** • List the important physical characteristics, mannerisms, and personality traits, especially those that make your subject unique or worth reading about. (Remember: Show, don't tell. Include people and action in your writing and let them "show" the reader what your subject is like.)

5. **Recall** • Add details (anecdotes and stories) recounting things your subject has said and done in the past. Try to recall at least one specific incident that reveals the kind of person your subject really is.

6. **Compare** • Compare (and contrast) your subject to other people. Who is he or she most like? A little bit like? Not at all like? What object, thing, place, word, sport, or plant could she or he be compared to?

7. **Analyze** • Ask others about your subject and notice how they react to your questions. Their reactions can tell you (and your reader) about the kind of person your subject truly is. What are his or her strengths and weaknesses? How does he or she influence others?

8. **Evaluate** • Determine why this person is important to you, to others, to the community.

possible
topics

I know a special person, a person who . . .

is clever/funny	is a living legend	is a little weird
is stubborn	is always happy	is afraid of nothing
is helpful/kind	is a perfectionist	is always talking
is very talented	is a complainer	is always around
is phony	is very patriotic	is always in trouble

⟨137⟩ Writing About a Place

Whenever possible, write about a place you know well, one that left a distinct impression on you, or one that is an important part of your life. Follow the steps in the writing process and gather enough details to make your writing interesting to you and your reader. The suggestions below should help get you started.

1. **Observe** • Continue gathering details by observing (firsthand, in books, in pictures) your subject and the people, events, and feelings that contribute to making this place unique. Notice the way people react to it and what their general attitude seems to be.

2. **Investigate** • Talk to others about this place, its past, its future. Talk to the place. *(Talk to a place?)* Why not. Try something like this: "If this place could talk, what would it say?" Or wonder out loud or on paper: "I wonder what this place thinks, feels, hears . . ."

3. **Define** • Determine what type of place it is you are writing about (land, landmark, building, etc.) and to what degree it is or is not like other places of the same type. What is its function or purpose?

4. **Describe** • Describe the age, size, shape, color, and other important physical features. Where is it located, or where does it spend most of its time? What is its most outstanding feature? Show, don't tell. Include people and action in your writing (including yourself) to show the reader what this place is really like—what it feels, smells, tastes, and sounds like—as well as how it looks.

5. **Recall** • Add information you remember from the past. Stories or anecdotes are especially important.

6. **Compare** • Compare (and contrast) your subject to other places. What other place is it most like? A little bit like? Sometimes like? Not at all like?

7. **Analyze** • Talk to other people about your subject. What do they remember or how do they feel about this place? Does it remind them of other places? In what way? What are its strengths, its weaknesses? What is its future?

8. **Evaluate** • Why is this place important to you, to others, to the community? What would things be like if this place were no longer there?

possible topics

your favorite classroom	the stadium before a concert
your favorite hangout	a shoreline or beach
a nursing home	the principal's office
the school library	the park after a picnic
the dentist's office	an unusual hole on a golf course
a deserted house	a polluted river
an auto salvage yard	a music store

138 Writing About an Object

As with any type of writing, select a subject that interests you. Do some free writing or clustering about your subject to find a focus, an angle, or a slant that you think might make it more interesting for your reader. Continue other prewriting activities, until you have gathered enough information to get you started. The suggestions below may also help.

1. **Observe** • Observe the object closely to determine how it works. Also notice how other people use this object and how they feel about it.

2. **Investigate** • Ask other people about their experiences, attitudes, and feelings about this object. Read about it.

3. **Define** • What class or category does this object fall into? How is this object similar to or different from other objects in this same category?

4. **Describe** • Describe the color, size, shape, and texture of your subject (but don't overdo it). Describe the important parts and how they fit together. (Remember: Showing is better than telling.) Surround your object with people, action, and places so that the reader can get a true picture of your subject and its importance.

5. **Recall** • Try to remember an interesting incident or story involving this object that will help the reader better understand your subject.

6. **Compare** • What other objects is your subject most like, least like, not at all like? What person (or type of person) does it remind you of? What season? What foreign country?

7. **Analyze** • Try to find out when this object was discovered, built, first used, etc. What are its strengths and weaknesses? What changes would you make in it if you were able?

8. **Evaluate** • Why is this object important? Does it have any practical, aesthetic (artistic), or historical value?

Once you have gathered enough detail, begin writing. Think of an unusual way to approach your subject. How about a news report, fairy tale, parody, TV drama, rap poem . . . ? You can always go back to a more traditional form if your new approach doesn't work out.

possible topics

a video game	a favorite movie	a picture
a school bus	a special coat	a favorite shirt
a book	a favorite food	a certain clock
a tool	a musical instrument	a uniform
a closet	an unusual building	a car or bike
a camera	a billboard	a drawing
a poster	a pet	a story

"Knowledge is of two kinds. We know a subject ourselves, or we know where we can find information upon it."

—Samuel Johnson

Searching for Information

139   As a writer, you can draw on two types of material. The first type includes your own personal experiences, ideas, and knowledge; the second consists of the ideas, experiences, and knowledge of other people. You can collect information from other people in several ways: (1) by observing, listening to, and talking with them; (2) by reading what they have written in books, articles, and newspapers; (3) by listening to or observing what they have recorded on tapes, films, CDs, and other media. Most of your collecting can be done in two convenient locations—at the library or at a computer.

140 Using the Library

Collecting information in the library is like detective work: it requires time, thought, and an inspired use of clues. As an information detective, one of your best informants is the librarian. A trained expert in the storage and retrieval of information, the librarian can help you find the information that you will put together to "make your case" in writing.

141 Using the Computer

Collecting information with a computer can be even more rewarding—and convenient—than using a library. In fact, if you have access to a modem and a phone line, you can tap into the resources of nearly every library in the country. You can exchange information with other students (and some experts) via one of the hundreds of bulletin boards now available. Interactive and CD-ROM programs make it possible for you to search through large volumes of materials in minutes. Note • If you don't have a personal computer, you may be able to find one you can use in your school or public library.

what's ahead? In this section of your handbook, you'll find guidelines and advice on using the library and the computer to find information. In addition, you'll receive useful tips on how to better use a reference book, dictionary, and thesaurus.

142 Finding Books

To find books in a library, you need to use a catalog. Library catalogs take two forms. One form is a cabinet with many small drawers and alphabetically arranged cards. This traditional form of catalog is called a **card catalog**. The other form of catalog can be found at a computer terminal. This is the computerized or **on-line catalog**.

143 The Card Catalog

The **card catalog** is an index (listing) of nearly all the materials in the library. The most common type of card catalog is a "dictionary catalog" in which subject, author, and title cards are filed alphabetically. Each book has at least three entry cards: one for the general subject, one for the author's name, and one for the title. There are also one or more cards for additional subjects. Once you've found your title, copy down the call number.

Sample Catalog Cards

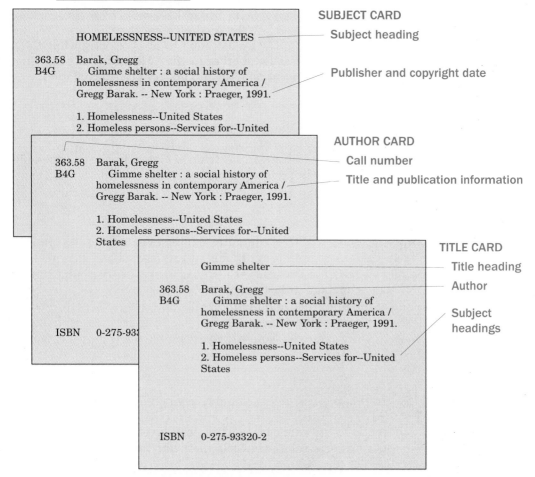

SUBJECT CARD

HOMELESSNESS--UNITED STATES ── Subject heading

363.58 Barak, Gregg
B4G   Gimme shelter : a social history of ── Publisher and copyright date
homelessness in contemporary America /
Gregg Barak. -- New York : Praeger, 1991.

1. Homelessness--United States
2. Homeless persons--Services for--United

AUTHOR CARD

363.58 Barak, Gregg ── Call number
B4G   Gimme shelter : a social history of
homelessness in contemporary America / ── Title and publication information
Gregg Barak. -- New York : Praeger, 1991.

1. Homelessness--United States
2. Homeless persons--Services for--United
States

TITLE CARD

Gimme shelter ── Title heading

363.58 Barak, Gregg ── Author
B4G   Gimme shelter : a social history of
homelessness in contemporary America /
Gregg Barak. -- New York : Praeger, 1991. ── Subject headings

ISBN   0-275-93   1. Homelessness--United States
2. Homeless persons--Services for--United
States

ISBN   0-275-93320-2

144 The Computerized Catalog

The computerized or on-line catalog can make finding information easier and faster. What follows is a typical start-up screen and some basic guidelines to get you started.

```
Welcome to the Rapid City Public
Access On-line Catalog
Databases:
    1. author, title, subject searching
    2. general periodical index
    3. information about system libraries
To make a selection, type a number and
then press [RETURN]>>>
```

Let's say you need to find a book. By simply typing in the number 1, you are ready to begin. After making a series of choices, you may come up with a screen that looks like the one shown below. Either print out the screen or write down the information you need (perhaps the title and call number).

Sample On-Line Entry

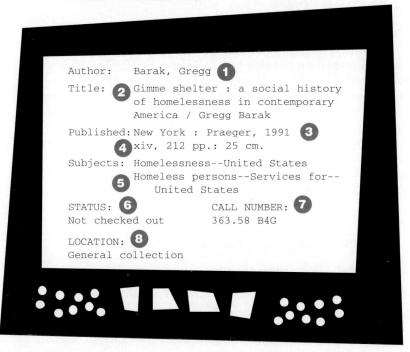

```
Author:    Barak, Gregg  1
Title:  2 Gimme shelter : a social history
           of homelessness in contemporary
           America / Gregg Barak
Published: New York : Praeger, 1991  3
        4 xiv, 212 pp.: 25 cm.
Subjects:  Homelessness--United States
        5  Homeless persons--Services for--
              United States
STATUS:  6            CALL NUMBER:  7
Not checked out        363.58 B4G

LOCATION:  8
General collection
```

1 Author's name

2 Title heading

3 Publisher and copyright date

4 Descriptive information

5 Subject heading(s)

6 Library status

7 Call number

8 Location information

145 Keyword Searching

Probably the greatest advantage of using an on-line catalog lies in your ability to do **keyword searching**. This means that you need to know only part of the title or author's name in order to find the work.

For example, suppose you are searching for the title *Gimme Shelter.* You remember only the word *Shelter.* If you look in the traditional card catalog under *Shelter,* you will not find this work. However, if your computerized library system has the appropriate software, you need only select *keyword searching.* From there, you might select "title search" and type in "Shelter" or "find Shelter," and the computer will find the book. Similarly, if you can remember only part of an author's name, the computer can help you. Both of these types of title and author searches are forms of keyword searching.

146 Keyword Subject Searching

On-line catalogs also offer advantages for subject searching. Suppose you are searching for information on bats. You select "subject," type in the word *bats,* and instantly gather a huge number of entries. That's similar to what you can do using the traditional card catalog. With a computer, however, this list is only the beginning.

Broadening a Search

Once you're in the subject field, you can find even more entries, by choosing *keyword searching, advanced keyword searching,* or *expert keyword searching.* Then you might type in a command such as "bats **or** insects." The computer will search for records that contain either of these terms and offer hundreds or perhaps even thousands of possibilities.

Narrowing a Search

Sometimes, however, too many possibilities is also a problem. To solve this problem, keyword searching enables you to limit possibilities. Two ways to do this are by using the words "and" and "not." For example, suppose you are looking for information about dragonflies, but you are interested only in dragonflies preserved in amber. In this case, you might type in "dragonflies **and** amber." The computer would gather only those records containing both terms. Similarly, suppose you were looking for information about civil wars; however, the U.S. Civil War is not of interest to you. In this case, you would type in "civil wars **not** United States." The computer would gather only those records about civil wars in countries other than the United States.

Terms for Broadening or Narrowing a Search

AND: find records that contain more than one term / bats and radar

OR: find records that contain either term / teen or adolescent

NOT: exclude records that contain a term / oils spills not Exxon Valdez

147 The Dewey Decimal System

You can use either the card catalog or the on-line catalog to help you identify books (and other library materials) related to your research. To find a book on the library shelves, you will need to use the **call number** listed on the catalog card or on-line entry. This call number refers to the classification plan used to arrange books. The most common plan used in high schools and public libraries is the Dewey Decimal classification system.

148 Major Subject Classes

As you can see in the following chart, the **Dewey Decimal System** divides books into 10 main subject classes numbered from 000-999.

Dewey Decimal System Major Subject Classes

000-099	**General Works** ● These works include encyclopedias and handbooks.
100-199	**Philosophy**
200-299	**Religion** ● Mythology is also shelved here.
300-399	**Social Sciences** ● Books about education, government, law, and economics carry these numbers.
400-499	**Languages** ● Look here for dictionaries and books about grammar.
500-599	**Sciences** ● Here are books about biology, chemistry, and other sciences, as well as books about math.
600-699	**Technology** ● Look here for books about engineering, medicine, cooking, and inventions.
700-799	**Arts and Recreation** ● Shelved here are books about painting, music, and other arts, as well as books about sports and games.
800-899	**Literature** ● Look here for poetry, plays, famous speeches, and essays.
900-999	**History, Travel, Biography, and Geography**

149 Divisions of the Class Number

These 10 subject classes are subdivided into divisions, each with its own number. The divisions are then divided into as many sections and subsections as needed. Each of these divisions has its own number, as shown below.

Divisions of the Dewey Decimal Class Number

900	History	Class
970	History of North America	Division
973	History of the United States	Section
973.7	History of the U.S. Civil War	Subsection
973.74	History of Civil War Songs	Subsection

150 Locating Books by Call Number

In addition to its class number, a **call number** contains the first letter of the author's last name. It *may* also contain a cutter number assigned by the librarian to help in shelving the book and the first letter of the title's first significant word. The call number determines where a book is located in the library.

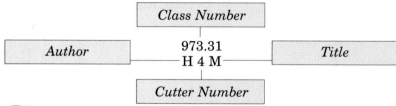

Class Number
973.31

Author			Title

H 4 M

Cutter Number

The exceptions to this classification system are fiction books and the individual biography. Fiction is usually kept in a separate section of the library where the books are arranged by the author's last name. (Classic books, however, are listed and shelved in the literature section.) Biographies are arranged on separate shelves by the last name of the person written about.

151 Searching the Shelves

When you go to the shelves to get your book, you must remember to look carefully at the call numbers. Because some call numbers contain several decimal points and are longer than others, they can easily distract you into looking in the wrong place for your book. For instance, the call number 973.2 is located on the shelf after a book with the call number 973.198. (See the illustration below.) Also, you will most likely find several books with the same Dewey Decimal number. Whenever this happens, the books are arranged alphabetically by author abbreviation.

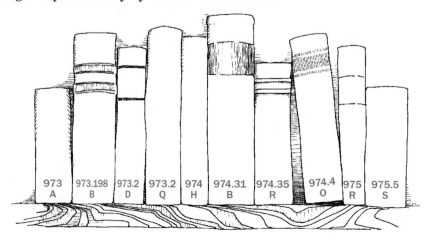

| 973 | 973.198 | 973.2 | 973.2 | 974 | 974.31 | 974.35 | 974.4 | 975 | 975.5 |
| A | B | D | Q | H | B | R | O | R | S |

152 Finding Articles in Periodicals

The best tool for locating articles in periodicals (magazines and journals) is the journal indexes that can be found in the reference or periodical section of the library. The most widely used journal index is the **Readers' Guide to Periodical Literature**. Some libraries also carry an electronic version of this index. Other libraries carry a similar computer index called the **General Periodicals Index**.

153 Readers' Guide to Periodical Literature

If you are looking for information on a current topic, the *Readers' Guide* will direct you to specific magazine articles. It will also help you find magazine articles from years ago. To use a hard copy of this index, simply select a volume that covers the appropriate year(s) and search alphabetically for the subject or author that interests you. You will avoid unnecessary work and frustration by checking your library's current list of periodicals. This way you won't spend time recording information about articles from periodicals your library may not have.

Look closely at the sample page from the *Readers' Guide*. Pay careful attention to the following points:

- Articles are arranged alphabetically by subject and author; the title of the article is listed under one of these two entries.

- Each subject entry is divided into subtopics whenever there are several articles on the same subject listed together.

- The *Readers' Guide* is cross-referenced, giving other subject headings where you may find additional articles on related topics.

154 Locating Articles

In some libraries, you must give a library staff person a *call slip* listing the title, date, and volume number for each of the periodicals you are interested in. A member of the staff will get these issues for you. In other libraries, periodicals are shelved so that you can locate specific issues yourself. Check with your librarian if you are not sure how periodicals are arranged in your library.

155 Sample Readers' Guide Page

"SEE ALSO" REFERENCE

PAGE NUMBER(S)

VOLUME

NAME OF MAGAZINE

NAME OF AUTHOR

SUBTOPIC

DATE

"SEE" CROSS-REFERENCE

TITLE OF ARTICLE

SUBJECT ENTRY

AUTHOR ENTRY

ENVIRONMENTAL MOVEMENT
See also
Conservation of resources
Environmental associations
Industry and the environment
Minorities and the environment
Field observations [interview with W. Berry] J. Fisher-
Smith. il por *Orion* v12 p50-9 Aut '93
Pacific Northwest
Reconciling rural communities and resource conservation
[Pacific Northwest; with editorial comment by Timothy
O'Riordan] K. Johnson. bibl f il *Environment* v35
p inside cover, 16-20+ N '93
Vancouver Island (B.C.)
Brazil of the North? [battle over logging in Vancouver
Island's Clayoquot Sound area] C. A. White. il *Canada
and the World* v59 p8-9 S '93
ENVIRONMENTAL POLICY
See also
Air pollution—Laws and regulations
Genetic research—Environmental aspects
Industry and the environment
The compensation game [takings cases] F. Williams.
il por *Wilderness* v57 p28-33 Fall '93
Images of home [population and the environment] C. A.
Douglas. il *Wilderness* v57 p10-22 Fall '93
Unfunded federal environmental mandates. P. H. Abelson.
Science v262 p1191 N 19 '93
International aspects
The best environment of 1993. il *Time* v143 p74 Ja 3 '94
Public opinion
Of global concern: results of the Health of the planet sur-
vey [cover story] R. E. Dunlap and others. bibl f il
Environment v35 p6-15+ N '93
United States
See Environmental policy
ENVIRONMENTAL RACISM *See* Minorities and the
environment
ENVIRONMENTAL REGULATIONS *See* Environmental
policy
ENVIRONMENTAL SYSTEMS PRODUCTS INC.
Playing favorites [L Weicker fires L. Goldberg over
Connecticut state contract for auto emissions testing]
C. Byron. il pors *New York* v27 p12-13 Ja 10 '94
ENVIROTEST SYSTEMS CORPORATION
Playing favorites [L. Weicker fires L. Goldberg over
Connecticut state contract for auto emissions testing]
C. Byron il pors *New York* v27 p12-13 Ja 10 '94
EPHRON, NORA
about
Sleepless in Seattle's Nora Ephron [interview] C. Krupp. il
por *Glamour* v91 p147-8 Ag '93
EPIDEMICS
See also
AIDS (Disease)

156 Finding Reference Books

If you've asked the librarian some questions, used encyclopedias, or searched some of the periodical indexes, you may already be familiar with the reference section of your library. This is the place to go for quick facts and information. The following list includes useful reference titles:

Statesman's Yearbook is an annual publication devoted to the nations of the world. It includes facts about government, geography, population, religion, education, social welfare, and so on. A bibliography follows each entry.

The World Almanac and Book of Facts and **Information Please Almanac, Atlas and Yearbook** are two extremely useful annual publications. They contain extensive information on the United States and other countries, a review of the past year's events, weights and measures, maps, history, statistics, and many other kinds of general information.

Current Biography is published monthly and annually. Each article includes a photo of the individual, a biographical sketch, and information concerning the person's birth date, address, occupation, etc.

The Negro Almanac is a reference work about African-Americans. It covers a wide range of topics in the social sciences and includes many articles, illustrations, statistical tables and charts on various aspects of African-American life, history, and culture.

The Handbook of North American Indians provides an encyclopedic summary of what is known about the prehistory, history, and cultures of the native peoples of North America. Each volume contains essays written by specialists on Indian life.

The McGraw-Hill Encyclopedia of Science and Technology includes many articles written by leading authorities in each field. Articles are grouped by major subject areas. There is an annual yearbook.

Congressional Quarterly Weekly is a reliable news service providing weekly summaries of the actions and developments in Congress.

Facts on File is a weekly news digest published in loose-leaf format. It is arranged by such subject headings as world, national, and foreign affairs, Latin America, finance, economy, arts, science, etc. Indexes are published bimonthly. Maps and tables are included.

Bartlett's Familiar Quotations contains 20,000 quotations arranged in chronological order from ancient times to the present.

extend

The list above contains a small sampling of the many books available in the reference section. With a little effort, you're bound to find just the right book, one that fits your topic perfectly.

157 Using the Dictionary

A dictionary can help you gather many different types of information. (All are illustrated on the following page.)

Spelling Not knowing how to spell a word can make it difficult to find in the dictionary, but not impossible. You will be surprised at how quickly you can find most words by following their sounded-out spelling.

Capital letters If you need to know whether a certain word is capitalized, it will probably be faster and more accurate to look it up in the dictionary than to ask a friend who thinks he or she knows.

Syllabication Besides locating meaning and pronunciation, the dictionary is most often used to determine where you can divide a word.

Pronunciation To remember a word and its meaning it is helpful to know its correct pronunciation. The dictionary gives you the pronunciation of each word next to its meaning. It also lists a key to the pronunciation markings at the bottom of the page.

Parts of speech The dictionary uses nine abbreviations for the parts of speech.

n.	noun	**v.t.**	transitive verb	**adj.**	adjective
pron.	pronoun	**interj.**	interjection	**adv.**	adverb
v.i.	intransitive verb	**conj.**	conjunction	**prep.**	preposition

Etymology Many entries also contain etymologies, or word histories. You may find interesting information here about how the word entered the language. In most cases, you can find an explanation of the abbreviations used in the etymologies by reading the pages in the front of your dictionary.

Restrictive labels Subject labels tell you that a word has a special meaning when used in a particular field (mus. for music, med. for medicine, zool. for zoology, etc.). Usage labels tell you how a word is used (slang, colloq. for colloquial, dial. for dialect, etc.). Geographic labels tell you in which region of the country (N.E. for New England, West, South, etc.) the definition applies.

Synonyms and antonyms Even though the best place to look for synonyms and antonyms is in a thesaurus (159), a dictionary will often list and label synonyms and antonyms after a word's meaning.

Illustrations If a definition is difficult to make clear with words alone, a picture or drawing is used.

Meaning Even though you probably know how to look up the meaning of a word, it is not quite as easy to figure out what to do with all those meanings once you have found them. Some dictionaries list their meanings chronologically, which means the oldest meaning of the word is given first, then the newer or technical versions. Others place the most common meaning first. So, you can see the danger of simply taking the first meaning listed—it may not be the meaning you are after at all.

⬤158 Sample Dictionary Page

GUIDE WORDS

SYLLABICATION AND
PARTS OF SPEECH

MEANING

SPELLING OF VERB FORMS

SPELLING AND CAPITAL LETTERS

ILLUSTRATION

PRONUNCIATION

ETYMOLOGY (History)

ACCENT MARK

SYNONYMS

USAGE

PRONUNCIATION KEY

---

mixer • mock   747

¹**mo•bile** \'mō-bəl, -ˌbīl, *also* -ˌbēl\ *adj* [ME *mobyll*, fr. MF *mobile*, fr. L *mobilis*, fr. *movere* to move] (15c) **1** : capable of moving or being moved: MOVABLE <a - missile launcher> **2 a** : changeable in appearance, mood, or purpose <- face> **b** : VERSATILE **3** : relating to a mobile—**mo•bil•i•ty** \mō-'bil-ət-e\ *n*

²**mo•bile** \'mō-ˌbēl\ *n* (1936) : a construction or sculpture frequently of wire and sheet metal shapes with parts that can be set in motion by air currents; *also* : a similar structure (as of paper or plastic) suspended so that it moves in a current of air

-mobile *comb form* [auto*mobile*] **1**: motorized vehicle <snow*mobile*> **2**: automotive vehicle bringing services to the public <blood*mobile*> <book*mobile*>

mobile home *n* (1949) : a dwelling structure built on a steel chassis and fitted with wheels that is intended to be hauled to a usu. permanent site—compare MOTOR HOME

mo•bi•li•za•tion \ˌmō-bə-lə-'zā-shən\ *n* (1799) **1** : the act of mobilizing **2** : the state of being mobilized

mo•bi•lize \'mō-bə-ˌlīz\ *vb* **-lized; -liz•ing** *vt* (1838) **1 a** : to put into movement or circulation <- financial assets> **b** : to release (something stored in the organism) for bodily use **2 a** : to assemble and make ready for war duty **b** : to marshal (as resources) for action <- support for a proposal> - *vi* : to undergo mobilization

Mö•bi•us strip \ˌmœ-bē-əs-, ˌmə(r), ˌmō-\ *n* [August F. *Möbius* † 1868 Ger. mathematician] (1904) : a one-sided surface that is constructed from a rectangle by holding one end fixed, rotating the opposite end through 180 degrees, and applying it to the first end

Möbius strip

mob•oc•ra•cy \mä-'bä-kre-sə\ *n* (1754) **1** : rule by the mob **2** : the mob as a ruling class— **mob•o•crat** \'mä-bə-ˌkrat\ *n* — **mob•o•crat•ic** \ˌmä-bə-'kra-tik\ *adj*

mob•ster \'mäb-stər\ *n* (1917) : a member of a criminal gang

moc•ca•sin \'mä-kə-sən\ *n* [Virginia Algonquian *mockasin*] (ca. 1612) **1 a** : a soft leather heelless shoe or boot with the sole brought up the sides of the foot and over the toes where it is joined with a puckered seam to a U-shaped piece lying on top of the foot **b** : a regular shoe having a seam on the forepart of the vamp imitating the seam of a moccasin **2 a** : WATER MOCCASIN **b** : a snake (as of the genus *Natrix*) resembling a water moccasin

moccasin flower *n* (1680) : any of several lady's slippers (genus *Cypripedium*); esp : a once common woodland orchid (*C. acaule*) of eastern No. America with pink or white moccasin-shaped flowers

mo•cha \'mō-kə\ *n* [*Mocha*, Arabia] (1773) **1 a** (1) : a superior Arabian coffee consisting of small green or yellowish beans (2) : a coffee of superior quality **b** : a flavoring made of strong coffee infusion or of a mixture of cocoa or chocolate with coffee **2** : a pliable suede-finished glove leather from African sheepskins **3** : a dark chocolate-brown color

¹**mock** \'mäk, 'mȯk\ *vb* [ME, fr. MF *mocquer*] *vt* (15c) **1** : to treat with contempt : DERIDE **2** : to disappoint the hopes of **3** : DEFY, CHALLENGE **4 a** : to imitate (as a mannerism) closely : MIMIC **b** : to mimic in sport or derision - *vi* : JEER, SCOFF *syn* see RIDICULE, COPY — **mock•er** *n* — **mock•ing•ly** \'mä-kiŋ-le, 'mȯ\ *adv*

²**mock** *n* (15c) **1** : an act of ridicule or derision : JEER **2** : one that is an object of derision or scorn **3** : MOCKERY **4 a** : an act of imitation **b** : something made as an imitation

³**mock** *adv* (ca. 1619) : in an insincere or counterfeit manner – **usu. used in combination** <*mock*-serious>

\ə\abut \'ʳ\kitten, F table \ər\further \a\ash \ā\āce \ä\cot, cart
\aù\out \ch\chin \e\bet \ē\easy \g\go \i\hit \ī\ice \j\job \ŋ\sing
\ō\go \ȯ\law \ȯi\boy \th\thin \t̷h\the \ü\loot \ù\foot \y\yet
\zh\vision \ȧ, k, ʳ, œ, ͧœ, ü̵, ʳ\see Guide to Pronunciation

---

159 Using the Thesaurus

A thesaurus is, in a sense, the opposite of a dictionary. You go to a dictionary when you know the word but need the definition. You go to a thesaurus when you know the definition but need the word. For example, you might want a word that means *fear*, the kind of fear that causes more worry than pain. You need the word to complete the following sentence:

Joan experienced a certain amount of _____ over the upcoming exam.

If you have a thesaurus in dictionary form, simply look up the word *fear* as you would in a dictionary. If, however, you have a traditional thesaurus, you must first look up your word in the alphabetical INDEX at the back of the thesaurus. You might find this entry for fear in the index:

FEAR 860
Fearful painful 830
timid 862

The numbers after *fear* are GUIDE NUMBERS, not page numbers. (Guide numbers are similar to the topic numbers in your handbook.) For instance, if you look up number 860 in the body of the thesaurus, you will find a long list of synonyms for the word *fear*. These include *fearfulness, timidity, diffidence, apprehensiveness, solicitude, anxiety, misgiving, mistrust, suspicion,* and *qualm*. You select the word *anxiety,* and your sentence becomes

Joan experienced a certain amount of <u>anxiety</u> over the upcoming exam.

---

259 PERSONAL AFFECTIONS 859-861

860. FEAR—*N.* **fear,** timidity, diffidence, apprehensiveness, fearfulness, solicitude, anxiety, care, apprehension, misgiving, mistrust, suspicion, qualm, hesitation.

trepidation, flutter, fear and trembling, perturbation, tremor, restlessness, disquietude, funk *[colloq.]*.

fright, alarm, dread, awe, terror, horror, dismay, consternation, panic, scare; stampede *[of horses]*.

V. **fear,** be afraid, apprehend, dread, distrust; hesitate, falter, wince, flinch, shy, shrink, fly.

tremble, shake, shiver, shudder, flutter, quake, quaver, quiver, quail.

frighten, fright, terrify, inspire (*or* excite) fear, bulldoze *[colloq.]*, alarm, startle, scare, dismay, astound; awe; strike terror, appall, unman, petrify, horrify.

Adj. **afraid,** frightened, alarmed, fearful, timid, timorous, nervous, diffident, fainthearted, tremulous, shaky, afraid of one's shadow, apprehensive; aghast, awe-struck, awe-stricken, horror-stricken, panic-stricken.

861. [absence of fear] COURAGE—*N.* courage, bravery, valor, resoluteness, boldness, spirit, daring, gallantry, intrepidity, prowess, heroism, chivalry, audacity, rashness, dash, defiance, confidence, self-reliance; manhood, manliness, nerve, pluck, mettle, grit, virtue, hardihood, fortitude, firmness, backbone.

160 Using a Book

Knowing the parts of a book can help you find information easily and quickly. Note that an appendix, a glossary, a bibliography, and an index are typically found only in nonfiction books.

The **title page** is usually the first printed page in a book. It gives you (1) the full title of the book, (2) the author's name, (3) the publisher's name, and (4) the place of publication.

The **copyright** page follows the title page. Here you will find the year the copyright was issued (usually the same year the book was published).

The **preface** (also called foreword, introduction, or acknowledgement) comes before the table of contents and gives you an idea of what the book is about, who may have been involved in writing it, and why it was written.

The **table of contents** is one section most of you are familiar with since it shows you the major divisions of the book (units, chapters, and topics). It comes right before the body and helps you locate major topics or subjects covered in the book.

The **body** of the book, which follows the table of contents, is the main text of the book.

An **epigraph** is a quotation at the beginning of a chapter or division to suggest what the theme or central idea is going to be.

A **footnote** is a note placed at the bottom of a page that either gives the source of the information used in the text or adds useful information.

An **appendix** may follow the body. This section provides extra information, often in the form of maps, charts, tables, diagrams, letters, or documents.

A **glossary**, the dictionary portion of the book, may follow the appendix. It is an alphabetical listing of technical terms, foreign words, or special words, with an explanation or definition for each.

The **index** is an alphabetical listing of all the important topics in the book. Though similar to the table of contents, the index is a much more detailed list. It tells you on which pages of the book you will find the specific information you need.

The **bibliography** is a list of sources used by the author, as well as suggestions for further reading.

 **a closer look** There are two kinds of bibliographies—one lists the sources used when writing a book or paper; the other lists titles that are related to the subject. Be sure to take advantage of both bibliographies as you search for information.

161 Surfing for Information

Using Software: Like the library, the computer can offer you a world of information. One way is through the use of software programs, either your own personal programs or those available at schools or libraries. Reference material on CD-ROM can be especially helpful when you need background information for a quick overview of your topic.

Networking: A second way to gain information is to be part of a local area network (LAN). People in businesses and universities are often linked by LANS so that they are able to trade information or access it from a central computer. Some schools also have computers that are linked by LANS.

Accessing Other Services: A third way to access information with a computer is through your own personal modem. With a modem, you can hook up to other individual computers or huge networks of computers. Through a modem you may be able to access your local library's on-line catalog. If you have a modem, you can also purchase an on-line service (America On-line, Prodigy, Compu-Serve, etc.) that can offer you everything from the latest news and weather reports to reference books to university research. Through on-line services, you can also access the Internet and its thousands of smaller network connections.

162 Internet

Right now, the Internet is the most complex vehicle on the information superhighway. It links thousands of computers all over the world. Users "surf" the Internet, looking for a wide array of information, leaving messages, exchanging ideas, offering many types of shareware, and suggesting solutions to problems.

If you have access to the Internet, you may find it to be the most exciting way to search for information. In particular, you may want to access a subset of computers on the Internet called the World-Wide Web. Because databases on the web are linked, you can use navigational tools to highlight information in one location that you want to explore in more detail in other parts of the web.

the bottom line

Many software packages are now being developed and refined to help you find your way in this rapidly swelling ocean of information. So, keep yourself up on what's going on—and, then, "Catch a wave!"

"Research is to see what everybody else has seen, and to think what nobody else has thought."

—Albert Szent-Gyorgyi

Writing the Research Paper

163　　A research paper is a carefully planned essay that has been thoroughly investigated and analyzed by the writer. Research papers are written to share new information or prove a point. What sets them apart from other essays is the amount of information gathered and used in the writing. A research paper may include ideas from books, magazines, newspapers, computer files, or interviews. (Any ideas borrowed from different sources are credited to the original writer or speaker.) Most research papers are at least five pages in length and may include a title page, an outline, the actual essay, and a Works Cited or bibliography page.

164 What does it mean to be a researcher?

To William Least Heat-Moon, author of *Blue Highways*, it meant packing up his van and traveling the back roads of America, the "blue highways." It meant setting out on a personal quest, living and learning on the open road. To Joanne Hauser, a student researcher, it meant four weeks' worth of reading, interviewing, observing, and volunteering so she could evaluate the day-care services in her city. It meant becoming an active member in her community.

Becoming a researcher can mean the same to you as it did to these two individuals. It can be a process that helps you better understand the world around you. This can be the goal of all your research projects, in school and on your own, now and in the future.

what's ahead? This section of your handbook provides you with everything you need to write a research paper, from prewriting through the final documenting of your sources. Included are clear step-by-step instructions and helpful models. (This chapter follows the MLA style sheet, the most popular research-paper form in use today.)

165 Research Update

Traditionally, student researchers headed straight for their libraries to find secondary sources of information (books, magazines, etc.) for their research papers. Today, students are encouraged to work with both primary and secondary sources of information when conducting research.

Primary sources include interviews, observations, questionnaires, and so on. The researcher is personally involved in gathering facts, finding examples, and forming ideas. This process makes the whole research experience more meaningful and satisfying.

166 I-Search vs. Re-Search

One method of research that focuses almost entirely on primary sources of information is the I-Search paper. An I-Search paper begins with an individual's own natural curiosity about something. One person may wonder if he or she has what it takes to become an emergency-room nurse. Another may wonder about the risks and rewards of bungee jumping.

Once a personal need is identified, an I-Searcher then sets out in search of information and answers through visits and interviews. Magazines and books are used only when recommended by someone during an interview or visit. (People first, books second.) An I-Search paper becomes the story of an individual's own searching adventure, a story that naturally includes original thoughts and genuine feelings.

167 A Personalized Approach

Here's what we recommend for your next research paper:

Get Involved. Start by selecting a subject that really interests you, and then carry out your research personally, using both primary and secondary sources.

Keep a Journal. Consider writing in a journal during your research. Thinking and writing about your work will help you make sense of new information, refocus your thinking, and evaluate your progress.

Personalize It. Present the results of your searching and writing in a personal way that sounds like it comes from you. The more your research paper comes from your own thinking, the more satisfied you and your readers will be.

Follow the Steps. Finally, we recommend that you follow the 20 steps suggested on the following pages.

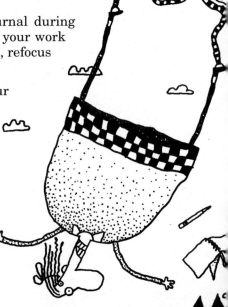

Steps in the Process

> "My idea of research is to look at the thing from all sides; the person who has seen the animal, how the animal behaves, and so on."
>
> —Marianne Moore

PREWRITING

168

1. Select an interesting subject.

Meaningful research projects start with a personal need to know or learn about something. *Which used car has the best repair record? What are the best career opportunities for young people today? What are the real risks, rewards, and costs involved in bungee jumping?* Select a general subject that suits your interests and seems practical for the time and resources available. Just make sure the subject you choose gets your teacher's approval.

2. Gather some general information.

Once you've selected a general subject, talk with people who may know something about your subject. Teachers in your school may be able to provide basic information about your subject, or they may direct you to local experts. Then do some exploratory reading in reference books, magazines, and newspapers. Look for videos, CDs, and other electronic information.

Note • Ask an aide to help you find the basic sources of information in the media center or local library. Some computer databases may be available to you, as well as the usual resources: The *Readers' Guide to Periodical Literature, New York Times* and *Washington Post* indexes, an on-line or traditional card catalog, vertical files, and so on. (Also see 139-162.)

3. Limit your subject.

As you read about your subject, ask questions such as *What do I really want to know about this subject? What makes it worth investigating? What interests me the most about it?* These types of questions help you focus on the part of your subject you will want to research. Put this central idea into words by developing a **focus** or **thesis statement**—a sentence or two that state what you plan to research. Or state your focus in the form of a research question. A two-part question is the focus, or thesis, in the second model research paper (285): "Who are these people we call 'the homeless,' and what are the reasons for their predicament?"

INSIDE info

Don't be surprised if your thesis changes as you do your research. You will probably consider a number of focuses before you settle upon the one you will finally use for your paper.

169 Searching for Information

4. Prepare a preliminary bibliography.

Continue to look for information related to your focus, or thesis, especially in sources containing up-to-date facts. Often, you can find additional good sources by checking the bibliographies in material you've already reviewed. Then make a list of the materials available on your subject. Put this information into a computer or on 3- by 5-inch bibliography cards arranged in alphabetical order by the authors' last names. If the name of an author is not known, alphabetize by the first word in the title (not including *A, An,* or *The*). Either number each entry in your computer list, or number each card in the upper right-hand corner.

Sample Bibliography Card

> Chambers, Rick. "No Place to Lay ②
>   Their Heads." The Church
>   Herald 16 Sept 1988: 9-11

Sample Note Card

> Homeless--personal close-up   ②
>
> A man sleeping on a New York sidewalk
> during the noon hour has a sign at his
> feet that reads: "Won't you help me?
> I'm cold and homeless and lonely. God
> Bless You."
>   (p. 11)

5. Take notes.

As you begin reading the material listed in your bibliography, take notes on ideas and write down quotations relating to the focus of your research.

- ◉ Keep notes on cards of the same size and style (4- by 6-inch cards are recommended).
- ◉ Write main ideas, significant details, and quotations on your cards along with the page numbers where this information can be found. Also place the number of the related bibliography entry in the upper right-hand corner.
- ◉ Use abbreviations and short phrases.
- ◉ Place quotation marks around word-for-word quotes.
- ◉ Use the ellipsis (. . .) when you leave words out of a quotation. Use brackets around words you add to a quotation. (See 184.)
- ◉ Use a diagonal (/) to indicate where a quotation has gone from one page to another in the original source. This will prove useful later when you are citing the exact pages of a quotation in your paper.
- ◉ Look up unfamiliar words in your reading. If you find that a particular word is important, copy its definition onto a note card.
- ◉ Give each card a descriptive heading, a word or phrase to highlight the main idea of that note card.

170 Note Taking: A Closer Look

Summarize ● To summarize, reduce what you have read to a few important points using your own words.

Paraphrase ● To paraphrase, restate what you have read using your own words. Use this method when you are trying to retrace the thinking of one of your sources. Put quotation marks around only key words or phrases you borrow directly from the sources. (See 180-184.)

Quote Directly ● To quote someone directly, record the statement or idea word for word and put quotation marks around this information.

6. Collect information from primary sources.

If possible, collect firsthand information by conducting interviews, passing out questionnaires or surveys, or making on-site observations.

171 Designing a Writing Plan

7. Write your working outline.

Organize your note cards into their most logical order and use them to construct a working outline. Your descriptive headings may be used as main points and subpoints in your outline. (See 249.)

8. Continue developing your research.

Search for any additional information that may be needed to develop your focus, or thesis. Also be sure to review the thesis statement you wrote in Step 3 to see if your thoughts about it have changed.

9. Revise your outline.

Revise your working outline as needed when you find new information.

> "... having something to say means having a good stock of facts."
> —Rudolph Flesch

172 WRITING THE FIRST DRAFT

10. Write the introduction.

The introduction should do two things. The first part should say something interesting, surprising, personal, or dramatic about your subject to gain your readers' attention. (See the list below for ideas.) The second part should identify the specific focus, or thesis, of your research.

- Start out with a revealing story or quotation.
- Give important background information.
- Offer a series of interesting or surprising facts.
- Provide important definitions.
- State your reason for choosing this subject.

11. Write the body.

The next step is to write the main part of your research paper, the part that supports or proves your thesis. There are two ways to proceed. You may write freely and openly, or you may work systematically, carefully following your notes and working outline.

173 Writing Freely and Openly

One way to go about writing the body of your research paper is to put your outline and note cards aside and write as much as you can on your own. Refer to your note cards only when you need a quotation, specific facts, or figures.

After you have completed this first writing, review your outline and note cards to see if you have missed or misplaced any important points. Then continue writing, filling in or reorganizing ideas as you go along. (You may continue in this fashion—writing and reviewing—until you have all of the basic ideas on paper.)

174 Writing Systematically

You may also write the body of your paper more systematically—carefully following your working outline and note cards right from the start. Begin by laying out the first section of note cards (those covering the first main topic in your working outline, or related cards you simply want to deal with first). Then write a general statement that covers the main topic of these cards. Using the note cards you have in front of you, add supporting facts and details. Repeat this process until you have dealt with all the main topics in your outline, or until you have covered each section of note cards.

175 # Writing Tips

- Use your own words as much as possible. Direct quotations should be used only when the point being made is stated exactly as you want it to be.

- Present your ideas honestly and clearly. If you feel strongly about your research and have something meaningful to say, you are more likely to write an interesting paper.

- Avoid fragments, abbreviations, or informal expressions ("you know," "no way," "forget it") in your writing. Work to achieve a style that is semiformal.

- Drop statements that you cannot find enough facts and details to support.

12. Write the conclusion.

The final section, or **conclusion**, of your paper should leave the reader with a clear understanding of the importance of your research. Review the important points you have made and draw a final conclusion. In a more personal approach, you may discuss how your research has strengthened or changed your thinking about your subject; or you may explain what you have learned from your research.

"Only the hand that erases can write the true thing."

—Meister Eckhart

176 ## REVISING

13. Revise your first draft at least two times.

Revise once to make sure all of the main points have been covered and effectively supported. Revise a second time to make sure all of your sentences are clear and smooth reading. (See "A Guide to Revising" in the writing process section of your handbook for help.)

14. Document your sources.

Give credit for ideas and direct quotations that you have used from different sources. (See 185-196 for guidelines.) Also make sure you have copied the ideas and quotations accurately. Then assemble the Works Cited section (bibliography), listing all of the sources you have cited in your paper. (See 197-240 for appropriate style guidelines.)

"[Good] writing is concise. A sentence should contain no unnecessary words, a paragraph no unnecessary sentences, for the same reason that a drawing should have no unnecessary lines and a machine no unnecessary parts."

—William Strunk

177 PREPARING THE FINAL PAPER

15. Edit your final revision.

Check and correct punctuation, capitalization, usage, and grammar. (See "The Proofreader's Guide" for help.)

16. Prepare your final copy.

If you use a word processor, try to print with a letter-quality printer and use a fresh ribbon if necessary. Leave a margin of one inch on all sides, except for page numbers. Double-space your entire paper, including long quotations and the Works Cited section. (See 246-265 for examples.)

17. Arrange and number your pages.

Begin numbering with the first page of the essay and continue through the Works Cited section. Type your last name before each page number. Place the page numbers in the upper right-hand corner, one-half inch from the top and even with the right-hand margin.

18. Add your title.

A title page is not required in the MLA guidelines for a research paper. Simply type your name, the teacher's name, the course title, and the date in the upper-left corner of the first page of the paper. (Begin one inch from the top and double-space throughout.) Center the title (double-space before and after); then type the first line of the paper. (See 250.)

If your instructor requires a title page, center the title one-third of the way down from the top of the page; then, center your name, the instructor's name, and any additional information two-thirds of the way down. (See 256.)

19. Type your final outline.

If a final outline is required, make sure it follows the final version of your paper. Use either a topic or sentence outline (as your instructor requires). (See 249 and 259.) Double-space throughout your outline; if it is more than one page in length, number its pages with small Roman numerals.

20. Proofread your paper for typing errors.

Check the final draft from beginning to end. When you submit your research paper, it should be as error free as you can possibly make it.

"Everyone has a right to an opinion, but no one has a right to be wrong about the facts."

—**Anonymous**

Writing Responsibly

178   A research paper—like any other type of meaningful writing—should be a personal process of discovering new information. Once you've gathered the information, you need to go about the business of making it part of your own thinking. Study points on which your sources agree and disagree about related issues, and decide which ones offer the best arguments and why. Determine how these findings stand up to your own thinking. Research will become your own when you

- ◉ believe in the subject,
- ◉ give yourself enough time to learn about it,
- ◉ get actively involved and research your topic thoroughly,
- ◉ and make the primary voice in your writing your own!

Note • Research will not become your own when you simply piece together the ideas of others and call it a research paper.

179 Avoiding Plagiarism

When you make research your own, your writing will sound like you. That is exactly what you want. But what you don't want is to mislead people into thinking that all these ideas are your own. If you do, you may be guilty of **plagiarism**—the act of presenting someone else's ideas as your own.

In *word-for-word plagiarism*, a researcher repeats the exact words of a source without giving the necessary credit. *Paraphrase plagiarism* occurs when a researcher says basically the same thing as an original source with just a few words changed. In *spot plagiarism,* a researcher uses only a source's key words or phrases as his or her own without giving credit.

You owe it to your sources, your readers, and yourself to give credit for the ideas you use, unless the ideas are widely accepted as "common knowledge." Information is considered common knowledge if most people already know it, or if it can be found in nearly any basic reference book on the subject. (The fact that there are 365 days in the year is common knowledge; the fact that it rained 210 days in Seattle during 1990 is not.)

180 Writing Paraphrases

When you write a report or research paper, you need to support your ideas with information from other sources and give credit to those sources. There are two ways to do this: either quote directly or paraphrase what other people have written. When you **paraphrase**, you use your own words to restate the author's ideas. You include the exact words of the author when necessary and put quotation marks around them.

Below you'll find some helpful guidelines, followed by two model paraphrases that could have been used in a research paper. One model is a basic paraphrase; the other is a paraphrase containing a direct quotation.

Quick Guide

1. Skim the selection first to get the overall meaning. (Concentrate on just the main ideas, not the details.)

2. Read the selection carefully, paying particular attention to key words and phrases. (Check the meaning of unfamiliar words.)

3. Try listing the main ideas on a piece of paper—without looking at the selection.

4. Review the selection another time so that you have the overall meaning clearly in mind as you begin to write.

5. Write your paraphrase, using your own words to restate the author's ideas. Keep the following points in mind as you write:

   ● Stick to the essential information.
   ● State each important idea as clearly and concisely (briefly) as possible.
   ● Put quotation marks around key words or phrases taken directly from the source. (See 184.)
   ● Arrange the ideas into a smooth, logical order. (Your version of the author's views should be as easy to read as the original—maybe easier.)

6. Check your summary for accuracy by asking these questions:

   ● Have I kept the original writer's ideas and point of view clear in my paraphrase? Have I quoted where necessary?
   ● Have I cut enough of the original? Too much?
   ● Could another person get the author's main idea by simply reading my paraphrase?

181 **Original Source**

The human brain, once surrounded by myth and misconception, is no longer such a mystery. It is now understood to be the supervisory center of the nervous system, and, as such, it controls all voluntary (eating and thinking) and most involuntary behavior (blinking and breathing).

The brain functions by receiving information from nerve cells that are located throughout the body. Recent research has provided a clear picture of exactly what happens when information first reaches the brain. It has been discovered that the cells that receive the information in the cortex of the brain are arranged in a regular pattern in columns. The columns are, in turn, arranged into a series of "hypercolumns." Each cell within each column has a specific responsibility to perceive and analyze certain kinds of incoming information. Within the columns, the analysis of this information follows a formal sequence.

Eventually, the information is relayed to the higher centers of the brain where a complete picture is assembled. The brain then evaluates the information and either sends a return message or stores the information for later use. The return message travels through the body in the form of electrical and chemical signals via the billions of nerve cells (neurons). When the message reaches its destination, the muscles or glands respond with the appropriate reaction.

182 **Basic Paraphrase**

The human brain controls all voluntary and most involuntary behavior. The process begins when the brain receives information from nerve cells located throughout the body. This information is received by brain cells arranged in a series of columns with each cell having a specific responsibility to analyze certain kinds of incoming information. After the information has been analyzed, it is sent to the higher centers of the brain where a complete picture is put together. The brain then evaluates the information and either stores it for later use or sends a return message to the muscles and glands, which react appropriately ("The Brain" 26).

183 **Paraphrase with Quotation**

The human brain controls all voluntary and most involuntary behavior. The process begins when the brain receives information from nerve cells located throughout the body. "The cells that receive the information in the cortex of the brain are arranged in a regular pattern in columns. . . . Each cell within each column has a specific responsibility to . . . analyze certain kinds of incoming information" ("The Brain" 26). After the information has been analyzed, it is sent to the higher centers of the brain where a complete picture is put together. The brain then evaluates the information and either stores it for later use or sends a return message to the muscles and glands, which react appropriately.

184 Using Quoted Material

Quick Guide

A quotation can be a single word or an entire paragraph. Choose quotations carefully, keep them as brief as possible, and use them only when they are interesting, revealing, or necessary in the development of your text. A paper that is quotation heavy usually means a writer has not done much independent thinking. When you do quote material directly, be sure that the capitalization, punctuation, and spelling are the same as that in the original work. Any changes you make should be clearly marked for your readers.

Short Quotations

If a quotation is four typed lines or fewer, work it into the body of your paper and put quotation marks around it.

Long Quotations

Quotations of more than four typed lines should be set off from the rest of the writing by indenting each line 10 spaces and double-spacing the material. Do not use quotation marks.

In quoting two or more paragraphs, indent the first line of each paragraph three spaces. (Leave two spaces after a longer quotation before you cite a parenthetical reference.) Generally, a colon is used to introduce quotations set off from the text. (See "Quotation Marks" in the index for more.)

Quoting Poetry

Three lines of verse or fewer should be worked into your writing and punctuated with quotation marks. Use a diagonal (/) between lines of verse in your text. For verse quotations of four lines or more, indent each line 10 spaces and double-space. Do not use quotation marks.

To show that you have left out a line or more of verse, make a line of spaced periods the approximate length of a complete line of the poem.

Partial Quotations

If you want to leave out part of the quotation, use an ellipsis to signify the omission. An ellipsis (. . .) is three periods with a space before and after each one. (See "Ellipsis" in the index.)

Note • Anything you take out of a quotation should not change the author's original meaning.

Adding to Quotations

Use brackets [like this] to signify any material you add within a quotation to help clarify its meaning.

"Adam was the only man who, when he said a good thing, knew that nobody had said it before him."

—Mark Twain

Citing Sources

185 Parenthetical References

The *MLA Handbook for Writers of Research Papers* suggests giving credit in the body of your research paper rather than in footnotes or endnotes. To give credit, simply insert the appropriate information (usually author and page number) in parentheses after the words or ideas borrowed from another source. Place them where a pause would naturally occur to avoid disrupting the flow of your writing (usually at the end of a sentence).

> At the man's feet is a sign that reads: "Won't you help me? I'm cold and homeless and lonely. God Bless You" (Chambers 11).

Keep two points in mind when citing sources: First, indicate as precisely as you can where you found this information. (Use page numbers, volume numbers, acts, chapters, etc.) Second, make sure all of your sources are listed in the Works Cited section of your paper.

186 One Author: Citing a Complete Work

No parenthetical reference is needed if you identify the author in your text. (See the first entry below.) However, you must give the author's last name in a parenthetical reference if it is not mentioned in the text. (See the second entry below.) A parenthetical reference could begin with an editor, a translator, a speaker, or an artist instead of the author if that is how the work is listed in the Works Cited section.

With Author in Text (This is the preferred way of citing a complete work.)

> In No Need for Hunger, Robert Spitzer recommends that the U.S. government develop a new foreign policy to help Third World countries overcome poverty and hunger.

Without Author in Text

> No Need for Hunger recommends that the U.S. government develop a new foreign policy to help Third World countries overcome poverty and hunger (Spitzer).

187 One Author: Citing Part of a Work

List the necessary page numbers in parentheses if you borrow words or ideas from a particular work. Leave a space between the author's last name and the page reference. No punctuation is needed.

With Author in Text

Bullough writes that genetic engineering was dubbed "eugenics" by a cousin of Darwin's, Sir Francis Galton, in 1885 (5).

Without Author in Text

Genetic engineering was dubbed "eugenics" by a cousin of Darwin's, Sir Francis Galton, in 1885 (Bullough 5).

188 Two or Three Authors

Give the last names of every author in the same order that they appear in the Works Cited section. (The correct order of the author's names can be found on the title page of the book.)

Students learned more than a full year's Spanish in ten days using the complete supermemory method (Ostrander and Schroeder 51).

189 More Than Three Authors

Give the first author's last name as it appears in the Works Cited section followed by *et al.* or *and others* with no punctuation in between.

According to Guerin and others, Huck Finn reflects "those same nightmarish shadows that even in our own time threaten to obscure the American Dream" (149).

190 Corporate Author

If a book or other work was written by a committee or task force, it is said to have a *corporate* author. If the corporate name is long, include it in the text (rather than in parentheses) to avoid disrupting the flow of your writing. Use a shortened form of the name in the text and in references after the full name has been used at least once. For example, *Task Force* may be used for *Task Force on Education for Economic Growth* after the full name has been used at least once.

The thesis of the Task Force's report is that economic success depends on our ability to improve large scale education and training as quickly as possible (14).

191 An Anonymous Book (Work)

When there is no author listed, give the title or a shortened version of the title as it appears in the Works Cited section. (No page numbers are needed for single-page articles or nonprint sources.)

The Information Please Almanac states that drinking water can make up 20 percent or more of a person's total exposure to lead (572).

192 Two or More Works by the Same Author

Give the author's last name (unless it appears in the text), the title or a shortened version of the title, and the page reference.

> The average person will have taken more than 2,600 quizzes, tests, and exams if he or she finishes college (Von Oech, Whack 21).

193 One or More Works in a Reference

Cite each work as you normally would; separate the references with a semicolon.

> Both poet-teachers strongly believe in the benefits of dream writing for beginning writers (Koch 137; Ziegler 34).

194 Indirect Source

If you cite an indirect source—someone's remarks published second-hand—give the abbreviation *qtd. in* (quoted in) before the indirect source in your reference.

> Paton improved the conditions in Diepkloof [a prison] by "removing all the more obvious aids to detention. The dormitories are open at night: the great barred gate is gone" (qtd. in Callan xviii).

195 Literary Works: Verse Plays and Poems

Cite verse (plays and poems) by divisions (act, scene, canto, book, part) and lines, using Arabic numerals for the various divisions unless your teacher prefers Roman numerals. Use periods to separate the various parts. If you are citing lines only, use the word *line* or *lines* in your first reference and numbers only in additional references.

> When she learns that Romeo is a Montague, Juliet exclaims, "My only love, sprung from my only hate! / Too early seen unknown, and known too late!" (1.5.138-139).

Note • A diagonal is used to show where each new line of verse begins.

Verse quotations of more than three lines should be indented 10 spaces and double-spaced. Each line of the poem or play begins a new line of the quotation; do not run the lines together or separate them with diagonals (/). Diagonals are used to separate lines only when you are quoting within the main text of your paper.

> Elizabeth Bishop's poem "The Fish" contains layer upon layer of specific details:
>
>> He was speckled with barnacles,
>> Five rosettes of lines
>> and infested
>> with tiny white sea-lice,
>> and underneath two or three
>> rags of green weed hung down. (16-21)

196 **Literary Works: Prose**

To cite literary prose works, list more than the page reference if the work is available in several editions. Give the page reference first, and then add a chapter, section, or book number in abbreviated form after a semicolon.

> In Cry the Beloved Country, Alan Paton presents Steven Kumalo as "a man who lives in a world not made for him, whose own world is slipping away, dying, being destroyed, beyond recall" (14; ch. 3).

When you are quoting prose that takes more than four typed lines, indent each line of the quotation 10 spaces and double-space it. In this case, you put the parenthetical citation (the pages and chapter numbers) *outside* the end punctuation mark of the quotation itself. Skip two spaces before you begin the citation.

> Kumalo would describe the land as he wanted his sister to remember it, beautiful and inviting. Then suddenly his missing son would darken his thoughts and feelings about the land:
>
> > And then in one fraction of time the hills with the deep melodious names stood out waste and desolate beneath the pitiless sun, the streams ceased to run, the cattle moved thin and listless over the red and rootless earth. It was a place of old women and mothers and children, from each house something was gone. His voice would falter and die away, and he would fall silent and muse. (61; ch. 10)

the
bottom
line

When you give credit to your sources within the research paper, follow these guidelines:

- ◉ Insert the appropriate information (usually author and page number) in parentheses after the words or ideas borrowed from another source.

- ◉ Place your parentheses where a pause would naturally occur (usually at the end of a sentence).

- ◉ Make sure all the sources you cite in your paper are also listed on the Works Cited page.

197 **Works Cited**

The Works Cited section lists all of the sources you have cited in your text. It does not include any sources you may have read or studied but did not refer to in your paper (that's a bibliography). Begin your list of works cited on a new page (the next page after the text), and number each page, continuing the numbering from the last page of the text. The guidelines that follow describe the form of the Works Cited section in detail.

198 **The Works Cited Section**

Quick Guide

1. Type the page number in the upper right-hand corner, one-half inch from the top of the page.

2. Center the title *Works Cited* one inch from the top. Double-space before the first entry.

3. Begin each entry flush with the left margin. If the entry runs more than one line, indent additional lines five spaces.

4. Double-space each entry; also double-space between entries.

5. List each entry alphabetically by the author's last name. If there is no author, use the first word of the title (disregard *A, An, The*).

6. A basic entry for a book would be as follows:

    Guillermo, Kathy Snow. Monkey Business. Washington, DC: National

    Press Books, 1993.

    Note • For both books and periodicals, leave two spaces after the author and after the title. Leave a single space between other items of the publication information.

7. A basic entry for a periodical (a magazine) would be as follows:

    Murr, Andrew. "The High Cost of Defense." Newsweek 21 Mar.

    1994: 70.

8. Check the following pages for specific information on other kinds of entries.

Model Works Cited Entries: Books

The entries that follow illustrate the information needed to cite books, sections of a book, pamphlets, and government publications.

199 **One Author**

> Shaw, Arnold. Black Popular Music in America: From the Spirituals,
>
> Minstrels, and Ragtime to Soul, Disco, and Hip-Hop. New York:
>
> Schirmer Books, 1986.

200 **Two or Three Authors**

> Bystydzienski, Jill M., and Estelle P. Resnik. Women in Cross-Cultural
>
> Transitions. Bloomington, IN: Phi Delta Kappa Educational
>
> Foundation, 1994.

201 **More Than Three Authors**

> Marine, April, et al. Internet: Getting Started. Englewood Cliffs, NJ:
>
> PTR Prentice Hall, 1994.

202 **A Single Work from an Anthology**

> Rich, Adrienne. "Re-Forming the Crystal." Contemporary American
>
> Poetry. Ed. A. Poulin, Jr. 3rd ed. Boston: Houghton Mifflin
>
> Company, 1980. 396.

Note • If you cite a complete anthology, begin the entry with the editors.

> Poulin, A., Jr., ed. Contemporary American Poetry. 3rd ed. Boston:
>
> Houghton Mifflin Company, 1980.

203 Two or More Books by the Same Author

List the books alphabetically according to title. After the first entry, substitute three hyphens for the author's name.

Von Oech, Roger. A Kick in the Seat of the Pants. New York: Perennial-

Harper, 1986.

- - -. A Whack on the Side of the Head. New York: Warner, 1983.

204 A Corporate Group Author

Task Force on Education for Economic Growth. Action for Excellence.

Washington: Education Commission of the States, 1983.

205 An Anonymous Book

The World Almanac Book of the Strange. New York: New American

Library, 1977.

Note • The Bible is considered an anonymous book. Documentation should read exactly as it is printed on the title page. (Translations and editions of the Bible vary, which is why you must be precise.)

The Jerusalem Bible. Garden City, NY: Doubleday, 1966.

The English Revised Bible with the Apocrypha. n.p.: Oxford UP and

Cambridge UP, 1989.

206 A Multivolume Work

Ziegler, Alan. The Writing Workshop. Vol. 2. New York: Teachers and

Writers, 1984.

Note • If you cite two or more volumes in a multivolume work, give the total number of volumes after the title.

Israel, Fred L., ed. Major Peace Treaties of Modern History, 1648-1967.

4 vols. New York: Chelsea, 1967.

207 An Introduction, a Preface, a Foreword, or an Afterword

Callan, Edward. Introduction. Cry, the Beloved Country. By Alan Paton.

New York: Macmillan, 1987. xv-xxvii.

Note • Give only the author's last name after *By* if he is the author of the piece cited and the complete work.

Buscaglia, Leo F. Introduction. Love. By Buscaglia. New York:

Fawcett Crest, 1972. 9-12.

208 Cross-References

To avoid unnecessary repetition when citing two or more entries from a larger collection, you may cite the collection once with complete publication information (see Hall). The individual entries (see Abbey and Baldwin) can then be cross-referenced by listing the author, title of the piece, editor of the collection, and page numbers.

Abbey, Edward. "The Most Beautiful Place on Earth." Hall 225-41.

Baldwin, James. "Notes of a Native Son." Hall 164-83.

Hall, Donald, ed. The Contemporary Essay. New York: Bedford-St.

Martin's, 1984.

209 An "Edition"

An edition refers to the particular publication you are citing, as in the 3rd edition. But "edition" also refers to the work of one person that is prepared by another person, an editor.

Shakespeare, William. Macbeth. Ed. Sylvan Barnet. New York: Signet-

NAL, 1963.

210 A Translation

Turgenev, Ivan Sergeevich. Fathers and Sons. Trans. Michael R. Katz.

New York: W. W. Norton, 1994.

211 An Article in a Reference Book

It is not necessary to give full publication information for familiar reference works (encyclopedias and dictionaries). For these titles, list only the edition (if available) and the publication year. If an article is initialed, check the index of authors (in the opening section of each volume) for the author's full name.

"Euthanasia." Merriam-Webster's Collegiate Dictionary. 10th ed. 1993.

"Costume." Encyclopedia Americana. 1985 ed.

Vorhaus, Louis J. "Bursitis." Collier's Encyclopedia. 1993 ed.

212 Pamphlet with No Author or Publication Information Stated

If known, list the country of publication [in brackets]. Use N.p. (no place) if the country is unknown.

Pedestrian Safety. [United States]: n.p., n.d.

Note • In the entry, n.p. (after the colon) means "no publisher given"; n.d. means "no date of publication given."

213 Signed Pamphlet

Treat a pamphlet as you would a book.

> Grayson, George W. The North American Free Trade Agreement. New
>
> York: Foreign Policy Association, Inc., 1993.

214 Government Publications

State the name of the government (country, state, etc.) followed by the name of the agency.

> United States. Federal Trade Commission. Shopping by Mail or Phone.
>
> Washington: GPO, 1994.

215 A Book in a Series

Give the series name and number (if any) before the publication information.

> Bishop, Jack. Ralph Ellison. Black Americans of Achievement. New
>
> York: Chelsea House, 1988.

216 A Publisher s Imprint

The name of a publisher's imprint appears above the publisher's name on the title page. Give the imprint followed by a hyphen and the name of the publisher (Signet-NAL).

> Solzhenitsyn, Alexander. One Day in the Life of Ivan Denisovich. Trans.
>
> Ralph Parker. New York: Signet-NAL, 1963.

Note • If more than one city is listed for a publisher, list the first one.

217 A Book with a Title Within a Title

If the title contains a title normally in quotation marks, keep the quotation marks and underline the entire title.

> Harte, Bret. "The Outcasts of Poker Flat" and Other Stories. New York:
>
> Signet-NAL, 1961.

Note • If the title contains a title normally underlined, do not underline it in your entry, as in this example: A Tale of Two Cities as History.

218 A Reference Book on CD-ROM

If you use an encyclopedia or other reference book recorded on CD-ROM, use the form below.

> Software Tool Works Multimedia Encyclopedia. CD-ROM.
>
> Novato, CA: Software Tool Works, 1991.

Model Works Cited Entries: Periodicals

The entries that follow illustrate the information and arrangement needed to cite periodicals.

219 **Signed Article in a Magazine**

Tully, Shawn. "The Universal Teenager." Fortune 4 Apr. 1994: 14-16.

220 **Unsigned Article in a Magazine**

"Speak, Hillary." The New Republic 28 Mar. 1994: 9.

221 **An Article in a Scholarly Journal**

Cartwright, David E. "The Last Temptation of Zarathustra." Journal of

the History of Philosophy 31 (1993): 49-69.

Note • Journals are usually issued no more than four times a year. Number 31 refers to the volume. The issue number is not needed if the page numbers in a volume continue from one issue to the next. If the page numbers start over with each issue, then put a period between the volume number and issue number: 31.2.

222 **Signed Newspaper Article**

Stanley, Alessandra. "Russians Find Their Heroes in Mexican TV Soap

Operas." New York Times 20 Mar. 1994, national ed.: 1.

Note • Cite the edition of a major daily newspaper (if given) after the date (20 Mar. 1994, national ed.: 1). To cite an article in a lettered section of the newspaper, list the section after the page number. (For example, 4A would refer to page 4 in section A of the newspaper.) If the sections are numbered, however, use a comma after the year; then indicate sec. 1, 2, 3, etc., followed by a colon and the page number.

223 Unsigned Newspaper Article

> "African Roots of American Music Traced at Westchester College
>
> Program." Amsterdam News [New York] 29 Jan. 1994, sec. 1:21.

Note • If the unsigned article is an editorial, put *Editorial* after the title. Also, if the city of publication is included in the newspaper's name, you do not have to add it in brackets.

224 A Letter to the Editor

> Epsy, Mike. Letter. "Abolishing the Farmer's Home Administration."
>
> Washington Post 5 Mar. 1994, 5A.

225 A Review

> Drew, Bettina. "Hollywood on Wry." Rev. of Delusions of Grandma, by
>
> Carrie Fisher. Chicago Tribune 10 Apr. 1994, sec. 1:5.

Note • If you cite the review of a work by an editor or a translator, use *ed.* or *trans.* instead of *by.*

226 Published Interview

> Orbison, Roy. "Roy Orbison: 1936-1988." By Steve Pond. Rolling
>
> Stone 26 Jan. 1989: 22+.

Note • Type the word *Interview* after the interviewee's name if the interview is untitled.

227 A Title or Quotation Within an Article's Title

> Merrill, Susan F. " 'Sunday Morning' Thoughts." English Journal 76.6
>
> (1987): 63.

Note • Use single quotation marks around the shorter title if it is a title normally punctuated with quotation marks.

228 A Periodical on a Computer Information Service

> O'Connell, Loraine. "Busy Teens Feel the Beep." Orlando Sentinel 7
>
> Jan. 1993: E1+. Rpt. in Youth, Vol. 4. Ed. Eleanor C. Goldstein,
>
> Boca Raton, FL: Social Issues Resources Series, Inc., 1993.
>
> Art. 41.

Note • The information you need for this type of entry is provided by the computer service.

Model Works Cited Entries: Other Print and Nonprint Sources

229 Computer Software

> Wordstar Professional. Vers. 4. Computer software. MicroPro, 1987.
>
> IBM PC-DOS 2.0, 256KB, disk.

230 Television and Radio Programs

If your reference is primarily to the work of an individual, cite that person before the title. Otherwise, other pertinent information (writer, director, producer, narrator, etc.) may be given after the main title of the program (underlined).

> "An Interview with Elton John." Barbara Walters Special. ABC. WISN,
>
> Milwaukee. 21 Mar. 1994.

231 Recordings

> Shocked, Michelle. Arkansas Traveler. Polygram Records, Inc.,
>
> D110521, 1992.

Note • D110521 refers to the catalog number. The person cited first in a recording (the composer, conductor, performer, etc.) depends on the emphasis you want in the entry. If citing jacket notes, give the author's name, the title of the material (if given), and the words *Jacket notes* before the regular bibliographic information.

232 Recorded Interview

> Orbison, Roy. "Roy Orbison: 1936-1988." By Steve Pond. Rolling
>
> Stone. 26 Jan. 1989: 22+.

233 **Films**

If it is important, cite the size and length of the film (for example: 16 mm, 32 min.) after the date.

> Rebel Without a Cause. Dir. Nicholas Ray. With James Dean, Natalie
>
> Wood, Sal Mineo, and Dennis Hopper. Warner, 1955.

234 **Filmstrips, Slide Programs, and Videotapes**

Cite the medium (filmstrip, slide program, etc.) after the title.

> Going Back, A Return to Vietnam. Videocassette. Virginia Productions,
>
> 1982. 55 min.

235 **Published Letters**

> Bottomley, Edwin. "To Father." 6 Dec. 1843. An English Settler in
>
> Pioneer Wisconsin: The Letters of Edwin Bottomley. Ed. Milo M.
>
> Quaife. Madison: State Historical Society, 1918. 60-62.

Note • "To Father" and 6 Dec. 1843 refer to the cited letter.

236 **Letter Received by the Author (Yourself)**

> Thomas, Bob. Letter to the author. 10 Jan. 1989.

237 **Personal Interview**

> Brooks, Sarah. Personal interview. 15 Oct. 1993.

Note • If you spoke to your interviewee by phone, cite the entry this way: Telephone interview.

238 **Maps and Charts**

> Wisconsin Territory. Map. Madison: Wisconsin Trails, 1988.

239 **Cartoons**

> Trudeau, Garry. "Doonesbury." Cartoon. Chicago Tribune 23 Dec.
>
> 1988, sec. 5:6.

240 **Lectures, Speeches, and Addresses**

> Angelou, Maya. Address. Opening General Sess. NCTE Convention.
>
> Adam's Mark Hotel, St. Louis. 18 Nov. 1988.

Note • If known, give the speech's title in quotation marks instead of the label *Address, Lecture,* or *Speech.*

241

Abbreviations for Research Papers

anon.	anonymous
bk., bks.	book(s)
©	copyright
chap., ch., chs.	chapter(s)
comp.	compiler, compiled, compiled by
ed., eds.	editor(s), edition(s), or edited by
e.g.	for example; *exempli gratia*
et al.	and others; *et alii*
et seq.	and the following; *et sequens*
ex.	example
f., ff.	and the following page(s)
fig., figs.	figure(s)
GPO	Government Printing Office, Washington, DC
ibid.	in the same place as quoted above; *ibidem*
i.e.	that is; *id est*
ill., illus.	illustration, illustrated by
introd.	(author of) introduction, introduced by, introduction
l., ll.	line(s)
loc. cit.	in the place cited; *loco citato*
MS, MSS	manuscript(s)
narr., narrs.	narrated by, narrator(s)
n.d.	no date given
no., nos.	number(s)
n. pag.	no pagination
n.p.	no place of publication and/or no publisher given
op. cit.	in the work cited; *opere citato*
p., pp.	page(s)
pub. (or publ.), pubs.	published by, publication(s)
rev.	revised by, revision, review, reviewed by
rpt.	reprinted (by), reprint
sc.	scene
sec., secs.	section(s)
sic	thus (used with brackets to indicate an error is that way in the original)
tr., trans.	translator, translation
v., vv. (or vs., vss.)	verse(s)
viz.	namely; *videlicet*
vol., vols.	volume(s): capitalize when used with Roman numerals

242 **Other Forms of Documentation**

Use the guide below and the model notes on the following page **only if** you have been instructed to use footnotes or endnotes in your research paper instead of parenthetical references. Endnotes appear at the end of a text on a separate page; footnotes appear at the bottom of the pages in the text. The first endnote or footnote to a work contains the publication information found in the Works Cited section or bibliography. Second and later references to a particular work contain less information. (See 244-245.)

Information to Include

Endnotes and footnotes contain all the information a reader would need to locate the source:

- ● . . . . **author's name**
- ● . . . . the **title** of the work
- ● . . . . **publication facts** (publisher, place, and date)
- ● . . . . specific **page reference** of the source

Using Footnotes and Endnotes

243 Quick Guide

1. Number notes consecutively throughout a paper.

2. Place numbers at the end of a sentence or a clause to help maintain the flow of ideas.

3. Raise note numbers slightly above the typed line; leave one space after the number.

4. Indent the first line of each endnote or footnote five spaces.

5. For endnotes, center the title *Notes* one inch from the top of the endnote page. Double-space, indent five spaces, and type the note number slightly above the line. Leave one space and enter the reference. Additional lines in each note should be flush with the left-hand margin. Double-space throughout.

6. For footnotes, double-space twice between the last line of the text on a page and the first footnote. Single-space each entry and double-space between them. If a note continues to the next page, type a line one double space below the text. Double-space again and continue the footnote.

Model Footnotes and Endnotes

244 ## First References

The model notes below illustrate the information needed the first time you refer to a source:

Book by One Author

^{1} Arnold Shaw, Black Popular Music in America: From the Spirituals, Minstrels, and Ragtime to Soul, Disco, and Hip-Hop (New York: Schirmer Books, 1986) 34.

Book by Two or Three Authors

^{2} Jill M. Bystydzienski and Estelle P. Resnik, Women in Cross-Cultural Transitions (Bloomington, IN: Phi Delta Kappa Educational Foundation, 1994) 23.

Article in a Magazine

^{3} Shawn Tully, "The Universal Teenager," Fortune 4 Apr. 1994: 14-16.

Newspaper Article

^{4} Alessandra Stanley, "Russians Find Their Heroes in Mexican TV Soap Operas," New York Times 20 Mar. 1994, national ed.: 1.

Television and Radio Programs

^{5} "An Interview with Elton John," Barbara Walters Special, ABC, WISN, Milwaukee, 21 Mar. 1994.

Personal Interview

^{6} Sarah Brooks, personal interview, 15 Oct. 1993.

245 ## Second and Later References

If a work has been fully documented in an endnote or a footnote, succeeding references need only include the author's last name (or the title if no author) and the pages cited.

Book by One Author

^{7} Shaw 45.

^{8} Shaw 13-17.

Note • Simply repeat the necessary information—the author or title and page numbers—even when you are referring to the same work two or more times in a sequence.

"Put it before them briefly so they will read it, clearly so they will appreciate it, . . . and, above all, accurately so they will be guided by its light."

—Joseph Pulitzer

Student Models

246   Before you put your final research paper together, you may want to check your work against other student models. On the following pages, you will find two student papers. The first model uses only secondhand sources (a book, a magazine, and a computer program); the second model uses first-hand or primary sources (interviews), along with books and magazines.

247 **The Return of the Buffalo**

    The writer of this research paper introduces his topic with a brief history and ends his first paragraph with his topic or thesis statement: "The buffalo, once endangered, has returned." The writer then discusses the word "buffalo" and begins the body of his paper—a history of the sudden disappearance and slow return of the American buffalo. Throughout the paper, the writer includes references to the three sources he used when doing his research. Those same three sources are listed on a Works Cited page at the end of the paper.

248 **Helping the Homeless**

    The second research paper is different from the first in two important ways: 1) It includes primary sources (interviews by the student) as well as secondary sources. 2) It deals with an important issue of the day (homelessness) and proposes a possible solution to the problem.

    The writer begins her introductory paragraph with the story of a homeless person and ends it with her thesis: "Who are these people we call 'the homeless,' and what are the reasons for their predicament?" She begins to answer this complex question by paraphrasing a person she had interviewed. She goes on to cite several studies that support her position that the current housing system isn't working. She ends her paper by calling on the readers—and the federal government—to help the homeless.

249 Title Page and Outline

If you are instructed to include a title page and/or an outline with your paper, you can use the samples below as your guide. (Also see 256 and 257.)

TITLE PAGE

The Return of the Buffalo

Kendall McGinn

Mr. Gilding

History

20 Feb. 1995

RESEARCH
PAPER OUTLINE

The Return of the Buffalo

Introduction—What are American buffalo and what happened to them?

I. American buffalo thrived (1700-1800)
   A. Discovered by French *voyageurs*
   B. Millions roamed the Great Plains
   C. Native people depended on buffalo

II. American buffalo almost destroyed (1800-1900)
   A. Europeans and Native Americans clashed
   B. Open season declared on buffalo
   C. Native people's livelihood destroyed

III. American buffalo "returns" (late 1800's to present)
   A. Rancher begins raising buffalo (1881)
   B. Today many raise buffalo for meat

IV. Raising (growing) buffalo
   A. Benefits
   B. Problems

V. Future of American buffalo
   A. Buffalo-meat industry expanding
   B. Plans for vast wildlife preserve

Conclusion—The American buffalo population is growing again, because people intervened to save their animal brother.

McGinn 1

Kendall McGinn

Mr. Gilding

History

Feb. 20, 1995

The Return of the Buffalo

At one point in the early twentieth century, it seemed that the American buffalo, *Bison bison*, would continue to exist only in pictures or on the buffalo nickel. Its population of 100 million around 1700 had been reduced to 1,000 by 1889. Today, that number has increased to nearly 200,000 (Hodgson 71). The buffalo, once endangered, has returned.

The American bison roamed the Great Plains of North America undisturbed when the French *voyageurs* first encountered them. Knowing they were not true buffalo like the African or Asian buffalo, the French called these bison *les boeufs,* the oxen. The English altered that word to *buffle,* and later to *buffalo.*

Before the Europeans came to North America, the native people of the North American plains and the buffalo were one *Pte Oyate,* or Buffalo Nation. The big bull *tantanka* was life itself. These Native Americans followed the herds and used the buffalo for food, clothing, shelter, religious ceremonies, and medicine. A Lakota leader summed up this unity between human and animal: "When the Creator made the buffalo, he put power in them. When you eat the meat, that power goes into you, heals the body and spirit" (qtd. in Hodgson 69).

During the expansion of the United States, a cultural clash occurred, and the Europeans practically destroyed the buffalo. By the year 1800, it was reported that there were about 30 million buffalo left in the United States. In 1876, Representative James Throckmorton of Texas

McGinn 2

repeated the administration's policy: "There is no question that, so long as there are millions of buffaloes in the West, so long as the Indians cannot be controlled, even by the strong arm of the Government, I believe it would be a great step forward in the civilization of the Indians and the preservation of peace on the border if there was not a buffalo in existence" (qtd. in Hodgson 71). It was open season on buffalo in the late 1800's as millions were killed by Easterners simply for the sport of it.

With the buffalo almost gone, the Native Americans' livelihood had been destroyed ("Buffalo"). They were forced onto Indian reservations, and the remaining buffalo were corralled and placed in government parks or zoos. Since then, Native Americans have worked hard to gain rights, and today they pass along their proud heritage to future generations. The Pte Oyate, however, is far from the Buffalo Nation it once was. Will the great buffalo *tantanka* ever rule again?

In 1881, French-Canadian rancher Fred Dupree helped ensure the buffalo's survival by starting his own herd from five calves he had captured north of the Cheyenne River. These calves, from the great Black Hills buffalo of South Dakota, would be the ancestors of thousands. Dr. Jim Shaw of Oklahoma State University says, "Most of today's buffalo descend from 77 animals in five founding herds" (qtd. in Hodgson 80).

The American buffalo is making a comeback today mainly because of ranchers who are raising them for consumption. Before this practice began, the herds numbered only 25,000 head as late as 1950. By comparison, the 1994 buffalo population had reached 200,000. People now are literally "growing" bison on farms and ranches across the nation as a cash crop.

Sometimes a reference is listed by title instead of the author. No page number is needed here, because the article is from a nonprint source.

The writer offers just enough statistics to help the reader understand the subject.

At a glance, a handy chart shows the decline and return of the buffalo.

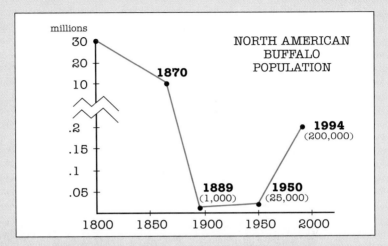

millions

NORTH AMERICAN BUFFALO POPULATION

30
20
10

1870

.2
.15
.1
.05

1994
(200,000)

1889
(1,000)

1950
(25,000)

1800   1850   1900   1950   2000

The buffalo is "returning" to North America in ever-increasing numbers. Cable Network News owner Ted Turner and his actress wife, Jane Fonda, raise almost 10,000 buffalo on their Montana and New Mexico ranches. "I guess I've gone buffalo batty," Turner says. Both he and his wife support the raising of buffalo as an excellent source of low-fat meat and as a way to help save this once endangered species (Hodgson 75).

Buffalo ranchers are, in fact, learning that raising buffalo has certain benefits over raising cattle. For instance, buffalo won't overeat. Their sharp hooves break up the hard soil, helping the land hold valuable water. Their very presence on the land increases grass production; and because they are wild, buffalo are even less dependent on humans than cattle are. The buffalo is a large, tough mammal, and this helps it adapt to almost any situation or climate. Buffalo living in Florida seem just as happy as those living in Alaska. In Hawaii, they even survived Hurricane Iniki in 1992. Hawaiian rancher Bill Mowry recalls how the buffalo "loved every minute of it." He adds, "I was huddled in the basement;

A humorous quotation adds interest to a factual report.

they were lying down chewing their cuds" (qtd. in Hodgson 71-72).

Despite the benefits, raising wild buffalo is surely no easy task. Author Roger Caras states that both male and female are "testy, nervous, and easily tempted into a charge or a fight" (464). This nervous animal, on the average, weighs from 2,000 to 3,000 pounds and measures six feet from hooves to shoulder and 12 feet from head to tail (Caras 466). A sign in Yellowstone Park states: "THESE ANIMALS MAY APPEAR TAME BUT ARE WILD, UNPREDICTABLE, AND DANGEROUS." More than 50 tourists since 1983 have been gored by these large beasts when they violated the buffalo's space (Hodgson 71). Still, with proper knowledge, ranchers are willing to take the risks, and buffalo are found today in ever-growing numbers on ranches, farms, and private holdings throughout North America.

Breeding and caring for buffalo has been successful, but it hasn't been easy. Standards had to be set so breeders would not treat buffalo like cattle. Zoologists have proven that attempting to make bison docile seriously endangers the species, and they warn growers that the aggressive-behavior trait is essential ("Buffalo"). It is what makes the buffalo, a buffalo.

Buffalo growers face other problems. For example, some cattle ranchers are angry about having these wild animals right next to their land. They know that buffalo infected with *Brucella abortus* bacterium could infect their cattle. The buffalo can handle the infection, but the cattle cannot. Also, inbreeding is always a concern. Much care must be taken to breed animals that contain a variety of ancestors to keep them strong (Caras 469).

The buffalo business continues to expand, however.

Only a page number is needed in this reference, because the author is mentioned in the sentence itself.

Having thoroughly covered the benefits, the writer fairly addresses the problems buffalo growers face.

McGinn 5

From the rancher to the restaurant owner, profits and jobs are being created along the way. Denver restaurant owner Sam Arnold serves 50,000 buffalo dinners a year. He also sells buffalo delicacies such as tongue, bone marrow, and hump, all of which go for premium prices. As the public discovers the practical reasons for the new buffalo-meat industry, as well as the tastiness of this low-fat meat, more and more buffalo meat is being purchased. Sam Arnold recalls, "I first tried to sell the buffalo tongue as an hors d'oeuvre at $1.75 and no takers. So I priced it at $6.75, set a limit of two to a customer, and sold out every night" (qtd. in Hodgson 80).

Finally, perhaps the most enterprising scheme is that of land-use planner Frank Popper and his geographer wife, Deborah. They would like to turn the vast, open areas of the West into a nature preserve much like Africa's Serengeti National Park. They would call it the Buffalo Commons. Earliest plans propose the use of a 10,000-acre tract of eastern Montana that would one day support 75,000 buffalo, 150,000 deer, 40,000 elk, and 40,000 pronghorn sheep (Hodgson 85).

The grave nineteenth-century destruction—almost elimination—of one of the world's magnificent mammals, the American buffalo *Bison bison,* was checked in time. It will be a wonder of science, and perhaps a symbol of the future harmony between humans and animals, that the American buffalo will flourish again. Lakota teacher Harry Charger tells his people, "Brother Buffalo kept us from starving, kept us clothed, kept us housed, kept us company. He paid the price, and now we sustain him" (qtd. in Hodgson 89).

The final paragraphs predict a positive future for the buffalo.

A quotation from a descendant of those affected most by the buffalo's near demise ends the report.

McGinn 6

Works Cited

"Buffalo." <u>Software Tool Works Multimedia Encyclopedia</u>.

Computer software. Novato, CA: Software Tool

Works, 1991. CD-ROM.

Caras, Roger A. <u>North American Mammals</u>. New York:

Galahad Books, 1992.

Hodgson, Bryan. "Buffalo: Back Home on the Range."

<u>National Geographic</u> Nov. 1994: 65-89.

The second and third lines are indented.

The sources cited in the paper are listed in alphabetical order.

Helping the Homeless

Center title one-third from top.

Amy Douma

Mr. VanderMey

English 202

Dec. 11, 1988

Center other information two-thirds from top. Double-space.

Center title
one inch
from top.
Double-space
throughout.

In the outline,
ideas of equal
importance are
stated in the
same way.
Here, for
example, the
three main
parts of the
paper (I., II.,
III.) are stated
as participial
phrases.

Helping the Homeless

Introduction—Who are the homeless and why are they so?

I. Classifying the homeless

    A. Unemployed males

    B. Entire family units

II. Addressing the causes

    A. National housing shortage

    B. Ineffective federal programs and policies

        1. Temporary Emergency Food Assistance Program

        2. Voucher System

        3. Rent-Control System

III. Alleviating the problem

    A. Acceptance of responsibility for the problem at the federal level

        1. Reduction in funding for housing during Reagan administration

        2. Drop in housing production

    B. Establishment of proper housing

        1. Maintenance of temporary and transitional shelters

        2. Construction of permanent housing

    C. Regular review of facilities

Conclusion—The homeless need help immediately from the federal government.

Name and page number are one-half inch from top; title is centered.

Writer uses a detailed description to get the reader emotionally involved with the topic.

This question provides the focus for the paper.

Writer paraphrases comments from a personal interview, part of her "field research."

Douma 1

Helping the Homeless

On a chilly February afternoon, an old man sits sleeping on the sidewalk outside a New York hotel while the lunchtime crowd shuffles by. At the man's feet is a sign which reads: "Won't you help me? I'm cold and homeless and lonely. God Bless You" (Chambers 11). Imagine, if you can, the life this man leads. He probably spends his days alone on the street begging for handouts, and his nights searching for shelter from the cold. He has no job, no friends, and nowhere to turn. Although most Americans would like to believe that cases like this are rare, the National Coalition for the Homeless estimates that as many as 3 million citizens of our country share this man's lifestyle (Tucker 34). Who are these people we call "the homeless," and what are the reasons for their predicament?

According to Pastor Walker, the director of the Gospel Missions Shelter in Sioux City, Iowa, most of the homeless are unemployed males, and from 40 to 50 percent have alcohol or drug-related problems. Walker also points out, however, that the image of the "typical" homeless person is changing. He says, for instance, that the average age of the homeless has dropped from fifty-five to thirty in the last ten years (Walker interview). National studies also show that America's homeless population is changing. A recent study by the U.S. Conference of Mayors, for example, found that one-third of the homeless population consists of families with small children, and 22 percent of the homeless have full- or part-time jobs (Mathews 57). Statistics seem to show that more and more of the homeless are entire families who have simply become the victims of economic hardship.

Douma 2

Why are these people still on the streets, despite the billions of dollars that are spent on the homeless each year? Some blame the national housing shortage, pointing out that there are not enough homes to fill the country's need for shelter (Marcuse 426). Further study of the problem, however, suggests that government programs and policies are more likely to blame. The current government programs fall into several categories. Some are handout programs designed to provide food or clothing to all of the needy, not just the homeless. An example of this type of program is the Temporary Emergency Food Assistance Program, created by the federal government in 1981 to make surplus agricultural products available to those in need. Other programs, such as the experimental voucher program and the rent-control system, are intended to provide housing for low-income families that need shelter. Despite the good intentions behind these programs, however, none of them have provided sufficient help for the homeless.

Why have these programs been ineffective in cutting down on homelessness? In some cases, the answer is that the programs are not designed to fit the special needs of the homeless. It was estimated in October of 1986, for instance, that 99 percent of the food supplied by the Temporary Emergency Assistance Program had gone to those who were not homeless. The reason? As Anna Kondratas of the Department of Agriculture says, "When you're homeless, you don't carry around a five-pound block of cheese" (qtd. in Whitman 34). Food programs like these are valuable only to those who already have a place to store and prepare the food they are given. The homeless, therefore, are unable to take full advantage of these programs.

This question shifts the reader's attention from who the homeless are . . . to the causes of their homelessness.

Writer blends examples and comments.

The question serves as a transition and signals a closer look at the problem.

This quotation is found in a secondary source.

Douma 3

Not all programs set up to make housing available to those with low incomes have been effective, either. An example is the voucher system, a federal program created in 1983, which allows low-income families to live wherever they can find housing, regardless of cost. The only requirement is that families must pay at least 30 percent of their incomes in rent. Although this system has been successful in finding shelter for some needy families, it is not a long-term solution to homelessness. One problem is that most families who use the voucher system pay a lower percent of their income for rent than those who rent apartments on their own. Therefore, a family could "raise" its income simply by becoming "homeless" (Coulson 16). The second problem with the program is that it needs a much greater housing supply to be effective. Says Democratic Congressman Thomas Downey of Long Island, "The voucher system would make sense if there were housing, but there is just not enough. It doesn't in any way address the problem" (qtd. in Hull 23).

The program that has had the worst results, however, is the rent-control system, which now covers approximately 12 percent of America's housing. Rent control is a program set up by local governments to limit the amount of rent that a landlord can charge his tenants. It dates back to World War II, when New York tenants became worried about rent increases following the war. In 1947, these tenants persuaded politicians to extend the rent limits to permanent housing. Since that time, nine states and many major cities, such as Los Angeles and Washington, D.C., have adopted rent-control policies (Fleetwood 19).

At first glance, it would appear that rent control

Writer uses a lengthy paraphrase.

Discussion of "rent control," placed last in the series of failed government programs, will be developed most extensively.

should benefit the homeless, making sure that low-rent housing is available. The problem is that most of this housing is rented by those in the middle and upper class. Most of these tenants like living in these cheaper apartments and do not plan to move. This results in a condition known as "housing gridlock," in which no one moves out of the low-rent housing. Seymour Durst, a developer-philosopher from Manhattan, describes the situation this way: "We've got plenty of low-income housing in New York. We've just got upper-income people living in it" (qtd. in Tucker 43).

This situation has had a drastic effect on the poor of New York City. Unless they can find a rent-controlled apartment, they are forced into housing at middle- to upper-income prices. Some estimate that this means these people are paying 20 to 100 percent more for housing than they would have without the rent-control program ("Then There's Rent"). Those who can't afford these higher rent payments are often left without a place to live. Such abuses of the rent-control program are contributing to the problem of homelessness rather than fixing it.

Throughout the nation, rent control has had effects similar to those in New York. According to William Tucker, a writer who has done a great deal of research on the subject, rent control adds to the number of homeless a city will have, regardless of location. For example, homelessness in Santa Monica, California, is so common that the city is called "The Homeless Capital of the West Coast." The only thing that makes this city different from others in the same area is its extremely strict rent-control policy. Other cities in Tucker's study that have rent-control programs also have a much higher

---

Writer provides an explanatory phrase, adding to the reader's understanding of "who" this quoted source is.

This parenthetical reference is for a one-page article with no author.

Writer establishes the authority of her source in an explanatory phrase.

Douma 5

The source is named in text, so only the page number is cited in parentheses.

This question shifts the reader's attention from the causes of homelessness to possible solutions.

Statistics are used to support claims.

rate of homelessness than the national average. In fact, Tucker reports that where rent control is practiced, homelessness is 250 percent greater than in cities without rent control (41).

Since these government programs have not solved the problem of homelessness, what should be done instead? There is no single answer to this question, but the most promising solution consists of three steps. First of all, the federal government must accept responsibility for providing shelter for the homeless. During the Reagan administration, the federal government attempted to shift this burden to state and local governments by slashing federal funds for housing. Between the years of 1981 and 1987, Reagan cut the housing budget from $30 billion to $7.3 billion, expecting local governments and private contributions to make up the difference (Mathews 58). Unfortunately, Reagan's plan has not worked as well as he expected. In New York City, for instance, only $500 million has been spent on the homeless since the cutbacks, while the need has been estimated at $12.5 billion (Chambers 11).

The decrease in funds is only half the problem; there has also been a major drop in housing production. Only 60,000 new housing units have been created in New York during the past three years, compared to 265,000 between the years 1960 and 1963. Many other cities have experienced similar cutbacks. In addition, some of the federal housing units built in the 1960's will soon be free from the rent restrictions placed on them at that time. The result will probably be a substantial raise in rent, which will put much of the current low-income housing out of the reach of the poor (Mathews 57-58). In order to avoid the drastic effects that these low-rent

Douma 6

housing shortages could cause, more housing must be created immediately. According to community groups, renewed federal support will be necessary to accomplish this task (Hull 22).

A second step necessary for helping the homeless is making sure that the proper type of housing is available. According to Peter Marcuse, a professor of urban planning at Columbia University, shelter for the homeless falls into three categories. The first and simplest type is the soup kitchen, a temporary emergency shelter that provides food and, sometimes, a place to sleep. Shelters of this type are especially important in places where little food is available or weather conditions are unfavorable. The second type of housing is the transitional shelter, which also provides housing only temporarily. Transitional housing is unique, however, in that it provides job counseling and other social services, which are intended to help the homeless rejoin society. The third type of shelter is permanent housing, the type of shelter most likely to bring about an end to homelessness (428). Permanent shelter could be provided by constructing low-cost, prefabricated housing modules, or by renovating buildings that no one presently lives in (Coulson 16). Unfortunately, most current housing programs rely on temporary soup kitchens, as they are the least expensive to build and maintain. Although soup kitchens have an important role to play, more transitional and permanent housing will be necessary for the homeless to fully readjust to society.

The final step to ending homelessness is forming an organization that will check to see that shelter residents are satisfied with their facilities and surroundings. This function should be coupled with psychiatric care for those

Writer summarizes types of shelter, using key transitional words "first," "second," and "third."

Since the source was named at the beginning of the paragraph, only the page number is placed in parentheses.

Writer offers support for "final step," anticipating objections: "Studies have shown. . . ."

who are not yet ready to rejoin society. Studies have shown that neglecting the personal care of the homeless often makes all other efforts to help them useless. These people often return to living on the streets unless they are offered some type of support group (Whitman 27). This check-up work could be done either by a government agency or by one of the existing social groups. This third step must be included in any plan intended to end homelessness.

Writer concludes with a call to help the homeless who want help—and to do so with increased federal support.

When we talk about "ending" homelessness, however, we must remember that it is a problem that will never be truly eliminated. There will always be those who refuse any help offered to them, the ones who prize their "free" lifestyle above personal comfort. While we must respect the rights of such people, we cannot use them as an excuse to do nothing about the homeless. Most people living on the streets are there, not by choice, but because they have no alternative. It is these people that we must try to help immediately, with the support of the federal government. If we begin now, we may be able to make homelessness simply a matter of choice.

Works Cited

Chambers, Rick. "No Place to Lay Their Heads." The
 Church Herald 16 Sept. 1988: 9-11.

Coulson, C. "The $37,000 Slum." The New Republic 19
 Jan. 1988: 15-16.

Fleetwood, Blake. "There's Nothing Liberal about Rent
 Control." The Washington Monthly June 1986: 19-23.

Hull, Jennifer. "Building from the Bottom Up." Time 9
 Feb. 1987: 22-23.

Marcuse, Peter. "Why Are They Homeless?" The Nation 4
 Apr. 1987: 426-29.

Mathews, Tom. "What Can Be Done?" Newsweek 21 Mar.
 1988: 57-58.

"Then There's Rent Control." The New Republic 11 Apr.
 1988: 22.

Tucker, William. "Where Do the Homeless Come From?"
 National Review 25 Sept. 1987: 32-43.

Walker, Harry. Personal interview. 20 Dec. 1988.

Whitman, David. "Hope for the Homeless." U.S. News and
 World Report 29 Feb. 1988: 26-35.

"Works Cited"
is centered one
inch from
the top.

The second
lines are
indented five
spaces.

"For me it [the computer] was obviously the perfect new toy. I began playing on page 1—editing, cutting, and revising—and have been on a rewriting high ever since."

—William Zinsser

Writing with a Computer

266 When asked whether a computer helps them with their writing, most students answer *yes*. If you ask these students to explain their answer, they tell you that they stay at a piece of writing longer with a computer, that they experiment more, that they like the way they can move information around, and that they have a better attitude toward writing in general.

Teachers agree that computers help students with their writing, especially when it comes to writing research papers and other lengthy reports. Teachers will also say, however, that computers are better suited for certain parts of the writing process than they are for others. This section discusses the up side and the down side of computer-assisted writing. It also includes a list of the latest computer terms. We hope it helps.

267 PREWRITING

Up Side:

 Prewriting can be a breeze on a computer. For example, think about free writing. You can fill the screen any way you want and keep going as long as you want, without so much as having to flip over a sheet of paper. Also, if you type quickly, you can get ideas down faster by keyboarding than by writing.

 If you prewrite messily in longhand, using the computer can free you from worry about handwriting you (or your teacher) can't read later.

 Some people are more inventive in front of a screen. It may be that you have a different style of learning or creating. Using a computer may well free your thinking and help you get words on paper.

268 **Down Side:**

Some writers do less prewriting and planning when they are using a computer, partly because they aren't able to use some forms of prewriting, like clustering.

The monitor is too tempting for some writers; they constantly stop to read what they have written. *Solution:* Turn the resolution of the monitor down to stop yourself from deleting or editing.

Best Advice: Try it out! Find out whether prewriting on paper or prewriting on a screen is better for you. If you think it's simpler or easier to approach prewriting with paper and pen, you're not alone: many writers find this to be the case. At the same time, don't overlook the possibility that using a computer may help you get ideas down more quickly and effectively.

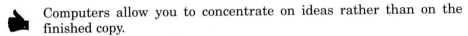

INSIDE   *Special Advisory:* Save your work at frequent intervals throughout a writing project. Before you turn off your computer, make a backup copy of your work on a disk.

269 **WRITING THE FIRST DRAFT**

Up Side:

Using a computer helps a writer stay with a piece of writing longer and develop it more thoroughly.

Computers allow you to concentrate on ideas rather than on the finished copy.

Drafting on a computer can make it easier for you to share ideas. You can simply print out a "hard copy" for your teacher or classmates to react to. As a result of this sharing, you also become more aware of a real audience.

Down Side:

Deleting sections of copy on a computer is very tempting for some writers. Most experts agree that it is important to save all of your ideas in early drafts. *Solution:* Don't push that "delete" key no matter what—at least not in your early drafts!

Best Advice: Do your drafting on your computer. If you can't resist the temptation to make a lot of changes during first drafts, turn down the brightness on your monitor and type "blind" for a while. Print out and share copies of what you've written.

270 **REVISING**

Up Side:

 A big plus for computer writing is the time and toil it saves you when writing or typing revision after revision, especially on longer essays and research papers.

 A computer makes revising easier because you can move, delete, and add large chunks of information by using a few simple commands. As a result, you no longer have to be afraid to try new things during revision.

 Group revision is also made easier with quick, clean printouts for everyone to read and react to.

Down Side:

 Some people are not as good at carefully rereading and evaluating writing on a screen as they are on paper. *Solution:* Simply print out the document, make the changes on paper, and then input them.

Best Advice: Use your computer for revising. Take advantage of the speed and ease of using a computer, but do slow down long enough to reflect on and rethink what you've written. (If you print out a copy of your work before you revise, you can easily undo any hasty revising later.)

271 **EDITING AND PROOFREADING**

Up Side:

 Because making changes is so easy, you can easily produce a clean final copy.

 Programs are available to help you prepare your writing for publication. The spell checkers and search-and-replace capabilities in some word-processing programs are especially helpful.

 Some programs make it simple to create the bibliography, table of contents, and index for a research paper.

Down Side:

 You may not see errors such as missing words, misplaced commas, or misspelled words as easily on a screen as on paper. Or, you may come to rely too much on your spell and grammar checkers. *Solution:* Watch as the computer does its work; then do a final read yourself.

Best Advice: Do your editing and proofreading on a computer. Clearly, the computer serves best in this final step of preparing a paper for publication.

272 Coming On-Line

If you are just getting into computers, you should find the following observations helpful:

- **Don't put your pens and paper into storage just because you are using a computer.** You will still do plenty of old-fashioned longhand during most of your writing projects. Many writers like to do their initial writing on paper and their revising and editing on computers. After a little experimenting, you can decide what works best for you.

- **To hunt and peck with a computer is slow and tedious, so you must know how to type.** There are keyboarding programs available to use on your computer if you can't take a basic typing or word-processing course in school.

- **Word-processing programs make a computer a hi-tech writing machine.** Programs are the software (disks, cartridges, cassettes, etc.) that instruct a computer to perform certain tasks. All word-processing programs allow you to enter, delete, add, and move data. Others will actually help you with your spelling, grammar, and research-paper work.

- **All word-processing programs come with step-by-step instructions.** Follow them carefully. When you do get stuck and you can't find your own answers, ask for help. It may seem difficult at first, but you'll soon be an expert!

- **Keep a written (or typed) copy of your writing handy.** That way, if your writing suddenly vanishes from your computer screen, you'll have a copy to fall back on. Remember: *Save!*

- **Give it a rest!** Staring at a monitor for a long period of time can cause eyestrain. Make sure that you adjust the contrast and brightness on your monitor so that it feels comfortable to your eyes. Also, make sure that the lighting in the room does not cause a glare on your screen. When your eyes begin to ache, save your text, and take a rest.

the .bottom line

Using a computer allows you to add some nice touches to your work:

- different typestyles for variety
- boldface or italics for emphasis
- indents and centering for page balance
- tables and charts for clarity
- uniform margins for neatness
- graphics for illustration

273 COMPUTER TERMS

Back-up: A duplicate copy of a program or file made to protect the original copy in case it is lost, stolen, or destroyed.

Binary: The number system commonly used by computers because the values 0 and 1 can easily be represented electronically in the computer.

Bit: (binary digit) The basic unit of computer memory; one binary digit.

Boot: To start up a computer system by loading a program into the memory.

Bug: An error in a computer program.

Bulletin board: A service that permits users to leave, store, or receive messages by computer modem.

Byte: Eight bits of information acting as a single piece of data.

CD-ROM: A compact disk that can hold large amounts of information, including moving video images.

Character: A letter or number used to display information on a computer screen or printer.

Chip: A small piece of silicon containing thousands of electrical elements. Also known as an integrated circuit.

Circuit board: A flat, rigid board inside a computer used to hold and electronically connect computer chips and other electrical elements.

Clear: To erase stored or displayed data.

Command: An instruction to a computer to perform a special task like "print."

Computer: A machine that can accept data, process it according to a stored set of instructions, and then output the results.

Computer program: A piece of software containing statements and commands that tell the computer to perform a task or function.

Configuration: A computer and all devices connected to it.

Control character: A character that is entered by holding down the control key while hitting another key. The control character "controls" or changes information that is printed or displayed.

CPU: (Central Processing Unit) The hardware portion of a computer. The "brain" of the computer that controls all other devices.

Crash: A term used to describe what happens when a computer or program stops working.

CRT: (Cathode Ray Tube) The computer screen; the electronic vacuum tube found in a TV.

Cursor: A pointer on the computer screen that shows you where the next character typed from the keyboard will appear.

Data: Information given to or produced by a computer.

Database: A program or collection of information that is organized in such a way that a computer can sort it quickly.

Debug: Remove errors from a computer program.

Device: A piece of computer hardware designed to perform a certain task. A monitor, printer, and disk drive are examples of computer devices.

Directory: The table of contents for all files on a disk.

Disk: A magnetic storage device used to record computer information. Each disk appears flat and square on the outside; inside, the disk is circular and rotates so that information can be stored on its many circular tracks.

Disk drive: The device that writes and reads information onto the disk.

Documentation: Writing and graphics that explain how to use and maintain a piece of hardware or software.

DOS: (Disk Operating System) A software system that allows a computer to operate by communicating with and controlling disk drives.

Download: To transfer programs or files from one computer to another.

Drag: To move the cursor across the screen by sliding the mouse.

Edit: To change an original document or program by adding, deleting, or replacing certain parts.

E-mail: (Electronic mail) A system that uses telecommunications to send messages from one computer to another.

Error: A programming mistake that will cause the program to run incorrectly or not run at all.

Error message: A message, displayed or printed, that tells you what error or problem is present in a program.

Execute: To run a computer program.

Exit: To leave or quit a program.

274

File: A collection of computer information stored under a single name.

Floppy disk: A storage device made of a thin, magnetically coated plastic.

Font: The style or kind of type a printer uses; most printers have several fonts or type-styles to choose from.

Footprint: The space on a desk or table taken up by a computer.

Format: To prepare a blank disk for use (also initialize).

Fuzzy: Approximate; not exact.

Graphics: Information that is displayed as pictures or images.

Hard copy: A printed copy.

Hardware: The electronic and mechanical parts of a computer system. A floppy disk is hardware; the program stored on it is software.

Icon: A small picture or graphic used to identify computer folders or files.

Input: Information placed into a computer from a disk drive, keyboard, or other device.

Instruction: Machine language that commands an action to be taken by the CPU of a computer.

Interactive: A computer system in which the operator and computer frequently exchange information.

Interface: The hardware and software that are used to link one computer or computer device to another.

K: (Kilobyte) A term used when describing the capacity of a computer memory or storage device. For example, 16K equals 16 x 1,024 or 16,384 bits of memory.

Keyboard: An input device used to enter information into a computer by striking keys that are labeled much like those on a typewriter.

Laser printer: A high-resolution printer that prints by laser. The more dots per inch (DPI) a laser printer has, the better the printout.

Library: A collection of computer programs.

List: A display or printout of a computer program or file.

Load: To take information from an external storage device and place or load it into a computer's memory.

LOGO: A language that combines pictures and words to teach programming to children.

Loop: A series of instructions that is repeated, usually with different data on each pass.

Main memory: The memory that is built into a computer.

Memory: The chips in the computer that store information and program instructions until they are needed.

Menu: A detailed list of choices presented in a program from which a user can select.

Microcomputer: A small computer using a microprocessor as its processing unit.

Modem: (modulator demodulator) A device that allows computers to communicate over telephone lines.

Monitor: A video screen on which information from a computer can be displayed.

Multimedia: A combination of text, graphics, video, voice, music, and animation.

Multiuser: A program that allows several computers to share information from the same source.

Network: A series of computers (or other devices) connected together.

Output: Information that a computer sends out to a drive, monitor, printer, or modem.

Peripheral: A device connected to a computer such as a plotter, disk drive, or printer.

Printout: A copy of a computer page or program printed on paper.

Processor: The part of the computer that receives language instructions and controls all other parts of the computer.

Program: A piece of software or set of instructions that tells the computer what to do.

Programmer: A person involved in the writing, editing, and production of a computer program.

Programming language: The language used when writing a computer program.

Prompt: A question on the screen that asks the user to put information into the computer.

RAM: (Random Access Memory) The part of the computer's memory where data, instructions, and results can be recorded and stored.

Resolution: The quality of the "picture" on a computer screen.

ROM: (Read-Only Memory) The part of the computer's memory containing the permanent instructions for the computer; new data cannot be recorded on this part of the computer's memory.

Save: To take a program or file from main memory and store it on disk, cassette, or hard drive for later use.

Scanner: A device used to "read" (scan) an image or picture and send it into a computer.

Sector: A fraction of the recording surface on a disk; a sector is a fraction of a track.

Software: Programs that tell a computer how to perform a certain task.

275 **Spreadsheet:** A program used to organize numbers and figures into a worksheet form so they are easier to read.

Statement: An instruction in a program that tells the computer to perform a specific task.

Storage: The main memory or external devices where information or programs can be stored.

String: A group of consecutive letters, numbers, and characters treated as one unit.

Subroutine: A group of statements that can be found and used from several different places in a main program.

System: The collection of hardware and software that work together to form a working computer.

Telecommunications: Sending and receiving information from one computer to another over phone lines, satellites, etc.

Terminal: A "computer" consisting of a keyboard and a monitor; it doesn't actually contain a computer (CPU) but shares a computer with other terminals.

Text: The words, letters, and numbers that can be read by an individual.

Track: A fraction of the recording surface on a disk. (A track can be compared to the space used by each song on an album.) The number of tracks on a disk varies.

User: A person using a computer.

Virus: A bug deliberately but secretly hidden in a computer system in order to wipe out stored information.

Word: A string of bits treated as a single unit by a computer.

Word processor: A program (or computer) that helps a user to write letters, memos, and other kinds of text.

Write-enable notch: The small, rectangular cutout in the edge of a disk's jacket used to protect the contents of a disk. If the notch is closed or covered by a write-protect tab, information cannot be written on the disk.

Write-protect: To cover up the write-enable notch (or opening), making it impossible for new information to be written on the disk. The information on the disk is now protected from being overwritten.

276 COMMAND STATEMENTS

DATA: Allows data to be stored in a computer program, then retrieved during the running of the program by the READ statement.

DIM: Saves space in memory for the size of an array you select.

END: The last statement in a program that stops the program and returns control of the computer to the user.

FOR: Allows the programmer to set up a loop that is to be repeated a specified number of times.

GOSUB: Causes the program to go to a subroutine. When a RETURN statement is made in the subroutine, the program returns to the line following the GOSUB statement.

GOTO: Causes the computer to go to a particular line in the program.

IF: A statement that tells the computer to go to the next line in the program if the argument following the IF statement is false or to go to a given line number if the argument is true.

INPUT: Allows the user to input information from the keyboard for use in a program.

LET: An optional instruction that can be used when a variable in a program is assigned a value. (Example: Let A=25.)

LIST: Displays or prints a copy of the program presently in the computer.

NEXT: Used with the FOR statement. When a NEXT statement is used in a program, the computer branches back to the FOR statement until the loop has been repeated a specific number of times.

PRINT: Instructs the computer to type or display information from a program.

READ: Instructs the computer to read the information in a DATA statement; takes information from a DATA statement and assigns the information to the variable(s) immediately following the READ statement.

REM: Allows the programmer to insert remarks and comments into a program that are used to make the program easier to understand.

RETURN: This command will instruct the computer to go back to the main part of the program. When encountered in a subroutine, this statement will cause the computer to branch to the first statement after the GOSUB command that sent the computer to the subroutine.

RUN: Causes the computer to "run" the program in memory.

THEN: Used with the IF statement. When the argument between the IF and THEN is true, the statements following the THEN statement are performed.

Forms of Writing

"Be yourself. Above all, let who you are, what you are, what you believe shine through every sentence you write, every piece you finish."

—John Jakes

Personal Writing: Writing from Within

277   Suppose your best friend, in all seriousness, said, "Instead of a movie tonight, let's do a little report writing." If you were any kind of friend at all, you would immediately dial 911 for help since no one in his or her right mind would ever make such a request. You write reports, summaries, and other such papers because they are assigned, not because you want to. They are important for many reasons; entertainment is not one of them.

There is one type of writing, however, that may have more to offer than most movies. It is called **personal writing**, or writing that comes from within, carried out because you have a personal need to explore or share your experiences.

278 Heady Stuff

Once you get into personal writing, you'll soon realize your thoughts and experiences are no more than starting points. You'll begin to turn these initial ideas inside out and see them in new ways. This might sound like heady stuff, but it really isn't. Personal writing is simply an effective way to examine your world.

what's ahead? This section in your handbook contains guidelines for writing in a journal (personal writing in the truest sense) and writing reminiscences (memory writing that is meant to be shared). Your experience with both forms will help you appreciate writing as a powerful learning tool.

> "A journal should, in fact, be clear proof that being you isn't boring, even on those days when we shrug and say, 'Nothing happened.'"
>
> —Peter Stillman

Journal Writing

279 Write on . . . and on . . . and on.

It doesn't take much to keep a journal: a notebook, a handy supply of your favorite pens or pencils (or a computer), and a promise on your part to write regularly.

The last point is the catch. Journal writing works best when it is done on a regular basis. Some writers do their journal writing early in the morning when they are fresh and alert. Others like to record their thoughts and feelings at the end of the day. Write when and where it feels comfortable to you—inside or outside of school. The important point is to get into a writing routine and stick to it.

Write about your experiences, freely recording thoughts and feelings as they come to mind. If nothing personal moves you to write, pick up on the actions of a friend, on something you have read in the newspaper, or on anything that catches your eye. But please don't say there is nothing to write about. That is just an excuse not to get started.

280 Writing to Explore

Meaning will come if you write regularly. You'll begin to enter the world of your inner thoughts; and in time, you'll feel a little different, a little sharper, as if your senses have been fine-tuned. A squeaky closet door will no longer go unnoticed. You'll begin to wonder how long it has been squeaky, why no one has fixed it, and what else is "squeaky" in your life.

The real fun starts when you begin to hit upon ideas that you want to explore further—and eventually turn into stories, poems, and essays to share. That is a sign of becoming a real writer, someone who values the power of the mind and the pen.

the bottom line

In the best of all worlds, journal writing will become a very important part of your life, right up there with good friends and good food. But we will settle for something far more practical and down to earth: That through journal writing you will begin to feel more comfortable with the physical act of writing and more confident in your ability to express yourself.

281 Journal Writing Tips

Think of your journal as a snapshot album, and you are a roving photographer capturing slices of life. Or think of it as a tape recorder, preserving (forever) the one-way conversations you have with a "silent partner." Or think of your journal in other ways—as a place to explore, reflect, experiment, and predict. It can be whatever you want it to be. Here are some tips that will help you get started . . . and keep going:

Try writing nonstop. This is how you will get the most mileage out of your writing. Your goal should be to write for at least 10-15 minutes at a time. If you get stuck during your writing, write "I'm drawing a blank" until something comes to mind.

Focus on ideas, not looks. The real satisfaction in keeping a journal is making new discoveries. Make that your goal. Don't worry about the appearance of your writing. Just make sure that it's readable.

Always date your entries. And make sure to read your entries from time to time. Underline interesting ideas, ideas that may seem unusual, surprising, or important. Continue writing about these thoughts in future entries.

Push an idea as far as you can. You'll never know what thoughts and feelings you will uncover unless you write about an idea from many different angles. (Keep asking yourself "Why?" as you write.)

Experiment in your writing. Write like your favorite author or like someone you know. Write in a foreign language or in jazzy street language. Write to laugh, or to give yourself a pep talk. Most important, write according to your own rules.

282 Other Types of Journals

Learning Log ● Writing in a learning log or subject journal helps you become more actively involved in your course work. It gives you an opportunity to make important concepts and ideas part of your own thinking. And in the end, it makes you a better student. (See "Writing to Learn" in the index for more.)

Response Journal ● Writing in a reader-response journal helps you make the most out of each reading experience—whether you are reading the newest title by one of your favorite authors or an article in a magazine, a short story in your literature anthology, or a chapter in your science textbook.

Dialogue Journal ● In a dialogue journal, you and a writing partner carry on a conversation (first one person writes, then the other) about experiences you have had, books you have read, ideas that you're not sure about, and so on. (Some students have found *team journals* to be an effective learning tool, a process in which four or five classmates regularly write entries about their course work in the same journal.)

> "Memories are not only statements about one life but a springboard to statements about all lives."
>
> —June Gould

283 Writing Reminiscences: Remembering and Sharing

Everyone of us has plenty of stories to tell about past experiences. I'm not talking about stories that belong in the *National Enquirer*—"I was attacked by giant lobsters!"—but real stories, everyday stories, shared honestly and sincerely. Think of all of the friends you've gained and lost, all of the highs and lows you've experienced, all of the different "firsts" you've lived through (your first serious injury, your first crush, etc.). You have so many real stories to tell, you could write a book.

We refer to writing about past experiences as reminiscence writing. (By definition, "reminiscing" is the process of sharing past experiences.) The best reminiscences help you see, hear, and feel experiences as they unfold. They contain specific details, dialogue, and action words. They have energy and life; they come close to the real thing.

Picture yourself sitting next to a friend who is telling you this great story. You are literally at the edge of your seat, waiting to hear what happens next. That is exactly how a reminiscence should make you feel as you read it. It should hold your attention from start to finish.

284 Basic Thinking and Writing Moves

Developing a personal reminiscence really involves two basic thinking and writing moves. You must first **recall** as much as you can about the experience (*who? what? when? where? why?* and *how?*). Then you have to decide on the most effective way to **share** this information. Your goal should be to re-create an experience rather than report on it. Your writing should have that special as-it-happened quality.

 What happens if you can't remember every last detail? Fill in the gaps with details that seem right. (Don't worry; all writers do this.)

285 Getting Started

Read the quick guide on the next page and the sample reminiscences in this section to get a better feel for effective memory writing. Then get ready to bring some of your experiences to life, following the guidelines for writing a reminiscence (287). Once you get started, you'll find it hard to stop.

"Writing is not apart from living. Writing is a kind of double living."
—Catherine Drinker Bowen

286 Reminiscence Writing

Quick Guide

All memory writing—no matter if you are recalling one specific incident or a series of related incidents—shares the following characteristics.

Starting Point: Reminiscence writing begins when you identify a memorable experience—something that happened over a relatively short period of time—that you would like to explore or develop.

Purpose: Writing about past experiences satisfies your desire or need to share part of your past. It helps you establish who you are in the world. (On another level, the purpose is to inform or entertain your readers.)

Form: Think of a reminiscence as a story with the details unfolding one after another. There should be little need for introductions or explanations. (Try to start right in the middle of the action when you write.)

Audience: In most cases, you will be addressing your immediate audience—your classmates, peers, and perhaps your family members.

Voice: To make your reminiscence come alive, use your best storytelling voice. Include plenty of dialogue, description, and action words. Take your readers back in time and help them see, hear, and feel the experience as you remember it.

Point of View: Obviously, the first person (I) point of view is used in reminiscences because you are writing about personal experiences.

The Big Picture

Personal reminiscence writing is the process of tapping into your past, of recalling and sharing memories. Your goal is to tell good stories, not to dwell on the importance of different times in your past.

Personal Writing·················· *Here's what I remember or feel . . .*

287 Guidelines for Writing a Reminiscence

From the Beginning . . .

Discussion: In a basic reminiscence, you share an incident or event from your past that happened over a relatively short period of time. This incident might have taken only a few minutes, or perhaps it extended over a few hours or the better part of a day. You might focus on an emotional experience, a silly incident, a serious or solemn event, or a frightening few minutes. Be sure to include enough specific details to make your writing come alive for your readers. Refer to the steps below and the models that follow to help you with your writing.

Searching and Selecting

1. **Selecting** • You should have little trouble thinking of a subject to write about. You're simply looking for an incident that appeals to you personally and that will have some appeal to your readers.

2. **Reviewing** • Review your journal entries for ideas. Or focus your attention on a specific time in your past and list related ideas as they come to mind. Then again, you might want to talk about the "old days" with a friend or classmate.

Generating the Text

3. **Collecting** • Write freely about your subject to see how much you already know about it. Then gather additional details if necessary, by talking to other people about the incident or by searching your own memory for more ideas.

4. **Focusing** • State a possible focus or approach for your writing (you might want to surprise your readers, or have them share your feelings related to the experience). Then plan accordingly, organizing details that support this focus.

Writing and Revising

5. **Writing** • Write your first draft freely, working in details according to the planning you may have done.

6. **Revising** • Carefully review, revise, and refine your writing before sharing it. Remember that your goal is to re-create this incident in living color for your readers.

Evaluating

Is the writing focused around a specific incident or event?

Does the writing contain effective supporting details?

Does the writing sound sincere and honest?

Will readers appreciate the treatment of this subject?

288 Personal Reminiscence

In this model, student writer Laura Baginski shares an entertaining incident involving herself (obviously), her mother, and a tomato. Pay special attention to Ms. Baginski's attitude throughout the piece. (This model appeared in the June 1992 commemorative issue of the *High School Writer*, a monthly publication of student writing.)

Tomato on the Brain

One day I was hanging upside down from my knees on my monkey bars. I glanced around the yard. Hanging there, the world was completely rearranged; the trees looked like feather dusters, the basket of vegetables underneath me seemed to replace the clouds, and my dog seemed to be flying. My mother was laboriously caring for her precious yet weed-infested garden. She worked in such jerking, hummingbird-like movements that watching her from an upside-down position was a special and amusing treat.

Wiping sweat off her brow, she peered at me over her shoulder and shook her head. "You know, if you hang upside down like that, all the blood rushing to your brain will make your head blow up."

I smiled. A challenge. This was what I had been waiting for. The sheer excitement of the possibility of my head exploding motivated me to hang there longer.

After five minutes, my temples began to throb. My heart felt like a big lump of pain and seemed to weigh at least 200 pounds. My entire body was numb. I could feel all the blood rushing to my brain like a flash flood. My mother's wise warnings jabbed and replayed over and over in my mind. I was suddenly gripped with the realization that my head was indeed going to blow up.

I tried to get down, but paralysis seized me. In a panic, I closed my eyes and envisioned fragments of my head strewn around the yard. I saw myself transformed into fertilizer for my mother's garden, my severed eyes and nose in my father's tomato patch, dripping off the lilac patch, flowing down the fence. . . .

Suddenly, darkness washed over me and I was falling, sinking . . . until my head struck something offering little resistance. The impact jolted me out of my trance.

As my eyes tried to focus, I reached my hand to my head, checking to see how much of it was left. What my hand discovered was soft, mushy, brain-like. Struck with terror, I brought my trembling hand to my focusing eyes. It was oozing, it was red, it was . . . it was . . . a tomato! @

The main focus of the writing is a specific childhood experience.

The writer goes to extremes in describing her dangerous situation.

The drama increases until the messy end of the incident.

289 Reminiscence of a Person

It's natural for writers to reminisce about important people in their lives, people who have had a strong influence on them—mothers, fathers, friends, teachers, and so on. But writers may also find it important to reminisce about people they hardly know, people they may have encountered only once in their lives. That is what student writer Sara Berner does in this reminiscence of a person.

The Woman

There she was, going into the grocery store right in front of my family. She was the most interesting lady I had ever encountered. I was only about seven years old at the time. We were living in Colorado.

She pushed a cartload of things going into the store. I was confused because I had always thought that people came out of stores with stuff. Then again, the things she had in her cart weren't exactly "store bought."

The woman looked to be in her forties. She had on three sweaters, a stocking cap on her head, a large trench coat, sweatpants, gloves, two different socks, and old boots with no shoelaces. She seemed lost, I thought, and very dirty. Her face was wrinkled, and her hair was graying. Her eyes were droopy and seemed very sad. She hung her head, looking at no one when she walked. She looked as if she had just finished a hard day's work.

Then all of a sudden a man walked up to the lady and dragged her out of the store. I really didn't know why because she wasn't bothering anyone. My mom told me not to stare. She said that the woman was homeless and probably didn't have any money. She was a bag lady, carrying everything she owned in her cart. I couldn't understand how this woman could have almost nothing.

That night I kept thinking about the bag lady, trying to imagine how she lived from day to day. Where did she sleep? What did she eat? Did she have a family? I also realized for the first time that there probably were many other bag people in the world. I had been completely blind to this side of life. It was so far removed from my own comfortable experience. All I could do was wonder why some people had to live like that, and why no one helped them. Now, 10 years later, I still wonder. @

The reminiscence starts right in the middle of the action.

The woman's appearance is recalled in great detail.

The writer's questions and concerns reflect the importance of this experience.

❷❾⓿ Reminiscence of School Life

Memories of school life—all of the many experiences related to teachers, classmates, and classrooms—are popular subjects for reminiscences. The following reminiscence comes from *The Land Remembers* by Ben Logan. Logan apparently had the utmost respect for his teacher, always referring to her as "Teacher" with a capital *T*. (From *The Land Remembers* by Ben Logan. Copyright © 1975 by Ben T. Logan. Reprinted by permission of NorthWord Press/Heartland Press.)

"Quiet!"

An opening generalization about "outrage" leads into the specific reminiscence.

. . . One of the things Teacher taught us was that outrage is something you should have and should show. Teacher showed us that when we laughed at Tom Withers. She showed it on a day when I was so lost in a book I didn't know my sixth-grade arithmetic class had gone to the front of the room. I heard Teacher speak my name. She was right at my elbow. I realized she had spoken several times. I jumped to my feet, dropping the book, and hurried to the front. The others laughed. Teacher straightened up with the fallen book. Her face was white.

"Quiet!" she yelled.

The use of dialogue and realism add intensity to the reminiscence.

She marched to the front of the room. I had never seen her look so angry before. "Don't ever let me hear you do that again!" she thundered. "Don't ever let me hear you laugh at somebody because they are that interested in a book!"

Everyone was looking at me. I was embarrassed and hung my head.

Teacher smiled suddenly. "What was so interesting?"

"The monarch butterfly," I said.

"Tell us."

I tried to repeat what I had found, still not quite believing it myself. All my life I had seen the big orange monarchs perched on the summer flowers. They especially liked milkweed. In the fall they vanished along with all the other butterflies. I had thought they were killed by frost. The book said they did not die. They flew south, like the birds, migrating all the way from Wisconsin to the Gulf of Mexico, a thousand miles away. They laid their eggs there. Those eggs became new monarchs, and in spring they flew north again. The thought of those beautiful and fragile butterflies, migrating like bright-colored flowers, was more vivid than any fairy tale.

The author *shows* readers that Teacher is someone to be obeyed.

I stopped speaking. Teacher opened the book, read a moment, and nodded. "That's what it says. And I think it is an accurate book."

She walked back to my desk and put the book down. Then sixth-grade arithmetic began. . . . @

291 Extended Reminiscence

Sometimes a reminiscence focuses on an important extended period of time in the writer's life, a time of great joy or sadness or change. In this extended reminiscence, Malcolm X recalls a very disturbing time when his family began to lose control of their own lives. (From *The Autobiography of Malcolm X* by Malcolm X with Alex Haley. Copyright © 1964 by Alex Haley and Malcolm X. Copyright © 1965 by Alex Haley and Betty Shabazz. Reprinted by permission of Random House, Inc.)

The Autobiography of Malcolm X

The writer's thoughts and feelings are presented clearly and forcefully.

. . . My mother began to buy on credit. My father had always been very strongly against credit. "Credit is the first step into debt and back into slavery," he had always said. And then she went to work herself. She would go into Lansing and find different jobs—in housework, or sewing— for white people. They didn't realize, usually, that she was a Negro. A lot of white people around there didn't want Negroes in their houses.

She would do fine until in some way or other it got to people who she was, whose widow she was. And then she would be let go. I remember how she used to come home crying, but trying to hide it, because she had lost a job that she needed so much.

Once, when one of us—I cannot remember which—had to go for something to where she was working, and the people saw us, and realized she was actually a Negro, she was fired on the spot, and she came home crying, this time not hiding it.

The reminiscence highlights important events during this time.

When the state Welfare people began coming to our house, we would come from school sometimes and find them talking with our mother, asking a thousand questions. They acted and looked at her, and at us, and around in our house, in a way that had about it the feeling—at least for me—that we were not people. In their eyesight we were just things, that was all.

My mother began to receive two checks—a Welfare check and, I believe, a widow's pension. The checks helped, but they weren't enough, as many of us as there were. When they came, about the first of the month, one always was already owed in full, if not more, to the man at the grocery store. And, after that, the other one didn't last long.

The mother's reactions to the welfare checks are clearly described.

We began to go swiftly downhill. The physical downhill wasn't as quick as the psychological. My mother was, above everything else, a proud woman, and it took its toll on her that she was accepting charity. And her feelings were communicated to us.

She would speak sharply to the man at the grocery store for padding the bill, telling him that she wasn't ignorant, and he didn't like that. She would talk back sharply to the state Welfare people, telling them that she was a grown woman, able to raise her children, that it wasn't necessary for them to keep coming around so much, meddling in our lives. And they didn't like that.

But the monthly Welfare check was their pass. They acted as if they owned us, as if we were their private property. As much as my mother would have liked to, she couldn't keep them out. She would get particularly incensed when they began insisting upon drawing us older children aside, one at a time, out on the porch or somewhere, and asking us questions, or telling us things—against our mother and against each other.

Time and experience helped the writer better understand his mother's actions.

We couldn't understand why, if the state was willing to give us packages of meat, sacks of potatoes and fruit, and cans of all kinds of things, our mother obviously hated to accept. We really couldn't understand. What I later understood was that my mother was making a desperate effort to preserve her pride—and ours. . . .

Pride was just about all we had to preserve. . . . ℰ

Related Forms

There are many ways to think and write about your past experiences. Experiment with some of these types of reminiscing to gain a full appreciation of memory writing.

Related Reminiscence

Share two or three related experiences from your past. Maybe your older brothers or sisters played tricks on you when you were little. Maybe you did some wild and crazy things in your old neighborhood. (Try to make the experiences work together in a unified whole; include only the most important details related to each experience.)

"Unpeopled" Reminiscence

Share a memory about an unforgettable object or place from an earlier time in your life. Help your readers feel why the object or place is unforgettable. (Writing an "unpeopled" reminiscence is really a matter of linking a place or an object from your past to a strong feeling.)

Reminiscence of a Group

Think back to all of the groups you have been associated with. Consider long-term groups like your family and friends as well as short-term groups like teams or clubs. Then re-create a specific memory related to one of these groups. Try to capture the group's special flavor.

Personal Essay

Develop an essay about an important experience or time in your past. Write to inform and/or entertain your readers as well as to get them thinking. A personal essay should be part recollection and part reflection.

extend

For a rich resource of reminiscences, read autobiographies written by individuals who really interest you. Pay special attention to the childhood experiences they share. Note specifically how they begin particular reminiscences, how much detail and dialogue they use, how they arrange all of their ideas, and so on. Then experiment with some of these techniques in your own memory writing.

"I don't pick subjects so much as they pick me. Ideas seem to present themselves to me all the time."

—Andy Rooney

Subject Writing: Searching and Reporting

294   Let's page through a current issue of *Rolling Stone* magazine and review its main stories. The summer music scene and old and new rockers in the news are highlighted in summary reports. Two longer reports follow, one on old-style punk rock and another on President Clinton's national service program. A profile of comedian Jerry Seinfeld appears next, followed by an extended interview with Thurston Moore, a guitarist for a group called Sonic Youth. Also included is a photojournalist's shocking eyewitness account of the death and destruction in Rwanda.

295 Real-World Writing

    What do these articles have in common? They are all examples of **subject writing**, writing carried out to share information about newsworthy people, places, and events. We classify descriptions, interviews, reports, profiles, and eyewitness accounts as subject writing. It is the type of writing you find in all current magazines, addressing the needs and interests of specific audiences. The best subject writing contains important information and personality; it educates and entertains.

what's ahead?   Read the quick guide on the next page and the writing examples in this section to learn more about subject writing. You will find everything from a description of a person to a firsthand experience, from an interview report to a historical profile. Also included is a set of basic writing guidelines (297) that will help you with all of your subject writing.

> "Never underestimate your readers' intelligence or overestimate their information."

296 Subject Writing

Quick Guide

All subject writing—no matter if you are describing a firsthand experience or compiling a report—shares the following characteristics.

Starting Point: Subject writing begins with your interest in a person, place, event, or idea. ("I'd like to interview that old guy I see every day after school, learn firsthand about bungee jumping, spend some time reading about the new . . .")

Purpose: The purpose is to investigate subjects of current interest and report on the findings. (On another level, the purpose is to inform your readers.)

Form: Subject writing follows many different patterns of organization. A description may look very closely at a subject's actions or appearance, point by point. An interview report may be set up in a basic question-and-answer format. An eyewitness account will present the details of an event chronologically, and so on.

Audience: In most cases, you will be speaking to your classmates and peers. (Your interests are their interests.)

Voice: Speak to your readers sincerely and honestly about your subject; keep them interested and entertained.

Point of View: Use the first-person point of view (I) when you have a strong personal attachment to your subject (especially in eyewitness accounts, firsthand experiences, extended experiences, etc.). In most other cases, use the third-person point of view (he, she, they).

The Big Picture

Subject writing shares what you learn about people and places. It is different from personal reminiscence writing, which shares your memories.

Personal Writing ·············· *Here's what I remember or feel . . .*

Subject Writing ················ *Here's what I learned about . . .*

297 **Guidelines for Subject Writing**

Writing in the Real World

Discussion: Write an article (description, report, profile, etc.) about an interesting person, place, or event. The effectiveness of your writing will depend upon your ability to collect information about your subject. You will need to conduct interviews, make visits, engage in hands-on experiences, and/or read articles. Read the examples (298-309) and refer to the basic guidelines below to help you with your writing.

Searching and Selecting

1. **Searching** • Use the following questions to begin your subject search: Who would you like to describe or get to know better? What places would you like to visit or learn about? What current events or topics would you like to investigate?

2. **Choosing** • Once you have identified two or three possible subjects, ask yourself two additional questions: Which of these subjects best meets the needs and interests of my readers? Will it be difficult to find information about any of these subjects?

Generating the Text

3. **Recording** • With a subject in mind, explore your thoughts about it in a free writing. This will help you to determine what you already know about your subject and what you need to find out.

4. **Collecting** • Plan and carry out your investigation. Schedule interviews and visits, read articles, and so on. (Take good notes!)

5. **Reviewing** • Decide on a focus for your writing—a main point about your subject that you would like to emphasize. Then plan your writing, selecting and organizing details that support this focus.

Writing and Revising

6. **Writing** • Write your first draft freely, working in details according to your planning. ("Speak" honestly and naturally.)

7. **Revising** • Review your first draft, making sure that you have included all of the important facts and that you have presented your information in an interesting way. Make the necessary changes.

Evaluating

Does your writing present a complete and detailed look at your subject?

Does it move smoothly and clearly from one idea to the next?

Will readers appreciate the way you have presented your subject?

298 Description of a Person

When describing a person, writers usually focus on one or two specific parts of the total person. They think in terms of physical features, personality traits, and/or mannerisms. In the following model, student writer Janae Sebranek focuses on her subject's physical features and mannerisms.

"Pretty good deal, hey kid?"

The description of the boy is built upon a brief encounter.

The ferry crew hauled the thick wet ropes on board as the giant boat motor roared and spun beneath the deck. As they worked, a small, blue-jeaned boy stood inside the safety gate, watching every movement of the crew members, all the time pulling his sweatshirt hood up and down over his head. When two of the men pushed through the gate toward the cab, the boy plunged his chubby hands into his pockets and strode alongside them.

"Do you do this every day?" he asked, breathing rapidly while trying to keep up. They looked down at the deep, dark eyes of the tiny Native American boy.

"Yeah," the blond one replied. "I get paid, too. Pretty good deal, hey kid?" He nudged his buddy and they exchanged glances. The dark one laughed.

The writer tries to enter the boy's mind.

"We'll see you around, kid," the blond said while patting the young boy on his head. They disappeared into the cabin and the boy stumbled just outside the door. He turned and faced the water for a moment, lost in thought. What was going through his mind at that moment? Maybe he was thinking about something more remote and adventurous, like stories told to him about his ancestors crossing these waters to the islands. Maybe he thought about the ferry crew traveling back and forth every day between the islands. Maybe he was thinking about working on the ferry when he grew up, hauling in ropes and talking to little boys. As he stood there, his hair was tousled about in the wind and his dark eyes shone.

Words like "snapped" and "weaving" help readers see the subject.

Then suddenly he snapped back into action by turning and weaving a path among the passengers, who were all lost in their own thoughts while staring out into the water. @

299 Eyewitness Account

In an eyewitness account, a writer shares the details of an event he or she has recently witnessed. In the following model, student writer Ron St. Germain describes a fire that destroyed a neighbor's house. Note how powerful verbs and sensory details effectively re-create the scene for the readers. ("One Hot Night" appeared in *Kaleidoscope,* [Amesbury Middle School], 1991.)

One Hot Night

It was three o'clock when my mother came screaming into the hall waking us up. She told us to grab the dog and to get out of the house for safety. As I ran down the stairs, the temperature rose; and as I opened the side door, I was hit with a blast of hot air and the sound of bottle rockets and exploding glass. I saw my neighbor's sleek red motorcycle pop and shrapnel shoot in all directions as the bright blaze engulfed the once shiny and beautiful Honda.

My family gathered in the front yard and watched with our neighbors as the house across the street went up in flames. No one spoke as the fire trucks came up the hill with lights flashing but no sirens on. The firefighters got the hoses attached together faster than lightning, but couldn't get any water pressure. The fire spread through the old house as the flames melted the black Toyota's brakes. It came rolling at our house with flames billowing from the windows, hood, and muffler. Luckily, it stopped as the rear wheel hit a fire hose.

Minutes later the water pressure from another hydrant was high and the flames started to die. More people gathered in horror as the smoke flew to the edge of the sky and made my eyes tear. It was getting hard to breathe and I was getting burned by the ashes as they flew by. As morning approached, two other cars parked in the charred garage slowly melted. The sun rose but no one could see it because of the thick screen of ash and smoke.

My friends and I sat and watched on the lawn as the last of the flames were extinguished. The firefighters then grabbed axes and charged into the house, cutting holes in the roof. They threw out mattresses and clothing that were smoldering. They found a guitar case and brought it down. A minute later, down came the black-filmed keys to the case. We all gathered around as the firefighter unlocked it. There lay a metallic blue guitar with only some water damage. They also found a jar of jewelry cleaner with a diamond ring at the bottom of the pink liquid.

I got mad at the people who walked or drove slowly by and stared at the house as the owners sat crying, wearing their only possessions.

After a few hours of sleep my friends and I took up a collection for our three homeless neighbors. That night, I wrapped the two hundred twenty-three dollars to present to them the next day. @

The event is recalled in great detail from the opening idea to the closing sentence.

Notice that the writing is organized around the writer's actions before, during, and after the fire.

(300) Summary Report

Summary reports in magazines and newspapers provide an invaluable service to the reading public by providing scaled-down versions of detailed stories. In the following professional model, writer Steven Findlay provides a summary report related to a conference on AIDS research. (This report first appeared in the August 3, 1992, issue of *U.S. News & World Report*. Copyright 1992, *U.S. News & World Report*. It is reprinted with permission.)

The Shock of the New

The main point of this summary report—a new virus causing an AIDS-like illness—is clearly identified in the first paragraph.

Again and again, AIDS has provided powerful lessons in how little is really known about the mysterious world of viruses. Scientists and AIDS activists—including protesters angry about the high cost of treatment and the low investment in research—who convened last week in Amsterdam for the Eighth International Conference on AIDS were reminded anew of their frustrating ignorance. The meeting was rocked by reports of a possible new virus causing an AIDS-like illness. Health officials rushed to gather information, put the finding in context and calm public fears. There was no threat to the blood supply, they promised. And even if it was a new virus, it did not seem to be spreading rapidly or to be easily transmitted through sex. But by week's end, as some scientists sounded notes of urgency, the World Health Organization was planning a special meeting within the next month to probe the finding. "This problem will be very, very actively pursued," pledged Anthony Fauci, head of AIDS research at the U.S. National Institutes of Health.

The facts and details related to this new finding are outlined in the second paragraph.

What is known now is this: Between 24 and 30 people in the United States and Europe have developed the AIDS-like illness, but their blood has shown no signs of HIV, the virus that causes AIDS. Three separate teams of U.S. researchers say they have detected the presence of a new virus in the blood of a dozen of these people. The teams were not claiming to have found the same virus, though, and other leading AIDS experts and virologists cautioned that complete testing has not been done to rule out known viruses. One explanation is that the researchers are seeing an AIDS-like disease caused by a rare virus—perhaps a mutated animal virus—that has been around for a long time but never previously identified. Another is that some or all of the people with the AIDS-like illness are infected with a mutant form of HIV not detectable with current blood tests. Indeed, other researchers reported at the meeting that a new and unusual strain of HIV appears to be spreading rapidly among heterosexuals in Thailand. For all the gains in understanding AIDS, scientists admitted at the conference's closing sessions that a vaccine, much less a cure, remains an elusive goal. @

301 Firsthand Experience

In a report of a firsthand experience, a writer shares the details related to an event she or he has recently participated in. In this model, student writer Jon Eric Jacobson recalls a recent time when he was trapped in a walk-in freezer. Note how clearly he recalls this brief experience, detail by detail.

Frozen Bagel, Anyone?

The opening lines establish the time and the place of the experience.

I put myself in a very dangerous situation, all for a bag of bagels. Now, that statement may seem a little exaggerated, but it is true.

It happened on a Sunday afternoon at about 12:30 p.m. with one-half hour of brunch left at Grand Island Resort. I noticed that the bagel tray was empty, so I got the keys to the freezer and headed for the basement. I had never been in the walk-in freezer before, but I thought nothing of it. I opened the door, dropped the keys in my pocket, walked in, and shut the door tightly behind me. Then I began hunting for bagels. A few seconds later I decided there were none to be found, so I returned to the door and gave the latch a gentle push—nothing. A shiver crept up my spine. I quickly joked it away.

Action words like "pushed," "kicked," and "rammed" help create suspense.

I gave a slightly harder push—no response. I then decided to use a little force. I pushed, kicked, and rammed—nothing! I pushed and pulled the safety latch with all my might. The door was so solid, just like the other three walls in the freezer.

By that time, I was becoming exhausted by all the futile lunges against the unyielding door, but I still continued to pound. I finally stuck my hands in my pockets to warm them up. I pulled the key ring out. These were the keys to open the freezer from the outside. I wondered if someone had another set, or was I truly sealed in. I banged even harder.

The writer lets his thoughts ("I wondered if . . .") and his actions ("I still continued to pound . . .") tell his story for him.

I knew I would get out; someone had to open the door. But when? All around me, I noticed frozen shrimp, crab legs, and lobsters. I realized that I couldn't even eat. My hands were now turning numb. I took the insulation cover off the light. The only source of heat was a 60-watt light bulb. It offered little warmth. I continued to pound.

Suddenly, I heard a noise outside. I pounded louder than ever. The door swung open. A blast of hot air enveloped me. All around me there was light, and there was the smiling face of Kirk Krempel. I went up to the kitchen and told my story to the cooks. They sat me in front of the ovens. Jokingly, one of them said, "By the way, the safety latch on that door is broken."

The clock said 1:05 and brunch was over. We didn't even need the bagels. ℮

302 Interview Report

A report of this type is based on the facts and details a writer has gathered while interviewing someone. The following report by student writer Dumary Lewis follows the basic question/answer format, reflecting the interview as it happened. (This report, adapted from a WBAI radio interview, first appeared in *New Youth Connections: The Magazine Written By and For New York Youth,* September/October 1991. It is reprinted with permission.)

The opening paragraphs provide the necessary background information.

Matty Rich—Straight to Success

Matty Rich, 19 (otherwise known as Matthew Richardson), grew up in the run-down, drug-infested projects of Red Hook, Brooklyn, and has seen it all. At 17, he decided to make a movie based on his experiences—from the violent death of his best friend Lamont to the senseless killing of his aunt and uncle.

Straight Out of Brooklyn was written, produced, and directed by Matty Rich (he also acts in it) and came out last spring in theaters all over the country. The movie deals with disturbing issues of racial and social discrimination. I talked to Matty about how he did it.

What motivated you to do the movie? How did you get started?

When I was 17—when everyone had been destroyed, when my best friend died in prison, when my aunt and uncle died on my birthday, when I saw my brother beaten by 10 guys with bats on the Fourth of July—at the age of 17, I told my mother that I wanted to do this movie, not about my life but the whole situation in the Black community.

The writer of this interview relies exclusively on the remarks of the subject to develop this report.

She gave me some film books, took some from the library, got some here, some there; I had about fifty-some books. Don't misquote me or nothin' like that. I'm not no bookworm. I used to hang out with the boys, but at night they didn't know I was reading.

My mom told me she had a credit card and a little money in the bank. My sister had a credit card too. She told me to go through this three week writing program at New York University. It was just a side thing of the college. It wasn't a college class or anything like that. I went there to put all my work into script form, to learn the whole structure of doing [movie] script writing.

Black People Made This Movie

After that, I cast the actors. I put an ad in *Backstage* and got 2,000 Black actors to come out and rehearse and audition for me. I cast my actors and for six months I had them in my room, my bathroom, my living room, my kitchen. We worked heavily.

After six months these guys said, "Wait a minute. We love you and all, but we are tired of eating chicken wings and collard greens in your house. We got to shoot this movie."

[I still didn't have enough money.] So, I went on WLIB radio. I didn't go there saying I need $5, give me $10, come on $15, come on community, come on I need some money. No. I said I was selling $5,000 shares. I said this movie would be a mirror where people could say: "That's my son." "That's my father." "That's my mother." "That's my daughter."

Two days later, I got $77,000. Not from lawyers, not from doctors, but from [regular] Black folk. People who gave me their life savings. Black people made this movie. This wasn't made by Paramount. This wasn't made by Columbia. This was made by the community.

How did your relationship with your mother contribute to your success?

Being the youngest and the closest to my mother, I figured if I fell between the cracks—like all my friends who died, who were depressed, who were angry, who got destroyed, who were sick on the street looking at a 40-ounce [bottle] of Old English, talking to themselves because they're so angry and are denied the opportunity for an education—if I fell between the cracks, I would hurt my mother more than I would hurt myself. So I decided to look at the long goal and not the short goal. The short goal was getting money quick quick quick and dying quick quick quick . . .

What is it that you do that is so different from other teens? What's the secret of your success?

I look like you, I talk like you, I got a stupid car with a booming system just like you, but the difference is I use my brain.

The number one killer in the Black community is your emotion. You talk about my mother—bang. You step on my foot—bang. That's emotion. You [have to] take that negative energy and turn it into something positive . . .

You can't let those negative forces come into your game and your dream. Society says, "Oh, Matty, you got to go to school for four years. Oh, you got to go to school for another four years."

A lot of young people growing up in the inner city may not have the money to go to college. Maybe now they can look at me and say, "You see Matty Rich—he took that negative anger and put it towards something positive. He didn't go to school."

I'm not telling people not to go to school, but I did it my way and you can do it your way. You might have to go to school to do whatever you like to do. It may take you four years, even eight. But that doesn't mean you have to wait. You can start right now. @

Brackets added by the writer give the reader information that the speaker assumed was understood.

The subject's remarks about success bring the report to an effective closing.

304 Character Profile

In a character profile a writer tries to discover as much as possible about another person. The results of this research are presented in a report discussing a special part of the subject's life. The following character profile reflects Karina Sang's effort to learn about her grandfather and her Chinese heritage. Her father's stories are Ms. Sang's primary source of information. (This article first appeared in *New Youth Connections: The Magazine Written By and For New York Youth,* November 1991.)

 INSIDE

In the process of developing a profile, a writer may employ a number of different gathering techniques, including reading, interviewing, observing, corresponding, and reflecting.

Grandfather's Journey From China to Santo Domingo

I have often wondered about my Chinese grandfather. He died before I was born, and my family has never really said much about him. Someday I would like to go to China and find what is left of my Chinese family. But for now, I have to be satisfied with the few stories my father has told me.

The writer highlights important events in her grandfather's life.

My grandfather left China for Santo Domingo in 1916 with two relatives. His father had been a wealthy merchant, and two of his sons decided to go in search of new horizons. They settled in the Dominican town of Bonao and opened a restaurant called "Sang Lee Long." Even though it had a Chinese name, the restaurant served Dominican food and was very popular.

My grandfather's name was Luis Sang. He never told anyone in our family his Chinese name. He had gone through an arranged marriage in China and left his wife and two sons behind when he moved to the Dominican Republic. In his new country he married again and had 10 children: 7 daughters and 3 sons. My father was one of them.

Grandfather's restaurant got most of its business from travelers. But when the old highway that had united the south of the Dominican Republic with the capital closed in late 1959, Bonao was isolated. As a result, my grandfather's restaurant went bankrupt. He stayed home after that and never opened another restaurant.

305

Details
include the
grandfather's
interests and
personality.

He Played Dominoes and Drank Rum

Over the years, my grandfather had acquired Dominican customs. He liked to hunt, play dominoes and poker, and drink Dominican rum. He was accepted by the Dominican society.

In 1961, he read newspapers that protested the actions of the country's dictator, Rafael Trujillo. He believed so much in the opposition that he wanted to participate in politics, but he couldn't because he wasn't a citizen.

He suffered a heart attack in 1968. His doctor told him he didn't have much time left, three months at the most. He lived another year doing everything the doctor had forbidden. He ate pork, drank, played poker, and smoked. "He died January 26, 1969," says my father in a proud voice, "but the fruits he left behind are still here and I'm part of them."

The writer's
need to know
about her
heritage is
contrasted with
her father's
disinterest.

My father does not feel a connection to his Chinese heritage. It may be because he was never taught anything about that culture. Unlike my father, I do feel a connection to my Chinese heritage. I keep asking questions about my grandfather's life and wait for the day I can visit Canton, China, to learn more about him. ℮

306 Extended Experience

An extended-experience paper focuses on related events (taking place over a period of days, weeks, or months) from the writer's recent past. Going to the state basketball tournament is a possible subject, as is a week's worth of algebra class or a vacation or trip. The writing should give an overview of the entire time and then describe a few key moments. In the following model, Elizabeth Weisenburger shares, through journal entries, some of her experiences as an exchange student living with a host family in Ecuador.

Ecuador

The writer's opening remarks set the scene for the journal entries that follow.

On a cold August morning, the stars blanketed the night sky over the pueblo town on the outskirts of Quito, Ecuador. I stood on the street corner, shaking underneath my wool sweater, waiting for my A.F.S. host father to bring around the car so that we could leave for my trip home to my family in Santa Barbara, California. I was not alone, for already many of the townsfolk were out on the streets, selling fruits or heading out for the day's work. As they passed by, they observed me with a strange curiosity, noticing my fair skin and blonde hair. Men whistled and called in my direction. I stood unmoved; I was used to being different. Time was passing slowly, and the sun was starting to rise over the sloping mountains. Growing weary, I grabbed my bag and searched for my journal that I had kept over my two-month stay, hoping to appear busy and pass the time more quickly.

.........**June 27, 1991.** The mountains encompassing the modest A.F.S. campsite tower up towards the sky as clouds creep up their green slopes. The sight of it is soothing because at the moment butterflies are fluttering about my stomach as if they were multiplying by the hundreds! I am leaving for Quito tomorrow to meet my host family and I am anxious, facing the unpredictable and the unknown. My head is spinning with questions! How will I greet them? Will they like me?

The entries highlight aspects of everyday life with the writer's host family.

.........**June 28, 1991.** I'm sitting here in my host parents' room watching television. My father has fallen asleep, after watching the soccer game; my mother soon followed. I just arrived and am already unsure of why I am here. I feel so alone. I haven't met my brother or sister yet.

.........**July 4, 1991.** I made French toast this morning for my family. It was an American treat and they praised its taste. Afterward we all went to my parents' room, hopped under the bed covers, and watched an old rerun of *Happy Days* dubbed in Spanish. I have never felt such a strength of family unity. I feel as though I have lived with them for ages, the way they treat me as their own.

.........**July 12, 1991.** Language charades have become a great asset. The language barrier is a tough wall to climb, and I get easily frustrated, saying foolish things I did not mean to say.

307

I really think it has humbled me, though; I am so grateful when I can finally say what I want and be able to joke.

.........**July 17, 1991.** I just arrived home from a large family dinner. I sat silent most of the time at the table, unable to express what I wanted to say in Spanish, able only to make small talk. It is frustrating at times, and I feel so excluded when I am not able to be included in all the conversations. I feel like I'm on the outside of their world looking in.

.........**July 25, 1991.** Walking to the market and home is an adventure in itself. Today as I walked through a very nice residential area, I passed by an Indian woman and her children. They had enormous baskets tied onto their backs. The woman couldn't even look up. I had not noticed that the young boy was carrying something. It was a baby, slung onto his back. None of them had shoes on. I will never forget the boy's eyes as he looked up to me. He was carrying such a heavy burden at such a young age! What kind of life does he have in front of him? I can't do anything for him.

> The writer's perceptive thoughts and comments bring the journal entries to life.

.........**August 1, 1991.** I am beginning to feel as if I belong here more and more each day. Today I bargained at Ipiales, an open market. I got down to the prices my host mother would have paid, which are very low. So, I'm feeling very accomplished in that a gringo like me could get such a ganga, or bargain, from the natives.

.........**August 5, 1991.** Last night I was invited to a party. The counselors at A.F.S. had said something about "Latin time." It was last night that I discovered what "Latin time" was. People here are very kicked back with time. My Ecuadorian friends told me they would pick me up at 8:00 p.m.; they really meant around "9:30-ish." I was very mad when they came but soon realized that it is completely cultural. The party made up for it. It is amazing how I had the best time of my life with only a little music and dancing. There are so many deep-rooted feelings that go into dancing; I got swept away. Dancing suddenly became a way of socializing and meeting people.

.........**August 16, 1991.** Today I embarked on a trip into a world unknown to me. It was 8:00 a.m. when the old steam train pulled out of the station. The train was overflowing with people who had their livestock and produce, so we had to board on the tin roof of the train. Four young boys sat next to me. They were dirty but in good humor, and they stared at my belongings with great interest. As we pulled out of the mountains, we stopped at small stations along the way. The open flatlands were scattered with rickety huts on stilts. Young children ran around naked. I promise no longer to complain about my mother's meatloaf after thinking about what these kids have for dinner. . . .

> The writing comes full circle, connecting with the opening remarks.

The blank journal that I arrived with in Ecuador had been filled. I closed it and put it in my backpack as my host father drove up and we left for the airport. In many respects, however, that journal will never be closed. ℮

308 Historical Profile

A historical profile presents a detailed report on a person, place, or event from the past. As student writer John Nichols researched epitaphs in his local cemetery, he made many interesting discoveries about the pioneers who settled in his hometown.

And When I Die . . .

At the outset, the writer explains his personal interest in cemeteries.

I've always had a feeling for cemeteries. It's hard to explain any further than that, except to say history never seems quite as real as it does when I walk between rows of old gravestones.

I know there's a cemetery in Concord, Massachusetts, where Ralph Waldo Emerson, Louisa May Alcott, and Henry David Thoreau are buried within a few feet of each other. The story behind that burying ground is pretty obvious, and no doubt quite romantic. When I first began looking into the prospects of doing an article on the Union Grove Cemetery, I was afraid I wouldn't find anything too interesting. My fears were unfounded.

I soon found that within a mile of my home was the grave of a Revolutionary War veteran and one of a man who may very well have been Abraham Lincoln's bodyguard on the night he was shot. I also found the graves of less famous but equally interesting people, many of whose gravestones are as beautiful as the artwork you might find in a museum.

Then, in the cemetery's older section, I found the graves of the Cadwell family. The Cadwells were early Union Grove area settlers. If you were to view their graves on Memorial Day (when the American Legion places flags by the graves of veterans), you'd quickly get the impression that the Cadwells believed strongly in supporting America's military efforts. Phineas Cadwell, the oldest member of the family to emigrate from New York to Wisconsin in 1850, fought in the Revolutionary War.

A real sense of local history emerges with the details about the Cadwell family.

Phineas, who the family Bible claimed was "enticed" into the army at age 18, served under Washington and rose to the rank of corporal. By the time he reached Wisconsin, he was totally blind and seldom ventured from the family home. Still, he kept an interest in the affairs of his nation, especially the slavery situation. The inscription on his tombstone reads: "Oh my country, how sure I loved thee. In my youth I fought for, sought, and saw thy prosperity. Free all thy sons. May thy Freedom be universal and perpetual. I leave thee."

309

The writer expands the coverage of his report by including stories about some of the other settlers in the community.

Phineas' son, Ebenezer, served in the War of 1812. He was a captain in the New York Militia for four months in 1814, during the closing days of the war. Like so many veterans of the War of 1812, he received no real compensation for his service until the late 1840's when he was awarded 40 acres of land near Union Grove (in what now is the town of Paris). Ebenezer brought his father, mother, wife, and children to live on that land.

Two other Cadwells, also buried in the cemetery, carried on the family tradition of service to their country. Both Erastmus and Walter fought in the Civil War. Erastmus was Union Grove's first blacksmith. He entered the Union Army in 1864 after meeting Abraham Lincoln in Racine. It seemed Erastmus was so impressed with Lincoln, he immediately joined Company A of the 22nd Wisconsin Infantry. Erastmus died in Tennessee near the end of the war, and his body was brought back to Wisconsin for burial.

Thirty-three other Civil War veterans are buried in the cemetery. Fordyce Lincoln, veteran of the Blackhawk War, and Earl McCormick, who served in the Spanish-American War, were also laid to rest there, as was Harley Osborne who fought in World War II as a member of the Canadian Army.

More than just soldiers' graves make up the Union Grove Cemetery, though. It provides a strong tie with Union Grove's past. While John Dunnam, the village's first settler, was not buried there, many other pioneers were. Among them was Gideon Morey, the town's first store owner and postmaster. The graves of the village's presidents and local officials, its shop owners, blacksmiths, and printers are there—all with unique and wonderful names—from Miles Hulett, the only Racine County sheriff from Union Grove, to Menzo Bixby, the first Union Grove boy to die on foreign shores.

A thought about cemeteries as "living" history concludes this article.

It is in its cemetery that much of Union Grove remains alive. Beneath its grounds lies our past, and on its stones, our history, as telling as any book or article. ℮

Related Forms

To sharpen your reporting skills, experiment with some of the ideas for subject writing listed below. (In a very general sense, they are arranged according to level of difficulty.)

Secondhand Story

Share a memorable story told to you by someone you know very well—a grandparent, neighbor, etc. This story should come from the past, from a different time and place.

Description of a Place

Describe a specific place or location that has left a strong impression on you. Help your readers see, hear, and feel this place.

Compiled Report from Multiple Interviews

Compile a report based on multiple interviews related to a current subject (smoking, dating, etc.). Obviously, the key to this type of writing is gathering information from a number of different people.

Observation Report

Record all of the sights, sounds, and smells related to a specific location that you visit. Then share these sensory impressions.

Compiled Report from Multiple Sources

Consult various sources (magazines, newspapers, pamphlets, etc.) to gather information about a timely subject. Then compile the results of your investigation in an informational summary report.

Case Study

Share the story of one individual whose experiences speak for the experiences of a larger group of people (disaster victims, recent immigrants, groupies, etc.). The effectiveness of a case study depends upon your ability to conduct interviews, make firsthand observations, and gather timely information from print materials.

Venture Report

Provide an in-depth report on a specific occupation or business. Base the information in your report on interviews, job-site visits, and other types of direct contact.

Personal Research Report

Present the detailed story of your investigation into a subject of personal interest (a new form of technology, a current fad, etc.). This type of report is usually divided into four parts: *what I already knew about my subject, what I wanted to find out, what I discovered,* and *what I learned from the experience.*

"Fact and fiction, fiction and fact. Shapeshifting into one another . . ."

—Gail Godwin

Creative Writing: Inventing and Imagining

311   Let's say you write a story about an old tree house in your backyard (this is fact). Let's also say that you include two main characters in your story—two friends who built the tree house (this, too, may be true). The main part of your story tells how these two friends meet many years later and talk about their work (this is the fiction part).

This example illustrates how creative writing often works. "Fact and fiction, fiction and fact," blend together to form imaginative pieces of writing. A memory may develop into a poem, an image (like a tree house) may be the driving force behind a story, a recent experience may be portrayed in a play.

Remember: Creative writing is the process of inventing, the process of making something new and different, something made-up. But it also has solid roots in the real-world experiences and memories of the writer—fact and fiction, blending together.

what's ahead?

Read the quick guide on the next page and the example poems, stories, and play scripts in this section to learn more about creative writing. (As you will see, many of the examples clearly spring from the writers' experiences and memories.) Also included are basic writing guidelines and tips for all three types of creative writing.

312 Creative Writing
Quick Guide

The following characteristics are fundamental to all creative writing.

Starting Point: Creative writing begins when you ask yourself, What can I create (or make) out of a certain feeling, image, or memory? (The anger you feel about some of the guys in your neighborhood may lead to a rap poem. The image of an old tree house may lead to a story about the builders.)

Special Note: Most creative writers would say that they don't actively search for subjects. Instead, subjects usually find them.

Purpose: Creative writing fulfills a writer's need to imagine, invent, and explore. It is a process that satisfies the creative spirit. (On another level, it is meant to delight, entertain, and move the readers.)

Form: To our way of thinking, any form of writing that comes from your imagination, that contains some element of fiction, is creative. A brief imaginary dialogue is a form of creative writing, as is a one-act play, an invented journal entry, or a science fiction story.

Audience: You may or may not have an audience in mind when you develop a creative piece. A rap poem may be intended for your peers; a short story, for young readers. Each situation will be different. However, if the finished product is good, it will speak to a wide range of readers.

Voice and Point of View: How the writing sounds (voice) and how the ideas are communicated (point of view) will differ from poem to poem and from story to story. (See "Point of view" in the index.)

Special Note: Creative writing often takes on a life of its own (as the poem or story moves ahead, the writer simply follows along).

The Big Picture

Creative writing requires a higher level of thinking than many types of writing. It challenges writers to reshape what they know into something new and inventive.

Writing Reminiscences ·········· *Here's what I remember . . .*

Subject Writing ················· *Here's what I learned about . . .*

Creative Writing ················· *Here's what I imagine . . .*

313 **Guidelines for Poetry Writing**

Creating "Imaginary Gardens"

Discussion: When you write poetry, you try to get at the emotional heart or core of a memory, belief, feeling, image, or dream. Since poetry is so compact, special attention must be given to every word and phrase. As you will see in the models in this section, each poem has its own special look and tone. Use the guidelines that follow and the models to help you develop your own poems. (Also refer to "Poetry, Terms" in the index for additional help.)

Searching and Selecting

1. **Searching** • Write freely and rapidly in 5- to 10-minute bursts to see what thoughts and feelings come to mind. Also review your journal entries for ideas. Be on the lookout for interesting sights and sounds in your community, as well as for intriguing concepts and events in your reading.

   Remember: All you are looking for is an initial thought burst—a memory, a feeling, or an idea that will get you started on your poem.

Generating the Text

2. **Collecting** • List words and phrases that come to mind when you think about a possible subject. (Push yourself!) As your list grows, look for words or phrases that stand out. They will help you focus your thinking about your subject. Continue listing until you feel a poem emerging.

3. **Forming** • The way your poem looks is really up to you. Some poems are written in basic list form. Others are written according to specific guidelines (sonnets, ballads, etc.). Still others take on a certain shape (a circle, a tumbling of words). Study the poems in this section and in other books for ideas.

Writing and Revising

4. **Writing** • As you develop your poem, remember the importance of word choice. Experiment with special comparisons (metaphors, personification, etc.) and special sounds (alliteration, repetition, etc.). Also experiment with the arrangement of ideas in your poem.

5. **Revising** • Keep working on your poem until every word, phrase, and line says exactly what you want it to say.

Evaluating

Do all of the pieces work together to form a unified whole or to express a creative idea?

Has proper attention been given to specific word choice, figurative language, and form?

314 Memory Poem

In this memory poem, writer Lisa Prusinski investigates her own feelings toward a childhood friend named Steven. (This poem originally appeared in the December/January 1992 issue of *Merlyn's Pen: The National Magazine of Student Writing.* It is reprinted by permission of *Merlyn's Pen.*)

The poem has a very personal tone, as if written directly to Steven.

To Steven, My Childhood Friend

In June we went crayfishing;
You broke my pail.
You made me red-faced and angry
Cheating in Monopoly,
Scribbling in my coloring book.
I tried hard to be your friend,
But you wrecked my Lego house in one blow.

For your birthday, a mud puddle day in July,
We gave you a T-shirt that read
"Joe Cool"
Next to a picture of Snoopy;
You lived up to it well
Standing on a swing like a mighty warrior.
Never were you content with peace—

The writer includes a number of visual details, making it easy to see Steven.

Blocking the sidewalk with your Bigwheel
Creating havoc.
I wished and wished that you would go away,
And late one afternoon
I heard the rumor goin' round the block
That your dad was transferred
To Indiana
I rejoiced:
No more broken Barbie Dolls or fixed games of tag.

For the remaining part of that dusty August
The neighborhood was quiet and still;
We were restless and antsy,

Using a detail from the poem's beginning, the writer comes full circle for a strong ending.

Only hushed Monopoly games
And calm-weathered days in Lego-land.
No more art contests or anticipated Bigwheel warfare.
No one knocking on our doors
With invitations
To crayfish anymore. ℮

315 Found Poetry

A found poem is created by working with existing words and phrases on signs and bumper stickers, in titles and headlines, and so on. Common street signs are the source of this model by teacher and writer Ken Taylor. The choice of signs and the positions of the words on the page say something about the pace and quality of modern life as seen by the author.

The poem's title is a play on words.

The arrangement of words provides visual clues to the poem's intent.

Note that the found items have been repeated, run together, and broken apart.

Life Signs

GO! GO!   STOP!

ENTER DO NOT ENTER EXIT WAIT!

WAIT WAIT WAIT WAIT WAIT WAIT WAIT WAIT

WALK   WALK DO NOT RUN

WRONG WAY   ONE WAY   NO THRU PASSAGE   NO

WAY?

NO NO NO NO NO

STOPPINGSTANDINGPARKINGSMOKINGLOITERING

EXIT

ENTRANCE?   NOT AN ENTRANCE

SLIPPERY

WHEN

WET PAINT

SILENCE. ℮

316 ## Statement Through Poetry

Poems, like essays, can express strongly felt statements or beliefs. The words and images in this type of poem must vividly convey the importance of the message. In "Tell Him Why," Lisa Frederick presents a forceful message that builds rhythmically in rap-lyric style. (The poem originally appeared in *New Youth Connections: The Magazine Written By and For New York Youth,* May 1992. It is reprinted with permission.)

Tell Him Why

Excuse me, do I know you? Do you know me?
Yes, I do know you. You're the brother hanging
   on the corner with nothing to do.

Now you have nerve telling me about myself
When you have empty pockets on the right and emptier
   pockets on the left

Just because I ignore your hisses, ain't no need for disses
I'll treat you like a mister if you treat me like a missus

I'm telling you this 'cause I'm sick and tired
There's a difference between being heckled
   and being admired

You know what I'm talking about, you do it every day
You want the attention so be attentive to what you say

It's lewd, it's crude, it's downright rude

But in your head you're thinking, "What the heck"
And when a sista walks by you give her no respect

I'm a young female and I'm Black too
And in this day and age, that's two strikes against you.

So don't give me no stress because you fail to impress
If my own people give me nothing, others will give
   me still less

Give us what we deserve: a lot of respect, a lot of love
'Cause you know I'm right when I say you need us
When you entered this world, it was a woman you saw first
Behind every good man stands a better woman
So give us what we ask, ain't no big task

The opening lines of this poem immediately establish the female speaker's demand for respect for herself and her gender.

The use of internal and end rhyme helps create the poem's rhythm, or beat.

317

And if you fall off the track we'll be there to pick up
   the slack
With us you won't lack, 'cause sista's got your back

But I can't help you if you won't help yourself, so get those
   want ads off the shelf

Don't get me wrong, honey, it's not all about the money
Whoever said life was a joke won't find this funny:

Think you look cute with a beeper and a Malcolm X hat
But I don't think Malcolm would speak to a sista like that

He would know that we're dignified, full of pride,
   classified, bona fide and refined

He would've also stated that we're educated, complicated,
   understated, underrated, and underestimated

Unashamed, unclaimed, untamed, unchanged,
   understanding, undemanding . . . but still disrespected

We're used, bruised and left confused

So . . . my brown bag drinking, big mouth braggin, 1,000
   gold chain wearing, imaginary B.M.W. driving, Jafarian
   belt hoopin, bead wearing, Rastafarian talking, wannabe
   down with culture brother
(you know it's true, at least one applies to you)

When you see us walking by and you say "hi"
Don't get mad 'cause we don't reply

It's just something in our culture that we miss
I know Isis and Nefertiti weren't spoken to like this

Oh, you don't see our crowns but we did come down from a
   nation of queens and kings
Just think of us as royalty in jeans

A lot of love you can expect
If you just give your sista her respect ❧

The use of repetition ("understated, underrated . . .") and the poet's direct manner of addressing her male counterparts create a forceful expression.

Related Forms

Listed below are three traditional forms of poetry. Work with one or more of these forms to gain a more complete appreciation of the poetry-writing process.

Ballad

Traditionally, ballads have been written about great adventures, triumphs, or tragedies. Modern ballads may address more contemporary themes like social injustice and greed. Traditional ballads are written in quatrains (four-line verses). The first and third lines usually have four accented beats per line. The second and fourth lines usually have three accented beats per line. The second and fourth lines must rhyme.

> ***Ballad of Scull Rock*** (first stanza)
> We miners long ago did find
> the skull rock on the lake.
> The silver lay in open veins,
> all shining for the take.

Blank Verse

Blank verse is unrhymed poetry with a regular rhythm. The lines in blank verse are 10 syllables in length. Every other syllable, beginning with the second syllable, is accented.

> ***Birches*** (first three lines)
> When I see birches bend to left and right
> Across the lines of straighter darker trees,
> I like to think some boy's been swinging them.

Haiku

Haiku is a form of Japanese poetry that has three lines; the first line has five syllables, the second has seven syllables, and the third has five syllables. The subject of haiku has traditionally been nature.

> Behind me the moon
> Brushes shadows of pine trees
> Lightly on the floor.

319 Guidelines for Writing Fiction

Searching for a Story

Discussion: Create a piece of fiction using a memory, experience, current event, image, or feeling as your starting point. Build your writing around interesting characters, around description and dialogue, and around conflict and suspense. Use the guidelines that follow and the models in this section to help you with your writing.

Searching and Selecting

1. **Searching** • Think of faces, places, problems, sounds, smells, or dreams from the past and present. **Remember:** You're looking for seeds or elements for a story—maybe a setting or problem to build a story around, or an interesting personality to start with. Let's say you spent a lot of time by a river when you were young. A river could be the setting for your story. And let's also say that both good and bad things happened there. Those happenings could spark ideas for your story.

2. **Reviewing** • Review your journal for entries exploring some of your experiences. Or try free writing or listing to gather ideas.

Generating the Text

3. **Focusing** • Begin organizing your thoughts for a story. In most stories there are *people* in a *place* doing some *activity* and a *conflict*, or *problem*, occurs. You should be able to identify at least two of the italicized elements before you begin your first draft.

4. **Planning** • Keep things simple. Start with a few characters (perhaps only one or two), a basic setting, and one problem to deal with. Then see what you can make of it.

Writing and Revising

5. **Writing** • Write your first draft freely, using your planning and organizing notes as a general guide. Don't expect everything to fall into place immediately. Stories usually come together piece by piece.

6. **Revising** • Carefully review your first draft for the basic flow and development of the story line. (Things shouldn't happen too quickly or predictably.) Also have at least one classmate review your work. Revise and refine accordingly.

Evaluating

Does the finished piece exhibit the qualities of a well-made story—character development, conflict, and suspense?

Has proper attention been given to description and dialogue?

320 Fictionalized Journal Entry

You can put an imaginative twist on journal writing by creating entries as if they were written by a made-up character, or by someone you have read about or observed. The two fictionalized journal entries provided here come from "Up on Fong Mountain" by Norma Fox Mazer. These entries explore the main character's thoughts, feelings, and actions. ("Up on Fong Mountain," from *Dear Bill, Remember Me? and Other Stories* by Norma Fox Mazer. Copyright © 1976 by Norma Fox Mazer. Used by permission of the Dell Books, a division of Bantam Doubleday Dell Publishing Group, Inc.)

A brief introduction explains why Jessie writes in a journal.

In addition to what she says about herself, Jessie's responses to other people reveal something about her own personality.

Up on Fong Mountain

TO: All Students Taking English 10
MEMO FROM: Carol Durmacher
DATE: February 3
"That favorite subject, Myself."—James Boswell

Wednesday, March 26

Mom thinks she and I are alike. She's always saying it. (She thinks Dad and Anita are alike, she says they are both very good-looking. True. While she and I are both chunky and sandy-haired.) But Mom doesn't say boo to Dad, she's always very sweet to him. (Actually she's sort of sweet to everybody.) I'm not like her in that way at all. I'm not sweet. In that regard, I'm more like my father than Anita is. I became aware of this because of BD. I have been noticing that he likes things his own way. Most of the time he gets it. I have noticed, too, that I don't feel sweet about this at all!

March 29, Sat. afternoon

BD came over last night and said we were going bowling. I said why didn't we do something else, as we went bowling last week. He said he liked bowling and what else was there to do, anyway? I said we could go roller skating. BD laughed a lot. I said what's the problem with roller skating. I like roller skating. (Which I do.) BD said, "Jessie, why are you being so picky? Why are you being so hard to get along with?" I thought, Right! Why am I? And we went bowling. And then, later, I realized, just like that, he had talked me out of what I wanted to do and into what he wanted to do. @

321 Story Based on a Memory

A memory of a person or place can serve as an effective starting point for fiction writing. The memory of writer Chris Noble's summer visits to Maine is the driving force behind this story. The author notes that there is no similarity between the parents in the story and his own. Uncle Joe is also a creation of the writer's imagination.

Uncle Joe

At the end of the dock, his back tanning to a dark brown in the noonday sun, his feet dangling in the water, sat a small boy. He was perhaps twelve years old.

"Alex." A voice interrupted his reverie. The boy looked back over his shoulder. It was Uncle Joe. Uncle Joe was really no uncle at all; he was just the man who lived in the next cabin. Usually, he kept to himself, but he knew how Alex felt about fishing. "I thought you might want to go fishing," suggested Uncle Joe.

"I don't know," said Alex, the conflict showing in his face.

"Come on," urged Uncle Joe. "There's nothing wrong with fishing. Especially on a day like this." He craned his neck up and lifted his eyes to the blue sky. "It'd be a shame to pass up a beautiful day like today."

"Okay," Alex said. "But we can't be too long," he added with a manufactured air of responsibility. Secretly, he rejoiced. Uncle Joe had taught him to fish several summers ago, but his parents had discouraged any further excursions.

As the boy climbed into the boat, the man unloaded his gear into the bow and began to undo the ropes which held the vessel in place. Uncle Joe stepped deftly into the boat, teetered slightly, and sat down. In one smooth motion, he pushed off. Alex watched, his chin cupped in his hands, his elbows resting on his knees, as Uncle Joe started to row out toward the middle of the lake.

"My parents don't like you very much," Alex said.

"Parents are sometimes hard to figure out," Uncle Joe answered. "They're like fishermen," he said, looking off to the horizon. "Sometimes they just hold on too tight. Sooner or later, the line snaps—just like that."

Soon, they glided into a patch of reeds on the far side of the lake. Uncle Joe slowed the boat and took out his pole, freeing the hook. Alex followed suit and soon the two were casting at a regular pace, stopping only to clear weeds from their hooks.

Suddenly, Alex's pole jerked; the line pulled taut. Uncle Joe, who had been reeling in a cast, dropped his rod immediately. "Alex, let out some slack, but not too much. I think you've got one!" Alex obeyed. "Okay," said the old man,

---

The central conflict of the story comes into focus with the invitation to go fishing.

Uncle Joe uses a fishing simile to state the central theme of the story.

The detailed description of catching the fish demonstrates the bond between the boy and the old man.

excitement in his voice, "now reel 'er in." With effort, Alex began to draw the line in. Majestically, the fish jumped, twisting and turning, brilliant in the sun. For the man, and for the boy, too, it was a religious moment—the mass of muscle and desire soaring, defying gravity, in total abandon, and finally crashing back down into the deep from which it sprang. In that moment, Alex forgot everything but the beauty of that freedom, the joy and the exhilaration. And in that split second, his hand slipped from the reel.

Reality rushed back in. The fish began to pull the line out at a terrible speed. "Quick!" shouted Uncle Joe. "You're gonna lose him!" And just at the moment when he gave up the fish for lost, the old man reached calmly across and grabbed the line. The fine cord cut instantly into his calloused fingers and blood beaded on the fishing line. But the reel slowed, and Alex, though horrified, had the presence of mind to catch hold of it. It took another fifteen minutes to reel the length of cord in and net the fish—a three-pound bass.

The sun sank low as Uncle Joe rowed back. Alex's father was waiting on the dock when they returned, his hands on his hips, his face twisted somewhere between concern and rage. He said nothing as the boat coasted into a landing.

"Get out of the boat, Alex," his father ordered. Alex climbed out. "And throw that dirty thing back in the water. What would your mother say?"

"But, Dad. . . ."

"It's all right, Alex," said Uncle Joe. "Do as your father says."

"But it's dead. It won't do any good to let it go now."

"That all depends," said Uncle Joe, "on whose good you mean."

The story ends on an uncertain note, leaving the reader to wonder about the final outcome.

Alex let his bass drop into the water. The fish floated on the surface for a few moments, its mouth gaping. Then, slowly, it dipped, tilted, and sank beneath the darkening shroud of the endless waves. ℗

323 Patterned Fiction

Knowing something about the basic patterns of fiction will help you write effective stories. (See the next page for a list of four common patterns.) The following model presents a very concise interplay between a boy named Frank and his friends. Notice that this story follows the *choice* pattern, in which the main character must make an important decision near the end of the story.

Taking Heat

Frank stood by the tall, green electrical boxes pleading with the others. "Come on. It will be a riot!" Spruce branches, waving under a full moon, threw a mask of shadow over his face. He yanked at the padlock.

"Vinnie. Your old man got a crowbar, don't he? What say we jack this thing?"

Ernie, the littlest, looked terrified. "No, Frank," he said, holding up his hands.

"Ah, pip-squeak, what do you know? Get the bar, Vinnie."

Vinnie looked uncertain. "But it says, 'Danger: High Voltage.'"

"That's just to scare little twerps like Ernie."

Dave sided with Vinnie. "I don't know, Frank. I don't think we should."

"Come on, ya wing nuts. It's Halloween. We break the lock. We hit the switch to the girls' dorm. Everything goes black. We hit 'em with the eggs. And we beat it, while the college kids blame each other. Trick or treat, major league!"

"Frank," said Ernie, nearly moaning, "don't."

"Are you still here, you maggot?" Frank tucked Ernie's head under his arm and rapped on it with his knuckles.

Ernie wriggled loose and jumped back, red in the face. "Frank! You want to fry? My cousin tried that two years ago. He got burned to death. I went to his funeral. The kid who tried to save him died too. And a third kid was in critical condition!"

Frank hardly seemed to listen. "I'm not a moron like your cousin, Ernie. Come on, you guys. Say we do it? I'll take the heat."

"No, Frank," said Dave.

"No, Frank," said Vinnie.

They all began to walk away, following Ernie. Frank followed reluctantly, looking smaller in the bare moonlight. He called after them: "Well, what's your plan? What's a Halloween in your book? Bobbing for apples? You guys stink!" ℮

Note • "Taking Heat" could be part of a more involved story. What might have happened before and after this interplay?

Throughout the story, dialogue is used to establish the characters and create the drama.

Notice how Frank's friends help him make his decision.

Patterns of Fiction

The following patterns are not necessarily based on any hard-and-fast rules that must be followed from start to finish during the story-writing process. Think of them more as general approaches to story writing. After reviewing this information, you may think of many great ideas for stories.

324 The Quest (Return)

In a quest, the main character sets out in search of something and ultimately returns after various adventures, having achieved success or gained new wisdom. (A freshman sets out to make the basketball team and succeeds against significant odds.)

Sample Stories:
"A Worn Path" by Eudora Welty
"By the Waters of Babylon" by Stephen Vincent Benét
(Any of the heroic myths)

325 The Initiation

A main character (usually a younger person) is faced with a new situation that tests his or her abilities or beliefs. How the character deals with this situation determines which direction or course his or her life will take. (A young boy learns something about life by losing a horse that he worships.)

Sample Stories:
"The Bluest Eye" (Chapter One) by Toni Morrison
"The Red Pony" by John Steinbeck

326 The Union

In this pattern, a boy and girl grow fond of each other, but their parents or some other authority figure comes between them. The couple usually gets together in the end after overcoming various obstacles. (A teenaged girl and the young migrant worker she likes have to work around her parents to meet.)

Sample Stories:
"Hoods I Have Known" by Sondra Spatt
"Horsetrader's Daughter" by D. H. Lawrence

327 The Choice

The main character must make a choice or decision near the end of this type of story. Making this decision is the high point of the action. (An out-of-work laborer must decide if he should work for someone he hates—someone who hurt him in the past.)

Sample Stories:
"The Ones Who Walk Away From Omelas" by Ursula LeGuin
"Lather and Nothing Else" by Hernando Tellez
"Taking Heat" (included on the previous page)

328 Uncharted Fiction

In uncharted fiction, an object, image, interesting thought, or dream is used as a starting point for a story. A writer simply picks up on this idea to see what he or she can make of it one step at a time. This seems to have happened to Amy Honecker as she developed the following story. ("Angel Song" first appeared in *Espial IV: The Mental Omelette,* a Troy [Mich.] High School literary magazine. It is reprinted with permission.)

The story's main character is identified and the setting is established in the brief opening paragraphs.

Angel Song

The theater was empty, yet the curtain was drawn. The excitement that had existed only minutes before was now ebbing away, as if it had been turned off. Christian looked out and imagined all the fans, his fans, still there. But they were gone.

He walked carefully among the jungle of metal and cords that was the stage and stood behind his keyboards. *I can't believe it's over,* he thought. He ran his hands over the keys lovingly.

And then Christian began to play. The song came easily to him, he had been hearing it in his mind over and over since the tour had begun. It belonged to him alone; he shared it with no one. Just once he wanted to keep a song for himself.

But there still seemed to be something missing, something intangible that he couldn't discern about the harmony, something he longed to complete but knew he couldn't.

The sweet sound of his music became water flowing around him. The notes flowed into a cascade of harmony. He closed his eyes and felt the song carry him away . . .

"You were very good tonight."

The introduction of a second character—"You were very good tonight"—quickly turns the direction of the story.

The music ceased, and Christian fell back to earth. He opened his eyes to the harsh lights and reality of the stage. His heart ached to be away from it, away from this life.

He shaded his eyes with a hand to find the owner of the voice and was stunned by the result. "The band's at the party, backstage. . . ."

The softly accented voice interrupted. "And you are out here. How strange," the girl said, walking forward to join him behind the synthesizers.

She had been in the front row earlier. Her hair fell in soft waves of honey to frame a delicately chiseled face with large, almond-shaped eyes.

Chris noted immediately that this wasn't an ordinary groupie. She didn't hide behind the hair-sprayed style that he was so used to seeing. This girl had no need for any of that; she was vibrantly, naturally beautiful.

329

Readers learn about the mysterious Darelinia through her conversation with Christian.

This surreal, dreamlike story contains two interesting characters, a tightly knit and intriguing plot, and an effective closing scene.

Shaking himself out of the trance, he managed to repeat himself.

"There's a party backstage, you know."

The girl flashed him a smile. "I know. I just don't wish to be there," she replied, eyes dancing.

Definitely not an ordinary groupie, he thought, forcing his voice to work again. "Why not?"

She tilted her head slightly, and her hair fell to the side. "Because you are out here, and I would much rather listen to you play," she answered.

"Oh, really?" *Don't be caustic, Chris,* he reprimanded himself, and corrected his tone. "Why?"

Her eyes grew wide and luminous. "You have such great style, Christian."

"Look, it was just one show."

"Oh, I have been watching you for a while," she said. "You must not have noticed me before."

He couldn't believe that for a moment. One look at that face—*No way, I know I'd remember those eyes!*

Her smile widened at his troubled expression. "Do not worry. You do not remember me because I did not wish to be remembered."

Christian was silent for a moment, staring at long fingers that danced on black and white tiles. Artist's hands—

"Who are you?" he asked suddenly.

"Who am I?" she laughed. "Who are any of us? My name is Darelinia, but who I will be remains to be seen. You may call me 'Dare' if it pleases you, Christian Rilke."

"Chris," he corrected absently, now staring at her. "Why have you been watching me, Darelinia?"

"That is neither here nor there," she muttered, turning away from him.

It was as if night had fallen. Then the sun returned with her golden hair glowing like rays of light.

"Play for me," she whispered, pleading with her eyes.

How can I refuse? Christian put his fingers to the keys and began to play. Elation came with the song; the music surrounded him and lifted him up. His eyes shut out the light again.

Her voice entered the melody like sweet rain in the desert. She sang with words that were foreign, yet joined his song to become one harmony.

They floated above the world together, the world that loved him for his music and not for him. *I don't ever want to go back—*

And the world, as Christian Rilke knew it, disappeared.

Related Forms

If you'd like to experiment with various approaches to fiction, here are additional forms you can try:

Fictionalized Imitations

Imitate one of your favorite authors out of respect and admiration for her or his style. The purpose of such an exercise is to learn about or experiment with new writing techniques. The actual situation for your writing can be as basic or complex as you want to make it. However, make sure that your imitation forms a meaningful whole (a story, character sketch, dialogue, etc.).

Special Note: If your imitation is intentionally critical (in a comical or exaggerated way), it is called a parody.

Fiction from Fact

Write a story using a brief news article as your starting point. Look for human-interest stories that tell about minor thefts, accidents, embarrassing moments, winning streaks, etc. Develop your story by expanding upon (or changing) the basic facts stated in the article.

Genre Writing

Write a story based on your understanding of a particular genre or story type: science fantasy, science fiction, mystery, urban fiction, etc. (If you like to read science fiction, it would follow that you would also like to write stories of this type.) Basic features of the four common story types are listed below:

Science Fantasy: set in imaginary and unpredictable worlds, draws heavily on mythic or supernatural elements, the fantastic is commonplace, includes cartoon-like violence and little logic.

Science Fiction: set in the future, exists in the realm of scientific possibilities, logical, realistic within context of the story line

Mystery: focuses on who committed a crime (or how or why it was committed), revolves around main character as crime solver, all important clues worked into the story line

Urban Fiction: urban setting, characters in conflict with the environment, naturalistic in tone and outlook (man or woman vs. environment), starkly real

331 Guidelines for Script Writing

Act and Interact

Discussion: Write a script exploring a specific conflict in the life of one or two characters. Develop your script into a one-act play, including stage directions and actions. (Or, if that seems too involved, develop an interesting dialogue between two characters.) Refer to the guidelines below and the model scripts in this section for help with your writing.

Searching and Selecting

1. **Searching** • The best ideas for plays are often found in everyday situations. You and a family member may have an ongoing disagreement about your "future." Someone you know may be heading for big trouble. Keep your eyes and ears open for ideas.

2. **Creating** • If you can't find an idea, then invent one. (How about a girl trying out for the varsity football team, or an elderly gentleman who suddenly can't remember where he lives?) **Remember:** You are only looking for a starting point, a situation to build a script around.

Generating the Text

3. **Planning** • Identify who will be involved in the situation (the main characters) and how this situation complicates their lives (the problem). Then decide how your play will start (who will be doing what and where). Be open-minded and flexible at this point.

Writing and Revising

4. **Writing** • Introduce the situation and characters in the opening part of your script. Then let the rest of the play build naturally by listening to and imagining your characters as you write. (See 335 for additional tips.)

5. **Revising** • Read your first draft at least two times. During the first reading, pay close attention to the basic story line. (Are there any missing parts?) During the second reading, listen for the sound and flow of the dialogue. Revise and refine accordingly. (Add stage directions as needed.)

Evaluating

Does the play (or dialogue) focus on a specific problem? Does it build in suspense?

Do the characters have distinctive personalities? Is their conversation realistic?

Does the piece come to an effective conclusion?

332 Dialogue Writing

In this model, a dialogue (or conversation) develops between a younger brother, who is in the midst of an "educational crisis," and his older sister. The interchanges between the brother and sister provide insights into their personalities. (Note that this dialogue is written in script form.)

What Can I Say?

Liz: You are in deep trouble, Little Bro. So what are you going to tell Mom?

Billy: Mom? What about Dad?

Liz: Dad? He's easy. But, you know Mom.

Billy: Yeah, she'll make me feel awful. And . . .

Liz: But, how could you fail? I don't think Blodgett's failed two people in the last twenty years.

Billy: You sure are a big help.

Liz: Why don't you try to see if Blodgett will let you make up the work?

Billy: I already asked. He said no.

Liz: How much work do you owe?

Billy: Kind of all of it.

Liz: All of it! You didn't hand in anything the whole marking period?

Billy: I did all of the in-class work, but no important assignments.

Liz: You went the entire marking period and never handed in a single assignment. How could you do that?

Billy: I just sort of got behind, and thought I could catch up, and you know Blodgett never says anything.

Liz: What did you tell him when you went to see him?

Billy: I said that I owed some assignments and I wondered if he'd let me do some extra work to make them up. And he said, how did I think I could make up so much work right before grades were to come out.

Liz: And what did you say?

Billy: I said well maybe I could write a book report or something.

Liz: Oh, real good!

Billy: And he got a little mad. And then I said, that I, that I'd been having some real tough personal problems, a death in the family.

Liz: What? Who died?

Billy: Uh, Grandma.

Liz: Come on! And what did he say?

Billy: Well, he, you know, I mean, he said he wondered why he hadn't heard about this before . . .

Liz: And?

Billy: I don't think he bought it at all . . . and, what can I say?

Liz: Obviously not a whole lot. I don't believe you!

Billy: So, what am I going to tell Mom and Dad?

Liz: That, Little Bro, is one very interesting question. @

The opening lines establish a semi-humorous tone for the dialogue.

Note how Liz's comments reflect her amazement at her brother's situation.

As the dialogue continues, the brother's "story" becomes more unbelievable.

333 Play Writing

Student playwrights Nathan E. Slaughter and Jim Schweitzer worked together to write "When Time Dies," a one-act play. Provided below is the opening part of this play.

When Time Dies

Characters:
DOCTOR, a psychologist
SUSAN GRUNWALD, a college student
MICHAEL P. LIEGL, a college student

Setting: Scene opens in a small room with one door that is stage right. The room is rather bleak looking and has two chairs in the middle. One is cushioned, the other is not. There is a large observation mirror stage left. The door opens and three characters enter together, the doctor behind the other two. He is dressed in a white coat and wears small, round glasses. The other two are dressed plainly and in the same colors. The doctor leads them to the chairs.

> Details of the setting lead into the beginning of the play.

DOCTOR: Well, now. If you would have a seat in one of the chairs, we will begin the experiment.

MIKE: Could you please explain one more time what will take place? There's no chance of physical trauma, is there?

DOCTOR: *(chuckles)* No, it is not set up to affect you physically. This is strictly a psychological experiment. We are interested in the human responses to external stimuli. We are here to study your minds. Body study takes place in anatomy labs . . . and on the beach. I assure you that you are safe.

MIKE: Good. Good. I'm glad.

DOCTOR: I'm sure you are. Now, please, sit down. *(Mike offers Susan the cushioned chair and she accepts. They sit down.)* We will be right on the other side of the mirror here *(motioning to the audience).* Now, you, Susan, will be in here for five minutes. Every minute there will be a light letting you know that another minute has elapsed. At the end of the time period, I or one of my colleagues will reenter the room to let you know that your portion of the experiment has ended. Then, Michael, you will be left in here for another five minutes following Susan's exit. When your time has ended, I or a colleague will enter to notify you.

> The audience learns about the experiment along with the actors.

MIKE: All right.

SUSAN: Is there anything else we need to know?

334

DOCTOR: As a matter of fact, there is something I need. *(He points at their wrists.)* I need to take your watches to ensure the success of the experiment. *(They take off the watches and hand them to the doctor.)* Thank you. *(The doctor leaves. There is an ominous, echoing click as the door locks. Both people turn to look at it, then return to their original positions, nervously.)*

SUSAN: Well . . . this should be . . . uh . . . fun!

MIKE: Yeah, a real riot in L.A. A veritable scream.

SUSAN: *(uneasy)* Well, introductions are in order, I suppose.

MIKE: Yeah, sure. We're going to know each other for five minutes. Please, tell me your name!

SUSAN: *(sweetly ignoring his cynicism)* My name is Susan Grunwald.

MIKE: I'm Mike. Michael P. Liegl, to be exact.

SUSAN: What does the "P" stand for?

MIKE: I didn't ask your middle name.

SUSAN: It's Anne. Now, what does the "P" stand for?

MIKE: Protection. Privacy. Pretentious. Pick your poison.

SUSAN: Look, you could be just a little nicer.

MIKE: I'm nervous enough as it is. I'm here to complete a bet, all right? This is not my idea of fun . . . , Sue.

SUSAN: Fine. *(A few seconds pass.)* So, I understand that you are a college student also.

MIKE: How did you know that?

SUSAN: The experiment is on college-age test subjects.

MIKE: Oh, yeah.

SUSAN: So where do you go?

MIKE: I go to—*(A red light flashes.)* What was that? Did you see that?

SUSAN: I think it was the light telling us that one minute has passed. Wow, that was rather quick. *(sarcastically)* I suppose time flies when you're having fun.

MIKE: I guess so. *(sarcastically)* Well, then, I suppose we'd better have more fun, so the time will pass even faster. So, what do you want to do when you get out of college . . . ?

[As the play continues, Mike becomes increasingly nervous. Then, when Susan's part of the experiment is completed, Mike is confronted with different stimuli, which cause him to become totally paranoid. Near the end of the play, he passes out in exhaustion. At that point, the doctor enters the room, ignores Mike, and, as the lights go down, reads his clinical notes about the subject's behavior.] ❧

The opening dialogue between Mike and Susan establishes clear differences in their personalities.

There is no movement on stage in this part of the play; all attention is focused on the characters' words.

335 Playwriting Tips

Make sure to pay special attention to each of the following elements as you write your play scripts.

Dialogue: Conversation is at the core of playwriting. The characters' words move the action along. How they speak reveals something about their identity. (Clues to voice or delivery can be included in stage directions.)

Conflict: Make sure your play is built around a believable conflict, or problem, one that makes sense in the lives of the main characters. (The conflict should make life increasingly difficult for the main characters until the play reaches a breaking point, or climax.)

Stage Directions: Indicate the time and place of the action, entrances and exits, and so on through stage directions. They can also be used to indicate what the characters are doing on stage. (However, try not to complicate a play with too many stage directions.)

Form: Make sure to follow the accepted format for your play, beginning with the title and following with a list of characters and an explanation of the setting *before* the first words are spoken. (See the example play.)

336

Related Forms

If you enjoy writing scripts, here are two more forms to try:

Monologue

Have a character you create carry on a one-way conversation. The challenge of this type of writing is to have your character reveal something important about his or her personality during the conversation. Make sure that your monologue forms a complete whole, with a beginning, middle, and ending, so readers understand what is going on. (You often find monologues in longer pieces of writing—in plays, short stories, or novels. A monologue in a play is called a soliloquy.)

Ad Script

Create a television (or radio) ad script for a real or imagined product. To get started, determine what your product can do, how it can do it better than related products, and what kind of story would best sell this to your audience. Tell a very brief story, one that covers either 30 or 60 seconds. ***Remember:*** In advertising, it's important to capture your audience's attention immediately.

Note • There are special types of stage directions to consider for ad scripts: *Add Graphic, Add Music, Blend In, Cut To, Fade In, Fade Out, Insert, Quick Shot,* and so on.

"I think somehow, we learn who we really are and then live with that decision."

—Eleanor Roosevelt

Reflective Writing: Exploring and Speculating

337   To illustrate the word "alienation," student writer Mike Varveris shared a story about a classmate who had trouble fitting in. To examine the problem of teenage drinking, Jeff Koczwara focused on four main causes. To sort out her feelings about her boyfriend, Sue Chong presented opposing points of view (her own and her steady's) related to an important issue.

All three examples are forms of **reflective writing**, writing that examines or comments upon some part of the writer's experience. Think of this type of writing as a form of self-study in which the writer "reflects" upon different aspects of life (experiences, beliefs, current events, etc.) to better understand what they mean and why they might be important.

338 The Writer's Stance

The writer of a reflective essay says: I've written about a subject that I find important, interesting, or just plain fun. You might not agree with what I say about this subject, but that's okay. We are all entitled to our opinions. What matters to me is that you find my essay interesting, that it gets you thinking about my subject, and that it helps you understand me a little better.

what's ahead?   Read the quick guide on the next page and the writing examples in this section to learn more about reflective writing. You'll find a wide variety of essays included here, each one providing a little different slant on reflective writing. Then refer to the writing guidelines (340) to help you get started on your own essays.

(339) Reflective Writing

Quick Guide

All reflective writing—no matter if it examines a past experience, comments upon the present state of things, or explores the future—shares the following characteristics:

Starting Point: Reflective writing begins with a personal question, a personal need to examine some part of your experience. ("Why all this fuss about virtual reality?")

Purpose: The purpose is to examine, explain, or comment upon some part of life. (On another level, the purpose is to inform readers and to get them thinking.)

Form: What your writing looks like—its beginning, middle, and end—depends upon your thoughts about your subject. Your writing may simply reflect your thoughts about a subject as they naturally come to mind. Or your writing may be more tightly structured with a thesis statement, supporting paragraphs, and so on.

Audience: When writing reflectively, you are usually speaking to your classmates and peers. (They are the ones who can most directly relate to your experiences and comments.)

Voice: Speak openly and honestly in reflective writing. It should sincerely "reflect" your thoughts and feelings.

Point of View: In most cases you should use the first-person (I) point of view in reflective writing. (No surprise here. Reflective writing is based on *personal* exploration and discovery.)

The Big Picture

Reflective writing is really thinking on paper—the process of searching for meaning and value in experience.

Writing Reminiscences ·········· *Here's what I remember . . .*

Subject Writing ··············· *Here's what I learned about . . .*

Creative Writing ··············· *Here's what I imagine . . .*

Reflective Writing ············ *Here's what I think . . .*

340 Guidelines for Reflective Writing

From My Point of View

Discussion: When you write reflectively, you tap into (and clarify) your feelings, concerns, and beliefs about subjects of personal importance. In one case, you may explore the value of one of your experiences; in another case, you may examine or comment upon something that you have witnessed or read. Use the guidelines below and the models that follow to help you get started on your writing.

Searching and Selecting

1. **Reviewing** • Anything that is part of your life—questions, problems, experiences, or observations—is a potential writing idea. (Many of the ideas you write about in your journal can serve as starting points for reflective essays.)

2. **Searching** • Leave no scrap of paper unturned for ideas. Think of letters and notes to friends. Study issues of local and national importance in the newspaper. Consider books you have read as well as common or uncommon sights in your community.

Generating the Text

3. **Collecting** • Free-write about a potential subject, letting your ideas take you where they will. (Write for at least 10-15 minutes.)

4. **Assessing** • Carefully study your free writing. Look for parts that you like and want to explore further. Also look for any emerging idea that could serve as the focus for your essay. Continue gathering, focusing, and organizing your thoughts as needed.

Writing and Revising

5. **Writing** • Write your first draft freely, allowing your own personality to come through in your writing. Use any planning and organizing you have done as a general guide for your writing.

6. **Revising** • Read through your first draft two or three times. Ask a classmate to read it as well. Make sure to add information if your subject is not completely developed; also make sure that all of the parts are arranged in the best order.

Evaluating

Is the writing focused around one idea?

Does the writing sound honest and sincere?

Does the writing form an effective whole, moving smoothly and clearly from one point to the next?

Will readers appreciate the treatment of the subject?

341 Essay of Illustration

In an essay of illustration, you use an experience in your life (or in the life of someone you know) to prove a point or illustrate an idea. In the following model, Tristan Ching describes her actions during a very frightening experience to prove that she would, in the future, make a dependable college roommate.

On writing assessment tests, you are often asked to write about the importance of a personal experience, or to use a personal experience to prove a point.

In a Note to My Future College Roommate

The main point of the essay is identified in the first paragraph.

I get along with most people, but please don't tell me you have a harmless pet snake named Fangs. I hate spiders, lizards, and anything else that goes bump in the night. Now wait! Before you beg the housing office for a new roommate, let me also say that I can be counted on to protect you should the need arise.

The experience that illustrates the main point is developed in great detail.

I first stayed in the dorm as a fourteen-year-old summer ballet student. About halfway through the session, my roommate woke me very late one night. For a change, I woke up right away. Even without my glasses I could see her big eyes as she pointed to the door. There was a scratching sound outside. "Grab something," I whispered. She snatched a pair of scissors while I reached for a bottle of 409. If our visitor succeeded in entering, I planned on squirting some cleaner in his eyes. Suddenly I remembered . . . dial 2222 for the campus police. I crept to the phone while the intruder yelled and banged at the door. When the police arrived, they took him away, and we slept happily ever after.

The final comments reinforce the writer's position.

I don't have a black belt in karate, but I did manage to stay calm under pressure. (That's strange, considering I'm not that calm when I'm not under pressure.) Anyway . . . remember your bottle of 409, and we'll be just fine. ☺

342 Pet Peeve

A pet peeve presents a writer's humorous or sensible reaction to a common, everyday annoyance. In the following essay, student writer Kris Hirsig details the frustration involved in losing a button at the worst possible time.

Button, Button, Who's Got the Button?

Sharing details of time and place increases the urgency of a minor problem.

Darn it! There goes a button, and you're already fourteen minutes late for work. Why does a button hang in there month after month and then at the most inconvenient time let loose? And why is it that when the button falls to the floor, it always rolls under the dresser where it blends in perfectly with the carpet?

Each step in the repair process seems to create new difficulties.

After retrieving the button, the search begins for a needle and thread. As you might expect, the needle and thread are never where they should be, especially now that you're in a hurry. Finally, you locate the sewing tin and begin to pry it open. A stubbed fingernail or two later, you are ready to go. So, with a needle in one hand and the wrong-colored thread in the other, you begin to attempt the impossible—getting that tiny piece of thread through an even tinier hole in the needle. After several awkward attempts, you decide that the only way you're going to thread this needle is to use a larger needle.

You feel pretty smart when the thread passes through the new needle on the first try. Such a simple solution! You knot the thread, hold the button in place, and insert the needle into the back of the first hole. You begin to pull the needle through, but for some reason it stops. You pull again—harder. You pick up the shirt, turn it inside out, and examine the back of the button. You can't help but moan out loud. But then, how could you have known the larger needle was too thick to pass through the hole in the button? So much for simple solutions.

In the end, the narrator seizes upon a different approach to the problem.

Still, a solution is near . . . in this case, as near as the closet door. You open the door, grab the first shirt you see, quickly inspect the buttons for durability, and swing your arm through the sleeve. Who says you have to know how to sew on a button to survive in today's world? ✑

343 Essay of Explanation

In an essay of explanation, a writer explains his or her beliefs about an important subject. In this student model, Jeff Koczwara explores the causes of teenage drinking. You will notice that the essay is based on some strongly felt beliefs about this serious problem.

 INSIDE info

This type of writing is sometimes called an essay of enumeration because a writer may identify, or enumerate, the number of points to be covered. (*There are four main reasons why . . .*)

The focus of this essay is identified in the opening paragraph.

A Shot: The All-Too-Common Cure

Drinking is a serious problem affecting millions of people in America. There are, of course, many individual business people, housewives, and workers who come home and relax with a drink or two. For some, these occasional drinks pose no threat; but for others, they lead to serious drinking problems, and eventually to alcoholism, a deadly disease that ruins lives and causes undue suffering. No group seems to be more negatively influenced by drinking than teenagers. They often use and abuse alcohol for all of the wrong reasons.

First, there's the universal understanding that teenagers rebel against anything. Some teens who drink do it to get back at their families, or possibly their friends. It is a way for them to say "in your face" to a particular group or individual. It seems as though many teens will start doing the first thing they are told not to do; and if they are asked to do something constructive, well . . . slim chance, unless they will directly benefit. I saw a girl I know at McDonald's, and she was drunk. When I asked her why she was drinking, because it was so unlike her, she said, "This will really tick my mom off bad."

Each paragraph addresses a specific cause of teenage drinking.

Contrary to the first cause, in which teens rebel, the second has to do with going along with the crowd. Drinking for teens may be their ticket to acceptance. They need to feel part of the group, and if the only way to achieve that is to have a drink, then so be it. Peer pressure can be an incredibly powerful factor in teen drinking. I personally know someone who drinks so he will be accepted by the "in crowd." Members of this group do not talk to him much during the week, except to discuss plans for the weekend, and generally shun him if he isn't drinking. This person wants to belong, and he feels drinking is the only way to do that.

Another reason for teen drinking is that teens like the feeling, the "buzzing," and they say they have more fun when they drink. While drinking, otherwise-shy people can say and do things that they would not normally do. I was with a friend at a party, and it was fairly packed. My friend is quite shy, but he wanted to meet a girl that I had been talking to. I refused to introduce the two, and said he ought to do all the talking for himself. A few other friends joined us, but we failed to persuade him to go talk to the girl. By chance, some whiskey fell into our hands, and my friend started to become more outgoing after several shots. He did go talk to her, and did ask her out. I knew what her reply would be before he said a word, even though he was laughing as he wobbled back across the room. Drinking is a force that, for some people, breaks down personality barriers allowing them to do things they would ordinarily consider unthinkable.

The main reason for teen drinking, however, and the one most likely to lead to serious problems, is escapism. Alcohol can provide an escape from family, friends, personal relationships, anything upsetting. A guy I work with is a good case in point. He gets in a fight with his parents, and he heads straight for the bottle. He comes home from work or school tired and frustrated, and he goes to the bottle. Recently things had not been too stable with his girlfriend, who was complaining about his drinking. He made a date with another girl, but he didn't really want to break up with his girlfriend. His mind was in a total state of confusion, and he was tired of thinking about it, so out came the bottle. It would not be so bad if his was an isolated case, but too many teens would rather watch the ceiling spin than think out their problems.

Drinking is an all-too-common factor or influence in the lives of many teenagers. The first three reasons discussed here would seldom lead to a serious drinking problem. Teens generally grow out of their rebellious stage, and they usually feel less influenced by others as time passes. The "buzzing" feeling gets old, too, and loses its glamour for most individuals. The one reason that remains a constant threat is drinking to escape from problems. The first drink that a person takes to escape reality is the drink that may eventually shut the door on that person's life. A life seen through the bottom of a bottle is a life headed for trouble. ℮

In most cases the writer supports his main ideas with references to young drinkers that he personally knows.

In the closing, the writer reviews the main points in his essay and leaves readers with a disturbing image of teenage drinking.

345 ## Essay of Opposing Ideas

An essay of opposing ideas presents the value or strength of two points of view about a particular subject. If you're speaking from personal experience, the opposing ideas will presents themselves naturally as you tell your story. That is just what student writer Sue Chong did in the following example. (This essay "works" because the writer speaks honestly about a subject that is very important to her.)

He Said I Was Too American

My boyfriend Kevin and I went out for a year and, during that time, we fought until we got sick of it. We fought about the stupid things all couples fight about, but the main thing that came between us was something that other couples probably don't have to deal with. We constantly argued about whether I was too Americanized.

Kevin and I both came to the United States from Korea five years ago. Although we had this in common, we had different points of view on everything. He would ask me why I couldn't be like other Korean girls. If I were a "real" Korean girl, I would listen to him when he told me to do something, depend on him for most things, and think his way instead of my way. When I didn't agree with him, we would have another fight. To me, he was too Korean and too narrow-minded. He refused to accept any culture except his own, and he always thought his way was the only way.

I eat Korean food, speak Korean, have respect for my parents as Koreans have, and I celebrate Korean holidays and traditional days. I even joined the Korean Club in school, so that I can observe my customs with Korean friends.

During the past five years, however, I have come to love certain customs from other cultures. For example, I see the way my Hispanic friends greet people with affection. They kiss and hug when they say "hello," and I love this. (In Korea, people are much more formal; they just shake hands and bow to each other out of respect.) So I started kissing my friends on the cheek, too.

Kevin didn't like this, and he told me so. He even asked me to stop it. I didn't want to, so I did it anyway but not as much. Later on, he told me not to kiss and hug other people. I asked him why, and he told me that he didn't like it and that other Koreans didn't act the way I did. He couldn't accept it.

Korean men like to tell their wives and girlfriends what to do. He would always tell me how to dress and how to act

The opening introduces the players in the conflict and the source of their opposing ideas.

The author provides specific examples of conflicts arising out of being Korean and trying to become more American.

in front of others. He wanted me to stay next to him all the time. I would complain that I was not his little toy and that he couldn't just order me around.

When I would go against his wishes, Kevin would say, "Why are you so Americanized?" I didn't know how to respond to his question. He said I must be ashamed of my country and my culture to act the way I did. I was shocked, and it hurt me deeply. I was not ashamed of my country or culture. I am proud of being a Korean. I just want to accept other cultures, too.

I can't deny that I sometimes act like an American, trying to be more independent and outgoing than other Korean girls. But I still act like a Korean, too. I want to go with the flow, and that doesn't mean that I don't like my own culture. I am trying to balance two cultures. Through my boyfriend, I got a chance to think about who I really am. I realized that I am a Korean and an American, too. @

The closing provides a thoughtful analysis of the conflict.

347 Essay of Experience

In an essay of experience, a writer reflects upon an experience or set of circumstances that has provided a new perspective on life. Writer Robert Fulghum discusses his experiences with "sink gunk" in this entertaining essay. (From *It Was On Fire When I Lay Down On It* by Robert Fulghum. Copyright © 1988, 1989 by Robert Fulghum. Reprinted by permission of Villard Books, a division of Random House, Inc.)

 INSIDE info

An essay of experience often follows the *before and after* pattern of organization: "Before I used to think . . . , but now I . . ."

"Dinner Dandruff"

The writer's friendly tone, humor, and graphic descriptions naturally draw readers into the essay.

AFTER THE DISHES ARE WASHED and the sink rinsed out, there remains in the strainer at the bottom of the sink what I will call, momentarily, some "stuff." A rational, intelligent, objective person would say that this is simply a mixture of food particles too big to go down the drain, composed of bits of protein, carbohydrates, fat, and fiber. Dinner dandruff.

Furthermore, the person might add that not only was the material first sterilized by the high heat of cooking, but further sanitized by going through the detergent and hot water of the dishpan, and rinsed. No problem.

But any teenager who has been dragooned into washing dishes knows this explanation is a lie. That stuff in the bottom of the strainer is toxic waste—deadly poison—a danger to health. In other words, about as icky as icky gets.

By focusing on sink gunk, the writer sets the reader up for the weighty lesson he provides in the end.

One of the very few reasons I had any respect for my mother when I was thirteen was because she would reach into the sink with her bare hands—BARE HANDS—and pick up that lethal gunk and drop it into the garbage. To top that, I saw her reach into the wet garbage bag and fish around in there looking for a lost teaspoon BAREHANDED—a kind of mad courage. She found the spoon in a clump of coffee grounds mixed with scrambled egg remains and the end of the vegetable soup. I almost passed out when she handed it to me to rinse off. No teenager who wanted to live would have touched that without being armed with gloves, a face mask, and stainless-steel tongs. . . .

I lobbied long and hard for a disposal and an automatic dishwasher, knowing full well that they had been invented so that nobody would ever have to touch the gunk again.

Never mind what any parent or objective adult might tell me, I knew that the stuff in the sink drainer was lethal and septic. It would give you leprosy, or something worse. If you should ever accidentally touch it, you must never touch any other part of your body with your fingers until you had scalded and

The writer creates an imaginary graduation speech to announce that being an adult is not what teenagers imagine.

soaped and rinsed your hands. Even worse, I knew that the stuff could congeal and mush up and mutate into some living thing that would crawl out of the sink during the night and get loose in the house.

Why not just use rubber gloves, you ask? Oh, come on. Rubber gloves are for sissies. Besides, my mother used her bare hands, remember. My father never came closer than three feet to the sink in his life. My mother said he was lazy. But I knew that he knew what I knew about the gunk. . . .

My father, however, would take a plunger to the toilet when it was stopped up with even worse stuff. I wouldn't even go in the room when he did it. I didn't want to know.

But now. Now, I am a grown-up. And have been for some time. And I imagine making a speech to a high school graduating class. First, I would ask them, How many of you would like to be an adult, an independent, on-your-own citizen? All would raise their hands with some enthusiasm. And then I would give them this list of things that grown-ups do:

-clean the sink strainer
-plunge out the toilet
-wipe runny noses
-clean up the floor when the baby throws strained spinach
-clean ovens and grease traps and roasting pans
-empty the kitty box and scrape up the dog doo
-carry out the garbage
-pump out the bilges
-bury dead pets when they get run over in the street

I'd tell the graduates that when they can do these things, they will be adults. Some of the students might not want to go on at this point. But they may as well face the truth.

It can get even worse than the list suggests. My wife is a doctor, and I won't tell you what she tells me she has to do sometimes. I wish I didn't know. I feel ill at ease sometimes being around someone who does those things. And also proud.

A more serious tone establishes the real worth and meaning of cleaning up the gunk.

A willingness to do your share of cleaning up the mess is a test. And taking out the garbage of this life is a condition of membership in community.

When you are a kid, you feel that if they really loved you, they wouldn't ever ask you to take out the garbage. When you join the ranks of the grown-ups, you take out the garbage because you love them. And by "them" I mean not only your own family, but the family of humankind.

The old cliche holds firm and true.

Being an adult is dirty work.

But someone has to do it. @

349 Personal Commentary

In a personal commentary, a writer makes a brief reflective statement about life. The subject of a commentary may relate to popular culture (like dating or dining out), or it may relate to something more fundamental (like health and safety). Nightly newscasts often include commentaries. In this example, Irma Johnson comments on magazines aimed at teenage girls.

Like most good commentaries, this one stems from the personal experiences of the commentator.

The writer makes the point that magazines *create* as much as *reflect* the thinking of their readers.

The writer cites many examples to illustrate her point.

Wanna Life? Get a Boyfriend!

I used to be an avid reader of teen magazines. From when I was 10 until I was 13, I devoured *Seventeen* and *YM* every month. I was just becoming a teenager and I wanted to know how I was supposed to act and what I was supposed to do. The magazines had everything I was interested in (or thought I was interested in)—information on clothes, make-up, and boys.

The magazines told me that to be normal and happy I had to look good and have a boyfriend. But I wasn't as pretty or as thin as the models. I wasn't dating yet either. Every time I read another article on how to deal with your boyfriend, I would feel as if there were something wrong with me. The feeling that I didn't quite measure up stayed with me for years.

Eventually, I matured and realized that I was perfectly normal and that the magazines were giving me a wrong message. Looking back, I'm glad that I didn't start dating then. I realize now that if I was so easily influenced by some dumb magazines, I probably wasn't ready.

BOYS, BOYS, BOYS

Teen magazines haven't changed since then. The August issue of *YM* had an article on how to get guys to commit; an article on guys' biggest dating disasters; and two girls' opinions on whether they would date a guy that their best friend had a crush on.

In the August issue of *Seventeen* there was a fashion spread on sweaters featuring a girl who is distressed because her boyfriend is going away to college. In the August *Sassy,* I found an article called "Chronic Long Distance Boyfriend Distress." What I didn't find was even one article on girls who don't have boyfriends and don't want them.

As if that weren't enough, two of these magazines devoted entire issues to guys. *Seventeen*'s July "Boy Crazed" issue had more than 10 articles and photo spreads about guys. There was a quiz to help you rate your boyfriend, a photo spread that followed two boy-crazy girls on their hunt for Mr. Right, and an article about the winners of *Seventeen*'s "Best Boyfriend Contest" featuring quotes from their lucky girlfriends and pictures of the happy couples.

YM's April "Major Guy Issue" had about the same number of articles and photo spreads on the subject, including "How to Survive the First 60 Days of a Relationship" and a quiz to help you figure out whether your relationship is healthy or harmful.

JUST FOR FUN

By printing so many articles on how to relate to guys, these magazines are giving teenage girls the impression that dating should be a major part of their lives. If it's not, there must be something wrong with them.

Where are the articles on resisting peer pressure to date or how to have a successful friendship? Not in *Seventeen* or *YM!*

Instead, these magazines give us articles like "100 Guys Talk—What 100 Guys Had to Say about Love, Sex, Dating and You" (April *YM*); "Real Back to School Clothes . . . Rated by Real Guys" (August *YM*); "Why Guys Love Long Hair" (July *Seventeen*); and monthly columns like "Guy Talk" in *Seventeen* and "What He Said" in *Sassy*. In short, guys' opinions on everything—especially clothes and dating. Articles like these tell us that what guys want is very important and that we should keep their likes and dislikes in mind when we decide what clothes to buy, how to wear our hair, and how to act. Girls' opinions, on the other hand, are limited to letters and reader polls. Why don't they have girls rate outfits?

. . . A magazine can inflict an enormous amount of pressure on teenage girls—especially younger teens who don't really know what they want. Younger girls view teen magazines as handbooks on how to be a teenager. I know I did. Teen magazines can influence how girls act as much as they influence how girls should look. They shouldn't, but they do. @

Note all of the specific facts and details presented in this commentary.

The writer's main point about teen magazines is clearly expressed in the closing.

351 Essay of Reflection

In an essay of reflection, a writer focuses on an important aspect of his or her past, carefully examining the subject in order to form new understanding about its significance. In this example, Joe Fletcher reflects upon a special teacher he had when he was in middle school. Note that the writer directs his comments specifically to this teacher.

The opening paragraph establishes the focus of the writing.

The writer recalls in detail, and with great respect, Mr. Schyvinck's special style of teaching.

Dear Mr. Schyvinck,

Throughout life, people are always influenced in some way by others. This influence is what causes individuals to grow mentally. It has been no different for me. I have met a wide variety of people in my life and have learned from each of them. The one person that sticks out in my mind as having had the most influence on me, however, is you.

One reason why I took such a strong liking to you is that my parents had recently gotten a divorce, and I was coming out of a turbulent sixth-grade year. I needed something to fill the emptiness I was feeling. You were there for me. You had a way of making me feel good about myself, who I was and what I did. The little talks that you had with us really touched on some things that I needed to hear. I remember one day you told us that we should not be overly concerned when people ridicule us. You said that the important thing is that we like who we are. You restored some confidence in me that I had thought I had lost for good.

One of your better qualities was your ability to connect a story with a meaningful lesson in life. You told us about your son who was trying out for some major league baseball team. During the tryouts, he went out of his way for a fly ball and ended up crashing into the fence. I think he hurt himself, but because of the extra effort he put forth, he made the team. You had many stories like this that inspired us to do our best.

You worked with all of us to make us better students, never leaving anyone out. You would make sure that everyone answered a question or added something to class each day. You would go around the room and ask each student a question or how he or she felt about something. You showed that you really did care if we learned. You would always stress doing more than just an average job, that we would not get very far if we were not willing to put forth that extra effort.

Throughout the year you remained a great teacher, always fair. You pushed us to do our homework and do it better. You could not stand students being lazy (which I was before I had you). If kids in the class would not do anything, you would make them work. You would ask the students questions and have them diagram sentences as a class until you were sure

There is a directness and clarity of expression in this letter that can only come from careful writing and rewriting.

they knew what they were doing. Remember Paul? One day while we were diagramming sentences, you noticed him staring out the window. You made Paul diagram the next sentence on the chalkboard, incorporating him into the class. You worked with him and in a way made it fun so that he would want to work. This impressed me.

At the end of the year, we were all anxious to see what our grades were. You gave us these index cards that had our grades on them. I looked at mine, and then I turned the card over and read the words, "Don't Just Get By!" You told us to bring the cards back senior year when we graduate and you would give us a dollar.

Before I had you as a teacher, I was just an average student. Then I started applying what you were teaching us to all of my classes. I started trying harder to do the best that I could, and my grades improved significantly. Ever since our year together, I have been a 4.0 student or close to it.

Your approach affected not only my grades, but my whole outlook on life. You told us that we live life only once so we should try to live it to the fullest. Before I had you, I was a lazy, chubby kid, content to spend my free time, even in the summer, just staying inside and watching TV. You told us that if we did not like the way our lives were going that we should change them. I did not like the way mine was going, so I changed it. The summer after I had you I became more active. I stayed outside a lot more and went to my friends' houses more often. I began riding my bike often, and I slimmed down and gained muscle (you probably would have made a great exercise instructor).

A natural method of development— before, during, and after having Mr. Schyvinck as a teacher— provides the necessary structure for the writing.

Ever since our seventh-grade year, I have looked at that time as a turning point in my life. I credit most of those changes to you and your indispensable advice. Without your constant encouragement, I am sure that I would still be just getting by. Many years from now, I will still look back on my childhood and reflect on the timeless lessons that you were generous enough to share with me.

I'm looking forward to graduating next year and moving on to college, but I am especially anxious to meet with you and cash in on that card that I have been hanging on to for the last four years. Along with this letter, I will finally get the chance to thank you in person for giving me the desire to do the best I can.

Best wishes,
Joe Fletcher

Related Forms

As you can see in this list, there are many ways to reflect upon experiences, ideas, and issues. Make sure to experiment with many of these forms in your own essay writing.

Dialogue of Ideas

Discuss two different points of view in dialogue form. All you need to include is the basic give-and-take of a conversation. First one person says something about the subject; then the other person responds. Back and forth you go until the conversation comes to a natural stopping point. (This form is really a simplified version of an essay of opposing ideas.)

Editorial

An editorial is a brief persuasive essay expressing an opinion about a timely and important topic. Editorials usually call for a specific course of action. (An editorial writer might argue that the school student council does not represent the entire student body after a controversial council action.) It's important to come quickly to your point, speak with authority, and present a clear, forceful case. A 200-word editorial is appropriate for high-school newspapers.

Satiric Essay

Use exaggeration, distortion, and irony to comment on a subject (a particular behavior or point of view) that you disapprove of. (You could, for example, greatly exaggerate and distort the value of study halls to show what you really think about them.) A satirist attempts to argue indirectly rather than through direct commentary.

Essay of Speculation

Study a current trend, cultural attitude, or present-day technology, and write about the effect it might have in the future. Your speculations must take into account as many variables as possible—including past patterns and experiences, current research, and logical outcomes.

Position Paper

Present your position on an issue of local, national, or global importance. A position paper should offer reasons for your position, provide alternative points of view, and, in closing, reaffirm your main point. A position paper requires extensive research and reflection. It is very carefully planned and may require documentation. (See "Citing Sources" in the index for help.)

"Nothing in life is to be feared. It is only to be understood."

—Madame Curie

Academic Writing: Informing and Analyzing

354 ***Define the universe and give three examples.*** This assignment almost looks and sounds real, doesn't it? But define the universe? I don't think so. This message was, in fact, scrawled on a wall somewhere by a clever student, or former student, poking fun at school-related writing. It is graffiti.

Of course, your **academic writing** is very serious business, assigned to help you collect and organize your thoughts about different subjects you are studying. In a science class you may be asked to explain how a complex process works. In a history class you may be asked to analyze the causes and effects of an important event, and in an English class you may be asked to define an abstract term. Writing is the most effective way to prove to yourself and to your teachers that you really understand a subject, that you have made it part of your own thinking.

355 The Ultimate End

The best academic writing sounds like the writer knows what he or she is talking about. (It speaks with authority.) It flows logically from one point to the next. (It speaks coherently.) It carefully follows the standard conventions of grammar, usage, and punctuation. (It speaks clearly.) It is the end product of a lot of careful planning, writing, and revising.

what's ahead? Read the quick guide on the next page to learn more about academic writing. On the pages that follow, you will find guidelines and examples for many important forms of academic writing, including essays of explanation, comparison, cause and effect, definition, and argumentation. Whenever you are asked to write about important concepts in any of your classes, turn to this section for help.

356 Academic Writing
Quick Guide

All forms of academic writing share the following characteristics:

Starting Point: Academic writing begins when you are assigned to gather, organize, and present your thoughts about a course-related subject.

Purpose: The general purpose of academic writing is to present information that displays a clear understanding of a subject. The specific purpose will vary from assignment to assignment. It may be to inform, explain, compare, identify causes and effects, define, propose solutions, or argue for or against.

Form: Think in terms of the traditional essay form—*thesis statement, supporting paragraphs,* and *closing remarks*—when developing academic writing. In other words, work deductively: state your main idea (thesis) early and then follow with examples and details that support it. This approach makes complicated ideas easier to understand.

Audience: Academic writing is intended for your teachers and classmates. (They are the individuals most interested in your ideas and learning.)

Voice: A semiformal voice is used in most academic writing. To use this voice, carefully choose your words for clarity and avoid slang terms and popular expressions.

Point of View: Use third-person point of view (he, she, they) in academic essays, unless the writing clearly focuses on your personal experiences.

The Big Picture

Academic writing is based on analysis, the process of breaking ideas down to increase your understanding of them. Careful study is to academic writing what imagination is to creative writing and intuition is to reflective writing.

Creative Writing ···················· *Here's what I imagine . . .*

Reflective Writing ············· *Here's what I think . . .*

Academic Writing ··············· *Here's what I understand . . .*

357 **Writing the Essay to Explain a Process**

"The first thing you do . . ."

Discussion: In this type of essay, you explain how a process works or how to make or do something. Your goal is to speak clearly, in a helpful voice, so that readers can easily follow the explanation or directions. Provided below are basic guidelines to help you develop your writing. Also note the example essay on the following page.

Searching and Selecting

1. Selecting • You may choose to explain an everyday procedure (how to program a VCR). Or you may be asked to explain an important process related to the work in one of your classes (how the HIV virus affects the immune system).

2. Reviewing • Review your class notes or texts for ideas. If you are searching for an everyday procedure, think of the jobs, hobbies, and talents you have. Brainstorm for ideas with your classmates.

Generating the Text

3. Recording • List related facts and details about your subject as they come to mind, or write an instant version of the finished product to see how much you already know about your subject—and how much you need to find out.

4. Collecting • Collect additional information and details accordingly.

5. Organizing • If necessary, organize the information you have collected before you write your first draft. Also think about the main feeling or impression you want to express about your subject.

Writing and Revising

6. Writing • Write your first draft freely, working in details according to your planning—or according to the steps as you know them.

7. Revising • As you review your first draft, make sure you have included all of the necessary information and that it is in the right order. Also have at least one of your classmates check your work. Revise and refine accordingly.

Evaluating

Does the explanation form a meaningful whole? Does each step lead the reader clearly and logically to the next?

Are main points supported by specific details and examples?

Will readers appreciate the treatment of this subject?

358 Essay to Explain a Process

Christopher Fait's essay explains how the healing process works after someone experiences a minor scrape or cut. As you will see, this is not an easy process to explain since many things seem to happen at the same time.

Only Skin Deep

The opening line identifies the subject of the explanation.

Whenever you experience a minor scrape or cut, the body's healing process is immediately called into action. In a simple wound, the first and second layers of skin are severed along with tiny blood vessels called capillaries. As these vessels bleed into the wound, platelets work with fibrinogens to form a clot. This blood clot, with its fiber network, begins to join the edges of the wound together. In less than 24 hours, a scab forms as the clot dries out.

Transitions like "While this is happening" and "In addition" guide the reader through this process.

While this is happening, phagocytes, cells that eat waste and foreign matter, enter the wound from surrounding blood vessels. In addition, cells from the first layer of skin begin to divide and multiply, forming a bridge over the wound. Within three days, in a shallow or clean cut, the bridge of new skin (which is forming under the scab) is complete. The new skin is protected by the phagocytes, which keep the area free from infection-causing materials.

If the wound is somewhat wide, special cells called fibroblasts help build new fibers, or scar tissue, to bridge the gap between the wound's edges. It may take up to 10 days for the scar tissue to be formed, completing the healing process.

The concluding remarks add to the reader's understanding of the process.

In a healthy body, a simple wound heals in a fairly short period of time, from three to 10 days. The healing process is similar to normal skin replacement. (Cells from deeper in the skin are constantly moving up to replace old cells as they naturally wear out.) Things simply happen faster when there is a wound. There is minimum scarring and little discomfort during the healing of most minor cuts and scrapes. @

359 # Writing the Essay to Compare

A Balancing Act

Discussion: Compare two subjects (people, books, ideas, events, experiments, products, etc.) in such a way that both you and your readers better understand the similarities and/or differences between them. Use the guidelines below and the example that follows to help you develop your writing.

Searching and Selecting

1. **Selecting** • The subjects for your writing will depend on the unit you are studying or the class in which these guidelines are being used. Keep in mind that the subjects must be related in some *important* way and must be of some interest to you and your readers.

2. **Reviewing** • If no subjects come readily to mind, review your class notes or your text for ideas. Or try writing freely about your course work, noting potential subjects—people, ideas, or events—as they come to mind.

Generating the Text

3. **Collecting** • Gather ideas and details related to your subjects and enter them onto a Venn diagram. (See "Venn diagram" in the index.)

4. **Assessing** • Review your collecting to determine how much you already know about your subjects and how much you need to find out. Continue collecting if necessary.

5. **Focusing** • State a possible focus for your work; then organize or plan your writing accordingly. (You might do a point-by-point comparison of the subjects, or address each subject separately.)

Writing and Revising

6. **Writing** • Write your first draft, working in details and ideas according to your planning and organizing.

7. **Revising** • As you review your first draft, make sure you have made all of the main points of comparison between the two subjects. Also make sure that you have arranged this information in the best possible order. Revise accordingly.

Evaluating

Is the writing organized so readers can understand the similarities and differences between the two subjects?

Are main points supported by specific details and examples?

Does the writing form a meaningful whole, moving smoothly from the opening paragraph to the closing thoughts?

Will readers appreciate the treatment of the two subjects?

360 Essay to Compare

The following essay by Joseph Lucarelli compares the main characters in two great American novels, *The Adventures of Huckleberry Finn* and *The Red Badge of Courage*. The writer focuses his attention on the important decisions made by each character.

Huck and Henry: Two Roads to Adulthood

The focus of this comparison is clearly stated in the opening paragraph.

There comes a time in all of our lives when we reach a major crossroad and must choose a direction that will affect us for a long time to come. In *The Adventures of Huckleberry Finn* and *The Red Badge of Courage*, the main characters, Huck and Henry, reach such a crossroad, and their stories reveal the effects of their choices.

Both stories contain a part in which each main character decides to run: Huck from his drunken father and Henry from his first major battle. Huck's decision to run leads to wonderful adventure and a growing respect for his traveling partner, Jim. Henry's decision leads to fear, anger, and constant uncertainty.

Each paragraph addresses a separate point of comparison between the two characters.

Each story also has a part in which each character must decide whether to help a man in need or not. In Huck's case, the slave Jim has escaped and needs help to get off the very island that Huck is hiding on. Huck helps Jim get some food. Jim repairs a raft and they begin their journey down the Mississippi toward Cairo, a free black town. Henry, on the other hand, does something much different. His man in need is the wounded soldier Henry meets in chapter 11. The tattered soldier approaches Henry and in a friendly way asks him where he was hit. This annoys Henry and at the end of the chapter, he leaves the poor man to die alone.

At the end of *Huck* and in the middle of *Red Badge*, each youth must decide whether or not to return after running. Tom Sawyer's Aunt Sally decides to adopt Huck and "civilize" him. Since Huck despises learning, using utensils, and wearing nice, clean clothes, he decides to "light out for the territory." Because of his wound and hunger, Henry decides to return to camp and accept his comrades' ridicule. Instead, though, he is welcomed back with open, sensitive arms.

Finally, each youth is forced to confront the reality of death. Huck's case is the death of his father. Those who have read *Huck* know that this death can only make his life better. But Henry's life becomes more difficult after witnessing the strange, imp-like death dance of his lifetime friend, Jim Conklin, which haunts him for life.

The closing remarks tie all of the points of comparison together.

Both Huck and Henry start out on the road to adulthood under very difficult circumstances. Huck starts out as a runaway on the Mississippi, and Henry starts out as a young soldier in a war. Both of their lives are changed permanently because of their difficult journeys. @

361 ## Writing the Cause/Effect Essay

Meaningful Relationships

Discussion: Write an essay analyzing the cause (causes) and/or the effect (effects) of a timely situation (civil unrest in a country, lead poisoning, etc.). Make sure that you establish a logical relationship between the cause and the effect as you develop your work. Use the guidelines below and the example that follows to help you shape your essay.

Searching and Selecting

1. **Reviewing** • Think about recent experiences, conversations, newscasts, and headlines for possible ideas. A cause/effect essay could focus on an improved situation in your school or community. It could focus on a recent development in medicine or science, an exciting discovery, a milestone in history or politics.

2. **Searching** • If this assignment relates to the work in one of your classes, review your texts and class notes for possible subjects. Look for situations, events, and discoveries that seem to have made a difference (for better or worse).

Generating the Text

3. **Collecting** • Once you have a subject in mind, determine what you already know about it and what you need to find out. Collect additional information accordingly. (Take accurate notes of facts, figures, and direct references.)

4. **Focusing** • Establish a specific focus or purpose for your writing as well as an effective order for presenting your ideas. (The example essay focuses on the main cause of the civil war in Lebanon.)

Writing and Revising

5. **Writing** • Develop your first draft according to your planning. Don't, however, be afraid to follow a new line of thinking if one begins to emerge.

6. **Revising** • Review, revise, and refine your writing before sharing it with others. (Make sure each paragraph or main point supports your focus.)

Evaluating

Has the cause/effect relationship been effectively addressed?

Has sufficient supporting detail been included?

Does the writing contain an effective opening and closing?

Does the writing form a meaningful whole?

362 Cause/Effect Essay

In the following model, student Mohamad Bazzi discusses how cultural and religious differences have divided his country. This writing is a clear, logical cause/effect essay. Note how examples in the essay work to clarify and support the writer's main idea. (This article first appeared in *New York Connections: The Magazine Written By and For New York Youth,* November 1991. It is reprinted with permission.)

Ethnocentrism Destroyed My Country

Multicultural education is vital to a society made up of many different peoples. But there must also be some common culture which binds everyone together. Otherwise, we become so involved in our own culture and people that we can't get along with anyone else. My homeland is a good example of what happens to a society in which different groups isolate themselves to the extreme.

The opening paragraph presents a clear backdrop against which the rest of the essay is developed.

Ever since I was born there in 1975, a bloody civil war has ravaged Lebanon. One of the main causes of the war is ethnic and religious segregation. Beirut, the Lebanese capital, is divided into two sectors: east and west. East Beirut is for the Christians, while West Beirut is where the Moslems live. Until recently, few ever dared to cross the "green line" which divides the city (I've never been to East Beirut). Everyone knew on which side of the line he or she belonged. The segregation cuts even deeper, however. Within each religion there are different denominations and sects. Catholics and Maronites are the two major Christian groups, while most Moslems are either Sunnis or Shiites. These groups also fight amongst themselves.

The writer points to ethnocentrism as the main cause of Lebanon's problems (and to civil war as the effect).

In Beirut, schools barely a dozen miles apart teach as if they were on opposite sides of the globe. Lebanon's many religious sects give children a vastly different, ethnocentric education. Each group runs the schools in its own little area of town. The curriculum is tailored to the beliefs and needs of that particular faction, and rarely is anything about Lebanon's other sects ever mentioned (except perhaps for lessons in hate).

History is taught within the context of that group's heritage and not the common Lebanese culture. Certain subjects that offend religious beliefs are prohibited. Students are also discouraged from studying subjects that a rival faction finds useful. Since most Christians study French (Lebanon's second language), for example, Moslem youths are discouraged from doing so.

All in all, Lebanese schools—and society—teach their young to see themselves as parts of groups distinct from and at odds with every other group. They teach them that they have absolutely nothing in common with someone who prays differently. Is it any wonder then, with all of its divisiveness and blind, ethnocentric passion, that a country like Lebanon has lost over 100,000 people in a gruesome civil war that's as old as I am? ℮

363 Writing the Essay of Definition

"Words don't mean; people do."

Discussion: Write an extended definition of a commonly used term or concept that is not easily defined. It may be that the term is complicated (stock market, apartheid, cancer) or that it means different things to different people (love, courage, fairness). Consider the following approaches in developing your definition: dictionary definitions, personal definitions, negative definitions (telling what it is not), explanations, comparisons, quotations, and so on. Use the guidelines below and the example essay that follows to help you develop your writing.

Searching and Selecting

1. **Selecting** • It's very important that you select a term or concept that is complex enough to require some real thought on your part; likewise, it should prompt your reader to think as well.

2. **Reviewing** • If no subject comes to mind, write freely about your course work, about current events, or about your personal experiences. (Also consider terms people either misuse or use too freely.)

Generating the Text

3. **Collecting** • Gather details about your subject from dictionaries, interviews, song lyrics, personal anecdotes, newspapers, etc.

4. **Organizing** • Decide how you want to arrange the details. You may want to begin with a dictionary definition and end with a negative definition, or begin with a personal anecdote and end with how most people feel. Try a number of approaches.

Writing and Revising

5. **Writing** • Be sure to identify your term clearly very near the beginning of your writing. Also be sure to help your reader understand why it's important to know more about this term.

6. **Revising** • As you review your first draft, decide if it offers your reader something new or different to think about. If not, look for a more creative approach.

Evaluating

Is your definition clearly supported in a variety of ways?

Have you included enough specific examples, anecdotes, comparisons?

Is your writing organized logically?

364 Essay of Definition

In the following essay, student writer Martina Lowry defines, explains, and clarifies the meaning of the word "tact." Note that she does an excellent job of summarizing the definition in her concluding paragraph.

Break It to 'Em Gently

There is a boy in my gym class (I'll call him Bill) who has unbearably yellow, scummy teeth that gross everyone out. Recently, another boy told Bill that he "should go Ajax" his teeth. Bill was crushed. Had the other boy been thinking, he would have realized that there is a better way to handle such a situation. He could have handled it with tact. Tact is the sensitive handling of situations which require conveying a potentially hurtful truth.

If a person isn't sensitive to another's feelings, there is no way he can be tactful. Children are especially vulnerable and must be handled sensitively. Yesterday, my 5-year-old brother proudly announced that he had cleaned the screen on our television set. Unfortunately, he used Pledge furniture polish, which produced a smeared, oily film on the television screen. My mother smiled and thanked him for his efforts—and then showed him how to clean the screen properly. Her sensitivity enabled my brother to keep his self-respect. Yet, sensitivity alone does not make tact. It is possible for someone to be sensitive but not be tactful.

A tactful person not only expresses herself sensitively, but truthfully as well. Doctors, for example, must be truthful. If her patient is paralyzed, a tactful doctor will tell the truth—but she will express it with sensitivity. She may try to give the patient hope by telling of new healing techniques under study or of advanced programs for handicapped people. A doctor should use tact with patients' relatives as well. Instead of bluntly saying, "Your husband is dead," a doctor should say, "I'm sorry . . ." or, "He's no longer suffering pain." These are tactful ways of expressing the truth.

Tact should not be confused with trickery. Trickery occurs when a nurse is about to give a patient an injection and says, "This won't hurt a bit." Trickery occurs in the courtroom when a lawyer phrases his question so as to get the witness to say something he never meant to say. An admiring audience might say, "How tactful he is, this lawyer!" Clever he may be, but tactful he is not.

Sensitivity, truthfulness, and careful thought are all necessary components of tact. No one component will do; they must all be utilized in situations where people's feelings are at stake. Tact is a wonderful skill to have, and tactful people are usually admired and respected. Without tact our society would nurture insensitivity and disregard for others. @

The first paragraph ends with a basic definition of "tact."

A basic pattern of stating an element of tact, followed by an example, is set in the second paragraph.

The closing lines not only summarize the essay, but also emphasize the importance of tact in society.

365 # Writing an Essay of Argumentation

"Now this is the way I see it . . ."

Discussion: *First,* choose a topic for which you are able to write the following: (a) a proposition or main point that you will argue for, (b) argument(s) supporting your proposition, (c) argument(s) opposing your proposition. *Second,* look for information (evidence) with which to build arguments for and against your proposition. And *third,* use the information to write an essay that convinces your readers that your proposition is right. Use the guidelines below and the example that follows to help you develop your essay. (Also see "Thinking Logically" in the index for more.)

Searching and Selecting

1. **Searching** • Review your texts or class notes for possible topics. Also think of related issues or problems you hear debated locally or nationally. (Focus on subjects that are serious, specific, timely, and debatable.)
2. **Selecting** • Test a possible topic in the following way: (a) identify a reasonable point or proposition to argue for, (b) list one argument supporting this proposition, and (c) list one argument opposing it.

Generating the Text

3. **Collecting** • Look in books, magazines, or newspapers for information. Take notes, especially on strong arguments supported by the opinions of authorities and by factual evidence. Label arguments "pro" (for your proposition) or "con" (against).
4. **Assessing** • Check the best pro and con arguments. If you need to change your main point in order to defend it more effectively, do that now. Then decide on the best arrangement of your ideas. (Consider saving your best pro argument for last.)

Writing and Revising

5. **Writing** • Develop your argument using your planning as a guide. If you become stuck, ask a classmate to be your ear: read your proposition and talk through your argument.
6. **Revising** • Review, revise, and refine your argument before presenting it to your readers. Have a classmate review your writing as well.

Evaluating

Is the proposition reasonable and clearly stated?

Are supporting arguments logical, clear, and convincing? Are opposing arguments dealt with?

Given the supporting arguments, is the conclusion valid?

366 Essay of Argumentation

Student writer Jennifer Nanna's essay presents a well-organized argument about the U.S. government's decision to intervene in the Persian Gulf Crisis in 1990. (This model first appeared in *Moments* [1991], a collection of student writing from Badger High School in Lake Geneva, Wisconsin.) *Note:* This essay was written before Desert Storm.

Price of War

Throughout history, disease, poverty, crime, and war have plagued Americans. For the most part, these ills of society are difficult to control. Regardless of the precautions Americans take to rid themselves of these misfortunes, they affect (excluding war) every town in every part of America. One of the more serious conflicts that Americans have faced is war. Recently, for example, when Iraq invaded Kuwait on August 2, 1990, the United States was faced with the choice to ignore it or intervene. On August 3, the United States chose to intervene in the Persian Gulf Crisis. However, it is in the United States' best interest to take a defensive position and avoid an all-out war with Iraq.

Although America's reputation would be enhanced as a world power if the United States won the war against Iraq, it is not certain by any means that this would actually happen. Iraq has one of the largest armies in the world, numbering over one million soldiers. This compares with the 400,000 U.S. servicemen in the gulf.

While it may seem that the Iraqi soldiers are tired after fighting Iran for nine years, the truth is that this lengthy war hardened many boys into seasoned soldiers. Also, the Arab nations view death differently than Americans. Americans perceive death with fear and apprehension, whereas the Arabs would go to any length to fight for what they believe. For the Iraqis, death is more of an obstacle than a final outcome. They won't hesitate to kill. This is a paramount point to remember, considering Iraq is expected to develop the technology for the nuclear bomb in eight to nine months.

Many Americans think the price of oil will continue to escalate if Americans don't go to war to settle this crisis. This, however, is a narrow viewpoint that is unlikely to happen. As soon as the first shot is fired in the gulf, Hussein has threatened to push a button that will blow up the oil rigs in Kuwait. This catastrophe will lead to an expensive and lengthy operation to rebuild the oil wells.

The writer clearly states her position.

Arguments opposing this position are addressed early.

A strong pro argument (the killing) is introduced here.

The pro arguments continue in this section.

Furthermore, if we fail at war, our reputation as one of the top three world powers may deteriorate. In the eyes of the other two world powers, China and Russia, and others, we may appear "soft." As Americans it is our duty to realize that we cannot successfully be world policemen, which is evident by our past mistakes. In 1950, we felt the need to come to South Korea's rescue, and, as a result, the United States and South Korea lost 580,000 men. In 1958, again it seemed our responsibility to come to South Vietnam's aid, and we came out of the war without victory and with 55,000 deaths. In both wars, the question was asked: Why are we here? If we go to war with Iraq, many Americans will be angry at the lack of direction from President Bush and become indifferent towards the war.

In addition to this, we as Americans must think about the financial state of our country. After the rapid growth in the 1980's, our economy has slumped into a recession that has forced Americans to be more frugal. Meanwhile, millions of dollars are being sent to our soldiers in the Middle East. Already, Operation Desert Shield has cost 17.5 million dollars. While our allies profess their utmost support in stopping madman Hussein, it is the United States that is paying for 90 percent of the effort. This drainage of resources is increasing our high national debt.

The "loss of life," the "killing," is again presented as the author's strongest argument against all-out war with Iraq.

And most important of all, many innocent men and women will go to war fighting for a cause they can't understand, striving to put their finger on why they are over there. If the United States engages in war, devoted soldiers will be brutally killed over something that could have been resolved through negotiation. This is the real tragedy of war—the loss of each and every life.

The author clearly restates her position, along with her three strongest pro arguments.

Thus, it is up to the United States to take a defensive position and avoid an all-out war with Iraq in the upcoming months. Our nation cannot afford to fall as one of the top three world powers. Our nation cannot afford the extreme cost of such an event. And finally, our nation cannot afford to lose thousands of men and women to war, where even they can not see the reason. The trauma and holocaust of a war with Iraq would make the problems of society, such as disease, poverty, and crime, pale in comparison. ℮

368 Writing a Problem/Solution Essay

"A problem well stated is a problem half solved."

Discussion: Write an essay in which you analyze a problem and present one or more solutions. Choose a problem related to the work in one of your classes or related to the world around you, and analyze it completely before suggesting possible solutions. Use the guidelines below and the example that follows to help you develop your writing.

Searching and Selecting

1. **Reviewing** • If your assignment is related to a specific subject, review your text and class notes for possible topics. Also consider brainstorming for ideas with a small group of classmates.

2. **Searching** • Otherwise, think about the things students complain most about: crowded classrooms, peer pressure, school spirit, jobs, grades, discrimination, safety. Could you discover a solution for any of these problems? What about a problem that's developed recently around your neighborhood, at your school, or in your personal life? What about environmental issues, politics, or other areas that affect your world? What is being done to address these problems? Do you have suggestions or solutions?

Generating the Text

3. **Forming** • After you've selected a problem, write it out in the form of a clear statement. Then analyze it thoroughly, exploring the problem's parts, history, and causes. Weigh possible solutions. Try listing reasons why solutions might work, or why they might not.

4. **Assessing** • Make sure you are dealing with a manageable problem and that you have enough background material to write intelligently about it. (You may need to gather more facts and statistics to establish the problem or propose solutions.)

Writing and Revising

5. **Writing** • Once you have assessed the problem, write your first draft. Discuss the problem and possible solutions as clearly and completely as you can.

6. **Revising** • Carefully review your first draft for clarity and logic. Also have a classmate review your work. Revise accordingly.

Evaluating

Have you found a real solution to a real problem?

Is your writing interesting? Your opening engaging? Your conclusion logical?

Will readers understand and appreciate your essay?

369 Problem/Solution Essay

In this essay Monica Bermudez discusses the problem of overcrowded classrooms. Some people believe that schools alone hold the key to solving this problem, but as this writer suggests, everyone needs to become involved. (This article is reprinted with permission from *New Youth Connections: The Magazine Written By and For New York Youth,* December 1991.)

The writer describes the scene in overcrowded classrooms (the problem) and suggests two main causes.

Effects of overcrowding are discussed.

Overcrowded Classrooms:
Do You Ever Feel Like a Teen Sardine?

You know the scene, the first week of school and your classes are packed. You walk in a little late only to find that all the seats have been taken, so you have to stand. Usually they manage to find a seat for you by the second week (even if they have to take it from another overcrowded class).

Sometimes it's because the program office has screwed up and [has] accidentally given you a class you took last term or a class you didn't ask for. But most of the time there are just too many students and not enough teachers or classrooms. Immigration is one big factor in why schools are so jammed. But the main reason is that there is no money. At Humanities HS, for instance, Jan Zubiarr, 15, has 38 people in his math class, four over the limit set by the teachers' union contract.

"Lots of people don't have seats," he said. "It's not fair."

The school has room for 1,702 students but last year 1,860 registered. This means that the school was at what the board of education calls "109% utilization." (If 1,702 had registered it would have been 100% utilized—full to capacity.)

No Place to Sit Down

Students from several high schools all had the same complaint: with so many kids in one room, the time for learning is being taken up just getting the class together. "We deserve 41 minutes [of education]," said Nancy Alfaro, 16, of Grover Cleveland HS, "and not spend half of it finding out where people sit."

Students also complained that there aren't enough supplies to go around. Amy Herget, 16, also from Cleveland, says in her classes not only are people always standing, there aren't enough books either. (Cleveland is 111% utilized.) Another problem is that with so many people in one class, the teacher just doesn't have time for all of them. Claudia Ramos, a senior at Richmond Hill HS (129% utilized), is planning to pursue a career in the fashion industry. With 40 people in her fashion design class, she says it's hard to get the teacher to look at her work. "It bothers me. I feel I'm getting less attention . . . a lot of kids are getting short-changed on their education."

Overcrowding Causes Tension and Violence

Noreen Connell, executive director of the Educational Priorities Panel (EPP), an organization working to improve public education in New York City, says, "Overcrowding also affects morale." A 1989 EPP report on overcrowding said that "the school's atmosphere can become tense and, in some cases, violent."

Overcrowding can also contribute to the dropout rate. The EPP report found that schools with the greatest number of students at risk of dropping out are also the most overcrowded. And schools which are predominately Black and Latino are consistently more crowded than those with a large white population.

Many schools have tried to adapt by creating "double sessions." At Bushwick HS, which is 170% utilized—serving almost twice as many students as it should be—this means that the 11th and 12th grades start their day at 7:50 and end at 2:00. The 9th and 10th grades start at 9:15 and finish at 3:30. But this often prevents students from participating in after-school activities.

Temporary Solutions

Rose T. Diamond, director of strategic planning at the New York City Board of Education's Division of School Facilities, said some schools are moving administrative offices out of their buildings to make more space for students. During our interview, Diamond got a phone call about two school districts fighting over classroom space. Her solution was to use another place such as the auditorium or gym. This has been the common remedy around the city, and not a great one, many teens say.

Meanwhile, the board of education has a five-year plan to build new schools and add and lease new space. By the year 1995, they say they will need to make room for almost 50,000 more students. In Queens they will be building West Queens HS, which will accommodate 2,500 students. Townsend Harris (also Queens) will house 1,000 students. In Port Richmond HS, on Staten Island, there will be room for 800 more. "Solving this problem," Ms. Diamond says, "is the chancellor's top priority." In the meantime, she says we should "try to be patient and understand."

But Connell doesn't think so. She says that teens are a great "political force" and they should write letters to their legislators and invite them to "observe overcrowding first-hand." She recommends that teens "tell as many people as possible how bad things really are." @

The writer shows that the impact of overcrowding affects everyone.

Present solutions offer little relief. Successful solutions will involve the students themselves.

"In school, writing mistakes are graded. In the work world, there are no grades—but also no forgiveness for poor writing."

—Jim Franken, Electrical Contractor

Business Writing

371   All organizations—IBM, the Farmer's Co-op, the Buffalo Bills—need people who can write well. Whether you end up an engineer or a nurse, a lab technician or a social worker, your writing helps you *get* a job and *do* your job.

Why the big deal about writing? It's very simple. In a world which depends so much on information and technology, organizations need people who can present information and ideas clearly When you're on the job, you're no longer writing for a teacher but for a living.

372 The Advantages of a Written Message

To write or not to write: that's the question. Speaking (face-to-face or over the phone) is useful when (1) you want immediate feedback, (2) the subject requires special tact, or (3) you are interested in building up a professional relationship. On the other hand, a written message . . .

- gives you time to think about, organize, and edit what you want to say.
- communicates a specific message that doesn't wander like a phone conversation or informal dialogue.
- provides both the sender and the receiver with a copy of important details—why the message was sent and what action should be taken. The result: an official record.
- generally carries more weight—is taken more seriously—than the spoken word.
- can be sent to many people conveniently.

what's ahead? The sections that follow explore three important topics: (1) Writing a Business Letter, (2) Writing to Get a Job, (3) Writing on the Job.

Business Writing
373 Quick Guide

All business writing—no matter if you are writing a letter, a résumé, or a memo—share the following characteristics.

Starting Point: Business writing begins when you have a need to make contact with another person to conduct some form of commerce. ("I would like to apply for, request, or . . . ")

Purpose: The purpose is to discuss, announce, clarify, or confirm a specific business-related matter. (On another level, the purpose is to begin or continue some action pertaining to the matter.)

Form: In business writing, it's important to follow the basic standards of form and style (as outlined in this chapter). People in the workplace don't have time for surprises. They want letters and memos to be presented in recognizable formats so they are easy to follow. Writing in the business world is a highly structured and functional form of communication.

Audience: In most cases, you are speaking to one specific individual (or group) about one particular form of business. Always provide your audience with the necessary information to act upon your request, concern, or announcement.

Voice: Speak clearly, concisely, and courteously in business writing. Think of your writing as one part of a direct and sincere conversation with your reader.

Point of View: Use the first-person (I) point of view in person-to-person communication and the third-person (she, he, they) in most general messages and memos.

The Big Picture

Business writing is the process of sharing work-related information in a standardized format (letter, résumé, memo, etc.). The writer must know why he or she is writing (the specific message) and how the writing should be presented (the correct form).

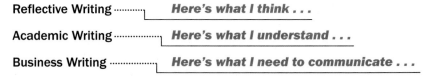

Reflective Writing ············ *Here's what I think . . .*

Academic Writing ·············· *Here's what I understand . . .*

Business Writing ·············· *Here's what I need to communicate . . .*

374 Writing a Business Letter

> "Writing a letter should be like having a conversation with a friend—it needs to be open and honest."
> —Shirley Born, Loan Officer

Letters are workplace workhorses that help you apply for a job, spell out a complaint, order supplies, or make a sales pitch. Well-written letters are true *correspondence*, an exchange between people; but poorly-written ones are *letter bombs*, exploding in the reader's face.

How do you write effective letters? Simple. Pay close attention to the following tips on prewriting, organization, style, form, revising, folding, and addressing.

Prewriting Tips

- Think first about your reader. How well do you know her or him? How will she or he feel about your message?
- Think about your purpose. Write out your reason for writing—what you want the reader to know or do—and keep it in front of you.
- Collect the information you will need. Think about the best way to order and present it.

375 Effective Letter Organization

As a general rule, organize your letters into three parts:

Situation: The opening introduces the message by stating the subject and purpose. It answers the reader's question, "Why are you writing?"

Explanation: The middle of the letter presents the information and ideas at the heart of the message—the details. It answers the question, "What's it all about?"

Action: The conclusion focuses on outcomes—what you want the reader to do, when, and how. It answers the question, "What's next?"

376 Effective Letter Style

Be conversational. Your letter should sound like one person speaking to another. Be plain and simple in the words you choose but avoid slang.

Be courteous. You accomplish nothing positive by talking down to, aggravating, or blowing off steam at your reader.

Avoid formal, wordy, cliched, and insensitive language. The table later in this section (380) gives examples of each.

377 Form of the Business Letter

A letter must be professional and look professional—neatly typed or printed on good quality paper. (See the guidelines below.)

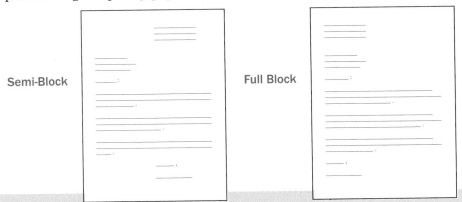

Semi-Block

Full Block

Letter-Writing Guidelines

- Use a consistent style: semi-block or full block.
- Avoid worn-out ribbons and poor dot-matrix printers.
- Use margins left and right, top and bottom, from 1 to 1.5 inches.
- Center the letter vertically (top to bottom) on the page.
- Present your information completely and in the correct order so that your reader can file or reply to the letter easily.

378 Parts of the Business Letter

The **heading** gives the writer's complete address, either in the letterhead (company stationery) or typed out, plus the date.

The **inside address** gives the reader's name and address.

- ⊚ If you're not sure who to address or how to spell a person's name, you could call the company for the information.
- ⊚ If the person's title is a single word, place it after the name and a comma. A longer title goes on a separate line.

The **salutation** begins with *Dear* and ends with a colon, not a comma.

- ⊚ Use Mr. or Ms. plus the person's last name, unless you are well acquainted. Do not guess at Miss or Mrs.
- ⊚ If you can't get the person's name, replace the salutation with *Dear* or *Attention:* plus the title of an appropriate reader, such as *Customer Service Department, Sales Manager*, or *Personnel Manager*. DO NOT use *Dear Sir* or *Gentlemen*.

379 The **body** should consist of single-spaced paragraphs with double-spacing between paragraphs. (Do not indent the paragraphs.)

◉ If the body continues on a second page, put the reader's name at the top left, the number 2 in the center, and the date at the right margin.

For the **complimentary closing**, use *Sincerely, Yours sincerely,* or *Yours truly* followed by a comma. Capitalize only the first word.

The **signature** includes the writer's handwritten name plus the typed name.

◉ When someone types the letter for the writer, that person's initials appear (in lowercase) beside the writer's initials (in capitals).

◉ If a document (brochure, form, copy, etc.) is enclosed with the letter, the word *Enclosure* or *Encl.* appears below the initials.

◉ If a copy of the letter is sent elsewhere, type the letters *cc:* plus the person's or department's name beneath the enclosure line.

Heading	Savannah Chamber of Commerce 105 E. Bay Rd. Savannah, GA 31404-0012 October 19, 1993
	Four to Seven Spaces
Inside Address	Ms. Charlotte Williams, Manager Belles Lettres Books The Delta Mall Savannah, GA 31404-0012
	Double Space
Salutation	Dear Ms. Williams:
	Double Space
	Welcome to the Savannah business community. As the Chamber's Executive Director, I'd like to thank you for opening your store in Delta Mall.
Body	Belles Lettres is a welcome addition to the town's economy, especially with the store's emphasis on Southern authors. I wish you success. For this reason I encourage you to join the Chamber of Commerce. Membership gives you a voice in your community's development and access to promotional materials. I've enclosed a brochure about our work in the community.
	If you decide to join, I could set up a ribbon-cutting ceremony within two weeks. You would meet other members of the Chamber and receive some useful news coverage. I look forward to hearing from you.
	Double Space
Complimentary Closing	Yours sincerely,
Signature	*Ardith Lein* **Four Spaces**
	Ardith Lein
	Double Space
Initials **Enclosure** **Copies**	AL:nk Encl. membership brochure cc: Peter Sanchez

380   Expressions to Avoid in Business Writing

Formal and Awkward Phrasing: Replace with simpler, contemporary language.

problem	solution
at the present writing	presently, right now
you are hereby advised	I'm writing to let you know
indisposed	busy
ceased functioning	quit working

Wordy and Repetitive Phrasing: Replace with more concise wording.

problem	solution
in the near future	soon
due to the fact that	because
on a daily basis	daily
absolutely essential	essential
be in agreement with	agree
over and done with	finished
bring together	join

Cliches: Because they're worn out, don't use them. Replace them with clear, simple statements.

problems	more problems
at this point in time	as a matter of fact
in view of the fact	better late than never
token of our appreciation	it has come to my attention
I regret to inform you	par for the course

Insensitive Language: Eliminate words insensitive to gender, race, or class. Use neutral or positive terms. (For a complete treatment of gender sensitivity in language, see "Sexism, Avoiding" in the index.)

problem	solution
foreign	international
foreigner	Canadian, Brazilian, etc.
lower class	working class
Negro	African-American
Indian	Native American

381 **Proofreading a Business Letter**

Organization

☐ 1. The letter states its purpose clearly, right away.

☐ 2. The explanation gives the reader complete and accurate details.

☐ 3. The letter clearly states what you want the reader to do.

Wording and Tone

☐ 4. The letter avoids expressions that are wordy, cliched, vague, or sexist.

☐ 5. The letter begins, continues, and ends with a courteous tone.

Form and Appearance

☐ 6. The letter follows consistently either Semi-Block or Full Block format.

☐ 7. The letter is neatly typed or printed with no smudges or obvious corrections.

☐ 8. The margins are correct and even, spacing is correct, and the message is centered on the page.

☐ 9. The letter is signed in blue or black ink, and the signature is readable.

Punctuation

☐ 10. A comma separates the city and state, but not the state and ZIP code.

☐ 11. A colon is used after the salutation (except after an *Attention* line) and a comma after the complimentary close.

Capitalization

☐ 12. The names of streets, cities, and people are capitalized.

☐ 13. The month in the heading is capitalized.

☐ 14. The title of the reader, the name of the department, and the company in the inside address are capitalized.

☐ 15. The word *Dear* and all nouns in the salutation are capitalized, but only the first word of the complimentary close is capitalized.

Spelling

☐ 16. The reader's name is spelled correctly in both the inside address and the salutation.

☐ 17. The numbered street names from one to ten are spelled out, but figures are used for higher numbers.

☐ 18. The names of cities, streets, and months are spelled out. Any of the abbreviations used are correct.

382 Folding the Letter

An 8½" by 11" letter should be mailed in a standard-sized 4⅛" by 9½" envelope.

- ◉ Fold the bottom edge so that the paper is divided into thirds.
- ◉ Fold the top third of the letter down and crease the edges firmly.
- ◉ Insert the letter (with the open end at the top) into the envelope.

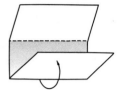

383 Addressing the Business Envelope

Address the letter correctly so it can be delivered promptly. Make sure that the destination and return addresses match the heading and inside address on the letter. The return address goes in the upper left corner, the destination address in the center.

REP OLYMPIA SNOWE
2464 RAYBURN BLDG
WASHINGTON DC 20515-0001

MR LOUIS FREEN
DIRECTOR
FEDERAL BUREAU OF INVESTIGATION
10TH ST & PENNSYLVANIA AVE NW
WASHINGTON DC 20535-0001

Sample addresses:

ATTN MANAGER TRAINING
MCDONALDS CORP
1 MCDONALDS PLZ
OAKBROOK IL 60521-1900

MS TERESA CHANG
GOODWILL INDUSTRIES OF AMERICA
9200 WISCONSIN AVE
BETHESDA MD 20814-3896

Official USPS Envelope Guidelines

1. Capitalize everything in the address and leave out ALL punctuation.
2. Use the list of common abbreviations found in the National ZIP Code Directory. (See "Abbreviations" in the handbook index.) Use numerals rather than words for numbered streets and avenues (9TH AVE NE, 3RD ST SW).
3. If you know the ZIP + 4 code, use it. You can get ZIP + 4 information by phoning one of the Postal Service's ZIP Code information units.

384 The Letter of Inquiry (or Request)

An inquiring mind is curious. Out of curiosity, a person writes a letter of inquiry to check things out—to seek information about a job, product, service, policy, or procedure. Writing a letter of inquiry or request involves detective work. You need to follow clues to get the facts. Ask yourself these questions:

- ◉ Exactly what do I want or need? Why? By when?
- ◉ Where can I get it? From whom?
- ◉ Am I being realistic or expecting too much?

If your letter is exact, you might get exactly the information you need. In fact, listing the specific questions you need answered or the items you want makes your reader's job even easier.

---

456 Seventh Ave. N.E.
Cedar City, UT 84720-1697
17 September 1994

Utah Jazz
301 W. South Temple
Salt Lake City, UT 84101

Appropriate reader to address

Attention: Public Relations Department

I'm writing for information about attending a Utah Jazz home game between December 7 and 24.

Request stated in first sentences

As the captain of the Cedar City Crusaders basketball team, I've been asked to set up a team trip. We would like to attend a weekend game and a practice, if possible. Could you send me the following:

1. ticket prices for a group of 12-15,

Specific details put in list

2. a schedule of home games and practices between December 7 and 24, and

3. directions on how and when to book tickets.

Closing looks forward to action

I would appreciate the information by October 1. I look forward to your reply.

Sincerely,

Jenny Smithers

Jenny "Sky" Smithers

385 The Letter of Complaint

A letter of complaint should be written clearly and concisely. It is especially important to include all the essential information surrounding the complaint.

- ◉ Begin your letter with a brief description of the **product** (or service), including the brand name, model number, and where and when you bought the product.
- ◉ Also include a description of just what the **problem** is, when you first noticed it, and what you think may be the **cause** of the problem.
- ◉ If you have already tried to resolve the problem, explain what you did, who you talked to, and what the result of that **action** was.
- ◉ Finally, suggest what action you would like the reader to take to find a **solution** to the problem.

2020 Sunnyside Ave. N.E.
Buffalo, NY 14222
15 October 1994

Best of 70's Rock
2951 Washington Blvd.
Buffalo, NY 14206

Dear Salesperson:

Product Information

Last August Channel 14 advertised copies of a special recording called "Best of 70's Rock." I decided to get the recording for my dad's birthday, and on August 8 I sent you a letter and check ordering a copy on CD.

**Problem/
Action Taken**

About the 2nd week of September I received the cashed check from the First Bank, but I didn't receive the CD from Channel 14. I called your station asking why you cashed my check without sending the CD.

Cause of Problem

Rita told me that you cashed the check promptly according to company policy, but that you didn't send the CD because it was backordered. She said that she expected a new shipment later in the week. She promised that when the shipment came in, she would send out my order "pronto."

Well, "pronto" took a month. Today the "Best of 70's Rock" arrived one week *after* my dad's birthday. In addition, you sent a cassette copy, not a CD!

Solution Desired

I'm frustrated. I'm returning the cassette along with a copy of my canceled check. Please do the following: 1) send me a check for $21.84 ($19.95 refund + $1.85 return postage = $21.84); 2) stop sending any more advertising about your special offers.

Sincerely,

Kenya Tabotto

Kenya Tabotto

Encl. cassette and copy of check

386 Writing to Get a Job

> "We want employees who can think, can use a computer, and can write well."
> —Nan Van Andel, Amway Corporation

An employer probably will meet something you've written before meeting you. Your job application form, your résumé, or your application letter will make the first impression, either helping or hurting your chances for getting a job.

387 Writing a Résumé

The word *résumé* comes from the French *resumer*, which means to summarize. A résumé is a one-page summary of you! It includes these parts:

- ◉ ....**personal data** about you

- ◉ ....your job **objective** (job you want to have)

- ◉ ....details about your **education**

- ◉ ....your work **experience**

- ◉ ....your **achievements** or abilities

Your résumé is a vivid word picture of you. Its purpose is to interest the employer so he or she will call you for an interview. A résumé is not a brag rag! Instead of *telling* about yourself, you *show* what skills and knowledge you have and the responsibilities you have carried.

Tips

- ● Design each résumé to fit a particular job.
- ● Be specific—use numbers, dates, names.
- ● First, present information that is the most impressive or most important to the job for which you are applying. This guideline will determine whether to put experience or education first.
- ● Use everyday language and short, concise phrases.
- ● Use the techniques of boldface, underline, white space, and indentations to make your résumé readable.
- ● Get someone else's reaction before typing the final copy.
- ● Proofread carefully for spelling, punctuation, and typographical errors.

388 Sample Résumé

LEE R. EPSTEIN
207 S. 40th Pl., Mt. Vernon, WA 98273-3129
(206) 424-2518

JOB OBJECTIVE: Full-time automobile mechanic in car dealership

EDUCATION: A.A., Large Engine Repair, Northwest
Technical College, expected May 1995

Mt. Vernon High School—Graduated May,
1993
Course highlights:
Auto Mechanics I, II
Small Engine Repair
Power Mechanics

EXPERIENCE:

1993-Present   Auto mechanic and gas station attendant,
Parman Texaco Service
Many customers request me to do their work
88% customer satisfaction,
1993 Customer Evaluations
Own automotive tools

1992-Present   Restored three stock cars
Upon request, displayed 1980 Buick Regal at
Cascade Mall on July 24, 1993
Sold two cars at 50% profit

ACHIEVEMENTS:

1990-1992   Member, Mt. Vernon High School Automotive
Club

1992   1976 Oldsmobile Cutlass Supreme took 3rd
place in the "A" feature, Charger Division,
Skagit County Fair

REFERENCES: Available upon request.

389 The Letter of Application

Your letter of application (or cover letter) introduces you to an employer and often highlights information on an accompanying résumé. The goal for writing a letter of application is to convince the employer to invite you for an interview. Before writing the actual letter, answer these questions:

- What job are you applying for?
- How did you find out about the job?
- What are the employer's needs? (List)
- How can you fill these needs?

Then write the letter as a brief business letter. Remember to keep your tone enthusiastic and positive.

207 S. 40th Pl.
Mt. Vernon, WA 98273-3129
September 28, 1994

Mr. Joe Lombardi
Joe's Chevrolet and Pontiac
540 Main Ave.
Mt. Vernon, WA 98273-4997

Dear Mr. Lombardi:

Ms. Sanchez, your office manager, mentioned that you need an auto mechanic in your shop. The enclosed résumé will show you that automotive repair has been my occupation and my recreation.

A successful dealership like yours depends on its reputation. My record of high customer satisfaction at Parman Texaco Service and my experience with automotive parts show that the quality of my work would support your reputation.

Please contact me at my home to arrange an interview at your convenience. I am usually home after 4 p.m., and my number is 424-2518. Thank you for your consideration, and I look forward to meeting you.

Sincerely,

Lee R. Epstein

Lee R. Epstein

In the **salutation**, address a specific person. If you don't know the person's name, write "Dear Personnel Manager."

In the **introduction**, state the job for which you are applying and where you found out about the job. State your chief qualification (your #1 selling point!).

In the **body**, explain what you can do for the employer—how your skills can meet the organization's needs.

In the **conclusion**, request an interview. Thank the reader for her or his time and consideration.

390 Interviewing for the Job

Your letter of application and résumé are pictures of you. If the employer likes the pictures and wants a closer look at the real thing, he or she will ask you to come for an interview. Here are some tips to help you get ready:

What to do before the interview

Think about yourself
What are your goals? Strengths? Weaknesses?

Think about the employer
Why is the organization interested in you?
What are the business's goals? Size? Products? Services? Plans?

Think about the interview
What questions can you expect: Strengths? Weaknesses? Reason for seeking the job?
What materials may the employer want to see: Work samples? Portfolio?

Think about the job
What does the job involve? What are the hours? Wages? Opportunities for advancement?

How to respond during the interview

Be attentive
Introduce yourself to the office staff and say why you're there.
Complete forms neatly and quietly.
Shake hands and look the interviewer in the eye.
Listen carefully.

Be clear
Answer questions clearly and briefly.
Restate questions in your own words if you are unsure what the interviewer means.
State your strengths and how you use them.

Ask about the job
What is the job description? Salary? Benefits? Work schedule? Opportunities for advancement?

What to do after the interview

Tell when and where you can be reached.
Shake hands and thank each person involved in the interview.
Write a follow-up letter.

391 Writing the Follow-Up Letter

Your application and résumé have gotten you an interview, and that interview went well. Now what? Pace the floor and chew your nails? No! Put your hands to work. A day or two after the interview you should send a follow-up letter. A good follow-up message contains the following:

- A thank-you comment.
- A statement confirming your interest in the job and your value as an employee, with specific reference to the interview.
- A statement about your willingness to answer further questions.
- Your phone number and times you're available.

207 S. 40th Pl.
Mt. Vernon, WA 98273-3129
October 2, 1994

Mr. Joe Lambardi
Joe's Chevrolet and Pontiac
540 Main Ave.
Mt. Vernon, WA 98273-4997

Dear Mr. Lombardi:

Thank-you comment

Thank you for the interview yesterday. I enjoyed meeting you, the mechanics, and other staff members.

Confirming interest in the job

After touring your showroom and service area, I'm convinced that my training and experience, especially my experience in the automotive parts department, would make me an asset to your team.

Follow-up information

I appreciate your considering me for the position of auto mechanic. If you have any further questions, I shall continue to be available at your convenience. I can be reached at home after 4 p.m. at 424-2518.

Sincerely,

Lee R. Epstein

Lee R. Epstein

392 Writing on the Job

> "Law enforcement officers hate to write. Writing is one of the least emphasized but most important aspects of our work."
>
> —Dan Altena, Deputy Sheriff

Writing at work is a practical activity, and practically everyone does it. In fact, usually the higher you advance in an organization, the more writing you will do. In addition, the quality of your writing will be one of the things that determines how high—or far—you go. Below are some helpful guidelines and characteristics to get you started:

Writing Guidelines

- Reply to others promptly and pay attention to deadlines.
- Use the form and style the company uses, but also be creative.
- Be honest with your readers and work hard to help them understand ideas and information.
- Show respect for the people you write to by being sensitive to their culture, gender, religion, etc.
- Become familiar with new ways of communicating information: E-mail, fax, voice mail, electronic bulletin boards, desktop publishing.
- Be a team writer. A lot of writing in the workplace happens in groups, so learn how to collaborate.

393 Characteristics of Good Writing

Concise:

Good writing makes its point quickly and accurately—no toxic waste here, only well-chosen words and efficient thinking.

Clear:

Like a clean pane of glass, workplace writing should be transparent with no hidden messages or cloudy meanings.

Organized:

Workplace writing is attractive and easy to read, like a store with clearly labeled aisles.

Reader-Specific:

Good writing pays close attention to the reader—like a good tailor who knows suits but also knows what suits the client.

394 Writing Messages

Messages in the workplace must be taken carefully and given promptly. Remember, each message you write well will help establish your reputation as an efficient, dependable worker.

A message is a simple kind of memo that requires two things: 1) Being polite and professional on the phone. 2) Getting down all the facts correctly. Double-check numbers and spellings with the caller, and use the 5 W's as a checklist:

- ⦿ **Who** is the message for? Who is the message from?
- ⦿ **What** is the message?
- ⦿ **When** is the meeting or appointment mentioned in the message? When was the message written?
- ⦿ **Where** is the receiver of the message to go? or call back?
- ⦿ **Why** is the message important—what's the purpose?

After you've taken the message, deliver it promptly, using whatever medium is appropriate for the receiver. You can, for example, either fill out a standard message form by hand or use electronic mail (E-mail).

Standard Message Form

MESSAGE _____

To: Mr. Smith	Date: Sept. 6, 1994 Time: 10:00 a.m.

From:
    Elinor Stacey of the Daily Press

Telephone:
- ☐ Telephone
- ☐ Called to see you
- ☑ Returned your call
- ☐ Please call
- ☐ Will call again
- ☐ URGENT

Message: There will be no problem in rescheduling your interview. She will meet you at the dump site on Thursday, Sept. 15, at 9:00 a.m.

By: Steve Killberg

E-Mail Message

```
Date:    12 Jul 1994  09:07:39
From:    nkramer@greenway.com
To:      lfeather@greenway.com
Subject: message fom polanski
Priority: normal

b polanski of crossing boundaries
called at 9 a.m. today

1. she'll send seminar materials by
UPS this a.m.
2. will FAX a sem. outline and prep.
instructions by this afternoon.
```

395 Writing Memos

A memorandum is a written message sent from one person to other people in the same organization. As such, it is less formal than a letter. A memo can vary in length from a sentence or two to a four-or-five page report.

Memos are written to create a *flow of information* within an organization—asking and answering questions, describing procedures and policies, reminding people about appointments and meetings. Here are some guidelines for writing memos:

- ◉ Write memos only when necessary.
- ◉ Send them only to those who need them.
- ◉ Distribute them through appropriate media—paper, interoffice mail, fax, bulletin boards, E-mail.
- ◉ Make your subject line precise so that the topic is clear and the memo is easy to file.
- ◉ Get to the point: 1) state the subject, 2) give necessary details, 3) state the response you want.

The **subject line** clarifies the memo's purpose.

The memo's **point** is stated right away.

Details the reader needs are **listed** rather than buried in a paragraph.

The writer looks foward to a **positive result** for the reader.

Greenway Medical Laboratories

Date:	16 July 1994
To:	Sales Staff
From:	Lois Whitefeather, Director of Personnel
Subject:	Cross-Cultural Training Seminar for International Sales Effort

Next Thursday, July 22, Brenda Polanski from Crossing Boundaries Consultants will talk to us about the connection between culture and business. The information we learn will help us meet out goals for market expansion. Here are the details:

Time:	8:30 to 4:00 p.m. Noon to 1:00 - group lunch
Place:	East End Conference Room
Preparation:	(1) Read the attached article, "Ethnic Difference: Business Headache or Opportunity?"

(2) Write a paragraph about an encounter, positive or negative, with a person of a race or culture different from your own.

Your participation in this seminar will help you relate to all clients—locally, nationally, and internationally.

396 Writing Instructions

> "When writing instructions, don't assume anything. If the reader knew what to
> do, he wouldn't need instructions."
>
> —Dennis Walstra, Plumbing Contractor

"Put whatchamacallit A into whosit B, turn 62.5 degrees, and crank it
with a grummle wrench." Ugh! Help!

Do instructions frustrate you? You're not alone. Poorly written instructions can be a real problem. This is especially true when your job depends
upon instructions day after day. Good instructions explain how to complete a
process using a clear, step-by-step procedure. Nothing is left to chance. Here
are some guidelines for you to follow:

397 How do you write helpful instructions?

Know your goal	What result do you want? The machine assembled, the parcel delivered, the food prepared? Spell it out and keep the goal in front of you.
Know your reader	What does the reader already know and need to know about the process? Does he or she understand technical terms? Develop your instructions around the reader's needs.
Know the process	How well do you as the writer know the process? Make sure you know it backward and forward.
Organize the steps	**Part 1:** an introduction that gives an overview of the whole process and states the end goal. **Part 2:** a list of required parts, equipment, or tools. **Part 3:** a step-by-step walk-through of the process.
Write the steps	Use clear, exact verbs that tell the reader what to do; also, use precise terms for parts, tools, and measurements.
Clarify the steps	Because readers work back and forth between the task and the instructions, your writing must be easy to get in and out of. Number the steps and use graphics to help the reader.
Test the steps	Allow a couple of days to pass after you write the instructions. Then pretend you are a beginner and follow the directions. Ask a friend to do the same. Then revise your instructions as necessary.

Writing About Literature

"The books that help you the most are those that make you think the most."

—Theodore Parker

Personal Responses

398 How do you normally react after seeing a great movie or hearing an outstanding concert? Do you feel like talking to someone about the experience, or more like mellowing out in a quiet corner? If you're like most people, you can't wait to talk about it. You need an immediate outlet for all of the thoughts and feelings popping into your head. ("You won't believe what happened when . . . " "I've never seen anything like . . .") Movies and music can do that to you.

Are you just as quick—or ready—to share your thoughts about a good book? Probably not. For one thing, it may not always be easy to describe in words why you like it. Books can be complex, containing many different levels of meaning. For another thing, the "whys" are often very personal, developing slowly from chapter to chapter in your reading. Instead of going bonkers over a good book, your reaction is likely to be more thoughtful and inward.

399 The Reading/Writing Connection

This may be why books, as well as other types of literature, are written about as much as they are talked about. Writing makes it possible for you to put your thoughts about a book at arm's length so you can explore them more carefully. It allows you to respond to the text on a personal level—to agree with it, question it, and study it. **Personal responses to reading** can be anything from entries in a journal to letters to the authors, from imaginary dialogues to personal essays.

what's ahead? On the next page, you will find a basic set of guidelines that will help you form personal responses to literature. The pages that follow contain examples of three different types of personal responses plus a set of reader-response questions for journal writing. Whenever you find the need to explore your thoughts and feelings about literature, turn to this chapter for help.

400 Guidelines for Responding to Reading

Discussion: Write a thoughtful personal response to a book, poem, play, or short story. Your response may be a letter to the author or to one of the characters, a journal entry (or entries) focusing on a certain part of your reading, an imaginary dialogue with one of the characters, a poem expressing a specific thought or feeling about the text, or an essay (paragraph) exploring your personal connection to your reading. Use the guidelines below and the examples that follow to help you with your writing.

Searching and Selecting

1. **Selecting** • Choose a piece of literature that you have recently read on your own or as part of your classroom work. (Make sure that you know the text well.)

2. **Reading** • You may also read a new book, short story, or poem. Ask your teacher and classmates for their recommendations.

Generating the Text

3. **Collecting** • Generate some initial thoughts and feelings about your subject through exploratory free writing. (See 402 for possible starting points.)

4. **Reviewing** • Review your free writing for ideas you want to develop further. Perhaps there are some thoughts you would like to explore in journal entries or in a letter to the author. Or maybe you identified some personal connections between the text and your own life. You could explore these connections in a brief essay. Then again, an idea for a poem might have developed in your exploratory writing.

Writing and Revising

5. **Writing** • Develop your writing freely and naturally as thoughts come to mind—or according to any planning you may have done.

6. **Revising*** • Carefully review your work, first for the overall flow of your ideas, and then for the effectiveness of the individual parts (paragraphs, sentences, and words). Have a classmate review your work as well. Revise and refine accordingly.

   *The revising notes address personal responses that will be shared (not personal journal entries).

Evaluating

Does the writing clearly communicate a thoughtful response to a piece of literature?

Has proper attention been given to accuracy and detail?

Does the writing form a meaningful whole, moving smoothly and clearly from beginning to end?

401 Responding in a Journal

Responding to a Novel: This response to *The Adventures of Huckleberry Finn* is based on the following question: What connections are there between the book and your life? (See a complete list of these questions on the next page.) One of Huck's actions serves as a starting point for the entry.

The writing sounds as if it were part of a conversation.

> Huck takes a great risk when he decides to help Jim escape. But to turn him in goes against some very basic beliefs that he can't really explain. (I guess this is what makes Huck such a likable character—his natural goodness and "uncivilized" approach to life.) I think there is a little bit of Huck Finn, the risk taker, in me. Take my choice of friends. I know that my parents and some of my teachers don't approve of the crowd I hang around with. (No names will be mentioned.) But they don't see and know my friends like I do . . .

Responding to an Essay: This sample entry is a freely written response to an essay about acid rain. As you will see, the writer is clearly trying to sort out his or her thoughts about the reading material.

In journals, asking questions is as important as finding answers.

> What a crazy world! We expect big plants to provide us with good jobs; we expect basic creature comforts like heat and light in our homes; we love cars and can't wait to drive them on our freeways. Yet scientists are saying that the acid rain produced by factories, power plants, and cars may be wrecking the very buildings and freeways that make city life possible. And what's really bad is the effect it has on rural and wilderness areas. Many of our lakes, streams, and rivers are just dead bodies of water. So do we give up our jobs and our cars? Do we . . . ?

402 Starting Points for Journal Writing

The following reader-response questions will help you react personally and honestly to the books you read. This list is not meant to cover all of the issues that might concern you, and it should be used only when you need a starting point for writing. Your own thoughts and feelings are always the best source of ideas for journal writing.

Making Connections

1. What were your feelings after reading the opening chapter(s) of this book? After reading half of the book? After finishing the book?
2. Did this book make you laugh? Cry? Cringe? Smile? Cheer? Explain.
3. What connections are there between the book and your life? Explain.
4. What is the most important word in the book? The most important passage? The most important event or feeling? Explain.
5. Who should or shouldn't read this book? Why?

Points of Interest

6. What are the best parts of the book? Why? What are the worst parts? Why?
7. Do you like the ending of the book? Why or why not? Do you think there is more to tell? What do you think might happen next?
8. What came as a surprise in the book? Why?
9. What parts of the book seem most believable or unbelievable? Why?
10. What makes you wonder in this book? What confuses you?

Strictly in Character

11. In what ways are you like any of the characters? Explain.
12. Do any of the characters remind you of friends, family members, or classmates? Explain.
13. Which character would you like to be in this book? Why?
14. What would you and your favorite character talk about in your first conversation? Begin the conversation.

Careful Reflection

15. Do you think the title fits the book? Why or why not?
16. What was the author saying about life and living through this book?
17. Has this book helped you in any way? Explain.
18. How have you changed after reading this book? Explain.
19. What do you know now that you didn't know before?
20. What questions in this book would you like answered?

Special Note: You can use this same list to react to other forms of literature (plays, poems, short stories, etc.). Simply change the questions to meet your needs: *What were your feelings after reading the opening scene(s) of this play? After reading half of the play? After finishing it?* (Question #1)

④⓪③ Responding in a Letter to the Author

In this letter to author Maya Angelou, student writer Kate Keefe shares her thoughts and feelings about Ms. Angelou's book *All God's Children Need Traveling Shoes*. Note that Ms. Keefe makes many personal connections between the book and her own life.

Madbury, New Hampshire
September 30, 1992

Ms. Maya Angelou
Ghana, Africa

Dear Ms. Angelou,

After I had read *I Know Why the Caged Bird Sings,* I was very anxious to read *All God's Children Need Traveling Shoes* because your first book left me wondering about how your life and your son's life continued to be.

The reason that *All God's Children Need Traveling Shoes* appealed to me was because in social studies I have studied about black civil rights, and so many of the people that you mention in your book were familiar and of interest to me. Although I think that probably your book appeals mostly to an older age group because a lot of people my age still don't know much about this time in history. It was worthwhile reading for me because it made me aware that the black civil rights movement in the United States was not something that was only affecting our country, but was a worldwide situation.

There was one thing that I was confused about, Ms. Angelou. You did not want blacks to be treated unjustly, and yet you treated Kojo, your "small boy," unjustly until you found out that his parents were wealthy. I had a hard time understanding this. Or, maybe I just misunderstood.

But mostly, Ms. Angelou, your book taught me the importance of pride in yourself—even when life is not easy. I understand much better now what black pride is, and how important returning to Africa was in your search for yourself, because really, we are all searching for ourselves. Your book's ending showed me the journey that blacks must travel. You wrote: "Despite the murders, rapes, and suicides, we have survived. The middle passage and the auction blocks have not erased us. Not humiliation, nor lynchings, individual cruelties, nor collective oppression has been able to eradicate us from the earth. We have come through despite our own ignorance and gullibility, and the ignorance and rapacious greed of our assailants." When I read those words, I could understand not only your struggle, but also my own struggle to be what I want to be.

Sincerely,
Kate Keefe ℮

The writer explains her motive for reading *All God's Children Need Traveling Shoes.*

The writer parallels her own search for identity with Ms. Angelou's.

④④④ Responding in a Dialogue

In this response paper, writer Travis Taylor creates an imaginary conversation between himself and Archie Costello from *The Chocolate War* by Robert Cormier. Through this conversation, the writer attempts to understand Archie's disturbing actions.

Dialogue with Archie Costello

Me: I don't think anyone who knows you, likes you at all. Doesn't that bother you?

Archie: Not particularly. Why should it?

Me: Well, don't you like anybody?

Archie: Oddly enough I think I could have liked Jerry Renault.

Me: How could you have liked him? You did everything you could to destroy the kid.

Archie: I said that I could have liked him, not that I did like him.

Me: Could you explain that?

Archie: I probably could, but you probably wouldn't even begin to understand.

Me: Try me.

Archie: Okay. You see, I wanted Jerry to beat me, but I knew he couldn't. But there was always that little chance, you see?

Me: No.

Archie: Well, I told you, you wouldn't understand.

Me: Now let me get this straight. You could have liked Jerry, but you didn't because you beat him and wound up controlling almost the whole school afterward.

Archie: Basically, yes.

Me: Okay, I'll bite. Why?

Archie: Because if Jerry had beaten me, then he would have proved I'm wrong. I mean everybody is so predictable. Everybody wants their little bit of power. The teachers want power over the students. The upperclassmen want power over the underclassmen. Parents want power over their kids. Everyone wants a little power, so they can forget that they don't really have any power at all. I thought Jerry might be different, because he wasn't interested in power. And that was how he might have won. But since he didn't want to fall in line and play the power game, everybody jumped on his head. All I had to do was set things up and give the kids and Brother Leon a chance to do what they already wanted to do anyhow—squash Jerry. So, he just got taken out of the game. And now he'll be just like everyone else. Or else he'll stay on the sidelines. Either way it doesn't matter. I won.

Me: Yeah, I guess that's what I was afraid of. ℮

Note that the conversation is written in script form, much like a scene from a play.

Archie's explanation provides an effective self-analysis of his actions.

"There are books of which the backs and covers are by far the best parts."

—Charles Dickens

Writing a Book Review

405   Everyone has his or her own personal tastes. While you may love Mexican food (hot and healthy), your best friend may have a passion for Italian food (rich and robust). While you may dig blues, your brother may be devoted to heavy metal. While you may go for action movies, a classmate may enjoy romantic comedies.

     The same holds true for the books you read. While you may enjoy science fiction or science fantasy, the next person may enjoy murder mysteries or modern dramas. One way to share your personal taste in literature is to review some of the books you read. A **book review** is a brief essay expressing your personal opinion about a book's value or worth. Reviews are usually published in newspapers or magazines.

406 A Winning Combination

     An effective book review is informative and enjoyable to read. It highlights important parts of the book without giving the whole story away. It provides comparisons between the subject of the review and similar books. It helps readers decide if they, in fact, should read the book themselves. And it presents all of the information in interesting and creative ways.

what's ahead? On the next page, you will find a set of guidelines that will help you write your own book reviews. Also included in this chapter are two sample book reviews, the first one reviewing a novel and the second one reviewing a nonfiction book. The information in this chapter will also help you review movies, videos, concerts, and other art forms.

407 Guidelines for Writing a Book Review

Discussion: Write a review of a book or another form of literature suitable for a school publication. Keep in mind that a review is based on your personal response to your subject; however, simply stating that something was good or bad is not enough. You will need to support your feelings with thoughtful explanations and specific references to the book itself. Express your opinion about the value or worth of your subject in order to help your readers decide whether or not to read this book. Use the guidelines below and the models that follow to help you with your review.

Searching and Selecting

1. **Reviewing** • The subject of your review should be a book that you have recently read, a book that you have strong feelings (positive or negative) about.

2. **Brainstorming** • If you're having trouble selecting a subject, brainstorm for ideas with a small group of classmates. If you still have no luck, read a new book to review.

Generating the Text

3. **Collecting** • Gather your initial thoughts and feelings about your subject through free writing. (If you like the way your free writing develops, consider it a first draft and continue working with it.) If, on the other hand, you would like to proceed more carefully, begin by developing one list identifying your subject's strengths and another list identifying any significant weaknesses. Continue exploring and collecting ideas as needed.

4. **Designing** • Read through your initial gathering, making some basic decisions about the organization and design of your writing. Remember that you can't say everything. A book review usually provides a few basic comments about the subject and then addresses two or three strengths and weaknesses in detail.

Writing and Revising

5. **Writing** • Develop your first draft according to your planning and organizing. Make sure that you hook your reader's interest with your opening paragraph.

6. **Revising** • Review, revise, and refine your writing until you feel it is ready for publication. (Your writing should present a lively, personal analysis of your subject.)

Evaluating

Is the review appropriate for a school (or other) publication?
Do you speak with authority and make specific references to your subject?
Will readers appreciate the treatment of the subject?

④⓪⑧ Model Review: Fiction

The subject of Andrea Facey's book review is the novel *Native Son* by Richard Wright. As you will see, this review does not give the whole story away. Instead, it helps readers decide if they should read the book. (This review originally appeared in *New Youth Connections: The Magazine Written By and For New York Youth,* September/October 1991. It is reprinted with permission.)

Trapped Between Two Worlds

The first part of the review "sets the scene" for readers.

Set in Chicago during the Depression of the 1930s, Richard Wright's novel *Native Son* is the story of one young black man's struggle to survive in a racist society.

The main character, Bigger Thomas, is the man of the house and his family expects him to bring home the bacon. But Bigger only cares about whether he has food to eat, a roof over his head, and clothes on his own back.

Bigger hates white people. He curses and mocks them behind their backs. In one conversation with his friend Gus, he describes how blacks and whites live in two different worlds:

"We live here and they live there," he says. "We black and they white. They got things and we ain't. They do things and we can't. It's just like living in jail. Half the time I feel like I'm on the outside of the world peeping in through a knot-hole in the fence."

THE "WHITE" SIDE OF THE FENCE

Throughout the book, Bigger tries to escape that feeling of being trapped. He gets a taste of life on the other side of the fence when he starts working as a chauffeur for Mr. Dalton, a white millionaire who tries to "help out" black people.

One event in the book is described in great detail.

The day he arrives at the Daltons' is supposed to be the day his troubles end; instead, it is the beginning of a chain of events that will destroy his life.

In one scene, Bigger meets Mr. Dalton's daughter, Mary, and her friend Jan. They treat him like a person, not like a servant. They ask him to call them by their first names, to look at them when they speak to him, and to shake their hands. They even invite Bigger to sit down to dinner with them.

But Bigger is afraid they are trying to trick him. By the end of the evening, Mary is drunk and cannot get up the stairs to her room so Bigger carries her. The next thing he knows, he is trapped in the white girl's bedroom, aware that no one will believe his explanation for why he is there. The things he does to try to escape only get him into more trouble.

The book's value is discussed in the final paragraph.

This book shows how prejudice affects people, the way segregation has a way of closing in on them, and what some people will do to find a way out. Everyone who wants to better understand racism in this society should read it. ⊚

409 Model Review: Nonfiction

Why do you read reviews? You want to know whether a new book, movie, CD, or video is worth the investment of time and money. Professional writer and editor Anne Brady cuts right to the heart of the matter in her refreshingly honest book review of *Second Ascent* by Alison Osius. (This review first appeared in the February 1992 issue of *Sassy Magazine*. Reprinted with permission of *Sassy Magazine*. Copyright © 1992 by Sassy Publishers, Inc.)

The opening grabs the reader's attention.

The writer packs a summary of the entire book into two sentences.

Both the good and the bad are addressed in this brief review.

Second Ascent

If you don't skip the first five chapters of this book, you probably won't make it to number six, and you'd be missing something. (If you're into rock climbing, however, you'll enjoy those first chapters a lot more than I did.)

This is the inspiring story of Hugh Herr, a rock climber who at age 17 had both his legs amputated below the knee after they had been destroyed by frostbite during a climb on New Hampshire's Mt. Washington. This guy is incredibly focused and was back climbing within weeks after receiving his first set of prosthetic legs, and has since devoted a lot of his time to improving prostheses. As I was reading, I kept wondering if I'd deal as well. And that's the strength of this book. It made me think about what things are really important to me, and reminded me that you need to focus and work hard to achieve them.

Beware, though, *Second Ascent* gets a little ponderous at times; author Alison Osius recounts many of Herr's rock climbs in exhaustive detail. I had trouble following—and caring. But if you're a serious athlete, or just need a push to get your rear end in gear, then you'll appreciate this. @

"For although literature can never replace actual human interaction, it can deepen the understanding that comes from sharing in the common struggle for human dignity and freedom."

—Coretta Scott King

Writing a Literary Analysis

410 A personal response to literature explores your thoughts and feelings about a piece of literature. A review discusses why a particular book or series of stories may or may not be worth reading. A **literary analysis** presents your thoughtful interpretation or understanding of a literary work. It is the most challenging form of writing about literature.

411 Starting Out

The starting point (and the foundation) for meaningful analysis is your honest response to a piece of literature. You may like how the story line develops in a novel. Or you may be interested in the actions of the main character in a short story or play. Then again, you may wonder why a writer spends so much time developing a certain image in a poem. Any one of these features could lead to an effective analysis. How you work with or explore an initial idea is the real challenge.

Base the ideas in your analysis on a close and careful reading of the piece of literature. Make sure to connect all of your main points with specific references to the text. And present the results of your work in a carefully planned essay containing a focus statement, supporting paragraphs, and closing remarks.

what's ahead? On the next page, you will find a set of basic guidelines that will help you write a literary analysis. On the pages that follow, you will find two sample analyses, the first one examining a classic novel and the second one examining an important poem. Also included in this chapter is a list of possible starting points for literary analyses (415) and a set of helpful writing tips (416). Whenever you are asked to analyze a piece of literature (novel, poem, short story, essay, etc.), turn to this chapter for help.

412 Guidelines for Writing a Literary Analysis

Discussion: Develop a close analysis of a specific literary work (short story, poem, novel, play, or essay). The focus of your analysis depends on the length and complexity of your subject. A short poem may be analyzed line by line for more than one element (perhaps style and theme); whereas the analysis of a longer work should focus on a specific aspect of the plot, setting, theme, characterization, or style. Use the guidelines below and the models that follow to help you develop your analysis.

Searching and Selecting

1. **Searching** • Your teacher may already have a selection in mind for your analysis. If not, look for a literary work that "speaks" to you. Perhaps it has taught you something or makes you smile, or wonder.

2. **Selecting** • If no subject comes to mind, ask your classmates for their recommendations. You might also ask your teacher if the activity could be expanded to include other artistic works like movies, paintings, or live performances.

Generating the Text

3. **Reviewing** • Make sure that you have a good understanding of your subject. Reread the text (or at least parts of it) if necessary, and review your class notes if the text was covered in class.

4. **Noting** • Think about different features of the text that you might write about. Are you drawn to a specific character? Would you like to analyze one of the themes or messages? Do you like how the writing sounds? (See 415 for ideas.)

5. **Focusing** • State a possible focus for your analysis—a sentence or two expressing the main point you want to emphasize in your writing. Plan and organize your writing accordingly. (Make sure that you can support your focus with direct references to the literary work.)

Writing and Revising

6. **Writing** • Develop a first draft, working in ideas and details according to your planning and organizing. Make sure that the opening paragraph attracts your readers and identifies the focus of your analysis. (See 416 for more writing tips.)

7. **Revising** • Carefully review your first draft. Look for parts that are unclear, incomplete, or confusing. Revise and refine accordingly.

Evaluating

 Does the work present a thoughtful and thorough analysis?

Is the purpose of the analysis clearly in focus?

Are the main ideas in the writing supported by direct references to the text?

413 Literary Analysis: Novel

In this analysis, student writer Elizabeth Delaney explores the element of fear in William Golding's novel *Lord of the Flies.* Throughout this analysis, Ms. Delaney maintains her focus on the "beast" created by the boys on the island, exploring the significance of the beast's development in the text as well as in terms of our own human nature.

The Beast of Fear

In William Golding's novel *Lord of the Flies,* the boys allow themselves to be terrorized by the beast because deep down they want it to exist. By creating a physical object to represent everything they are afraid of, the boys can base their fears on something tangible and distant, rather than something close and personal.

When they first arrive on the island, the boys have many implied fears: fear of being left on the island, fear of being on their own without adult assistance, fear of what may be occurring in the war from which they have fled, and perhaps even fear of not making a good show at being British. Consequently they all rapidly embrace the concept of the beast, for it is a way to externalize their fears. What the boys want is something they can fear in good conscience, some evil which does not stem from a past, present, or future in their own personal experience; so they place their fear outside themselves and believe in a beast.

Jack sums up the reason why externalized fear is so much easier to deal with than internal fear when he says, "If there was a snake we'd hunt it and kill it." It's a simple question of power. The boys never would have consciously thought that they were responsible for the incarnation of the beast, but they did believe they could be responsible for its demise or destruction. If the beast is something which can be destroyed, there is the potential for everything turning out suddenly all right, the possibility that all the evil which the boys perceive on their island could be purged with the removal of this one creature. In one sense Jack's cause is a noble one: purifying the world in which he resides of evil. However, he goes about looking for the beast in all the wrong places, and as a result, the boys commit several horrible crimes. In fact, part of Golding's message is that to "fancy thinking the Beast was something you could hunt and kill" is really catering to the true inner beast itself.

The development of the beast in *Lord of the Flies* is not an unusual one. We are always looking for a beast, a scapegoat, to destroy to solve our problems. And, as the Nazis set out to exterminate the Jews and Stalin the freedom of the individual, the boys create the beast as a safety net, an outside evil that protects them from the knowledge of their true nature as fallen creatures, "beasts" themselves. ℮

The first sentence states the thesis.

The concept of the "beast" is carefully examined.

In the final paragraph, the writer connects the beast in this book to the world at large.

414 Literary Analysis: Poem

This literary analysis by teacher and writer Ken Taylor explores Adrienne Rich's interpretations of *loneliness* in the poem "Song." As you will see, this analysis displays a clear and complete understanding of the poem.

"Song" by Adrienne Rich

The meaning and a great deal of the impact of Adrienne Rich's short poem, "Song," lies in the way the poet defines and interprets loneliness.

For most of us, "loneliness" carries a sad connotation (feeling). The word implies an unwanted isolation or separation from others. *Webster's New World Dictionary* gives the second meaning for "lonely" as "unhappy at being alone." That is not how loneliness is presented in "Song."

In the first stanza of the poem, the narrator compares her "loneliness" to that of an airplane which ". . . rides lonely and level/ on its radio beam, aiming/across the Rockies/for the blue-strung aisles/of an airfield on the ocean." The plane is alone, but it is going somewhere, toward the "blue-strung aisles/of an airfield on the ocean." Aiming for such a destination seems positive, and good, and almost magical. Loneliness in this stanza is anything but unhappy; instead, it is full of purpose and direction.

The second stanza, which describes a woman driving across country by herself, reinforces the idea of an individual who has chosen to be "lonely" for a purpose and indicates that real loneliness would be found in the "little towns she might have stopped / and lived and died in, lonely." In this line the narrator suggests that loneliness is not necessarily a condition of being physically separate from other people; she implies that any one of the small towns mentioned would have left her spiritually "lonely" because of their very sameness and drabness. She could have stopped at any one of them, but chooses not to. She seems much too full of purpose and control to give in to small-town loneliness.

The third stanza with its description of a person "waking first, of breathing/dawn's first cold breath on the city/of being the one awake/in a house wrapped in sleep" suggests a healthy sense of solitude and an equal sense of one's "differentness." Everyone else is sleeping. The narrator alone is awake to breathe "dawn's first cold breath on the city," awake and alive to the new day that the sleepers are missing.

The final stanza celebrates the poet's sense of her potential. She compares herself to an ice-bound rowboat on a wintry day, a boat ". . . that knows what it is, that knows it's neither/ice nor mud nor winter light/but wood, with a gift for burning." Like the rowboat, the speaker knows who she is. And like the rowboat's "gift for burning," the poet also has the "gift" to exert her individuality against those forces that would appear to shape or limit her. @

A standard dictionary definition of loneliness establishes a starting point for the analysis.

The writer works through the poem stanza by stanza, discussing the different shades of loneliness as suggested by the poet.

415 Ideas for Literary Analyses

The ideas listed below will help you choose a specific focus for your analysis.

Theme: You can write about the main idea, or theme, presented in your selection. (The questions listed here will help you think about the theme.)

● Does the author seem to be saying something about ambition or courage or greed or jealousy or happiness ?

● Does the selection show you what it is like to experience racism, loneliness, etc.?

● Does the author say something about a specific historical event?

Characterization: You could also write about one or more of the characters in your selection.

● How does the main character change from the beginning to the end?

● What forces or circumstances make one of the characters act in a certain way? (Consider the setting, the conflict, other characters, etc.)

● What are the most revealing aspects of one of the characters? (Consider his or her thoughts, words, and actions.)

● Does the main character have a confidant, someone he or she relies on? (How important or reliable is this person?)

Plot: Certain aspects of the action or story line may also lead to analysis.

● What external conflicts affect the main character? (Consider conflicts with other characters, the setting, objects, etc.)

● What internal conflicts make life difficult for the main character? (Consider the thoughts, feelings, and ideas that affect him or her.)

● How is suspense built into the story? (Consider the important events leading up to the climax.)

● Are there any twists or reversals in the plot? (What do they add to the story?)

Setting: You may want to analyze the role of the setting in the story.

● What effect does the setting have on the characters?

● Has the setting increased your knowledge of a specific time and place?

● Is the setting new and thought provoking? (This question is especially important in science fiction.)

Style: Special attention in an analysis can also be given to the author's style of writing—the words and phrases he or she uses.

● How does the writing—descriptive phrases, comparisons, etc.—create a main feeling or tone in the selection?

● Is dialogue or description used effectively? (Provide example and explain.)

● Is there an important symbol that adds meaning to the selection? (How is this symbol represented in different parts?)

● Has special attention been given to figures of speech like metaphors, similes, and personification? (What do these devices add to the writing?)

416 Tips for Writing an Analysis

Writing the Opening ● Your opening paragraph should hook your reader's attention and identify the focus of your analysis. Use the suggestions listed below to help you get started on your opening.

1. Summarize your subject very briefly. Include the title, author, and the type of book (or other literature form). This can be done with a statement of "what and how" about the book.

   > In his novel *Lord of the Flies,* William Golding writes about [what?] the evil side of man [how?] by describing the actions of a group of young boys who are marooned on a deserted island.

2. Start with a quotation from the book and then comment upon its importance (think in terms of the focus of your analysis).

3. Begin with an explanation of the author's purpose and how well you think he or she achieves this purpose.

4. Open with a few general statements about life that relate to the focus of your analysis.

   > "There comes a time when everyone has to . . ."

5. Begin with a general statement about the type of literature you are analyzing. Then discuss your subject within this context.

   > "The best science fiction always seems believable and logical within the context of the story line. This certainly is true in . . ."

Writing the Body ● Develop or support your focus in the body, or main part, of the analysis. To make sure that you effectively explain each main point in your analysis, follow these three steps:

1. State each main point so that it clearly relates to the focus of your analysis.

2. Support each main point with specific details or direct quotations from the text you are analyzing.

3. Explain how each of these specific details helps prove your point.

Special Note: Try to organize your writing so that each new paragraph deals with a separate main point.

Writing the Closing ● In the final paragraph, tie all of the important points together and make a final statement about the main focus of your analysis. (Give your readers something to think about, something that will keep your analysis alive long after it has been read.)

417 Literary Terms

Action is what happens in a story: the events or conflicts. If the action is well organized, it will develop into a pattern or plot.

Allegory is a story in which people, things, and actions represent an idea or generalization about life; allegories often have a strong moral or lesson.

Allusion is a reference in literature to a familiar person, place, thing, or event.

Analogy is a comparison of two or more similar objects, suggesting that if they are alike in certain respects, they will probably be alike in other ways as well.

Anecdote is a short summary of a funny or humorous event. Abe Lincoln was famous for his anecdotes, especially this one:

> Two fellows, after a hot dispute over how long a man's legs should be in proportion to his body, stormed into Lincoln's office one day and confronted him with their problem. Lincoln listened intently to the arguments given by each of the men and after some reflection rendered his verdict: "This question has been a source of controversy for untold ages," he said, slowly and deliberately, "and it is about time it should be definitely decided. It has led to bloodshed in the past, and there is no reason to suppose it will not lead to the same in the future.
>
> "After much thought and consideration, not to mention mental worry and anxiety, it is my opinion, all side issues being swept aside, that a man's lower limbs, in order to preserve harmony of proportion, should be at least long enough to reach from his body to the ground."

Antagonist is the person or thing working against the protagonist, or hero, of the work.

Autobiography is an author's account or story of her or his own life.

Biography is the story of a person's life written by another person.

Caricature is a picture or imitation of a person's features or mannerisms exaggerated as to be comic or absurd. (See illustration.)

418 <u>Character sketch</u> is a short piece of writing that reveals or shows something important about a person or fictional character.

<u>Characterization</u> is the method an author uses to reveal or describe characters and their various personalities.

<u>Climax</u> is the high point, or turning point, in a story—usually the most intense point.

<u>Comedy</u> is literature that deals with life in a humorous or satiric manner. In comedy, human errors or problems appear funny. Comedies end on a happy note.

<u>Conflict</u> is the problem or struggle in a story that triggers the action. There are five basic types of conflict:

Person vs. Person: **One character in a story has a problem with one or more of the other characters.**

Person vs. Society: **A character has a problem with some element of society: the school, the law, the accepted way of doing things, and so on.**

Person vs. Self: **A character has a problem deciding what to do in a particular situation.**

Person vs. Nature: **A character has a problem with some natural happening: a snowstorm, an avalanche, the bitter cold, or any other element of nature.**

Person vs. Fate (God): **A character has to battle what seems to be an uncontrollable problem. Whenever the problem seems to be a strange or unbelievable coincidence, fate can be considered the cause of the conflict.**

<u>Context</u> is the set of facts or circumstances surrounding an event or a situation in a piece of literature.

<u>Denouement</u> is the final solution or outcome of a play or story.

<u>Dialogue</u> is the conversation carried on by the characters in a literary work.

<u>Diction</u> is an author's choice of words based on their correctness, clearness, or effectiveness.

Archaic **words are words that are old-fashioned and no longer sound natural when used, as "I believe thee not" for "I don't believe you."**

Colloquialism **is an expression that is usually accepted in informal situations and certain locations, as in "He really grinds my beans."**

Jargon **(technical diction) is the specialized language used by a specific group, such as those who use computers:** *override, interface, download.*

Profanity **is language that shows disrespect for someone or something regarded as holy or sacred.**

Slang **is the language used by a particular group of people among themselves; it is also language that is used in fiction and special writing situations to lend color and feeling:** *awesome, chill out.*

Trite **expressions are expressions that lack depth or originality, or are overworked or not worth mentioning in the first place.**

Vulgarity **is language that is generally considered common, crude, gross, and, at times, offensive. It is used in fiction to add realism.**

419 **Didactic** literature instructs or presents a moral or religious statement. It can also be, as in the case of Dante's *Divine Comedy* or Milton's *Paradise Lost*, a work that stands on its own as valuable literature.

Drama is the form of literature known as *plays*; but drama also refers to the type of serious play that is often concerned with the leading character's relationship to society.

Dramatic monologue is a literary work (or part of a literary work) in which a character is speaking about him- or herself as if another person were present. The speaker's words reveal something important about his or her character.

Empathy is putting yourself in someone else's place and imagining how that person must feel. The phrase "What would you do if you were in my shoes?" is a request for one person to empathize with another.

Epic is a long narrative poem that tells of the deeds and adventures of a hero.

Epigram is a brief, witty poem or saying often dealing with its subject in a satirical manner.

"There never was a good war or a bad peace" —Ben Franklin

Epitaph is a short poem or verse written in memory of someone.

Epithet is a word or phrase used in place of a person's name; it is characteristic of that person: *Alexander the Great, Material Girl, Ms. Know-it-all.*

Essay is a piece of prose that expresses an individual's point of view; usually, it is a series of closely related paragraphs that combine to make a complete piece of writing.

Exaggeration (hyperbole) is overstating or stretching the truth for special effect: "My shoes are killing me!"

Exposition is writing that is intended to make clear, or explain, something that might otherwise be difficult to understand; in a play or novel, it would be that portion that helps the reader to understand the background or situation in which the work is set.

Fable is a short, simple story that teaches a lesson. It usually includes animals that talk and act like people.

Falling action is the action of a play or story that works out the decision arrived at during the climax. It ends with the resolution.

Farce is literature based on a highly humorous and highly improbable plot.

Figurative language is language used to create a special effect or feeling. It is characterized by figures of speech or language that compares, exaggerates, or means something other than what it first appears to mean. (See "Figure of speech," 420.)

420 **Figure of speech** is a literary device used to create a special effect or feeling by making some type of interesting or creative comparison. The most common types are *antithesis, hyperbole, metaphor, metonymy, personification, simile,* and *understatement.*

> **Antithesis** is an opposition, or contrast, of ideas: "It was the best of times, it was the worst of times, it was the age of wisdom, it was the age of foolishness . . ."
>
> — Charles Dickens, *A Tale of Two Cities*

> **Hyperbole** (hi-pur´ ba-li) is an exaggeration, or overstatement: "I have seen this river so wide it had only one bank."
>
> —Mark Twain, *Life on the Mississippi*

> **Metaphor** is a comparison of two unlike things in which no word of comparison (*as* or *like*) is used: "A green plant is a machine that runs on solar energy."
>
> —*Scientific American*, April 1988

> **Metonymy** (ma-tón a-mi) is the substituting of one word for another that is closely related to it: "The White House has decided to provide a million more public service jobs." (*White House* is substituting for president.)

> **Personification** is a literary device in which the author speaks of or describes an animal, object, or idea as if it were a person:

"The rock stubbornly refused to move."

> **Simile** is a comparison of two unlike things in which a word of comparison (*like* or *as*) is used: "She stood in front of the altar, shaking like a freshly caught trout."
>
> —Maya Angelou, *I Know Why the Caged Bird Sings*

> **Understatement** is stating an idea with restraint (holding back) to emphasize what is being talked about. Mark Twain once described Tom Sawyer's Aunt Polly as being "prejudiced against snakes." Since she could not stand snakes, this way of saying so is called understatement.

421 **Flashback** is returning to an earlier time (in a story) for the purpose of making something in the present more clear.

Foil is someone who serves as a contrast or challenge to another character.

Foreshadowing is giving hints and clues of what is to come later in a story.

Genre refers to a category or type of literature based on its style, form, and content. The mystery novel is a literary genre.

Gothic novel is a type of fiction that is usually characterized by gloomy castles, ghosts, and supernatural or sensational happenings—creating a mysterious, chilling, and sometimes frightening story. Mary Shelley's *Frankenstein* is probably the best known gothic novel still popular today.

Hubris, derived from the Greek word *hybris,* means "excessive pride." In Greek tragedy, hubris is often viewed as the flaw that leads to the downfall of the tragic hero.

Imagery is the words or phrases a writer selects to create a certain picture in the reader's mind. Imagery is usually based on sensory details.

> "The sky was dark and gloomy, the air was damp and raw, the streets were wet and sloppy."
>
> —Charles Dickens, *The Pickwick Papers*

Impressionism is the recording of events or situations as they have been impressed upon the mind. Impressionism deals with feelings, emotions, and vague thoughts; realism deals with objective facts. In "A Child's Christmas in Wales," Dylan Thomas shares his boyhood impressions of winter:

> ". . . we waited to snowball the cats. Sleek and long as jaguars and horrible-whiskered, spitting and snarling, they would slink and sidle over the white back-garden walls, and the lynx-eyed hunters, Jim and I, fur-capped and moccasined trappers from Hudson Bay, off Mumbles Road, would hurl our deadly snowballs at the green of their eyes. The wise cats never appeared."
>
> —Dylan Thomas

Irony is using a word or phrase to mean the exact opposite of its literal or normal meaning. There are three kinds of irony:

> **dramatic** irony, in which the reader or the audience sees a character's mistakes or misunderstandings, but the character himself does not.
>
> **verbal** irony, in which the writer says one thing and means another: "The best substitute for experience is being sixteen."
>
> irony of **situation**, in which there is a great difference between the purpose of a particular action and the result.

Local color is the use of details that are common in a certain region of the country.

> "Mama came out and lit into me for sitting there doing nothing. Said I was no-count and shiftless and why hadn't I gathered eggs and . . ."
>
> —Olive Ann Burns, *Cold Sassy Tree*

422

Malapropism is the type of pun, or play on words, that results when two words become jumbled in the speaker's mind. The term comes from a character in Sheridan's comedy, *The Rivals*. The character, Mrs. Malaprop, is constantly mixing up her words, as when she says "as headstrong as an allegory [she means alligator] on the banks of the Nile."

Melodrama is an exaggerated, sensational form of drama (as in television soap operas) characterized by heavy use of romance, suspense, and emotion.

Mood is the feeling a piece of literature arouses in the reader: happiness, sadness, peacefulness, etc.

Moral is the particular value or lesson the author is trying to get across to the reader. The "moral of the story" is a common phrase in Aesop's fables.

Motif is a term for an often-repeated idea or theme in literature. In *The Adventures of Huckleberry Finn*, Huck is constantly coming into conflict with the "civilized" world. This conflict becomes a motif throughout the novel.

Myth is a traditional story that attempts to explain a natural phenomenon or justify a certain practice or belief of a society.

Narration is writing that relates an event or a series of events: a story.

Narrator is the person who is telling the story.

Naturalism is an extreme form of realism in which the author tries to show the relation of a person to the environment or surroundings. Often, the author finds it necessary to show the ugly or raw side of that relationship.

Novel is a lengthy fictional story with a plot that is revealed by the speech, action, and thoughts of the characters.

Novella is a prose work longer than the standard short story, but shorter and less complex than a full-length novel.

Oxymoron is a combination of contradictory terms as in *jumbo shrimp*.

Parable is a short, descriptive story that illustrates a particular belief or moral.

Paradox is a statement that seems contrary to common sense yet may, in fact, be true: "The coach considered this a good loss."

Parody is a form of literature intended to mock a particular literary work or its style; a comic effect is intended.

Pathos is a Greek root meaning *suffering* or *passion*. It usually describes the part in a play or story that is intended to bring out pity or sorrow from the audience or reader.

Picaresque novel is a novel consisting of a lengthy string of loosely connected events. It usually features the adventures of a rogue, or scamp, living by his wits among the middle class. Mark Twain's *Huckleberry Finn* is a picaresque novel.

423 **Plot** is the action or sequence of events in a story. It is usually a series of related incidents that builds and grows as the story develops. There are five basic elements in a plot line.

Plot line is the graphic display of the action or events in a story: *exposition, rising action, climax, falling action,* and *resolution.*

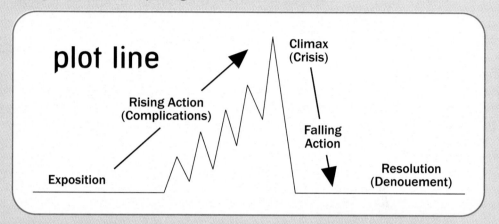

Poetic justice is a term that describes a character "getting what he deserves" in the end, especially if what he deserves is punishment. The purest form of poetic justice is when one character plots against another but ends up being caught in his own trap.

Poetry is an imaginative response to experience reflecting a keen awareness of language. There are many elements used in writing effective poetry.

Point of view is the vantage point from which the story is told. In the **first-person** point of view, the story is told by one of the characters: "I don't know what I'm doing tonight. What about you?" In the **third-person** point of view, the story is told by someone outside the story: The simple fact is he lacked confidence. He would rather do something he wasn't all that crazy about doing than risk looking foolish.

Protagonist is the main character or hero of the story.

Pseudonym (also known as "pen name") means "false name" and applies to the name a writer uses in place of his or her given name. Mark Twain was a pseudonym for Samuel Langhorne Clemens.

Pun is a word or phrase that is used in such a way as to suggest more than one possible meaning. Words used in a pun are words that sound the same (or nearly the same) but have different meanings: "I really don't mind going to school; it's the principal (principle) of the thing."

Quest features a main character who is seeking to find something or achieve a goal. In the process, this person encounters and overcomes a series of obstacles. In the end, he or she returns, having gained knowledge and experience as a result of the adventures.

424 **Realism** is literature that attempts to represent life as it really is.

Reminiscence is writing based on the writer's memory of a particular time, place, or incident. Memoir is another term for reminiscence.

Renaissance, which means "rebirth," is the period of history following the Middle Ages. This period began late in the fourteenth century and continued through the fifteenth and sixteenth centuries. Milton (1608-1674) is often regarded as the last of the great Renaissance poets. The term now applies to any period of time in which intellectual and artistic interest is revived or reborn.

Resolution, or denouement, is the portion of the play or story where the problem is solved. It comes after the climax and falling action and is intended to bring the story to a satisfactory end.

Rising action is the series of conflicts or struggles that build a story or play toward a climax.

Romance is a form of literature that presents life as we would like it to be rather than as it actually is. Usually, it has a great deal of adventure, love, and excitement.

Romanticism is a literary movement with an emphasis on the imagination and emotions.

Sarcasm is the use of praise to mock someone or something, as in "He's a real he-man," "She's a real winner," or "No one cuts pizza like Clyde."

No one cuts pizza like Clyde.

Satire is a literary tone used to ridicule or make fun of human vice or weakness, often with the intent of correcting, or changing, the subject of the satiric attack.

Setting is the time and place in which the action of a literary work occurs.

425 **Short story** is a brief fictional work. It usually contains one major conflict and at least one main character.

Slapstick is a form of low comedy that makes its appeal through the use of exaggerated, sometimes violent action. The "pie in the face" routine is a classic piece of slapstick.

Slice of life is a term that describes the type of realistic or naturalistic writing that accurately reflects what life is really like. This is done by giving the reader a sample, or slice, of life.

Soliloquy is a speech delivered by a character when he or she is alone on stage.

Stereotype is a pattern or form that does not change. A character is "stereotyped" if she or he has no individuality and fits the mold of that particular kind of person.

Stream of consciousness is a style of writing in which the thoughts and feelings of the writer are recorded as they occur.

Structure is the form or organization a writer uses for her or his literary work. There are a great number of possible forms used regularly in literature: parable, fable, romance, satire, farce, slapstick, and so on.

Style is how the author uses words, phrases, and sentences to form his or her ideas. Style is also thought of as the qualities and characteristics that distinguish one writer's work from the work of others.

Symbol is a person, a place, a thing, or an event used to represent something else: the dove is a symbol of peace. Characters in literature are often symbols of good or evil.

Theme is the statement about life a particular work is trying to get across to the reader. In stories written for children, the theme is often spelled out clearly at the end. In more complex literature, the theme will not be so clearly spelled out.

Tone is the overall feeling, or effect, created by a writer's use of words. This feeling may be serious, mock-serious, humorous, satiric, and so on.

Total effect is the general impression left with the reader by a literary work.

Tragedy is a literary work in which the hero is destroyed by some character flaw and by forces beyond his or her control.

Tragic hero is a character who experiences an inner struggle because of a character flaw. That struggle ends in the defeat of the hero.

Transcendentalism is a philosophy that requires human beings to go beyond (transcend) reason in their search for truth. An individual can arrive at the basic truths of life through spiritual insight if he or she takes the time to think seriously about them.

426 Poetry Terms

Alliteration is the repetition of initial consonant sounds in words such as "rough and ready." An example of alliteration (from "Runaway Warning" by Anne-Marie Oomen) is underlined below:

> "Our gang paces the pier like an old myth . . ."

Assonance is the repetition of vowel sounds without the repetition of consonants.

> "My words like silent rain drops fell . . ."   —Paul Simon, "Sounds of Silence"

Ballad is a poem in verse form that tells a story.

Blank verse is an unrhymed form of poetry that normally consists of ten syllables in which every other syllable, beginning with the second, is stressed. Since blank verse is often used in very long poems, it may depart from the strict pattern from time to time.

Caesura is a pause or sudden break in a line of poetry.

Canto is a main division of a long poem.

Consonance is the repetition of consonant sounds. Although it is similar to alliteration, consonance is not limited to the first letters of words:

> " . . . and high school girls with clear skin smiles . . ."
> —Janis Ian, "At Seventeen"

Couplet is two lines of verse the same length that usually rhyme.

End rhyme is the rhyming of words that appear at the ends of two or more lines of poetry.

Enjambment is the running over of a sentence or thought from one line to another.

Foot is the smallest repeated pattern of stressed and unstressed syllables in a poetic line. (See "Verse.")

Iambic: an unstressed followed by a stressed syllable (repeat)
Anapestic: two unstressed followed by a stressed syllable (interrupt)
Trochaic: a stressed followed by an unstressed syllable (older)
Dactylic: a stressed followed by two unstressed syllables (openly)
Spondaic: two stressed syllables (heartbreak)
Pyrrhic: two unstressed syllables (Pyrrhic seldom appears by itself.)

Free verse is poetry that does not have a regular meter or rhyme scheme.

Haiku is a form of Japanese poetry that has three lines; the first line has five syllables, the second has seven syllables, and the third has five syllables. The subject of the haiku has traditionally been nature, as in the following poem:

> Behind me the moon
> Brushes shadows of pine trees
> Lightly on the floor.

Heroic couplet (closed couplet) consists of two successive rhyming lines that contain a complete thought.

Internal rhyme occurs when the rhyming words appear in the same line of poetry: "You break my eyes with a look that buys sweet cake."

Lyric is a short verse that is intended to express the emotions of the author; quite often these lyrics are set to music.

Meter is the patterned repetition of stressed and unstressed syllables in a line of poetry.

Onomatopoeia is the use of a word whose sound suggests its meaning, as in *clang, buzz,* and *twang.*

Refrain is the repetition of a line or phrase of a poem at regular intervals, especially at the end of each stanza. A song's refrain may be called the chorus.

Repetition is the repeating of a word or phrase within a poem or prose piece to create a sense of rhythm: "His laugh, his dare, his shrug / sag ghostlike . . . "

Rhyme is the similarity or likeness of sound existing between two words. *Sat* and *cat* are perfect rhymes because the vowel and final consonant sounds are exactly the same.

Rhymed verse is verse with end rhyme; it usually has regular meter.

Rhythm is the ordered or free occurrences of sound in poetry. Ordered or regular rhythm is called meter. Free occurrence of sound is called free verse.

Sonnet is a poem consisting of fourteen lines of iambic pentameter. There are two popular forms of the sonnet, the Italian (or Petrarchan) and the Shakespearean (or English).

> **Italian (Petrarchan) sonnet** has two parts: an octave (eight lines) and a sestet (six lines), usually rhyming abbaabba, cdecde. Often a question is raised in the octave and answered in the sestet.
>
> **Shakespearean (English or Elizabethan) sonnet** consists of three quatrains and a final rhyming couplet. The rhyme scheme is *abab, cdcd, efef, gg.* Usually, the question or theme is set forth in the quatrains while the answer or resolution appears in the final couplet.

Stanza is a division of poetry named for the number of lines it contains:

Couplet: two-line stanza	**Sestet:** six-line stanza
Triplet: three-line stanza	**Septet:** seven-line stanza
Quatrain: four-line stanza	**Octave:** eight-line stanza
Quintet: five-line stanza	

Verse is a metric line of poetry. It is named according to the kind and number of feet composing it: iambic pentameter, anapestic tetrameter . . . (See "Foot.")

Monometer: one foot	**Pentameter:** five feet
Dimeter: two feet	**Hexameter:** six feet
Trimeter: three feet	**Heptameter:** seven feet
Tetrameter: four feet	**Octometer:** eight feet

Reading and Study Skills

"Reading is to the mind what exercise is to the body."

—Richard Steele

Reading Strategies

428   Over the years, you've spent a lot of time "reading." In the early grades, reading meant learning patterns and sounds, how words work together to form sentences, and then how sentences work together to form paragraphs and stories. Now, the word *reading* has an entirely different meaning for you. Rather than "learning to read," most of your time is spent "reading to learn." Reading now means studying, note taking, summarizing, reviewing, and so on.

429 Reading to Learn

From now on, most of the reading you will do in school will be reading to learn, or study-reading. Your goal will be to read, remember, and use the main ideas of each assignment in order to write a report, take part in a discussion, or take a test. Luckily, there are a number of strategies that can help you do this more efficiently, from SQ3R to mapping to acronyms. And they're not as difficult or mysterious as they sound.

what's ahead?   Throughout this section of your handbook, you will be introduced to strategies, guidelines, and organizers to help you improve your reading and study skills:

Reading Strategies

Improving Vocabulary Skills

Reading Charts and Graphs

Improving Classroom Skills

Writing to Learn

Test-Taking Skills

430 Guidelines for Reading to Learn

The guidelines that follow will help you put together a personal learning plan, one that may include several new reading and study strategies.

Before you read . . .

◉ Know exactly what the reading assignment is, when it is due, and what you have to do to complete it.

◉ Gather all the materials you may need to complete your assignment (notebook, handouts, reference books, etc.).

◉ Decide how much time you will need to complete the assignment and when and where (library, study hall, home) you will do it.

◉ Try to avoid doing your studying or reading when you are overly hungry or tired; take breaks only after completing an assignment or a major part of it.

As you read . . .

◉ Know your textbooks and what they contain; use the index, glossary, and special sections.

◉ Use a specific approach to your study-reading—KWL, SQ3R, mapping, or graphic organizers, for example. (See 431-435.)

◉ Preview each page before you begin reading to get an overall picture of what the selection is about; if there are questions that go with the assignment, look them over before you begin reading.

◉ Read the titles and headings and use them to ask yourself questions about what may be coming up next.

◉ Try to figure out the main idea of each paragraph and the supporting details that are worth remembering. Notice words or phrases in *italics* or **boldface**.

◉ Look closely at maps, charts, graphs, and other illustrations to help you understand and remember important information.

◉ Take good notes of everything you read—summarize, outline, star, underline, or highlight important information.

◉ Use all of your senses when you read. Try to imagine what something looks, feels, and tastes like; draw illustrations.

◉ Remember that some reading assignments are much more difficult than others. Read difficult material slowly; reread if necessary.

After you read . . .

◉ Try hard to figure out difficult material by rereading first; then, if necessary, ask someone for an explanation.

◉ Always summarize difficult material out loud (either to yourself or to someone else); make note cards or flash cards to study later.

◉ Keep a list of things you want to check on or ask your teacher about.

431 Strategies for Reading to Learn

Much of the reading you will be asked to do in school will involve study-reading, reading that you are expected to remember for a discussion, test, or project. There are many strategies you can use for these assignments. Among the most popular are KWL, mapping, graphic organizers, and SQ3R.

432 KWL

To use the KWL strategy, all you need to do is set up a chart similar to the one below and fill it in each time you read. It may seem too simple to be of much help, but you will be surprised by how helpful it can be.

K	W	L
List what you **KNOW**	List what you **WANT** to know	List what you **LEARNED**

433 Mapping

When you use this strategy, you actually draw a map of the material you are reading. Mapping is much like clustering; but in mapping, the ideas come from the reading, not from your personal experiences. Simply place the subject of your reading in the center and "map" out the details as you read.

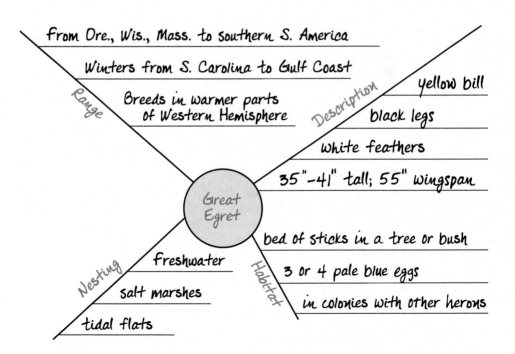

434 Graphic Organizers

A third study-reading strategy is the "graphic organizer." Simply draw and fill in one of the following organizers as you read or study. (*Remember:* You can change any of these organizers to fit your needs.)

Describing: Write the subject you want to describe in the circle. List the important details on the spokes as you read.

Finding Cause and Effect: Simply fill in the causes on the first set of lines and the effects on the bottom set.

Cause
_____

_____
_____
_____

↓

Effect
_____

_____
_____
_____

Finding Sequence: If the material you are studying has a definite sequence, list the facts and details in order beneath it.

Topic _____

1 _____

2 _____

3 _____

4 _____

Comparing and Contrasting: Write the two things you want to compare or contrast on the top lines. Then list all the ways they are similar; next list all the ways they differ. (Also see "Venn diagram" in the index.)

_____   _____

Similarities

_____
_____
_____

Differences

↔

_____
↔
_____
↔

_____   _____

Identifying a Problem/Solution: List the problems on the left, the solutions on the right.

Problem   Solution

→

_____   _____

_____   _____

_____   _____

_____   _____

Finding Examples: List the main topic in the center and the examples that relate to it on all sides.

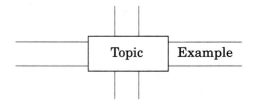

435 SQ3R

Another popular technique for study-reading is the SQ3R method. SQ3R stands for the five steps in the study-reading process: *Survey, Question, Read, Recite,* and *Review.*

Survey:

The first step in the SQ3R study method is survey. When you "survey" a reading assignment, you try to get a general picture of what the assignment is about. To survey, you must look briefly at each page, paying special attention to the headings, chapter titles, illustrations, and boldfaced type. It is also a good idea to read the first and last paragraphs. This should give you a good overall picture or survey.

Question:

As you do your survey, you should begin to ask yourself questions about the reading material—questions that you hope to find the answers to as you read. One quick way of doing this is to turn the headings and subheadings into questions. Asking questions will make you an "active" rather than a "passive" reader. It will keep you involved in the subject and keep you thinking about what may be coming up next.

Read:

Read the assignment carefully from start to finish. Look for main ideas in each paragraph or section. Take notes as you read, or stop from time to time to write a brief summary. Read the difficult parts slowly. (Reread them if necessary.) Use context clues to help you figure out some of the most difficult passages. (See 440-443.) Look up unfamiliar words or ideas. Use your senses to imagine what each subject in your assignment looks, feels, sounds, tastes, or smells like.

Recite:

One of the most valuable parts of the SQ3R method is the reciting step. It is very important that you recite out loud what you have learned from your reading. (Whisper quietly to yourself if you are in a public place.) It is best to stop at the end of each page, section, or chapter to answer the *who, what, when, where, why,* and *how* questions. By reciting this information out loud, you can test yourself on how well you understand what you have read. You may then go back and reread if necessary. Even if you understand the material well, reciting it out loud will help you remember it much longer.

Review:

The final step in the SQ3R study method is the review step. You should review or summarize what you have read as soon as you finish. If you have some questions to answer about the assignment, do them immediately. If you have no questions to answer, summarize the assignment in a short writing. You may also make an outline, note cards, flash cards, illustrations, etc., to help you review and remember what you have read. (Also see 436-439.)

Memory Strategies

In addition to using a study-reading plan, there are several specific memory strategies that you can use to help you remember your reading material.

436 Association

The association method is a memory strategy in which each idea being studied is associated with a more memorable word, picture, or idea. For example, if you were supposed to remember the first 10 amendments to the Constitution (the Bill of Rights), you would begin by setting up an association for the first amendment. What do most people "see" when they visualize the early colonists who helped set up the Bill of Rights? Pilgrims (religion), Benjamin Franklin (printing press), Patrick Henry (speech), Boston Tea Party (protest or petition)? You, of course, may see an entirely different set of images.

437 Acronym

Another way to remember facts is to use an acronym, a "word" created by using the first letter(s) of several related words. (VISTA, for example, is an acronym for Volunteers In Service To America.) To create an acronym for the Bill of Rights, you would use the first letter(s) of the words *press, religion, petition,* and *speech.* One possibility is the word (acronym) **preps**, which is made up of the "re" from religion and the first letter from the other three. The first amendment can easily be associated with firsts, beginnings, or preparations; the acronym *preps* can then be used to help you remember the first four basic rights, which are? Without looking!

438 Strange Sentences

A slightly different version of the acronym technique is to compose a sentence which is silly or strange enough that you will have no trouble remembering it. Say, for example, that you needed to remember the countries of Central America and match them to their places on a map. These countries are (from top to bottom) Mexico, Belize, Guatemala, Honduras, El Salvador, Nicaragua, Costa Rica, and Panama. Your sentence would have to contain words beginning (in order) with M . . . b . . . g . . . h . . . e . . . n . . . c . . . p. Want to give it a try? How about, "My brother George has extremely noisy car pipes"? Anything equally strange will work.

439 Rhymes, Songs, Jingles, and Raps

Anything that has rhyme and rhythm is easier to remember than a straight list of facts. Remember either of these? *"I before e, except after c . . ."* *"In 1492, Columbus sailed . . ."* Put your imagination (and talent) to work: Compose rhymes, songs, jingles, and raps to help you remember ideas and facts. You'll be surprised and pleased with the results.

Related Reading Strategies

440 ## Using Context Clues

One of the biggest challenges for readers in high school and beyond is handling new or difficult words and concepts. A strategy that will help you sharpen your word-attack skills and improve your overall reading ability is using context clues. (The *context* of a word is its environment, or the words that surround it.) The chart that follows lists six types of context clues. Look them over. Then use them the next time you run across an unfamiliar word or idea.

441 ## Types of Context Clues

1. Clues supplied through **synonyms:**

Carol is fond of using **trite**, worn-out expressions in her writing. Her favorite is "You can lead a horse to water, but you can't make him drink."

2. Clues contained in **comparisons and contrasts:**

As the trial continued, the defendant's guilt became more and more obvious. With even the slightest bit of new evidence against him, there would be no chance of **acquittal**.

3. Clues contained in a **definition or description:**

Peggy is a **transcriptionist**, a person who makes a written copy of a recorded message.

4. Clues that appear in a **series:**

The **dulcimer**, fiddle, and banjo are all popular among the Appalachian Mountain people.

5. Clues provided by the **tone and setting:**

The streets filled instantly with **bellicose** protesters who pushed and shoved their way through the frantic bystanders. The scene was no longer peaceful and calm as the marchers had promised it would be.

6. Clues derived from **cause and effect:**

Since nobody came to the first voluntary work session, attendance for the second one is **mandatory** for all the members.

442 Direct and Indirect Clues

Context clues are made up of synonyms, definitions, descriptions, and several other kinds of specific information helpful to understanding the meaning of a passage or a particular word. In addition, clues can help strengthen and deepen the meaning of words you already know. Context clues can help explain how something works, where or when an event takes place, what the purpose or significance of an action is, and on and on.

Some context clues are not so direct as the six types listed on the previous page. They might be examples, results, or general statements rather than direct definitions or descriptions. Still, indirect clues can be very helpful. The more clues you find, the closer you can get to the specific meaning of a word and—more importantly—to the overall meaning of the passage itself.

 Context clues do not always appear immediately before or after the word you are studying. In a lengthy piece of writing, the clues might appear several paragraphs later (or earlier). Be aware of all clues—whenever they appear.

443 Now You Try It

See how well you can apply context clues. Look carefully at the bold-faced words in the passage below taken from Jack London's *Call of the Wild.* Then look for direct and indirect context clues to help you understand the meaning of those words. In addition to the clues available in this single paragraph, any reader of this novel would have the advantage of having read the first 46 pages. Taken together, there is a good chance the reader could figure out the meaning of at least some of the boldfaced words. See how your efficiency improves now that you understand more about context clues.

They made Sixty Miles, which is a fifty-mile run, on the first day; and the second day saw them booming up the Yukon well on their way to Pelly. But such splendid running was achieved not without great trouble and **vexation** on the part of Francois. The **insidious** revolt led by Buck had destroyed the **solidarity** of the team. It no longer was as one dog leaping in the traces. The encouragement Buck gave the rebels led them into all kinds of petty **misdemeanors**. No more was Spitz a leader greatly to be feared. The old awe departed, and they grew equal to challenging his authority. Pike robbed him of half a fish one night and gulped it down under the protection of Buck. Another night Dub and Joe fought Spitz and made him forego the punishment they deserved. And even Billee, the good-natured, was less good-natured, and whined not half so **placatingly** as in former days. Buck never came near Spitz without snarling and bristling **menacingly**. In fact, his conduct approached that of a bully, and he was given to swaggering up and down before Spitz's very nose. @

444 Reading a Poem

A poet once said that "a poem should not mean, but be." That may sound a bit odd at first, but if you think about it, it just might point you in the right direction when it comes to reading a poem. Maybe thinking about what a poem "is" and what it "does" might be a better way to approach a poem than regarding it as a puzzle or riddle to be solved for some concealed "meaning."

It might also help to remember that poems don't jump fully formed into a poet's mind. Poems (at least most of them) are created gradually. A poet may work on a poem for days or weeks before it is "complete." Just as the creation of a poem comes through gradual change and growth, the reading of a poem should also be viewed as a process. You shouldn't expect to grasp everything a poem has to offer in one reading, especially if the poem is lengthy or complex. Below are some strategies to help get you started in the process.

First Reading

- Read the poem all the way through at your normal reading speed.
- Try to gain an overall impression of the poem. (Don't stop to analyze individual lines or sections.)
- Respond by jotting down your immediate reaction to the entire poem. (Basically, this reaction will be your thoughts or first feelings.)

Second Reading

- Read the poem again—out loud, if possible. (Pay attention to the "sound effects" of the poem—both of individual words and overall.)
- Read slowly and carefully—word by word, syllable by syllable—observing the punctuation, spacing, and special treatment of words and syllables.
- Note examples of sound devices in the poem—alliteration, assonance, rhyme, etc. (This will help you understand the proper phrasing and rhythm of the poem.)
- Try to guess what the poem is saying or where the poem is going.

Third Reading

- Try to identify the type of poem you're reading. (Does this poem follow the usual pattern of that particular type? If not, why not?)
- Determine the literal sense of the poem. (What is the poem about? What does the poem seem to say about its subject?)
- Look carefully for figurative devices in the poem. (How do these devices—metaphors, similes, personification, symbols, etc.—support the literal level of the poem?)

Putting It All Together

- Give the poem as many additional readings as necessary.
- Do a 10-minute free writing. Write down everything you can about the poem. (Relate what you've read to what you know or have experienced.)

445 Reading a Novel

Reading a novel as a class assignment is different from reading a novel for your own enjoyment. This doesn't mean you won't enjoy your reading. In fact, you may find that you get more out of the experience because you are putting more into it. With practice, you will find that you can apply the same kind of concentration to all the books you read. These suggestions should help:

1. **Be certain you understand the reading "schedule"**; if your teacher sets certain "due dates" for portions of the reading, write them down.

2. **Make your own "due dates" for assignments.** If your teacher has assigned a novel with the statement "This is due in three weeks," just use common sense: read one-third of the novel each week.

3. **Find a good place to read:** somewhere that's quiet and away from distractions. But don't get too comfortable! Choose a straight-backed chair (not an easy chair), preferably at a desk or table, with a good light. Keep pens and pencils at hand so that you can take notes as you read.

4. **Look over your questions.** If your teacher has provided you with a list of questions to consider as you read, look them over before you begin your assignment. This will give you an idea of the things you should be looking for as you read. Then, read! Go straight through the assignment without stopping to look anything up or to write out any answers.

5. **Think about what you've read** after you've finished a fair portion, and ask yourself if you could summarize what you've understood so far. If you can, great! If you can't, you've read too far without concentrating sufficiently. Pause for a moment to refresh your brain (not too long!) and continue reading. If you find yourself becoming more and more confused, put a light pencil question mark next to whatever you don't understand. You can always go back later and work on it. Your first priority should be to get to the end of the assignment.

INSIDE info

If the assignment seems fairly long, you can divide it up into smaller chunks and deal with one piece at a time.

6. **Take a break.** Once you've made it to the end of the assignment, get away for a few minutes. Then go back to your chair, sit down, and read (or skim) the material again. Now is the time to look up words you don't know, work out the answers to any questions you may have had in the initial reading, and make connections between characters, plot developments, etc. (If you have assigned questions, take time to answer them.)

7. **Ask yourself questions.** As you do your final "reading," keep your mind alert by asking yourself questions like these: "What's going on here?" "Who are these characters?" "Why are they behaving this way?" Keeping a reading log is a good way to keep track of your questions. The whole point is to concentrate and get involved with your reading.

"Words are one of our chief means of adjusting to all the situations of life. The better control we have over words, the more successful our adjustment is likely to be."

—Bergen Evans

Improving Vocabulary Skills

Increasing your vocabulary—the words you understand and use comfortably—will improve your reading, writing, and speaking skills. As your vocabulary grows, your reading rate and comprehension level will naturally grow, too. Here are a few tips for adding words to your working vocabulary.

446 "Picking Up" a Vocabulary

Using context clues can certainly help you to figure out the meanings of new words as you read. Often, you can use context clues to "pick up" new words in everyday life, too. Try this: listen for unfamiliar words on television and the radio as well as in classrooms and conversations. Examine the lyrics of popular songs for unfamiliar words, too. Figure out their meanings by using context clues contained in the phrases and sentences surrounding the unfamiliar words. (See 440-441.)

447 Using a Dictionary

If you're unsure whether or not the context clues have led you to the correct definition of a certain word, check a dictionary. Read over (and think about) all of the definitions listed for that word, not just the one you need at the moment. By knowing all of its meanings, you'll deepen your understanding of the word.

Once you're sure that you understand what the word means, use it in your own writing and speaking. Using a word makes it your word. You'll remember what it means only if you practice using it.

448 Using Word Parts

Another extremely useful tool for building your reading vocabulary is the ability to chop unfamiliar words into pieces so that you can examine each part of the word, namely the *prefix, suffix,* and *root.* To do this chopping, you need to know how each part works. Here are some examples.

449 Prefixes

A **prefix** is a word part that is added to the beginning of a base word:

Base Word	Prefix	New Word
typical	a	atypical

The prefix *a* means "not." Knowing this meaning will help you understand and remember that *atypical* means "not typical."

450 Suffixes

A **suffix** is a word part that is added to the ending of a base word:

Base Word	Suffix	New Word
assist	ant	assistant

The suffix *ant* means "the performers or agent of a task." Knowing this meaning will help you remember that *assistant* means "someone who assists."

451 Roots

A **root** is a base upon which a word is built:

Root Word	Meaning	Word
bibl	*"book"*	bibliography
graph	*"write"*	

Knowing that the root *bibl* means "book" and *graph* means "write" will help you to remember that *bibliography* means "a written list of books."

452 A Study Plan

You already know and use many common prefixes, suffixes, and roots every day. To increase your speaking and writing vocabulary, study the meanings of those prefixes, suffixes, and roots that are not familiar to you. The following pages contain nearly 500 of them! Scan down one of the pages until you come to a word part that is "new." Learn its meanings and at least one of the sample words listed.

the **bottom** line

By learning two or three new word parts a day (and a word that each is used in), you will soon become an expert. For example, by learning that *hydro* means "water," you have a good start at adding all these words to your vocabulary: *hydrogen, hydrofoil, hydroid, hydrolysis, hydrometer, hydronaut, hydrophobia, hydroplane,* and *hydrosphere.*

453 Prefixes

Prefixes are those "word parts" that come *before* the root word (pre = before). Depending upon its meaning, a prefix changes the intent, or sense, of the base word. As a skilled reader, you will want to know the meanings of the most common prefixes and then watch for them when you read.

a, an [not, without] amoral (without a sense of moral responsibility), atypical, atom (not cutable), apathy (without feeling), anesthesia (without sensation)

ab, abs, a [from, away] abnormal, abduct, absent, avert (turn away)

acro [high] acropolis (high city), acrobat, acronym, acrophobia (fear of height)

ambi, amb [both, around] ambidextrous (skilled with both hands), ambiguous, amble

amphi [both] amphibious (living on both land and water), amphitheater

ante [before] antedate, anteroom, antebellum, antecedent (happening before)

anti, ant [against] anticommunist, antidote, anticlimax, antacid

be [on, away] bedeck, belabor, bequest, bestow, beloved

bene, bon [well] benefit, benefactor, benevolent, benediction, bonanza, bonus

bi, bis, bin [both, double, twice] bicycle, biweekly, bilateral, biscuit, binoculars

by [side, close, near] bypass, bystander, by-product, bylaw, byline

cata [down, against] catalog, catapult, catastrophe, cataclysm

cerebro [brain] cerebral, cerebrum, cerebellum

circum, circ [around] circumference, circumnavigate, circumspect, circular

co, con, col, come [together, with] co-pilot, conspire, collect, compose

coni [dust] coniosis (disease that comes from inhaling dust)

contra, counter [against] controversy, contradict, counterpart

de [from, down] demote, depress, degrade, deject, deprive

deca [ten] decade, decathlon, decapod (ten feet)

di [two, twice] divide, dilemma, dilute, dioxide, dipole, ditto

dia [through, between] diameter, diagonal, diagram, dialogue (speech between people)

dis, dif [apart, away, reverse] dismiss, distort, distinguish, diffuse

dys [badly, ill] dyspepsia (digesting badly), dystrophy, dysentery

em, en [in, into] embrace, enslave

epi [upon] epidermis (upon the skin, outer layer of skin), epitaph, epithet

eu [well] eulogize (speak well of, praise), euphony, eugenics

ex, e, ec, ef [out] expel (drive out), ex-mayor, exorcism, eject, eccentric (out of the center position), efflux

extra, extro [beyond, outside] extraordinary (beyond the ordinary), extracurricular, extrovert

for [away or off] forswear (to renounce an oath)

fore [before in time] forecast, foretell (to tell beforehand), foreshadow

hemi, demi, semi [half] hemisphere, demitasse, semicircle (half of a circle)

hex [six] hexameter, hexagon

homo [man] Homo sapiens, homicide (killing man)

hyper [over, above] hypersensitive (overly sensitive), hyperactive

hypo [under] hypodermic (under the skin), hypothesis

il, ir, in, im [not] illegal, irregular, incorrect, immoral

in, il, im [into] inject, inside, illuminate, illustrate, impose, implant, imprison

infra [beneath] infrared

inter [between] intercollegiate, interfere, intervene, interrupt (break between)

intra [within] intramural, intravenous (within the veins)

intro [into, inward] introduce, introvert (turn inward)

macro [large, excessive] macrodent (having large teeth), macrocosm

mal [badly, poorly] maladjusted, malnutrition, malfunction, malady

meta [beyond, after, with] metaphor, metamorphosis, metaphysical

mis [incorrect, bad] misuse, misprint

miso [hate] misanthrope, misogynist

454

mono [one] monoplane, monotone, monochrome, monocle

multi [many] multiply, multiform

neo [new] neopaganism, neoclassic, neologism, neophyte

non [not] nontaxable (not taxed), nontoxic, nonexistent, nonsense

ob, of, op, oc [toward, against] obstruct, offend, oppose, occur

oct [eight] octagon, octameter, octave, octopus

paleo [ancient] paleoanthropology (pertaining to ancient man), paleontology (study of ancient life-forms)

para [beside, almost] parasite (one who eats beside or at the table of another), paraphrase, paramedic, parallel, parody

penta [five] pentagon (figure or building having five angles or sides), pentameter, pentathlon

per [throughout, completely] pervert (completely turn wrong, corrupt), perfect, perceive, permanent, persuade

peri [around] perimeter (measurement around an area), periphery, periscope, pericardium, period

poly [many] polygon (figure having many angles or sides), polygamy, polyglot, polychrome

post [after] postpone, postwar, postscript, posterity

pre [before] prewar, preview, precede, prevent, premonition

pro [forward, in favor of] project (throw forward), progress, promote, prohibition

pseudo [false] pseudonym (false or assumed name), pseudo, pseudopodia

quad [four] quadruple (four times as much), quadriplegic, quadratic, quadrant

quint [five] quintuplet, quintuple, quintet, quintile

re [back, again] reclaim, revive, revoke, rejuvenate, retard, reject, return

retro [backward] retrospective (looking backward), retroactive, retrorocket

se [aside] seduce (lead aside), secede, secrete, segregate

self [by oneself] self-determination, self-employed, self-service, selfish

sesqui [one and a half] sesquicentennial (one and one-half centuries)

sex, sest [six] sexagenarian (sixty years old), sexennial, sextant, sextuplet, sestet

sub [under] submerge (put under), submarine, subhuman, substitute, subsoil

suf, sug, sup, sus [from under] suffer, sufficient, suggest, support, suspect, suspend

super, supr [above, over, more] supervise, superman, supernatural, supreme

syn, sym, sys, syl [with, together] synthesis, synchronize (time together), synonym, sympathy, symphony, system, syllable

trans, tra [across, beyond] transoceanic, transmit (send across), transfusion, tradition

tri [three] tricycle, triangle, tripod, tristate

ultra [beyond, exceedingly] ultramodern, ultraviolet, ultraconservative

un [not, release] unfair, unnatural, unbutton

under [beneath] underground, underlying

uni [one] unicycle, uniform, unify, universe, unique (one of a kind)

vice [in place of] vice president, vice admiral, viceroy

455

Numerical Prefixes

Prefix	Symbol	Multiples and Submultiples	Equivalent	Prefix	Symbol	Multiples and Submultiples	Equivalent
tera	T	10^{12}	trillionfold	centi	c	10^{-2}	hundredth part
giga	G	10^{9}	billionfold	milli	m	10^{-3}	thousandth part
mega	M	10^{6}	millionfold	micro	u	10^{-6}	millionth part
kilo	k	10^{3}	thousandfold	nano	n	10^{-9}	billionth part
hecto	h	10^{2}	hundredfold	pico	p	10^{-12}	trillionth part
deka	da	10	tenfold	femto	f	10^{-15}	quadrillionth part
deci	d	10^{-1}	tenth part	atto	a	10^{-18}	quintillionth part

456 **Suffixes**

Suffixes come at the end of a word. Very often a suffix will tell you what kind of word it is part of (noun, adverb, adjective, etc.). For example, words ending in *-dom* are usually nouns, *-ly* words are usually adverbs, and words ending in *-able* are usually adjectives. Study these suffixes carefully.

able, ible [able, can do] capable, agreeable, edible, visible (can be seen)

ade [result of action] blockade (the result of a blocking action), lemonade

age [act of, state of, collection of] salvage (act of saving), storage, forage

al [relating to] sensual, gradual, manual, natural (relating to nature)

algia [pain] neuralgia (nerve pain)

an, ian [native of, relating to] African, Canadian (native of Canada)

ance, ancy [action, process, state] assistance, allowance, defiance, truancy

ant [performing, agent] assistant, servant

ary, ery, ory [relating to, quality, place where] dictionary, bravery, dormitory

ate [cause, make] liquidate, segregate (cause a group to be set aside)

cian [having a certain skill or art] musician, beautician, magician, physician

cule, ling [very small] molecule, ridicule, duckling (very small duck), sapling

cy [action, function] hesitancy, prophecy, normalcy (function in a normal way)

dom [quality, realm, office] freedom, kingdom, wisdom (quality of being wise)

ee [one who receives the action] employee, nominee (one who is nominated), refugee

en [made of, make] silken, frozen, oaken (made of oak), wooden, lighten

ence, ency [action, state of, quality] difference, conference, urgency

er, or [one who, that which] baker, miller, teacher, racer, amplifier, doctor

escent [in the process of] adolescent (in the process of becoming an adult), obsolescent, convalescent

ese [a native of, the language of] Japanese, Vietnamese

esis, osis [action, process, condition] genesis, hypnosis (a sleeplike condition), neurosis, osmosis

ess [female] actress, goddess, lioness

et, ette [a small one, group] midget, octet, baronet, majorette

fic [making, causing] scientific, specific

ful [full of] frightful, careful, helpful

fy [make] fortify (make strong), simplify, amplify

hood [order, condition, quality] manhood, womanhood, brotherhood

ic [nature of, like] metallic (of the nature of metal), heroic, poetic, acidic

ice [condition, state, quality] justice, malice

id, ide [a thing connected with or belonging to] fluid, fluoride

ile [relating to, suited for, capable of] juvenile, senile (related to being old), missile

ine [nature of] feminine, genuine, medicine

ion, sion, tion [act of, state of, result of] contagion, aversion, infection (state of being infected)

ish [origin, nature, resembling] foolish, Irish, clownish (resembling a clown)

ism [system, manner, condition, characteristic] alcoholism, heroism, Communism

ist [one who, that which] artist, dentist, violinist

ite [nature of, quality of, mineral product] Israelite, dynamite, graphite, sulfite

ity, ty [state of, quality] captivity, clarity

ive [causing, making] abusive (causing abuse), exhaustive

ize [make] emphasize, publicize, idolize

less [without] baseless, careless (without care), artless, fearless, helpless

ly [like, manner of] carelessly, fearlessly, hopelessly, shamelessly

ment [act of, state of, result] contentment, amendment (state of amending)

ness [state of] carelessness, restlessness

oid [resembling] asteroid, spheroid, tabloid, anthropoid

ology [study, science, theory] biology, anthropology, geology, neurology

ous [full of, having] gracious, nervous, spacious, vivacious (full of life)

ship [office, state, quality, skill] friendship, authorship, dictatorship

some [like, apt, tending to] lonesome, threesome, gruesome

tude [state of, condition of] gratitude, aptitude, multitude (condition of being many)

ure [state of, act, process, rank] culture, literature, rupture (state of being broken)

ward [in the direction of] eastward, forward, backward

y [inclined to, tend to] cheery, crafty, faulty

457 Roots

Knowing the root of a difficult word can go a long way toward helping you figure out its meaning—even without a dictionary. Because improving your vocabulary is so important to success in all your classes (and beyond school), learning the following roots will be very valuable.

acer, acid, acri [bitter, sour, sharp] acerbic, acidity (sourness), acrid, acrimony

acu [sharp] acute, acupuncture

ag, agi, ig, act [do, move, go] agent (doer), agenda (things to do), agitate, navigate (move by sea), ambiguous (going both ways), action

ali, allo, alter [other] alias (a person's other name), alibi, alien (from another place), alloy, alter (change to another form)

alt(us) [high, deep] altimeter (a device for measuring heights), altitude

am, amor [love, liking] amiable, amorous, enamored

anni, annu, enni [year] anniversary, annually (yearly), centennial (occurring once in 100 years)

anthrop [man] anthropology (study of mankind), misanthrope (hater of mankind), philanthropy (love of mankind)

anti(co) [old] antique, antiquated, antiquity

arch [chief, first, rule] archangel (chief angel), architect (chief worker), archaic (first; very early), monarchy (rule by one person), matriarchy (rule by the mother)

aster, astr [star] aster (star flower), asterisk, asteroid, astronomy (star law), astronaut (star traveler; space traveler)

aud, aus [hear, listen] audible (can be heard), auditorium, audio, audition, auditory, audience, ausculate

aug, auc [increase] augur, augment (add to; increase), auction

auto, aut [self] automobile (self-moving vehicle), autograph (self-writing), automatic (self-acting), autobiography, author

belli [war] rebellion, belligerent (warlike or hostile)

bibl [book] Bible, bibliography (writing, list of books), bibliomania (craze for books), bibliophile (book lover)

bio [life] biology (study of life), biography, biopsy (cutting living tissue for examination)

brev [short] abbreviate, brevity, brief

cad, cas [to fall] cadaver, cadence, caducous (falling off), cascade

calor [heat] calorie (a unit of heat), calorify (to make hot), caloric

cap, cip, cept [take] capable, capacity, capture, reciprocate, accept, except, forceps

capit, capt [head] decapitate (to remove the head from), capital, captain, caption

carn [flesh] carnivorous (flesh-eating), incarnate, reincarnation

caus, caut [burn, heat] caustic, cauldron, cauterize (to make hot; burn)

cause, cuse, cus [cause, motive] because, excuse (to attempt to remove the blame or cause), accusation

ced, ceed, cede, cess [move, yield, go, surrender] procedure, proceed (move forward), cede (yield), concede, intercede, precede, recede, secede (move aside from), success

centri [center] concentric, centrifugal, centripetal, eccentric (out of center)

chrom [color] chrome, chromosome (color body in genetics), Kodachrome, monochrome (one color), polychrome

chron [time] chronological (in order of time), chronometer (time-measured), chronicle (record of events in time), synchronize (make time with, set time together)

cide, cise [cut down, kill] suicide (self-killer), homicide (man, human killer), pesticide (pest killer), germicide (germ killer), insecticide, decide (cut off uncertainty), precise (cut exactly right), incision, scissors

cit [to call, start] incite, citation, cite

civ [citizen] civic (relating to a citizen), civil, civilian, civilization

clam, claim [cry out] exclamation, clamor, proclamation, reclamation, acclaim

clud, clus, claus [shut] include (to take in), conclude, recluse (one who shuts himself away from others), claustrophobia (abnormal fear of being shut up, confined)

cognosc, gnosi [know] recognize (to know again), incognito (not known), prognosis (forward knowing), diagnosis

cord, cor, cardi [heart] cordial (hearty, heartfelt), concord, discord, courage, encourage (put heart into), discourage (take heart out of), core, coronary, cardiac

corp [body] corporation (a legal body), corpse, corpulent

cosm [universe, world] cosmos (the universe), cosmic, cosmopolitan (world citizen), cosmonaut, microcosm, macrocosm

458 **crat, cracy** [rule, strength] democratic, autocracy

crea [create] creature (anything created), recreation, creation, creator

cred [believe] creed (statement of beliefs), credo (a creed), credence (belief), credit (belief, trust), credulous (believing too readily, easily deceived), incredible

cresc, cret, crease, cru [rise, grow] crescendo (growing in loudness or intensity), concrete (grown together, solidified), increase, decrease, accrue (to grow)

crit [separate, choose] critical, criterion (that which is used in choosing), hypocrite

cur, curs [run] current (running or flowing), concurrent, concur (run together, agree), incur (run into), recur, occur, courier, precursor (forerunner), cursive

cura [care] curator, curative, manicure (caring for the hands)

cycl, cyclo [wheel, circular] Cyclops (a mythical giant with one eye in the middle of his forehead), unicycle, bicycle, cyclone (a wind blowing circularly; a tornado)

deca [ten] decade, decalogue, decathlon

dem [people] democracy (people-rule), demography (vital statistics of the people: deaths, births, etc.), epidemic (on or among the people)

dent, dont [tooth] dental (relating to teeth), denture, dentifrice, orthodontist

derm [skin] hypodermic (injected under the skin), dermatology (skin study), epidermis (outer layer of skin), taxidermy (arranging skin; mounting animals)

dict [say, speak] diction (how one speaks, what one says), dictionary, dictate, dictator, dictaphone, dictatorial, edict, predict, verdict, contradict, benediction

doc [teach] indoctrinate, document, doctrine

domin [master] dominate, dominion, predominant, domain

don [give] donate, condone

dorm [sleep] dormant, dormitory

dox [opinion, praise] doxy (belief, creed, or opinion), orthodox (having the correct, commonly accepted opinion), heterodox (differing opinion), paradox (contradictory)

drome [run, step] syndrome (run together; symptoms) hippodrome (a place where horses run)

duc, duct [lead] induce (lead into, persuade), seduce (lead aside), produce, reduce, aquaduct (water leader or channel), viaduct, conduct, conduit, subdue, duke

dura [hard, lasting] durable, duration, endurance

dynam [power] dynamo (power producer), dynamic, dynamite, hydrodynamics

endo [within] endoral (within the mouth), endocardial (within the heart), endoskeletal

equi [equal] equinox, equilibrium

erg [work] energy, erg (unit of work), allergy, ergophobia (morbid fear of work), ergometer, ergograph

fac, fact, fic, fect [do, make] factory (place where workmen make goods of various kinds), fact (a thing done), manufacture, amplification, confection

fall, fals [deceive] fallacy, falsify

fer [bear, carry] ferry (carry by water), coniferous (bearing cones, as a pine tree), fertile (bearing richly), defer, infer, refer

fid, fide, feder [faith, trust] confidante, Fido, fidelity, confident, infidelity, infidel, federal, confederacy

fila, fili [thread] filament (a threadlike conductor heated by electrical current), filter, filet, filibuster, filigree

fin [end, ended, finished] final, finite, finish, confine, fine, refine, define, finale

fix [fix] fix, fixation (the state of being attached), fixture, affix, prefix, suffix

flex, flect [bend] flex (bend), reflex (bending back), flexible, flexor (muscle for bending), inflexibility, reflect, deflect

flu, fluc, fluv [flowing] influence (to flow in), fluid, flue, flush, fluently, fluctuate (to wave in an unsteady motion)

form [form, shape] form, uniform, conform, deform, reform, perform, formative, formation, formal, formula

fort, forc [strong] fort, fortress (a strong point), fortify (make strong), forte (one's strong point), fortitude

fract, frag [break] fracture (a break), infraction, fragile (easy to break), fraction (result of breaking a whole into equal parts), refract (to break or bend)

gam [marriage] bigamy (two marriages), monogamy, polygamy (many spouses or marriages)

gastr(o) [stomach] gastric, gastronomic, gastritis (inflammation of the stomach)

gen [birth, race, produce] genesis (birth, beginning), genetics (study of heredity), eugenics (well-born), genealogy (lineage by race, stock), generate, genetic

geo [earth] geometry (earth measurement), geography (earth-writing), geocentric (earth-centered), geology

germ [vital part] germination (to grow), germ (seed; living substance, as the germ of an idea), germane

gest [carry, bear] congest (bear together, clog), congestive (causing clogging), gestation

459 **gloss, glot** [tongue] glossary, polyglot (many tongues), epiglottis

glu, glo [lump, bond, glue] glue, agglutinate (make to hold in a bond), conglomerate (bond together)

grad, gress [step, go] grade (step, degree), gradual (step-by-step), graduate (make all the steps, finish a course), graduated (in steps or degrees), progress

graph, gram [write, written] graph, graphic (written; vivid), autograph (self-writing; signature), photography (light-writing), graphite (carbon used for writing), phonograph (sound-writing), bibliography, telegram, diagram

grat [pleasing] congratulate (express pleasure over success), gratuity (mark of favor, a tip), grateful, ingrate (not thankful)

grav [heavy, weighty] grave, gravity, aggravate, gravitate

greg [herd, group, crowd] gregarian (belonging to a herd), congregation (a group functioning together), segregate (tending to group aside or apart)

helio [sun] heliograph (an instrument for using the sun's rays to send signals), heliotrope (a plant that turns to the sun)

hema, hemo [blood] hemorrhage (an outpouring or flowing of blood), hemoglobin, hemophilia

here, hes [stick] adhere, cohere, cohesion

hetero [different] heterogeneous (different in birth), heterosexual (with interest in the opposite sex)

homo [same] homogeneous (of same birth or kind), homonyn (word with same name or pronunciation as another), homogenize

hum, human [earth, ground, man] humus, exhume (to take out of the ground), humane (compassion for other humans)

hydr, hydra, hydro [water] dehydrate (take water out of; dry), hydrant (water faucet), hydraulic, hydraulics, hydrogen, hydrophobia (fear of water)

hypn [sleep] hypnosis, Hypnos (god of sleep), hypnotherapy (treatment of disease by hypnosis)

ignis [fire] ignite, igneous, ignition

ject [throw] deject, inject, project (throw forward), eject, object

join, junct [join] adjoining, enjoin (to lay an order upon; to command), juncture, conjunction, injunction, conjunction

juven [young] juvenile, rejuvenate (to make young again)

lau, lav, lot, lut [wash] launder, lavatory, lotion, ablution (a washing away), dilute (to make a liquid thinner and weaker)

leg [law] legal (lawful; according to law), legislate (to enact a law), legislature, legitimize (make legal)

levi [light] alleviate (lighten a load), levitate, levity (light conversation; humor)

liber, liver [free] liberty (freedom), liberal, liberalize (to make more free), deliverance

liter [letters] literary (concerned with books and writing), literature, literal, alliteration, obliterate

460 **loc, loco** [place] locality, locale, location, allocate (to assign; to place), relocate (to put back into place), locomotion (act of moving from place to place)

log, logo, ology [word, study, speech] catalog, prologue, dialogue, logogram (a symbol representing a word), zoology (animal study), psychology (mind study)

loqu, locut [talk, speak] eloquent (speaking well and forcefully), loquacious (talkative), colloquial (talking together; conversational or informal), soliloquy, locution

luc, lum, lus, lun [light] translucent (letting light come through), lumen (a unit of light), luminary (a heavenly body; someone who shines in his profession), luster (sparkle; shine), Luna (the moon goddess)

magn [great] magnify (make great, enlarge), magnificent, magnanimous (great of mind or spirit), magnate, magnitude, magnum

man [hand] manual, manage, manufacture, manacle, manicure, manifest, maneuver, emancipate

mand [command] mandatory (commanded), remand (order back), mandate

mania [madness] mania (insanity; craze), monomania (mania on one idea), kleptomania, pyromania (insane tendency to set fires), maniac

mar, mari, mer [sea, pool] marine (a sailor serving on shipboard), marsh (wetland, swamp), maritime (relating to the sea and navigation), mermaid (fabled marine creature, half fish)

matri [mother] matrimony (state of wedlock), maternal (relating to the mother), matriarchate (rulership of women), matron

medi [half, middle, between, halfway] mediate (come between, intervene), medieval (pertaining to the Middle Ages), mediterranean (lying between lands), mediocre, medium

mega [great] megaphone (great sound), megalopolis (great city; an extensive urban area including a number of cities), megacycle (a million cycles), megaton

mem [remember] memo (a note; a reminder), commemoration (the act of remembering by a memorial or ceremony), memento, memoir, memorable

meter [measure] meter (a metric measure), voltameter (instrument to measure volts), barometer, thermometer

micro [small] microscope, microfilm, microcard, microwave, micrometer (device for measuring small distances), omicron, micron (a millionth of a meter), microbe (small living thing)

migra [wander] migrate (to wander), emigrant (one who leaves a country), immigrate (to come into the land to settle)

mit, miss [send] emit (send out, give off), remit (send back, as money due), submit, admit, commit, permit, transmit (send across), omit, intermittent (sending between, at intervals), mission, missile

mob, mot, mov [move] mobile (capable of moving), motionless (without motion), motor, emotional (moved strongly by feelings), motivate, promotion, demote, movement

mon [warn, remind] monument (a reminder or memorial of a person or event), admonish (warn), monitor, premonition (forewarning)

mor, mort [mortal, death] mortal (causing death or destined for death), immortal (not subject to death), mortality (rate of death), mortician (one who prepares the dead for burial), mortuary (place for the dead, a morgue)

morph [form] amorphous (with no form, shapeless), metamorphosis (a change of form, as a caterpillar into a butterfly), morphology

multi [many, much] multifold (folded many times), multilinguist (one who speaks many languages), multiped (an organism with many feet), multiply

nat, nasc [to be born, to spring forth] innate (inborn), natal, native, nativity, renascence (a rebirth; a revival)

neur [nerve] neuritis (inflammation of a nerve), neuropathic (having a nerve disease), neurologist (one who practices neurology), neural, neurosis, neurotic

nom [law, order] autonomy (self-law, self-government), astronomy, gastronomy (stomach law; art of good eating), economy

nomen, nomin [name] nomenclature, nominate (name someone for an office)

nov [new] novel (new; strange; not formerly known), renovate (to make like new again), novice, nova, innovate

nox, noc [night] nocturnal, equinox (equal nights), noctilucent (shining by night)

numer [number] numeral (a figure expressing a number), numeration (act of counting), enumerate (count out, one by one), innumerable

omni [all, every] omnipotent (all-powerful), omniscient (all-knowing), omnipresent (present everywhere), omnivorous

onym [name] anonymous (without name), pseudonym (false name), antonym (against name; word of opposite meaning), synonym

prefixes—suffixes—roots

oper [work] operate (to labor; function), cooperate (work together), opus (a musical composition or work)

ortho [straight, correct] orthodox (of the correct or accepted opinion), orthodontist (tooth straightener), orthopedic (originally pertaining to straightening a child), unorthodox

pac [peace] pacifist (one for peace only; opposed to war), pacify (make peace, quiet), Pacific ocean (peaceful ocean)

pan [all] Pan-American, panacea (cure-all), pandemonium (place of all the demons; wild disorder), pantheon (place of all the gods in mythology)

pater, patr [father] paternity (fatherhood, responsibility, etc.), patriarch (head of the tribe, family), patriot, patron (a wealthy person who supports as would a father)

path, pathy [feeling, suffering] pathos (feeling of pity, sorrow), sympathy, antipathy (against feeling), apathy (without feeling), empathy (feeling or identifying with another), telepathy (far feeling; thought transference)

ped, pod [foot] pedal (lever for a foot), impede (get the feet in a trap, hinder), pedestal (foot or base of a statue), pedestrian (foot traveler), centipede, tripod (three-footed support), podiatry (care of the feet), antipodes (opposite feet)

pedo [child] orthopedic, pedagogue (child leader; teacher), pediatrics (medical care of children)

pel, puls [drive, urge] compel, dispel, expel, repel, propel, pulse, impulse, pulsate, compulsory, expulsion, repulsive

pend, pens, pond [hang, weigh] pendant (a hanging object), pendulum, suspend, appendage, pensive (weighing thought)

phil [love] philosophy (love of wisdom), philanthropy, philharmonic, bibliophile, Philadelphia (city of brotherly love)

phobia [fear] claustrophobia (fear of closed spaces), acrophobia (fear of high places), aquaphobia (fear of water)

phon [sound] phonograph, phonetic (pertaining to sound), symphony (sounds with or together)

photo [light] photograph (light-writing), photoelectric, photogenic (artistically suitable for being photographed), photosynthesis (action of light on chlorophyll to make carbohydrates)

plac, plais [please] placid (calm, peaceful), placebo, placate, complacent (pleased)

plu, plur, plus [more] plural (more than one), pluralist (a person who holds more than one office), plus (indicating that something more is to be added)

pneuma, pneumon [breath] pneumatic (pertaining to air, wind, or other gases), pneumonia (disease of the lungs)

pod (see ped)

poli [city] metropolis (mother city; main city), police, politics, Indianapolis, megalopolis, Acropolis (high city, upper part of Athens)

pon, pos, pound [place, put] postpone (put afterward), component, opponent (one put against), proponent, expose, impose, deposit, posture (how one places oneself), position, expound, impound

pop [people] population (the number of people in an area), populous (full of people), popular

port [carry] porter (one who carries), portable, transport (carry across), report, export, import, support, transportation

portion [part, share] portion (a part; a share, as a portion of pie), proportion (the relation of one share to others)

prehend [seize] apprehend (seize a criminal), comprehend (seize with the mind), comprehensive (seizing much, extensive)

prim, prime [first] primacy (state of being first in rank), prima donna (the first lady of opera), primitive (from the earliest or first time), primary, primal, primeval

proto [first] prototype (the first model made), protocol, protagonist, protozoan

psych [mind, soul] psyche (soul, mind), psychiatry (healing of the mind), psychology, psychosis (serious mental disorder), psychotherapy (mind treatment), psychic

punct [point, dot] punctual (being exactly on time), punctuation, puncture, acupuncture

reg, recti [straighten] regiment, regular, rectify (make straight), correct, direct, rectangle

ri, ridi, risi [laughter] deride (mock; jeer at), ridicule (laughter at the expense of another; mockery), ridiculous, derision

rog, roga [ask] prerogative (privilege; asking before), interrogation (questioning; the act of questioning), derogatory

rupt [break] rupture (break), interrupt (break into), abrupt (broken off), disrupt (break apart), erupt (break out), incorruptible (unable to be broken down)

sacr, sanc, secr [sacred] sacred, sacrosanct, sanction, consecrate, desecrate

salv, salu [safe, healthy] salvation (act of being saved), salvage, salutation

sat, satis [enough] satient (giving pleasure, satisfying), saturate, satisfy (to give pleasure to; to give as much as is needed)

462

sci [know] science (knowledge), conscious (knowing, aware), omniscient (knowing everything)

scope [see, watch] telescope, microscope, kaleidoscope (instrument for seeing beautiful forms), periscope, stethoscope

scrib, script [write] scribe (a writer), scribble, inscribe, describe, subscribe, prescribe, manuscript (written by hand)

sed, sess, sid [sit] sediment (that which sits or settles out of a liquid), session (a sitting), obsession (an idea that sits stubbornly in the mind), possess, preside (sit before), president, reside, subside

sen [old] senior, senator, senile (old; showing the weakness of old age)

sent, sens [feel] sentiment (feeling), consent, resent, dissent, sentimental (having strong feeling or emotion), sense, sensation, sensitive, sensory, dissension

sequ, secu, sue [follow] sequence (following of one thing after another), sequel, consequence, subsequent, prosecute, consecutive (following in order), second (following first), ensue, pursue

serv [save, serve] servant, service, subservient, servitude, preserve, conserve, reservation, deserve, conservation, observe

sign, signi [sign, mark, seal] signal (a gesture or sign to call attention), signature (the mark of a person written in his own handwriting), design, insignia (distinguishing marks), significant

simil, simul [like, resembling] similar (resembling in many respects), assimilate (to make similar to), simile, simulate (pretend; put on an act to make a certain impression)

sist, sta, stit [stand] assist (to stand by with help), persist (stand firmly; unyielding; continue), circumstance, stamina (power to withstand, to endure), status (standing), state, static, stable, stationary, substitute (to stand in for another)

solus [alone] solo, soliloquy, solitaire, solitude

solv, solu [loosen] solvent (a loosener, a dissolver), solve, absolve (loosen from, free from), resolve, soluble, solution, resolution, resolute, dissolute (loosened morally)

somnus [sleep] insomnia (not being able to sleep), somnambulist (a sleepwalker)

soph [wise] sophomore (wise fool), philosophy (love of wisdom), sophisticated (world wise)

spec, spect, spic [look] specimen (an example to look at, study), specific, spectator (one who looks), spectacle, aspect, speculate, inspect, respect, prospect, retrospective (looking backward), introspective, expect, conspicuous

sphere [ball, sphere] sphere (a planet; a ball), stratosphere (the upper portion of the atmosphere), hemisphere (half of the earth), spheroid

spir [breath] spirit (breath), conspire (breathe together; plot), inspire (breathe into), aspire (breathe toward), expire (breathe out; die), perspire, respiration

string, strict [draw tight] stringent (drawn tight; rigid), strict, restrict, constrict (draw tightly together), boa constrictor (snake that constricts its prey)

stru, struct [build] construe (build in the mind, interpret), structure, construct, instruct, obstruct, destruction, destroy

sume, sump [take, use, waste] consume (to use up), assume (to take; to use), sump pump (a pump that takes up water), presumption (to take or use before knowing all the facts)

tact, tang, tag, tig, ting [touch] tactile, contact (touch), intact (untouched, uninjured), intangible (not able to be touched), tangible, contagious (able to transmit disease by touching), contiguous, contingency

tele [far] telephone (far sound), telegraph (far writing), telegram, telescope (far look), television (far seeing), telephoto (far photography), telecast, telepathy (far feeling)

tempo [time] tempo (rate of speed), temporary, extemporaneously, contemporary (those who live at the same time), pro tem (for the time being)

ten, tin, tain [hold] tenacious (holding fast), tenant, tenure, untenable, detention, retentive, content, pertinent, continent, obstinate, contain, abstain, pertain, detain

tend, tent, tens [stretch, strain] tendency (a stretching; leaning), extend, intend, contend, pretend, superintend, tender, extent, tension (a stretching, strain), pretense

terra [earth] terrain, terrarium, territory, terrestrial

test [to bear witness] testament (a will; bearing witness to someone's wishes), detest, attest (bear witness to), testimony

the, theo [God, a god] monotheism (belief in one god), polytheism (belief in many gods), atheism, theology

therm [heat] thermometer, therm (heat unit), thermal, thermos bottle, thermostat, hypothermia (subnormal temperature)

thesis, thet [place, put] antithesis (place against), hypothesis (place under), synthesis (put together), epithet

prefixes–suffixes–roots

463

tom [cut] atom (not cutable; smallest particle of matter), appendectomy (cutting out an appendix), tonsillectomy, dichotomy (cutting in two; a division), anatomy (cutting, dissecting to study structure)

tort, tors [twist] torture (twisting to inflict pain), retort (twist back, reply sharply), extort (twist out), distort (twist out of shape), contort, torsion (act of twisting, as a torsion bar)

tox [poison] toxic (poisonous), intoxicate, antitoxin

tract, tra [draw, pull] tractor, attract, subtract, tractable (can be handled), abstract (to draw away), subtrahend (the number to be drawn away from another)

trib [pay, bestow] tribute (to pay honor to), contribute (to give money to a cause), attribute, retribution, tributary

turbo [disturb] turbulent, disturb, turbid, turmoil

typ [print] type, prototype (first print; model), typical, typography, typewriter, typology (study of types, symbols), typify

ultima [last] ultimate, ultimatum (the final or last offer that can be made)

uni [one] unicorn (a legendary creature with one horn), unify (make into one), university, unanimous, universal

vac [empty] vacate (to make empty), vacuum (a space entirely devoid of matter), evacuate (to remove troops or people), vacation, vacant

vale, vali, valu [strength, worth] equivalent (of equal worth), valiant, validity (truth; legal strength), evaluate (find out the value), value, valor (value; worth)

ven, vent [come] convene (come together, assemble), intervene (come between), venue, convenient, avenue, circumvent (come or go around), invent, convent, venture, event, advent, prevent

ver, veri [true] very, aver (say to be true, affirm), verdict, verity (truth), verify (show to be true), verisimilitude

vert, vers [turn] avert (turn away), divert (turn aside, amuse), invert (turn over), introvert (turn inward), convertible, reverse (turn back), controversy (a turning against; a dispute), versatile (turning easily from one skill to another)

vic, vicis [change, substitute] vicarious, vicar, vicissitude

vict, vinc [conquer] victor (conqueror, winner), evict (conquer out, expel), convict (prove guilty), convince (conquer mentally, persuade), invincible (not able to be conquered)

vid, vis [see] video (television), evident, provide, providence, visible, revise, supervise (oversee), vista, visit, vision

viv, vita, vivi [alive, life] revive (make live again), survive (live beyond, outlive), vivid, vivacious (full of life), vitality, vivisection (surgery on a living animal)

voc [call] vocation (a calling), avocation (occupation not one's calling), convocation (a calling together), invocation (calling in), evoke, provoke, revoke, advocate, provocative, vocal

vol [will] malevolent, benevolent (one of goodwill), volunteer, volition

volcan, vulcan [fire] volcano (a mountain erupting fiery lava), volcanize (to undergo volcanic heat), Vulcan (Roman god of fire)

volvo [turn about, roll] revolve, voluble (easily turned about or around), voluminous (winding), convolution (a twisting or coiling)

vor [eat greedily] voracious, carnivorous (flesh-eating), herbivorous (plant-eating), omnivorous (eating everything), devour (eat greedily)

zo [animal] zoo (short for zoological garden), zoology (study of animal life), zoomorphism (attributing animal form to God), zodiac (circle of animal constellations), protozoa (one-celled animals)

464

The Human Body

capit	head	gastro	stomach	osteo	bone
card	heart	glos	tongue	ped	foot
corp	body	hema	blood	pneuma	breathe
dent	tooth	man	hand	psych	mind
derm	skin	neur	nerve	spir	breath

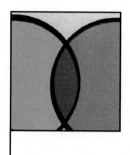

Reading Charts and Graphs

465   Graphs, tables, diagrams, and maps all have something in common: They're all "information pictures." They express information in pictures (visually) rather than in words (verbally). They may contain a few words, but most of the information is expressed visually. These information pictures, often called charts, can help us in a variety of ways.

466 The Big Picture

A good chart can make complex information easy to understand. It can show in one picture what it might take hundreds of words to tell. Remember the old saying: *One picture is worth a thousand words.* That's why a chart makes a big impression: It doesn't just tell; it shows.

So when will I ever have to read a chart, you ask? Well, imagine trying to find your favorite store in the new mega-mall without that handy map with the arrow that says You Are Here! Or let's say you finally get your driver's license. You hop into your new 4-wheel drive machine for a fun-run to Mexico, but you don't have a map. How many times would you have to stop and ask for directions? Or imagine trying to put together a new bookcase without diagrams that show each step—and one that shows what the finished product should look like!

what's ahead?

The basic job of all charts is the same: to show you how things relate to one another. Different kinds of charts show different kinds of relationships. This section will help you understand and read the most common kinds of charts: graphs (line, pie, bar, stacked bar), tables (schedule, distance), diagrams (picture, line), and maps (weather).

467 Graphs

Graphs are popular forms of charts because they are easy to create and read. Graphs are pictures of information, not pictures of things you can see. The most common kinds are line graphs, pie graphs, and bar graphs.

468 Line Graph ● A line graph shows how things change over time. It starts with an L-shaped grid. The horizontal line of the grid stands for passing time (seconds, minutes, years, centuries, etc.). The vertical line of the grid shows the subject of the graph. The graph below is a double-line graph showing the number of deaths due to firearms compared to deaths due to motor vehicles.

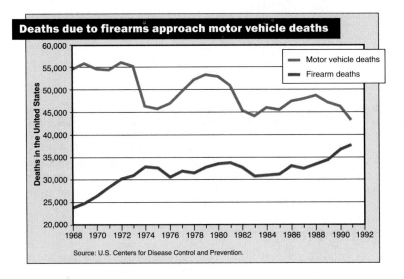

Deaths due to firearms approach motor vehicle deaths

Source: U.S. Centers for Disease Control and Prevention.

469 Pie Graph ● A pie graph shows proportions and how each proportion, or part, relates to the other parts as well as to the whole "pie." In the sample pie graphs below, you can see at a glance how electric power is produced, both in the United States and in the world.

Electric Power Sources Worldwide

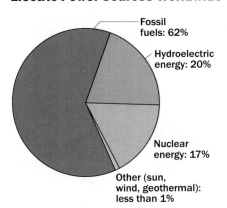

Fossil fuels: 62%
Hydroelectric energy: 20%
Nuclear energy: 17%
Other (sun, wind, geothermal): less than 1%

U.S. Electric Power Sources

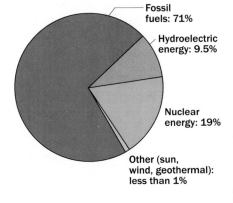

Fossil fuels: 71%
Hydroelectric energy: 9.5%
Nuclear energy: 19%
Other (sun, wind, geothermal): less than 1%

470 **Bar Graph** ● A bar graph uses bars (sometimes called columns) to stand for the subjects of the graph. Unlike line graphs, they do not show how things change over time. A bar graph is like a snapshot that shows how things compare at one point in time.

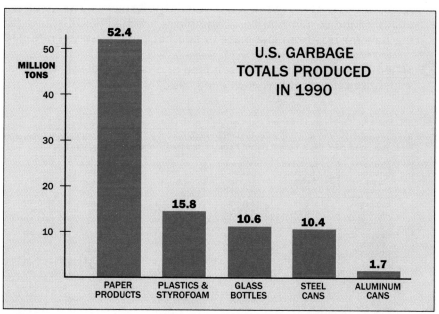

471 **Stacked Bar Graph** ● A stacked bar graph is a special kind of bar graph that gives more detailed information than a regular bar graph. Besides comparing the bars, it compares parts within the bars themselves.

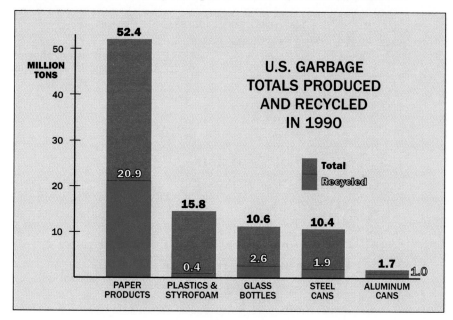

472 Tables

Tables organize words and numbers so that it's easy to see how they relate to one another. Most tables have rows (going across) and columns (going down). Rows contain one kind of information, while columns contain another kind of information. Examples are schedules, distance tables (showing how far it is from one place to another), and conversion tables.

473 Schedule ● One of the most common and useful tables is the schedule. Read schedules *very* carefully; each one is a little bit different.

MILWAUKEE TO O'HARE BUS SCHEDULE

Reading schedules: Find the time you want to arrive at O'Hare in the right-hand column. Read straight across to your left on the same line to your pickup point; that is the time you will leave from that point. (Disregard all other times.)

Lv **Marquette University Library** 1415 Wisconsin Ave.	Lv **Milwaukee** Amtrak Station 5th & St. Paul Sts.	Lv **Milwaukee** United Limo 4960 S. 13th St.	Lv **Mitchell Field Airport**	Lv **Racine Jct.** Colony Inn I-94 & Hwy. 20	Lv **Kenosha Jct.** Burger King I-94 & Hwy. 50	Ar **O'Hare Airport** Upper Level - All Airlines
4:30 AM	4:45 AM	5:00 AM	5:10 AM	5:25 AM	5:40 AM	6:40 AM
5:45 AM	6:00 AM	6:15 AM	6:25 AM	6:40 AM	6:55 AM	7:55 AM
8:30 AM	8:45 AM	9:00 AM	9:10 AM	9:25 AM	9:40 AM	10:40 AM
11:05 AM	11:20 AM	11:35 AM	11:45 AM	Noon	12:15 PM	1:15 PM
12:30 PM	12:45 PM	1:00 PM	1:10 PM	1:25 PM	1:40 PM	2:40 PM
1:45 PM	2:00 PM	2:15 PM	2:25 PM	2:40 PM	2:55 PM	3:55 PM
4:15 PM	4:30 PM	4:45 PM	4:55 PM	5:10 PM	5:25 PM	6:25 PM
7:15 PM	7:30 PM	7:45 PM	7:55 PM	8:10 PM	8:25 PM	9:25 PM

474 Distance Table ● Another common kind of table is a distance or mileage table. To read a distance table, find the place you're starting from and the place you're going to. Then, find the place where the row and the column meet—that's how far it is from one place to the other.

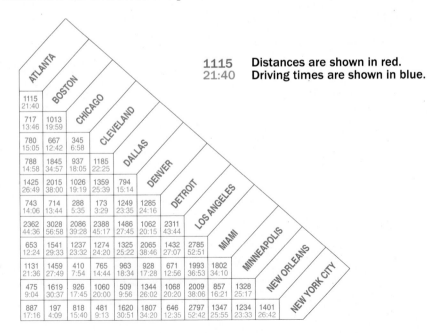

1115
21:40

Distances are shown in red.
Driving times are shown in blue.

475 Diagrams

A diagram is a drawing designed to show how something is constructed, how its parts relate to one another, or how it works. The two most common types of diagrams are the picture diagram and the line diagram.

476 Picture Diagram ● A picture diagram is just that—a picture or drawing of the subject being discussed. Often, some parts are left out of the diagram to emphasize the parts the writer wants to show. For example, the diagram below shows the parts of the brain responsible for certain functions.

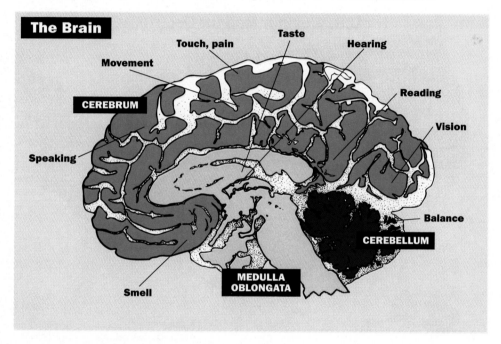

477 Line Diagram ● Another type of diagram is a line diagram. A line diagram uses lines, symbols, and words to help you picture things that you can't actually see. The diagram below helps you to see how nuclear fission works in a nuclear reactor.

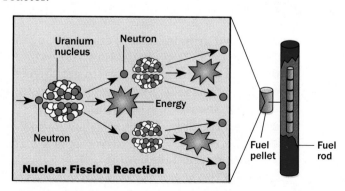

478 Maps

Of all the "information pictures" we use on a regular basis, maps are probably the most useful. Road maps, mall maps, political maps (see 802-818), and weather maps all play an important part in our daily lives.

479 **Weather Map** • Weather maps are typical of all maps—they contain an outline of a country, state, or city. But they also contain a language of words, lines, and symbols that are unique to weather maps. Study the one below, using the key as your guide.

U.S. Weather Map for Dec. 10, 1994

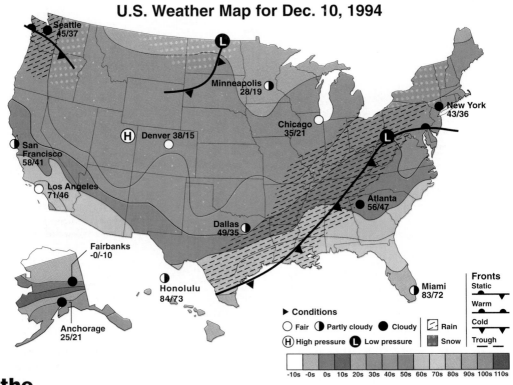

the bottom line

Although no two graphs, tables, diagrams, or maps are exactly alike, there are some general guidelines you can use:

- Read the title or caption (to get the big picture).
- Read the labels or column headings (to get a better idea of what the chart is covering).
- Read the data (to get specific information).
- Read the paragraph above or below the chart (to provide background information).
- Read the key or footnotes (to clarify the details).

"A good listener is not only popular everywhere, but after awhile he gets to know something."

—Wilson Mizner

Improving Classroom Skills

480   Doing well in school means doing well individually and as a group member. To do well individually, you need to manage your time and complete assignments—among other things. To be successful in the classroom, you need to listen to others, observe, respond, ask questions, and so on. In other words, you need to be actively involved. You can't just sit back and let it happen. Learning requires a strong personal commitment.

481 The Learning Team

Inside the classroom, you're part of a learning team. Your teacher heads up the learning team and introduces the concepts to be studied. Your texts—books, videos, discussions—provide you with the information you need to understand the concepts. Your job is to supply the enthusiasm and effort. To do this, you need to pay close attention to all of what is going on. You need to listen carefully, participate in class discussions, and generally be a good team member. Without that personal commitment, no teacher or textbook can make learning happen.

what's ahead? This section of your handbook emphasizes those skills you need to be successful in the classroom, both as an individual and as a member of a group:

Listening Strategies

Note-Taking Skills

Group Skills

Managing Your Time

Completing Assignments

482 Listening Strategies

Someone (probably an English teacher) once observed that there must be a reason for two ears and only one mouth. Yet, even with two ears, listening is one of the least understood and underpracticed learning skills. Why? First, listening is not something we do automatically. We all hear, but most of us have to be reminded to listen. Second, listening requires us to concentrate on what another person is saying, and concentrating is work.

Lots of things can interfere with listening. Some distractions, like outside noise or the temperature of a room, may be out of your control. But other things, like staying up too late, overeating before a class, or daydreaming, are within your power to change. Poor listening habits are hard to change. What you need is a positive attitude and some guidelines. Here are the guidelines.

Guidelines for Improving Listening Skills

Listen actively . . .

- ◉ **Challenge yourself.** To get the most out of what you are hearing, you must motivate yourself to listen well.

- ◉ **Prepare to listen.** Think ahead about what you may hear and keep an open mind about the speaker and the topic.

- ◉ **Keep a goal in mind.** Take time to figure out why you are listening (to gather information for tests, to learn how to . . . , etc.).

- ◉ **Listen carefully.** Listen not only to what the speaker is actually saying but also to what the speaker is implying (saying between the lines). The speaker's voice, facial expression, and gestures can tell you what's really important.

- ◉ **Listen for directions;** then follow them carefully. Listen to the speaker's transitions or signal words for the next major point or idea.

- ◉ **Listen for the speaker's plan.** Often a speaker uses a specific sequence in presenting main points. Try to figure out what that plan is.

- ◉ **Separate fact from opinion;** listen for bias or opinion disguised as fact. (See "Fallacies of Thinking" in the index.)

- ◉ **Listen actively;** avoid daydreaming and other poor listening habits.

Think and write . . .

- ◉ **Think about what is being said.** How does this material relate to you? What can you associate it with in your personal life to help you remember? How might you use the information in the future?

- ◉ **Listen with pen in hand.** Take notes and ask questions.

- ◉ **Put the speaker's statements into your own words.** Identify each main point and draw conclusions about the importance of each.

- ◉ **Summarize the entire talk in one or two sentences.** This summary can serve as the final "test" of whether or not you understood what was said.

483 Note-Taking Skills

Note taking is a skill worth knowing. It is an active approach to learning —or at least it should be. Taking notes gets you personally involved in the learning process and helps you focus on the most important information. It changes information you would otherwise have only heard about into ideas you have actively worked with and thought about. This active involvement will make learning and remembering easier and more meaningful. (See the guidelines on the following page and "Writing to Learn," 494.)

 Memory experts tell us that the average person forgets at least half of what he or she learns within 24 hours of learning it. These same experts also tell us that the more personally involved we are in the learning process, the more likely we are to understand and remember what we have learned.

484 Using a Note-Taking Guide

One way to make note taking more active is to use your reading assignment notes as a classroom note-taking guide. Follow your notes during the classroom review of the reading material. As you do, you will be prepared to answer any questions your teacher may ask and take additional notes as well. Simply follow along and jot down anything that helps to clarify or adds to your understanding of the material. By combining your reading and classroom notes in this way, you should end up with one set of well-organized study notes.

Note • Use the left two-thirds of your paper for reading notes; use the right one-third for class notes.

Chapter 10: "The Disinherited"	
Outlined Reading Assignment	Class Notes
I. The Clash of Cultures	Early settlers had
A. Pioneer attitude toward	few problems; as
Native Americans	more trappers and
1. Inferior beings	hunters moved in,
a. Lacked "civilization"	conflicts started.
b. Lacked "religion"	Native Americans
2. Easily exploited	labeled "pagans";
a. Swindled in trades	anti-Indian
b. Set against other tribes	sentiment followed.
3. No property rights	
a. A "squatter" on govt. land	Some argued that
b. False promises	because Native
c. Forced off land	Americans did not
B. Native American reaction	have the right to
to treatment	vote, they could not
1. Attitudes	own property.
a. Disappointment	
b. Bitterness	
2. Resulting Action	
a. Move	Serious clashing of
1) To designated areas	the cultures
2) Further west	followed.
b. Defend	
c. Attack	

485 Guidelines for Improving Note-Taking Skills

Be attentive . . .

- **Listen for any special instructions,** rules, or guidelines your classroom teacher may have regarding notebooks and note taking.
- **Write the date and the topic** of each lecture or discussion at the top of each page of notes.
- **Write your notes in ink,** and as neatly as time will allow; leave space in the margin for working with your notes later.
- **Begin taking notes immediately.** Don't wait for something new or earth-shaking before you write your first note.
- **Relate the material** you are noting to something in your life by writing a brief personal observation or reminder.

Be concise . . .

- **Summarize the main ideas,** listing only the important details. *Remember,* taking good notes does *not* mean writing down everything.
- **Write as concisely as you can.** Write your notes in phrases and thoughts rather than complete sentences.
- **Use abbreviations,** acronyms, and symbols (U.S., avg., in., ea., lb, vs., @, #, $, %, &, +, =, w/o, etc.).
- **Develop your own shorthand method.** (Example: CW for Civil War)
- **Draw simple illustrations,** charts, or diagrams in your notes whenever they will make a point clearer.

Be organized . . .

- **Write a title or heading** for each new topic covered in your notes.
- **Listen for transitions** or signal words to help you organize your notes. Number all related ideas and information presented in time sequence.
- **Ask questions** when you don't understand.
- **Use a special system of marking** your notes to emphasize important information (underline, star, check, indent).
- **Label** or indicate in some way **information** that is related by cause and effect, by comparison or contrast, or by any other special way.

Be smart . . .

- **Always copy down** (or summarize) what the teacher puts on the board or an overhead projector.
- **Circle those words or ideas** that you will need to ask about or look up later.
- **Don't let your notes sit** until it is time to review for a test. Read over the notes you have taken within 24 hours and recopy, highlight, or summarize as necessary. (Use a colored marker to highlight key notes.)
- **Share your note-taking techniques,** abbreviations, or special markings with others; then learn from what they share with you.

486 Group Skills

Groups happen everywhere—on the job, in the neighborhood, in the classroom. Without them, a lot of important work would never get done. Some groups form spontaneously (sandbagging ahead of a surging river). Some groups are assigned (your writing group). And some groups stay together for years (the Grateful Dead).

Maybe you think that you're not the group type; but like it or not, you're already a member of several groups. And you'll be a member of many more in the years to come. As a member of any group, you have a responsibility to yourself and to all the other members. So it's a good idea to learn about group skills. The following guidelines will help:

487 Understanding Groups

Forming • The key to being a successful group member is to put forth the effort it takes to form a good working group. This doesn't happen overnight, so it's important to understand the stages groups often go through:

Stage 1 - During the first stage, there is a general lack of understanding about the purpose and direction of a group as each individual tries to find his or her place in the group.

Stage 2 - This stage is often a period of discouragement, conflict, and frustration; members find it difficult to adjust to their places and roles in the group.

Stage 3 - The group begins to develop harmony, first by avoiding conflict. Members begin to listen and observe, and soon they feel more comfortable in the group.

Stage 4 - Finally, the group develops a sense of purpose and begins working together. Members start to respond to and clarify one another's ideas. Leaders emerge and efficient work begins.

488 Becoming Actively Involved

Listening • It's important to have a positive attitude toward your work. It will help you listen carefully and accurately whenever someone in the group speaks. It will also help you focus on the words and ideas rather than on the person. As you listen, ask yourself how this person's ideas relate to the group's work and goals. And it's always a good idea to take notes as you listen, saving your questions for discussion after the speaker stops. Keep interruptions to an absolute minimum; if you must add something to what a speaker is saying, do so courteously.

Proposing • The longer you work with your classroom group, the more comfortable you'll feel about proposing a useful idea or opinion. If what you propose builds on the ideas of someone else in the group, make that known by giving credit to the person and showing consideration for others' feelings. Use "I statements" whenever you propose ideas, to let the listeners know that you accept responsibility for what you say.

Challenging • From time to time, you may want to challenge the ideas of others in your group. Make sure, however, that you challenge the ideas, not the person. Instead of saying, "I disagree with you," say, "I don't agree with your first point because . . . " Make sure that you have a good reason for challenging an idea, and make sure that you base your challenge on accurate information.

Questioning • Asking good questions is perhaps the most important of all group skills. It not only keeps group members thinking about what they say, but it also keeps them focused on the task at hand. When you ask a question, try to connect it to an idea that was previously made. You might, for example, say, "Josie, it seems to me that your point about . . . is very important, but I'm not sure I understand . . . " When a group gets bogged down or loses direction, a good question can help members refocus. You might, for example, say, "Tom, what do you think about Josie's last observation?"

Deciding • It's also important to understand how groups make decisions and that decisions made by a group can be as democratic (or autocratic) as its members like. Here are some of the ways decisions are reached by groups:

Leader's Choice	The group leader makes decisions based on choices offered by group members.
Consensus	Group members continue to discuss choices until everyone in the group agrees.
Research	Members can agree to get additional information before making a decision.
Gallup Poll	A vote or survey taken of individuals outside the group is conducted to guide the group's decision.
Expert's Choice	An expert is invited to make the decision for the group.
Voting	Group members vote on a list of choices.

489 Managing Your Time

One of the biggest obstacles to succeeding is failing to plan. Managing your time requires planning. Almost everyone has failed to plan at one time or another and suffered the consequences. When we don't manage our time, it manages us. You may find the following suggestions helpful:

Making Progress

1. **Turn big jobs into smaller ones.** Successful people will tell you that they often divide up their big jobs into smaller, more manageable steps. Spreading a project over a reasonable period of time will reduce the pressure that comes from letting everything go until the last minute. Tackle your tasks as they need to be done, and develop a process for working through the big jobs. Then follow your plan.

2. **Keep a weekly schedule.** If you haven't started a personal calendar to keep track of appointments and assignments, what are you waiting for? You'll have your day at a glance and be twice as likely to keep the appointments you write down. Design your planner to meet your needs; the more personalized you make it, the more likely you'll use it.

   Note • Planners and calendars can be purchased at a reasonable cost if that seems easier than making your own. Also, most word-processing programs have built-in note pads and calendars.

3. **Make lists.** Making a daily list of things to do may strike you as overdoing it at first, but you'll soon change your mind. You'll also rest easier at night, knowing that you've got the next day covered.

4. **Plan your study time.** Good advice, but most of us seldom take it. Good planning means having everything you need where you need it. Schedule your study time as early in the day as you can, take short breaks, keep snacks to a minimum, interact with the page by asking questions (out loud, if no one objects), and summarize what you've learned before turning out the light.

5. **Stay flexible.** Plans do change and new things can pop up daily. Be realistic, willing to change those events that can be changed and exercising patience for those that cannot. You'll save yourself lots of wear and tear if you remain flexible and upbeat.

490 Completing Assignments

In and out of school, assignments are a fact of life. They won't go away. Depending on your situation, you may find assignments more difficult these days, and study time more scarce. The following guidelines should help you organize your thinking about completing assignments.

Planning Ahead

1. It's your responsibility to know exactly what the assignments are, when they're due, and what you must do to complete them successfully.

2. Decide how much time you'll need to complete each assignment. Then set aside the time in your daily schedule. Each time you organize this way, you'll find that you've gotten better at estimating the time you need.

3. Decide where you'll study (library, study hall, home) and work in relative quiet. Be comfortable while you study, but don't get too comfortable.

4. Gather your materials ahead of time. Unless you really like going out at 11 p.m. to buy a pencil at the convenience store, keep a supply of the things you'll need. Check to make sure you have the right books and reference materials, paper, pencils, pens, etc., before you settle in to study.

If you are having trouble getting started on your assignments, try doing them at the same time and place each day. This will help you control the urge to wait until you are "in the mood" before starting. Also, try to avoid doing your assignments when you are overly hungry or tired.

Getting It Done

◉ **Go over your directions carefully.** Look up any words you are unsure of and write down the meaning of each.

◉ **Keep track of those things you need to check with your teachers about.** All learning is an attempt to solve a problem. You must clearly understand the problem before you can solve it.

◉ **Use a study strategy.** Using the KWL or SQ3R method will help you complete the reading and studying parts of your assignments.

◉ **Make a deal with yourself.** Plan a break after you have completed major segments of the assignment, and then stick to it. Hold all calls, and don't answer the door. (Families are good at running interference.)

◉ **Show pride in your work.** Complete your assignments, and turn them in on time. Welcome the suggestions your teachers may give for future improvement.

"The man who has ceased to learn ought not to be allowed to wander around loose."

—**M. M. Coady**

Writing to Learn

491   *Writing about a particular topic to understand and remember it better.* That's what writing to learn is all about. It's really that simple. When you write to learn, you are *not* trying to show how well you can write or how much you already know about a topic; you are writing to learn more.

492 The Process

    When you write to learn, you write freely and naturally. Usually, writing-to-learn activities are short, spontaneous, and exploratory. They are almost never graded or corrected for mechanical errors. Some educators now believe that writing to learn is the best way to truly learn anything, from math to music. This chapter will provide you with a variety of writing-to-learn strategies that you can try out in the weeks and months ahead.

493 The Benefits

    Once you commit yourself to writing to learn, you will benefit in a number of important ways:

Interest ·················┐ You will develop a greater interest in learning.

Understanding ·····┐ You will improve your ability to understand and remember.

Thinking ············┐ You will become a better, more creative thinker.

Attitude ········┐ You will approach your classes with a more positive attitude.

Learning ·················┐ You will gain a lifelong learning technique.

494 Learning Logs

One of the most effective writing-to-learn activities is the learning log. A learning log gets you actively involved in your course work and gives you the opportunity to explore important ideas freely and naturally. This free flow of ideas and questions promotes true learning. (Use the guidelines for journal writing, 279, to get you started in your learning log; then refer to the list that follows for writing ideas.)

Guidelines for Keeping a Learning Log

1. **Write about class activities**—anything from a class discussion to an important exam. Consider what was valuable, confusing, interesting, humorous, etc.

2. **Discuss new ideas and concepts.** Consider how this new information relates to what you already know.

3. **Evaluate your progress in a particular class.** Consider your strengths, your weaknesses, your relationship with members of the class.

4. **Discuss your course work with a particular audience:** a young child, a foreign exchange student, an object, an alien from another planet.

5. **Question what you are learning.** Dig deeply into the importance of the concepts presented. (One way to do this is to write a dialogue.)

6. **Confront ideas that confuse you.** Back them into a corner until you finally understand the problem.

7. **Plan the activities for tomorrow's class.** Perhaps you could develop a mock essay test. Answer one or more of the questions yourself.

8. **Keep a record of your thoughts and feelings.** This can be especially helpful during an extended lab or research assignment.

9. **Start a glossary** of important and interesting vocabulary words. Use these words in your log entries.

10. **Argue for or against a topic.** The topic can be anything that comes up in a discussion, in your reading, or in a lecture.

Personal Note Taking

If you plan to use your learning log for reading notes, here's one method you can use. Begin by dividing a page in half. On the left side, record notes from your reading, and on the right side, record comments or questions. This written dialogue makes note taking more meaningful and provides you with material for class discussion. Here are examples of the types of comments you can make:

- ◉ a reaction to a particular point which you strongly agree or disagree with
- ◉ a question about a concept that confuses you
- ◉ a paraphrase of a difficult or complex idea
- ◉ a discussion of the importance or significance of the material
- ◉ a comment on what memory or feeling a particular idea brings to mind

495 Writing-to-Learn Activities

Writing to learn is essentially exploratory writing. What form your writing takes is strictly up to you, as long as it encourages thinking and learning. You might be perfectly satisfied with free, nonstop writing; others might find clustering or listing meaningful. Still others might enjoy a variety of writing activities similar to those that follow.

Admit slips ● Admit slips are brief pieces of writing in which you "admit" something about what is being studied. An admit slip can be a summary of last night's reading, a question about class material, a request for the teacher to review a particular point, or anything else you may have on your mind. (Admit slips are turned in to the teacher.)

Bio-poems ● Writing bio-poems forces you to select precise language to fit the form. Bio-poems also encourage creative and other higher-level thinking. A bio-poem follows this pattern:

Line **1.** First name

Line **2.** Four traits that describe the character

Line **3.** Relative ("brother," "sister," "daughter," etc.) of _____

Line **4.** Lover of _____ (list three things or people)

Line **5.** Who feels _____ (three items)

Line **6.** Who needs _____ (three items)

Line **7.** Who fears _____ (three items)

Line **8.** Who gives _____ (three items)

Line **9.** Who would like to see _____ (three items)

Line **10.** Resident of _____

Line **11.** Last name

Note ● Even though this bio-poem is set up to describe a person or literary character, it can also be used to describe a complex term such as *inflation, photosynthesis,* etc.

496 **Debates** ● Try splitting your mind into two "persons." Have one side debate (disagree with) your thinking on a subject, and have the other side defend it. Keep the debate going as long as you can.

Dialogues ● In a dialogue, you create an imaginary conversation between yourself and a character (a historical figure, for example) or between two characters (from a story, for example). Dialogue can bring information to life, helping you to better understand a particular subject or historical period.

Dramatic scenarios ● In a dramatic scenario, you project yourself into a unit of study and develop a scenario (plot) that can be played out in writing. If the unit is World War II, for example, you may put yourself in President Truman's shoes the day before he decided to drop the first atomic bomb.

Exit slips ● Write a short piece at the end of class in which you summarize, evaluate, or question something about the day's lesson. Turn in your exit slip to your teacher before you leave the classroom.

First thoughts ● You can benefit greatly from writing your immediate impressions about a topic you are preparing to study. These writings will help you focus on the task at hand and prepare you for what's ahead.

How-to writing ● Write instructions or directions on how to perform a certain task. This will help you to clarify and remember the information.

Instant versions ● In an instant version of a paper or report, you pretend to compose a final draft long before you are ready. Writing instant versions can help you clarify ideas and find a focus. It also helps you discover how much you know (or don't know) about the subject.

Nutshelling ● Try writing down, in one sentence, the importance or relevance of something you've heard, seen, or read.

Picture outlines ● Instead of using a traditional outline format, organize your thoughts into a picture outline. For example, a lecture on the makeup and function of a particular organ might work well as a picture outline.

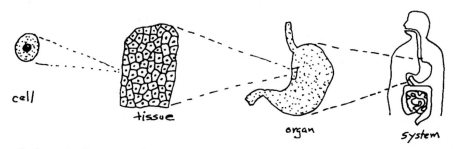

cell

tissue

organ

system

Predicting ● Stop at a key point in a lesson and write what you think will happen next. Predicting works especially well with lessons that have a strong cause and effect relationship.

497 **Pointed questions** ● Keep asking yourself *why* in your writing. Keep pressing the question until you can't push it any further.

Role-playing ● Imagine yourself in a different role (a reporter, a historical or fictional character, an animal, etc.) and write about a topic from that point of view.

Stop-n-write ● At any point in a reading assignment, stop and write. This allows you to evaluate your understanding of the topic and to reflect on what you've just read.

Summarizing ● An excellent way to learn about a subject is to summarize it in your own words, relating it to your own life whenever possible.

Textbook Summary

Cholesterol, a fatty substance found in human tissues, is primarily produced by the body. Some cholesterol enters the body as food. An important part of the membranes of every cell in the body, cholesterol is a building block in the production of bile acids (aid digestion) and hormones (chemical substances affecting many activities in the body). Though all cells can produce cholesterol, most is produced by liver cells. Special molecules called lipoproteins transport cholesterol from the liver throughout the body via the bloodstream. There are three types of lipoproteins: high-density lipoprotein (HDL), low-density lipoprotein (LDL), and very low-density lipoprotein (VLDL). Even though the body requires cholesterol, high levels of LDL- and VLDL-cholesterol (those high in saturated fats) have been linked to arteriosclerosis (hardening of the arteries) that results when fatty deposits that contain cholesterol collect on the inner walls of the blood vessels, narrowing them. This condition increases risk of stroke or heart attack.

Personal Summary

I remember hearing only bad things about cholesterol. I knew a man who had been on a low-cholesterol diet for many years. He still had high levels of "bad" cholesterol in his blood. Why does the body produce something that can cause such serious problems as heart attacks? Then I heard there's good cholesterol and that eating certain things can affect the production of the "good" cholesterol instead of the "bad." So why doesn't a diet low in LDL- and VLDL-cholesterol automatically mean only HDL or good cholesterol will be produced?

Unsent letters ● Write a letter to anyone (or anything) on a topic related to the subject being studied. Unsent letters allow you to personalize the subject matter and share those thoughts with another person—real or imagined.

take note For additional writing-to-learn activities, see Journal Writing, Free Writing, Clustering, Listing, and Imaginary Dialogue (017-018). Also see Structured Questions and Offbeat (Unstructured) Questions (022).

498 The Paraphrase

A paraphrase is a summary written in your own words. It states fully and clearly (in language of the simplest kind) the meaning of a piece of writing. Because it often includes your interpretation, a paraphrase can actually be longer than the original. Below you'll find some guidelines and a model for this type of writing to learn.

Guidelines for Writing a Paraphrase

1. **Skim** the entire selection.
2. **Read** the selection carefully, noting key words and ideas.
3. Try to **list** the main idea(s) of the selection without looking at it.
4. Now go back and **reread** each line.
5. **Summarize** each idea (line by line if necessary) in a clear statement.

Original:

Nothing Gold Can Stay

Nature's first green is gold,	(1)
Her hardest hue to hold.	(2)
Her early leaf's a flower;	(3)
But only so an hour.	(4)
Then leaf subsides to leaf,	(5)
So Eden sank to grief,	(6)
So dawn goes down to day.	(7)
Nothing gold can stay.	(8)

—Robert Frost

Paraphrase:

The first growth of spring is more gold in color than green.	(1)
But this golden shade of green doesn't last very long.	(2)
The first leaf is actually a blossom or flower,	(3)
but it remains for only a very short time.	(4)
Then the buds and blossoms give way to full, green leaves.	(5)
In the same way, the Garden of Eden was taken away;	(6)
and dawn's glow gives way to the harsher light of day.	(7)
Nothing in nature—especially those things most beautiful— lasts forever.	(8)

499 Writing a Summary

In the day-to-day process of learning, you'll often be asked to write summaries—in your own words—of something you've read. Summarizing is another of the many ways you can write and learn at the same time. Being able to write summaries can greatly increase your ability to understand and remember what you have read.

To write a good summary, you must first understand what you've read (or heard). This may require a second or even a third reading. Then you need to select the most important ideas and combine them into clear, concise sentences. In most cases your summary should be no more than one-third as long as the original. Follow the guidelines below and the model on the next page.

Guidelines for Writing a Summary

◉ **Skim** the selection first to get the overall meaning.

◉ **Read** the selection carefully, paying particular attention to key words and phrases. (Check the meaning of any words you're unsure of.)

◉ **List** the main ideas on your paper—without looking at the selection!

◉ **Review** the selection a final time so that you have the overall meaning clearly in mind as you begin to write.

◉ **Write** a summary of the major ideas, using your own words except for those "few" words in the original that cannot be changed. Keep the following points in mind as you write:

● Your opening (topic) sentence should be a clear statement of the main idea of the original selection.

● Stick to the essential information. Names, dates, times, places, and similar facts are usually essential; examples, descriptive details, and adjectives are usually not.

● Try to state each important idea in one clear sentence.

● Arrange your ideas into the most logical order.

● Use a concluding sentence that ties all of your points together and brings the summary to an effective end.

◉ **Check** your summary for accuracy and conciseness by asking yourself the following questions:

● Have I included all the main ideas?

● Have I cut or at least combined most of the descriptive details?

● Could another person get the main idea of the selection by simply reading my summary?

take note If you are summarizing material that is especially complicated or difficult, you may want to *personalize* your writing by relating it to things in your own life. (See Summarizing, 497.)

500 Student Model

The summary below is a good example of what you need to do when you condense scientific or textbook information. Notice that the opening sentence contains both a definition of the topic and a statement of the purpose or point of the summary. The writer goes on to list all the essential information and ends with a strong concluding sentence that brings the summary into final focus.

Original Text

"Acid rain" is precipitation with a high concentration of acids. The acids are produced by sulfur dioxide, nitrogen oxide, and other chemicals that are created by the burning of fossil fuels. Acid rain is known to have a gradual, destructive effect on plant and aquatic life.

The greatest harm from acid rain is caused by sulfur dioxide, a gas produced from coal. As coal is burned in large industrial and power plant boilers, the sulfur it contains is turned into sulfur dioxide. This invisible gas is funneled up tall smokestacks and released into the atmosphere some 350-600 feet above the ground. As a result, the effects of the gas are seldom felt immediately. Instead, the gas is carried by the wind for hundreds and sometimes thousands of miles before it floats back down to earth. For example, sulfur dioxide produced in Pennsylvania at noon on Monday may not show up again until early Tuesday when it settles into the lakes and soil of rural Wisconsin.

Adding to the problem is the good possibility that the sulfur dioxide has undergone a chemical change while in flight. By simply taking on another molecule of oxygen, the sulfur dioxide could be changed to sulfur trioxide. Sulfur trioxide, when mixed with water, creates sulfuric acid—a highly toxic acid. If the sulfur trioxide enters a lake or stream, the resulting acid can kill fish, algae, and plankton. This, in turn, can interrupt the reproductive cycle of other life-forms, causing a serious imbalance in nature. If the sulfuric acid enters the soil, it can work on metals such as aluminum and mercury and set them free to poison both the soil and water.

Damage from acid rain has been recorded throughout the world, from the Black Forest in Germany to the lakes in Sweden to the sugar maple groves in Ontario, Canada. The result is a growing concern among scientists and the general public about the increasing damage being done to the environment by acid rain.

Model Summary

"Acid rain," the term for precipitation that contains a high concentration of harmful chemicals, is gradually damaging our environment. The greatest harm from acid rain is caused by sulfur dioxide, a gas produced from the burning of coal. This gas, which is released into the atmosphere by industries using coal-fired boilers, is carried by the wind for hundreds of miles. By the time this gas has floated back to earth, it has often changed from sulfur dioxide to sulfur trioxide. Sulfur trioxide, when mixed with water, forms sulfuric acid—a highly toxic acid. This acid can kill both plant and aquatic life and upset the natural balance so important to the cycle of life.

"To treat your facts with imagination is one thing; to imagine your facts is another."

—John Burroughs

Taking Tests

501   The key to doing well on tests is being well prepared. This is true of any kind of test you have to take—essay, objective, or standardized. You must begin with a solid test-taking plan, so that you keep your wits about you and reduce "test anxiety."

Your plan should include a system for organizing the test material, reviewing it (perhaps with a partner), remembering it, and, finally, using it on the test itself. You need to review the important names, dates, places, and concepts, but more importantly, you need to think about how all of these facts and figures fit together—what they add up to. Having a good overall plan will keep you on track and give you the best possible test results.

Even though it is easier said than done, there are a number of steps you can take to improve your ability to do well on tests. Studying the guidelines and models in this chapter is a good first step.

what's ahead?

The following chapter provides a number of guidelines, tips, and models for you to follow as you begin working to improve your test-taking skills. Here are the topics covered:

Taking the Essay Test

Taking an Objective Test

Guidelines for Taking Tests

Taking a Standardized Test

502 Taking the Essay Test

One of the most common (and most challenging) tests in high school is the essay test. It's a test you'll be called on to do over and over again. And there are certain skills or strategies you should know if you hope to do well. Writing a good essay test answer is more than just writing—it's reading, thinking, planning, analyzing, judging, etc.

Too many students make the error of thinking the best way to answer an essay question is to write down everything and anything about the topic as fast as they can. Clearly, this is not the best way to approach an essay test. Your goal is to write well, not simply to fill as many pages as possible. You have to take time to think about the essay test question and to organize an appropriate answer. If you don't, you'll probably be disappointed in the results.

The poor results many students experience on essay tests do not necessarily stem from a lack of knowledge about the subject, but rather from a lack of basic skills needed to write a good answer.

503 Understanding the Question

The first step in correctly handling an essay test question is to read the question several times until you are sure you know what the teacher is asking. As you read, you must pay special attention to the **key words** found in every essay question. Your ability to understand and respond to these key words is a basic skill necessary to handling the essay question. For example, if you are asked to *contrast* two things on a test and you *classify* them instead, you have not given the teacher the information requested. Your score will obviously suffer.

Key Words

A list of key terms, along with a definition and an example of how each is used, can be found below and on the next two pages. Study these terms carefully. It is the first step to improving your essay test scores.

Classify: To **classify** is to place persons or things (especially animals and plants) together in a group because they are alike or similar. In science there is an order that all groups follow when it comes to classifying or categorizing: *phylum* (or *division*), *class, order, family, genus, species,* and *variety.*

Compare: To **compare** is to use examples to show how things are similar and different, with the greater emphasis on similarities.

> "Compare the British and American forms of government."

Contrast: To **contrast** is to use examples to show how things are different in one or more important ways.

> "Contrast the views of the North and South on the issue of states' rights."

504 **Define:** To **define** is to give a clear, concise definition or meaning for a term. Generally, to define consists of identifying the class to which a term belongs and telling how it differs from other things in that class. (See 546.)

> "Define what is meant by the term *filibuster*."

Describe: To **describe** is to give a written sketch or impression of the topic.

> "Describe Scout's appearance on the night of the Halloween party."

Diagram: To **diagram** is to explain with lines or pictures—a flowchart, a map, or some other graphic device. Generally, a good diagram will include labels that point out the important points or parts. (See 475-477.)

> "Diagram the levels of authority and responsibility of our town's government officials."

Discuss: To **discuss** is to talk about an issue from all sides. A discussion answer must be carefully organized so that you stay on track.

> "Discuss the long-range effects of the atomic bomb on the people of Hiroshima."

Evaluate: To **evaluate** is to make a value judgment, to give the pluses and minuses backed up with evidence (facts, figures, instances, etc.).

> "Evaluate the contributions of the automobile to the average American's overall standard of living."

Explain: To **explain** is to bring out into the open, to make clear, to analyze. This term is similar to *discuss* but places more emphasis on cause-effect relationships or step-by-step sequences. (See 506-508.)

> "Explain the immediate effects of the atomic bomb on Hiroshima."

Illustrate: To **illustrate** is to show by means of a picture, a diagram, or some other graphic aid. At times, however, you may use specific examples or instances to illustrate a law, rule, or principle.

> "Illustrate the relationship between the Senate and the House of Representatives."

Justify: To **justify** is to tell why a position or point of view is good or right. A justification should be mostly positive, meaning you stress the advantages over the disadvantages.

> "Justify the U.S.A.'s intervention in Cuban-Russian relations during Kennedy's administration."

List: To **list** is to itemize or write down a series of related words or ideas.

> "List three examples of naturalism in Jack London's *Call of the Wild*."

Outline: To **outline** is to organize a set of facts or ideas by listing main points and subpoints. A good outline shows at a glance how topics or ideas fit together or relate to one another. (See "Outlining" in the index.)

> "Outline the events in the Tom Robinson affair."

505 **Prove:** To **prove** means to bring out the truth by giving evidence and facts to back up your point.

> "Attempt to prove that capital punishment is not an effective deterrent to crime."

Relate: To **relate** is to show how two or more things are connected in some important way. (Don't confuse this use of the word with the verb *relate* meaning simply "to tell," as in "He related the story of his life.")

> "Relate the invention of the cotton gin to the spread of slavery into the territories of the West during the early 1800's."

Review: To **review** is to reexamine or to summarize the key characteristics or major points of the topic. Generally speaking, a review presents material in the order in which it happened or in decreasing order of importance.

> "Review the steps leading to the founding of the United States."

State: To **state** means to present a brief, concise statement of a position, fact, or point of view.

> "State your reasons for having taken the position you now hold on the issues of states' rights versus federal power."

Summarize: To **summarize** is to present the main points of an issue in a shortened form. Details, illustrations, and examples are usually not given.

> "Summarize Lincoln's reasons for issuing the Emancipation Proclamation."

Trace: To **trace** is to present—in step-by-step sequence—a series of facts that are somehow related. Usually, the facts are presented in time order.

> "Trace the events leading up to the attempted secession of several Southern states from the Union."

506 Planning and Writing the Essay Test Answer

In addition to a basic understanding of the key words, you must also understand the process of writing the essay answer.

1. Read the question several times. (Pay special attention to the key word being used in the question.)

2. Rephrase the question into a topic sentence (thesis statement) with a clear point. Note ● It often works well to drop the question's key word from your thesis statement.

> **Question:** *Explain* the immediate effects of the atomic bomb on Hiroshima.

> **Thesis statement:** The immediate effects of the atomic bomb on Hiroshima were devastating.

3. Outline the main points you plan to cover in your answer. Time will probably not allow you to include all supporting details in your outline.

4. Write your essay (or paragraph). Begin with your thesis statement (or topic sentence). Add whatever background information may be needed, and then follow your outline, writing as clearly as possible.

507 Sample Essay Answer

One-Paragraph Answer ● If you feel that only one paragraph is needed to answer the question, use the main points of your outline as supporting details for your thesis statement. (Your thesis statement now serves as the topic sentence of your single-paragraph answer.)

> **Question:** Explain the immediate effects of the atomic bomb on Hiroshima.

> *The immediate effects of the atomic bomb on Hiroshima were devastating.* The initial explosion and violent wind that followed toppled train cars, stone walls, and bridges as far as two miles away from the impact area. Of the 90,000 buildings in Hiroshima, an estimated 62,000 were destroyed in an instant. Buildings near the center of the explosion were ignited at once by the tremendous heat (estimated at 6,000 degrees C) that was generated by the splitting atoms. Away from the impact area, the splintered wreckage was ignited by exposed wiring and overturned cooking stoves. By late afternoon of the first day, very nearly every building in Hiroshima was burning. As the fires raged, huge drops of "black rain," created by heat, dust, and radiation, began to fall on the city. The radioactive "fallout" polluted the air and water, adding to the problems of those who had survived the blast and fires. Before the day had ended, the devastation from the bomb was nearly complete. Very little of Hiroshima remained.

508 **Multi-Paragraph Answer** ● If the question is too complex to be handled in one paragraph, your opening paragraph should include only your thesis statement and any essential background information. Begin your second paragraph by rephrasing one of the main points from your outline into a suitable topic sentence. Support this topic sentence with examples, reasons, or other appropriate details. (Additional paragraphs should be handled in the same manner as paragraph two.) If time permits, add a summary or concluding paragraph to bring all of your thoughts to a logical close. By adding or changing an appropriate word or two, your original thesis statement can be used as a closing sentence for your essay answer.

I. The Explosion
   A. A "noiseless flash"
   B. A wave of pressure
II. The Fire
   A. Ignited by bomb
   B. Ignited by exposed wiring
III. The Fallout
   A. Black rain
   B. Contamination

The immediate effects of the atomic bomb on Hiroshima were devastating.

The initial explosion of the atomic bomb on Hiroshima has often been described by those who survived it as a "noiseless flash." The bomb that was dropped on this island city was equal in power to 13,000 tons of TNT; incredibly, no explosion was heard by the residents of Hiroshima. Instead, they recall an enormous flash of blinding light followed by a tremendous wave of pressure. The wave and the violent wind that followed did an unbelievable amount of damage. Train cars, stone walls, and bridges as far as two miles away from the impact area were toppled. Of the 90,000 buildings in Hiroshima, an estimated 62,000 were destroyed in an instant. In that same instant, the smoke and dust carried by the wind turned day into night.

The darkness quickly gave way to light as fires sprang up throughout the city. Buildings near the center of the explosion were ignited at once by the tremendous heat (estimated at 6,000 degrees C) that was generated by the splitting atoms. Away from the impact area, it was simply a matter of time before the splintered wreckage was ignited by exposed wiring and overturned cooking stoves. By late afternoon of the first day, very nearly every building in Hiroshima was ablaze.

As the fires raged, additional effects of the bomb became evident. Huge drops of "black rain" began to fall. The explosion had lifted tremendous amounts of smoke, dust, and fission fragments high into the atmosphere over Hiroshima. Soon a condensed moisture, blackened by the smoke and dust and contaminated with radiation, began to fall like rain on the city. The radioactive "fallout" polluted the air and water, adding to the problems of those who had survived the blast and fires.

Before the day had ended, the devastation from the bomb was nearly complete. Very little of Hiroshima remained.

Taking an Essay Test

509 Quick Guide

1. **Make sure you are ready for the test both mentally and physically.** (See the "Guidelines for Taking Tests," 511.)

2. **Listen carefully to the final instructions of the teacher.**

   ◉ How much time do you have to complete the test?

   ◉ Do all the questions count equally?

   ◉ May you use any aids such as a dictionary or handbook?

   ◉ Are there any corrections, changes, or additions to the test?

3. **Begin the test immediately and watch the time carefully.** Don't spend so much time answering one question that you run out of time before answering the others.

4. **Read all the essay questions carefully, paying special attention to the key words.** (See 503-505.)

5. **Ask the teacher to clarify any question (or key word) you may not understand.**

6. **Rephrase each question into a controlling idea** (thesis statement or topic sentence) **for your essay answer.**

7. **Think before you write.** Jot down all the important information and work it into a brief outline. Do this on the back of the test sheet or on a piece of scrap paper.

8. **Use a logical pattern of organization and a strong topic sentence for each paragraph.**

9. **Write concisely without using abbreviations or nonstandard language.**

10. **Write about those areas of the subject you are most sure of first; then work on the remaining areas as time permits.**

11. **Keep your test paper neat with reasonable margins.** Neat-ness is always important, and readability is a must, especially on an exam.

12. **Revise and proofread as carefully and completely as time permits.**

510 Taking an Objective Test

True/False

- Read the entire question before answering. Often the first half of a statement will be true or false, while the second half is just the opposite. For an answer to be true, the entire statement must be true.
- Read each word and number carefully. Pay special attention to names, dates, and numbers that are similar and could easily be confused.
- Be especially careful of true/false statements that contain words like *all, every, always, never,* etc. Very often these statements will be false.
- Also watch for statements that contain more than one negative word. *Remember:* Two negatives make a positive. (Example: It is unlikely ice will not melt when the temperature rises above 32 degrees F.)
- Remember that if one part of the statement is false, the whole statement is false.

Matching Test

- Read through both lists quickly before you begin answering. Note any descriptions that are similar and pay particular attention to the details that make them different.
- When matching word to phrase, read the phrase first and look for the word it describes.
- Cross out each answer as you find it—unless you are told that the answer can be used more than once.
- If you get stuck when matching word to word, determine the part of speech of each word. If the word is a verb, for example, match it with another verb.
- Fill in the blanks with capital letters rather than lowercase letters since they are less likely to be misread by the person correcting the test.

Multiple Choice Test

- Read the directions very carefully to determine whether you are looking for the correct answer or the best answer. Also check to see if some questions can have two (or more) correct answers.
- Read the first part of the question very carefully, looking for negative words like *not, never, except, unless,* etc.
- Try to answer the question in your mind before looking at the choices.
- Read all the choices before selecting your answer. This is especially important on tests where you must select the best answer, or on tests where one of your choices is a combination of two or more answers. (Example: **c.** Both a and b **d.** All of the above **e.** None of the above)
- As you read through the choices, eliminate those that are obviously incorrect; then go back and reconsider the remaining choices carefully.

511 Guidelines for Taking Tests

Organizing and Preparing Test Material

1. Ask the teacher to be as specific as possible about what will be on the test.
2. Ask how the material will be tested (true/false, multiple choice, essay).
3. Review your class notes and recopy those sections that are most important.
4. Get any notes or materials you may have missed from the teacher or another student.
5. Set up a specific time(s) to study for an exam and schedule other activities around it.
6. Look over quizzes and exams you took earlier in that class.
7. Prepare an outline of everything to be tested to get an overview of the unit.
8. Prepare a detailed study sheet for each part of your outline.
9. Attempt to predict test questions and write practice answers for them.
10. Set aside a list of questions to ask the teacher or another student.

Reviewing and Remembering Test Material

1. Begin reviewing early. Don't wait until the night before the test.
2. Whenever possible, relate the test material to your personal life or to other subjects you are taking.
3. Look for patterns of organization in the material you study (cause/effect, comparison, chronological, etc.).
4. Use maps, lists, diagrams, acronyms, rhymes, or any other special memory aids.
5. Use flash cards or note cards and review with them whenever time becomes available.
6. Recite material out loud whenever possible as you review.
7. Skim the material in your textbooks, noting key words and ideas; practice for the test by summarizing the importance of these ideas.
8. Study with others only after you have studied well by yourself.
9. Test your knowledge of a subject by teaching or explaining it to someone else.
10. Review especially difficult material just before going to bed the night before the exam.

512 Taking a Standardized Test

One kind of test that will continue to come up throughout high school is the standardized test. These tests are set up to measure your skills, progress, and achievement in nearly every subject—grammar and language, science, social studies, mathematics, reading, etc. The questions on most standardized tests follow a certain style or format. Knowing a little about these questions can help you prepare for your next standardized test, as will the guidelines below and the models on the following page.

Standardized Tests
Quick Guide

1. **Listen carefully to the instructions.** Most standardized tests follow very strict guidelines; there is a clear procedure for you to follow and a definite time limit.

2. **Skim the test.** Take a quick look at the entire test to make sure you have all the pages—and that you understand what you need to do with each section.

3. **Read the directions carefully.** Don't assume you know what the test is asking for just by the way it looks. Most standardized tests have specific directions for each section, and no two sections are exactly alike.

4. **Plan your time.** Many tests are broken down into time frames, allowing you a certain amount of time for each section. If not, you will have to plan your time based on the number of questions, the difficulty level, and your own strengths and weaknesses.

5. **Answer the easy questions first.** Skip questions you're totally in the dark about; go back to them later.

6. **Read all the choices.** Don't answer a question until you've read all the choices; many choices are purposely worded alike to test your true understanding.

7. **Make educated guesses.** Unless you're told not to, select an answer for every question. First eliminate choices that are obviously incorrect; then use logic to guess between the remaining answers.

8. **Double-check your answers.** As time permits, check each of your answers to make sure you haven't made any foolish mistakes or missed any questions.

Note • Mark your answer sheet correctly and clearly. If you need to change an answer, erase it completely. Also make sure you keep your place and that your answers end up next to the correct numbers.

513 Vocabulary

The vocabulary section of standardized tests usually contains two types of questions: synonym and antonym questions. Synonym questions will test your ability to find words that are the same in meaning; antonym questions, the opposite in meaning.

Synonym BIBLIOPHILE (A) soldier (B) artist (C) lover of books (D) music lover (E) child

Antonym PRELUDE (A) forerunner (B) ending (C) interruption (D) test (E) conference

Note • One way to figure out the meanings of unfamiliar words is to look for familiar prefixes, suffixes, or roots (*biblio* means *book; pre* means *before*).

Analogies

Analogies test your ability to figure out relationships. You need to first look at the pair of words you are given (WARM : HOT) and decide how they are related. Then read the choices and decide which pair of words has the same relationship as the first two. (The colon between the word pair means *is to;* the double colon means *as.*)

Analogy WARM : HOT : : (A) gray : black (B) high : low (C) cold : frozen (D) sad : silly

Multiple Choice

The key to multiple choice questions is to read the directions carefully. (The example below requires finding the sentence error.) Always read all the choices before selecting your answer. Eliminate those responses that are obviously not correct; then go back and consider the remaining choices.

Multiple Choice 1. I enjoy eating in a good restaurant and
                         A   B
  to go to a movie afterward. No error.
     C   D   E

Reading Comprehension

Often, you will be asked to read a passage and answer questions about it. Here are some guidelines that can help you handle these kinds of questions more efficiently:

1. Read the questions before you read the passage.
2. Read the passage carefully, but as quickly as possible.
3. Read all the choices before choosing the best answer.

Speaking and Thinking

"Half the world is composed of people who have something to say and can't and the other half who have nothing to say and keep on saying it."

—Robert Frost

Speech Skills

514   "This is speech class," announced Mr. Cook, leaning forward, his fingers gripping the lip of the lectern. "And during this semester you will all give informational, persuasive, extemporaneous, impromptu, and manuscript speeches. Why? Because sometime later in life you will have to do these things."

Teacher-talk! I thought. I mean, who's ever going to say to me, "Hey, kid, I wancha ta do an info-suasive, entemp-tu, promp-to speech. Okay?"

515 That was then . . .

That was then . . . high school. But this is now . . . after 26 years in education and business. And you know what? I was partly right! People in the workplace don't use the words *manuscript, extemporaneous,* and *impromptu.* People in the workplace don't talk that way about speeches.

However, Mr. Cook was also right. Every day people give the kinds of speeches he assigned. It's just that on the job, people talk about speeches in terms of what the speech does, rather than the speaker's delivery method. In the workplace, people refer to a speech as "an explanation," "a report," "some instructions," "a presentation," "an introduction," or "a little talk."

what's ahead?

You, too, will give speeches on the job. And more important for now, you'll give speeches in school. To help you prepare, this section of your handbook explains the process of preparing and presenting a speech:

Preparing to Speak

Writing the Speech

Rehearsing and Delivering the Speech

516 Preparing to Speak

You give a speech in order to communicate something to an audience. That takes time—yours and theirs. Use that time well by first taking time out to think.

Think about your audience by asking . . .

◉ What are their ages, backgrounds, interests, and needs?

◉ Will my audience be large or small, familiar or unfamiliar?

Think about the occasion by asking . . .

◉ Who asked me to speak and why?

◉ Where will I speak, and is the occasion formal or informal?

◉ What else is happening at this event? What comes before and after my speech?

◉ How much time do I have?

Think about your purpose by asking . . .

◉ Am I going to inform my audience? Give them information about a person, topic, or process?

◉ Am I going to persuade them? Convince them to do something or believe something?

◉ Am I going to entertain them? Help them relax and enjoy themselves?

Note • Your purpose will often be more than one of these, but you still need to decide which one is most important.

Think about your topic by asking . . .

◉ Am I required to speak on a specific topic? A general subject area? A topic of my own choosing?

◉ What topic do I already know something about or have an interest in? (Also see 021.)

◉ Where can I find possible topics if no personal topics come to mind? (See 017 and 132.)

◉ Where can I find . . .

the bottom line

Once you've thought about your audience, the occasion, and your purpose, you should be able to put together a purpose or thesis statement. You can begin the statement with a simple "My purpose is . . ." and follow with one of the three specific purposes (to inform, to persuade, to entertain). Finish your statement with your specific topic.

"My purpose is to persuade my audience that high-school study halls are inefficient and should be done away with."

517 Choosing the Method for Delivering the Speech

There are three basic methods for delivering a speech. The method you choose depends on your purpose and the time you have to prepare the speech. (See 526-528.)

518 **Impromptu** Use this method when you've had little or no time to prepare. Sometimes you may be able to jot down a few words to help you present your ideas in an orderly way, but basically you will speak "off the cuff," putting your speech together as you give it. Here are some basic characteristics of the impromptu speech:

- Sounds informal and "live."

- A confident, experienced speaker can be smooth and effective, but an inexperienced speaker may appear tense, stiff, and disorganized.

- Allows speaker to shape the speech in response to audience's laughter or applause.

- Little preparation needed.

- Tends to lack evidence and sources.

519 **Outline** Use this method when you have more time and want to shape the speech more carefully. Write out the main ideas you plan to talk about in outline form, not word for word. You may choose to write the outline on note cards and then use the cards when you give the speech. (See 118-119 for more on "Outlining.")

- Speaker can prepare speech, giving him or her more confidence than impromptu.

- Like impromptu, speaker can use eye contact and gestures freely.

- Like impromptu, allows freedom to adapt speech in response to audience.

- Sounds conversational: more formal than impromptu, but less formal than manuscript.

520 **Manuscript** When you want precision and formality, use this method. Write out exactly what you plan to say. Then (1) memorize and recite the speech, (2) read it to your audience, or (3) get very familiar with the manuscript so you can keep eye contact with the audience, glancing at your paper only on occasion.

- Lets speaker choose exact words of speech—nothing is changed or forgotten during delivery.

- Gives nervous or shy speaker confidence.

- Speaker can time speech exactly.

- When done effectively, the method can be precise, formal, and powerful.

- When writing is weak, or speaker has little eye contact, method can be stiff.

521 Writing the Speech

The way you gather information, organize your ideas, and write them down depends primarily on (1) the kind of speech you're giving and (2) your method of delivery. For example, if you're giving a 10-minute impromptu speech during a business meeting, you probably will have no time to gather information and only a few minutes to outline your thoughts.

On the other hand, if you're giving an informational speech at an industrial convention, you may have six months to search for information, to write out the speech in manuscript form, and to rehearse the delivery.

However, the first step in writing any speech is searching for information. For help on how and where to find information, look in the index under "Searching for Information." After collecting your facts and details, organize them into a speech with an introduction, a body, and a conclusion.

522 Introduction

The introduction of a speech is like the nose of an airplane. The nose sets the course and leads the plane off in a specific direction. A good introduction sets the direction of your speech by

◉ getting the attention of your audience,

◉ introducing your topic,

◉ stating your central idea, or purpose,

◉ briefly identifying the main points, and

◉ making your audience eager to hear what else you have to say.

Start-Up Techniques

To get the audience's attention and focus it, use one or more of the following techniques:

● An amazing fact or a startling statement

● A funny story or an attention-grabbing illustration

● A short demonstration or colorful visual aid

● A series of questions or a short history of the topic

● A strong statement about why the topic is important to you and your audience

523 Body

The body of a speech is like the cargo bay of an airplane. While the nose sets the course and the tail stabilizes the plane, it's the cargo bay—the middle of the plane—that carries the baggage from liftoff to landing.

The body of your speech is like that. It carries the cargo, the main arguments and supporting evidence.

As a result, the way you organize information in the body is very important. In fact, the organization must be so effective that the audience understands the information after hearing it only once! Six popular ways to organize the body are listed below.

Order of Importance: Arrange information according to its importance: least to greatest, or greatest to least.

> Speech listing reasons for buying a new drill press for the machine shop

Chronological Order: Arrange information according to the time order in which events take place.

> Instructions for sending a message on an E-mail system

Comparison/Contrast: Give information about subjects by comparing them (showing similarities) and contrasting them (showing differences).

> Proposal for choosing one fax machine rather than another

Cause and Effect: Give information about a situation or problem by showing (1) what causes the problem and (2) the effects of the problem.

> Report on what causes mail service to slow down during the holidays

Order of Location: Arrange information about subjects according to where things are located in relation to each other.

> A walking tour of your school for a group of senior citizens

Problem/Solution: Describe a problem and then present a solution to solve it.

> Presentation showing how an asphalt product seals cracks in concrete streets

524 Conclusion

Just as the tail of an airplane helps steer the whole plane, the conclusion of your speech helps focus the whole speech. A good conclusion helps your audience understand

◉ what they have heard,

◉ why it's important, and

◉ what they should do about it.

Note • To write a conclusion that does all three, you may want to (1) restate your central idea (or thesis statement) and (2) use some of the attention-getting devices listed earlier in the introduction (522).

525 Rehearsing and Delivering the Speech

Good writers understand the need for revising. They do it because it helps them write well. Similarly, good speakers understand that preparing the script, revising, and rehearsing are necessary steps in the speaking process. How you prepare the script for delivery depends on your delivery method.

526 **Impromptu:** For an impromptu speech, think about your purpose and write an abbreviated outline that includes the following:

- Your opening sentence
- Two or three phrases, each of which summarizes one main point
- Your closing sentence

> I. Opening sentence
> II. Phrase #1
>   Phrase #2
>   Phrase #3
> III. Closing sentence

527 **Outline:** For an outline speech, one that you have time to research and prepare, think carefully about your topic, purpose, and audience. Then outline your speech as follows:

- Opening statement in sentence form
- All main points in sentence form
- Supporting points written as phrases
- Quotations written in full
- All supporting numbers, technical details, and sources listed
- Closing statement in sentence form
- Notes indicating visual aids you plan to use

> I. Introduction
>   A. Point with support
>   B. Point (purpose or thesis)
> II. Body (with 3-5 main points)
>   A. Main point with details
>   B. Main point with details
>   C. Main point with details
> III. Conclusion
>   A. Point, including restatement of thesis
>   B. Point, possibly a call to action

528 **Manuscript:** For a manuscript speech, write the finished copy neatly, following these guidelines:

- Pages double-spaced
- Pages or cards numbered
- Abbreviations used only when you plan to say them (FBI, but not w/o)
- All sentences on same page, not running from one page to the next
- All difficult words marked for pronunciation
- Script marked for interpretation (See copy-marking symbols on next page.)

Save Now or Pay Later

Imagine that you've just finished school, gotten a good job, worked hard all week, and this $1.00 bill represents your whole paycheck. *[hold up dollar bill]* As your employer, I'm about to hand you the check when I stop, tear off about 20% like this, give it to Uncle Sam and say, "Here is my employee's income tax." Then I tear off another 30% like this, give that to Uncle Sam, too, and say, "And here is her Medicare and Social Security tax."

529 Rehearsing the Speech

Rehearse the speech until you're comfortable with it. Ask a family member or friend to listen and give you feedback, or use a tape recorder or video recorder so you can hear and see yourself. Practice these techniques:

- Stand, walk to the lectern carefully, and arrange your notes on it.
- Face the audience with your head up and back straight.
- Speak loudly and clearly.
- Don't rush. Take your time and glance at your notes when you need them.
- Think about what you're saying so your audience hears the feeling in your voice.
- Talk with your hands—use gestures that help you communicate.
- Talk with your eyes and facial expressions by looking at the audience as you speak.
- Check whether audiovisual equipment is working.
- Use the equipment while speaking.
- Conclude the speech by picking up your notes and walking carefully to your seat.

530 Marking for Interpretation

As you decide what changes you need to make, note them on your speech copy. This applies to changes in delivery technique as well. Noting delivery techniques on your paper is called "marking your copy" and involves using a set of symbols to represent voice patterns. These special symbols will remind you to pause in key places during your speech or to emphasize a certain word or phrase. Below is a sample list of copy-marking symbols.

Copy-Marking Symbols
Inflection *(arrows)* .... for a rise in pitch, for a drop in pitch.
Emphasis *(underlining or boldface)* ....for additional <u>drive</u> or **force**.
Color *(curved line or italic)* ....for additional feeling or *emotion*.
Pause *(dash, diagonal, ellipsis)* ....for a pause—or / break . . . in the flow.

take note

When it's time to deliver the speech, remember who you are. You are an important person who has thought about a topic and has something worthwhile to say. Speak loudly, clearly, and confidently.

531 Model Speech

"Save Now or Pay Later" is a persuasive speech by student writer Burnette Sawyer. Burnette's topic is the failing Social Security system. Her purpose is to show her classmates that they can't depend on Social Security to provide their retirement needs. Watch how she builds her argument by showing the audience how the problem affects them personally. (Also notice her use of *italics* to add vocal color and **boldface** to add emphasis.)

Save Now or Pay Later

Speaker begins with an imaginary anecdote, or story.

Imagine that you've just finished school, gotten a job, worked hard all week, and this $1.00 bill represents your whole paycheck. *[hold up dollar bill]* As your employer, I'm about to hand you the check when I stop, tear off about 20% like this, give it to Uncle Sam and say, "Here is my employee's income tax." Then I tear off another 30% like this, give that to him, too, and say, "And here is her Medicare and Social Security tax."

Speaker tears dollar bill to emphasize her point.

Finally, I give you this half and say, "Here, hard worker, this is your *whole paycheck.*"

Does that sound like science fiction?

An allusion to a famous person is used to add believability.

Senator Alan Simpson doesn't think so. In the last issue of *Modern Maturity,* he says that unless legislation changes the Social Security system, *our generation* will have to pay 20% of our paychecks as income tax, and 30% as Social Security tax. That means we can keep just **50%** of what we earn.

Appeal to fear is used to keep audience interested.

But the news gets **worse.** Remember this 30% that we paid to Social Security? *[hold up piece of dollar bill]* Well, that won't be enough money for us to live on when we get to be 65 in the year 2043. Remember that year, 2043—we'll get back to that soon.

Speaker states problem and solution.

What's the problem? The Social Security system *can't insure* our financial security. What's the solution? We have to start our own savings plans, and the *earlier* the *better.*

Ever since it started back in 1935, the Social Security system has never been *secure.* While the system has been "fixed" a number of times, the fix-it jobs haven't done the job. For example, writer Keith Carlson points out that in 1983 Congress raised payroll taxes, extended the retirement age, and said that the system would be in good financial shape until 2056.

But then, says Carlson, *just nine years later,* a report came out saying that Congress had been *wrong.* The report

532

Irony is used to emphasize the year the system may run dry.

The speaker uses a quotation to support her point.

The speaker uses a chart to help make her point clear.

The conclusion repeats the point of the speech, and calls the audience to action.

said that Social Security money wouldn't even last until 2056—it would run out by 2043. Remember that year, 2043? *That's* the year we're supposed to retire—at age 65!

Do you think this news is bad? Just two months ago, the *AARP Bulletin* reported on the Bipartisan Commission on Entitlement and Tax Reform. This commission warned that entitlement programs like Social Security are growing so fast they could "bankrupt the country" by the year 2029—when we're **only 52!**

Will the U.S. government take the action necessary to secure the Social Security system? *Don't count on it.* As Senator Simpson, a member of the Bipartisan Commission said in *Modern Maturity,* "We've been playing political chicken with the federal budget for decades."

So what should we do? Run for Congress and change the system? That's not a bad idea except the track record for Social Security shows that one more fix-it job won't fix the system. Besides, we have to be 30 years old to be U.S. senators, and we have to start our own retirement plans long before then.

In fact, in his book, *Retirement 101,* Willard Enteman says that we should start a personal savings plan the day we get our first checks. In sociology class last week, Mr. Christians made the same point. He gave us this graph *[hold up graph]* which shows that if our goal is to save $100,000 by age 65, we better start *early* before saving gets too expensive.

You can see that if we start here, when we're 25, we can reach $100,000 by saving just $29 a month. If we wait until here, when we're 35, we'll have to save $68 a month. If we wait until here, when we're 45, we'll have to put away $170 a month. And if we wait until we're 55, we'll need $547 a month.

Look at the difference. To reach $100,000 by age 65 would cost $29 a month if we start at 25, and $547 a month if we start at 55.

What's my point? The Social Security system *can't promise us* financial security when we retire.

What's the solution? We have to start our own savings plans—and the *earlier* we start, the *easier* it will be to reach our goals.

533 A Closer Look at Style

More than any other president of recent times, John F. Kennedy is remembered for the appealing style and tone of his speeches. By looking at sample portions of his speeches, you should get a better feel for how style and tone can help strengthen the spoken word. (The tone of each sample is listed above the excerpt and labeled as an **appeal**—a word that reflects both the writer's personal feelings and attitudes, and the feelings he or she hopes the audience will also experience.)

534 **Allusion** is a reference in a speech to a familiar person, place, or thing.

Appeal to the Democratic Principle

One hundred years of delay have passed since *President Lincoln* freed the slaves, yet their heirs, their grandsons, are not fully free (Radio and Television Address, 1963).

535 **Analogy** is a comparison of an unfamiliar idea to a simple, familiar one. The comparison is usually quite lengthy, suggesting several points of similarity. An analogy is especially useful when attempting to explain a difficult or complex idea.

Appeal to Common Sense

In our opinion the German people wish to have one united country. If the Soviet Union had lost the war, the Soviet people themselves would object to a line being drawn through Moscow and the entire country defeated in war. We wouldn't like to have a line drawn down the Mississippi River . . . (Interview, November 25, 1961).

536 **Anecdote** is a short story told to illustrate a point.

Appeal to Pride, Commitment

Frank O'Connor, the Irish writer, tells in one of his books how as a boy, he and his friends would make their way across the countryside and when they came to an orchard wall that seemed too high and too doubtful to try and too difficult to permit their voyage to continue, they took off their hats and tossed them over the wall—and then they had no choice but to follow them. This nation has tossed its cap over the wall of space, and we have no choice but to follow it. Whatever the difficulties, they will be overcome (San Antonio Address, November 21, 1963).

537 **Antithesis** is balancing or contrasting one word or idea against another, usually in the same sentence.

Appeal to Common Sense, Commitment

Let us never negotiate out of fear. But let us never fear to negotiate (Inaugural Address, 1961).

Mankind must put an end to war, or war will put an end to mankind (Address to the U.N., 1961).

538 **Irony** is using a word or phrase to mean the exact opposite of its literal meaning, or to show a result that is the opposite of what would be expected or appropriate; an odd coincidence.

Appeal to Common Sense

They see no harm in paying those to whom they entrust the minds of their children a smaller wage than is paid to those to whom they entrust the care of their plumbing (Vanderbilt University, 1961).

539 **Negative definition** is describing something by telling what it is *not* rather than, or in addition to, what it is.

Appeal for Commitment

. . . members of this organization are committed by the Charter to promote and respect human rights. Those rights are not respected when a Buddhist priest is driven from his pagoda, when a synagogue is shut down, when a Protestant church cannot open a mission, when a cardinal is forced into hiding, or when a crowded church service is bombed (United Nations, September 20, 1963).

540 **Parallel structuring** is the repeating of phrases or sentences that are similar (parallel) in meaning and structure; **repetition** is the repeating of the same word or phrase to create a sense of rhythm and emphasis.

Appeal for Commitment

Let every nation know, whether it wishes us well or ill, that we shall *pay any price, bear any burden, meet any hardship, support any friend, oppose any foe,* in order to assure the survival and the success of liberty (Inaugural Address, 1961).

541 **Quotations,** especially of well-known individuals, can be effective in nearly any speech.

Appeal for Emulation or Affiliation

At the inauguration, Robert Frost read a poem which began "the land was ours before we were the land's"—meaning, in part, that this new land of ours sustained us before we were a nation. And although we are now the land's—a nation of people matched to a continent—we still draw our strength and sustenance . . . from the earth (Dedication Speech, 1961).

542 **Rhetorical question** is a question posed for emphasis of a point, not for the purpose of getting an answer.

Appeal to Common Sense, Democratic Principle

"When a man's ways please the Lord," the Scriptures tell us, "he maketh even his enemies to be at peace with him." And is not peace, in the last analysis, basically a matter of human rights—the right to live out our lives without fear of devastation—the right to breathe air as nature provided it— the right of future generations to a healthy existence (Commencement Address, 1963)?

543 Speech Terms

Acoustics: The science of sound or the way the walls, floor, ceiling, and other parts of a room react to sound. The quality of speech sounds depends in part on the acoustics of the room in which they are produced.

Ad Lib: Making up or composing the words to a speech as you deliver it.

Articulation: The uttering of speech sounds in a clear, distinct manner.

Cadence: The rhythm or flow of a speech. Your goal is to make your cadence as smooth as possible.

Climax: The high point or peak in a speech.

Color: The emotional treatment given certain key words in a speech to convey the special meaning or connotation of those words. The volume and pitch of the voice are changed to add color.

Commentary: An organized group of remarks or observations on a particular subject; an interpretation, usually of an important social issue.

Continuity: The state or quality of being continuous or unbroken. A speech with continuity will move smoothly from the introduction through the conclusion by use of effective linking or transitional devices.

Editorial: A carefully organized piece of writing in which an opinion is expressed.

Emphasis: Giving more attention to a particular word or phrase than to the others. This can be done by varying the volume, pace, pitch, or color of the voice.

Enunciation: The clearness or crispness of a person's voice. If a speaker's enunciation is good, it will be easy to understand each word he or she says.

Eye Contact: The communicating a speaker does with his or her eyes during a speech. It is very important that a speaker establish sincere eye contact with the audience so that full communication can take place.

Force (Drive): The amount of pressure or punch behind the speaker's voice; the *loudness*.

Gesture: The motion a speaker uses to emphasize a point. Hand and body gestures are usually effective additions to a speech, although they can also be visual distractions and take away from the speaker's effectiveness. You should keep gestures as natural as possible and not overuse them.

Impromptu: A speech given with little time for preparation.

Inflection: The rising and falling in the pitch of the voice.

Interpretation: The act of figuring out or explaining the meaning of a piece of writing.

Manuscript: The written copy of the speech used during a presentation.

Monotonous: A voice that is unchanging in inflection or color; *dull.*

Oratory: The art of public speaking.

Pace: The rate of movement or overall speed of a speech.

Pause: The momentary stopping in a speech to give additional emphasis to a particular word, phrase, or idea.

Pitch: The highness or lowness of a voice. By properly varying the pitch of the voice, the speaker can emphasize or color the words in the script.

Presence: The sense of closeness of the speaker to the audience. If a speaker is sincere and open with the audience, he or she is more likely to be believed.

Projection: Directing or throwing the voice so it can be heard at a distance; speaking loudly.

Rate: The speed (fastness or slowness) of the speech.

Repetition: The repeating of words or phrases to add a sense of balance and rhythm to a piece of writing, as in Lincoln's Gettysburg Address: ". . . of the people, by the people, and for the people."

Resonance: The prolonging of a sound through vibration. In the speech process, the resonance is amplified by the chest, throat, and nose.

Speech: The process of communicating with the voice through a combination of breathing, resonating, and articulating.

Stage Fright: The tension or nervousness a speaker feels when he or she is preparing to deliver or is actually delivering a speech.

"Every good thought you think is contributing its share to the ultimate result of your life."

—Grenville Kleiser

Thinking in All Your Classes

Have you ever been asked to compare two things in an English paper or on a history test? Easier said than done, right? Or how about defining or classifying a *simple* term in science class? Not so simple? The truth is, thinking can be hard work, especially in some of your tougher classes.

Not to worry. There are many strategies that you can use to carry out your most challenging thinking. For example, you can use a Venn Diagram to help you compare two things. And you can use "definition expanders" to define an important term.

what's ahead?

In addition to comparing and defining, this chapter will help you learn how to classify, make decisions, solve problems, and ask questions.

Thinking Operations

Defining Terms

Comparing and Contrasting

Classifying

Thinking Creatively

Methods of Thinking

Asking Questions

545 Thinking Operations

When you are asked to . . .	You should be ready to . . .

Know

recall	define
list	label
name	identify
record	memorize

Recall what you've learned
- to list details
- to identify or define terms
- to collect information
- to remember information

Comprehend

understand	show
review	restate
cite	explain
summarize	describe

Show that you understand what you've learned
- by giving examples
- by restating the important details
- by explaining how something works

Apply

utilize	select
choose	model
illustrate	organize
locate	demonstrate

Use what you've learned
- to select the most important details
- to organize information
- to make something work
- to show how something works

Analyze

classify	compare
divide	contrast
edit	characterize
tell why	map
examine	break down

Break material down to understand it better
- by examining and putting each part into the correct group
- by making connections between this and other things: cause and effect, comparison, contrast, etc.

Synthesize

combine	develop
speculate	invent
design	blend
compose	propose
create	formulate
predict	imagine

Reshape material into a new form
- by inventing a better way of doing something
- by redesigning or blending the old and the new
- by predicting or hypothesizing (making an educated guess)

Evaluate

judge	rate
recommend	measure
argue	persuade
evaluate	assess
criticize	convince

Judge the worth of the material
- by assessing its strengths and weaknesses (pluses and minuses)
- by evaluating its clearness, accuracy, value, etc.
- by judging its value/worth

Defining Terms

546 The Sentence Definition

The simplest way to define a term is to summarize its meaning in a single sentence, much the way a dictionary does. To build a defining sentence, you must first name the term. Then put the term into a class of objects similar to it. Finally, mention the special characteristics that make this term different from other objects in its class. Here's an example:

TERM .... The canines

CLASS .... are the teeth

SPECIAL
CHARACTERISTICS .... in the front corners of the mouth for cutting and tearing.

Note • A good definition doesn't place the word you are trying to define in the definition itself. For example, do not say, "A calculator is an electronic device used to calculate numbers."

547 The Paragraph Definition

A sentence definition is bare-bones stuff. Usually we need more information (explanations and examples) to show how something looks, acts, or fits in among other things before we truly understand it. There are many kinds of details you can add to a definition sentence to expand it into a paragraph or an essay. The following paragraph definition uses several methods of expansion, all of which are included in the list below.

The canines are the long, sharp teeth found in the front corners of the upper and lower rows of teeth, between the incisors and bicuspids. Because they are long and strong and deeply rooted, they have several functions. First, even though canines do not chew food, they guide the jaw during the chewing process. Second, they shape the face. They can also serve as anchors for other teeth when a dentist puts in bridgework. And finally, as the name "canine" suggests, they work like the teeth of a dog to cut and tear food—and to bite.

Definition Expanders

- Tell what people say about it.
- Give a dictionary definition.
- Describe it in detail.
- Add your personal experiences.
- Compare it to something.
- Tell what it is not.
- Explain the different kinds.
- Use a quotation.

548 Comparing and Contrasting

If you're like most people, you are constantly comparing and contrasting one thing to another: music groups, foods, cars, clothing—even classes. The strategies that follow will help you improve your comparing and contrasting skills and show you how to use them in all your school subjects. Here are some sample situations where you might need to use comparison and contrast:

- ◉ **History:** Review two different reports of Columbus's "discovery" of America.
- ◉ **English:** Write a comparison/contrast paper on two stories or poems you've read.
- ◉ **Science:** Answer an essay test question that asks you to compare a plant cell with an animal cell.
- ◉ **Math:** Compare a trapezoid to a parallelogram.

549 Choosing Two Things to Compare

If you have the freedom to choose, use this checklist to help you make a decision about which two things to compare:

- ✔ Choose two things you're **really interested in**.
- ✔ Choose two things **you know about** (or can find out about).
- ✔ Choose two things that **can be compared**. (See the box below.)
- ✔ **Have a good reason** for comparing the two.

It's important for you to know that not just *anything* can be compared. Two things can be compared only if they are two types of the same thing. They can't be compared (1) if they are two different types of things or (2) if one is an example of the other. (See the chart below and "The Venn Diagram" on the next page.)

A & B	Can Be Compared As	Can't Be Compared
Eagle & Falcon	**Types of Birds**	
Eagle & Otter	**Types of Animals**	
Eagle & Flag	**Types of Symbols**	
Eagle & Rainforest		**Two different types of things**
Eagle & Birds		**Eagle is an example of a bird**

550 The Venn Diagram

Once you've chosen two things to compare, list the details about each in a Venn diagram. First, list everything that fits only your first subject (the eagle) in area **A**; do the same for your second subject (the falcon) in area **B**. Then, list everything A and B have in common in area **C**.

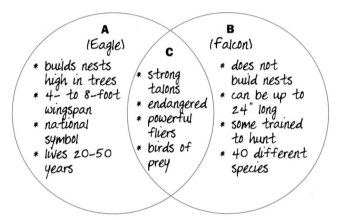

551 Organizing Your Comparison

Once you've listed all your details, you need to choose a plan for organizing your comparison. Your three choices are *whole vs. whole* (for shorter subjects), *topic by topic* (for more complicated subjects), and *similarities and differences* (for summarizing).

PLAN 1: Whole vs. Whole

- First discuss all of subject A.
- Then discuss all of subject B. As you discuss B, remind the reader of points you want to contrast with A.
- End with a conclusion that emphasizes the greatest similarity or difference.

PLAN 2: Topic by Topic

- List several topics for comparison between subject A and subject B. Arrange the topics in a meaningful order.
- Under each topic, first discuss A, then compare B.
- End by emphasizing the overall picture or the most important point of comparison or contrast.

PLAN 3: Similarities and Differences

- First tell why you want to show similarities and differences between A and B.
- Discuss all the similarities first.
- Then discuss the differences, ending with the one you want to emphasize. (If you want to emphasize the similarities, place them last.)

552 Classifying

Classifying may not sound like fun, but try living—or writing—without it! To think and speak clearly, you need to be able to "lump" and "split." To lump means to bunch similar things together into a single category and give the category a name. To split means to take a big lump, or class, and break it into smaller lumps, or subclasses.

For example, we can lump all those furry, barking, slobbering, floppy-eared quadrupeds together and call them "dogs." But we could split all dogs into at least two subclasses: wild and tame. For fun, we could split tame dogs into two sub-subclasses: serious (like pit bulls) and silly (like Pekingese).

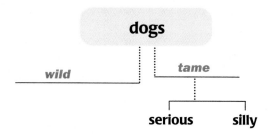

553 Writing Classification Paragraphs

When would you most likely be asked to *lump* or *split*? Probably in a science class where classifying is an everyday activity, especially in biology. On a science test, for example, you might be asked to write a short paragraph classifying things within a group (trees, for example) according to their uses. You might also be asked to support your classifications with an example of each. Here's what that paragraph might look like:

> Trees can be classified in several ways based on their function or use. They are used most commonly for lumber or building products. Pine and oak are among the most popular for this purpose. Trees, especially pine and other fast-growing trees, are also used for erosion control and wind barriers. They are planted in rows on the tops and sides of steep hills. Besides these uses, trees are considered extremely valuable for landscaping purposes where they provide shade, color, and screening for homes and businesses. Among the most popular are evergreens, maples, honey locusts, and birch. Obviously, trees have many other uses as well—just ask a bird . . . or a kid.

554 Thinking Creatively

The best creative thinkers see things differently than the people around them. They see challenges rather than problems. They set aside all the rules, all the scorecards, all of what is usually expected, and begin to imagine "What would happen if . . . ?" If you sometimes find it hard to imagine, to go beyond the correct or obvious answer, maybe the suggestions below will help.

- **What if** a certain person, place, thing, or idea did not exist today? What if it suddenly appeared 100 years before its time? (What if the airplane had not yet been invented? What if it had been invented before the Civil War?)

- **What if** the world were different in some important way? (What if the sun were to shine only two hours a day? Twenty hours a day? What if it rained only twice a year? Every day?)

- **What if** two people, things, or ideas that are usually separate were brought together? (Parents and rock musicians? Tomatoes and ice cream?)

- **What if** you were to change just one important thing about an object or machine? (Change the ink in every pen to green? Cut the gas tanks on all cars to one-fourth their current size?)

- **What if** a certain object could talk? (Your shoe? Your house? A new-born baby?)

- **What if** a certain object were made of another material? (Metal car tires? Grass clothes? Cardboard furniture?)

- **What if** a certain person, place, object, or idea were the opposite of what he, she, or it is now? (Homes became schools? Cars became helicopters? Forward became backward?)

- **What if** a certain object were suddenly scarce or plentiful? (What if there were suddenly very little paper? Plenty of money?)

- **What if** a certain object were a totally different size? (Two-foot pens? Twelve-foot baskets?)

- **What if** . . .

555 The Creative Mind in Action

Without creativity, you might look at an ordinary object like a pencil and think, "There's a pencil. Something to write with. It looks brand-new. It's probably worth less than a dime." But if you look at the same pencil with a creative mind—not just look at it, but look at it carefully, from every angle imaginable—you may set all sorts of mental imagery in motion. Here's proof:

The No. 2 Pencil Meets a Creative Mind

- First, notice the parts: lead point, hexagonal wooden barrel painted yellow, words "Dixon Ticonderoga 1388—2 Soft" stamped along one side in green ink on gold, triple-striped green and yellow metal collar holding a powdery pink eraser, not yet rubbed raw.
- Imagine the manufacturing process—the wood gluers, the planers, the slicers, the paint vats, the dryers, the stamps, and so on.
- Think of the tree the wood was once a part of. Where did it grow? Where on the tree was this pencil's wood located? Where are the other parts of the tree now?
- Imagine being the paint. Now imagine being covered all over with yellow paint and stamped with green and gold letters.
- See the pencil as a bridge stretching between two places. What are they?
- Imagine the pencil as a pillar. What is it holding up?
- Who will hold this pencil before it is worn to a nub? What will be the most important thing ever written with it? What will be the funniest thing?
- How strong is it? How much weight would be needed to break it? The weight of a safe? Of a hamster? A frying pan? A six-year-old boy? A rainbow trout?
- Now it is being used as a pointer. Who is pointing it and what are they pointing at? Why?
- Imagine an occasion when this pencil might be given as a gift. What is the occasion?
- If the pencil could think, what would it be thinking as it is locked away in a drawer? As it is being used to write a letter?
- Listen to the sounds it makes—what do they remind you of?
- Bite it—what does it taste like?
- Roll the pencil around in your fingers—what does its texture bring to mind?

the bottom line

Get the idea? What other new ways of experiencing the pencil can you think of? Always be on the alert, thinking of new ways to look at old objects and ideas. It's an excellent way to learn—in all your classes.

556 Methods of Thinking

Different people solve problems in different ways. In the classroom, your teacher may ask you to use a specific method. If not, here are some of the possibilities you can use to make your thinking more efficient.

Decision-Making Method

I magine the outcome or result.

D efine your goal.

E xplore (list) your options.

C hoose two or three best options.

I nvestigate the chosen options; try each one out.

D ecide on the best option.

E valuate your choice.

Problem-Solving Method

I dentify the problem.

D escribe the problem.

E xplore possible solutions or actions.

A dopt the best plan or solution.

L ook at the effects or results.

The Scientific Method

I dentify the problem.

M ake observations.

A dvance a hypothesis, or educated guess.

G ather data and test it against your hypothesis.

I nvestigate further, observing and collecting more data.

N ote data and draw possible conclusions.

E stablish a single conclusion.

557 Asking Questions

To get the most out of your classes, you need to think—to think well, you need to ask questions. The basic questions to ask are the 5 W's and H: *Who? What? When? Where? Why?* and *How?* To go beyond the basic questions, see the chart below. It will get you started. You can then adapt the chart to fit people, places, events, and any other subject you come across.

	Description	Function	History	Value
P R O B L E M S	What is the problem? What type of problem is it? What are its parts? What are the signs of the problem?	Who or what is affected by it? What new problems may it cause in the future?	What is the current status of the problem? What or who caused it? What or who contributed to it?	What is its significance? Why? Why is it more (or less) important than other problems? What does it symbolize or illustrate?
P O L I C I E S	What type of policy is it? How broad is it? What are its most important features? What are its parts?	What is the policy designed to do? What is needed to make it work? What will be its effects?	What brought this policy about? What are the alternatives to this policy?	Is the policy workable? What are its advantages and disadvantages? Is it practical? Is it a good policy? Why or why not?
C O N C E P T S	What is the concept? What does it look like? What are its parts? Who or what is it related to?	Who has been influenced by this concept? Why is it important? How does it work?	When did it originate? How has it changed over the years? How may it change in the future?	What practical value does it have? Why is it superior (or inferior) to similar concepts? What is its social worth?

"The best argument is that which seems merely an explanation."
—Dale Carnegie

Thinking Logically

558   Thinking logically means thinking sensibly. It means going beyond your knee-jerk reaction or the first answer that pops into your head. It means looking at all sides of a question, proposing reasonable and sensible solutions, and then supporting the solutions with good reasons, interesting examples, and solid evidence. In fact, the only kind of thinking that will hold up under careful examination by your audience is logical thinking—thinking that is reasonable, reliable, and above all, believable.

So how do you go about making your thinking believable and, therefore, acceptable to your audience? Generally speaking, you must organize, support, and present your points *so well* that your audience will find it difficult to disagree with or question what you've said or written. This chapter can help you do just that.

what's ahead?

To begin thinking more logically, you can follow the guidelines under "Becoming a Logical Thinker" on the next two pages. You can also check the reliability of your thinking against the "Fallacies of Thinking" later in the chapter (565-574).

Becoming a Logical Thinker

559 Quick Guide

The steps below cover the logical thinking process from start to finish. Look each step over carefully and try to get the big picture. (Also look carefully at "Making and Supporting a Point" on the next page.) Then apply what you've learned the next time you need to use logic in an argument, a debate, or a persuasive essay.

1. **Decide on your purpose** and state it clearly on the top of your paper.

2. **Gather information** on the topic.

3. **Focus on a central point** that you feel you can support or prove. (This is called "making a claim." See 560.)

4. **Add "qualifiers"** as necessary to strengthen your claim. (See 561.)

5. **Define any terms** that may be unclear.

6. **Support your points** with evidence that is both interesting and reliable. (See 562.)

7. **Explain your evidence** and why your audience should accept it.

8. **Consider any objections** your audience could have to your explanation.

9. **Make concessions**; admit that some of your arguments may be weak. (See 563.)

10. **Point out weaknesses** in the arguments on the other side of the issue, the arguments you do not accept.

11. **Restate your point** or central claim.

12. **Urge your audience** to accept your viewpoint.

Note ● You will probably not use every one of these steps, or stages, each time you set out to prove a point. Each situation is different and, in addition to logic, requires some creative thinking and common sense.

Making and Supporting a Point

560 **Making Claims** ● Making a strong point, or "claim," is essential to the logical thinking process. Claims fall into three main groups: *claims of fact, claims of value,* and *claims of policy.*

Claims of fact state or claim that something is true or not true.

> Television violence causes violent behavior in children.

Claims of value state that something has or does not have worth.

> The Bigfoot Cross-Trainer is the best all-around shoe for the money.

Claims of policy assert that something ought to be done or not done.

> We need a law to prevent any more farmland from being turned into suburban housing.

561 **Using Qualifiers** ● Qualifiers are terms that make a claim more flexible. Note the difference between the two claims below:

> Teachers ignore students' excuses.

> **Some** teachers **tend to** ignore students' excuses.

The second claim is easier to defend because it makes a qualified claim, rather than an all-or-nothing claim. Here are some other useful qualifiers:

almost	if . . . then . . .	maybe	probably
frequently	in most cases	might	sometimes
often	likely	often	usually

562 **Adding Support** ● Your central claim needs evidence for support; the more kinds of evidence you offer, and the stronger the evidence, the stronger your argument will be. Here are some kinds of evidence you might use:

Observation:	"I personally observed the audience reaction to the movie."
Statistics:	"According to *Entertainment Weekly,* over 2 million people saw the movie in the first week."
Comparison:	"The movie was almost as moving as *Schindler's List.*"
Expert Testimony:	"Siskel and Ebert gave it two thumbs up."
Experience:	"I've seen it three times."
Demonstration:	"The movie begins with a wide shot of . . ."
Analysis:	"The plot hinges on a secret that . . ."
Prediction:	"Early predictions are that it will be nominated . . ."

563 **Making Concessions** ● Concessions are "points" that you let the other side score. When your argument has some true weaknesses, it is usually best to admit it. Giving away points will not weaken your argument; in fact, a concession often adds believability to your overall claim. Here are some useful expressions for making concessions:

admittedly	granted	I cannot argue with
even though	I agree that	while it is true that

564 Using Evidence and Logic

An argument is a chain of reasons that a person uses to support a claim or conclusion. To use argument well, you need to know both how to draw logical conclusions from sound evidence and how to recognize and avoid false arguments, or logical fallacies.

The logical fallacies described in this section are the bits of fuzzy or dishonest thinking that crop up often in our own speaking and writing, as well as in advertisements, political appeals, editorials, and so on. You should first read them through so that you can recognize them in the things you read or hear. Then avoid them in your own writing and thinking.

Fallacies of Thinking

565 Appeal to Ignorance

One commits this logical fallacy by claiming that since no one has ever proved a claim, it must therefore be false. Appeals to ignorance unfairly shift the burden of proof onto someone else.

> Show me one study that proves seat belts save lives.

566 Appeal to Pity

This fallacy may be heard in courts of law when an attorney begs for leniency because his client's mother is ill, his brother is out of work, his cat has a hair ball, and blah, blah, blah. The strong tug on the heartstrings can also be heard in the classroom when the student says to the teacher, "May I have an extension on this paper? I worked till my eyeballs fell out, but it's still not done."

> Imagine what it must have been like. If anyone deserves a break, he does.

567 Bandwagon

Another way to avoid using logic in an argument is to appeal to everyone's sense of wanting to belong or be accepted. By suggesting that everyone else is doing this or wearing that or going there, you can avoid the real question—"Is this idea or claim a good one or not?"

> Everyone on the team wears high-tops. It's the only way to go.

568 Broad Generalization

A broad generalization takes in everything and everyone at once, allowing no exceptions. For example, a broad generalization about voters might be, "All voters spend too little time reading about a candidate and too much time being swayed by 30-second sound bites." It may be true that quite a few voters spend too little time reading about the candidates, but it is unfair to suggest that this is true of all voters. Here's another example of a broad generalization:

> All teenagers spend too much time watching television.

569 Circular Thinking

This fallacy consists of assuming, in a definition or an argument, the very point you are trying to prove. Note how circular this sort of reasoning is:

> I hate Mr. Baldwin's class because I'm never happy in there. (But what's wrong with the class?)

570 Either-Or Thinking

Either-or thinking consists of reducing a solution to two possible extremes: "America: Love It or Leave It." "Put up or shut up." This fallacy of thinking eliminates every possibility in the middle.

> Either this community votes to build a new school or the quality of education will drop dramatically.

571 Half-Truths

Avoid building your argument with evidence or statements that contain part of the truth, but not the whole truth. These kinds of statements are called half-truths. They are especially misleading because they leave out "the rest of the story." They are true and dishonest at the same time.

> The new recycling law is bad because it will cost more money than it saves. (Maybe so; but it will also save the environment.)

572 Oversimplification

Beware of phrases like "It all boils down to . . ." or "It's a simple question of . . ." Almost no dispute among reasonably intelligent people is "a simple question of . . ." Anyone who feels, for example, that capital punishment "all boils down" to a matter of protecting society ought to question a doctor, an inmate on death row, the inmate's family, a sociologist, a religious leader, etc.

> Capital punishment is a simple question of protecting society.

573 Slanted Language

By choosing words that carry strong positive or negative feelings, a person can distract the audience, leading them away from the valid arguments being made. The philosopher Bertrand Russell once illustrated the bias involved in slanted language when he compared three synonyms for the word *stubborn:* "I am *firm*. You are *obstinate*. He is *pigheaded*."

> No one in his right mind would ever do anything that dumb.

574 Testimonial

You can take Dr. Carl Sagan's word on the composition of Saturn's rings, but the moment he starts pushing exercise machines, watch out! If the testimonial or statement comes from a recognized authority in the field, great. If it comes from a person famous in another field (sports hero, singer, actor), it can be misleading.

> Sports hero: "I've tried every cold medicine on the market, and—believe me—nothing works like Comptrol."

Proofreader's Guide

"It's not wise to violate the rules until you know how to observe them."

—T.S. Eliot

Marking Punctuation

Period

575 A **period** is used to end a sentence that makes a statement or that gives a command that is not an exclamation.

(Statement) One does not sell the earth upon which the people walk.

—Crazy Horse of the Oglala Sioux

(Mild command) Never find your delight in another's misfortune.

—Publilius Syrus

(Request) Please read your punctuation rules carefully.

Note • It is not necessary to place a period after a statement that has parentheses around it and is part of another sentence.

I believe his murderer (for what purpose, God can alone tell) is still lurking in his victim's room.

—Robert Louis Stevenson, *Dr. Jekyll and Mr. Hyde*

576 A period should be placed after an initial or **abbreviation**.

Mr.   Sen.   D.D.S.   Ph.D.   M.D.   Jr.   B.C.   p.m.   U.S.
Edna St. V. Millay   Booker T. Washington   F. Scott Fitzgerald

Note • When an abbreviation is the last word in a sentence, use only one period at the end of the sentence.

Grace picked up her clothes, fed her boxer, put away her CD's, did her homework, etc.

577 A period is used as a decimal point.

The Sierra pickup had been designed from the wheels up at a cost of $2.8 billion.

—Tim Cahill, *Road Fever*

Using the Ellipsis

578 Quick Guide

1 An **ellipsis** (three periods) is used to show that one or more words have been omitted in a quotation. (When typing, leave one space before and after each period.)

(Original)

We the people of the United States, in order to form a more perfect Union, establish justice, insure domestic tranquility, provide for the common defense, promote the general welfare, and secure the blessings of liberty to ourselves and our posterity, do ordain and establish this Constitution for the United States of America.

–Preamble, U.S. Constitution

(Quotation)

"We the people . . . in order to form a more perfect Union . . . establish this Constitution for the United States of America."

2 If words from a quotation are omitted at the end of a sentence, the ellipsis is placed after the period which marks the conclusion of the sentence.

"Five score years ago, a great American, in whose symbolic shadow we stand, signed the Emancipation Proclamation. . . . But one hundred years later, we must face the tragic fact that the Negro is still not free."

—Martin Luther King, Jr., "I Have a Dream"

Note • If the quoted material is a complete sentence (even if it was not complete in the original), use a period, then an ellipsis.

(Original)

I am tired; my heart is sick and sad. From where the sun now stands I will fight no more forever.

–Chief Joseph of the Nez Percé

(Quotations)

"I am tired. . . . From where the sun now stands I will fight no more forever."

or

"I am tired. . . . I will fight no more. . . ."

3 An ellipsis may be used to indicate a pause.

Ever since old Pastor Bill was in our church, I've remembered these . . . these potlucks.

—Ben Hawkinson, student writer

I brought my trembling hand to my focusing eyes. It was oozing, it was red, it was . . . it was . . . a tomato!

—Laura Baginski, student writer

Comma

579 A **comma** may be used between two independent clauses that are joined by coordinating conjunctions such as these: *but, or, nor, for, yet, and, so.*

> I would have liked to speak to him, *but* I did not know what to say.

> Our clothes had been left behind in the other block, *and* we had been promised other outfits.
> **—Elie Wiesel, *Night***

Note • Do not confuse a sentence with a compound verb for a compound sentence.

> I *had* to burn her trash and then *sweep* up her porches and halls.
> **—Anne Moody, *Coming of Age in Mississippi***

580 Commas are used to separate individual words, phrases, or clauses in a series. (A series contains at least three items.)

> I'd never known anything about having *meat, vegetables,* and *a salad.*
> **(Three nouns in a series)**

> I *took her for walks, read her stories,* and *made up games for her to play.*
> **(Three verb phrases in a series)**
> **—Anne Moody, *Coming of Age in Mississippi***

Note • Do not use commas when the words in a series are connected with *or, nor,* or *and.*

> Her fingernails are pointed *and* manicured *and* painted a shiny red.
> **—Carson McCullers, "Sucker"**

581 Commas are used to separate adjectives that *equally* modify the same noun. (Notice in the examples below that no comma separates the last adjective from the noun.)

> I can still remember how my heart started beating when I walked into the *dark, little* room.
> **—Lisa Servais (student), "Me . . . Afraid?"**

> The brief day drew to a close in a long, slow twilight.
> **—Jack London, "To Build a Fire"**

---

inside info

To determine whether adjectives modify equally (and should be separated by commas), use these two tests:

1 Shift the order of the adjectives; if the sentence is clear, the adjectives modify equally. (If *several* and *large* were shifted in the example below, the sentence would be unclear.)

2 Insert *and* between the adjectives; if the sentence reads well, use a comma when *and* is omitted. (If *and* were inserted in the sentences below, it would not read well.)

> He threw down *several large* pieces on top of the snow.
> **—Jack London, "To Build a Fire"**

582 Commas are used to enclose an explanatory word or phrase.

> Matthew, younger by two years, had always been more daring than I.
> —Benjamin Baker

583 A specific kind of explanatory word or phrase called an **appositive** identifies or renames a preceding noun or pronoun. (Do not use commas with *restrictive appositives*. A restrictive appositive is essential to the basic meaning of the sentence. See the second example below and 587.)

> Benson, *our uninhibited and enthusiastic Yorkshire terrier,* joined our family on my sister's fifteenth birthday. Benson is a devoted friend to Baxter, *our older Yorkie.* (**appositive**)
> —Chad Hockerman, student writer

> Twenty-one-year-old student *Edna E. Rivera* almost had a nose job but changed her mind. (**restrictive appositive**)
> —Andrea Lo & Vera Perez

584 Commas are used to separate contrasted elements within a sentence.

> I laughed, not at my two colleagues, but at people who spend time worrying about what clothes they should wear.
> —Liu Zongren, *Two Years in the Melting Pot*

585 A comma should separate an adverb clause or a long modifying phrase from the independent clause that follows it.

> In the oddest places and at the strangest times, my grandmother can be found knitting madly away.

Note • A comma is usually omitted if the phrase or adverb clause follows the independent clause.

My grandmother can be found knitting madly away in the oddest places and at the strangest times.

586 Commas are used to enclose **nonrestrictive** phrases and clauses. Nonrestrictive phrases or clauses are those that are not essential or necessary to the basic meaning of the sentence. **Restrictive** phrases or clauses—phrases or clauses that *are* needed in the sentence because they restrict or limit the meaning of the sentence—*are not* set off with commas. Compare the following examples with their nonrestrictive and restrictive phrases.

> This woman, *whose hands were once large enough to hold my entire body,* does not now reach as high as my daughter's shoulder. (**nonrestrictive**)
> —Kim Chernin, *In My Mother's House*

> My hair, *which was already prickling,* began to rise upon my head. (**nonrestrictive**)
> —Mary Renault, *The Bull from the Sea*

Note • The two italicized clauses in the examples above are merely additional information; they are nonrestrictive (not required). If the clauses were left out of the sentences, the meaning of the sentences would remain clear. Clauses are restrictive if they are necessary to the sense of the sentence.

> Most Muslim women *who come here* change like me and become more liberated. (**restrictive**)
> —Fariba Nawa, student writer

> The man *who strikes first* admits that his ideas have given out. (**restrictive**)
> —Chinese proverb

---

a closer look Compare the following restrictive and nonrestrictive phrases:

> The novelist *Sinclair Lewis* was the first American to win a Nobel Prize for literature. (***Sinclair Lewis* is required; do not use commas.**)

> Sinclair Lewis, *a novelist,* was the first American to win a Nobel Prize for literature. (***A novelist* is not required; use commas.**)

587 Commas are used to set off items in an address and items in a date.

> Send your letter before January 1, 1996, to President Clinton, 1600 Pennsylvania Avenue NW, Washington, DC 20006.

Note • No comma is placed between the state and ZIP code. Also, no comma is needed if only the month and year are given: *January 1996*.

588 Commas are used to set off the exact words of the speaker from the rest of the sentence.

> "We can look as we walk," Kost murmured on the other side of him. "I, too, would like to stay in this place."
> —Robert Murphy, "Planet of the Condemned"

589 Commas are used to separate a **vocative** from the rest of the sentence. (A vocative is the noun that names the person/s spoken to.)

> I told you, *Mama,* you don't have to iron perma-prest.
> —Jeanne A. Taylor, "A House Divided"

590 A comma is used to separate an interjection or a weak exclamation from the rest of the sentence.

> *Yeah,* and like I can lie with the best of them.
> —**John Oliver Killens, *The Cotillion***

591 Commas are used to set off a word, phrase, or clause that interrupts the movement of a sentence. Such expressions usually can be identified through the following tests: (1) They may be omitted without changing the substance or meaning of a sentence. (2) They may be placed nearly anywhere in the sentence without changing the meaning of the sentence.

> For me, *well,* it's just a good job gone!
> —**Langston Hughes, "A Good Job Gone"**

> As a general rule, the safest way to double your money is to fold it and put it in your pocket.

592 Commas are used to separate a series of numbers in order to distinguish hundreds, thousands, millions, etc.

> 1,101   25,000   7,642,020

593 Commas are used to enclose a title or initials and names that follow a surname.

> Until Martin, Sr., was fifteen, he never had more than three months of schooling in any one year. —**Ed Clayton, *Martin Luther King: The Peaceful Warrior***

> Hickok, J. B., and Cody, William F., are two popular Western heroes.

594 A comma may be used for clarity or for emphasis. There will be times when none of the traditional comma rules call for a comma, but one will be needed to prevent confusion or to emphasize an important idea. Use a comma in either case.

> What she does, does matter to us. **(clarity)**

> He saw only dreams and memories, and heard music. **(emphasis)**
> —**Langston Hughes, "Home"**

---

inside
info

Do not use a comma that could cause confusion. There should be no comma between the subject and its verb or the verb and its object. Also, use no comma before an indirect quotation. (The commas circled below should not be used.)

> My English teacher always said◯Hemingway was a bit difficult.
> **(misuse of a comma before an indirect quotation)**

> But I liked◯*The Sun Also Rises.*
> **(misuse of a comma between a verb and its object)**

Semicolon

595 A **semicolon** is used to join two or more independent clauses that are not connected with a coordinating conjunction. (In other words, each of the clauses could stand alone as a separate sentence.)

> I did not call myself a poet; I told people I wrote poems.
>
> —Terry McMillan, "Breaking Ice"

Note • The exception to this rule occurs when the two clauses are closely related, short, or conversational in tone. Then a comma may be used.

> To rule is easy, to govern is difficult.

596 A semicolon is used *before* a conjunctive adverb when the word connects two independent clauses in a compound sentence. A comma should follow the adverb in this case. (Common conjunctive adverbs are these: *also, besides, for example, however, in addition, instead, meanwhile, then,* and *therefore.*)

> The old man seldom thought about the old white and blue dishes on the table; however, they seemed very important to him at this moment.
>
> — Lisa Servais, student writer

597 A semicolon is used to separate independent clauses that are long or contain commas.

> I fill this sacred pipe with the bark of the red willow; but before we smoke it, you must see how it is made and what it means.
>
> —John G. Neihardt, *Black Elk Speaks*

598 A semicolon is used to separate groups of words that already contain commas.

Every Saturday night my brother gathers up his things—goggles, shower cap, and snorkel; bubble bath, soap, and shampoo; tapes, stereo, and rubber duck—and heads for the tub.

Colon

599 A **colon** may be used after the salutation of a business letter.

Dear Justice Ginsberg: Dear Governor Symington:

600 A colon is used between the parts of a number indicating time.

8:30 p.m.   9:45 a.m.   10:10 p.m.

601 A colon may be used to emphasize a word, phrase, clause, or sentence that explains or adds impact to the main clause.

He's been a prisoner here longer than anyone else: thirty-three years.

—Wilbert Rideau, *Life Sentences*

I live two lives: one at home within my community and one outside in the society.

—Fariba Nawa, student writer

602 A colon is used to introduce a list.

We shared the same fundamental needs: family, friends, a familiar culture.

—Liu Zongren, *Two Years in the Melting Pot*

---

inside info

A colon should not separate a verb from its object or complement, and it should not separate a preposition from its object.

Incorrect: Dave likes: comfortable space and time to think.

Correct: Dave likes two things: comfortable space and time to think.

Incorrect: There was a show on the radio this morning: about stress and laughter.

Correct: This morning there was a show on the radio about an interesting subject: stress and laughter.

---

603 The colon is used to distinguish between title and subtitle, volume and page, and chapter and verse in literature.

Writers INC: A Guide to Writing, Thinking, & Learning

Encyclopedia Americana IV: 211

Psalm 23:1-6

604 A colon may be used to formally introduce a sentence, a question, or a quotation.

It was John F. Kennedy who said these words: "Ask not what your country can do for you. Ask what you can do for your country."

Hyphen

605 The **hyphen** is used to make a compound word.

>   great-great-grandfather   mother-in-law   three-year-old
>
>   And they pried pieces of baked-too-fast sunshine cake from the roofs of their
>   mouths and looked once more into the boy's eyes.
>
>   —Toni Morrison, *Song of Solomon*

Note • Don't use a single hyphen when a dash (two hyphens) is required.

606 A hyphen is used to join a capital letter to a noun or participle.

>   T-shirt   U-turn   V-shaped

607 The hyphen is used to join the words in compound numbers from *twenty*-*one* to *ninety-nine* when it is necessary to write them out. (See 678.)

>   On this day in 1955, a forty-two-year-old woman was on her way home from
>   work.
>   —Robert Fulghum, *It Was On Fire When I Lay Down On It*

608 A hyphen is used between the elements of a fraction, but not between the numerator and denominator when one or both are already hyphenated.

>   four-tenths   Five-sixteenths   (7/32) seven thirty-seconds

609 Use hyphens when two or more words have a common element that is omitted in all but the last term.

>   We have cedar posts in four-, six-, and eight-inch widths.

610 A hyphen is usually used to form new words beginning with the prefixes *self, ex, all, great,* and *half.* It is also used to join any prefix to a proper noun, a proper adjective, or the official name of an office. A hyphen is used with the suffix *elect.*

>   half-eaten   great-grandson   ex-mayor
>   post-Depression   governor-elect   mid-May
>
>   Self-trust is the essence of heroism.
>
>   —Ralph Waldo Emerson

Note • Use a hyphen with other prefixes or suffixes to avoid confusion or awkward spelling.

>   re-cover (not *recover*) the sofa   shell-like (not *shelllike*) shape

611 The hyphen is used to join numbers indicating the life span of a person and the score in a contest or vote.

>   In 1954 Attorney Thurgood Marshall (1908-1993) argued the winning side of
>   the 9-0 Supreme Court decision that school segregation is unconstitutional.

612 The hyphen is used to separate a word at the end of a line of print. A word may be divided only between syllables, and the hyphen is always placed after the syllable at the end of the line—never before a syllable at the beginning of the following line.

Guidelines for Using the Hyphen

1. Always leave enough of the word at the end of the line so that the word can be identified.

2. Never divide a one-syllable word: *rained, skills, through.*

3. Avoid dividing a word of five letters or less: *paper, study, July.*

4. Never divide a one-letter syllable from the rest of the word: *omit-ted,* not *o-mitted.*

5. Always divide a compound word between its basic units: *sister-in-law,* not *sis-ter-in-law.*

6. Never divide abbreviations or contractions: *shouldn't,* not *should-n't.*

7. When a vowel is a syllable by itself, divide the word after the vowel: *epi-sode,* not *ep-isode.*

8. Avoid dividing a number written as a figure: *1,000,000;* not *1,000,-000.* (If a figure must be broken, divide it after one of the commas.)

9. Avoid dividing the last word in a paragraph.

10. Never divide the last word in more than two lines in a row.

613 Use the hyphen to join two or more words that serve as a single adjective (a single-thought adjective) before a noun.

> In real life I am a large, big-boned woman with rough, man-working hands.
> —Alice Walker, "Everyday Use"

Note • When words forming the adjective come after the noun, do not hyphenate them.

> In real life, I am large and *big boned.*

Also note • When the first of these words is an adverb ending in *ly*, do not use a hyphen; also, do not use a hyphen when a number or letter is the final element in a one-thought adjective.

> *freshly painted* barn (adverb ending in *-ly*)

> *grade A* milk (letter is the final element)

> He had coarse hair combed back from an *oddly crescent* hairline.
> —E. L. Doctorow, *Ragtime*

Dash

614 The **dash** is used to indicate a sudden break or change in the sentence.

> At dark, shadowy intersections, I could cross in front of a car stopped at a traffic light and elicit the thunk, thunk, thunk, thunk of the driver—black, white, male, female—hammering down the door locks.
>
> —Brent Staples, "Night Stalker"

Note • A dash is indicated by two hyphens--without spacing before or after-- in all handwritten and typed material.

615 A dash is used to set off an introductory series from the clause that explains the series.

> Health, friends, family—where would we be without them?

616 A dash is used to show interrupted or faltering speech in dialogue.

> Why, hello, dear—yes, I understand—no, I remember—oh, I want to—of course I won't—why, no, I—why, yes, I—it was so nice to talk with you again, dear.

617 A dash may also be used to show that words or letters are missing.

> Mr.—won't let us marry.   —Alice Walker, *The Color Purple*

618 A dash may be used to emphasize a word, series, phrase, or clause.

> He's the kind of man who picks his friends—to pieces.   —Mae West

Little did Belthar know that his invention—the wheel of fortune—would change the course of human history.

Question Mark

619 A **question mark** is used at the end of a direct question.

> What can I know? What ought I to do? What may I hope?
> —**Immanuel Kant**

> Since when do you have to agree with people to defend them from injustice?
> —**Lillian Hellman**

620 No question mark is used after an indirect question.

> I asked her if she'd ever met with the angel who whispered to her mother at cooking time.
> —**Gina M. Camodeca, "Kelli"**

621 When two clauses within a sentence both ask questions, one question mark is used.

> When you come home late, does your mother greet you with, "Do you know what time it is?"

622 The question mark is placed within parentheses to show uncertainty.

> This August will be the 25th anniversary (?) of Woodstock.

623 A short question within parentheses—or set off by dashes—is punctuated with a question mark.

> You must consult your handbook (what choice do you have?) when you need to know a punctuation rule.

> Maybe somewhere in the pasts of these humbled people, there were cases of bad mothering or absent fathering or emotional neglect—what family surviving the '50s was exempt?—but I couldn't believe these human errors brought the physical changes in Frank.
> —**Mary Kay Blakely,** *Wake Me When It's Over*

Exclamation Point

624 The **exclamation point** is used to express strong feeling. It may be placed after a word, a phrase, or a sentence. (The exclamation point should be used sparingly.)

> "That's not the point," said Wangero. "These are all pieces of dresses Grandma used to wear. She did all this stitching by hand. Imagine!"
> —**Alice Walker, "Everyday Use"**

> Su-su-something's crawling up the back of my neck!
> —**Mark Twain,** *Roughing It*

> She was on tiptoe, stretching for an orange, when they heard, "HEY YOU!"
> —**Beverly Naidoo,** *Journey to Jo'burg*

Quotation Marks

625 **Quotation marks** are used to punctuate titles of songs, poems, short stories, lectures, courses, episodes of radio or television programs, chapters of books, unpublished works, and articles found in magazines, newspapers, or encyclopedias. (For punctuation of other titles, see 632.)

> "Even Flow" **(song)**
>
> "A Song for Emily" **(short story)**
>
> "Twentieth Century Women Writers" **(course title)**
>
> "Warm Welcome in Tokyo" **(magazine article)**
>
> "Lady in the Cupboard" **(chapter in a book)**
>
> "Force of Nature" **(television episode from** *Star Trek: The Next Generation***)**

Note ● In titles, capitalize the first word, the last word, and every word in between *except* articles, short prepositions, and short conjunctions. (See 658.)

626 Quotation marks also may be used (1) to distinguish a word that is being discussed, (2) to indicate that a word is slang, or (3) to point out that a word is being used in a special way.

> (1) A commentary on the times is that the word "honesty" is now preceded by "old-fashioned."
> > **—Larry Wolters**
>
> (2) I drank a Dixie and ate bar peanuts and asked the bartender where I could hear "chanky-chank," as Cajuns call their music.
> > **—William Least Heat Moon,** *Blue Highways*
>
> (3) In order to be popular, he works very hard at being "cute."

Note ● Italics (underlining) may be used in place of quotation marks for each of these three functions.

627 Periods and commas are always placed inside quotation marks.

> "Dr. Slaughter wants you to have liquids, Will," Mama said anxiously. "He said not to give you any solid food tonight."
> > **—Olive Ann Burns,** *Cold Sassy Tree*

628 An exclamation point or a question mark is placed inside quotation marks when it punctuates the quotation; it is placed outside when it punctuates the main sentence.

> What do you suppose it means when a vampire says, "Well, of course, you're welcome to stay the night"?

629 Semicolons or colons are always placed outside quotation marks.

> I wrote about Wallace Stevens' "Thirteen Ways of Looking at a Blackbird"; "Sunday Morning" was too deep for me.

Marking Quoted Material

1 **Quotation marks** are placed before and after direct quotations. Only the exact words quoted are placed within quotation marks.

> "Why, when I was a little girl," she began, "there was always plenty to do." **—Elizabeth Beling, student writer**

2 Quotation marks are placed before and after a quoted passage. Any word or punctuation mark that is not part of the original quotation must be placed inside brackets.

> **(Original)** First of all, it must accept responsibility for providing shelter for the homeless.

> **(Quotation)** "First of all, it [the federal government] must accept responsibility for providing shelter for the homeless."
> **—Amy Douma, "Helping the Homeless"**

Note • If you quote only part of the original passage, be sure to construct a sentence that is both accurate and grammatically correct.

> The report goes on to say that the federal government "must accept responsibility for providing shelter for the homeless."

3 If more than one paragraph is quoted, quotation marks are placed before each paragraph and at the end of the last paragraph (Example A). Quotations that are more than four lines on a page are usually set off from the text by indenting ten spaces from the left margin ("block form"). Quotation marks are placed neither before nor after the quoted material unless they appear in the original (Example B).

Example A

> " _____
> _____
> _____ .
> " _____
> _____
> _____ .
> " _____ ."

Example B

> _____
> _____
> _____
> _____
> _____ .
> _____

4 Single quotation marks are used to punctuate a quotation within a quotation. Double and single quotation marks are alternated in order to distinguish a quotation within a quotation within a quotation.

> Sarah said, "I never read 'The Raven'!"

> I said, "Did you hear her say, 'I never read "The Raven" '?"

Italics (Underlining)

631 **Italics** is a printer's term for a style of type that is slightly slanted. In this sentence the word *happiness* is typed in italics. In material that is handwritten or typed on a machine that cannot print in italics, each word or letter that should be in italics is underlined.

> In <u>The Road to Memphis</u>, racism is a contagious disease. **(typed)**

> Mildred Taylor's *The Road to Memphis* exposes racism. **(printed)**

632 Italics are used to indicate the titles of magazines, newspapers, pamphlets, books, plays, films, radio and television programs, book-length poems, ballets, operas, lengthy musical compositions, record albums, CD's, legal cases, and the names of ships and aircraft. (See 625.)

> <u>Young & Modern</u> **(magazine)**   <u>The Kitchen God's Wife</u> **(book)**
>
> <u>Schindler's List</u> **(film)**   <u>Home Improvement</u> **(television program)**
>
> <u>Romeo and Juliet</u> **(play)**   <u>Motorist's Handbook</u> **(pamphlet)**
>
> <u>New York Times</u> or New York <u>Times</u> **(newspaper)**

633 When one title appears within another title, punctuate as follows:

> "The <u>Fresh Prince of Bel-Air</u> Rings True" **(title of TV program in an article)**

634 Italics are used to indicate a foreign word that has not been adopted in the English language; it also denotes scientific names.

The <u>voyageurs</u> were hired by French businessmen to find new sources of fur. They found the <u>Costar Canadensis</u>, or North American beaver.

Parentheses

635 **Parentheses** are used to enclose explanatory or supplementary material that interrupts the normal sentence structure.

> Benson (our dog) sits in on our piano lessons (on the piano bench), much to the teacher's surprise and amusement.
> —**Chad Hockerman, student writer**

> One day he brought the teacher a dead chicken snake in a burlap sack, and a chicken was still inside the snake's belly (or whatever snakes call bellies).
> —**Willie Morris, *Good Old Boy***

636 Punctuation is placed within parentheses when it is intended to mark the material within the parenthetical. Also note that words enclosed by parentheses do not have to begin with a capital letter or end with a period—even though these words may express a complete thought.

> But Mom doesn't say boo to Dad; she's always sweet to him. (Actually she's sort of sweet to everybody.) —**Norma Fox Mazer, *Up on Fong Mountain***

> And, since your friend won't have the assignment (he was just thinking about calling *you*), you'll have to make a couple more calls to actually get it.
> —**Ken Taylor, "The Art and Practice of Avoiding Homework"**

Note • For unavoidable parentheses within parentheses (. . . [. . .] . . .), use brackets. Avoid overuse of parentheses by using commas instead.

Brackets

637 **Brackets** are used before and after material that a writer adds when quoting another writer.

> "Sometimes I think it [my writing] sounds like I walked out of the room and left the typewriter running." —**Gene Fowler**

Note • The brackets indicate that the words *my writing* are not part of the quotation but were added for clarification.

638 Place brackets around material that has been added by someone other than the author or speaker.

> "Congratulations to the astronomy club's softball team which put in, shall we say, a 'stellar' performance." [groans]

639 Place brackets around an editorial correction.

> "Brooklyn alone has eight percent of lead poisoning [victims] nationwide," said Marjorie Moore. —**Donna Actie, student writer**

640 Brackets should be placed around the letters *sic* (Latin for "as such"); the letters indicate that an error appearing in the quoted material was made by the original speaker or writer.

> "No parent can dessert [sic] his child without damaging a human life."

Apostrophe

641 An **apostrophe** is used to show that one or more letters have been left out of a word to form a contraction.

> don't - *o* is left out   she'd - *woul* is left out   it's - *i* is left out

Note • An apostrophe is also used to show that one or more letters or numbers have been left out of numerals or words that are spelled as they are actually spoken.

> class of '85 - *19* is left out   good mornin' - *g* is left out

642 An apostrophe and *s* are used to form the plural of a letter, a number, a sign, or a word discussed as a word.

> A - A's   C - C's   8 - 8's.
>
> You use too many *and*'s in your writing.

Note • When two apostrophes are called for in the same word, simply omit the second one.

> Follow closely the *do*'s and *don't*s (not *don't*'s) on the checklist.

643 The possessive form of singular nouns is usually made by adding an apostrophe and *s*.

> Spock's ears   John Lennon's assassination

Note • When a singular noun ends with an *s* or a *z* sound, the possessive may be formed by adding just an apostrophe. When the singular noun is a one-syllable word, however, the possessive is usually formed by adding both an apostrophe and *s*.

> Dallas' sports teams (or) Dallas's sports teams
>
> Kiss's last concert   my boss's generosity **(one-syllable word)**

644 The possessive form of plural nouns ending in *s* is usually made by adding just an apostrophe.

> Joneses' great-grandfather   bosses' office

---

inside info It will help you punctuate correctly if you remember that the word immediately before the apostrophe is the owner.

> girl's guitar **(girl is the owner)**   boss's office **(boss is the owner)**
>
> girls' guitar **(girls are the owners)**   bosses' office **(bosses are the owners)**

---

645 When possession is shared by more than one noun, use the possessive form for the last noun in the series.

> VanClumpin, VanDiken, and VanTulip's fish **(All three own the same fish.)**
>
> VanClumpin's, VanDiken's, and VanTulip's fish **(Each guy owns his own fish.)**

646 The possessive of a compound noun is formed by placing the possessive ending after the last word.

> his mother-in-law's**(singular)** career
> the secretary of state's**(singular)** spouse
>
> their mothers-in-law's**(plural)** husbands
> the secretaries of state's**(plural)** spouses

647 The possessive of an indefinite pronoun is formed by placing an apostrophe and s on the last word. (See 719.)

> everyone's   anyone's   somebody else's

648 An apostrophe is used with an adjective that is part of an expression indicating time or amount.

> yesterday's news   a day's wage   a month's pay

Diagonal

649 A **diagonal** (also called a slash) is used to form a fraction. Also place a diagonal between *and/or* to indicate that either is acceptable (avoid this use of the diagonal in formal writing).

> My shoe size is 5 1/2 unless I'm wearing running shoes; then it's 6 1/2.
>
> A large radio/tape player is a boombox, or a stereo or a box or a large metallic ham sandwich with speakers. It is not a "ghetto blaster."
>
> —Amoja Three Rivers, "Cultural Etiquette: A Guide"

650 When quoting more than one line of poetry, use a diagonal to show where each line of poetry ends.

> I go down. / Rung after rung and still / the oxygen immerses me / the blue light / the clear atoms / of our human air.
>
> —Adrienne Rich, "Diving Into the Wreck"

651

Punctuation Marks

´ Accent, acute	, Comma	( ) Parentheses
` Accent, grave	† Dagger	. Period
' Apostrophe	— Dash	? Question mark
* Asterisk	/ Diagonal/Slash	" " Quotation marks
{ or } Brace	¨(ü) Dieresis	§ Section
[ ] Brackets	… Ellipsis	; Semicolon
^ Caret	! Exclamation point	~ Tilde
¸(ç) Cedilla	‐ Hyphen	_____ Underscore
^ Circumflex	… Leaders	
: Colon	¶ Paragraph	

"Write freely and as rapidly as possible and throw the whole thing on paper. Never correct or rewrite until the whole thing is down."

—John Steinbeck

Checking Mechanics

Capitalization

 Capitalize all proper nouns and all proper adjectives (adjectives derived from proper nouns). The chart below provides a quick overview of capitalization rules. The pages following explain specific or special uses of capitalization.

Capitalization at a Glance

Days of the week	**Sunday, Monday, Tuesday**
Months	**June, July, August**
Holidays, holy days	**Thanksgiving, Easter, Hanukkah**
Periods, events in history	**Middle Ages, the Renaissance**
Special events	**the Battle of Bunker Hill**
Political parties	**Republican Party, Socialist Party**
Official documents	**Declaration of Independence**
Trade names	**Oscar Mayer hot dogs, Pontiac Sunbird**
Formal epithets	**Alexander the Great**
Official titles	**Mayor John Spitzer, Senator Feinstein**
Official state nicknames	**the Badger State, the Aloha State**
Geographical names	
Planets, heavenly bodies	**Earth, Jupiter, the Milky Way**
Continents	**Australia, South America**
Countries	**Ireland, Grenada, Sri Lanka**
States, provinces	**Ohio, Utah, Nova Scotia**
Cities, towns, villages	**El Paso, Burlington, Wonewoc**
Streets, roads, highways	**Park Avenue, Route 66, Interstate 90**
Sections of a country or continent	**the Southwest, the Far East**
Landforms	**the Rocky Mountains, the Sahara Desert**
Bodies of water	**Nile River, Lake Superior, Pumpkin Creek**
Public areas	**Yosemite, Yellowstone National Park**

653 Capitalize the first word in every sentence and the first word in a full-sentence direct quotation.

> **Hey**, remember that kid named Mary who has a little lamb?
>
> Well, last week she said, "**Oh**, Muttonface, why did you follow me?"

654 Capitalize the first word in each sentence that is enclosed in parentheses if that sentence comes before or after another complete sentence.

> Then Mary took that fuzzball right inside the school! (**Is** that weird or what?)

Note • Do *not* capitalize a sentence that is enclosed in parentheses and is located in the middle of another sentence.

> Well, just about everybody (**the** custodian who wiped up the puddle disagreed) thought the whole thing was a big joke.

655 Capitalize a complete sentence that follows a colon only if that sentence is a formal statement or a quotation. Also, capitalize the sentence following a colon if you want to emphasize that sentence.

> It was Ralph Waldo Emerson who made the following comment: "**What** you do speaks so loud that I cannot hear what you say."

656 Words that indicate particular sections of the country are proper nouns and should be capitalized; words that simply indicate direction are not proper nouns.

> Some sparrows stay in the **North**. (section of the country)
>
> They don't fly **south** because they're lazy. (direction)
>
> In fact, **northern** Minnesota sparrows are so lazy, they won't fly on weekends.

657 Capitalize races, nationalities, languages, and religions.

> African-American   Navajo   French   Catholic   Latino   Spanish   Muslim

658 Capitalize the first word of a title, the last word, and every word in between except articles (a, an, the), short prepositions, and short conjunctions. Follow this rule for titles of books, newspapers, magazines, poems, plays, songs, articles, films, works of art, pictures, and stories.

> *Going to Meet the Man*   *Chicago Tribune*   "Nothing Gold Can Stay"
>
> *A Midsummer Night's Dream*   "Jim Crow—a National Disgrace"

659 Capitalize the name of an organization, an association, or a team and its members.

> Tampa Bay Buccaneers   American Indian Movement
> Tucson High School Drama Club   Republican Party

660 Capitalize abbreviations of titles and organizations. (Some other abbreviations are also capitalized. See 681.)

> U.S.A.   NAACP   M.D.   Ph.D.   A.D.   B.C.   R.R.   No.

661 Capitalize the letters used to indicate form or shape.

> U-turn   I-beam   S-curve   A-bomb   T-shirt

662 Capitalize words like *father, mother, uncle,* and *senator* when they are parts of titles that include a personal name or when they are substituted for proper nouns (especially in direct address).

> Hi, **Uncle** Duane! (*Uncle* **is part of the name.**)
>
> My **uncle** has a new Harley.
>
> Did you know that **Senator** Proxmire owns a Harley?
>
> The **senator,** Bill Proxmire, is a cool guy.

Note ● To test whether a word is being substituted for a proper noun, simply read the sentence with a proper noun in place of the word. If the proper noun fits in the sentence, the word being tested should be capitalized; if the proper noun does not work in the sentence, the word should not be capitalized. (*Further note:* Usually the word is not capitalized if it follows a possessive—*my, his, our,* etc.)

> Did **Mom (Sue)** say we could go? (*Sue* **works in this sentence.**)
>
> Did your **mom (Sue)** say you could go? (*Sue* **does not work here; the word** *mom* **also follows the possessive** *your.*)

663 Words such as *sociology, history,* and *science* are proper nouns when they are the titles of specific courses, but are common nouns when they name a field of study.

> "Who teaches **History 202**?" **(title of a specific course)**
>
> "The same guy who teaches that **sociology** course." **(a field of study)**

Note ● The words *freshman, sophomore, junior,* and *senior* are not capitalized unless they refer to an entire class or are part of an official title.

> Rosa is a **senior** this year, so she'll be able to attend the **Senior** Banquet in the spring.

664 Nouns or pronouns that refer to the Supreme Being are capitalized. So are the word *Bible,* the books of the Bible, and the names for other holy books.

> **God**   **Him**   **Jehovah**   the **Lord**   the **Savior**   **Allah**
>
> **Bible**   **Book of Psalms**   **Ecclesiastes**   the **Koran**   the **Talmud**

665 Do *not* capitalize any of the following: (1) a prefix attached to a proper noun, (2) seasons of the year, (3) a common noun shared by (and coming after) two or more proper nouns, (4) words used to indicate direction or position, (5) the word *god* or *goddess* when referring to mythology, or (6) common nouns that appear to be part of a proper noun.

Capitalize	Do Not Capitalize
American	un-American
January, February	winter, spring
Lakes Erie and Michigan	Missouri and Ohio rivers
The South is quite conservative.	Turn south at the stop sign.
Are you going to the Junior Prom?	Only juniors are welcome.
Duluth Central High School	a Duluth high school
Governor Douglas Wilder	Douglas Wilder, our governor

Plurals

666 The **plurals** of most nouns are formed by adding *s* to the singular.

cheerleader – cheerleaders   wheel – wheels

667 The plurals of nouns ending in *sh, ch, x, s,* and *z* are made by adding *es* to the singular.

lunch – lunches   dish – dishes   mess – messes   fox – foxes

Note • Some nouns remain unchanged when used as plurals: *deer, sheep, salmon,* etc.

668 The plurals of common nouns that end in *y* (preceded by a consonant) are formed by changing the *y* to *i* and adding *es.*

fly – flies   jalopy – jalopies

669 The plurals of nouns that end in *y* (preceded by a vowel) are formed by adding only *s.*

donkey – donkeys   monkey – monkeys

Note • The plurals of proper nouns ending in *y* are formed by adding *s.*

670 The plurals of words ending in *o* (preceded by a vowel) are formed by adding *s.*

radio – radios   rodeo – rodeos   studio – studios

671 Most nouns ending in *o* (preceded by a consonant) are formed by adding *es.*

echo – echoes   hero – heroes   tomato – tomatoes

Exception: Musical terms always form plurals by adding *s;* consult a dictionary for other words of this type.

alto – altos   banjo – banjos   solo – solos   piano – pianos

672 The plurals of nouns that end in *f* or *fe* are formed in one of two ways: if the final *f* sound is still heard in the plural form of the word, simply add *s;* if the final sound is a *v* sound, change the *f* to *ve* and add *s.* (Note • Several words are correct with either ending.)

Plural ends with f sound: roof – roofs; chief – chiefs
Plural ends with v sound: wife – wives; loaf – loaves
Plural ends with either sound: hoof – hoofs, hooves

673 Many foreign words (as well as some of English origin) form a plural by taking on an irregular spelling; others are now acceptable with the commonly used *s* or *es* ending.

Foreign Words		English Words	
crisis	crises	child	children
criterion	criteria	goose	geese
radius	radii	die	dice

674 The plurals of symbols, letters, figures, and words considered as words are formed by adding an apostrophe and an *s*.

> I groaned when I opened my grade report and saw two C's and three B's.

> But Dad just yelled a lot of *wow*'s, *yippee*'s, and *way-to-go*'s.

Note • Some writers omit the apostrophe when the omission does not cause confusion.

> 1930's *or* 1930s   the three R's *or* Rs   YMCA's *or* YMCAs

675 The plurals of nouns that end with *ful* are formed by adding an *s* at the end of the word.

> three pailfuls   two tankfuls

Note • Do not confuse these examples with three *pails full* (when you are referring to three separate pails full of something) or two *tanks full*.

676 The plurals of compound nouns are usually formed by adding *s* or *es* to the important word in the compound.

> brothers-in-law   maids of honor   secretaries of state

677 Pronouns referring to a collective noun may be singular or plural. A pronoun is singular when the group (noun) is considered a unit. A pronoun is plural when the group (noun) is considered in terms of its individual components.

> The class prepared for its final exam. **(group as a unit)**

> The class prepared for their final exams. **(group as individuals)**

The class prepared for their final exams.

Numbers

678 Quick Guide

1 **Numbers** from one to nine are usually written as words; all numbers 10 and over are usually written as numerals.

> two   seven   nine   10   25   106   1,079

Exception: If numbers are used infrequently in a piece of writing, you may spell out those that can be written in no more than two words.

> ten   twenty-five   two hundred   fifty thousand

Note • Numbers being compared or contrasted should be kept in the same style.

> 8 to 11 years old *or* eight to eleven years old

2 Use numerals to express numbers in the following forms: money, decimal, percentage, chapter, page, address, telephone, ZIP code, time, dates, identification numbers, and statistics.

$2.39	26.2	8 percent
chapter 7	pages 287-89	July 6, 1945
44 B.C.	A.D. 79	4:30 P.M.
Highway 36	a vote of 23 to 4	24 mph

Exception: If numbers are used infrequently in a piece of writing, you may spell out amounts of money and percentages when you can do so in two or three words.

> nine cents   one hundred dollars   eight percent   thirty-five percent

Note • Always use numerals with abbreviations and symbols.

> 5'4"   8%   10 in.   3 tbsp.   6 lbs. 8 oz.   90° F

3 Use words to express numbers that begin a sentence.

> Fourteen students "forgot" their assignments.

Note • Change the sentence structure if this rule creates a clumsy construction.

> Clumsy: *Six hundred and thirty-nine* teachers were victims of the lay-off this year.
>
> Better: This year, 639 teachers were victims of the layoff.

4 Use words for numbers that precede a compound modifier that includes another number.

> The cats' chef prepared twelve 10-foot sub sandwiches for the picnic.
>
> Each sandwich contained twenty-one 12-centimeter mice.

Note • You may use a combination of words and numerals for very large numbers.

> 1.5 million   3 billion to 3.2 billion   6 billion

Abbreviations

679 An **abbreviation** is the shortened form of a word or phrase. The following abbreviations are always acceptable in both formal and informal writing:

Mr.   Mrs.   Miss   Ms.   Dr.   a.m.   p.m.   (A.M., P.M.)

Do not abbreviate the names of states, countries, months, days, units of measure, or courses of study in formal writing. Do not abbreviate the words *Street, Road, Avenue, Company,* and similar words when they are part of a proper name. Also, do not use signs or symbols (%, &, #, @) in place of words. The dollar sign is, however, appropriate when numerals are used to express an amount of money ($325).

680 Address Abbreviations

State Abbreviations

	Standard	Postal
Alabama	Ala.	AL
Alaska	Alaska	AK
Arizona	Ariz.	AZ
Arkansas	Ark.	AR
California	Calif.	CA
Colorado	Colo.	CO
Connecticut	Conn.	CT
Delaware	Del.	DE
District of Columbia	D.C.	DC
Florida	Fla.	FL
Georgia	Ga.	GA
Guam	Guam	GU
Hawaii	Hawaii	HI
Idaho	Idaho	ID
Illinois	Ill.	IL
Indiana	Ind.	IN
Iowa	Iowa	IA
Kansas	Kan.	KS
Kentucky	Ky.	KY
Louisiana	La.	LA
Maine	Maine	ME
Maryland	Md.	MD
Massachusetts	Mass.	MA
Michigan	Mich.	MI
Minnesota	Minn.	MN
Mississippi	Miss.	MS
Missouri	Mo.	MO
Montana	Mont.	MT
Nebraska	Neb.	NE
Nevada	Nev.	NV
New Hampshire	N.H.	NH
New Jersey	N.J.	NJ
New Mexico	N.M.	NM
New York	N.Y.	NY
North Carolina	N.C.	NC
North Dakota	N.D.	ND
Ohio	Ohio	OH
Oklahoma	Okla.	OK
Oregon	Ore.	OR
Pennsylvania	Pa.	PA
Puerto Rico	P.R.	PR
Rhode Island	R.I.	RI
South Carolina	S.C.	SC
South Dakota	S.D.	SD
Tennessee	Tenn.	TN
Texas	Texas	TX
Utah	Utah	UT
Vermont	Vt.	VT
Virginia	Va.	VA
Virgin Islands	V.I.	VI
Washington	Wash.	WA
West Virginia	W.Va.	WV
Wisconsin	Wis.	WI
Wyoming	Wyo.	WY

Canadian Provinces

	Standard	Postal
Alberta	Alta.	AB
British Columbia	B.C.	BC
Labrador	Lab.	LB
Manitoba	Man.	MB
New Brunswick	N.B.	NB
Newfoundland	N.F.	NF
Northwest Territories	N.W.T.	NT
Nova Scotia	N.S.	NS
Ontario	Ont.	ON
Prince Edward Island	P.E.I.	PE
Quebec	Que.	PQ
Saskatchewan	Sask.	SK
Yukon Territory	Y.T.	YT

Address Abbreviations

	Standard	Postal
Apartment	Apt.	APT
Avenue	Ave.	AVE
Boulevard	Blvd.	BLVD
Circle	Cir.	CIR
Court	Ct.	CT
Drive	Dr.	DR
East	E.	E
Expressway	Expy.	EXPY
Freeway	Fwy.	FWY
Heights	Hts.	HTS
Highway	Hwy.	HWY
Hospital	Hosp.	HOSP
Junction	Junc.	JCT
Lake	L.	LK
Lakes	Ls.	LKS
Lane	Ln.	LN
Meadows	Mdws.	MDWS
North	N.	N
Palms	Palms	PLMS
Park	Pk.	PK
Parkway	Pky.	PKY
Place	Pl.	PL
Plaza	Plaza	PLZ
Post Office	P.O.	PO
Box	Box	BOX
Ridge	Rdg.	RDG
River	R.	RV
Road	Rd.	RD
Room	Rm.	RM
Rural	R.	R
Rural Route	R.R.	RR
Shore	Sh.	SH
South	S.	S
Square	Sq.	SQ
Station	Sta.	STA
Street	St.	ST
Suite	Ste.	STE
Terrace	Ter.	TER
Turnpike	Tpke.	TPKE
Union	Un.	UN
View	View	VW
Village	Vil.	VLG
West	W.	W

681 Common Abbreviations

abr. abridge; abridgment
AC, ac alternating current
ack. acknowledge; acknowledgment
acv actual cash value
A.D. in the year of the Lord (Latin *anno Domini*)
AM amplitude modulation
A.M., a.m. before noon (Latin *ante meridiem*)
ASAP as soon as possible
avg., av. average
BBB Better Business Bureau
B.C. 1. before Christ 2. British Columbia
bibliog. bibliographer; bibliography
biog. biographer; biographical; biography
C 1. Celsius 2. centigrade 3. coulomb
c. circa (about)
cc cubic centimeter
cc. chapters
CDT, C.D.T. Central Daylight Time
cm. centimeter
c.o., c/o care of
COD, C.O.D 1. cash on delivery 2. collect on delivery
co-op. cooperative
CST, C.S.T. Central Standard Time
cu., c cubic
D.A. district attorney
d.b.a. doing business as
DC, dc direct current
dec. deceased
dept. department
disc. discount
DST, D.S.T. Daylight Saving Time
dup. duplicate
ea. each
ed. edition; editor
EDT, E.D.T. Eastern Daylight Time
e.g. for example (Latin *exempli gratia*)
EST, E.S.T. Eastern Standard Time
etc. and so forth (Latin *et cetera*)
ex. example
F Fahrenheit
FM frequency modulation
F.O.B., f.o.b. free on board
ft foot
g 1. gravity 2. gram
gal. gallon
gds. goods
gloss. glossary
GNP gross national product
hdqrs. headquarters

HIV human immunodeficiency virus
Hon. Honorable (title)
hp horsepower
Hz hertz
id. the same (Latin *idem*)
i.e. that is (Latin *id est*)
illus. illustration
inc. incorporated
IQ, I.Q. intelligence quotient
IRS Internal Revenue Service
ISBN International Standard Book Number
JP, J.P. justice of the peace
Jr., jr. junior
K 1. kelvin (temperature unit) 2. Kelvin (temperature scale)
kc kilocycle
kg kilogram
km kilometer
kn knot
kw kilowatt
l liter
lat. latitude
lb pound (Latin *libra*)
l.c. lowercase
lit. literary; literature
log logarithm
long. longitude
Ltd., ltd. limited
m meter
M.A. Master of Arts (Latin *Magister Artium*)
man. manual
Mc, mc megacycle
M.C., m.c. master of ceremonies
M.D. Doctor of Medicine (Latin *Medicinae Doctor*)
mdse. merchandise
mfg. manufacture; manufactured
mg milligram
mi. 1. mile 2. mill (monetary unit)
misc. miscellaneous
ml milliliter
mm millimeter
mpg, m.p.g. miles per gallon
mph, m.p.h. miles per hour
MS 1. manuscript 2. Mississippi (with ZIP code) 3. multiple sclerosis
Ms., Ms Title of courtesy for a woman
MST, M.S.T. Mountain Standard Time
NE northeast
neg. negative
N.S.F., n.s.f. not sufficient funds
NW northwest
oz, oz. ounce
PA public-address system
pct. percent
pd. paid

PDT, P.D.T. Pacific Daylight Time
Pfc, Pfc. private first class
pg., p. page
P.M., p.m. after noon (Latin *post meridiem*)
P.O. 1. Personnel Officer 2. purchase order 3. postal order; post office 4. also **p.o.** petty officer
pop. population
POW, P.O.W. prisoner of war
pp. pages
ppd. 1. postpaid 2. prepaid
PR, P.R. 1. public relations 2. Puerto Rico (with ZIP code)
psi, p.s.i. pounds per square inch
PST, P.S.T. Pacific Standard Time
PTA, P.T.A. Parent-Teachers Association
qt. quart
RD rural delivery
RF radio frequency
R.P.M., rpm revolutions per minute
R.S.V.P., r.s.v.p. please reply (French *répondez s'il vous plaît*)
SE southeast
SOS 1. international distress signal 2. any call for help
Sr. 1. senior (after surname) 2. sister (religious)
SRO, S.R.O. standing room only
ST standard time
St. 1. saint 2. strait 3. street
std. standard
SW southwest
syn. synonymous; synonym
tbs., tbsp. tablespoon
TM trademark
UHF, uhf ultra high frequency
V 1. *Physics:* velocity 2. *Electricity:* volt 3. volume
VA, V.A. Veterans Administration 2. Virginia (with ZIP code)
VHF, vhf very high frequency
VIP *Informal:* very important person
vol. 1. volume 2. volunteer
vs. versus
W 1. *Electricity:* watt 2. *Physics:* (also **w**) work 3. west
whse., whs. warehouse
wkly. weekly
w/o without
wt. weight
yd yard (measurement)

Acronyms and Initialisms

682 An **acronym** is a word formed from the first (or first few) letters of words in a set phrase. Even though acronyms are a form of abbreviation, they are not followed by a period(s).

radar – radio detecting and ranging

CARE – Cooperative for American Relief Everywhere

NASA – National Aeronautics and Space Administration

VISTA – Volunteers in Service to America

UNICEF – United Nations International Children's Emergency Fund

683 An **initialism** is similar to an acronym except that the initials used to form this abbreviation cannot be pronounced as a word.

CIA – Central Intelligence Agency

FBI – Federal Bureau of Investigation

FHA – Federal Housing Administration

684 Common Acronyms and Initialisms

AIDS	acquired immunodeficiency syndrome	**ORV**	off-road vehicle
CETA	Comprehensive Employment and Training Act	**OSHA**	Occupational Safety and Health Administration
CIA	Central Intelligence Agency	**PAC**	political action committee
FAA	Federal Aviation Administration	**PIN**	personal identification number
FBI	Federal Bureau of Investigation	**PSA**	public service announcement
FCC	Federal Communications Commission	**REA**	Rural Electrification Administration
FDA	Food and Drug Administration	**RICO**	Racketeer Influenced and Corrupt Organizations (Act)
FDIC	Federal Deposit Insurance Corporation	**ROTC**	Reserve Officers' Training Corps
FHA	Federal Housing Administration	**SADD**	Students Against Drunk Driving
FmHA	Farmers Home Administration	**SSA**	Social Security Administration
FTC	Federal Trade Commission	**SWAT**	Special Weapons and Tactics
IRS	Internal Revenue Service	**TDD**	telecommunications device for the deaf
MADD	Mothers Against Drunk Driving	**TMJ**	temporomandibular joint
NASA	National Aeronautics and Space Administration	**TVA**	Tennessee Valley Authority
NATO	North Atlantic Treaty Organization	**VA**	Veterans Administration
NYC	Neighborhood Youth Corps	**VISTA**	Volunteers in Service to America
OEO	Office of Economic Opportunity	**WAC**	Women's Army Corps
OEP	Office of Emergency Preparedness	**WAVES**	Women Accepted for Volunteer Emergency Service

Spelling Rules

685 Quick Guide

Rule 1: Write *i* before *e* except after *c*, or when sounded like *a* as in neighbor and weigh.

Examples: receive   perceive   relief

Exceptions: Eight of the exceptions are included in this sentence: **Neither sheik dared leisurely seize either weird species of financiers.**

When the *ie/ei* combination is not pronounced *ee*, it is usually spelled *ei*.

Examples: reign   foreign   weigh   neighbor

Exceptions: **fiery   friend   mischief   view**

Rule 2: When a one-syllable word (*bat*) ends in a consonant (*t*) preceded by one vowel (*a*), double the final consonant before adding a suffix that begins with a vowel (*batting*).

sum—summary   god—goddess

When a multi-syllable word (*control*) ends in a consonant (*l*) preceded by one vowel (*o*), the accent is on the last syllable (*con trol´*), and the suffix begins with a vowel (*ing*)—the same rule holds true: double the final consonant (*controlling*).

prefer—preferred   begin—beginning

forget—forgettable   admit—admittance

Rule 3: If a word ends with a silent *e*, drop the *e* before adding a suffix that begins with a vowel.

state—stating—statement   like—liking—likeness

use—using—useful   nine—ninety—nineteen

Note • You do not drop the *e* when the suffix begins with a consonant. Exceptions include *judgment, truly, argument,* and *ninth.*

Rule 4: When *y* is the last letter in a word and the *y* is preceded by a consonant, change the *y* to *i* before adding any suffix except those beginning with *i*.

fry—fries   hurry—hurried   lady—ladies

ply—pliable   happy—happiness   beauty—beautiful

When forming the plural of a word that ends with a *y* that is preceded by a vowel, add *s*.

toy—toys   play—plays   monkey—monkeys

686 Commonly Misspelled Words

A

ab-bre-vi-ate
a-brupt
ab-scess
ab-sence
ab-so-lute (-ly)
ab-sorb-ent
ab-surd
a-bun-dance
ac-cede
ac-cel-er-ate
ac-cept (-ance)
ac-ces-si-ble
ac-ces-so-ry
ac-ci-den-tal-ly
ac-com-mo-date
ac-com-pa-ny
ac-com-plice
ac-com-plish
ac-cor-dance
ac-cord-ing
ac-count
ac-crued
ac-cu-mu-late
ac-cu-rate
ac-cus-tom (ed)
ache
a-chieve (-ment)
ac-knowl-edge
ac-quaint-ance
ac-qui-esce
ac-quired
ac-tu-al
a-dapt
ad-di-tion (-al)
ad-dress
ad-e-quate
ad-journed
ad-just-ment
ad-mi-ra-ble
ad-mis-si-ble
ad-mit-tance
ad-van-ta-geous
ad-ver-tise-ment
ad-ver-tis-ing
ad-vice (n.)
ad-vis-able
ad-vise (v.)

ae-ri-al
af-fect
af-fi-da-vit
a-gain
a-gainst
ag-gra-vate
ag-gres-sion
a-gree-able
a-gree-ment
aisle
al-co-hol
a-lign-ment
al-ley
al-lot-ted
al-low-ance
all right
al-most
al-ready
al-though
al-to-geth-er
a-lu-mi-num
al-ways
am-a-teur
a-mend-ment
a-mong
a-mount
a-nal-y-sis
an-a-lyze
an-cient
an-ec-dote
an-es-thet-ic
an-gle
an-ni-hi-late
an-ni-ver-sa-ry
an-nounce
an-noy-ance
an-nu-al
a-noint
a-non-y-mous
an-swer
ant-arc-tic
an-tic-i-pate
anx-i-ety
anx-ious
any-thing
a-part-ment
a-pol-o-gize
ap-pa-ra-tus
ap-par-ent (-ly)
ap-peal

ap-pear-ance
ap-pe-tite
ap-pli-ance
ap-pli-ca-ble
ap-pli-ca-tion
ap-point-ment
ap-prais-al
ap-pre-ci-ate
ap-proach
ap-pro-pri-ate
ap-prov-al
ap-prox-i-mate-ly
ar-chi-tect
arc-tic
ar-gu-ment
a-rith-me-tic
a-rouse
ar-range-ment
ar-riv-al
ar-ti-cle
ar-ti-fi-cial
as-cend
as-cer-tain
as-i-nine
as-sas-sin
as-sess (-ment)
as-sign-ment
as-sist-ance
as-so-ci-ate
as-so-ci-a-tion
as-sume
as-sur-ance
as-ter-isk
ath-lete
ath-let-ic
at-tach
at-tack (ed)
at-tempt
at-tend-ance
at-ten-tion
at-ti-tude
at-tor-ney
at-trac-tive
au-di-ble
au-di-ence
au-thor-i-ty
au-to-mo-bile
au-tumn
aux-il-ia-ry

a-vail-a-ble
av-er-age
aw-ful
aw-ful-ly
awk-ward

B

bach-e-lor
bag-gage
bal-ance
bal-loon
bal-lot
ba-nan-a
ban-dage
bank-rupt
bar-gain
bar-rel
base-ment
ba-sis
bat-tery
beau-ti-ful
beau-ty
be-come
be-com-ing
be-fore
beg-gar
be-gin-ning
be-hav-ior
be-ing
be-lief
be-lieve
ben-e-fi-cial
ben-e-fit (-ed)
be-tween
bi-cy-cle
bis-cuit
bliz-zard
book-keep-er
bough
bought
bouil-lon
bound-a-ry
break-fast
breath (n.)
breathe (v.)
brief
bril-liant
Brit-ain

bro-chure
brought
bruise
budg-et
bul-le-tin
buoy-ant
bu-reau
bur-glar
bury
busi-ness
busy

C

caf-e-te-ria
caf-feine
cal-en-dar
cam-paign
can-celed
can-di-date
can-is-ter
ca-noe
can't
ca-pac-i-ty
cap-i-tal
cap-i-tol
cap-tain
car-bu-ret-or
ca-reer
car-i-ca-ture
car-riage
cash-ier
cas-se-role
cas-u-al-ty
cat-a-log
ca-tas-tro-phe
caught
cav-al-ry
cel-e-bra-tion
cem-e-tery
cen-sus
cen-tu-ry
cer-tain
cer-tif-i-cate
ces-sa-tion
chal-lenge
change-a-ble
char-ac-ter (-is-tic)
chauf-feur

687

chief
chim-ney
choc-o-late
choice
choose
Chris-tian
cir-cuit
cir-cu-lar
cir-cum-stance
civ-i-li-za-tion
cli-en-tele
cli-mate
climb
clothes
coach
co-coa
co-er-cion
col-lar
col-lat-er-al
col-lege
col-lo-qui-al
colo-nel
col-or
co-los-sal
col-umn
com-e-dy
com-ing
com-mence
com-mer-cial
com-mis-sion
com-mit
com-mit-ment
com-mit-ted
com-mit-tee
com-mu-ni-cate
com-mu-ni-ty
com-par-a-tive
com-par-i-son
com-pel
com-pe-tent
com-pe-ti-tion
com-pet-i-tive-ly
com-plain
com-ple-ment
com-plete-ly
com-plex-ion
com-pli-ment
com-pro-mise
con-cede
con-ceive
con-cern-ing
con-cert

con-ces-sion
con-clude
con-crete
con-curred
con-cur-rence
con-demn
con-de-scend
con-di-tion
con-fer-ence
con-ferred
con-fi-dence
con-fi-den-tial
con-grat-u-late
con-science
con-sci-en-tious
con-scious
con-sen-sus
con-se-quence
con-ser-va-tive
con-sid-er-ably
con-sign-ment
con-sis-tent
con-sti-tu-tion
con-tempt-ible
con-tin-u-al-ly
con-tin-ue
con-tin-u-ous
con-trol
con-tro-ver-sy
con-ven-ience
con-vince
cool-ly
co-op-er-ate
cor-dial
cor-po-ra-tion
cor-re-late
cor-re-spond
cor-re-spond-
    ence
cor-rob-o-rate
cough
couldn't
coun-cil
coun-sel
coun-ter-feit
coun-try
cour-age
cou-ra-geous
cour-te-ous
cour-te-sy
cous-in
cov-er-age
cred-i-tor

cri-sis
crit-i-cism
crit-i-cize
cru-el
cu-ri-os-i-ty
cu-ri-ous
cur-rent
cur-ric-u-lum
cus-tom
cus-tom-ary
cus-tom-er
cyl-in-der

D

dai-ly
dair-y
dealt
debt-or
de-ceased
de-ceit-ful
de-ceive
de-cid-ed
de-ci-sion
dec-la-ra-tion
dec-o-rate
de-duct-i-ble
de-fend-ant
de-fense
de-ferred
def-i-cit
def-i-nite (-ly)
def-i-ni-tion
del-e-gate
de-li-cious
de-pend-ent
de-pos-i-tor
de-pot
de-scend
de-scribe
de-scrip-tion
de-sert
de-serve
de-sign
de-sir-able
de-sir-ous
de-spair
des-per-ate
de-spise
des-sert
de-te-ri-o-rate

de-ter-mine
de-vel-op
de-vel-op-ment
de-vice
de-vise
di-a-mond
di-a-phragm
di-ar-rhe-a
di-a-ry
dic-tio-nary
dif-fer-ence
dif-fer-ent
dif-fi-cul-ty
di-lap-i-dat-ed
di-lem-ma
din-ing
di-plo-ma
di-rec-tor
dis-agree-able
dis-ap-pear
dis-ap-point
dis-ap-prove
dis-as-trous
dis-ci-pline
dis-cov-er
dis-crep-an-cy
dis-cuss
dis-cus-sion
dis-ease
dis-sat-is-fied
dis-si-pate
dis-tin-guish
dis-trib-ute
di-vide
di-vine
di-vis-i-ble
di-vi-sion
doc-tor
doesn't
dom-i-nant
dor-mi-to-ry
doubt
drudg-ery
du-al
du-pli-cate
dye-ing
dy-ing

E

ea-ger-ly
ear-nest
eco-nom-i-cal
econ-o-my
ec-sta-sy
e-di-tion
ef-fer-ves-cent
ef-fi-ca-cy
ef-fi-cien-cy
eighth
ei-ther
e-lab-o-rate
e-lec-tric-i-ty
el-e-phant
el-i-gi-ble
e-lim-i-nate
el-lipse
em-bar-rass
e-mer-gen-cy
em-i-nent
em-pha-size
em-ploy-ee
em-ploy-ment
e-mul-sion
en-close
en-cour-age
en-deav-or
en-dorse-ment
en-gi-neer
En-glish
e-nor-mous
e-nough
en-ter-prise
en-ter-tain
en-thu-si-as-tic
en-tire-ly
en-trance
en-vel-op (v.)
en-ve-lope (n.)
en-vi-ron-ment
equip-ment
equipped
e-quiv-a-lent
es-pe-cial-ly
es-sen-tial
es-tab-lish
es-teemed
et-i-quette
ev-i-dence

ommonly misspelled words

688

ex-ag-ger-ate
ex-ceed
ex-cel-lent
ex-cept
ex-cep-tion-al-ly
ex-ces-sive
ex-cite
ex-ec-u-tive
ex-er-cise
ex-haust (-ed)
ex-hi-bi-tion
ex-hil-a-ra-tion
ex-is-tence
ex-or-bi-tant
ex-pect
ex-pe-di-tion
ex-pend-i-ture
ex-pen-sive
ex-pe-ri-ence
ex-plain
ex-pla-na-tion
ex-pres-sion
ex-qui-site
ex-ten-sion
ex-tinct
ex-traor-di-nar-y
ex-treme-ly

F

fa-cil-i-ties
fal-la-cy
fa-mil-iar
fa-mous
fas-ci-nate
fash-ion
fa-tigue (d)
fau-cet
fa-vor-ite
fea-si-ble
fea-ture
Feb-ru-ar-y
fed-er-al
fem-i-nine
fer-tile
fic-ti-tious
field
fierce
fi-ery
fi-nal-ly
fi-nan-cial-ly

fo-li-age
for-ci-ble
for-eign
for-feit
for-go
for-mal-ly
for-mer-ly
for-tu-nate
for-ty
for-ward
foun-tain
fourth
frag-ile
fran-ti-cal-ly
freight
friend
ful-fill
fun-da-men-tal
fur-ther-more
fu-tile

G

gad-get
gan-grene
ga-rage
gas-o-line
gauge
ge-ne-al-o-gy
gen-er-al-ly
gen-er-ous
ge-nius
gen-u-ine
ge-og-ra-phy
ghet-to
ghost
glo-ri-ous
gnaw
gov-ern-ment
gov-er-nor
gra-cious
grad-u-a-tion
gram-mar
grate-ful
grat-i-tude
grease
grief
griev-ous
gro-cery
grudge
grue-some

guar-an-tee
guard
guard-i-an
guer-ril-la
guess
guid-ance
guide
guilty
gym-na-si-um
gyp-sy
gy-ro-scope

H

hab-i-tat
ham-mer
hand-ker-chief
han-dle (d)
hand-some
hap-haz-ard
hap-pen
hap-pi-ness
ha-rass
har-bor
hast-i-ly
hav-ing
haz-ard-ous
height
hem-or-rhage
hes-i-tate
hin-drance
his-to-ry
hoarse
hol-i-day
hon-or
hop-ing
hop-ping
horde
hor-ri-ble
hos-pi-tal
hu-mor-ous
hur-ried-ly
hy-drau-lic
hy-giene
hymn
hy-poc-ri-sy

I

i-am-bic
i-ci-cle
i-den-ti-cal
id-io-syn-cra-sy
il-leg-i-ble
il-lit-er-ate
il-lus-trate
im-ag-i-nary
im-ag-i-na-tive
im-ag-ine
im-i-ta-tion
im-me-di-ate-ly
im-mense
im-mi-grant
im-mor-tal
im-pa-tient
im-per-a-tive
im-por-tance
im-pos-si-ble
im-promp-tu
im-prove-ment
in-al-ien-able
in-ci-den-tal-ly
in-con-ve-nience
in-cred-i-ble
in-curred
in-def-i-nite-ly
in-del-ible
in-de-pend-ence
in-de-pend-ent
in-dict-ment
in-dis-pens-able
in-di-vid-u-al
in-duce-ment
in-dus-tri-al
in-dus-tri-ous
in-ev-i-ta-ble
in-fe-ri-or
in-ferred
in-fi-nite
in-flam-ma-ble
in-flu-en-tial
in-ge-nious
in-gen-u-ous
in-im-i-ta-ble
in-i-tial
ini-ti-a-tion
in-no-cence
in-no-cent

in-oc-u-la-tion
in-quir-y
in-stal-la-tion
in-stance
in-stead
in-sti-tute
in-sur-ance
in-tel-lec-tu-al
in-tel-li-gence
in-ten-tion
in-ter-cede
in-ter-est-ing
in-ter-fere
in-ter-mit-tent
in-ter-pret (-ed)
in-ter-rupt
in-ter-view
in-ti-mate
in-va-lid
in-ves-ti-gate
in-ves-tor
in-vi-ta-tion
ir-i-des-cent
ir-rel-e-vant
ir-re-sis-ti-ble
ir-rev-er-ent
ir-ri-gate
is-land
is-sue
i-tem-ized
i-tin-er-ar-y
it's (it is)

J

jan-i-tor
jeal-ous (-y)
jeop-ard-ize
jew-el-ry
jour-nal
jour-ney
judg-ment
jus-tice
jus-ti-fi-able

K

kitch-en
knowl-edge
knuck-le

commonly misspelled word

L

la-bel
lab-o-ra-to-ry
lac-quer
lan-guage
laugh
laun-dry
law-yer
league
lec-ture
le-gal
leg-i-ble
leg-is-la-ture
le-git-i-mate
lei-sure
length
let-ter-head
li-a-bil-i-ty
li-a-ble
li-ai-son
li-brar-y
li-cense
lieu-ten-ant
light-ning
lik-able
like-ly
lin-eage
liq-ue-fy
liq-uid
lis-ten
lit-er-ary
lit-er-a-ture
live-li-hood
liv-ing
log-a-rithm
lone-li-ness
loose
lose
los-ing
lov-able
love-ly
lun-cheon
lux-u-ry

M

ma-chine
mag-a-zine
mag-nif-i-cent

main-tain
main-te-nance
ma-jor-i-ty
mak-ing
man-age-ment
ma-neu-ver
man-u-al
man-u-fac-ture
man-u-script
mar-riage
mar-shal
ma-te-ri-al
math-e-mat-ics
max-i-mum
may-or
mean-ness
meant
mea-sure
med-i-cine
me-di-eval
me-di-o-cre
me-di-um
mem-o-ran-dum
men-us
mer-chan-dise
mer-it
mes-sage
mile-age
mil-lion-aire
min-i-a-ture
min-i-mum
min-ute
mir-ror
mis-cel-la-neous
mis-chief
mis-chie-vous
mis-er-a-ble
mis-ery
mis-sile
mis-sion-ary
mis-spell
mois-ture
mol-e-cule
mo-men-tous
mo-not-o-nous
mon-u-ment
mort-gage
mu-nic-i-pal
mus-cle
mu-si-cian
mus-tache
mys-te-ri-ous

N

na-ive
nat-u-ral-ly
nec-es-sary
ne-ces-si-ty
neg-li-gi-ble
ne-go-ti-ate
neigh-bor-hood
nev-er-the-less
nick-el
niece
nine-teenth
nine-ty
no-tice-able
no-to-ri-ety
nu-cle-ar
nui-sance

O

o-be-di-ence
o-bey
o-blige
ob-sta-cle
oc-ca-sion
oc-ca-sion-al-ly
oc-cu-pant
oc-cur
oc-curred
oc-cur-rence
of-fense
of-fi-cial
of-ten
o-mis-sion
o-mit-ted
o-pin-ion
op-er-ate
op-po-nent
op-por-tu-ni-ty
op-po-site
op-ti-mism
or-di-nance
or-di-nar-i-ly
orig-i-nal
out-ra-geous

P

pag-eant
paid
pam-phlet
par-a-dise
para-graph
par-al-lel
par-a-lyze
pa-ren-the-ses
pa-ren-the-sis
par-lia-ment
par-tial
par-tic-i-pant
par-tic-i-pate
par-tic-u-lar-ly
pas-time
pa-tience
pa-tron-age
pe-cu-liar
per-ceive
per-haps
per-il
per-ma-nent
per-mis-si-ble
per-pen-dic-u-
    lar
per-se-ver-ance
per-sis-tent
per-son-al (-ly)
per-son-nel
per-spi-ra-tion
per-suade
phase
phe-nom-e-non
phi-los-o-phy
phy-si-cian
piece
planned
pla-teau
plau-si-ble
play-wright
pleas-ant
pleas-ure
pneu-mo-nia
pol-i-ti-cian
pos-sess
pos-ses-sion
pos-si-ble
prac-ti-cal-ly
prai-rie
pre-cede

pre-ce-dence
pre-ced-ing
pre-cious
pre-cise-ly
pre-ci-sion
pre-de-ces-sor
pref-er-a-ble
pref-er-ence
pre-ferred
prej-u-dice
pre-lim-i-nar-y
pre-mi-um
prep-a-ra-tion
pres-ence
prev-a-lent
pre-vi-ous
prim-i-tive
prin-ci-pal
prin-ci-ple
pri-or-i-ty
pris-on-er
priv-i-lege
prob-a-bly
pro-ce-dure
pro-ceed
pro-fes-sor
prom-i-nent
pro-nounce
pro-nun-ci-a-
    tion
pro-pa-gan-da
pros-e-cute
pro-tein
psy-chol-o-gy
pub-lic-ly
pump-kin
pur-chase
pur-sue
pur-su-ing
pur-suit

Q

qual-i-fied
quan-ti-ty
quar-ter
ques-tion-naire
qui-et
quite
quo-tient

ommonly misspelled words

R

raise
rap-port
re-al-ize
re-al-ly
re-cede
re-ceipt
re-ceive
re-ceived
rec-i-pe
re-cip-i-ent
rec-og-ni-tion
rec-og-nize
rec-om-mend
re-cur-rence
ref-er-ence
re-ferred
re-hearse
reign
re-im-burse
rel-e-vant
re-lieve
re-li-gious
re-mem-ber
re-mem-brance
rem-i-nisce
ren-dez-vous
re-new-al
rep-e-ti-tion
rep-re-sen-ta-tive
req-ui-si-tion
res-er-voir
re-sis-tance
re-spect-a-bly
re-spect-ful-ly
re-spec-tive-ly
re-spon-si-bil-i-ty
res-tau-rant
rheu-ma-tism
rhyme
rhythm
ri-dic-u-lous
route

S

sac-ri-le-gious
safe-ty
sal-a-ry

sand-wich
sat-is-fac-to-ry
Sat-ur-day
scarce-ly
scene
scen-er-y
sched-ule
sci-ence
scis-sors
sec-re-tary
seize
sen-si-ble
sen-tence
sen-ti-nel
sep-a-rate
ser-geant
sev-er-al
se-vere-ly
shep-herd
sher-iff
shin-ing
siege
sig-nif-i-cance
sim-i-lar
si-mul-ta-ne-ous
since
sin-cere-ly
ski-ing
sol-dier
sol-emn
so-phis-ti-cat-ed
soph-o-more
so-ror-i-ty
source
sou-ve-nir
spa-ghet-ti
spe-cif-ic
spec-i-men
speech
sphere
spon-sor
spon-ta-ne-ous
sta-tion-ary
sta-tion-ery
sta-tis-tic
stat-ue
stat-ure
stat-ute
stom-ach
stopped
straight
strat-e-gy

strength
stretched
study-ing
sub-si-dize
sub-stan-tial
sub-sti-tute
sub-tle
suc-ceed
suc-cess
suf-fi-cient
sum-ma-rize
su-per-fi-cial
su-per-in-tend-ent
su-pe-ri-or-i-ty
su-per-sede
sup-ple-ment
sup-pose
sure-ly
sur-prise
sur-veil-lance
sur-vey
sus-cep-ti-ble
sus-pi-cious
sus-te-nance
syl-la-ble
sym-met-ri-cal
sym-pa-thy
sym-pho-ny
symp-tom
syn-chro-nous

T

tar-iff
tech-nique
tele-gram
tem-per-a-ment
tem-per-a-ture
tem-po-rary
ten-den-cy
ten-ta-tive
ter-res-tri-al
ter-ri-ble
ter-ri-to-ry
the-ater
their
there-fore
thief
thor-ough (-ly)
though
through-out

tired
to-bac-co
to-geth-er
to-mor-row
tongue
to-night
touch
tour-na-ment
tour-ni-quet
to-ward
trag-e-dy
trai-tor
tran-quil-iz-er
trans-ferred
trea-sur-er
tried
tru-ly
Tues-day
tu-ition
typ-i-cal
typ-ing

U

unan-i-mous
un-con-scious
un-doubt-ed-ly
un-for-tu-nate-ly
unique
u-ni-son
uni-ver-si-ty
un-nec-es-sary
un-prec-e-dent-ed
un-til
up-per
ur-gent
us-able
use-ful
using
usu-al-ly
u-ten-sil
u-til-ize

V

va-can-cies
va-ca-tion
vac-u-um
vague
valu-able

va-ri-ety
var-i-ous
veg-e-ta-ble
ve-hi-cle
veil
ve-loc-i-ty
ven-geance
vi-cin-i-ty
view
vig-i-lance
vil-lain
vi-o-lence
vis-i-bil-i-ty
vis-i-ble
vis-i-tor
voice
vol-ume
vol-un-tary
vol-un-teer

W

wan-der
war-rant
weath-er
Wednes-day
weird
wel-come
wel-fare
where
wheth-er
which
whole
whol-ly
whose
width
wom-en
worth-while
wor-thy
wreck-age
wres-tler
writ-ing
writ-ten
wrought

Y

yel-low
yes-ter-day
yield

691 | # Steps to Becoming a
Better Speller

1 **Be patient.** Learning to become a good speller takes time.

2 **Check the correct pronunciation of each word** you are attempting to spell. Knowing the correct pronunciation of each word is important to remembering its spelling.

3 **Note the meaning and history of each word** as you are checking the dictionary for pronunciation. Knowing the meaning and history of a word can provide you with a better notion of how and when the word will probably be used. This fuller understanding will help you remember the spelling of that particular word.

4 **Before you close the dictionary, practice spelling** the word. You can do this by looking away from the page and trying to "see" the word in your "mind's eye." Write the word on a piece of paper. Check the spelling in the dictionary and repeat the process until you are able to spell the word correctly.

5 **Learn some spelling rules.** The four rules in this handbook are four of the most useful, although there are others.

6 **Make a list of the words that you misspell.** Select the first 10 and practice spelling them.

> **STEP A:** Read each word carefully, then write it on a piece of paper. Look at the written word to see that it's spelled correctly. Repeat the process for those words that you misspelled.

> **STEP B:** When you have finished your first 10 words, ask someone to read the words to you so you can write them again. Again, check for misspellings. If you find none, congratulations! Repeat both steps with your next 10 words.

7 **Write often.** As noted educator Frank Smith said,

"There is little point in learning to spell if you have little intention of writing."

"The difference between the right word and the nearly right word is the same as that between lightning and the lightning bug."

—Mark Twain

⟨692⟩ Using the Right Word

a, an ● *A* is used before words that begin with a consonant sound; *an* is used before words that begin with a vowel sound.

a heap	a uniform	an idol
an urban area	an honor	a historian

accept, except ● The verb *accept* means "to receive or believe"; the preposition *except* means "other than."

> The principal accepted the boy's story about the broken window, but she asked why no one except him saw the ball accidentally slip from his hand.

adapt, adopt ● *Adapt* means "to adjust or change to fit"; *adopt* means "to choose and treat as your own" (a child, an idea).

> After a lengthy period of study, Malcolm X adopted the Muslim faith and adapted to its lifestyle.

affect, effect ● *Affect* means "to influence"; the verb *effect* means "to produce."

> Mark's giggle affected the preacher. Mark's giggle effected a pinch from his mom.

The noun *effect* means "the result."

> The effect of the pinch was a sore leg.

allusion, illusion ● *Allusion* is an indirect reference to something; *illusion* is a false picture or idea.

> The person who makes many allusions to his strength tries to reinforce the illusion that he's strong.

alot ● *Alot* is not one word; *a lot* (two words) is a vague descriptive phrase which should probably not be used too often.

> "You can observe a lot just by watching."
>
> — Yogi Berra

693 **already, all ready** ● *Already* is an adverb meaning "before this time" or "by this time." *All ready* is an adjective meaning "fully prepared."

> My three-year-old sister reads already. She is all ready to start school.

alright ● *Alright* is the incorrect form of *all right*. (Please note, the following are spelled correctly: *always, altogether, already, almost.*)

altogether, all together ● *Altogether* means "entirely." The phrase *all together* means "in a group" or "all at once."

> "There is altogether too much gridlock," complained the Democrats.
> All together, the Republicans yelled, "No way!"

among, between ● *Among* is used when speaking of more than two persons or things. *Between* is used when speaking of only two.

> It's between Jerome and Clifton. Among all of the boys in our class, they are the two that made it into the final round.

amount, number ● *Amount* is used for bulk measurement. *Number* is used to count separate units. (See also **fewer, less**.)

The amount of weight you lose depends on the number of carrot sticks you eat.

annual, biannual, semiannual, biennial, perennial ● An *annual* event happens once every year. A *biannual* event happens twice a year (*semiannual* is the same as *biannual*). A *biennial* event happens every two years. A *perennial* event is active throughout the year and continues to happen every year.

ant, aunt ● *Ant* is an insect. *Aunt* is a relative.

anyways ● This is the incorrect form of *anyway*. (Also watch out for *nowheres*.)

694 **ascared** ● *Ascared* is not standard English. Use either *scared* or *afraid.*

base, bass ● *Base* is the foundation or the lower part of something. *Bass* is a deep sound or tone. *Bass* (when pronounced like *class*) is a fish.

be, bee ● *Be* is the verb. *Bee* is the insect. *Bee* is also a neighborly work session.

berth, birth ● *Berth* is a space or compartment. *Birth* is the process of being born.

We give up our most comfortable berths through birth.

beside, besides ● *Beside* means "by the side of." *Besides* means "in addition to."

No other women besides Sandra Day O'Connor and Ruth Bader Ginsberg have sat beside men on the United States Supreme Court.

blew, blue ● *Blew* is the verb. *Blue* is the color.

board, bored ● *Board* is a piece of wood. *Board* is also an administrative group or council.

The school board approved the purchase of fifty 1- by 6-inch pine boards.

Bored may mean "to make a hole by drilling" or "to become weary out of dullness."

Watching television bored Joe, so he took his drill and bored a hole in the wall where he could hang his new clock.

brake, break ● *Brake* is a device used to stop a vehicle. *Break* means "to separate or to destroy."

I hope the brakes on my car never break.

bring, take ● *Bring* suggests the action is directed toward the speaker; *take* suggests the action is directed away from the speaker.

Mom says that she brings home the bacon, so I have to take out the garbage.

by, bye, buy ● *By* is the preposition. *Bye-bye* means "farewell." *Buy* means "to purchase."

The following message was posted in front of a small corner store: "Smart people buy; the others walk by!"

can, may ● *Can* suggests ability while *may* suggests permission.

"Can I go to the library?" literally means "Am I physically able to go to the library?"

"May I go to the library?" asks permission to go.

capital, capitol ● The noun *capital* refers to a city or to money. The adjective *capital* means "major or important." *Capitol* refers to a building.

The capitol building is in the capital city for a capital reason. The city government contributed capital for the building expense.

cent, sent, scent ● *Cent* is a coin; *sent* is the past tense of the verb "send"; *scent* is an odor or a smell.

For 32 cents, I sent my girlfriend a mushy love poem in a perfumed envelope. She adored the scent but hated the poem.

chord, cord ● *Chord* may mean "an emotion or feeling," but it also may mean "the combination of two or more tones sounded at the same time," as with a guitar chord. A *cord* is a string or rope.

695 **chose, choose** ● *Chose* (choz) is the past tense of the verb *choose* (chooz).

> Martin Luther King chose to write *The Strength to Love*—a book that says that choosing a nonviolent response to injustice takes strength.

coarse, course ● *Coarse* means "rough or crude"; *course* means "a direction or path taken." *Course* also means "a class or series of studies."

> The ladybug who taught the course "Insect Etiquette" said that only coarse mosquitoes fly over golf courses looking for bald golfers.

compare with, compare to ● Things of the same class are *compared with* each other; things of a different class are *compared to* each other.

> A man, compared with a woman, doesn't look so good; but then a man compared to a horse doesn't always look so good either.

complement, compliment ● *Complement* refers to that which completes or fulfills. *Compliment* is an expression of admiration or praise.

> Kimberly smiled, thinking she had received a compliment when Carlos said that her new Dodge Viper complemented her personality.

continual, continuous ● *Continual* refers to something that happens again and again; *continuous* refers to something that doesn't stop happening.

> Sunlight hits Peoria, Iowa, on a continual basis; but sunlight hits the world continuously.

counsel, council ● When used as a noun, *counsel* means "advice"; when used as a verb, *counsel* means "to advise." *Council* refers to a group that advises.

> The jackrabbit council counseled all rabbits to keep their tails out of the old man's garden. That's good counsel.

dear, deer ● *Dear* means "loved or valued"; *deer* are animals. (Please note, people will think you're strange if you write that you kissed your *deer* in the moonlight.)

desert, dessert ● *Desert* is barren wilderness. *Dessert* is food served at the end of a meal.

> The scorpion tiptoed through the moonlit desert, searching for dessert.

The verb *desert* means "to abandon"; the noun *desert* also may mean "deserved reward or punishment."

> The burglar's cover deserted him when the spotlight swung his way; his subsequent arrest was his just desert.

die, dye ● *Die* (dying) means "to stop living." *Dye* (dyeing) is used to change the color of something.

different from, different than ● Use *different from* in formal writing; use either form in informal or colloquial settings.

> She is as different from her sister as *Sassy* magazine is from *Time* magazine.

faint, feign, feint ● *Faint* means "without strength" or "to lose consciousness"; *feign* is a verb that means "to pretend or make up"; *feint* is a noun that means "a move or activity that is pretended or false."

> To avoid a tackler, the running back feigned a run one way and then cut quickly in another direction. The tackler grabbed nothing but air and fainted from the embarrassment.

696

farther, further ● *Farther* refers to a physical distance; *further* refers to additional time, quantity, or degree.

> The farther she walks down the path that is her life, the further she gets toward understanding her need to keep on walking.

fewer, less ● *Fewer* refers to the number of separate units; *less* refers to bulk quantity.

> Papa Bear growled when he found less porridge in his bowl, but Mama Bear smiled because he would gain fewer pounds.

for, fore, four ● *For* is a preposition meaning "because of" or "directed to"; *fore* means "earlier" or "the front"; *four* is the number 4.

> The four quick penalities served as a foreshadowing of what was in store for the visiting team.

good, well ● *Good* is an adjective; *well* is nearly always an adverb. (When used to indicate state of health, *well* is an adjective.)

The strange flying machines flew well. They looked good as they flew overhead.

heal, heel ● *Heal* means "to mend or restore to health." A *heel* is the back part of a human foot.

> Achilles was a young Greek soldier who died because a poison arrow pierced his heel and the wound would not heal.

healthful, healthy ● *Healthful* means "causing or improving health"; *healthy* means "possessing health."

> Healthful foods build healthy bodies.

hear, here ● You *hear* with your ears. *Here* means "the area close by."

697 **heard, herd** ● *Heard* is the past tense of the verb "hear"; *herd* is a large group of animals.

> The herd of grazing gazelles raised their heads when they heard the hyena laugh.

hole, whole ● A *hole* is a cavity or hollow place. *Whole* means "complete or entire."

immigrate, emigrate ● *Immigrate* means "to come into a new country or environment." *Emigrate* means "to go out of one country to live in another."

> Martin Ulferts immigrated to this country in 1882. He was only three years old when he emigrated from Germany.

imply, infer ● *Imply* means "to suggest or express indirectly"; *infer* means "to draw a conclusion from facts." (A writer or speaker *implies;* a reader or listener *infers.*)

> Dad implied I should drive more carefully, and I inferred he was concerned for both me and his new car.

it's, its ● *It's* is the contraction of "it is." *Its* is the possessive form of "it."

> It's fair to say that *Aladdin* still hasn't lost its appeal for my little sister even after 10 viewings.

knew, new ● *Knew* is the past tense of the verb "know." *New* means "recent or novel."

> I already knew that the zoo had acquired a number of new gnus.

know, no ● *Know* means "to understand or to realize." *No* means "the opposite of yes."

> Don't you know that no means no?

later, latter ● *Later* means "after a period of time." *Latter* refers to the second of two things mentioned.

> Later in the year 1965, Galen married Sam; the latter, Sam, is a woman.

lay, lie ● *Lay* means "to place." *Lay* is a transitive verb. (See 731.)

> If I lay another book on my reading table, I won't have room for anything else. Yesterday, I laid two books on the table. Over the last few days, I must have laid at least 20 books there.

Lie means to recline. *Lie* is an intransitive verb. (See 734.)

> The fat cat lies down.
> It lay down yesterday.
> It has lain down many, many times before.

lead, led ● *Lead* is the present tense of the verb meaning "to guide." The past tense of the verb is *led*. When the words are pronounced the same, *lead* is the metal.

> "Hey, Nat, get the lead out! Do I have to take you by the hand and lead you around the bases?"

learn, teach ● *Learn* means "to acquire information"; *teach* means "to give information."

> In *The Souls of Black Folk,* W. E. B. DuBois tried to teach us the tragedy of our age: that we have learned so little about each other.

698   leave, let ● *Leave* means "to allow something to remain behind." *Let* means "to permit."

> President Grant's 1868 request, "Let us have peace," indicated his naive belief that America was able to leave racism and bigotry behind.

lend, borrow ● *Lend* means "to give for temporary use"; *borrow* means "to receive for temporary use."

> I told Mom I needed to borrow $15 for a CD, but she said her lending service was for school supplies only.

like, as ● *Like* is a preposition meaning "similar to"; *as* is a conjunction. The conjunction "as" has several meanings. *Like* usually introduces a phrase; *as* usually introduces a clause.

> An egotist is someone who says, "If you want to be perfect like me, then think exactly as I think!"

loose, lose, loss ● *Loose* (loos) means "free, untied, unrestricted"; *lose* (looz) means "to misplace or fail to find or control"; *loss* (los) means "something that is lost."

mail, male ● *Mail* refers to letters or packages handled by the postal service (also voice mail and e-mail). *Male* refers to the masculine sex.

meat, meet ● *Meat* is food or flesh; *meet* means "to come upon or to encounter."

medal, metal ● *Medal* is an award. *Metal* is an element like iron or gold.

> Are the Olympic gold medals made out of solid gold metal?

miner, minor ● A *miner* digs in the ground for valuable ore. A *minor* is a person who is not legally an adult. A *minor* problem is one of no great importance.

> The use of minors as miners is no minor problem.

past, passed ● *Passed* is a verb. *Past* can be used as a noun, as an adjective, or as a preposition.

> That Escort passed my 'Vette. **(verb)**
> Many senior citizens hold dearly to the past. **(noun)**
> I'm sorry, but my past life is not your business. **(adjective)**
> Old Rosebud walked past us and never smelled the apples. **(preposition)**

peace, piece ● *Peace* means "tranquility or freedom from war." *Piece* is a part or fragment.

> Someone once observed that peace is not a condition, but a process—a process of building goodwill one piece, or one step, at a time.

personal, personnel ● *Personal* means "private." *Personnel* are people working at a particular job.

plain, plane ● *Plain* means "an area of land that is flat or level"; it also means "clearly seen or clearly understood."

> My instructor told me to check the map after I said it was not plain to me why the early settlers had trouble crossing the Rockies on their way to the Great Plains.

Plane means "flat, level, and even"; it is also a tool used to smooth the surface of wood.

> I used a plane to make the board plane and smooth.

699 **pore, pour, poor** ● A *pore* is an opening in the skin. *Pour* means "a constant flow or stream." *Poor* means "needy or pitiable."

> Tough exams on late spring days make my poor pores pour.

principal, principle ● As an adjective, *principal* means "primary." As a noun, it can mean "a school administrator" or "a sum of money." *Principle* means "idea or doctrine."

> His principal gripe is lack of freedom. **(adjective)**
> The principal expressed his concern about the open-campus policy. **(noun)**
> After 20 years, the amount of interest was higher than the principal. **(noun)**
> The principle of *caveat emptor* is "Let the buyer beware."

quiet, quit, quite ● *Quiet* is the opposite of noisy. *Quit* means "to stop." *Quite* means "completely or entirely."

> The library remained quite quiet until Mickie started hiccupping and couldn't quit.

quote, quotation ● *Quote* is a verb; *quotation* is a noun.

> "The quotation I used was from Woody Allen. You may quote me on that."

real, very, really ● Do not use *real* in place of the adverbs *very* or *really*.

> My mother's cake is usually very (not real) tasty. But this cake is really
> stale–I mean, it's just about fossilized.

right, write, wright, rite ● *Right* means "correct or proper"; it also refers to that which a person has a legal claim to, as in copyright. *Write* means "to inscribe or record." A *wright* is a person who makes or builds something. *Rite* is a ritual or ceremonial act.

> Did you write that it is the right of the shipwright to perform the rite of
> christening—breaking a bottle of champagne on the stern of the ship?

scene, seen ● *Scene* refers to the setting or location where something happens; it also may mean "sight or spectacle." *Seen* is part of the verb "see."

> An exhibitionist likes to be seen making a scene.

seam, seem ● *Seam* is a line formed by connecting two pieces. *Seem* means "to appear to exist."

> The ragged seams in his old coat seem to match the creases in his face.

set, sit ● *Sit* means "to put the body in a seated position." *Set* means "to place." *Set* is transitive; *sit* is intransitive.

> "How can you just sit there and watch as I set all these chairs in place?"

sight, cite, site ● *Sight* means "the act of seeing." *Cite* means "to quote" or "to summon." *Site* means "location or position."

> The building inspector cited the electrical contractor for breaking two city codes
> at a downtown job site.
> It was not a pretty sight when the two men started arguing.

sole, soul ● *Sole* means "single, only one"; *sole* also refers to the bottom surface of the foot. *Soul* refers to the spiritual part of a person.

> A blistered sole heals quickly, but a soul that is blistered may need time to
> heal.

700 **some, sum** ● *Some* refers to an unknown number or part. *Sum* means "the whole amount."

> A gunman held up some gas stations and stole the sum of their receipts.

stationary, stationery ● *Stationary* means "not movable"; *stationery* refers to the paper and envelopes used to write letters.

steal, steel ● *Steal* means "to take something without permission"; *steel* is a metal.

than, then ● *Than* is used in a comparison; *then* tells when.

> Then he cried and said that his big brother was bigger than my big brother. Then I cried.

their, there, they're ● *Their* is the possessive personal pronoun. *There* is an adverb used to point out location. *They're* is the contraction for "they are."

> They're quite a couple.
> Do you see them over there, with their matching jackets.

threw, through ● *Threw* is the past tense of "throw." *Through* means "passing from one side of something to the other."

Through seven innings, Egor threw just seven strikes.

to, too, two ● *To* is a preposition that can mean "in the direction of." *To* also is used to form an infinitive. *Too* means "also" or "very." *Two* is the number.

> The two divers were careful not to swim down to the sunken ship too quickly.

701 **vain, vane, vein** ● *Vain* means "valueless or fruitless"; it may also mean "holding a high regard for one's self." *Vane* is a flat piece of material set up to show which way the wind blows. *Vein* refers to a blood vessel or a mineral deposit.

> The weather vane indicates the direction of the wind. The blood vein determines the direction of flowing blood. The vain mind moves in no particular direction and is content to think only about itself.

waist, waste ● *Waist* is the part of the body just above the hips. The verb *waste* means "to lose through inaction" or "to wear away, decay"; the noun *waste* refers to material that is unused or useless.

> Her waist is small because she wastes no opportunity to exercise.

wait, weight ● *Wait* means "to stay somewhere expecting something." *Weight* refers to a degree or unit of heaviness.

ware, wear, where ● *Ware* refers to a product that is sold; *wear* means "to have on or to carry on one's body"; *where* asks the question, in what place? or in what situation?

> The designer boasted, "Anybody can wear my ware anywhere."

way, weigh ● *Way* means "path or route." *Weigh* means "to measure weight."

> Since our dog weighs too much, we now take him on walks all of the way around the park.

weather, whether ● *Weather* refers to the condition of the atmosphere. *Whether* refers to a possibility.

> Because of the weather forecast, Coach Pennington didn't know whether or not to schedule another practice.

who, which, that ● *Who* refers to people. *Which* refers to nonliving objects or to animals. (*Which* should never refer to people.) *That* may refer to animals, people, or nonliving objects.

who, whom ● *Who* is used as the subject of a verb; *whom* is used as the object of a preposition or as a direct object.

> To whom do we owe our thanks for these pizzas? And who ordered that one with pepperoni and pineapple?

who's, whose ● *Who's* is the contraction for "who is." *Whose* is the possessive pronoun.

> "Whose car are we using, and who's riding shotgun?"

wood, would ● *Wood* is the stuff that trees are made of; *would* is part of the verb "will."

> I would never have known that Mr. Hart had a wooden leg.

your, you're ● *Your* is a possessive pronoun. *You're* is the contraction for "you are."

> "Are your kisses always this short?"
> "No, only when you're standing on my feet."

Understanding Our Language

Parts of Speech

702 **Parts of speech** refers to the ways in which words are used in sentences. Words can be used in eight different ways; therefore, there are eight parts of speech: *noun, pronoun, verb, adjective, adverb, preposition, conjunction, interjection.*

703 # Noun

A **noun** is a word that is the name of something: a person, place, thing, or idea.

Mayor Maynard Jackson/mayor   Oregon/state   Home Alone 3/film
Richmond Memorial Hospital/hospital   Buddhism/religion

704 ## Classes of Nouns

The five classes of nouns are *proper, common, concrete, abstract,* and *collective.*

A **proper noun** names a particular person, place, thing, or idea. Proper nouns are always capitalized.

Wilma Rudolph   Jackie Robinson **(people)**   New York   Brooklyn **(places)**
Brooklyn Dodgers   World Series **(things)**   Christianity   Judaism **(ideas)**

A **common noun** is any noun that does not name a particular person, place, thing, or idea. Common nouns are not capitalized.

person   woman   president   baseball   government   park

A **concrete noun** names a thing that is tangible (can be seen, touched, heard, smelled, or tasted). Concrete nouns are either proper or common.

Flannery O'Connor   Grand Canyon   U-2   aroma   pizza

An **abstract noun** names an idea, a condition, or a feeling—in other words, something that cannot be touched, smelled, tasted, seen, or heard.

New Deal   greed   poverty   progress   freedom   hope

A **collective noun** names a group or unit.

United States   Portland Trailblazers   team   crowd   community

705 Forms of Nouns

Nouns are grouped according to their *number, gender,* and *case.*

706 Number of a Noun

Number indicates whether the noun is singular or plural.

A **singular noun** refers to one person, place, thing, or idea.

> actor   stadium   Canadian   bully   truth   child   person

A **plural noun** refers to more than one person, place, thing, or idea.

> actors   stadiums   Canadians   bullies   truths   children   people

707 Gender of a Noun

Gender indicates whether a noun is masculine, feminine, neuter, or indefinite.

> **Masculine:**   uncle   brother   host   men   bull   rooster   stallion
>
> **Feminine:**   mother   queen   hostess   women   cow   hen   filly
>
> **Neuter:**   tree   cobweb   fishing rod   closet   (without sex)
>
> **Indefinite:**   president   plumber   doctor   parent   (masculine or feminine)

708 Case of a Noun

Case tells how nouns are related to other words used with them. There are three cases: *nominative, possessive,* and *objective.*

Nominative case describes a noun used as the subject of a clause.

> The old **senator** pleaded with his colleagues to approve a freeze on nuclear weapons: "Even **survivors** are victims of a nuclear holocaust."

A noun is also in the nominative case when it is used as a *predicate noun* (or predicate nominative). A predicate noun follows a form of the *be* verb *(is, are, was, were, been)* and repeats or renames the subject.

> "Even the winner is a **loser** in a nuclear war," the senator added.
> (**Loser** renames *winner*.)

Possessive case describes a noun that shows possession or ownership.

> The younger **senator's** face curled into a smile as he spoke: "Nuclear weapons are **humanity's** salvation from war; fear of their use is our assurance that no one will dare to use them."

Objective case describes a noun used as a direct object, an indirect object, or an object of the preposition.

> A third senator spoke quietly. "The human race needs **peacemakers**, but even they can't promise **humanity** peace," he said.
> (*Peacemakers* is the direct object of *needs; humanity* is the indirect object of the verb *can promise.*)

> "Our best hope for **peace** lies within the **hearts** of the common **people**."
> (*Peace* is the object of the preposition *for; hearts* is the object of the preposition *within;* and *people* is the object of the preposition *of.*)

Pronoun

709 A **pronoun** is a word used in place of a noun.

> I, you, she, it, which, that, themselves, whoever, me, he, they, whatever, my, mine, ours

710 All pronouns have **antecedents**. An antecedent is the noun that the pronoun refers to or replaces.

> The **judge** coughed and reached for the glass of water. The water touched *his* lips before *he* noticed the **fly** *that* lay bathing in the cool liquid. (**Judge** is the antecedent of *his* and *he*; *fly* is the antecedent of *that*.)

Note • Each pronoun must agree with its antecedent in number, person, and gender. (See 772-774.)

711 **Pronouns** are distinguished according to their *type, class, number, gender, person,* and *case.* There are three **types**.

> **Simple**   I, you, he, she, it, we, they, who, what
>
> **Compound**   myself, yourself, himself, herself, ourself, itself, whatsoever
>
> **Phrasal**   one another, each other

There are five **classes** of pronouns: *personal, relative, indefinite, interrogative,* and *demonstrative.*

712 Forms of Personal Pronouns

The **form** of a personal pronoun indicates its number (singular or plural), its person (first, second, third), its case (nominative, possessive, or objective), and its gender (masculine, feminine, or neuter).

713 Number of a Pronoun

The **number** of a pronoun can be either singular or plural. Singular personal pronouns are these: I, you, he, she, it. Plural personal pronouns are these: we, you, they. Notice that the pronoun *you* can be singular or plural.

Larry, you need to keep all four tires on the road when turning. Are you still with us back there?

714 **Person of a Pronoun**

The **person** of a pronoun indicates whether that pronoun is speaking, is spoken to, or is spoken about.

> **First person** is used in place of the name of the speaker.
>
> "**I** am always right!"   —*Joe Bighead*, founder and president of the National Organization of Bigheads
>
> "**We** won't listen to anyone else!"   —motto of the three-member N.O.B.

> **Second person** is used to name the person or thing spoken to.
>
> "Joe, **you** [singular] are wrong."   —*Isabelle M. Right*, N.O.B. vice president
>
> "Isabelle and Joe, **you** [plural] are both wrong."
>   —*Uriah R. Wrong, N.O.B.* secretary/treasurer

> **Third person** is used to name the person or thing spoken about.
>
> I. M. Right elected **herself** vice president because **she** knew that **she** was the smartest Bighead.
>
> U. R. Wrong elected **himself** because **he** knew that **he** was the smartest.
>
> Neither I. M. Right nor U. R. Wrong voted for Joe because **they** knew that **he** was always wrong.

715 **Case of a Pronoun**

The **case** of each pronoun tells how it is related to the other words used with it. There are three cases: *nominative, possessive,* and *objective.*

> **Nominative case** describes a pronoun used as the *subject* of a clause. The following are nominative forms: I, you, he, she, it, we, they.
>
> **I** like myself when things go well.
> **You** must live life in order to love life.

A pronoun is also in the *nominative case* when it is used as a *predicate nominative.* A predicate nominative follows a form of the *be* verb (am, is, are, was, were, been), and it repeats the subject.

> "It is **I**," growled the big bad wolf from under Grandmother's bonnet.
> "It is **he**!" shrieked Little Red as she twisted his snout into a corkscrew.

> **Possessive case** describes a pronoun that shows possession or ownership. An apostrophe, however, is not used with a personal pronoun to show possession.
>
> my   mine   our   ours   his   her   hers   their   theirs   its   your   yours

> **Objective case** describes a pronoun used as the direct object, indirect object, or object of a preposition.
>
> Nathaniel hugged **me**. (***Me*** is the direct object of the verb *hugged*.)
>
> Benji told **me** a story. (***Me*** is the indirect object of the verb *told*.)
>
> Teddy Snappers, our dog, listened because the story was about **him**. (***Him*** is the object of the preposition *about*.)

716

Number, Person, and Case of Personal Pronouns

	Nominative Case	Possessive Case	Objective Case
First Person Singular	I	my, mine	me
Second Person Singular	you	your, yours	you
Third Person Singular	he she it	his her, hers its	him her it

	Nominative Case	Possessive Case	Objective Case
First Person Plural	we	our, ours	us
Second Person Plural	you	your, yours	you
Third Person Plural	they	their, theirs	them

717 ## Special Personal Pronouns

A **reflexive pronoun** is formed by adding *-self* or *-selves* to a personal pronoun. A reflexive pronoun can act as a direct object or an indirect object of the verb, the object of a preposition, or a predicate nominative.

He loves **himself**. **(direct object of *loves*)**

He gives **himself** birthday presents. **(indirect object of *gives*)**

He smiles at **himself** in the mirror. **(object of preposition *at*)**

He is truly **himself** only when he sleeps. **(predicate nominative)**

Note • A reflexive pronoun is called an **intensive pronoun** when it intensifies, or emphasizes, the noun or pronoun it refers to.

Leo **himself** taught his children to invest their lives in others.

The lesson was sometimes painful—but they learned it **themselves**.

718 ## Other Kinds of Pronouns

A **relative pronoun** relates one part of a sentence to a word in another part of the sentence. Specifically, a relative pronoun relates an adjective clause to the noun or pronoun it modifies. (The noun is underlined in each example below; the relative pronoun is in boldface.)

The girl **who** had been hit by a drunken driver regained consciousness and cried because she did not feel pain.

The accident, **which** had happened ten days earlier, had left her entire body paralyzed and numb.

719 An **indefinite pronoun** often refers to unnamed or unknown people or things.

The teacher stopped chewing, glanced at his sandwich, then glared at his snickering students and screamed, "**Whoever** put this caterpillar in here is in big trouble!" **(The antecedent of** *whoever* **is unknown.)**

720 An **interrogative pronoun** asks a question.

"**Who** is knocking on the door, and **what** do you want?" grunted Little Pig No. 1.

721 A **demonstrative pronoun** points out people, places, or things without naming them.

"**That** sounds too much like a growling stomach," whimpered Little Pig No. 2.

"And **those** don't look like Mommy's toenails under the door," squealed Little Pig No. 3.

722

Classes of Pronouns

Personal

I, me, my, mine / we, us, our, ours
you, your, yours / they, them, their, theirs
he, him, his, she, her, hers, it, its
myself, himself, herself, itself, yourself, themselves, ourselves

Relative

who, whose, whom, which, what, that

Indefinite Pronouns

all	both	everything	nobody	several
another	each	few	none	some
any	each one	many	no one	somebody
anybody	either	most	nothing	someone
anyone	everybody	much	one	something
anything	everyone	neither	other	such

Interrogative

who, whose, whom, which, what

Demonstrative

this, that, these, those

Verb

723 ## Forms of Verbs

A **verb** is a word that expresses action or state of being. A verb has different forms depending on its number (singular or plural); person (first, second, third); voice (active, passive); tense (present, past, future, present perfect, past perfect, future perfect); and mood (indicative, imperative, subjunctive).

724 ## Number of a Verb

Number indicates whether a verb is singular or plural. The verb and its subject both must be singular, or they both must be plural.

> One large **island floats** off Italy's "toe." **(singular)**

> Five small **islands float** inside Michigan's "thumb." **(plural)**

725 ## Person of a Verb

Person indicates whether the subject of the verb is **first**, **second**, or **third person** and whether the subject is **singular** or **plural**. Verbs usually have a different form only in third person singular of the present tense.

	Singular	Plural
First Person	I sniff	we sniff
Second Person	you sniff	you sniff
Third Person	he/she/it sniffs	they sniff

726 ## Voice of a Verb

Voice indicates whether the subject is acting or being acted upon.

Active voice indicates that the subject of the verb is acting—doing something.

> Ben Franklin **discovers** the secrets of electricity.

Passive voice indicates that the subject of the verb is being acted upon. A passive verb is a combination of a *be* verb and a past participle.

The secrets of electricity <u>are discovered</u> by Ben Franklin.

727 **Tense of a Verb**

Tense indicates time. Each verb has three principal parts: the *present, past,* and *past participle.* All six of the tenses are formed from these principal parts. The past and past participle of regular verbs are formed by adding *ed* to the present form. The past and past participle of irregular verbs are usually different words; however, some remain the same in all three principal parts. (See 736.)

Present tense expresses action that is happening at the present time, or action that happens continually, regularly.

> In September, sophomores **smirk** and **joke** about the "little freshies."

Past tense expresses action that is completed at a particular time in the past.

> They **forgot** that just ninety days **separated** them from freshman status.

Future tense expresses action that will take place in the future.

> They **will remember** in three years because they **will be** freshmen again.

Present perfect tense expresses action that began in the past but continues in the present or is completed at the present.

> Our boat **has weathered** worse storms than this one.

Past perfect tense expresses action that began in the past and was completed in the past.

> They **had supposed**, wrongly, that the hurricane would miss the island.

Future perfect tense expresses action that will begin in the future and be completed by a specific time in the future.

> By this time tomorrow, the hurricane **will have smashed** into the coast.

728

Tense	Active Voice		Passive Voice	
	Singular	**Plural**	**Singular**	**Plural**
PRESENT TENSE	I see you see he/she/it sees	we see you see they see	I am seen you are seen he/she/it is seen	we are seen you are seen they are seen
Past TENSE	I saw you saw he saw	we saw you saw they saw	I was seen you were seen he was seen	we were seen you were seen they were seen
Future TENSE	I shall see you will see he will see	we shall see you will see they will see	I shall be seen you will be seen he will be seen	we shall be seen you will be seen they will be seen
Present PERFECT	I have seen you have seen he has seen	we have seen you have seen they have seen	I have been seen you have been seen he has been seen	we have been seen you have been seen they have been seen
Past PERFECT	I had seen you had seen he had seen	we had seen you had seen they had seen	I had been seen you had been seen he had been seen	we had been seen you had been seen they had been seen
Future PERFECT	I shall have seen you will have seen he will have seen	we shall have seen you will have seen they will have seen	I shall have been seen you will have been seen he will have been seen	we shall have been seen you will have been seen they will have been seen

729 **Mood of a Verb**

The **mood** of the verb indicates the tone or attitude with which the statement is made.

> **Indicative mood** is used to state a fact or to ask a question.
>
> Can any theme capture the essence of the complex 1960's U.S. culture? President John F. Kennedy's directives (stated below) represent one ideal popular during the decade.

> **Imperative mood** is used to give a command.
>
> "Ask not what your country can do for you. Ask what you can do for your country."

> **Subjunctive mood** is no longer commonly used; however, it continues to be used by careful writers to express the exact manner in which their statements are meant.

> **1** Use the subjunctive *were* to express a condition that is contrary to fact.
>
> If I **were** you, I wouldn't giggle in front of Dad.

> **2** Use the subjunctive *were* after *as though* or *as if* to express doubt or uncertainty in the past.
>
> Dad looked as if he **were** about to ground you. Well . . . maybe not. Actually, he looked as though he **were** about to ring your neck!

> **3** Use the subjunctive *be* in "that clauses" to express necessity, parliamentary motions, or legal decisions.
>
> "It is moved and supported that no more than 6,000,000 quad **be used** to explore the planet Earth."
>
> "Ridiculous! Knowing earthlings is bound to help us understand ourselves! Therefore, I move that the sum **be amended** to 12,000,000 quad."
>
> "Stupidity! I move that all missions **be postponed** until we have living proof of life on Earth."

Classes of Verbs

730 **Auxiliary Verbs**

Auxiliary verbs, or helping verbs, help to form some of the **tenses** (727), the **mood** (729), and the **voice** (726) of the main verb. In the following examples, the auxiliary verbs are in boldface, and the main verbs are italicized.

> Two of Grandma Ulfert's fourteen children **had** *died* at birth.
>
> One child, Uncle Harry, **has** *been* severely retarded since birth.
>
> Grandma **will** *nurture* him until he dies because she loves all life.

			Common Auxiliary Verbs					
is	are	was	were	am	been	shall	will	would
did	must	can	may	have	had	has	do	should

731 **Transitive Verbs**

A **transitive** verb communicates action and is always followed by an object that receives the action and completes the meaning of the verb.

> The city council **passed** a strict noise ordinance.

Active voice • A transitive verb in the active voice directs the action from the subject to the object.

> The *students* **protested** the noise *ordinance* with a noisy demonstration.
> (*Ordinance* **receives the action of the verb *protested* from the subject *students*.**)

Passive voice • If a transitive verb is in the passive voice, the subject of the sentence receives the action. (In the example below, the the subject *ordinance* receives the action of the verb *was debated*.)

> The *ordinance* **was debated** by students and parents at a public meeting.

Note • The person or thing creating the action in a passive verb is not always stated. (It is not clear who did the overturning in the following example.)

> The *ordinance* **was overturned**.

732 A **direct object** receives the action of a transitive verb directly from the subject.

> The boy kicked his **skateboard** forward. (***Skateboard* is the direct object.**)

733 An **indirect object** receives the action of a transitive verb, but indirectly. An indirect object names the person (*or thing*) to whom (*or to what*) or for whom (*or for what*) something is done.

> Then he gave **me** a real show. (***Me* is the indirect object.**)

Note • When the word naming the indirect receiver of the action is contained in a prepositional phrase, it is no longer considered an indirect object.

> Then he put on a real show for **me**. (***Me* is the object of the preposition *for*.**)

734 **Intransitive Verbs**

An **intransitive verb** refers to an action that is complete in itself. It does not need an object to receive the action.

> He and his skateboard **flew** as one. Both **jumped** and **flipped** and **twisted**.

Note • Some verbs can be either *transitive* or *intransitive*.

> He had **pushed** himself to the limit. **(transitive)**
> He also **pushed** for recognition. **(intransitive)**

735 A **linking verb** is a special type of intransitive verb that links the subject to a noun or an adjective in the predicate.

> On his skateboard, the *boy* **felt** *cool*. *He* **was** *somebody*.

Common Linking Verbs

is	are	was	were	be	been	am	smell	look
seem	grow	become	appear	sound	taste	feel	remain	stand

736   ## Common Irregular Verbs and Their Principal Parts

Present Tense	Past Tense	Past Participle	Present Tense	Past Tense	Past Participle	Present Tense	Past Tense	Past Participle
am, be	was, were	been	freeze	froze	frozen	shine (polish)		
begin	began	begun	give	gave	given		shined	shined
bite	bit	bitten	go	went	gone	show	showed	shown
blow	blew	blown	grow	grew	grown	shrink	shrank	shrunk
break	broke	broken	hang (execute)			sing	sang, sung	sung
bring	brought	brought		hanged	hanged	sink	sank, sunk	sunk
burst	burst	burst	hang			sit	sat	sat
catch	caught	caught	(suspend)	hung	hung	slay	slew	slain
choose	chose	chosen	hide	hid	hidden, hid	speak	spoke	spoken
come	came	come	know	knew	known	spring	sprang,	
dive	dived	dived	lay	laid	laid		sprung	sprung
do	did	done	lead	led	led	steal	stole	stolen
drag	dragged	dragged	lie (recline)	lay	lain	strive	strove	striven
draw	drew	drawn	lie (deceive)	lied	lied	swear	swore	sworn
drink	drank	drunk	raise	raised	raised	swim	swam	swum
drive	drove	driven	ride	rode	ridden	swing	swung	swung
drown	drowned	drowned	ring	rang	rung	take	took	taken
eat	ate	eaten	rise	rose	risen	tear	tore	torn
fall	fell	fallen	run	ran	run	throw	threw	thrown
fight	fought	fought	see	saw	seen	wake	woke, waked	waked
flee	fled	fled	set	set	set	wear	wore	worn
flow	flowed	flowed	shake	shook	shaken	weave	wove	woven
fly	flew	flown	shine (light)			wring	wrung	wrung
forsake	forsook	forsaken		shone	shone	write	wrote	written

737   ## Special Verb Forms

A **verbal** is a word that is derived from a verb, has the power of a verb, but acts as another part of speech. Like a verb, a verbal may take an object, a modifier (adjective, adverb), and sometimes a subject; but unlike a verb, a verbal functions as a noun, an adjective, or an adverb. Three types of verbals are *gerunds, infinitives,* and *participles.*

> A **gerund** is a verb form that ends in *ing* and is used as a noun.
>
> > **Smoking** cigarettes rotted my lungs. **(subject)**
> >
> > I started **smoking** at fourteen. **(direct object)**
> >
> > The result of all that **smoking** is my cancer. **(object of the preposition)**

> An **infinitive** is a verb form that is usually introduced by *to*; the infinitive may be used as a noun, as an adjective, or as an adverb.
>
> > **To smoke** so much for so long has cost me greatly. **(subject)**
> >
> > If it had been illegal **to smoke** in public places twenty years ago, things might now be different. **(adverb)**
> >
> > The right **to smoke** in public is now in serious question. **(adjective)**

A **participle** is a verb form ending in *ing* or *ed*. A participle functions as a verb because it can take an object; a participle functions as an adjective because it can modify a noun or pronoun.

That man **smoking** the cigar is dangerous. The pile of **smoked** cigars grows deeper each day. (*Smoking* functions as an adjective because it modifies *man*. *Smoking* functions as a verb because it has an object, *cigar*. *Smoked* modifies the noun *cigars*; this participle does not have an object.)

Adjective

738 An **adjective** describes or modifies a noun or pronoun. Articles *a, an,* and *the* are adjectives.

The young driver peeked through **the big** steering wheel.
(*The* and *young* modify *driver*; *the* and *big* modify *steering wheel*.)

Adjectives can be common or proper. **Proper adjectives** are created from proper nouns and are capitalized.

Canada (proper noun) is a land of many cultures and climates.

Canadian (proper adjective) winters can be long and harsh.

Note ● Some words can be either adjectives or pronouns (*that, these, all, each, both, many, some,* etc.). These words are adjectives if they come before a noun and modify that noun; they are pronouns if they stand alone.

Joe made **both** goals. (*Both* modifies *goals*; it is an adjective.)

Both were scored in the final period. (*Both* stands alone; it is a pronoun.)

739 A **predicate adjective** follows a form of the *be* verb (or other linking verb) and describes the subject.

Late autumn seems **grim** to those who love summer.
(*Grim* modifies *autumn*.)

740 **The Forms of Adjectives**

Adjectives have three forms: *positive, comparative,* and *superlative.*

The **positive form** describes a noun or pronoun without comparing it to anyone or anything else.

Superman is **tough**. Superman is **wonderful**.

The **comparative form** (*-er*) compares two persons, places, things, or ideas.

Tarzan is **tougher** than Superman.

Tarzan is **more wonderful** than Superman.

The **superlative form** (*-est*) compares three or more persons, places, things, or ideas.

But I, Big Bird, am the **toughest** of all!

But I, Big Bird, am the **most wonderful** of all!

Adverb

741 An **adverb** modifies a verb, an adjective, or another adverb. An adverb tells *how, when, where, why, how often,* and *how much*.

> She kissed him **loudly**. (*Loudly* modifies the verb *kissed*.)

> Her kisses are **really** noisy. (*Really* modifies the adjective *noisy*.)

> The kiss exploded **very** dramatically. (*Very* modifies the adverb *dramatically*.)

Adverbs can be cataloged in four basic ways: *time, place, manner,* and *degree*.

Time. (These adverbs tell *when, how often,* and *how long*.)

> today, yesterday   daily, weekly   briefly, eternally

Place. (These adverbs tell *where, to where,* and *from where*.)

> here, there   nearby, yonder   backward, forward

Manner. (These adverbs often end in *ly* and tell *how* something is done.)

> precisely   regularly   regally   smoothly   well

Degree. (These adverbs tell *how much* or *how little*.)

> substantially   greatly   entirely   partly   too

Note • Some adverbs can be written with or without the *ly* ending. When in doubt, use the *ly* form.

> slow, slowly   loud, loudly   fair, fairly   tight, tightly   quick, quickly

742 ## The Forms of Adverbs

Adverbs have three forms: *positive, comparative,* and *superlative*.

The **positive form** describes a verb, an adjective, or another adverb without comparing it to anyone or anything else.

> Superman runs **fast**. Superman thinks **quickly**.

The **comparative form** (*-er*) compares two persons, places, things, or ideas.

> Tarzan runs **faster** than Superman.

> Tarzan thinks **more quickly** than Superman.

The **superlative form** (*-est*) compares three or more persons, places, things, or ideas.

> But I, Big Bird, run **fastest** of all!

> But I, Big Bird, think **most quickly** of all!

Positive	Comparative	Superlative
well	better	best
badly	worse	worst
fast	faster	fastest
remorsefully	more remorsefully	most remorsefully
passively	less passively	least passively

Preposition

743 A **preposition** is a word (or group of words) that shows the relationship between its object (a noun or a pronoun that follows the preposition) and another word in the sentence.

> To make a mustache, Natasha placed the hairy caterpillar **under** her nose. (*Under* shows the relationship between the verb *placed* and the object of the preposition *nose*. Note ● The first noun or pronoun following a preposition should be its object.)

> The drowsy insect clung obediently **to** the girl's upper lip. (*To* shows the relationship between the verb *clung* and the object of the preposition *lip*. Note that *girl's* is an adjective. Therefore, the first noun following *to* is *lip*.)

Note ● There are three kinds of prepositions: *simple* (at, in, of, on, with), *compound* (within, outside, underneath), and *phrasal* (on account of, on top of).

744 A **prepositional phrase** includes the preposition, the object of the preposition, and the modifiers of the object. A prepositional phrase may function as an adverb or as an adjective.

> Some people run **away from caterpillars**. (The phrase, functioning as an adverb, modifies the verb *run*.)

> However, little kids **with inquisitive minds** enjoy their company. (The phrase functions as an adjective modifying the noun *kids*.)

Note ● A **preposition** that lacks an object may be used as an adverb.

> Natasha never played with caterpillars **before**. (The object of the preposition is understood: before *today*. *Before* modifies *played*, a verb.)

745

LIST OF PREPOSITIONS

aboard	at	despite	in regard to	opposite	through
about	away from	down	inside	out	throughout
above	back of	down from	inside of	out of	till
according to	because of	during	in spite of	outside	to
across	before	except	instead of	outside of	toward
across from	behind	except for	into	over	under
after	below	excepting	like	over to	underneath
against	beneath	for	near	owing to	until
along	beside	from	near to	past	unto
alongside	besides	from among	notwithstanding	prior to	up
alongside of	between	from between	of	regarding	up to
along with	beyond	from under	off	round	upon
amid	but	in	on	round about	with
among	by	in addition to	on account of	save	within
apart from	by means of	in behalf of	on behalf of	since	without
around	concerning	in front of	onto	subsequent to	
aside from	considering	in place of	on top of	together with	

Conjunction

746 A **conjunction** connects individual words or groups of words.

> When we came back to Paris, it was clear **and** cold **and** lovely.
> (The conjunction *and* connects equal adjectives.)
> —Ernest Hemingway

Coordinating conjunctions connect a word to a word, a phrase to a phrase, or a clause to a clause. The words, phrases, or clauses joined by a coordinating conjunction must be *equal* or of the *same type*.

> I would sit in front of the fire **and** squeeze the peel of the little oranges into the edge of the flame **and** watch the sputter of blue that they made.
> (*And* connects equal phrases, each one part of the compound predicate.)
> —Ernest Hemingway

Correlative conjunctions are conjunctions used in pairs. (*either, or; neither, nor; not only, but also; both, and; whether, or; just, as; just, so; as, so*)

> **Neither** rain **nor** sleet **nor** dark of night shall keep them from their appointed rounds.

Subordinating conjunctions are words or groups of words that connect, and show the relationship between, two clauses that are *not* equally important. A subordinating conjunction connects a dependent clause to an independent clause in order to complete the meaning of the dependent clause.

> A brown trout will study the bait **before** he eats it. (The clause *before he eats it* is dependent. It depends on the rest of the sentence to complete its meaning.)

Kinds of Conjunctions

Coordinating: and, but, or, nor, for, yet, so

Correlative: either, or; neither, nor; not only, but also; both, and; whether, or; just, as; just, so; as, so

Subordinating: after, although, as, as if, as long as, as though, because, before, if, in order that, provided that, since, so, so that, that, though, till, unless, until, when, where, whereas, while

---

Note • Relative pronouns (718) and conjunctive adverbs (596) can also connect clauses.

Interjection

747 An **interjection** is included in a sentence in order to communicate strong emotion or surprise. Punctuation (often a comma or an exclamation point) is used to set an interjection off from the rest of the sentence.

> **Oh, no!** The TV broke. **Good grief!** I have nothing to do! **Yipes,** I'll go mad!

"The limits of my language stand for the limits of my world."
—**Ludwig Wittgenstein**

Using the Language
Constructing Sentences

748 A **sentence** is made up of one or more words that express a complete thought. (Note • A sentence begins with a capital letter; it ends with a period, a question mark, or an exclamation point.)

> It was mid-July on a Thursday night. School was out, right? "We've got nothing to do but relax," said one of the three boys. "Tonight belongs to us. We're in charge!"

749 A sentence must have a **subject** and **predicate** that express a complete thought. The subject is the element of the sentence about which something is said. The predicate is the element of the sentence that says something about the subject. (The primary part of a predicate is the word or words that function as a verb.)

> The boys passively flopped onto the couch. Almost instinctively they flipped on the tube.

Note • In the first sentence, *boys* is the subject—the sentence talks about the boys. *Flopped*, a verb, is the primary part of the predicate—it says something about the subject.

750 Either the subject or the predicate or both may be "missing" from a sentence, but both must be clearly **understood**.

> "What's on?" (*What* is the subject; the predicate is expressed by the contraction: *'s* for *is*.)

> "Nothing." (*Nothing* is the subject; the predicate *is* is understood.)

> "Shut up and turn the channel." (The subject *you* is understood; *shut up* and *turn* is the predicate.)

751 The Subject

The **subject** is always a noun, or a word or phrase that functions as a noun, such as a pronoun, an infinitive, a gerund, or a noun clause.

> The **jungle** around the muscled man exploded in flame and smoke. (**noun**)
>
> Perched on the lip of a rocky ravine, **he** looked out from his dusky inferno. (**pronoun**)
>
> **To run back toward the choppers** would bring death from above. (**infinitive phrase**)
>
> **Leaping into the ravine** would bring death from below. (**gerund phrase**)
>
> **That the dauntless hero was doomed** seemed inevitable. (**noun clause**)

A **simple subject** is the subject without the words that modify it.

> The younger **boy** grabbed the controller and switched to channel four.

A **complete subject** is the simple subject and all the words that modify it.

> **A muscular, heavily armed, sweating male** leaped out on the screen.

A **compound subject** is composed of two or more simple subjects.

> A rocket **launcher** and a twenty-millimeter **cannon** blazed at him from the two Apache choppers that hovered above.

752 The Predicate (Verb)

A **predicate** is the part of the sentence that says something about the subject.

> Then it **happened**!

A **simple predicate** is the predicate without the words that describe or modify it.

> Little people **can talk** faster than big people. (*Can talk* is the simple predicate; *faster than big people* describes how little people *can talk*.)

A **complete predicate** is the simple predicate and all the words that modify or explain it.

> Little people **can talk faster than big people**.

A **compound predicate** is composed of two or more simple predicates.

> Big people **talk** slowly but **eat** fast.

A **compound subject** and a **compound predicate** sometimes appear in the same sentence.

> Sturdy **tongues**, long **lips**, and thick **teeth say** sentences slowly but **chew** food quickly.

A **direct object** receives the action of the predicate. (See 732.)

> Chickens eat **oyster shells**. (The direct object, *oyster shells*, receives the action of *eat*. It answers the question *Chickens eat what*?)

The **direct object** may be **compound**.

> Chickens eat **oyster shells** and **grit**.

Using Phrases and Clauses

753 ## Phrases

A **phrase** is a group of related words that lacks either a subject or a predicate or both.

ran very fast **(The predicate lacks a subject.)**

the young colt **(The subject lacks a predicate.)**

down the steep slope **(The phrase lacks both a subject and a predicate.)**

The young colt ran very fast down the steep slope.

(Together, these three phrases present a complete thought.)

754 ## Types of Phrases

Phrases appear in several types: *noun, verb, verbal, prepositional, appositive,* and *absolute.*

A **noun phrase** consists of a noun and its modifiers; the whole phrase functions as a simple noun would.

The next kid in line has to sit on the dunking stool. **(subject)**

I could twist those skinny balloons into a **flying purple people eater**. **(object of preposition)**

A **verb phrase** consists of a verb and its modifiers.

Gina **quickly sat down on the tiny chair**.

(*Quickly, down,* and *on the tiny chair* all modify *sat;* the seven words combined make up the whole verb phrase.)

A **verbal phrase** is a phrase based on one of the three types of verbals: *gerund, infinitive,* or *participle.* (See 737.)

❶ A **gerund phrase** is based on a gerund and functions as a noun.

Heading a soccer ball is hard for a unicorn. **(subject)**

I was tired of his **popping our soccer balls**. **(object of preposition)**

❷ An **infinitive phrase** is based on an infinitive and functions as a noun, an adjective, or an adverb.

To err is human; **to forgive**, divine. **(*To err* and *to forgive,* used here as nouns, are subjects.)**

The old man installed iron bars on his windows **to stop intruders**. **(adverb modifying *installed*)**

Did he give his permission **to paint a mural on this wall**? **(adjective modifying *permission*)**

❸ A **participial phrase** consists of a past or present participle and its modifiers; the whole phrase functions as an adjective.

Scooping up the chihuahua, he took off for the end zone. **(adjective modifying the pronoun *he*)**

His voice, **cracked by fatigue**, sounded eighty years old. **(adjective modifying the noun *voice*)**

A **prepositional phrase** consists of a preposition, its object, and any modifiers.

> Zach won the wheelchair race **in spite of his broken wrist**. (adverb modifying the verb *won*)

> Reach for that catnip ball **behind the couch**. (adjective modifying *catnip ball*)

An **appositive phrase**, which stands beside another noun and renames it, consists of a noun and its modifiers. An appositive adds new information but does not modify any other word as an adjective would.

> My mother, **the woman with the strange face**, must have blinked as the shutter snapped. **(The appositive phrase, *the woman with the strange face*, renames *my mother*, though it does not modify the phrase.)**

An **absolute phrase** consists of a noun and a participle (plus the object of the participle and any modifiers). Because it has a subject and a verbal, an absolute phrase resembles a clause; however, the verbal does not have the tense and number found in the main verb of a clause.

> **Her whistle blasting repeatedly**, the lifeguard cleared the pool. (*Whistle* is the noun; *blasting* is a present participle modifying *whistle*.)

Note ● An absolute phrase can be placed anywhere within the sentence but has no direct grammatical relation with any part of it.

755 Clauses

A **clause** is a group of related words that has both a subject and a predicate.

An **independent clause** presents a complete thought and can stand alone as a sentence; a **dependent clause** does not present a complete thought and cannot stand alone as a sentence. Dependent clauses do, however, add important detail to a sentence.

> Sparrows make nests in cattle barns **(independent clause)** **so they can stay warm during the winter** **(dependent clause)**.

756 Types of Clauses

There are three basic types of dependent or subordinate clauses: *adverb, adjective,* and *noun.*

An **adverb clause** is used like an adverb to modify a verb, an adjective, or an adverb.

> **Unless I study hard**, I will not pass this test.

Note ● All adverb clauses begin with a subordinating conjunction. (See 746.)

An **adjective clause** is used like an adjective to modify a noun or pronoun.

> Tomorrow's test, **which covers the entire book**, is half essay and half short answers.

A **noun clause** is used in place of a noun.

> **Whatever essay questions are included on the test** will be from the last two chapters.

Using Sentence Variety

757 A **sentence** may be classified according to the type of statement it makes, the way it is constructed, and the arrangement of material within the sentence.

758 Kinds of Sentences

Sentences make different kinds of statements according to the mood of their main verbs: *declarative, interrogative, imperative, exclamatory,* or *conditional.*

Declarative sentences make statements. They tell us something about a person, a place, a thing, or an idea.

> The Statue of Liberty stands in New York Harbor.
>
> For nearly a century, it has greeted immigrants and visitors to America.

Interrogative sentences ask questions.

> Did you know that the Statue of Liberty is made of copper and stands over 150 feet tall?

Imperative sentences make commands. They often contain an understood subject (you).

> Go see the Statue of Liberty.
>
> After a few weeks of physical conditioning, climb its 168 stairs.

Exclamatory sentences communicate strong emotion or surprise.

> Climbing 168 stairs is not a dumb idea!
>
> Whatever happened to that old pioneering spirit, that desire to take a chance, to try something new, that never-say-die attitude that made America great!

Conditional sentences express wishes ("if . . . then" statements) or conditions contrary to fact.

> If you were to climb to the top of the statue, then you could share in the breathtaking feeling experienced by many recent immigrants.

759 Structure of a Sentence

A sentence may be *simple, compound, complex,* or *compound-complex* in structure, depending on the relationship between independent and dependent clauses in it.

A **simple sentence** may have a single subject or a compound subject. It may have a single predicate or a compound predicate. But a simple sentence has only one independent clause, and it has no dependent clauses. A simple sentence may, however, contain one or more phrases.

> My **back aches**. (single subject; single predicate)
>
> My **teeth** and my **eyes hurt**. (compound subject; single predicate)
>
> My **hair** and my **muscles are deteriorating** and **disappearing**. (compound subject; compound predicate)
>
> **I must be getting over the hill**. (single subject: *I;* single predicate: *must be getting;* phrase: *over the hill*)

A **compound sentence** consists of two independent clauses. The clauses must be joined by a coordinating conjunction, by punctuation, or by both.

> Energy is part of youth, **but** both are quickly spent.

> My middle-aged body is sore; my middle-aged face is wrinkled.

A **complex sentence** contains one independent clause (in italics) and one or more dependent clauses (in boldface).

> *People often say wise things,* **such as age is a state of mind**. (independent clause; dependent clause)

> *Youth seems past,* however, **when my back aches before the day is even half over**. (independent clause; two dependent clauses)

A **compound-complex sentence** contains two or more independent clauses (in italics) and one or more dependent clauses (in boldface).

> *My body is rather old, and age is not a state of mind,* **unless my bald head is an illusion**. (two independent clauses; dependent clause)

760 ## Arrangement of a Sentence

Depending on the arrangement of the words within a sentence and the placement of emphasis, a sentence may also be classified as *loose, balanced, periodic,* or *cumulative.*

A **loose sentence** expresses the main thought near the beginning and adds explanatory material as needed.

> **We bashed the piñata for 15 minutes without denting it**, although we at least avoided denting one another's craniums and, with masks raised, finally pried the candy out with a screwdriver.

A **balanced sentence** is constructed so that it emphasizes a similarity or contrast between two or more of its parts (words, phrases, or clauses).

> Joe's unusual security system **invited burglars** and **scared off friends**. (*Invited* contrasts with *scared off* and *burglars* contrasts with *friends.*)

A **periodic sentence** is one that postpones the crucial or most surprising idea until the end.

> Following my mother's repeated threats of being grounded for life, **I decided it was time to propose a compromise**.

A **cumulative sentence** places the general idea in the main clause and gives it greater precision with modifying words, phrases, or clauses placed before it, after it, or in the middle of it.

> Eyes squinting, puffy, always on alert, **he showed the effects of a week in the forest**, a brutal week, a week of staggering in circles driven by the baying of wolves. (The phrases *eyes squinting, puffy,* and *always on alert* look forward to the pronoun *he* in the main clause; the phrases after the word *forest* look back to the word *week* in the main clause.)

Getting Sentence Parts to Agree

761 Agreement of Subject and Verb

The subject and verb of any clause must agree in both **person** and **number**. There are **three persons: first person** *(I)*, **second person** *(you)*, and **third person** *(he, she, it)*. Checking sentences for agreement in **person** is simply a matter of reading carefully. (See 714.) Checking sentences for agreement in **number** (singular and plural) requires a much closer look. Read the following guidelines.

762 Agreement in Number

A verb must agree in number (singular or plural) with its subject.

> The **student was** proud of her quarter grades. (Both the subject *student* and the verb *was* are singular; they are said to agree in number.)

Note • Do not be confused by other words that come between the subject and verb.

> The **manager** as well as the players **is** required to display good sportsmanship. (*Manager*, not *players*, is the subject.)

763 Delayed subjects occur when the verb comes *before* the subject in a sentence. In these inverted sentences, the true *(delayed)* subject must be made to agree with the verb.

> There **are** many hardworking **students** in our schools.
> There **is** present among many students today a **will** to succeed.
> (*Students* and *will* are the true subjects of these sentences, not *there*.)

764 Compound subjects connected with *and* usually require a plural verb.

> **Strength** and **balance** are necessary for gymnastics.

765 Singular subjects joined by *or* or *nor* take a singular verb.

> **Neither** Bev **nor** Connie is going to the street dance.

Note • When one of the subjects joined by *or* or *nor* is singular and one is plural, the verb is made to agree with the subject nearer the verb.

> **Neither** Mr. Kemper **nor** his students are able to find the photographs.
> (The plural subject *students* is nearer the verb; therefore, the plural verb *are* is used to agree with *students*.)

766 The indefinite pronouns *each, either, neither, one, everybody, another, anybody, everyone, nobody, everything, somebody,* and *someone* are singular; they require a singular verb.

> Everybody is invited to the cafeteria for refreshments.

Note • Do not be confused by words or phrases which come between the indefinite pronoun and the verb.

> **Each** of the boys **is** (not **are**) required to bring a bar of soap on the first day of class.

767 The **indefinite pronouns** *all, any, half, most, none,* and *some* may be either singular or plural when they are used as subjects. These pronouns are singular if the number of the noun in the prepositional phrase is singular; they are plural if the noun is plural.

> **Half** of the bottles were missing.
> (*Bottles*, the noun in the prepositional phrase, is plural; therefore, the pronoun *half* is considered plural, and the plural verb *were* is used to agree with it.)
>
> **Half** of the movie was over by the time we arrived.
> (Because *movie* is singular, *half* is also singular.)

768 **Collective nouns** (*faculty, committee, team, congress, species, crowd, army, pair, assembly, squad*) take a singular verb when they refer to a group as a unit; collective nouns take a plural verb when they refer to the individuals within the group.

> The **faculty** is united in its effort to make this school a better place to be.
> (*Faculty* refers to a group as a unit; therefore, it requires a singular verb: *is.*)
>
> The **faculty** are required to turn in their keys before leaving for the summer.
> (In this example, *faculty* refers to the individuals within the group. If the word *individuals* were substituted for *faculty*, it would become clear that the plural verb *are* is needed in this sentence.)

769 Some nouns that are **plural in form** but singular in meaning take a singular verb: *mumps, measles, news, mathematics, economics, gallows, shambles.*

> **Measles** is still considered a serious disease in many parts of the world.

Exceptions: *scissors, trousers, tidings.*

> The scissors are missing again.

Note • Mathematical phrases usually take a singular verb.

> Three and three **is** six. Five times six **is** thirty.

770 When a **relative pronoun** (*who, which, that*) is used as the subject of a clause, the number of the verb is determined by the antecedent of the pronoun. (The antecedent is the word to which the pronoun refers.)

> This is one of the **books that are** required for geography class.
> (The relative pronoun *that* requires the plural verb *are* because its antecedent *books* is plural. To test this type of sentence for agreement, read the *of* phrase first: *Of the books that are . . .*)

771 When a sentence contains a form of the *to be* verb—and a noun comes before and after that verb—the verb must agree with the subject even if the *complement* (the noun coming after the verb) is different in number.

> The **cause** of his problem **was** his bad **brakes**. His bad **brakes were** the **cause** of his problem.

Agreement of a Pronoun and Its Antecedent

772 A pronoun must agree in number, person, and gender (sex) with its *antecedent*. (The *antecedent* is the word to which the pronoun refers.)

> **Bill** brought **his** gerbil to school.
>
> (The antecedent in this sentence is *Bill;* it is to *Bill* that the pronoun *his* refers. Both the pronoun and its antecedent are singular, third person, and masculine; therefore, the pronoun is said to agree with its antecedent.)

773 Use a singular pronoun to refer to such antecedents as *each, either, neither, one, anyone, anybody, everyone, everybody, somebody, another, nobody,* and *a person.*

> **One** of the rowboats is missing **its** (not **their**) oars.

Note • When *a person* or *everyone* is used to refer to both sexes or either sex, you will have to choose whether to offer optional pronouns or rewrite the sentence.

> A **person** must learn to wait **his** or **her** turn. **(optional pronouns)**
>
> **People** must learn to wait **their** turn. **(rewritten in plural form)**

774 Two or more antecedents joined by *and* are considered plural; two or more singular antecedents joined by *or* or *nor* are referred to by a singular pronoun.

> **Tom** and **Bob** are finishing **their** assignments.
>
> Either **Connie** or **Sue** left **her** headset in the library.

Note • If one of the antecedents is masculine and one feminine, the pronouns should likewise be masculine and feminine.

> Is either **Dave** or **Phyllis** bringing **his** or **her** frisbee?

Note • If one of the antecedents joined by *or* or *nor* is singular and one is plural, the pronoun is made to agree with the nearer antecedent.

> Neither the **manager** nor the **players** were crazy about **their** new uniforms.

775 Treating the Sexes Fairly

When you box people in or put them down just because of their sex, that is called "sexism." When you identify all human virtues with only one sex, or when you identify one sex with the whole human race, that, too, is sexism. And when you bring in sexual distinctions where they don't belong, that, too, is sexism. Sexism is unfair. And it hurts. Ask anyone who has been a victim of it.

To change our centuries-old habit of sexist thinking, we must try to change our language, for our traditional ways of speaking and writing have sexist patterns deeply imprinted in them. The assumptions built into our language teach even little children who they are and how they relate to others. For their sakes and our own, we must seek a language that implies equal value, equal potential, and equal opportunity for people of both sexes.

Portraying the Sexes in Writing . . .

776 **Don't** typecast all men as leaders, professionals, breadwinners, etc.; don't typecast all women as subordinates, homebodies, helpers, and dependents.

Do show both women and men as doctors and nurses, principals and teachers, breadwinners and housekeepers, bosses and secretaries, grocery-store owners and cashiers, pilots, plumbers, TV repairers, social workers, etc.

777 **Don't** associate courage, strength, brilliance, creativity, independence, persistence, and seriousness with only men and boys; don't associate emotionalism, passivity, and fearfulness with only women and girls.

Do portray people of both sexes along the whole range of potential human strengths and weaknesses.

778 **Don't** refer to women according to their physical appearance and to men according to their mental abilities or professional status:

> The admirable Dr. William Hicks and his wife Mary, an attractive former model, both showed up at the party.

Do refer to both on the same plane:

> Bill and Mary Hicks showed up at the party.

779 **Don't** use demeaning or sexually loaded labels when referring to women:

girl (for secretary)	career girl
the weaker sex	better half, little woman
chick, fox, bombshell, knockout	

Do use respectful terms rather than labels; consider what the woman herself might wish to be called:

secretary, Helen, Ms. Jones	professional woman, career person
wife, spouse	woman, girl, attractive woman, young woman

780 **Don't** take special notice when a woman does a "man's job" or vice versa:

      lady doctor   male nurse   coed

Do treat men's or women's involvement in a profession as normal, not exceptional:

      doctor   nurse   student

781 **Don't** portray women as the possessions of men:

      Fred took his wife and kids on a vacation.

Do portray women and men, husbands and wives, as equal partners:

      Fred and Wilma took their kids on a vacation.

Referring to Men and Women Together . . .

782 **Don't** give special treatment to one of the sexes:

      The men and the ladies came through in the clutch.

      Hank and Miss Jenkins

      Mr. Bubba Gumm, Mrs. Bubba Gumm

Do use equal language for both sexes:

      The men and the women came through in the clutch.

      Hank and Mimi

      Mr. Bubba Gumm, Mrs. Lotta Gumm

Referring to People in General . . .

783 **Don't** use "man words" to refer to all people or a person in general:

      mankind   man-hours

      man-made   the best man for the job

Do use nonsexist alternatives to man words:

      humanity   synthetic   employee hours   the best person for the job

784 **Don't** use only masculine pronouns (he, his, him) when you want to refer to a human being in general:

      A politician can kiss privacy good-bye when he runs for office.

Do use one of the several ways to avoid sexism:

      Reword the sentence: Running for office robs a politician of privacy.

      Express in the plural: Politicians can kiss privacy good-bye when they run for office.

      Offer optional pronouns: A politician can kiss privacy good-bye when he or she runs for office.

Addressing Your Reader ...

785 **Don't** assume that your reader is male:

You and your wife will be shocked at these prices.

After the morning shave, one feels a bit clearer in the head.

Do assume that your reader is either male or female:

You and your spouse (or loved one) will be shocked at these prices.

After the morning shower, one feels a bit clearer in the head.

786 **Don't** use a male word in the salutation of a business letter to someone you do not know:

Dear Sir: **Dear Gentlemen:**

Do address both if you're not sure whether the reader is male or female:

Dear Madam or Sir:

Dear Ladies and Gentlemen:

or address a position:

Dear Personnel Officer:

Dear Members of the Big Bird Fan Club:

Using Occupational Titles ...

787 **Don't** use "man words" for titles, even if the person in question is a male.

Do use neutral titles whenever possible. Do use equal language for both sexes.

What NOT to Do	What to DO
foreman	supervisor
chairman	chair; presiding officer; moderator
salesman	sales representative; sales clerk; salesperson
mailman	mail carrier; postal worker; letter carrier
insurance man	insurance agent
fireman	firefighter
businessman	executive; manager; businessperson
congressman	member of Congress; representative; senator

788 **Don't** use special titles to distinguish female workers from males.

Do use neutral terms for both men and women.

What NOT to Do	What to DO
steward, stewardess	flight attendant
usher, usherette	usher
policeman, policewoman	police officer
poet, poetess	poet
author, authoress	author
maid, houseboy	housekeeper, servant

Almanac

> "I find that a great part of the information I have was acquired by looking up something and finding something else on the way."
>
> —Franklin P. Adams

Tables and Charts

789 Manual Alphabet (Sign Language)

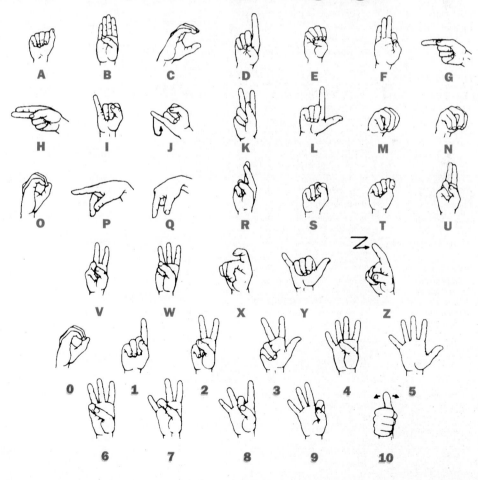

A Table of
(790) Common Parliamentary Procedures

Motion	Purpose	Needs Second	Debatable	Amend-able	Vote	May Interrupt Speaker	Subsidiary Motion Applied
I. ORIGINAL OR PRINCIPAL MOTION							
1. Main Motion (general) Main Motions (specific)	To introduce business	Yes	Yes	Yes	Majority	No	Yes
a. To reconsider	To reconsider previous motion	Yes	When original motion is	No	Majority	Yes	No
b. To rescind	To nullify or wipe out previous action	Yes	Yes	Yes	Majority or two-thirds	No	No
c. To take from the table	To consider tabled motion	Yes	No	No	Majority	No	No
II. SUBSIDIARY MOTIONS							
2. To lay on the table	To defer action	Yes	No	No	Majority	No	No
3. To call for previous question	To close debate and force vote	Yes	No	No	Two-thirds	No	Yes
4. To limit or extend limits of debate	To control time of debate	Yes	No	Yes	Two-thirds	No	Yes
5. To postpone to a certain time	To defer action	Yes	Yes	Yes	Majority	No	Yes
6. To refer to a committee	To provide for special study	Yes	Yes	Yes	Majority	No	Yes
7. To amend	To modify a motion	Yes	When original motion is	Yes (once only)	Majority	No	Yes
8. To postpone indefinitely	To suppress action	Yes	Yes	No	Majority	No	Yes
III. INCIDENTAL MOTIONS							
9. To raise a point of order	To correct error in procedure	No	No	No	Decision of chair	Yes	No
10. To appeal for decision of chair	To change decision on procedure	Yes	If motion does not relate to indecorum	No	Majority or tie	Yes	No
11. To suspend rules	To alter existing rules and order of business	Yes	No	No	Two-thirds	No	No
12. To object to consideration	To suppress action	No	No	No	Two-thirds	Yes	No
13. To call for division of house	To secure a countable vote	No	No	No	Majority if chair desires	Yes	Yes
14. To close nominations	To stop nomination of officers	Yes	No	Yes	Two-thirds	No	Yes
15. To reopen nominations	To permit additional nominations	Yes	No	Yes	Majority	No	Yes
16. To withdraw a motion	To remove a motion	No	No	No	Majority	No	No
17. To divide motion	To modify motion	No	No	Yes	Majority	No	Yes
IV. PRIVILEGED MOTIONS							
18. To fix time of next meeting	To set time of next meeting	Yes	No, if made when another question is before the assembly	Yes	Majority	No	Yes
19. To adjourn	To dismiss meeting	Yes	No	Yes	Majority	No	No
20. To take a recess	To dismiss meeting for specific time	Yes	No, if made when another question is before the assembly	Yes	Majority	No	Yes
21. To raise question of privilege	To make a request concerning rights of assembly	No	No	No	Decision of chair	Yes	No
22. To call for orders of the day	To keep assembly to order of business	No	No	No	None unless objection	Yes	No
23. To make a special order	To ensure consideration at specified time	Yes	Yes	Yes	Two-thirds	No	Yes

791 Multiplication and Division Table

A number in the top line (11) multiplied by a number in the extreme left-hand column (12) produces the number where the top line and side line meet (132).

A number in the table (208) divided by the number at the top of the same column (13) results in the number (16) in the extreme left-hand column. A number in the table (208) divided by the number at the extreme left (16) results in the number (13) at the top of the column.

1	2	3	4	5	6	7	8	9	10	11	12	13	14	15	16	17	18	19	20	21	22	23	24	25
2	4	6	8	10	12	14	16	18	20	22	24	26	28	30	32	34	36	38	40	42	44	46	48	50
3	6	9	12	15	18	21	24	27	30	33	36	39	42	45	48	51	54	57	60	63	66	69	72	75
4	8	12	16	20	24	28	32	36	40	44	48	52	56	60	64	68	72	76	80	84	88	92	96	100
5	10	15	20	25	30	35	40	45	50	55	60	65	70	75	80	85	90	95	100	105	110	115	120	125
6	12	18	24	30	36	42	48	54	60	66	72	78	84	90	96	102	108	114	120	126	132	138	144	150
7	14	21	28	35	42	49	56	63	70	77	84	91	98	105	112	119	126	133	140	147	154	161	168	175
8	16	24	32	40	48	56	64	72	80	88	96	104	112	120	128	136	144	152	160	168	176	184	192	200
9	18	27	36	45	54	63	72	81	90	99	108	117	126	135	144	153	162	171	180	189	198	207	216	225
10	20	30	40	50	60	70	80	90	100	110	120	130	140	150	160	170	180	190	200	210	220	230	240	250
11	22	33	44	55	66	77	88	99	110	121	132	143	154	165	176	187	198	209	220	231	242	253	264	275
12	24	36	48	60	72	84	96	108	120	132	144	156	168	180	192	204	216	228	240	252	264	276	288	300
13	26	39	52	65	78	91	104	117	130	143	156	169	182	195	208	221	234	247	260	273	286	299	312	325
14	28	42	56	70	84	98	112	126	140	154	168	182	196	210	224	238	252	266	280	294	308	322	336	350
15	30	45	60	75	90	105	120	135	150	160	180	195	210	225	240	255	270	285	300	315	330	345	360	375
16	32	48	64	80	96	112	128	144	160	176	192	208	224	240	256	272	288	304	320	336	352	368	384	400
17	34	51	68	85	102	119	136	153	170	187	204	221	238	255	272	289	306	323	340	357	374	391	408	425
18	36	54	72	90	108	126	143	162	180	198	216	234	252	270	288	306	323	340	360	378	396	414	432	450
19	38	57	76	95	114	133	152	171	190	209	228	247	266	285	304	323	342	361	380	399	418	437	456	475
20	40	60	80	100	120	140	160	180	200	220	240	260	285	300	320	340	360	380	400	420	440	460	480	500
21	42	63	84	105	126	147	168	189	210	231	252	273	294	315	336	357	378	399	420	441	462	483	504	525
22	44	66	88	110	132	154	176	198	220	242	264	286	308	330	352	374	396	418	440	462	484	506	528	550
23	46	69	92	115	138	161	184	207	230	253	276	299	322	345	368	391	414	437	460	483	506	529	552	575
24	48	72	96	120	144	168	192	216	240	264	288	312	336	360	384	408	432	456	480	504	528	552	576	600
25	50	75	100	125	150	175	200	225	250	275	300	325	350	375	400	425	450	475	500	525	550	575	600	625

792

Decimal Equivalents of Common Fractions

Fraction	Decimal	Fraction	Decimal	Fraction	Decimal	Fraction	Decimal	Fraction	Decimal
1/2	.5000	1/12	.0833	3/5	.6000	5/6	.8333	7/9	.7778
1/3	.3333	1/16	.0625	3/7	.4286	5/7	.7143	7/10	.7000
1/4	.2500	1/32	.0313	3/8	.3750	5/8	.6250	7/11	.6364
1/5	.2000	1/64	.0156	3/10	.3000	5/9	.5556	7/12	.5833
1/6	.1667	2/3	.6667	3/11	.2727	5/11	.4545	8/9	.8889
1/7	.1429	2/5	.4000	3/16	.1875	5/12	.4167	8/11	.7273
1/8	.1250	2/7	.2857	4/5	.8000	5/16	.3125	9/10	.9000
1/9	.1111	2/9	.2222	4/7	.5714	6/7	.8571	9/11	.8182
1/10	.1000	2/11	.1818	4/9	.4444	6/11	.5455	10/11	.9091
1/11	.0909	3/4	.7500	4/11	.3636	7/8	.8750	11/12	.9167

(793) Weights and Measures

Linear Measure

1 inch	=	2.54 centimeters
1 foot	=	12 inches
		0.3048 meter
1 yard	=	3 feet
		0.9144 meter
1 rod (or pole or perch)	=	5 $\frac{1}{2}$ yards or 16 $\frac{1}{2}$ feet
		5.029 meters
1 furlong	=	40 rods
		201.17 meters
1 (statute) mile	=	8 furlongs
		1,760 yards
		5,280 feet
		1,609.3 meters
1 (land) league	=	3 miles
		4.83 kilometers

Square Measure

1 square inch	=	6.452 sq. centimeters
1 square foot	=	144 square inches
		929 square centimeters
1 square yard	=	9 square feet
		0.8361 square meter
1 square rod	=	30 $\frac{1}{4}$ square rods
		25.29 square meters
1 acre	=	160 square rods
		4,840 square yards
		43,560 square feet
		0.4047 hectare
1 square mile	=	640 acres
		259 hectares
		2.59 square kilometers

Cubic Measure

1 cubic inch	=	16.387 cubic centimeters
1 cubic foot	=	1,728 cubic inches
		0.0283 cubic meter
1 cubic yard	=	27 cubic feet
		0.7646 cubic meter
1 cord foot	=	16 cubic feet
1 cord	=	8 cord feet
		3.625 cubic meters

Chain Measure
(Gunter's or surveyor's chain)

1 link	=	7.92 inches
		20.12 centimeters
1 chain	=	100 links or 66 feet
		20.12 meters
1 furlong	=	10 chains
		201.17 meters
1 mile	=	80 chains
		1,609.3 meters

(Engineer's chain)

1 link	=	1 foot
		0.3048 meter
1 chain	=	100 feet
		30.48 meters
1 mile	=	52.8 chains
		1,609.3 meters

Surveyor's (Square) Measure

1 square pole	=	625 square links
		25.29 square meters
1 square chain	=	16 square poles
		404.7 square meters
1 acre	=	10 square chains
		0.4047 hectare
1 square mile or		
1 section	=	640 acres
		259 hectares
		2.59 square kilometers
1 township	=	36 square miles
		9,324 hectares
		93.24 square kilometers

Nautical Measure

1 fathom	=	6 feet
		1.829 meters
1 cable's length (ordinary)	=	100 fathoms

(In the U.S. Navy 120 fathoms
or 720 feet = 1 cable's length;
in the British Navy 608 feet = 1 cable's length)

1 nautical mile	=	6,076.10333 feet; *by international agreement in 1954*
		10 cables' length
		1.852 kilometers
		1.1508 statute miles; *length of a minute of longitude at the equator*
1 marine league	=	3.45 statute miles
		3 nautical miles
		5.56 kilometers

1 degree of a great circle of the earth	=	60 nautical miles

Dry Measure

1 pint	=	33.60 cubic inches
		0.5505 liter
1 quart	=	2 pints
		67.20 cubic inches
		1.1012 liters
1 peck	=	8 quarts
		537.61 cubic inches
		8.8096 liters
1 bushel	=	4 pecks
		2,150.42 cubic inches
		35.2383 liters

Liquid Measure

4 fluid ounces *(see next table)*	=	1 gill
		7.219 cubic inches
		0.1183 liter
1 pint	=	4 gills
		28.875 cubic inches
		0.4732 liter
1 quart	=	2 pints
		57.75 cubic inches
		0.9463 liter
1 gallon	=	4 quarts
		231 cubic inches
		3.7853 liters

794

Apothecaries' Fluid Measure

1 minim	=	0.0038 cubic inch
		0.0616 milliliter
1 fluid dram	=	60 minims
		0.2256 cubic inch
		3.6966 milliliters
1 fluid ounce	=	8 fluid drams
		1.8047 cubic inches
		0.0296 liter
1 pint	=	16 fluid ounces
		28.875 cubic inches
		0.4732 liter

Circular (or Angular) Measure

1 minute (')	=	60 seconds (")
1 degree (°)	=	60 minutes
1 quadrant or 1 right angle	=	90 degrees
1 circle	=	4 quadrants
		360 degrees

Avoirdupois Weight
(The grain, equal to 0.0648 gram,
is the same in all three tables of weight)

1 dram or 27.34 grains	=	1.772 grams
1 ounce	=	16 drams
		437.5 grains
		28.3495 grams
1 pound	=	16 ounces
		7,000 grains
		453.59 grams
1 hundredweight	=	100 pounds
		45.36 kilograms
1 ton	=	2,000 pounds
		907.18 kilograms

Troy Weight
(The grain, equal to 0.0648 gram,
is the same in all three tables of weight)

1 carat	=	3.086 grains
		200 milligrams
1 pennyweight	=	24 grains
		1.5552 grams
1 ounce	=	20 pennyweights
		480 grains
		31.1035 grams
1 pound	=	12 ounces
		5,760 grains
		373.24 grams

Apothecaries' Weight
(The grain, equal to 0.0648 gram,
is the same in all three tables of weight)

1 scruple	=	20 grains
		1.296 grams
1 dram	=	3 scruples
		3.888 grams
1 ounce	=	8 drams
		480 grains
		31.1035 grams
1 pound	=	12 ounces
		5,760 grains
		373.24 grams

Miscellaneous

1 palm	=	3 inches
1 hand	=	4 inches
1 span	=	6 inches
1 cubit	=	18 inches
1 Bible cubit	=	21.8 inches
1 military pace	=	$2\frac{1}{2}$ feet

795

Additional Units of Measure

Astronomical Unit (A.U.): 93,000,000 miles, the average distance of the earth from the sun. Used in astronomy.

Board Foot (bd. ft.): 144 cubic inches (12 in. x 12 in. x 1 in.). Used for lumber.

Bolt: 40 yards. Used for measuring cloth.

Btu: British thermal unit. Amount of heat needed to increase the temperature of one pound of water by one degree Fahrenheit (252 calories).

Gross: 12 dozen or 144.

Knot: Not a distance, but the rate of speed of one nautical mile per hour.

Light, Speed of: 186,281.7 miles per second.

Light-year: 5,880,000,000,000 miles, the distance light travels in a year at the rate of 186,281.7 miles per second.

Pi (π): 3.14159265+. The ratio of the circumference of a circle to its diameter. For all practical purposes: 3.1416.

Roentgen: Dosage unit of radiation exposure produced by X rays.

Score: 20 units.

Sound, Speed of: Usually placed at 1,088 ft. per second at 32° F at sea level.

796 The Metric System

In 1975, the United States signed the Metric Conversion Act, declaring a national policy of encouraging voluntary use of the metric system. Today, the metric system exists side by side with the U.S. customary system. The debate on whether the United States should adopt the metric system has been going on for nearly 200 years, leaving the United States the only country in the world not totally committed to adopting the system.

The metric system is considered a simpler form of measurement. It is based on the decimal system (units of 10) and eliminates the need to deal with fractions as we currently use them.

Linear Measure

1 centimeter	=	10 millimeters
		0.3937 inch
1 decimeter	=	10 centimeters
		3.937 inches
1 meter	=	10 decimeters
		39.37 inches
		3.28 feet
1 decameter	=	10 meters
		393.7 inches
1 hectometer	=	10 decameters
		328 feet 1 inch
1 kilometer	=	10 hectometers
		0.621 mile
1 myriameter	=	10 kilometers
		6.21 miles

Volume Measure

1 cubic centimeter	=	1,000 cubic millimeters
		.06102 cubic inch
1 cubic decimeter	=	1,000 cubic centimeters
		61.02 cubic inches
1 cubic meter	=	1,000 cubic decimeters
		35.314 cubic feet

Capacity Measure

1 centiliter	=	10 milliliters
		.338 fluid ounce
1 deciliter	=	10 centiliters
		3.38 fluid ounces
1 liter	=	10 deciliters
		1.0567 liquid quarts
		0.9081 dry quart
1 decaliter	=	10 liters
		2.64 gallons
		0.284 bushel
1 hectoliter	=	10 decaliters
		26.418 gallons
		2.838 bushels
1 kiloliter	=	10 hectoliters
		264.18 gallons
		35.315 cubic feet

Square Measure

1 square centimeter	=	100 square millimeters
		0.15499 square inch
1 square decimeter	=	100 square centimeters
		15.499 square inches
1 square meter	=	100 square decimeters
		1,549.9 square inches
		1.196 square yards
1 square decameter	=	100 square meters
		119.6 square yards
1 square hectometer	=	100 square decameters
		2.471 acres
1 square kilometer	=	100 square hectometers
		0.386 square mile

Land Measure

1 centare	=	1 square meter
		1,549.9 square inches
1 are	=	100 centares
		119.6 square yards
1 hectare	=	100 ares
		2,471 acres
1 square kilometer	=	100 hectares
		0.386 square mile

Weights

1 centigram	=	10 milligrams
		0.1543 grain
1 decigram	=	10 centigrams
		1.5432 grains
1 gram	=	10 decigrams
		15.432 grains
1 decagram	=	10 grams
		0.3527 ounce
1 hectogram	=	10 decagrams
		3.5274 ounces
1 kilogram	=	10 hectograms
		2.2046 pounds
1 myriagram	=	10 kilograms
		22.046 pounds
1 quintal	=	10 myriagrams
		220.46 pounds
1 metric ton	=	10 quintals
		2,204.6 pounds

HANDY CONVERSION FACTORS

797

TO CHANGE	TO	MULTIPLY BY
acres	hectares	.4047
acres	square feet	43,560
acres	square miles	.001562
Celsius	Fahrenheit	*1.8
		*(then add 32)
centimeters	inches	.3937
centimeters	feet	.03281
cubic meters	cubic feet	35.3145
cubic meters	cubic yards	1.3079
cubic yards	cubic meters	.7646
degrees	radians	.01745
Fahrenheit	Celsius	*.556
		* (after subtracting 32)
feet	meters	.3048
feet	miles (nautical)	.0001645
feet	miles (statute)	.0001894
feet/sec.	miles/hr.	.6818
furlongs	feet	660.0
furlongs	miles	.125
gallons (U.S.)	liters	3.7853
grains	grams	.0648
grams	grains	15.4324
grams	ounces avdp.	.0353
grams	pounds	.002205
hectares	acres	2.4710
horsepower	watts	745.7
hours	days	.04167
inches	millimeters	25.4000
inches	centimeters	2.5400
kilograms	pounds advp. or t.	2.2046
kilometers	miles	.6214
kilowatts	horsepower	1.341
knots	nautical miles/hr.	1.0
knots	statute miles/hr.	1.151
liters	gallons (U.S.)	.2642
liters	pecks	.1135
liters	pints (dry)	1.8162
liters	pints (liquid)	2.1134
liters	quarts (dry)	.9081

TO CHANGE	TO	MULTIPLY BY
liters	quarts (liquid)	1.0567
meters	feet	3.2808
meters	miles	.0006214
meters	yards	1.0936
metric tons	tons (long)	.9842
metric tons	tons (short)	1.1023
miles	kilometers	1.6093
miles	feet	5,280
miles (nautical)	miles (statute)	1.1516
miles (statute)	miles (nautical)	.8684
miles/hr.	feet/min.	88
millimeters	inches	.0394
ounces advp.	grams	28.3495
ounces	pounds	.0625
ounces (troy)	ounces (advp.)	1.09714
pecks	liters	8.8096
pints (dry)	liters	.5506
pints (liquid)	liters	1.4732
pounds ap. or t.	kilograms	.3782
pounds advp.	kilograms	.4536
pounds	ounces	16
quarts (dry)	liters	1.1012
quarts (liquid)	liters	.9463
rods	meters	5.029
rods	feet	16.5
square feet	square meters	.0929
square kilometers	square miles	.3861
square meters	square feet	10.7639
square meters	square yards	1.1960
square miles	square kilometers	2.5900
square yards	square meters	.8361
tons (long)	metric tons	1.1060
tons (short)	metric tons	.9072
tons (long)	pounds	2,240
tons (short)	pounds	2,000
watts	Btu/hr.	3.4129
watts	horsepower	.001341
yards	meters	.9144
yards	miles	.0005682

798

ten ways to **measure** *when you don't have a ruler*

1. Many floor tiles are 12-inch by 12-inch squares.
2. U.S. paper currency is 6-1/8 inches long by 2-5/8 inches wide.
3. A quarter is approximately 1 inch wide.
4. A penny is approximately 3/4 of an inch wide.
5. A standard sheet of paper is 8-1/2 inches by 11 inches.

Each of the following items can be used as a measuring device by multiplying its length by the number of times it is used to measure an area in question.

6. A shoelace   7. A tie   8. A belt
9. Your feet—placing one in front of the other to measure floor area
10. Your outstretched arms from fingertip to fingertip

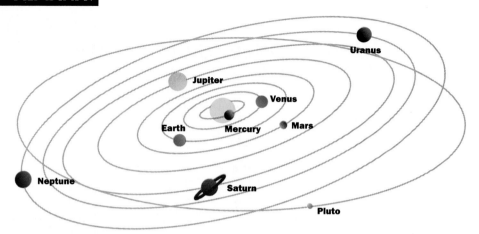

⑲⑨ Planet Profusion

Our solar system is located in the Milky Way Galaxy. Even though this galaxy contains approximately 100 billion stars, our solar system contains only one star—the sun. The sun, which is the center of our solar system, has 9 planets and a myriad of asteroids, meteors, and comets orbiting it. The planets are large, nonluminous bodies that follow fixed elliptical orbits about the sun. (See the illustration above.) The planets are divided into two categories: the terrestrial planets—Mercury, Venus, Earth, Mars, and Pluto—which resemble Earth in size, chemical composition, and density; and the Jovian planets—Jupiter, Saturn, Uranus, and Neptune—which are much larger in size and have thick, gaseous atmospheres and low densities. (See the table below.)

	Sun	Moon	Mercury	Venus	Earth	Mars	Jupiter	Saturn	Uranus	Neptune	Pluto
Orbital Speed (in mi. per second)		.6	29.8	21.8	18.5	15.0	8.1	6.0	4.1	3.4	2.9
Rotation on Axis	24 days 16 hrs. 48 min.	27 days 7 hrs. 38 min.	59 days	243 days	23 hrs. 56 min.	1 day 37 min.	9 hrs. 55 min.	10 hrs. 39 min.	16 to 28 hours	16 hrs.	6 days
Mean Surface Gravity (Earth=1)		0.16	0.38	0.9	1.00	0.38	2.87	1.32	0.93	1.23	0.03
Density (times that of water)	100 (core)	3.3	5.4	5.3	5.5	3.9	1.3	0.7	1.2	1.6	1.0
Mass (times that of Earth)	333,000	0.012	0.055	0.82	6×10^{21} metric tons	0.11	318	95	14.6	17.2	0.0026
Approx. Weight of a Human (in lbs.)		24	57	135	150	57	431	198	140	185	4.5
No. of Satellites	9 planets	0	0	0	1	2	16	23	15	8	1
Mean Distance to Sun (in millions of miles)		93.0	36.0	67.23	92.96	141.7	483.7	886.2	1,781	2,793	3,660
Revolution Around Sun		365.25 days	88.0 days	224.7 days	365.25 days	686.99 days	11.86 years	29.46 years	84.0 years	164.8 years	247.6 years
Approximate Surface Temp. (degrees Fahrenheit)	10,000° (surface) 27,000,000° (center)	lighted side 200° dark side -230°	-315°	850°	-126.9° to 136°	-191° to -24°	-236°	-285°	-357°	-400°	-342° to -369°
Diameter (in miles)	867,000	2,155	3,031	7,520	7,926	4,200	88,700	74,600	31,570	30,800	1,420

Periodic Table of the Elements

Key:

Atomic Number 1

Symbol .... H Hydrogen

Atomic Weight
(or Mass Number of most stable
isotope if in parentheses) 1.00797

Legend:
- Alkali metals
- Alkaline earth metals
- Transition metals
- Lanthanide series
- Actinide series
- Other metals
- Nonmetals
- Noble gases

1a	2a	3b	4b	5b	6b	7b	8	8	8	1b	2b	3a	4a	5a	6a	7a	0
1 **H** Hydrogen 1.00797																	2 **He** Helium 4.00260
3 **Li** Lithium 6.941	4 **Be** Beryllium 9.0128											5 **B** Boron 10.811	6 **C** Carbon 12.01115	7 **N** Nitrogen 14.0067	8 **O** Oxygen 15.9994	9 **F** Fluorine 18.9984	10 **Ne** Neon 20.179
11 **Na** Sodium 22.9898	12 **Mg** Magnesium 24.305											13 **Al** Aluminum 26.9815	14 **Si** Silicon 28.0855	15 **P** Phosphorus 30.9738	16 **S** Sulfur 32.064	17 **Cl** Chlorine 35.453	18 **Ar** Argon 39.948
19 **K** Potassium 39.0983	20 **Ca** Calcium 40.08	21 **Sc** Scandium 44.9559	22 **Ti** Titanium 47.88	23 **V** Vanadium 50.94	24 **Cr** Chromium 51.996	25 **Mn** Manganese 54.9380	26 **Fe** Iron 55.847	27 **Co** Cobalt 58.9332	28 **Ni** Nickel 58.69	29 **Cu** Copper 63.546	30 **Zn** Zinc 65.39	31 **Ga** Gallium 69.72	32 **Ge** Germanium 72.59	33 **As** Arsenic 74.9216	34 **Se** Selenium 78.96	35 **Br** Bromine 79.904	36 **Kr** Krypton 83.80
37 **Rb** Rubidium 85.4678	38 **Sr** Strontium 87.62	39 **Y** Yttrium 88.905	40 **Zr** Zirconium 91.224	41 **Nb** Niobium 92.906	42 **Mo** Molybdenum 95.94	43 **Tc** Technetium (98)	44 **Ru** Ruthenium 101.07	45 **Rh** Rhodium 102.906	46 **Pd** Palladium 106.42	47 **Ag** Silver 107.868	48 **Cd** Cadmium 112.41	49 **In** Indium 114.82	50 **Sn** Tin 118.71	51 **Sb** Antimony 121.75	52 **Te** Tellurium 127.60	53 **I** Iodine 126.905	54 **Xe** Xenon 131.29
55 **Cs** Cesium 132.905	56 **Ba** Barium 137.33	57-71* Lanthanides	72 **Hf** Hafnium 178.49	73 **Ta** Tantalum 180.948	74 **W** Tungsten 183.85	75 **Re** Rhenium 186.207	76 **Os** Osmium 190.2	77 **Ir** Iridium 192.22	78 **Pt** Platinum 195.08	79 **Au** Gold 196.967	80 **Hg** Mercury 200.59	81 **Tl** Thallium 204.383	82 **Pb** Lead 207.19	83 **Bi** Bismuth 208.980	84 **Po** Polonium (209)	85 **At** Astatine (210)	86 **Rn** Radon (222)
87 **Fr** Francium (223)	88 **Ra** Radium 226.025	89-103** Actinides (227)	104 **Unq**† Unnilquadium (261)	105 **Unp**†† Unnilpentium (262)	106 **Unh** Unnilhexium (263)	107 **Uns** Unnilseptium (262)		109 **Une** Unnilennium (266)									

*Lanthanides:

57 **La** Lanthanum 138.906	58 **Ce** Cerium 140.12	59 **Pr** Praseodymium 140.908	60 **Nd** Neodymium 144.24	61 **Pm** Promethium (145)	62 **Sm** Samarium 150.36	63 **Eu** Europium 151.96	64 **Gd** Gadolinium 157.25	65 **Tb** Terbium 158.925	66 **Dy** Dysprosium 162.50	67 **Ho** Holmium 164.930	68 **Er** Erbium 167.26	69 **Tm** Thulium 168.934	70 **Yb** Ytterbium 173.04	71 **Lu** Lutetium 174.967

**Actinides:

89 **Ac** Actinium 227.028	90 **Th** Thorium 232.038	91 **Pa** Protactinium 231.036	92 **U** Uranium 238.029	93 **Np** Neptunium 237.048	94 **Pu** Plutonium (244)	95 **Am** Americium (243)	96 **Cm** Curium (247)	97 **Bk** Berkelium (247)	98 **Cf** Californium (251)	99 **Es** Einsteinium (252)	100 **Fm** Fermium (257)	101 **Md** Mendelevium (258)	102 **No** Nobelium (259)	103 **Lw** Lawrencium (260)

†Other proposed names are kurchatovium (USSR) and hahnium (U.S.)
††Other proposed names are nielsbohrium (USSR) and rutherfordium (U.S.)

801 Traffic Signs

Red: Regulatory Signs

These signs are red to get your attention: they tell you to do (or *not* do) something. The red circle and stripe tells you NO.

White and Black: Information Signs

Informational signs are black and white and shaped like a square or rectangle. They provide basic information for pedestrians and drivers.

Yellow: Warning Signs

Yellow in color, these signs warn of a possible danger. Most warning signs are in the shape of a diamond.

Green: Directional or Guide Signs

These green signs give traffic directions or provide information on trail and bike routes.

Blue: Service Signs

These blue signs mean there are services nearby.

Orange: Construction Signs and Slow-Moving Vehicle Signs

Orange signs mean slow down and drive carefully.

"We are citizens of the world; and the tragedy of our times is that we do not know this."

—**Woodrow Wilson**

World Maps

802   As you know, the world has changed dramatically in the past several years. As global citizens it is up to each of us to stay on top of those changes. Just as we once tried to understand something about each of the 50 states, we must now work to understand each of the 170 countries in the world. The section that follows will give you the map skills you need to begin your work.

Using the Maps

803 ### Finding Direction

Mapmakers use special marks and symbols to show where things are or to give other useful information. Among other things, these marks and symbols show direction (north, south, east, and west). On most maps, north is at the top. But you should always check the **compass rose,** or directional finder, to make sure you know where north is. If there is no symbol, you can assume that north is at the top.

804 ### Finding Information

Other important marks and symbols are explained in a box printed on each map. This box is called the **legend**, or **key**. It is included to make it easier for you to understand and use the map. Below is the United States map legend. This legend also includes symbols for state capitals and state boundaries.

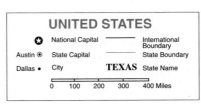

805 Measuring Distances

To measure distances on a map, use the **map scale**. (See the sample below.) Line up an index card or a piece of paper under the map scale and put a dot on your paper at "0." Now put other dots to mark off 100, 200, 300, and so on. Your paper can now be used to measure the approximate distance between points on the map.

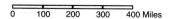

0   100   200   300   400 Miles

806 Locating Countries

Latitude and **longitude lines** are another helpful feature of most maps. Latitude and longitude refer to imaginary lines that mapmakers use. When used together, these lines can be used to locate any point on the earth.

Latitude

The imaginary lines that go from east to west around the earth are called lines of latitude. The line of latitude that goes around the earth exactly halfway between the North Pole and the South Pole is called the *equator*. Latitude is measured in degrees, with the equator being 0 degrees (0°). Above the equator, the lines are called *north latitude* and measure from 0° to 90° north (the North Pole). Below the equator, the lines are called *south latitude* and measure from 0° to 90° south (the South Pole). On a map, latitude numbers are printed along the left- and right-hand sides.

Longitude

The imaginary lines that run from the North Pole to the South Pole are lines of longitude. Longitude is also measured in degrees. The *prime meridian,* which passes through Greenwich, England, is 0° longitude. Lines east of the prime meridian are called *east longitude;* lines west of the prime meridian are called *west longitude.* On a map, longitude numbers are printed at the top and bottom.

the bottom line

The latitude and longitude numbers of a place are called its **coordinates**. In each set of coordinates, latitude is given first, then longitude. To locate a certain place on a map using its coordinates, find the point where the two lines cross. Take, for example, Australia, which has coordinates 25° S, 135° E. After finding the equator (0°), locate the line 25° south of that. Next, find the line of prime meridian (0°), and then the line 135° to its east. You will find Australia at the point where these two imaginary lines intersect.

807 Index to World Maps

Country	Latitude	Longitude
Afghanistan	33° N	65° E
Albania	41° N	20° E
Algeria	28° N	3° E
Andorra	42° N	1° E
Angola	12° S	18° E
Antigua and Barbuda	17° N	61° W
Argentina	34° S	64° W
Armenia	41° N	45° E
Australia	25° S	135° E
Austria	47° N	13° E
Azerbaijan	41° N	47° E
Bahamas	24° N	76° W
Bahrain	26° N	50° E
Bangladesh	24° N	90° E
Barbados	13° N	59° W
Belarus	54° N	25° E
Belgium	50° N	4° E
Belize	17° N	88° W
Benin	9° N	2° E
Bhutan	27° N	90° E
Bolivia	17° S	65° W
Bosnia-Herzegovina	44° N	18° E
Botswana	22° S	24° E
Brazil	10° S	55° W
Brunei	4° N	114° E
Bulgaria	43° N	25° E
Burkina Faso	13° N	2° W
Burundi	3° S	30° E
Cambodia	13° N	105° E
Cameroon	6° N	12° E
Canada	60° N	95° W
Cape Verde	16° N	24° W
Central African Republic	7° N	21° E
Chad	15° N	19° E
Chile	30° S	71° W
China	35° N	105° E
Colombia	4° N	72° W
Comoros	12° S	44° E
Congo	1° S	15° E
Costa Rica	10° N	84° W
Croatia	45° N	16° E
Cuba	21° N	80° W
Cyprus	35° N	33° E
Czech Republic	50° N	15° E
Denmark	56° N	10° E
Djibouti	11° N	43° E
Dominica	15° N	61° W
Dominican Republic	19° N	70° W
Ecuador	2° S	77° W
Egypt	27° N	30° E
El Salvador	14° N	89° W
Equatorial Guinea	2° N	9° E
Eritrea	17° N	38° E
Estonia	59° N	26° E
Ethiopia	8° N	38° E
Fiji	19° S	174° E
Finland	64° N	26° E
France	46° N	2° E
Gabon	1° S	11° E
The Gambia	13° N	16° W
Georgia	43° N	45° E
Germany	51° N	10° E
Ghana	8° N	2° W
Greece	39° N	22° E
Greenland	70° N	40° W
Grenada	12° N	61° W
Guatemala	15° N	90° W
Guinea	11° N	10° W
Guinea-Bissau	12° N	15° W
Guyana	5° N	59° W
Haiti	19° N	72° W
Honduras	15° N	86° W
Hungary	47° N	20° E
Iceland	65° N	18° W
India	20° N	77° E
Indonesia	5° S	120° E
Iran	32° N	53° E
Iraq	33° N	44° E
Ireland	53° N	8° W
Israel	31° N	35° E
Italy	42° N	12° E
Ivory Coast	8° N	5° W
Jamaica	18° N	77° W
Japan	36° N	138° E
Jordan	31° N	36° E
Kazakhstan	45° N	70° E
Kenya	1° N	38° E
Kiribati	0° N	175° E
North Korea	40° N	127° E
South Korea	36° N	128° E
Kuwait	29° N	47° E
Kyrgyzstan	42° N	75° E
Laos	18° N	105° E
Latvia	57° N	25° E
Lebanon	34° N	36° E
Lesotho	29° S	28° E
Liberia	6° N	10° W
Libya	27° N	17° E
Liechtenstein	47° N	9° E
Lithuania	56° N	24° E
Luxembourg	49° N	6° E
Macedonia	43° N	22° E
Madagascar	19° S	46° E
Malawi	13° S	34° E
Malaysia	2° N	112° E
Maldives	2° N	70° E
Mali	17° N	4° W
Malta	36° N	14° E
Mauritania	20° N	12° W
Mauritius	20° S	57° E
Mexico	23° N	102° W
Moldova	47° N	28° E
Monaco	43° N	7° E
Mongolia	46° N	105° E
Montenegro	43° N	19° E
Morocco	32° N	5° W
Mozambique	18° S	35° E
Myanmar	25° N	95° E
Namibia	22° S	17° E
Nauru	1° S	166° E
Nepal	28° N	84° E

Country	Latitude	Longitude
Netherlands	52° N	5° E
New Zealand	41° S	174° E
Nicaragua	13° N	85° W
Niger	16° N	8° E
Nigeria	10° N	8° E
Northern Ireland	55° N	7° W
Norway	62° N	10° E
Oman	22° N	58° E
Pakistan	30° N	70° E
Panama	9° N	80° W
Papua New Guinea	6° S	147° E
Paraguay	23° S	58° W
Peru	10° S	76° W
Philippines	13° N	122° E
Poland	52° N	19° E
Portugal	39° N	8° W
Qatar	25° N	51° E
Romania	46° N	25° E
Russia	60° N	80° E
Rwanda	2° S	30° E
St. Kitts & Nevis	17° N	62° W
Saint Lucia	14° N	61° W
Saint Vincent and the Grenadines	13° N	61° W
San Marino	44° N	12° E
Sao Tome and Principe	1° N	7° E
Saudi Arabia	25° N	45° E
Scotland	57° N	5° W
Senegal	14° N	14° W
Serbia	45° N	21° E
Seychelles	5° S	55° E
Sierra Leone	8° N	11° W
Singapore	1° N	103° E
Slovakia	49° N	19° E
Slovenia	46° N	15° E
Solomon Islands	8° S	159° E
Somalia	10° N	49° E
South Africa	30° S	26° E
Spain	40° N	4° W
Sri Lanka	7° N	81° E
Sudan	15° N	30° E
Suriname	4° N	56° W
Swaziland	26° S	31° E
Sweden	62° N	15° E
Switzerland	47° N	8° E
Syria	35° N	38° E
Taiwan	23° N	121° E
Tajikistan	39° N	71° E
Tanzania	6° S	35° E
Thailand	15° N	100° E
Togo	8° N	1° E
Tonga	20° S	173° W
Trinidad/Tobago	11° N	61° W
Tunisia	34° N	9° E
Turkey	39° N	35° E
Turkmenistan	40° N	55° E
Tuvalu	8° S	179° E
Uganda	1° N	32° E
Ukraine	50° N	30° E
United Arab Emirates	24° N	54° E
United Kingdom	54° N	2° W

Country	Latitude	Longitude
United States	38° N	97° W
Uruguay	33° S	56° W
Uzbekistan	40° N	68° E
Vanuatu	17° S	170° E
Venezuela	8° N	66° W
Vietnam	17° N	106° E
Wales	53° N	3° W
Western Samoa	10° S	173° W
Yemen	15° N	44° E
Yugoslavia	44° N	19° E
Zaire	4° S	25° E
Zambia	15° S	30° E
Zimbabwe	20° S	30° E

Topographic Tally Table

THE CONTINENTS

	Area (Sq Km)	Percent of Earth's Land
Asia	44,026,000	29.7
Africa	30,271,000	20.4
North America	24,258,000	16.3
South America	17,823,000	12.0
Antarctica	13,209,000	8.9
Europe	10,404,000	7.0
Australia	7,682,000	5.2

LONGEST RIVERS

	Length (Km)
Nile, *Africa*	6,671
Amazon, *South America*	6,437
Chang Jiang (Yangtze), *Asia*	6,380
Mississippi-Missouri, *North America*	5,971
Ob-Irtysk, *Asia*	5,410
Huang (Yellow), *Asia*	4,672
Congo, *Africa*	4,667
Amur, *Asia*	4,416
Lena, *Asia*	4,400
Mackenzie-Peace, *North America*	4,241

MAJOR ISLANDS

	Area (Sq Km)
Greenland	2,175,600
New Guinea	792,500
Borneo	725,500
Madagascar	587,000
Baffin	507,500
Sumatra	427,300
Honshu	227,400
Great Britain	218,100
Victoria	217,300
Ellesmere	196,200
Celebes	178,700
South (New Zealand)	151,000
Java	126,700

THE OCEANS

	Area (Sq Km)	Percent of Earth's Water Area
Pacific	166,241,000	46.0
Atlantic	86,557,000	23.9
Indian	73,427,000	20.3
Arctic	9,485,000	2.6

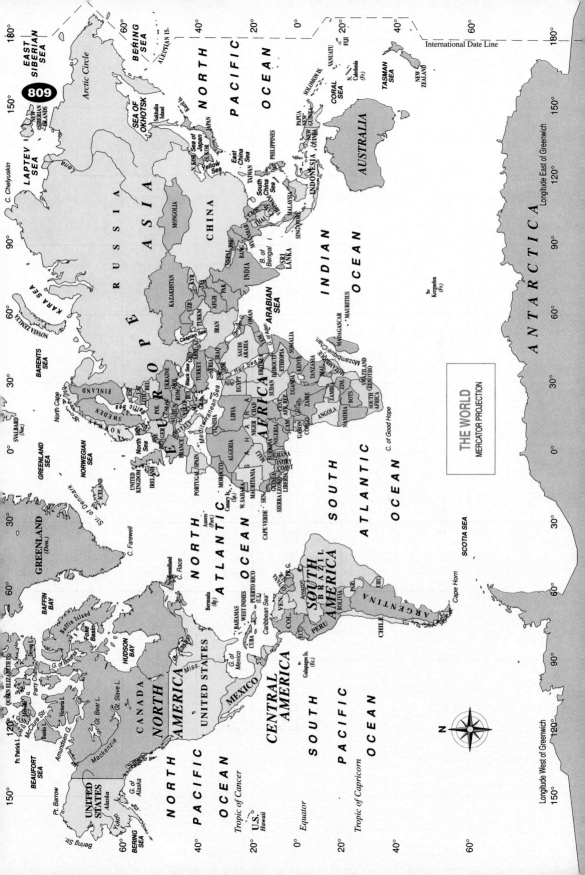

THE WORLD
MERCATOR PROJECTION

809

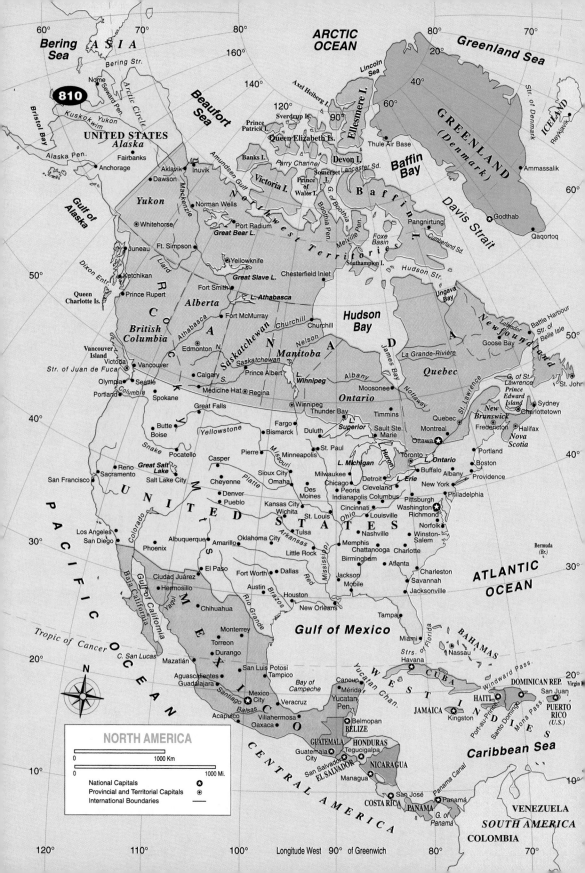

NORTH AMERICA

ARCTIC OCEAN

Bering Sea
Greenland Sea
Beaufort Sea

ASIA

Nome
Seward Pen.
Bering Str.
Arctic Circle
810
Kuskokwim
Yukon
Bristol Bay
Alaska Pen.

UNITED STATES
Alaska
Fairbanks
Anchorage

Gulf of Alaska

Lincoln Sea
Axel Heiberg I.
Prince Patrick I.
Sverdrup Is.
Queen Elizabeth Is.
Banks I.
Victoria I.
Parry Channel
Somerset I.
Prince of Wales I.
Devon I.
Lancaster Sd.
Thule Air Base

Baffin Bay

GREENLAND (Denmark)

ICELAND
Reykjavík
Ammassalik
Godthab
Qaqortoq

Davis Strait

Aklavik
Inuvik
Dawson

Yukon
Whitehorse
Norman Wells
Port Radium
Great Bear L.
Ft. Simpson
Yellowknife
Great Slave L.
Fort Smith
L. Athabasca

Juneau
Ketchikan
Prince Rupert
Queen Charlotte Is.
Dixon Ent.

Alberta
Fort McMurray
Athabasca
Edmonton
Calgary
Medicine Hat
Regina

British Columbia
Vancouver Island
Victoria
Vancouver
Str. of Juan de Fuca
Olympia
Seattle
Portland
Spokane

C A N A D A

Chesterfield Inlet
Churchill
Nelson
L. Winnipeg
Prince Albert
Saskatoon
Saskatchewan
Manitoba
Winnipeg
Thunder Bay

Melville Pen.
Boothia Pen.
G. of Boothia
Foxe Basin
Southampton I.
Hudson Str.
Ungava Bay

Hudson Bay

James Bay
La Grande-Rivière
Albany
Moosonee
Ontario
Timmins

Pangnirtung
Cumberland Sd.

Labrador
Battle Harbour
Str. of Belle Isle
Goose Bay
Newfoundland

Quebec

G. of St. Lawrence
Prince Edward Island
St. John's
Sydney
Charlottetown
New Brunswick
Fredericton
Halifax
Nova Scotia

Quebec
Montreal
Ottawa
St. Lawrence

Great Falls
Butte
Boise
Pocatello
Yellowstone
Snake
Great Salt Lake
Salt Lake City
Reno
Sacramento
San Francisco

U N I T E D

Fargo
Bismarck
Pierre
Sioux City
Cheyenne
Casper
Platte
Denver
Pueblo
Colorado
Missouri
Minneapolis
St. Paul
Duluth
Milwaukee
Des Moines
Omaha
Chicago
L. Michigan

L. Superior
Sault Ste. Marie
L. Huron
Toronto
L. Ontario
L. Erie
Detroit
Cleveland
Buffalo
Albany
Boston
Providence
New York
Philadelphia
Pittsburgh
Washington
Richmond

Portland

Los Angeles
San Diego
Phoenix
Albuquerque
Amarillo
Oklahoma City
El Paso
Fort Worth
Dallas

S T A T E S

Kansas City
Wichita
St. Louis
Tulsa
Arkansas
Ohio
Louisville
Nashville
Memphis
Little Rock
Chattanooga
Birmingham
Atlanta
Charlotte
Winston-Salem
Norfolk
Charleston
Savannah
Jacksonville

PACIFIC OCEAN

Tropic of Cancer

Ciudad Juárez
Hermosillo
Chihuahua
Monterrey
Torreon
Durango
Mazatlán
C. San Lucas
Baja California
Gulf of California
Yaqui

M E X I C O

Rio Grande
Brazos
Red
Austin
Houston
New Orleans
Jackson
Mobile
Tampa
Miami
Havana
Nassau

Gulf of Mexico

ATLANTIC OCEAN

Bermuda (Br.)
BAHAMAS

Aguascalientes
Guadalajara
San Luis Potosí
Tampico
Santiago
Balsas
Mexico City
Veracruz
Acapulco
Oaxaca
Villahermosa
Bay of Campeche
Cancún
Mérida
Yucatan Pen.
Yucatan Chan.
Belmopan
BELIZE

CUBA
Strs. of Florida
W E S T   I N D I E S
Windward Pass.
JAMAICA
Kingston
Port-au-Prince
HAITI
Santo Domingo
DOMINICAN REP.
San Juan
PUERTO RICO (U.S.)
Mona Pass.
Virgin Is.

GUATEMALA
Guatemala City
HONDURAS
Tegucigalpa
San Salvador
EL SALVADOR
Managua
NICARAGUA
San José
COSTA RICA
PANAMA
Panamá
Panama Canal
G. of Panama

Caribbean Sea

C E N T R A L   A M E R I C A

VENEZUELA
SOUTH AMERICA
COLOMBIA

0   1000 Km
0   1000 Mi.

✛ National Capitals
⊙ Provincial and Territorial Capitals
— International Boundaries

Longitude West 90° of Greenwich

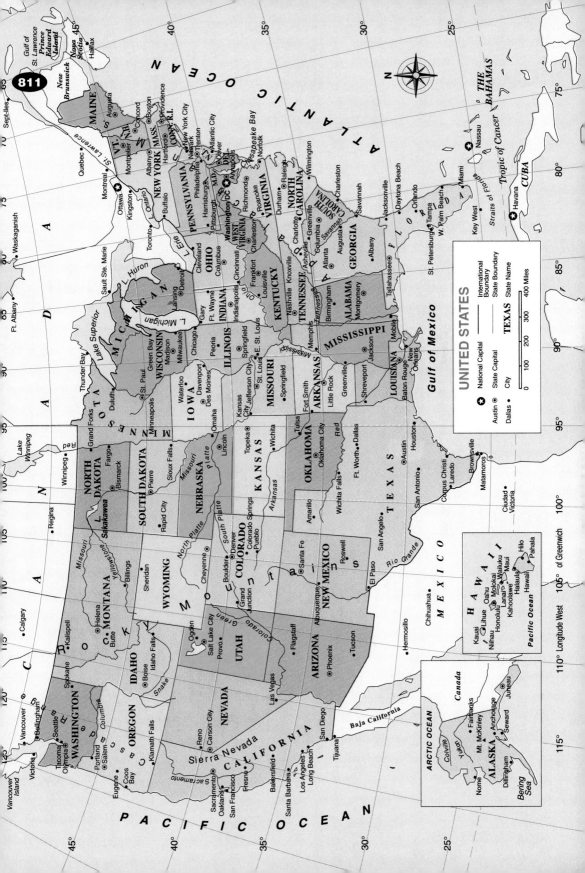

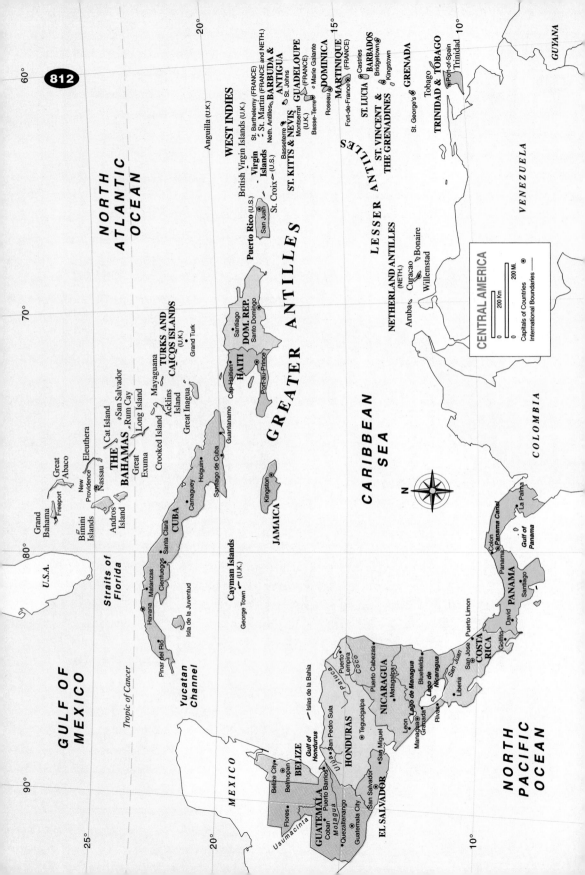

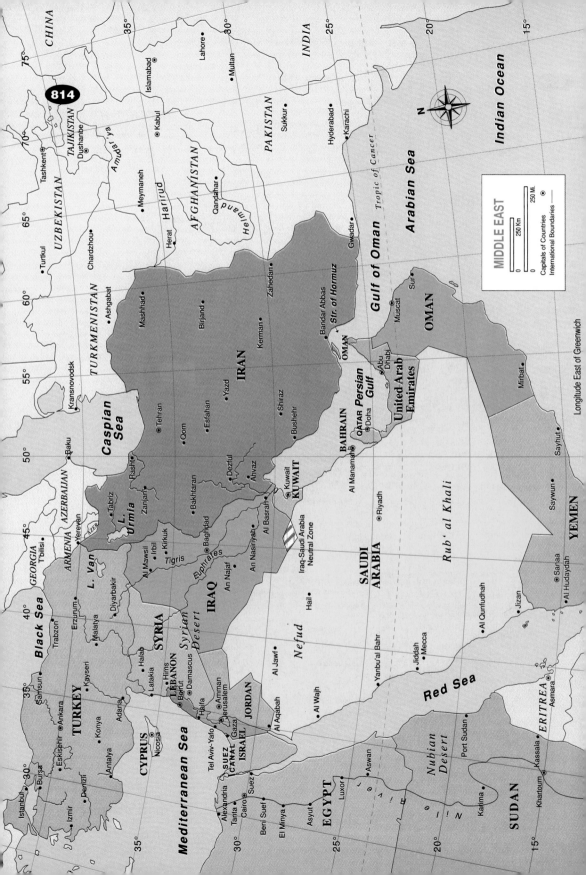

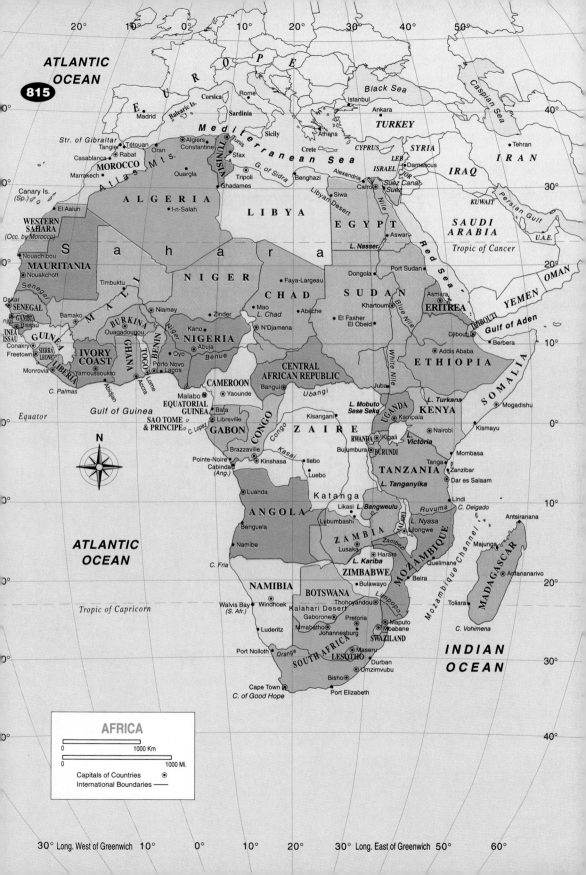

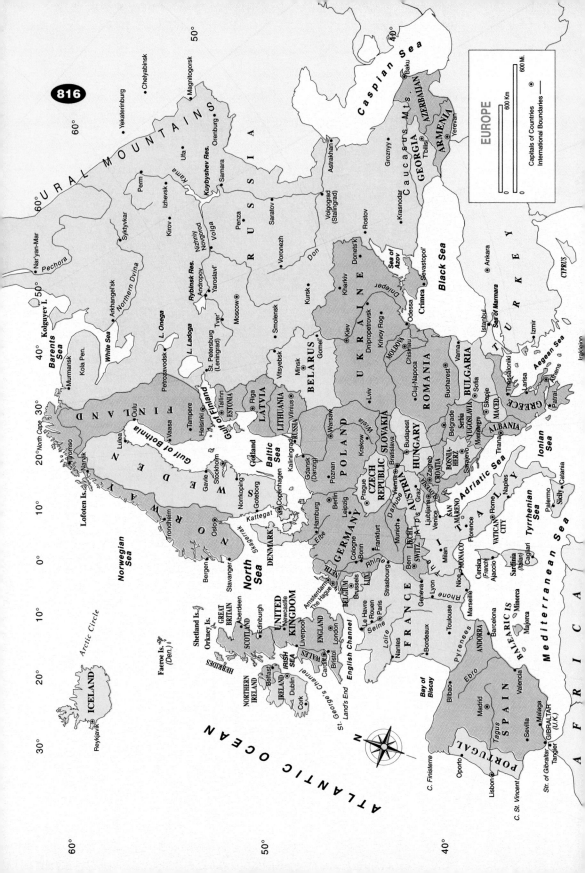

816

EUROPE

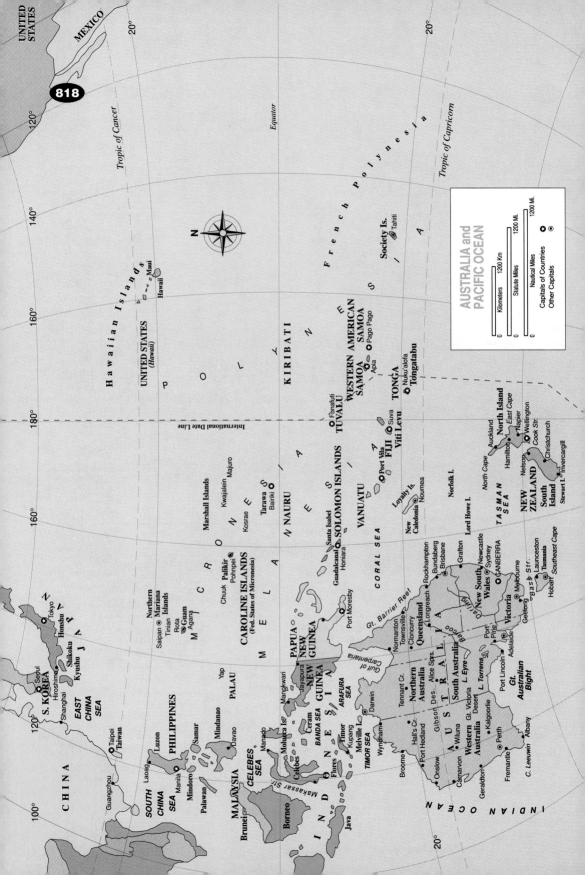

U.S. Constitution

819

Note ● *The original text of the Constitution has been edited to conform to contemporary American usage. The bracketed words have been added to help you locate information more quickly; they are not part of the Constitution.*

[Preamble]

We the people of the United States, in order to form a more perfect Union, establish justice, insure domestic tranquility, provide for the common defense, promote the general welfare, and secure the blessings of liberty to ourselves and our posterity, do ordain and establish this Constitution for the United States of America.

ARTICLE I
Section 1

[**Legislative powers given to Congress**] All legislative powers herein granted shall be vested in a Congress of the United States, which shall consist of a Senate and House of Representatives.

Section 2

1. [**Makeup of the House of Representatives**] The House of Representatives shall be composed of members chosen every second year by the people of the several States, and the electors in each State shall have the qualifications requisite for electors of the most numerous branch of the State Legislature.

2. [**Qualifications of Representatives**] No person shall be a Representative who shall not have attained to the age of twenty-five years, and been seven years a citizen of the United States, and who shall not, when elected, be an inhabitant of that State in which he shall be chosen.

3. [**Plan for sharing Representatives and direct taxes—census**] (Representatives and direct taxes shall be apportioned among the several States which may be included within this Union, according to their respective numbers, which shall be determined by adding to the whole number of free persons, including those bound to service for a term of years, and excluding Indians not taxed, three-fifths of all other persons.— *Amended by the 14th Amendment, section 2.)* The actual enumeration shall be made within three years after the first meeting of the Congress of the United States, and within every subsequent term of ten years, in such manner as they shall by law direct. The number of Representatives shall not exceed one for every thirty thousand, but each State shall have at least one Representative; and until such enumeration shall be made, the State of New Hampshire shall be entitled to choose three; Massachusetts, eight; Rhode Island and Providence Plantations, one; Connecticut, five; New York, six; New Jersey, four; Pennsylvania, eight; Delaware, one; Maryland, six; Virginia, ten; North Carolina, five; South Carolina, five; and Georgia, three.

4. [**Filling of vacancies in representation**] When vacancies happen in the representation from any State, the Executive Authority thereof shall issue writs of election to fill such vacancies.

5. [**Selection of officers; power of impeachment**] The House of Representatives shall choose their Speaker and other officers; and shall have the sole power of impeachment.

Section 3

1. **[The Senate]** (The Senate of the United States shall be composed of two Senators from each State, chosen by the Legislature thereof, for six years; and each Senator shall have one vote.—*Amended by the 17th Amendment, section 1.*)

2. **[Classification of Senators; filling of vacancies]** Immediately after they shall be assembled in consequence of the first election, they shall be divided as equally as may be into three classes. The seats of the Senators of the first class shall be vacated at the expiration of the second year, of the second class at the expiration of the fourth year, and of the third class at the expiration of the sixth year, so that one-third may be chosen every second year; and if vacancies happen by resignation, or otherwise (during the recess of the Legislature of any State), the Executive thereof may make temporary appointments (until the next meeting of the Legislature, which shall then fill such vacancies.—*Amended by the 17th Amendment.*)

3. **[Qualification of Senators]** No person shall be a Senator who shall not have attained to the age of thirty years, and been nine years a citizen of the United States, and who shall not, when elected, be an inhabitant of that State for which he shall be chosen.

4. **[Vice President to be President of Senate]** The Vice President of the United States shall be President of the Senate, but shall have no vote, unless they be equally divided.

5. **[Selection of Senate officers; President pro tempore]** The Senate shall choose their other officers, and also a President pro tempore, in the absence of the Vice President, or when he shall exercise the office of President of the United States.

6. **[Senate to try impeachments]** The Senate shall have the sole power to try all impeachments. When sitting for that purpose, they shall be on oath or affirmation. When the President of the United States is tried, the Chief Justice shall preside: and no person shall be convicted without the concurrence of two-thirds of the members present.

7. **[Judgment in cases of impeachment]** Judgment in cases of impeachment shall not extend further than to removal from office, and disqualification to hold and enjoy any office of honor, trust, or profit under the United States; but the party convicted shall nevertheless be liable and subject to indictment, trial, judgment, and punishment, according to Law.

Section 4

1. **[Control of congressional elections]** The times, places, and manner of holding elections for Senators and Representatives shall be prescribed in each State by the Legislature thereof; but the Congress may at any time by law make or alter such regulations, except as to the places of choosing Senators.

2. **[Time for assembling of Congress]** The Congress shall assemble at least once in every year, (and such meeting shall be on the first Monday in December, unless they shall by law appoint a different day.—*Amended by the 20th Amendment, section 2.*)

Section 5

1. **[Each House to be the judge of the election and qualifications of its members; regulations as to quorum]** Each House shall be the judge of the elections, returns, and qualifications of its own members, and a majority of each shall constitute a quorum to do business; but a smaller number may adjourn from day to day, and may be authorized to compel the attendance of absent members, in such manner, and under such penalties as each House may provide.

2. **[Each House to determine its own rules]** Each House may determine the rules of its proceedings, punish its members for disorderly behavior, and, with the concurrence of two-thirds, expel a member.

3. **[Journals and yeas and nays]** Each House shall keep a journal of its proceedings, and from time to time publish the same, excepting such parts as may in their judgment require secrecy; and the yeas and nays of the members of either House on any question shall, at the desire of one-fifth of those present, be entered on the journal.

4. **[Adjournment]** Neither House, during the session of Congress, shall, without the consent of the other, adjourn for more than three days, nor to any other place than that in which the two Houses shall be sitting.

Section 6

1. **[Pay and privileges of members of Congress]** The Senators and Representatives shall receive a compensation for their services, to be ascertained by law, and paid out of the Treasury of the United States. They shall in all cases, except treason, felony, and breach of the peace, be privileged from arrest during their attendance at the session of their respective Houses, and in going to and returning from the same; and for any speech or debate in either House, they shall not be

questioned in any other place.

2. **[Incompatible offices; exclusions]** No Senator or Representative shall, during the time for which he was elected, be appointed to any civil office under the authority of the United States, which shall have been created, or the emoluments whereof shall have been increased during such time; and no person holding any office under the United States shall be a member of either House during his continuance in office.

Section 7

1. **[Revenue bills to begin in House]** All bills for raising revenue shall originate in the House of Representatives; but the Senate may propose or concur with amendments as on other bills.

2. **[Manner of passing bills; veto power of President]** Every bill which shall have passed the House of Representatives and the Senate, shall, before it becomes a law, be presented to the President of the United States; if he approve, he shall sign it, but if not he shall return it, with his objections to that House in which it shall have originated, who shall enter the objections at large on their journal, and proceed to reconsider it. If after such reconsideration two-thirds of that House shall agree to pass the bill, it shall be sent, together with the objections, to the other House, by which it shall likewise be reconsidered, and if approved by two-thirds of that House, it shall become a law. But in all such cases the votes of both Houses shall be determined by yeas and nays, and the names of the persons voting for and against the bill shall be entered on the journal of each House, respectively. If any bill shall not be returned by the President within ten days (Sundays excepted) after it shall have been presented to him, the same shall be a law, in like manner as if he had signed it, unless the Congress by their adjournment prevent its return, in which case it shall not be a law.

3. **[Orders or resolutions to be passed by President]** Every order, resolution, or vote to which the concurrence of the Senate and House of Representatives may be necessary (except on a question of adjournment) shall be presented to the President of the United States; and before the same shall take effect, shall be approved by him, or being disapproved by him, shall be repassed by two-thirds of the Senate and House of Representatives, according to the rules and limitations prescribed in the case of a bill.

Section 8

[General powers of Congress] The Congress shall have the power:

1. **[Taxes, duties, imposts, and excises]** To lay and collect taxes, duties, imposts, and excises, to pay the debts and provide for the common defense and general welfare of the United States; but all duties, imposts, and excises shall be uniform throughout the United States; *(See the 16th Amendment.)*

2. **[Borrowing of money]** To borrow money on the credit of the United States;

3. **[Regulation of commerce]** To regulate commerce with foreign nations, and among the several States, and with the Indian tribes;

4. **[Naturalization and bankruptcy]** To establish a uniform rule of naturalization, and uniform laws on the subject of bankruptcies throughout the United States;

5. **[Money, weights, and measures]** To coin money, regulate the value thereof, and of foreign coin, and fix the standard of weights and measures;

6. **[Counterfeiting]** To provide for the punishment of counterfeiting the securities and current coin of the United States;

7. **[Post offices]** To establish post offices and post roads;

8. **[Patents and copyrights]** To promote the progress of science and useful arts, by securing for limited times to authors and inventors the exclusive right to their respective writings and discoveries;

9. **[Lower courts]** To constitute tribunals inferior to the Supreme Court;

10. **[Piracies and felonies]** To define and punish piracies and felonies committed on the high seas, and offenses against the law of nations.

11. **[War; allowing seizure and use of force]** To declare war, grant letters of marque and reprisal, and make rules concerning captures on land and water;

12. **[Armies]** To raise and support armies, but no appropriation of money to that use shall be for a longer term than two years;

13. **[Navy]** To provide and maintain a navy;

14. **[Land and naval forces]** To make rules for the government and regulation of the land and naval forces;

15. **[Calling out military]** To provide for calling forth the militia to execute the laws of the Union, suppress insurrections, and repel invasions.

16. **[Organizing, arming, and disciplining military]** To provide for organizing, arming, and disciplining the militia, and for

governing such part of them as may be employed in the service of the United States, reserving to the States, respectively, the appointment of the officers, and the authority of training the militia according to the discipline prescribed by Congress;

17. **[Legislation over District of Columbia]** To exercise exclusive legislation in all cases whatsoever, over such district (not exceeding ten miles square) as may, by cession of particular States, and the acceptance of Congress, become the seat of the Government of the United States, and to exercise like authority over all places purchased by the consent of the Legislature of the State in which the same shall be, for the erection of forts, magazines, arsenals, dockyards, and other needful buildings;—And

18. **[To enact laws necessary to enforce Constitution]** To make all laws which shall be necessary and proper for carrying into execution the foregoing powers, and all other powers vested by this Constitution in the Government of the United States, or in any department or officer thereof.

Section 9

1. **[Migration or importation of certain persons not to be prohibited before 1808]** The migration or importation of such persons as any of the States now existing shall think proper to admit, shall not be prohibited by the Congress prior to the year one thousand eight hundred and eight, but a tax or duty may be imposed on such importation, not exceeding ten dollars for each person.

2. **[Right to not be illegally imprisoned; exception]** The privilege of the writ of habeas corpus shall not be suspended, unless when in cases of rebellion or invasion the public safety may require it.

3. **[Bills that destroy civil rights or laws that punish people for something done before the law was made are prohibited.]** No bill of attainder or ex post facto law shall be passed.

4. **[Per person and other direct taxes]** No capitation, or other direct, tax shall be laid, unless in proportion to the census or enumeration herein before directed to be taken. *(See the 16th Amendment.)*

5. **[Exports not to be taxed]** No tax or duty shall be laid on articles exported from any State.

6. **[No favor to be given to ports of any State; interstate shipping]** No preference shall be given by any regulation of commerce or revenue to the ports of one State over those of another: nor shall vessels bound

to, or from, one State, be obliged to enter, clear, or pay duties in another.

7. **[Money, how drawn from treasury; financial statements to be published]** No money shall be drawn from the Treasury, but in consequence of appropriations made by law; and a regular statement and account of the receipts and expenditures of all public money shall be published from time to time.

8. **[Titles of nobility not to be granted; acceptance by government officers of favors from foreign powers]** No title of nobility shall be granted by the United States; and no person holding any office of profit or trust under them, shall, without the consent of the Congress, accept of any present, emolument, office, or title, of any kind whatever, from any king, prince, or foreign state.

Section 10

1. **[Limitations of the powers of the several States]** No state shall enter into any treaty, alliance, or confederation; grant letters of marque and reprisal; coin money; emit bills of credit; make anything but gold and silver coin a tender in payment of debts; pass any bill of attainder, ex post facto law, or law impairing the obligation of contracts, or grant any title of nobility.

2. **[State taxes and duties]** No State shall, without the consent of the Congress, lay any imposts or duties on imports or exports, except what may be absolutely necessary for executing its inspection laws: and the net produce of all duties and imposts, laid by any State on imports or exports, shall be for the use of the Treasury of the United States; and all such laws shall be subject to the revision and control of the Congress.

3. **[Further limits on powers of States]** No State shall, without the consent of Congress, lay any duty of tonnage, keep troops, or ships of war in time of peace, enter into any agreement or compact with another state, or with a foreign power, or engage in war, unless actually invaded, or in such imminent danger as will not admit of delay.

ARTICLE II
Section 1

1. **[The President; the executive power]** The executive power shall be vested in a President of the United States of America. He shall hold his office during the term of four years, and together with the Vice President, chosen for the same term, be elected, as follows:

2. **[Appointment and qualifications**

of presidential electors] Each State shall appoint, in such manner as the Legislature thereof may direct, a number of electors, equal to the whole number of Senators and Representatives to which the State may be entitled in the Congress: but no Senator or Representative, or person holding an office of trust or profit under the United States, shall be appointed an elector.

3. **[Original method of electing the President and Vice President]** (The electors shall meet in their respective States, and vote by ballot for two persons, of whom one at least shall not be an inhabitant of the same State with themselves. And they shall make a list of all the persons voted for, and of the number of votes for each; which list they shall sign and certify, and transmit sealed to the seat of the Government of the United States, directed to the President of the Senate. The President of the Senate shall, in the presence of the Senate and House of Representatives, open all the certificates, and the votes shall then be counted. The person having the greatest number of votes shall be the President, if such number be a majority of the whole number of electors appointed; and if there be more than one who have such majority, and have an equal number of votes, then the House of Representatives shall immediately choose by ballot one of them for President; and if no person have a majority, then from the five highest on the list the said House shall in like manner choose the President. But in choosing the President, the votes shall be taken by States, the representation from each State having one vote; a quorum for this purpose shall consist of a member or members from two-thirds of the States, and a majority of all the states shall be necessary to a choice. In every case, after the choice of the President, the person having the greatest number of votes of the electors shall be the Vice President. But if there should remain two or more who have equal votes, the Senate should choose from them by ballot the Vice President.—*Replaced by the 12th Amendment.*)

4. **[Congress may determine time of choosing electors and day for casting their votes]** The Congress may determine the time of choosing the electors, and the day on which they shall give their votes; which day shall be the same throughout the United States.

5. **[Qualifications for the office of President]** No person except a natural born citizen, or a citizen of the United States, at the time of the adoption of this Constitution, shall be eligible to the office of President; neither shall any person be eligible to that office who shall not have attained to the age of thirty-five years, and been fourteen years a resident within the United States. *(For qualifications of the Vice President, see the 12th Amendment.)*

6. **[Filling vacancy in the office of President]** (In case of the removal of the President from office, or of his death, resignation, or inability to discharge the powers and duties of the said office, the same shall devolve on the Vice President, and the Congress may by law provide for the case of removal, death, resignation or inability, both of the President and Vice President, declaring what officer shall then act as President, and such officer shall act accordingly, until the disability be removed, or a President shall be elected.—*Amended by the 20th and 25th Amendments.*)

7. **[Pay of the President]** The President shall, at stated times, receive for his services, a compensation, which shall neither be increased nor diminished during the period for which he shall have been elected, and he shall not receive within that period any other emolument from the United States, or any of them.

8. **[Oath to be taken by the President]** Before he enter on the execution of his office, he shall take the following oath or affirmation:—"I do solemnly swear (or affirm) that I will faithfully execute the office of President of the United States, and will to the best of my ability, preserve, protect, and defend the Constitution of the United States."

Section 2

1. **[The President to be Commander-in-Chief of army and navy and head of executive departments; may grant reprieves and pardons]** The President shall be Commander-in-Chief of the Army and Navy of the United States, and of the militia of the several States, when called into the actual service of the United States; he may require the opinion, in writing, of the principal officer in each of the executive departments, upon any subject relating to the duties of their respective offices, and he shall have power to grant reprieves and pardons for offenses against the United States, except in cases of impeachment.

2. **[President may, with agreement of Senate, make treaties, appoint ambassadors, etc.; appointment of lower officers, authority of Congress over]** He shall have power, by and with the advice and con-

sent of the Senate, to make treaties, provided two-thirds of the Senators present concur; and he shall nominate, and by and with the advice and consent of the Senate, shall appoint ambassadors, other public ministers and consuls, judges of the Supreme Court, and all other officers of the United States, whose appointments are not herein otherwise provided for, and which shall be established by law: but the Congress may by law vest the appointment of such inferior officers, as they think proper, in the President alone, in the courts of law, or in the heads of departments.

3. **[President may fill vacancies in office during recess of Senate]** The President shall have power to fill up all vacancies that may happen during the recess of the Senate, by granting commissions which shall expire at the end of their session.

Section 3

[President to give advice to Congress; may convene or adjourn it on certain occasions; to receive ambassadors, etc.; have laws executed and commission all officers] He shall from time to time give to the Congress information of the state of the Union, and recommend to their consideration such measures as he shall judge necessary and expedient; he may, on extraordinary occasions, convene both Houses, or either of them, and in case of disagreement between them, with respect to the time of adjournment, he may adjourn them to such time as he shall think proper; he shall receive ambassadors and other public ministers: he shall take care that the laws be faithfully executed, and shall commission all the officers of the United States.

Section 4

[All civil officers removable by impeachment] The President, Vice President, and all civil officers of the United States shall be removed from office on impeachment for, and conviction of, treason, bribery, or other high crimes and misdemeanors.

ARTICLE III
Section 1

[Judicial powers; how vested; term of office and payment of judges] The judicial power of the United States, shall be vested in one Supreme Court, and in such inferior courts as the Congress may from time to time ordain and establish. The judges, both of the supreme and inferior courts, shall hold their offices during good behavior, and shall, at stated times, receive for their services, a compensation, which shall not be diminished during their continuance in office.

Section 2

1. **[Authority of Federal courts]** (The judicial power shall extend to all cases, in law and equity, arising under this Constitution, the laws of the United States, and treaties made, or which shall be made, under their authority; to all cases affecting ambassadors, other public ministers and consuls; to all cases of admiralty and maritime jurisdiction; to controversies to which the United States, shall be a party; to controversies between two or more States; between a State and citizens of another State; between citizens of different States, between citizens of the same State claiming lands under grants of different states, and between a State, or the citizens thereof, and foreign states, citizens, or subjects.— *Amended by the 11th Amendment.*)

2. **[Original and appeal authority of Supreme Court]** In all cases affecting ambassadors, other public ministers and consuls, and those in which a State shall be party, the Supreme Court shall have original jurisdiction. In all the other cases before mentioned, the Supreme Court shall have appellate jurisdiction, both as to law and fact, with such exceptions, and under such regulations, as the Congress shall make.

3. **[Trial of all crimes, except impeachment, to be by jury]** The trial of all crimes, except in cases of impeachment, shall be by jury; and such trial shall be held in the State where the said crimes shall have been committed; but when not committed within any State, the trial shall be at such place or places as the Congress may by law have directed.

Section 3

1. **[Treason defined; conviction of]** Treason against the United States, shall consist only in levying war against them, or, in adhering to their enemies, giving them aid and comfort. No person shall be convicted of treason unless on the testimony of two witnesses to the same overt act, or on confession in open court.

2. **[Congress to declare punishment for treason; a condition]** The Congress shall have power to declare the punishment of treason, but no attainder of treason shall work corruption of blood, or forfeiture except during the life of the person attainted.

ARTICLE IV
Section 1

[Each State to respect the public acts and records of other States] Full faith and credit shall be given in each State to the public acts, records, and judicial proceedings of every other State. And the Congress may by general laws prescribe the manner in which such acts, records, and proceedings shall be proved, and the effect thereof.

Section 2

1. **[Privileges of citizens]** The citizens of each State shall be entitled to all privileges and immunities of citizens in the several States.

2. **[Extradition between the States]** A person charged in any State with treason, felony, or other crime, who shall flee from justice, and be found in another State, shall on demand of the Executive authority of the State from which he fled, be delivered up, to be removed to the State having jurisdiction of the crime.

3. **[Persons held to labor or service in one State, fleeing to another, to be returned]** (No person held to service or labor in one State, under the laws thereof, escaping into another, shall, in consequence of any law or regulation therein, be discharged from such service or labor, but shall be delivered up on claim of the party to whom such service or labor may be due.—*Eliminated by the 13th Amendment.*)

Section 3

1. **[New States]** New States may be admitted by the Congress into this Union; but no new State shall be formed or erected within the jurisdiction of any other State; nor any State be formed by the junction of two or more States, or parts of States, without the consent of the Legislatures of the States concerned as well as of the Congress.

2. **[Regulations concerning territory]** The Congress shall have power to dispose of and make all needful rules and regulations respecting the territory or other property belonging to the United States; and nothing in this Constitution shall be so construed as to prejudice any claims of the United States, or of any particular State.

Section 4

[Republican form of government and protection guaranteed the States] The United States shall guarantee to every State in this Union a Republican form of government, and shall protect each of them against invasion; and on application of the Legislature, or of the Executive (when the Legislature cannot be convened) against domestic violence.

ARTICLE V

[Ways in which the Constitution can be amended] The Congress, whenever two-thirds of both Houses shall deem it necessary, shall propose amendments to this Constitution, or, on the application of the Legislatures of two-thirds of the several States shall call a convention for proposing amendments, which, in either case, shall be valid to all intents and purposes, as part of this Constitution, when ratified by the Legislatures of three-fourths of the several States, or by conventions in three-fourths thereof, as the one or the other mode of ratification may be proposed by the Congress; provided that no amendment which may be made prior to the year one thousand eight hundred and eight shall in any manner affect the first and fourth clauses in the ninth Section of the first Article; and that no State, without its consent, shall be deprived of its equal suffrage in the Senate.

ARTICLE VI

1. **[Debts under the Confederation to be honored]** All debts contracted and engagements entered into, before the adoption of this Constitution, shall be as valid against the United States under this Constitution, as under the Confederation.

2. **[Constitution, laws, and treaties of the United States to be supreme]** This Constitution, and the laws of the United States which shall be made in pursuance thereof; and all treaties made, or which shall be made, under the authority of the United States, shall be the supreme law of the land; and the judges in every State shall be bound thereby, anything in the Constitution or laws of any State to the contrary notwithstanding.

3. **[Who shall take constitutional oath; no religious test as to official qualification]** The Senators and Representatives before mentioned, and the members of the several State Legislatures, and all executive and judicial officers, both of the United States and of the several States, shall be bound by oath or affirmation, to support this Constitution; but no religious test shall ever be required as a qualification to any office or public trust under the United States.

ARTICLE VII

[When ratified by nine States, Constitution to be considered adopted] The ratification of the conventions of nine States shall be sufficient for the establishment of this Constitution between the States so ratifying the same.

Amendments to the
826

CONSTITUTION
of the United States of America

AMENDMENT 1
[Freedom of religion, speech, of the press, and right of petition] Congress shall make no law respecting an establishment of religion, or prohibiting the free exercise thereof; or abridging the freedom of speech, or of the press; or the right of the people peaceably to assemble, and to petition the Government for a redress of grievances.

AMENDMENT 2
[Right of people to own arms] A well-regulated militia, being necessary to the security of a free State, the right of the people to keep and bear arms, shall not be infringed.

AMENDMENT 3
[Housing of troops] No soldier shall, in time of peace be quartered in any house, without the consent of the owner, nor in time of war, but in a manner to be prescribed by law.

AMENDMENT 4
[Searches of people or property require written permission of a judge] The right of the people to be secure in their persons, houses, papers, and effects, against unreasonable searches and seizures, shall not be violated, and no warrants shall issue, but upon probable cause, supported by oath or affirmation, and particularly describing the place to be searched, and the persons or things to be seized.

AMENDMENT 5
[Trials for crimes; fair payment for private property taken for public use] No person shall be held to answer for a capital, or otherwise infamous crime, unless on a presentment or indictment of a Grand Jury, except in cases arising in the land or naval forces, or in the militia, when in actual service in time of war or public danger; nor shall any person be subject for the same offense to be twice put in jeopardy of life or limb; nor shall be compelled in any criminal case to be a witness, against himself, nor be deprived of life, liberty, or property, without due process of law; nor shall private property be taken for public use, without just compensation.

AMENDMENT 6
[Right to speedy trial, witnesses, counsel] In all criminal prosecutions, the accused shall enjoy the right to a speedy and public trial, by an impartial jury of the State and district wherein the crime shall have been committed, which district shall have been previously ascertained by law, and to be informed of the nature and cause of the accusation; to be confronted with the witnesses against him; to have compulsory process for obtaining witnesses in his favor, and to have the assistance of counsel for his defense.

AMENDMENT 7
[Right of trial by jury] In suits at common law, where the value in controversy shall exceed twenty dollars, the right of trial by jury shall be preserved, and no fact tried by a jury, shall be otherwise re-examined in any court of the United States, than according to the rules of the common law.

AMENDMENT 8
[Fair bail, fines, and punishments] Excessive bail shall not be required, nor excessive fines imposed, nor cruel and unusual punishments inflicted.

AMENDMENT 9
[Reserved rights of people] The enumeration in the Constitution, of certain rights, shall not be construed to deny or disparage others retained by the people.

AMENDMENT 10
[Rights of States under Constitution] The powers not delegated to the United States by the Constitution, nor prohibited by it to the States, are reserved to the States, respectively, or to the people.

AMENDMENT 11
(The proposed amendment was sent to the states March 5, 1794, by the Third Congress. It was ratified Feb. 7, 1795. It changes Article III, Sect. 2, Para. 1.)
[States can't be sued in federal court] The judicial power of the United States shall not be construed to extend to any suit in law or equity, commenced or prosecuted

against one of the United States by citizens of another State, or by citizens or subjects of any foreign state.

AMENDMENT 12

(The proposed amendment was sent to the states Dec. 12, 1803, by the Eighth Congress. It was ratified July 27, 1804. It replaces Article II, Sect. 1, Para. 3.)

[Manner of electing President and Vice President by electors] (The electors shall meet in their respective states, and vote by ballot for President and Vice President, one of whom, at least, shall not be an inhabitant of the same state with themselves; they shall name in their ballots the person voted for as President, and in distinct ballots the person voted for as Vice President, and they shall make distinct lists of all persons voted for as President, and of all persons voted for as Vice President, and of the number of votes for each, which lists they shall sign and certify, and transmit sealed to the seat of the government of the United States, directed to the President of the Senate; the President of the Senate shall, in the presence of the Senate and House of Representatives, open all the certificates and the votes shall then be counted; the person having the greatest number of votes for President, shall be the President, if such number be a majority of the whole number of electors appointed; and if no person have such majority, then from the persons having the highest numbers not exceeding three on the list of those voted for as President, the House of Representatives shall choose immediately, by ballot, the President. But in choosing the President, the votes shall be taken by states, the representation from each State having one vote; a quorum for this purpose shall consist of a member or members from two-thirds of the states, and a majority of all the states shall be necessary to a choice. And if the House of Representatives shall not choose a President whenever the right of choice shall devolve upon them, before the fourth day of March next following, then the Vice President shall act as President, as in the case of the death or other constitutional disability of the President. The person having the greatest number of votes as Vice President, shall be the Vice President, if such number be a majority of the whole number of electors appointed, and if no person have a majority, then from the two highest numbers on the list, the Senate shall choose the Vice President; a quorum for the purpose shall consist of two-thirds of the whole number of Senators, and a majority of the whole number shall be necessary to a choice. But no person constitutionally ineligible to the office of President shall be eligible to that of Vice President of the United States.—*Amended by the 20th Amendment, sections 3 and 4.)*

AMENDMENT 13

(The proposed amendment was sent to the states Feb. 1, 1865, by the Thirty-eighth Congress. It was ratified Dec. 6, 1865. It eliminates Article IV, Sect. 2, Para. 3.)

Section 1

[Slavery prohibited] Neither slavery nor involuntary servitude, except as a punishment for crime whereof the party shall have been duly convicted, shall exist within the United States, or any place subject to their jurisdiction.

Section 2

[Congress given power to enforce this article] Congress shall have power to enforce this article by appropriate legislation.

AMENDMENT 14

(The proposed amendment was sent to the states June 16, 1866, by the Thirty-ninth Congress. It was ratified July 9, 1868. It changes Article 1, Sect. 2, Para. 3.)

Section 1

[Citizenship defined; privileges of citizens] All persons born or naturalized in the United States, and subject to the jurisdiction thereof, are citizens of the United States and of the State wherein they reside. No State shall make or enforce any law which shall abridge the privileges or immunities of citizens of the United States; nor shall any State deprive any person of life, liberty, or property, without due process of law; nor deny to any person within its jurisdiction the equal protection of the laws.

Section 2

[Apportionment of Representatives] Representatives shall be apportioned among the several States according to their respective numbers, counting the whole number of persons in each State, excluding Indians not taxed. But when the right to vote at any election for the choice of electors for President and Vice President of the United States, Representatives in Congress, the executive and judicial officers of a State, or the members of the Legislature thereof, is denied to any of the male inhabitants of such State, being twenty-one years of age, and citizens of the United States, or in any way abridged, except for participation in rebellion, or other crime, the basis of representation therein shall be reduced in the proportion which the number of such male citizens shall bear to the whole number of male citizens twenty-one years of age in such State.

Section 3
[Disqualification for office; removal] No person shall be a Senator or Representative in Congress, or elector of President and Vice President, or hold any office, civil or military, under the United States, or under any State, who, having previously taken an oath, as a member of Congress, or as an officer of the United States, or as a member of any State Legislature, or as an executive or judicial officer of any State, to support the Constitution of the United States, shall have engaged in insurrection or rebellion against the same, or given aid or comfort to the enemies thereof. But Congress may by a vote of two-thirds of each House, remove such disability.

Section 4
[Public debt not to be questioned; payment of debts which funded rebellion forbidden] The validity of the public debt of the United States, authorized by law, including debts incurred for payment of pensions and bounties for services in suppressing insurrection or rebellion, shall not be questioned. But neither the United States nor any State shall assume or pay any debt or obligation incurred in aid of insurrection or rebellion against the United States, or any claim for the loss or emancipation of any slave; but all such debts, obligations, and claims shall be held illegal and void.

Section 5
[Congress given power to enforce this article] The Congress shall have power to enforce, by appropriate legislation, the provisions of this article.

AMENDMENT 15
(The proposed amendment was sent to the states Feb. 27, 1869, by the Fortieth Congress. It was ratified Feb. 3, 1870.)

Section 1
[Right of certain citizens to vote established] The right of citizens of the United States to vote shall not be denied or abridged by the United States or by any State on account of race, color, or previous condition of servitude.

Section 2
[Congress given power to enforce this article] The Congress shall have power to enforce this article by appropriate legislation.

AMENDMENT 16
(The proposed amendment was sent to the states July 12, 1909, by the Sixty-first Congress. It was ratified Feb. 3, 1913.)

[Income taxes authorized] The Congress shall have power to lay and collect taxes on incomes, from whatever source derived, without apportionment among the several States, and without regard to any census or enumeration.

AMENDMENT 17
(The proposed amendment was sent to the states May 16, 1912, by the Sixty-second Congress. It was ratified April 8, 1913. It changes Article 1, Sect. 3, Para. 1 and 2.)

[Election of United States Senators; filling of vacancies; qualifications of electors] The Senate of the United States shall be composed of two Senators from each State, elected by the people thereof, for six years; and each Senator shall have one vote. The electors in each State shall have the qualifications requisite for electors of the most numerous branch of the State Legislatures.

When vacancies happen in the representation of any State in the Senate, the executive authority of such State shall issue writs of election to fill such vacancies: Provided, that the legislature of any State may empower the executive thereof to make temporary appointment until the people fill the vacancies by election as the legislature may direct.

This amendment shall not be so construed as to affect the election or term of any Senator chosen before it becomes valid as part of the Constitution.

AMENDMENT 18
(The proposed amendment was sent to the states Dec. 18, 1917, by the Sixty-fifth Congress. It was ratified by three-quarters of the states by Jan. 16, 1919, and became effective Jan. 16, 1920. It was repealed by the 21st Amendment.)

Section 1
[Making, selling, or transporting alcoholic beverages prohibited] After one year from the ratification of this article the manufacture, sale, or transportation of

intoxicating liquors within, the importation thereof into, or the exportation thereof from the United States and all territory subject to the jurisdiction thereof for beverage purposes is hereby prohibited.

Section 2

[Congress and the States have power to pass appropriate legislation to enforce this article] The Congress and the several States shall have concurrent power to enforce this article by appropriate legislation.

Section 3

[Provisions of article to take effect, when adopted by three-fourths of the States] This article shall be inoperative unless it shall have been ratified as an amendment to the Constitution by the legislatures of the several States, as provided in the Constitution, within seven years from the date of the submission hereof to the States by Congress.

AMENDMENT 19

(The proposed amendment was sent to the states June 4, 1919, by the Sixty-sixth Congress. It was ratified Aug 18, 1920.)

[Women gain the right to vote] The right of citizens of the United States to vote shall not be denied or abridged by the United States or by any State on account of sex.

[Congress given power to enforce this article] Congress shall have power to enforce this article by appropriate legislation.

AMENDMENT 20

(The proposed amendment, sometimes called the "Lame Duck Amendment," was sent to the states March 3, 1932, by the Seventy-second Congress. It was ratified Jan. 23, 1933; but, in accordance with Section 5, Sections 1 and 2 did not go into effect until Oct. 15, 1933. It changes Article 1, Sect. 4, Para. 2 and the 12th Amendment.)

Section 1

[Terms of President, Vice President, Senators, and Representatives] The terms of the President and Vice President shall end at noon on the twentieth day of January, and the terms of Senators and Representatives at noon on the third day of January, of the years in which such terms would have ended if this article had not been ratified; and the terms of their successors shall then begin.

Section 2

[Time of assembling Congress] The Congress shall assemble at least once in every year, and such meeting shall begin at noon on the third day of January, unless they shall by law appoint a different day.

Section 3

[Filling vacancy in office of President] If, at the time fixed for the beginning of the term of the President, the President-elect shall have died, the Vice President-elect shall become President. If a President shall not have been chosen before the time fixed for the beginning of his term, or if the President-elect shall have failed to qualify, then the Vice President shall have qualified; and the Congress may by law provide for the case wherein neither a President-elect nor a Vice President-elect shall have qualified, declaring who shall then act as President, or the manner in which one who is to act shall be selected, and such person shall act accordingly until a President or Vice President shall have qualified.

Section 4

[Power of Congress in Presidential succession] The Congress may by law provide for the case of the death of any of the persons from whom the House of Representatives may choose a President whenever the right of choice shall have devolved upon them, and for the case of the death of any of the persons from whom the Senate may choose a Vice President whenever the right of choice shall have devolved upon them.

Section 5

[Time of taking effect] Sections 1 and 2 shall take effect on the 15th day of October following the ratification of this article.

Section 6

[Ratification] This article shall be inoperative unless it shall have been ratified as an amendment to the Constitution by the legislatures of three-fourths of the several States within seven years from the date of its submission.

AMENDMENT 21

(The proposed amendment was sent to the states Feb. 20, 1933, by the Seventy-second Congress. It was ratified Dec. 5, 1933. It repeals the 18th Amendment.)

Section 1

[Repeal of Prohibition] The eighteenth article of amendment to the Constitution of the United States is hereby repealed.

Section 2

[Transportation of alcoholic beverages] The transportation or importation into any State, territory, or possession of the United States for delivery or use therein of intoxicating liquors, in violation of the laws thereof, is hereby prohibited.

Section 3
[Ratification] This article shall be inoperative unless it shall have been ratified as an amendment to the Constitution by convention in the several States, as provided in the Constitution, within seven years from the date of the submission thereof to the States by the Congress.

AMENDMENT 22
(The proposed amendment was sent to the states March 21, 1947, by the Eightieth Congress. It was ratified Feb. 27, 1951.)

Section 1
[Limit Presidential terms] No person shall be elected to the office of the President more than twice, and no person who has held the office of President, or acted as President for more than two years of a term to which some other person was elected President shall be elected to the office of the President more than once. But this article shall not apply to any person holding the office of President when this article was proposed by the Congress, and shall not prevent any person who may be holding the office of President, or acting as President, during the term within which this article becomes operative from holding the office of President or acting as President during the remainder of such term.

Section 2
[Ratification] This article shall be inoperative unless it shall have been ratified as an amendment to the Constitution by the legislatures of three-fourths of the several States within seven years from the date of its submission to the States by the Congress.

AMENDMENT 23
(The proposed amendment was sent to the states June 16, 1960, by the Eighty-sixth Congress. It was ratified March 29, 1961.)

Section 1
[Electors for the District of Columbia] The District constituting the seat of Government of the United States shall appoint in such manner as the Congress may direct:

A number of electors of President and Vice President equal to the whole number of Senators and Representatives in Congress to which the District would be entitled if it were a State, but in no event more than the least populous State; they shall be in addition to those appointed by the States, but they shall be considered, for the purposes of the election of President and Vice President, to be electors appointed by a State; and they shall meet in the District and perform such duties as provided by the twelfth article of amendment.

Section 2
[Congress given power to enforce this article] The Congress shall have the power to enforce this article by appropriate legislation.

AMENDMENT 24
(The proposed amendment was sent to the states Aug. 27, 1962, by the Eighty-seventh Congress. It was ratified Jan. 23, 1964.)

Section 1
[Poll tax barred in federal elections] The right of citizens of the United States to vote in any primary or other election for President or Vice President, for electors for President or Vice President, or for Senator or Representative in Congress, shall not be denied or abridged by the United States or any State by reasons of failure to pay any poll tax or other tax.

Section 2
[Congress given power to enforce this article] The Congress shall have the power to enforce this article by appropriate legislation.

AMENDMENT 25
(The proposed amendment was sent to the states July 6, 1965, by the Eighty-ninth Congress. It was ratified Feb. 10, 1967.)

Section 1
[Succession of Vice President to Presidency] In case of the removal of the President from office or of his death or resignation, the Vice President shall become President.

Section 2
[Vacancy in office of Vice President] Whenever there is a vacancy in the office of the Vice President, the President shall nominate a Vice President who shall take office upon confirmation by a majority vote of both Houses of Congress.

Section 3
[Vice President as Acting President] Whenever the President transmits to the

831 President pro tempore of the Senate and the Speaker of the House of Representatives his written declaration that he is unable to discharge the powers and duties of his office, and until he transmits to them a written declaration to the contrary, such powers and duties shall be discharged by the Vice President as Acting President.

Section 4
[Vice President as Acting President]
Whenever the Vice President and a majority of either the principal officers of the executive departments or of such other body as Congress may by law provide, transmit to the President pro tempore of the Senate and the Speaker of the House of Representatives their written declaration that the President is unable to discharge the powers and duties of his office, the Vice President shall immediately assume the powers and duties of the office as Acting President.

Thereafter, when the President transmits to the President pro tempore of the Senate and the Speaker of the House of Representatives his written declaration that no inability exists, he shall resume the powers and duties of his office unless the Vice President and a majority of either the principal officers of the executive department or of such other body as Congress may by law provide, transmit within four days to the President pro tempore of the Senate and the Speaker of the House of Representatives their written declaration that the President is unable to discharge the powers and duties of his office. Thereupon Congress shall decide the issue, assembling within forty-eight hours for that purpose if not in session. If the Congress, within twenty-one days after receipt of the latter written declaration, or, if Congress is not in session, within twenty-one days after Congress is required to assemble, determines by two-thirds vote of both Houses that the President is unable to discharge the powers and duties of his office, the Vice President shall continue to discharge the same as Acting President; otherwise, the President shall resume the powers and duties of his office.

AMENDMENT 26
(The proposed amendment was sent to the states March 23, 1971, by the Ninety-second Congress. It was ratified July 1, 1971.)

Section 1
[Voting for 18-year-olds] The right of citizens of the United States, who are 18 years of age or older, to vote shall not be denied or abridged by the United States or by any state on account of age.

Section 2
[Congress given power to enforce this article] The Congress shall have power to enforce this article by appropriate legislation.

AMENDMENT 27
(The proposed amendment was sent to the states September 25, 1789, by the First Congress. It was ratified May 7, 1992.)

No law, varying the compensation for the services of the Senators and Representatives, shall take effect, until an election of Representatives shall have intervened.

832
Order of Presidential Succession

1. Vice president
2. Speaker of the House
3. President pro tempore of the Senate
4. Secretary of state
5. Secretary of the treasury
6. Secretary of defense
7. Attorney general
8. Secretary of the interior
9. Secretary of agriculture
10. Secretary of commerce
11. Secretary of labor
12. Secretary of health and human services
13. Secretary of housing and urban development
14. Secretary of transportation
15. Secretary of energy
16. Secretary of education
17. Secretary of veterans affairs

833 U.S. Presidents and Vice Presidents

(*Did not finish term)

	Presidents			Vice Presidents	
1	George Washington	Apr. 30, 1789 -	Mar. 3, 1797	John Adams	1
2	John Adams	Mar. 4, 1797 -	Mar. 3, 1801	Thomas Jefferson	2
3	Thomas Jefferson	Mar. 4, 1801 -	Mar. 3, 1805	Aaron Burr	3
	Thomas Jefferson	Mar. 4, 1805 -	Mar. 3, 1809	George Clinton	4
4	James Madison	Mar. 4, 1809 -	Mar. 3, 1813	George Clinton	
	James Madison	Mar. 4, 1813 -	Mar. 3, 1817	Elbridge Gerry	5
5	James Monroe	Mar. 4, 1817 -	Mar. 3, 1825	Daniel D. Tompkins	6
6	John Quincy Adams	Mar. 4, 1825 -	Mar. 3, 1829	John C. Calhoun	7
7	Andrew Jackson	Mar. 4, 1829 -	Mar. 3, 1833	John C. Calhoun	
	Andrew Jackson	Mar. 4, 1833 -	Mar. 3, 1837	Martin Van Buren	8
8	Martin Van Buren	Mar. 4, 1837 -	Mar. 3, 1841	Richard M. Johnson	9
9	William H. Harrison*	Mar. 4, 1841 -	April 4, 1841	John Tyler	10
10	John Tyler	Apr. 6, 1841 -	Mar. 3, 1845		
11	James K. Polk	Mar. 4, 1845 -	Mar. 3, 1849	George M. Dallas	11
12	Zachary Taylor*	Mar. 5, 1849 -	July 9, 1850	Millard Fillmore	12
13	Millard Fillmore	July 10, 1850 -	Mar. 3, 1853		
14	Franklin Pierce	Mar. 4, 1853 -	Mar. 3, 1857	William R. King	13
15	James Buchanan	Mar. 4, 1857 -	Mar. 3, 1861	John C. Breckinridge	14
16	Abraham Lincoln	Mar. 4, 1861 -	Mar. 3, 1865	Hannibal Hamlin	15
	Abraham Lincoln*	Mar. 4, 1865 -	Apr. 15, 1865	Andrew Johnson	16
17	Andrew Johnson	Apr. 15, 1865 -	Mar. 3, 1869		
18	Ulysses S. Grant	Mar. 4, 1869 -	Mar. 3, 1873	Schuyler Colfax	17
	Ulysses S. Grant	Mar. 4, 1873 -	Mar. 3, 1877	Henry Wilson	18
19	Rutherford B. Hayes	Mar. 4, 1877 -	Mar. 3, 1881	William A. Wheeler	19
20	James A. Garfield*	Mar. 4, 1881 -	Sept. 19, 1881	Chester A. Arthur	20
21	Chester A. Arthur	Sept. 20, 1881 -	Mar. 3, 1885		
22	Grover Cleveland	Mar. 4, 1885 -	Mar. 3, 1889	Thomas A. Hendricks	21
23	Benjamin Harrison	Mar. 4, 1889 -	Mar. 3, 1893	Levi P. Morton	22
24	Grover Cleveland	Mar. 4, 1893 -	Mar. 3, 1897	Adlai E. Stevenson	23
25	William McKinley	Mar. 4, 1897 -	Mar. 3, 1901	Garret A. Hobart	24
	William McKinley*	Mar. 4, 1901 -	Sept. 14, 1901	Theodore Roosevelt	25
26	Theodore Roosevelt	Sept. 14, 1901 -	Mar. 3, 1905		
	Theodore Roosevelt	Mar. 4, 1905 -	Mar. 3, 1909	Charles W. Fairbanks	26
27	William H. Taft	Mar. 4, 1909 -	Mar. 3, 1913	James S. Sherman	27
28	Woodrow Wilson	Mar. 4, 1913 -	Mar. 3, 1921	Thomas R. Marshall	28
29	Warren G. Harding*	Mar. 4, 1921 -	Aug. 2, 1923	Calvin Coolidge	29
30	Calvin Coolidge	Aug. 3, 1923 -	Mar. 3, 1925		
	Calvin Coolidge	Mar. 4, 1925 -	Mar. 3, 1929	Charles G. Dawes	30
31	Herbert C. Hoover	Mar. 4, 1929 -	Mar. 3, 1933	Charles Curtis	31
32	Franklin D. Roosevelt	Mar. 4, 1933 -	Jan. 20, 1937	John N. Garner	32
	Franklin D. Roosevelt	Jan. 20, 1937 -	Jan. 20, 1941	John N. Garner	
	Franklin D. Roosevelt	Jan. 20, 1941 -	Jan. 20, 1945	Henry A. Wallace	33
	Franklin D. Roosevelt*	Jan. 20, 1945 -	Apr. 12, 1945	Harry S. Truman	34
33	Harry S. Truman	Apr. 12, 1945 -	Jan. 20, 1949		
	Harry S. Truman	Jan. 20, 1949 -	Jan. 20, 1953	Alben W. Barkley	35
34	Dwight D. Eisenhower	Jan. 20, 1953 -	Jan. 20, 1957	Richard M. Nixon	36
	Dwight D. Eisenhower	Jan. 20, 1957 -	Jan. 20, 1961	Richard M. Nixon	
35	John F. Kennedy*	Jan. 20, 1961 -	Nov. 22, 1963	Lyndon B. Johnson	37
36	Lyndon B. Johnson	Nov. 22, 1963 -	Jan. 20, 1965		
	Lyndon B. Johnson	Jan. 20, 1965 -	Jan. 20, 1969	Hubert H. Humphrey	38
37	Richard M. Nixon	Jan. 20, 1969 -	Jan. 20, 1973	Spiro T. Agnew	39
	Richard M. Nixon*	Jan. 20, 1973 -	Aug. 9, 1974	Gerald R. Ford	40
38	Gerald R. Ford	Aug. 9, 1974 -	Jan. 20, 1977	Nelson A. Rockefeller	41
39	James E. Carter	Jan. 20, 1977 -	Jan. 20, 1981	Walter Mondale	42
40	Ronald Reagan	Jan. 20, 1981 -	Jan. 20, 1985	George Bush	43
	Ronald Reagan	Jan. 20, 1985 -	Jan. 20, 1989	George Bush	
41	George Bush	Jan. 20, 1989 -	Jan. 20, 1993	J. Danforth Quayle	44
42	William J. Clinton	Jan. 20, 1993 -		Albert Gore, Jr.	45

834 Abraham Lincoln: Emancipation Proclamation
1863
By the President of the United States of America: A Proclamation

Whereas on the 22d day of September, A.D. 1862, a proclamation was issued by the President of the United States, containing, among other things, the following, to wit:

"That on the 1st day of January, A.D. 1863, all persons held as slaves within any State or designated part of a State the people whereof shall then be in rebellion against the Union States shall be then, thenceforward, and forever free; and the executive government of the United States, including the military and naval authority thereof, will recognize and maintain the freedom of such persons and will do no act or acts to repress such persons, or any of them, in any efforts they may make for their actual freedom.

"That the executive will on the 1st day of January aforesaid, by proclamation, designate the States and parts of States, if any, in which the people thereof, respectively, shall then be in rebellion against the United States; and the fact that any State of the people thereof shall on that day be in good faith represented in the Congress of the United States by members chosen thereto at elections wherein a majority of the qualified voters of such States shall have participated shall, in the absence of strong countervailing testimony, be deemed conclusive evidence that such State and the people thereof are not then in rebellion against the United States."

Now therefore, I, Abraham Lincoln, President of the United States, by virtue of the power in me vested as Commander-in-Chief of the Army and Navy of the United States in time of actual armed rebellion against the authority and government of the United States, and as a fit and necessary war measure for suppressing said rebellion, do, on this 1st day of January, A.D. 1863, and in accordance with my purpose so to do, publicly proclaimed for the full period of one hundred days from the first day above mentioned, order and designate as the States and parts of States wherein the people thereof, respectively, are this day in rebellion against the United States the following, to wit:

Arkansas, Texas, Louisiana (except the parishes of St. Bernard, Plaquemines, Jefferson, St. John, St. Charles, St. James, Ascension, Assumption, Terrebonne, Lafourche, St. Mary, St. Martin, and Orleans, including the city of New Orleans), Mississippi, Alabama, Florida, Georgia, South Carolina, North Carolina, and Virginia (except the forty-eight counties designated as West Virginia, and also the counties of Berkeley, Accomac, Northhampton, Elizabeth City, York, Princess Anne, and Norfolk, including the cities of Norfolk and Portsmouth), and which excepted parts are for the present left precisely as if this proclamation were not issued.

And by virtue of the power and for the purpose aforesaid, I do order and declare that all persons held as slaves within said designated States and parts of States are, and henceforward shall be, free; and that the Executive Government of the United States, including the military and naval authorities thereof, will recognize and maintain the freedom of said persons.

And I hereby enjoin upon the people so declared to be free to abstain from all violence, unless in necessary self-defense; and I recommend to them that, in all cases when allowed, they labor faithfully for reasonable wages.

And I further declare and make known that such persons of suitable condition will be received into the armed service of the United States to garrison forts, positions, stations, and other places, and to man vessels of all sorts in said service.

And upon this act, sincerely believed to be an act of justice, warranted by the Constitution upon military necessity, I invoke the considerate judgment of mankind and the gracious favor of Almighty God.

1500	1520	1540	1560	1580

UNITED STATES HISTORY

1492
Columbus reaches the West Indies.

1519
Magellan begins three-year voyage around the world.

1513
Ponce de León explores Florida; Balboa reaches Pacific.

1521
Cortez defeats Aztecs and claims Mexico for Spain.

1559
Spanish colony of Pensacola, Florida, lasts two years.

1565
Spain settles St. Augustine, Florida, first permanent European colony.

1570
League of the Iroquois Nations formed.

1588
England defeats the Spanish Armada and rules the seas.

1597
British Parliament sends criminals to colonies.

SCIENCE & INVENTIONS

1507
Book on surgery is developed.

1509
Watches are invented in Germany.

1530
Bottle corks are invented.

1531
Halley's Comet appears.

1545
French printer Garamond sets first type.

1543
Copernicus' theory proclaims a sun-centered universe.

1558
Magnetic compass invented by John Dee.

1585
Decimals introduced by Dutch mathematicians.

1590
First paper mill is used in England.

1596
Thermometer is invented.

LITERATURE & LIFE

1500
Game of bingo developed.

1503
Pocket handkerchiefs are first used.

1507
Glass mirrors are greatly improved.

1513
Machiavelli's *The Prince* published.

1517
Reformation begins in Europe.

1536
First songbook used in Spain.

1538
Mercator draws map with America on it.

1541
Michelangelo completes largest painting, "The Last Judgment."

1564
First horse-drawn coach used in England.

1580
First water closet designed in Bath, England.

1582
Pope Gregory XIII introduces the calendar still in use today.

1599
Copper coins made.

U.S. POPULATION: (NATIVE AMERICAN)   (SPANISH)

approximately 1,100,000   1,021

1600	1620	1640	1660	1680	1700

1607
England establishes Jamestown, Virginia.

1619
House of Burgesses is established in Virginia.

1654
First Jewish colonists settle in New Amsterdam.

1673
Marquette and Joliet explore Mississippi River for France.

1609
Henry Hudson explores the Hudson River and Great Lakes.

1620
Pilgrims found Plymouth Colony.

1634
Colony of Maryland is founded.

1664
The Dutch colony of New Netherlands becomes the English colony of New York.

1682
William Penn founds Pennsylvania.

1629
Massachusetts Bay Colony is established.

1608
Telescope is invented.

1641
First cotton factories open in England.

1668
Reflecting telescope invented by Sir Isaac Newton.

1682
Halley's Comet is studied by Edmund Halley and named for him.

1609
Galileo makes first observations with telescope.

1643
Galileo invents the barometer.

1671
First calculation machine invented.

1629
Human temperature measured by physician in Italy.

1650
First pendulum clocks developed by Huygens.

1687
Newton describes gravity and publishes *Principia Mathematica*.

1600
Shakespeare's plays are performed at Globe Theatre in London.

1636
Harvard is the first college in the colonies.

1685
First drinking fountain used in England.

1653
First postage stamps used in Paris.

1622
January 1 accepted as beginning of the year (instead of March 25).

1605
European diseases killing Native Americans (measles, TB, and smallpox).

1640
First book printed in the colonies.

1658
First colonial police force created in New Amsterdam.

1697
Tales of Mother Goose written by Charles Perrault.

(ENGLISH)

350	2,302	26,634	75,058	151,507

1700	1710	1720	1730	1740

UNITED STATES HISTORY

1700
France builds forts at Mackinac and Detroit to control fur trade.

1705
Virginia Act establishes public education.

1707
England (English) and Scotland (Scots) unite and become Great Britain (British).

1711
Tuscarora War fought in Carolina.

1718
France founds New Orleans.

Scotland

England

1733
James Oglethorpe founds Georgia.

1733
Molasses Act places taxes on sugar and molasses.

1735
Freedom of the press established during trial of John Peter Zenger.

1747
Ohio Company formed to settle Ohio River Valley.

SCIENCE & INVENTIONS

1701
Seed drill that plants seeds in a row is invented by Jethro Tull.

1712
Thomas Newcomen develops first practical steam engine.

1709
The pianoforte (first piano) is invented by Christofori Bartolommeo.

1728
First dental drill is used by Pierre Fauchard.

1732
Sedatives for operations discovered by Thomas Dover.

1735
Rubber found in South America.

1738
First cuckoo clocks invented in Germany.

1742
Benjamin Franklin invents efficient Franklin stove.

LITERATURE & LIFE

1700
The Selling of Joseph by Samuel Sewall is first protest of slavery.

1701
Yale University is founded.

1704
First successful newspaper in colonies, *Boston News-Letter*, is published.

1716
First hot-water home heating system developed.

1719
Robinson Crusoe written by Daniel Defoe.

1726
Gulliver's Travels written by Jonathan Swift.

1731
Ben Franklin begins first subscription library.

Poor Richard's Almanac printed.

1744
John Newbery publishes children's book, *A Little Pretty Pocket-Book*.

U.S. POPULATION: (ENGLISH COLONIES)

250,888	331,711	466,185	629,445	905,563

1750	1760	1770	1780	1790	1800

1750
The French and Indian War begins.

1750
Flatbed boats and Conestoga wagons begin moving settlers west.

1765
Stamp Act tax imposed on colonies.

1770
Boston Massacre occurs.

1763
Britain defeats France in French and Indian War.

1773
Boston Tea Party occurs.

1775
Revolutionary War begins.

1776
Declaration of Independence signed at Second Continental Congress on July 4.

1781
British surrender at Yorktown October 19.

1781
United colonies adopt Articles of Confederation as first government.

1787
U.S. Constitution is signed.

1794
U.S. Navy created.

1789
George Washington elected president.

1789
French Revolution begins.

1752
Benjamin Franklin discovers lightning is a form of electricity.

1758
Sextant for navigation is invented by John Bird.

1764
"Spinning Jenny" for cotton is invented by James Hargreaves.

1770
First steam carriage is invented by French engineer Nicholas Cugnot.

1781
Uranus, first planet not known to ancient world, is discovered.

1783
First balloon is flown by Frenchmen Joseph and Jacques Montgolfier.

1793
Eli Whitney invents cotton gin that takes seeds out of cotton.

1798
Eli Whitney invents mass production.

1752
First general hospital is established in Philadelphia.

1764
Mozart writes first symphony.

1757
Streetlights are installed in Philadelphia.

1769
Venetian blinds are first used.

1776
Paine prints *Common Sense*.

1782
The American bald eagle is first used as U.S. symbol.

1780
The waltz becomes popular dance.

1786
First ice-cream company in America begins production.

1790
Official U.S. census begins.

1790
Supreme Court meets for the first time.

1795
Food canning is introduced.

1,170,760	1,593,625	2,148,076	2,780,369	3,929,157

1800   1810   1820   1830   1840

UNITED STATES HISTORY

1800
Washington, D.C., becomes U.S. capital.

1803
Louisiana Purchase from France doubles U.S. size.

1804
Lewis & Clark explore Louisiana Territory and northwestern United States.

1812–1814
War of 1812 is fought between U.S. and Britain.

1819
U.S. acquires Florida from Spain.

1820
Missouri Compromise signed.

1821
Sierra Leone est. by U.S. for freed slaves.

1830
Indian Removal Act forces Native Americans west of Mississippi River.

1836
Texans defend the Alamo.

1838
Cherokee Nation forced west on "Trail of Tears."

1846
Mexican War begins.

1846
Brtitain cedes Oregon Country to U.S.

1848
Gold found in California.

SCIENCE & INVENTIONS

1800
The battery is invented by Count Volta.

1802
Steamboat is built by Robert Fulton.

1808
Chemical symbols are developed by Jöns Berzelius.

1816
Stethoscope invented by Reneé Laënnec.

1819
Hans Christian Oestad discovers electromagnetism.

1836
Samuel Morse invents telegraph.

1839
Bicycle is invented by Kirkpatrick Macmillan.

1841
Stapler is patented.

1844
Safety matches produced.

1846
Elias Howe invents sewing machine.

LITERATURE & LIFE

1800
Library of Congress is established.

1806
Gas lighting used in homes.

1812
Army meat inspector, "Uncle Sam" Wilson, becomes U.S. symbol.

1814
Sequoyah creates Cherokee alphabet.

1816
Niepce takes first photograph.

1820
Rip Van Winkle is written by Washington Irving.

1828
Webster's Dictionary is published.

1830
Mormon Church is founded.

1834
Louis Braille perfects a letter system for the blind.

1845
Thoreau moves to Walden Pond.

1849
Safety pin is invented.

U.S. POPULATION:

| 5,308,080 | 7,240,102 | 9,638,453 | 12,860,702 | 17,063,353 |

| **1850** | **1860** | **1870** | **1880** | **1890** | **1900** |

1853
National Council of Colored People is founded.

1860
Abraham Lincoln elected 16th president of the U.S.

1861
Civil War begins at Fort Sumter.

1869
Coast-to-coast railroad is finished in Utah.

1889
Jane Addams founds Hull House in Chicago to help immigrants.

1862
Lincoln proclaims abolition of slavery.

1876
U.S. Centennial celebrated.

1862
Merrimac-Monitor Battle.

1876
Custer is defeated at Little Big Horn.

1865
Lincoln is assassinated.

1898
U.S. defeats Spain in Spanish-American War.

1851
Isaac Singer produces sewing machine.

1860
Jean Lenoir builds internal combustion engine.

1874
Barbed wire introduced by Joseph Glidden.

1887
Radio waves produced by Hertz.

1876
Alexander Graham Bell invents telephone.

1893
First successful U.S. gasoline automobile is built.

1852
Elisha Otis invents elevator.

1865
Joseph Lister introduces antiseptic practices.

1877
Thomas Edison invents phonograph.

1896
Marconi invents wireless radio.

1857
Atlantic cable is completed.

1879
Edison makes incandescent light bulb.

1898
Curies discover radium.

1851
First World's Fair is held in London, England.

1864
Red Cross is established.

1876
National Baseball League established.

1883
Four U.S. time zones are established.

1892
"Pledge of Allegiance" is written by F. Bellamy.

1852
Uncle Tom's Cabin by Harriet Beecher Stowe strengthens anti-slavery movement.

1866
Hires introduces root beer.

1879
Ibsen's *Doll House* and Tolstoy's *War and Peace* published.

1888
Pneumatic bicycle tires invented by John Dunlop.

1873
Zipper invented by Whitcomb Judson.

1855
Alexander Parks produces first synthetic plastic.

1889
Roll film produced by George Eastman.

| 23,191,876 | 31,443,321 | 38,558,371 | 50,189,209 | 62,979,766 |

1900   1905   1910   1915   1920

UNITED STATES HISTORY

1900
First Olympics involving women held in Paris.

1903
Wrights' first successful airplane flight.

1909
National Association for the Advancement of Colored People (NAACP) is founded.

1913
Income Tax established.

1914
Panama Canal opens.

1914
World War I begins.

1917
United States enters World War I.

1917
Bolshevik Revolution starts in Russia.

1918
World War I ends.

1919
League of Nations founded.

1920
Prohibition begins.

1920
Women given vote.

SCIENCE & INVENTIONS

1901
Walter Reed discovers yellow fever is carried by mosquitos.

1904
New York City opens its subway system.

1905
Albert Einstein announces theory of relativity ($E=mc^2$) of time and space.

$$E=mc^2$$

1913
Henry Ford establishes assembly line for automobiles.

1915
Coast-to-coast telephone system established.

1921
Vaccine for tuberculosis is discovered.

1922
Insulin treatment diabetes discovere

1922
Farnswor develops electron scanner f television

LITERATURE & LIFE

1900
American Baseball League established.

1902
First Bowl game—Rose Bowl.

1903
First national wildlife refuge established.

1903
First World Series played.

1905
First nickelodeon movie theater established in Pittsburgh.

1907
Artists Picasso and Braque create cubism.

1913
Arthur Wynne invents the crossword puzzle.

1917
Doughnuts created for the soldier "doughboys" fighting in World War I.

KDKA

1920
First radio station, KDKA, founded in Pittsburgh.

1922
King Tut's tomb discovered.

U.S. POPULATION:

76,212,168   92,228,496   106,021,537

1925 1930 1935 1940 1945 1950

1927
Charles Lindbergh flies solo across the Atlantic Ocean.

1929
Wall Street stock market crashes.

1931
The 102-story Empire State Building completed as tallest in the world.

1933
President Franklin Roosevelt inaugurates New Deal to end Great Depression.

1933
Prohibition is repealed.

1939
Germany invades Poland to begin World War II.

1941
U.S. enters World War II after bombing of Pearl Harbor.

1945
World War II ends.

1945
United States joins the United Nations.

1948
Israel becomes a nation.

1949
Communists gain control in China.

1926
John Baird demonstrates his television system.

1926
Alexander Fleming develops penicillin.

1930
First analog computer invented by Vannevar Bush.

1929
Clarence Birdseye introduces frozen foods.

1935
Radar is invented.

1938
Modern-type ballpoint pens developed.

1938
First photocopy machine produced.

1939
First jet aircraft flown.

1940
Enrico Fermi develops nuclear reactor.

1947
Edwin Land invents Polaroid camera.

1947
Bell Lab scientists invent transistor.

1925
Potato chips are produced in New York City.

1927
Wings wins first Academy Award for motion pictures.

1927
First "talking movie," *The Jazz Singer*, made.

1931
"Star-Spangled Banner" becomes U.S. national anthem.

1936
Mitchell's *Gone with the Wind* is published.

1937
First full-length animated film, *Snow White*, is made.

1938
"War of the Worlds" broadcast on radio.

1939
Steinbeck's *Grapes of Wrath* is published.

1947
Jackie Robinson becomes the first black major league baseball player.

1947
Anne Frank's Diary is published.

123,202,624   132,164,569

1950	**1955**	**1960**	**1965**	**1970**

UNITED STATES HISTORY

1950
United States enters Korean War.

1953
Korean War ends.

1955
Rosa Parks refuses to follow segregation rules on Montgomery bus.

1955
Martin Luther King, Jr., begins organizing protests against black discrimination.

1959
Alaska becomes 49th state.

1959
Hawaii becomes 50th state.

1961
Alan Shepard becomes first U.S. astronaut in space.

1963
President John F. Kennedy assassinated in Dallas, TX.

1965
U.S. combat troops sent to Vietnam.

1965
Civil Rights Freedom March from Selma to Montgomery, Alabama.

1968
Martin Luther King, Jr., is assassinated.

1969
Neil Armstrong and Buzz Aldrin are first men to walk on moon.

1971
Eighteen-year-olds are given right to vote.

1974
President Richard Nixon resigns.

SCIENCE & INVENTIONS

1951
Fluoridated water discovered to prevent tooth decay.

1953
Watson and Crick map the DNA molecule.

1954
Jonas Salk discovers polio vaccine.

1957
Russia's Sputnik I satellite is launched.

1958
Stereo long-playing records are produced.

1960
First laser invented by Theodor Maiman.

1963
Cassette music tapes developed.

1967
Cholesterol discovered as a cause of heart disease.

1968
First U.S. heart transplant is performed by surgeon Norman Shumway.

1971
Space probe Mariner maps surface of Mars.

1972
DDT is banned.

1974
Sears Tower (110 stories) built in Chicago.

LITERATURE & LIFE

1950
Peanuts comic strip produced by Charles Schulz.

1951
Fifteen million American homes have television.

1953
Arthur Miller's *The Crucible* is published.

1955
Cat in the Hat produced by Theodor "Dr. Seuss" Geisel.

1957
Elvis Presley is the most popular rock 'n' roll musician in U.S.

1961
Peace Corps is established.

1962
Rachel Carson's *Silent Spring* is published.

1964
The Beatles appear on *The Ed Sullivan Show.*

1970
First Earth Day is observed.

1970
Dee Brown's *Bury My Heart At Wounded Knee* is published.

1970
Sesame Street television show with Jim Henson's Muppets begins.

U.S. POPULATION:

151,325,798   179,323,175   203,302,031

1975　　**1980**　　**1985**　　**1990**　　**1995**　　**2000**

1975
Vietnam
War ends.

1981
Sandra Day
O'Connor
becomes first
woman on
Supreme Court.

1981
U.S. hostages
returned from Iran
after 444 days.

1979
Iran
seizes
U.S.
hostages.

1983
Sally Ride becomes first
U.S. woman in space.

1986
Challenger
spacecraft
explodes, killing
entire crew.

1989
Berlin Wall is
torn down.

1991
Persian Gulf War begins.

1991
Restructuring of Soviet Union occurs.

1994
Earthquake rocks Los
Angeles, CA, killing
more than 50 people.

1994
110th and 111th elements
discovered.

1994
U.S. sends troops
to Haiti.

1976
Concorde
becomes
world's first
supersonic
passenger jet.

1977
Apple Computers
produce first
personal computer.

1979
Three-Mile
Island nuclear
accident occurs.

1981
Scientists
identify AIDS.

1983
Pioneer 10 space probe
passes Neptune and
leaves solar system.

1984
Compact
disks (CDs)
developed.

1988
NASA reports greenhouse effect is
caused by destruction of forests.

1991
Environmental Protection Agency
cites growing danger of
hole in Earth's ozone layer.

1993
Apple's Newton
Writing-Pad
computer introduced.

1976
Alex Haley's *Roots*
is published.

1976
U.S. Bicentennial
celebrated.

1977
Star Wars becomes
largest money-making
movie of all time.

1979
Yellow ribbons symbolize
support for return of U.S.
hostages in Iran.

1986
Martin Luther King
Day proclaimed
national holiday.

1988
Thirty million
U.S. school
children have
access to
computers.

1989
Amy Tan's
Joy Luck Club
is published.

1993
Connie Chung
is named first
woman to
co-anchor
a national
evening news
team.

C B S

1993
Jurassic Park features
new computer film-
making techniques.

226,542,203　　　　248,709,873